Global Marketing Strategies for the Promotion of Luxury Goods

Fabrizio Mosca
University of Turin, Italy

Rosalia Gallo
Universitat Autònoma de Barcelona, Spain

A volume in the Advances in Marketing, Customer Relationship Management, and E-Services (AMCRMES) Book Series

BUSINESS SCIENCE Reference
An Imprint of IGI Global

Published in the United States of America by
Business Science Reference (an imprint of IGI Global)
701 E. Chocolate Avenue
Hershey PA, USA 17033
Tel: 717-533-8845
Fax: 717-533-8661
E-mail: cust@igi-global.com
Web site: http://www.igi-global.com

Library of Congress Cataloging-in-Publication Data

Names: Mosca, Fabrizio, editor. | Gallo, Rosalia, editor.
Title: Global marketing strategies for the promotion of luxury goods / Fabrizio Mosca and Rosalia Gallo, editors.
Description: Hershey, PA : Business Science Reference, [2016] | Includes bibliographical references and index.
Identifiers: LCCN 2015050696| ISBN 9781466699588 (hardcover : alk. paper) | ISBN 9781466699595 (ebook : alk. paper)
Subjects: LCSH: Luxury goods industry. | Luxuries--Marketing. | Wealthy consumers.
Classification: LCC HD9999.L852 G596 2016 | DDC 658.8/02--dc23 LC record available at http://lccn.loc.gov/2015050696

This book is published in the IGI Global book series Advances in Marketing, Customer Relationship Management, and E-Services (AMCRMES) (ISSN: 2327-5502; eISSN: 2327-5529)

British Cataloguing in Publication Data
A Cataloguing in Publication record for this book is available from the British Library.

All work contributed to this book is new, previously-unpublished material. The views expressed in this book are those of the authors, but not necessarily of the publisher.

For electronic access to this publication, please contact: eresources@igi-global.com.

Advances in Marketing, Customer Relationship Management, and E-Services (AMCRMES) Book Series

Eldon Y. Li
National Chengchi University, Taiwan & California Polytechnic State University, USA

ISSN: 2327-5502
EISSN: 2327-5529

Mission

Business processes, services, and communications are important factors in the management of good customer relationship, which is the foundation of any well organized business. Technology continues to play a vital role in the organization and automation of business processes for marketing, sales, and customer service. These features aid in the attraction of new clients and maintaining existing relationships.

The Advances in Marketing, Customer Relationship Management, and E-Services (AMCRMES) Book Series addresses success factors for customer relationship management, marketing, and electronic services and its performance outcomes. This collection of reference source covers aspects of consumer behavior and marketing business strategies aiming towards researchers, scholars, and practitioners in the fields of marketing management.

Coverage

- Legal Considerations in E-Marketing
- E-Service Innovation
- Customer Relationship Management
- Database marketing
- Cases on CRM Implementation
- B2B marketing
- Electronic Services
- Data mining and marketing
- Mobile CRM
- Cases on Electronic Services

IGI Global is currently accepting manuscripts for publication within this series. To submit a proposal for a volume in this series, please contact our Acquisition Editors at Acquisitions@igi-global.com or visit: http://www.igi-global.com/publish/.

The Advances in Marketing, Customer Relationship Management, and E-Services (AMCRMES) Book Series (ISSN 2327-5502) is published by IGI Global, 701 E. Chocolate Avenue, Hershey, PA 17033-1240, USA, www.igi-global.com. This series is composed of titles available for purchase individually; each title is edited to be contextually exclusive from any other title within the series. For pricing and ordering information please visit http://www.igi-global.com/book-series/advances-marketing-customer-relationship-management/37150. Postmaster: Send all address changes to above address.

Titles in this Series

For a list of additional titles in this series, please visit: www.igi-global.com

Global Perspectives on Contemporary Marketing Education
Brent Smith (Saint Joseph's University, USA) and Amiram Porath (AmiPorCon Ltd, Israel)
Business Science Reference • copyright 2016 • 296pp • H/C (ISBN: 9781466697843) • US $190.00 (our price)

Competitive Social Media Marketing Strategies
Wilson Ozuem (University of Gloucestershire, UK) and Gordon Bowen (Regent's University London, UK)
Business Science Reference • copyright 2016 • 317pp • H/C (ISBN: 9781466697768) • US $195.00 (our price)

Product Innovation through Knowledge Management and Social Media Strategies
Alok Kumar Goel (CSIR Human Resource Development Centre, India) and Puja Singhal (Amity University, India)
Business Science Reference • copyright 2016 • 421pp • H/C (ISBN: 9781466696075) • US $205.00 (our price)

Fuzzy Optimization and Multi-Criteria Decision Making in Digital Marketing
Anil Kumar (ABV-Indian Institute of Information Technology & Management, India) and Manoj Kumar Dash (ABV-Indian Institute of Information Technology & Management, India)
Business Science Reference • copyright 2016 • 368pp • H/C (ISBN: 9781466688087) • US $200.00 (our price)

Trends and Innovations in Marketing Information Systems
Theodosios Tsiakis (Alexander Technological Educational Institute of Thessaloniki, Greece)
Business Science Reference • copyright 2015 • 454pp • H/C (ISBN: 9781466684591) • US $225.00 (our price)

Capturing, Analyzing, and Managing Word-of-Mouth in the Digital Marketplace
Sumangla Rathore (Sir Padampat Singhania University, India) and Avinash Panwar (Sir Padampat Singhania University, India)
Business Science Reference • copyright 2016 • 339pp • H/C (ISBN: 9781466694491) • US $200.00 (our price)

Strategic Customer Relationship Management in the Age of Social Media
Amir Khanlari (University of Tehran, Iran)
Business Science Reference • copyright 2015 • 332pp • H/C (ISBN: 9781466685864) • US $200.00 (our price)

Maximizing Commerce and Marketing Strategies through Micro-Blogging
Janée N. Burkhalter (Saint Joseph's University, USA) and Natalie T. Wood (Saint Joseph's University, USA & Edith Cowan University, Australia)
Business Science Reference • copyright 2015 • 380pp • H/C (ISBN: 9781466684089) • US $225.00 (our price)

IGI GLOBAL
DISSEMINATOR OF KNOWLEDGE
www.igi-global.com

701 E. Chocolate Ave., Hershey, PA 17033
Order online at www.igi-global.com or call 717-533-8845 x100
To place a standing order for titles released in this series, contact: cust@igi-global.com
Mon-Fri 8:00 am - 5:00 pm (est) or fax 24 hours a day 717-533-8661

Editorial Advisory Board

Table of Contents

Detailed Table of Contents

Due to the importance of the fragrances segment within the luxury market and the limited academic and professional literature available regarding the same, this chapter offers a detailed description of the basic characteristics of this segment. Therefore, based on the analysis of primary and secondary information (quantitative and qualitative) regarding the Spanish market, the key elements of luxury fragrance consumer behavior have been described, examining the principle explanatory factors leading to decision making processes for their purchase and use; in other words, the motivations to purchase and consume these products. This knowledge is decisive to permit luxury fragrance brands to appropriately design their global marketing strategies and formulate the appropriate marketing-mix.

This study attempts to fill in the gaps in the international marketing literature about international marketing entry decisions for luxury products. With this in mind, a macromarketing approach is used to segment countries according to the basic luxury consumption criteria based on the literature review. These criteria include population, GDP, GINI coefficient, total female labor force, and cultural dimensions. These indicators are listed for a total of 60 countries and multidimensional scaling analysis (MDS) is conducted to see whether some countries form groups. Finally, five groups are determined and are discussed for their luxury potentials.

Since the spread of digital environments has certainly helped to broaden the spectrum of possibilities for managing channels, while opening new areas of competitive confrontation, is to assume that new technologies have contributed to the definition of a hybrid environment in which pre- and post-digital-revolution habits coexist. The aim of the present chapter is to show how this kind of hybrid channels, want to meet the two requirements to communicate and sell - through the use of media platforms that appeal to each other, meet and complement each other – is nowadays managed and how it can be used in the future to reach business and awareness goals in luxury markets. The analysis has been based on ways through which global luxury goods firms integrate their communication and selling tools each other, by focusing the attention on web and social strategies.

years: a growing investment by luxury brands in direct distribution activities; the integration between distribution and communication activities; the development of the digital channel in luxury markets; and lastly, the growing integration between User Generated Content and distribution channels. As the distribution variable influences the constitution of brand identity, old and new distribution channels have to be differently articulated according to the exclusivity of the brand.

This chapter explores how the luxury sector has been affected by the fast fashion brands in the UK market. In particular, this chapter examines the effects of fast fashion activity on luxury brands and more specifically on how the marketing strategies of luxury brands have been drawn to the fast fashion model. Moreover, it analyzes how co-branding collaborations between luxury and fast fashion brands have positively affected consumer' perception of the luxury brands. The chapter is based on a theoretical review and two studies. Results provide insights for the international fashion business, showing how luxury fashion brands lean towards the fast fashion model and how co-branding collaborations between luxury and fast fashion brands are positive for luxury brands in terms of customer perception.

In this chapter the authors analyze the Moncler case using concepts link to the family business world. In the luxury industry family businesses are existing entities with a strong DNA created by a founder leader and guided by his vision across generations; the strong link between the founder's DNA, the company and the customers implies a high level of influence on how resources are managed and, consequently, it changes dynamics and results. In the rapid changing luxury industry's business environment it is necessary for the companies to maintain the DNA's heritage. To succeed it is necessary to innovate and to remain linked to the root of the past through innovation and evolution. Moncler perfectly shows how - from the successful vision of the founder to a deep crisis - is possible to reach a second life (with a new re-founder) appealing to the original values and DNA of the company.

Foreword

The marketing of luxury goods has become increasingly important over the years, and the number of universities and institutions addressing this concept has recently increased. Global luxury markets have grown, and they continue to grow, and the number of consumers who purchase high-end goods is very relevant. Luxury markets are characterized by the sum of global niches in which the process of internationalization began long ago.

Vast markets for high-symbolic-value goods serve as a large and global competitive arena where players that vie for the same category of consumers face off. The factors that have facilitated the development of an international presence are: the existence of a transnational segment of consumers who share similar characteristics, the global flattening of sociodemographic, lifestyle, and consumption factors, the uniformity of consumers' buying behaviors in the transnational segment, the gradual standardization of brand communication activities to achieve a consistent level of brand perception in all countries, the need to extend national niches toward similar niches at the global level, so as to ensure adequate market potential and the presence of economies of "replication" in distribution.

These prime factors have led to major international growth among all activities in firms' value chains.

In recent years, luxury goods markets have faced significant changes that have influenced both the dynamics of the competition, which are daring players, as well as their strategies.

This book provides a valuable window on the principal changes in luxury markets including the following: new geographical market development, such as in the Far East, India, and some parts of Africa (these countries are added to a list of already relevant countries that are involved in luxury goods consumption, such as the Emirates, Russia, and South America); new consumers are facing these luxury markets; there is diffusion of new media and new technologies in communication, which is characterized by a high degree of interaction; and the evolution of distribution channels is underway – these channels are moving toward new forms of integration that utilize both physical channels and digital ones.

With respect to new markets and new consumer development, we are facing a situation where increasing numbers of consumers are interested in luxury goods consumption. These consumers are not completely educated about global brands, but they are looking for products that are able differentiate themselves and/or guarantee unique experiences. Luxury players have to understand the factors that affect people who are making purchasing decisions, and they also have to be aware of the dynamics that characterize consumers' buying behaviors.

Concerning the diffusion of new digital technologies, in recent years, the increasing importance of the digital channel and the globalization of markets has changed both consumers' roles and the nature of the competitive landscape. This has forced firms to revise their strategies and implement multichannel marketing strategies to continue to operate in increasingly international markets that are characterized by increasingly more demanding and informed consumers.

The challenges in luxury markets are both difficult and interesting. People are working on them with enthusiasm, tenacity, and dedication to develop new methods of analysis and provide new solutions to keep up with the ever-changing threats. In this new age of global interconnectivity and interdependence, it is necessary to provide security practitioners, both professionals and students, with state-of-the art knowledge on the frontiers in luxury strategies with a focus on new media. This book is a good step in that direction.

Gaetano Aiello
University of Florence, Italy

Gaetano Aiello *is Dean, Department of Economics and Management since 2013; Full Professor of Retail Marketing at the University of Florence. He has been Research Fellow at the University of Florence since 1990. His research interests include brand management, international retailing, fashion and luxury marketing, SME marketing. His published research outputs have appeared in refereed international journals including Psicology & Marketing, Journal of Business Research, Journal of Brand Management, Journal of Marketing Trends, Journal of Global Scholars of Marketing Science, and also in Marketing Trends, EMAC, IMP, KSMS, AMS international conferences proceedings. He has been Visiting Professor at the Leibniz University of Hannover - Institute of Marketing and Management since 2008. He was Guest lecturer at Yonsei University of Seoul in 2011. He is a Member of Editorial Board of: Micro&Macro Marketing, Journal of Global Scholars of Marketing Science, Luxury Research Journal, Journal of Global Fashion Marketing, and Vice-President of AIDEA, Board Member of Italian Marketing Society, Member of EMAC, KSMS, AMS.*

Preface

The marketing of luxury goods has become increasingly important over the years, and the number of universities and institutions addressing this concept has recently increased. Global luxury markets have grown, and they continue to grow, and the number of consumers who purchase high-end goods is very relevant. Luxury markets are characterized by the sum of global niches in which the process of internationalization began long ago.

Vast markets for high-symbolic-value goods serve as a large and global competitive arena where players that vie for the same category of consumers face off. The factors that have facilitated the development of an international presence are:

1. The existence of a transnational segment of consumers who share similar characteristics;
2. The global flattening of sociodemographic, lifestyle, and consumption factors;
3. The uniformity of consumers' buying behaviors in the transnational segment;
4. The gradual standardization of brand communication activities to achieve a consistent level of brand perception in all countries;
5. The need to extend national niches toward similar niches at the global level, so as to ensure adequate market potential; and
6. The presence of economies of "replication" in distribution.

These prime factors have led to major international growth among all activities in firms' value chains.

Broader markets for high-symbolic-value goods can be considered as the sum of numerous niche markets, which are small when analyzed within the product sector to which they belong, but large in terms of turnover and the number of consumers they attract when considered on a global scale. This is another important reason why we cross-analyze marketing strategies; specifically, we do not focus exclusively on companies that specialize in fashion, watch making, or recreational boating.

Consumers of high-symbolic-value goods are transversely uniform in their preferences and buying behavior in each country. To simplify this idea, we can say that a senior executive of a multinational Dutch firm, as well as an Italian one, buy the same set of high-end goods and have similar purchasing models. The affluent consumers of Paris are certainly much more similar to affluent consumers in New York than to other segments of French consumers. Aging populations, declining birth rates, the increase in disposable income during retirement years, an increase in leisure time after age fifty, and the increase in female employment are phenomena that are common to all industrialized countries. Therefore, a trend toward the homogenization of consumption based on social class and age at the international level is only natural.

The competitiveness of a company that operates in markets for high-symbolic-value goods is endangered if the company is not in a position to market its goods and services in all countries around the world and, more specifically, both in mature areas and in emerging areas where there are customers with high disposable income to devote to consumption. If, until now, the main geographic areas of the market for high-symbolic-value goods have been Europe, Japan, and North America, the geographic area of emerging markets will be South East Asia, South America, Eastern Europe, and Africa.

The current process of globalization in luxury markets is not related to the relocation of manufacturing activities which, in many cases, are the subject of a reverse process of a return to the country of origin; rather, the phenomenon of globalization is related to distribution and communication activities. We are currently witnessing the gradual broadening of retail activities, often under direct control of the luxury firm, in emerging markets.

In this market, entry barriers are created with brands. To replicate a serially-produced high-end good is not difficult. The quality craftsmanship of the early phases of a firm's development soon gives way to high industrial quality, which is more easily imitated by competitors. The only real barrier is based on brand image. For companies that want to hold a significant market position, solidifying a brand's image involves developing a global presence and establishing a recognized and distinctive high-value brand.

Furthermore, there is also globalization of the value chain. This affects the ways in which businesses are organized to produce and sell their goods on the market. The activities of planning, product development, design, production, marketing, and distribution are carried out in different locations, and goods are distributed in all major global markets. The value chain of the enterprise and the value chain systems represented by the main business and its business partners are de-localized in many countries. Certain designers have long shifted their activities to different markets. For example, some firms that produce high-end apparel entrust their styling to Italy, production to Poland, and distribution to intermediaries in many geographic areas.

Concurrent with the globalization of value-chain activities, the last few years have witnessed an inverse process where manufacturing activities are redirected to global brands' countries of origin. This phenomenon has come about for economic reasons, primarily related to a general improvement in the competitiveness of the home country, as well as based on a number of marketing decisions. Consumers are paying more attention to the terms and conditions of production, and the link between the product and the skill systems of the territory of origin is a key success factor. For this reason, some firms (such as Brunello Cucinelli) have chosen not to relocate any phases of the value chain. Indeed, this tightly binds the design and production processes to the system and values of the region where the firm is located.

THE CHALLENGES

In recent years, luxury goods markets have faced significant changes that have influenced both the dynamics of the competition, which are daring players, as well as their strategies. The principal changes include the following: new geographical market development, such as in the Far East, India, and some parts of Africa (these countries are added to a list of already relevant countries that are involved in luxury goods consumption, such as the Emirates, Russia, and South America); new consumers are facing these luxury markets; there is diffusion of new media and new technologies in communication, which is characterized by a high degree of interaction; and the evolution of distribution channels is underway – these channels are moving toward new forms of integration that utilize both physical channels and digital ones.

With respect to new markets and new consumer development, we are facing a situation where increasing numbers of consumers are interested in luxury goods consumption. These consumers are not completely educated about global brands, but they are looking for products that are able differentiate themselves and/or guarantee unique experiences. Luxury players have to understand the factors that affect people who are making purchasing decisions, and they also have to be aware of the dynamics that characterize consumers' buying behaviors.

Concerning the diffusion of new digital technologies, in recent years, the increasing importance of the digital channel and the globalization of markets has changed both consumers' roles and the nature of the competitive landscape. This has forced firms to revise their strategies and implement multichannel marketing strategies to continue to operate in increasingly international markets that are characterized by increasingly more demanding and informed consumers.

Recourse to a plurality of channels has proven to be a necessity for luxury goods, especially because digital platforms now constitute communication channels in their own right. From this standpoint, the digital channel serves as a medium that interacts with demand, and it further adopts a hybrid connotation: it can perform functions that are informative, transactional, and relational, and it alternately or simultaneously uses both physical and virtual contact modes. Based on this perspective, multichannel management policies can contribute significantly to establishing a brand's loyalty of existing consumers while acquiring new market segments. Although luxury firms initially had some reservations about using the Web as a distribution channel – especially given that they did not think it would be able to reproduce customers' experiences from the physical point of sale, and that it created distance from buyers with high spending power – in recent years, the opportunities offered by the digital channel have become clear and numerous. In this way, the logic underlying the development of the digital channel for luxury players is one of integration with the physical channel; it is not to be viewed as a standalone distribution channel, but as one that completes and complements the physical channel.

The traditional store setting always plays a major role in the experience of buying luxury goods; however, the huge success of the digital channel has turned it into an inescapable channel for players in the market for high-symbolic-value goods. A Web strategy is thus essential for a luxury brand. The development of non-conventional marketing allows firms to engage with their consumers by focusing on the goal of transmitting the values of a specific brand through involvement, entertainment, and fun. Consumers become leading actors, and firms can develop measures of engagement, while taking advantage of word-of-mouth referrals, using both a proactive and dynamic approach.

Analyzing the evolution of consumer behavior during the purchasing process is particularly important for manufacturers and distributors because the Internet now enables two-way communication flow, thus transforming the classic approach to communication, which was characterized by a lack of interaction.

This digital channel has enabled firms to extend their market to new consumers who have different sociodemographic characteristics and are located in emerging countries. High-symbolic-value goods are traditionally considered incompatible with the digital channel; even today, some companies that maintain extreme brand positioning believe it inappropriate to develop distribution activities in the digital channel. Most luxury players have developed a direct presence in the digital space; this strategic distribution option has largely been successful. The digital channel is increasingly integrated with the activities of physical distribution, and this amalgamation makes it possible to enhance the consumer's shopping experience, while also maintaining long-term relationships.

The latest trend in brand development centers on the growing integration between UGC and the various distribution channels. Brand communication in luxury markets has undergone further development with social media marketing that has dovetailed into both the digital and physical distribution space. The consumer is ready, even in luxury markets, to receive information from a specific brand, to share that information, and to respond by liking the product and purchasing it in the digital or physical channel. This growing integration between distribution and effective communication (both online and offline) follows a circular approach, whereby information channels and their flows surround the consumer. This is one of the frontiers of marketing high-symbolic-value goods.

Channel integration in markets for luxury goods lies, in practice, in the introduction of innovative technologies to points of sale, in the integration between two-way communication activities in social networks, and in the physical channel of distribution. With regard to the first path of integration, the use of technology in luxury-brand stores clearly helps intensify consumers' feelings and stimulates their senses. New technologies make it possible to entertain customers, while enhancing the communication process.

The variety of communication options available online allows firms to send messages that are tailored to capture the attention of consumers because they are able to reflect these buyers' special interests and well-established habits. The Internet is thus a reliable medium to achieve this aim, and the effects of an online marketing campaign are easily traceable.1 Firms are now in a position to define and convey an offer in an integrated manner – that is, by using multichannel strategies. This involves developing a coordinated and comprehensive set of means and channels through which to reduce the gap between supply and demand.

Ultimately, it is an approach to managing customer relationships that tends to overcome the logistics of using a single channel (typically, the physical channel), thanks to the progressive growth of the economic weight of the service sector and to the increasing use of electronics and digital networks, which make it possible to extend beyond the logistical limits imposed by traditional points of sale.

Within this context, rapidly changing firms have reacted by adopting strategies that are focused on expanding their global presence. These firms have primarily developed hybrid distribution systems, both direct and indirect, but with increasing weight attributed to direct distribution. This growth not only pertains to the major global players in the luxury market, but also to medium-sized companies that have been able to establish themselves in global markets. These companies increase their attention to the use of the digital channel to market their products, as well as to integrate digital and physical distribution channels; this is a communication strategy that focuses on acquiring new consumers through social media.

The three sections of the present book aim to document the principal tendencies described above, with particular attention paid to purchasing behaviors, the progressive interaction between distribution channels and social media, and the major developments in distribution activities.

ORGANIZATION OF THE BOOK

This book is organized into three sections and twelve chapters. A brief description of each chapter follows.

Chapter 1 provides an overview of global consumer behavior in luxury goods markets. The discussion is based on the classic theories of consumers' decision-making processes, and the important factors affecting these processes. As global consumer behavior in luxury goods markets is greatly affected by cultural differences, Hofstede's cultural dimensions theory is used to explain the various consumption behaviors displayed by purchasers from different parts of the world. Past research findings are summarized, and examples of consumer behaviors and appropriate marketing strategies implemented by luxury brands are also presented to provide readers with a better understanding of this topic.

Chapter 2 analyzes the differences in consumer behavior and their attitudes toward luxury goods. The established bond between the consumer and the luxury brand, as derived from a psychological process, is strong and characterized by emotions. The luxury brand is a symbol of personal and social identity; it expresses the individual's personality and lifestyle, and strengthens the projection of self-image, status, and self-concept. This chapter analyzes the buyer's decision process, customer retention, and loyalty by focusing on the role of envy in purchase decisions associated with luxury goods, as this falls within the context of social comparison. Furthermore, advertising messages and their strategies (of which envy is commonly used) are also discussed. The personality of the luxury retail store will be analyzed. This chapter will review the most important scientific contributions in this field, paying special attention to research conducted in the area of neuromarketing and the neurobiology of beauty.

Chapter 3 focuses on the fragrances segment within the luxury market. The chapter offers a detailed description of the basic characteristics of this segment. Therefore, based on the analysis of primary and secondary information (quantitative and qualitative analyses) in the Spanish market, the key elements of luxury fragrance consumer behavior are described, examining the principal explanatory factors that lead to the decision-making processes underlying customers' purchases, as well as the motives that guide the purchase and consumption of these products. This knowledge will explain how luxury fragrance brands appropriately design their global marketing strategies and formulate suitable marketing mixes.

Chapter 4 attempts to fill the gaps in the international marketing literature regarding international marketing entry decisions for luxury products. With this in mind, a macro-marketing approach is used to segment countries according to basic luxury consumption criteria, which are based on a literature review. These criteria include population, gross domestic product (GDP), the GINI coefficient, the total female labor force, and cultural dimensions. These indicators are listed for a total of 60 countries and multidimensional scaling analysis (MDS) is conducted to determine whether some countries can be grouped together as cluster with similar characteristics. Finally, five groups are identified and are further discussed for their luxury goods purchase potential.

Chapter 5 analyzes the new ways in which global luxury players integrate their communication and sales tools to each other, centering their attention on Web and social strategies. Since the spread of digital environments has certainly helped broaden the spectrum of possibilities for managing channels – while also opening the door to new areas of competition – it is thus assumed that new technologies have contributed to the definition of a hybrid environment in which pre- and post-digital revolution habits coexist. The aim of this chapter is to show how this kind of hybrid channel (which aims to bridge communication and sales through the use of integrated media platforms) is currently managed, and how it can be used in the future to reach business and awareness goals in luxury markets.

Chapter 6 has two main objectives. First, it reviews the existing literature on content marketing and the main metrics used in this field. Second, it analyzes the degree of use and effectiveness of content marketing strategies by employing a number of tools and metrics to a sample of 218 luxury firms. The results of the study revealed that content marketing is regarded by luxury firms as a marketing communications strategy that provides valuable and helpful information to a clearly defined target audience with the aim of increasing sales. Luxury marketing strategies have undergone some major changes over the past couple of decades. The balance of power is moving away from luxury firms to luxury consumers, who are playing a more significant role than ever before. These challenges in global markets have sparked a growing interest by practitioners and academics in the content marketing field. Various metrics are now being adopted to measure this transition's impact on luxury firm performance.

Chapter 7 analyzes the relative importance of the different relationship platforms (physical and virtual) in the consumer experience of luxury brands, and it also aims to develop an understanding of how this experience has changed. On the one hand, the results are able to expand upon the theory of luxury branding; on the other, they are also able to highlight some key implications for luxury brand managers. Managing luxury brands nowadays is complex (Wiedmann & Hennigs, 2012). Luxury brands have built their foundation on the strategic use of physical platforms, enabling customers to experience points of sale, which have constituted an indispensable element for these firms' growth. Conversely, over the past 10 years, we have seen leading global luxury brands embrace virtual platforms in various ways to re-imagine consumer experiences. Blending these new elements together can present numerous challenges.

Chapter 8 investigates luxury fashion brands' interactions with consumers, especially on social media. The use of prescribers that identify consumer behavior has been a constant brand strategy, especially when a brand targets younger audiences. These individuals are large consumers of music and audio–visual entertainment products and, as fans, they show a high level of loyalty that leads them to copy the behaviors and consumption patterns of their idols. Furthermore, they are also big users of social media and the Internet, where they express their feelings, experiences, and opinions about their music idols, in addition to the brands and products they use. Technology not only empowers young people to access more information, but it also provides them with the possibility of generating their own content, thus highlighting the two roles played by the brand.

Chapter 9 sets out to explore the phenomenon of blogging and social media communities, and the impact these communities have on reference group culture, social identity, and the buying behavior of a target group of consumers – women aged 18–30 years old – who participate in the online beauty community. This research has examined the impact that participation in this community has had on the amount of money these consumers spend on beauty and skincare products, and the extent to which this behavior has influenced their attitude towards luxury products. The study confirmed findings from the existing literature, in that there does appear to be a connection between purchasing habits and the desire to be considered a member of the community. The study also revealed that regular participation in the community increases consumer knowledge of products, and can eventually lead to consumer expertise surpassing that of the sales staff.

Chapter 10 investigates how luxury global players manage their old and new distribution channels by integrating them together in the global market. It is clear that the distribution strategies implemented by firms operating in luxury markets are typical and specific with respect to firms in other markets, and they represent a source of competitive advantage. Four phenomena have characterized distribution in this area in recent years: a growing investment by luxury brands in direct distribution activities; the integration between distribution and communication activities; the development of the digital channel in luxury markets; and, lastly, the growing integration between UGC and distribution channels. Since distribution influences the constitution of brand identity, old and new distribution channels have to be differently articulated according to the exclusivity of the brand.

Chapter 11 explores how the luxury sector has been affected by the fast fashion brands in the UK market. In particular, this chapter is aimed at examining the effects of fast fashion activity on luxury brands and, more specifically, on how the marketing of luxury brands has been drawn to the fast fashion model. This chapter also analyzes how co-branding collaborations between luxury and fast fashion brands have positively affected consumers' perceptions of luxury brands. The results of this investigation provide insights into the international fashion business, showing how luxury fashion brands lean toward the fast fashion model and how co-branding collaborations between luxury and fast fashion brands are positive for luxury brands in terms of customers' perceptions.

Chapter 12 explores Moncler's case, an Italian family-owned, fast-growing luxury company. In the luxury industry, family businesses are entities with a strong DNA, where the business is created by a founder or leader and is guided by his or her vision across generations. The strong link between the founder's DNA, the company, and its customers implies a high level of influence on how resources are managed and, consequently, this changes the company's dynamics and results. In the rapidly changing luxury industry's business environment, it is necessary for companies to maintain the DNA's heritage. To succeed, it is necessary to innovate and remain linked to the roots of the past through innovation and evolution. Moncler perfectly illustrates how – ranging from the successful vision of the founder to the company's entrenchment in a deep crisis – it is possible to have a second life (with a new re-founder) that appeals to the original values and DNA of the company.

Fabrizio Mosca
University of Turin, Italy

Rosalia Gallo
Universitat Autònoma de Barcelona, Spain

Acknowledgment

The editors would like to acknowledge the help of all the people involved in this project and, more specifically, to the authors and reviewers that took part in the review process. Without their support, this book would not have become a reality.

First, the editors would like to thank each one of the authors for their contributions. Our sincere gratitude goes to the chapter's authors who contributed their time and expertise to this book.

Second, the editors wish to acknowledge the valuable contributions of the reviewers regarding the improvement of quality, coherence, and content presentation of chapters. Most of the authors also served as referees; we highly appreciate their double task.

Fabrizio Mosca
University of Turin, Italy

Rosalia Gallo
Universitat Autònoma de Barcelona, Spain

Section 1
New Trends in Consumer Behavior in Luxury Markets

Chapter 1
Global Consumer Behaviour in Luxury Goods Markets

Yuping Li
RMIT University, Australia

ABSTRACT

In this chapter, the author presents an overview on global consumer behaviour in luxury goods markets. The discussion is based on the classic theories of consumer decision-making process and the important factors affecting the decision-making process. As global consumer behaviour in luxury goods markets is greatly affected by cultural differences, Hofstede's cultural dimensions theory is used to explain the various consumption behaviours displayed by consumers from different parts of the world. Past research findings are summarised, examples of consumer behaviours and appropriate marketing strategies implemented by luxury brands are also presented to assist readers for a better understanding of the topic.

INTRODUCTION

The chapter aims to provide relevant theoretical frameworks and the latest empirical research findings in the area of global consumer behaviour in luxury goods markets.

The chapter focusses on the consumer decision-making process, as well as the internal (psychological) factors and external (social-cultural) factors which influence the process. Each area is examined from a global cross-cultural perspective, and luxury consumer behaviours from specific regions/countries are also discussed. Information and examples are sourced from consumer behaviour theories and existing literature.

BACKGROUND

Consumer behaviour is defined as 'the behaviours that consumers display in searching for, purchasing, using, evaluating and disposing of products and services that they expect will satisfy their needs" (Shiffman et. al, 2014).So luxury consumer behaviour means consumption behaviours related to luxury goods.

DOI: 10.4018/978-1-4666-9958-8.ch001

However "luxury goods" mean different things to different consumers in different countries. The understanding of luxury may also differ between individuals; it is situational, contingent and depends on the experience and individual needs of the consumer (Wiedmann, Hennigs & Siebels (2007).

Luxury brands constitute the highest level of prestigious brands and demonstrate several physical and psychological values; for instance, the act of use or display of a luxury product brings esteem for its owners (Vigneron & Johnson, 1999). Out of those two values psychological benefits are considered to be the main factor which distinguishes luxury products from non-luxury products (Nia & Zaichkowsky, 2000).

Over the last five years the luxury goods market has grown despite persistent economic turbulence and austerity approaches in many economies. The growth has been supported by the expansion of middle class in emerging economies. Based on Euromonitor's data (2013), Asia Pacific, Latin America, the Middle East and Africa contributed 19% to the global luxury goods market in 2013, and this is projected to grow to 25% by 2015. The growth is driven by the combined forces of urbanisation, economic expansion and the love of luxury (Deloitte, 2014). USA is by far the largest luxury goods market, followed by Japan, Italy, France and China (Euromonitor, 2013), but with the BRICs (Brazil, Russia, India and China) and other emerging economies being the key drivers of global luxury goods growth (Passport, 2013).

Research in the global luxury goods market has identified that the tastes of luxury consumers are constantly changing. Luxury brands need to respond to these changes in order to maintain their growth and market share. Bonding with the consumer is the key to the survival of luxury brands in an era where markets, products, services, marketing and distribution are always in a state of change (Khan, 2010).

Overall, the global market for luxury goods is maturing, stabilizing and consolidating, it is becoming more resilient to economic crises; more responsive to a global consumer base which has become more demanding and highly mobile; and it is less dependent on market booms for growth (D'Arpizio, 2014). Luxury goods have become available to a much wider range of consumers globally, and over the last decade the traditional conspicuous consumption model has been transformed into a new experiential way in which consumers define luxury (Wiedmann, Hennigs & Siebels, 2007). In mature luxury markets, such as Europe and the US, as well as in emerging markets such as China and India, middle class families with burgeoning incomes have begun to shop for brands that were previously regarded as out of reach (Catry, 2003), even the low-income individuals are purchasing luxury goods on occasions as for them the ownership of a luxury branded product represent an experience in status improvement.

This chapter explains the consumer decision-making process, which is extremely relevant to luxury goods, as they are high-involvement products. The chapter also discusses factors influencing the consumer decision-making process, which include social-cultural factors, psychological factors and situational factors, and how these factors and their influence vary depending on different cultures. Information on luxury consumer behaviours in some specific market regions/countries is also presented to facilitate understanding of this chapter.

The Consumer Decision-Making Process

The Five Stage Model initially proposed by Cox et al. (1983) is one of the most commonly used models of consumer decision making. It encompasses the five stages the purchaser will go through before making a final purchase decision.

The process covers the recognition of a problem or a need; search for information; evaluation of available alternatives; choice and making the purchase decision; and post-purchase evaluation. Core to this process is the fact that the purchase is generally of value in monetary terms, especially in the case of luxury goods - which are also called high-involvement purchases - so the consumer will take time and make efforts to assess the alternatives (Dudovskiy, 2013).

Factors Influencing the Consumer Decision-Making Process

Many factors influence consumer's decision making, according to Shiffman et al. (2014). These influential factors are grouped into three broad categories – social-cultural factors, psychological factors and situational factors.

Social-Cultural Factors

This group of *external factors* is very important in influencing the consumer decision-making process; it is particularly relevant to consumers from high collectivism societies, where family, peers and other external sources shape consumer perceptions and decisions.

Culture

Culture deals with a group's design for living, and is the result of many generations' solutions for survival, physically as well as psychologically. Because of its significant impact on human behaviour, culture has been widely linked to consumption (Yaprak, 2008). Cultural differences often cause variations in consumer behaviour within as well as across national borders (Hennigs et al., 2012). Wong and Ahuvia (1998) believe that the materialism in Asian societies may not reflect internal personal tastes, traits or goals as in Western societies; instead, it may reflect the orientation of social conformity in a hierarchical culture. In Asian countries interpersonal influence is strong, so people tend to endorse an interdependent sense of self that focuses on communal goals, norms and obligations (Markus & Kitayama, 1991).The needs consumers choose to satisfy and the manner in which their choices are made to satisfy those needs are a function of their cultures.

Geert Hofstede explains the fundamental differences between cultures using a cultural dimensions theory. After studying over 90,000 people in 66 countries, he found that the cultures of the countries varied along four basic dimensions:

- Power Distance Index (PDI).
- Individualism/Collectivism Index (IDV).
- Uncertainty Avoidance Index (UAI).
- Masculinity/Femininity Index (MAS).

Although later researchers added two more dimensions to the theory (Pragmatic/Normative (PRA); Indulgence/Restrain (IND)), the four original dimensions remain the foundation of the theory and have been widely used in cross-cultural studies.

Of the four dimensions, the Individualism/Collectivism Index may have the strongest impact on consumer behaviour in the purchase of luxury goods.

A high individualism society promotes self-interest and is very much "me' focused. This 'me" focus includes the members of immediate but not the extended family. On the other hand, a high collectivism society encourages people to integrate into strong, cohesive groups. This "we" culture means that everyone in the group (which could be the extended family, school or the organisation with which the person is employed) is protected from outsiders and the members of the group influence each other strongly (Hofstede, 2001).

Culture affects consumer decision making as it is a powerful force in regulating all human behaviour. Members of the same culture share the same values (Hofstede, 2001), and these values affect all stages of the decision-making process, particularly when the purchases are high-involvement such as of luxury goods.

Let's look at the first stage in the consumer decision-making process – needs recognition – and discuss how it is affected by cultural differences. Consumers in a high individualism society will purchase luxury products based on their hedonic and functional needs – for the appreciation of the exclusivity, craftsmanship or the history and story behind the brand. Consumers from individualistic cultures are more concerned about the performance of the product than the social status and the prestige of owning the brand (Nayeem, 2012). Research conducted in countries such as USA and Australia showed that consumers in these countries purchased luxury goods for personal gratification and indulgence (Unity marketing, 2014; Ganter, 2013); while consumers from strong collectivism societies will purchase luxury goods for their "show" value –conspicuous consumption in order to gain social recognition and prestige. The majority of consumers in China and India purchase luxury goods for these purposes (Ma, 2010, Puddick & Menon, 2012).

In the second stage of the consumer decision-making process, consumers search for information which will help them to make the purchase decision. In a high individualism society, where people are independent from others and in control of their surrounding environment, consumers are less likely to rely on others in their purchase decisions; they will mainly rely on internal knowledge derived from their personal experiences (Doran, 2002; Nayeem, 2012) or research information on their own by, for example, searching websites, talk to the sales person or go for a test drive. Whereas in a high collectivism society consumers will be more likely to seek the opinions of others regarding what information to collect and which types of sources are valuable to use. This is a consequence of consumers looking for social approval from others, in particular for highly visible and high involvement purchase decisions (Nayeem, 2012). This may involve asking their family, friends or work colleagues for their past experiences and opinions. Research conducted in Australia (Nayeem, 2012) to compare the information search stage of consumer behaviour for luxury automobiles between Asian born and Australian born consumers showed that Asian born consumers (from high collectivism cultures) mainly rely on family and friends for information, while Australian born consumers (from a high individualism culture) primarily depend on information searched online or through sales people.

Once consumers have collected sufficient information, they will need to evaluate and make a selection. In a high individualism society the criteria are more likely to be personal focused – for instance, whether the product fits in with the personal lifestyle, budget or appearance of the consumer; while in a high collectivism society the criteria will be more "other" focused – will the product impress other people, provide more social status or fit in with the group the consumer belongs to. Nagashima (1970) noted that wealthy Japanese bought German cars as these were associated with high social recognition and status.

The purchase decision is then made based on the outcome of the evaluation. The choice consumers make at this stage – the particular brand and product – is not only intended to provide the expected functional or performance benefits, but also can express consumers' backgrounds/values, personality, social status or affiliation (Nayeem, 2012). Consumers choose brands that reflect their own experience, values and, above all, aspirations (Wegrzyn, 2013). Purchasing luxury goods allows consumers to have an aspirational break – luxury embodies the epitome of consumers' desires and aspirations (Wegrzyn, 2013). Buying and using luxury goods helps consumers feel that they are breaking away from their mediocre daily lives and offer them a model of escapism (Wegrzyn, 2013). The brand, the style as well as the store are selected to satisfy the consumer's need and to meet their other selection criteria. In a high individualistic society, the brand may not necessarily be 'super luxury" as long as it suits the person; whereas in a high collectivism society the brand must be well recognised, preferably with a prominent display of logos; it may not suit the person but it serves to impress others (Nayeem, 2012).

The last stage of consumer decision making is also affected by cultural differences – cognitive dissonance may occur in a high individualism society due to concern about internal, personal factors such as fit, colour or mismatch to personal style; while in a high collectivism society doubt or anxiety may occur due to external factors such as friends'/family's disapproval of the purchase or a feeling of non-conformity with the group the person belongs to.

Based on Hefstede's cultural dimension theory (2013), economically more developed countries such as the UK (IDV 89), the USA (IDV 91) and Australia (IDV 90) have typical individualistic cultures; while economically less developed countries like China (IDV 20), Indonesia (IDV 14), Venezuelan (IDV 12) and Thailand (IDV 20) have highly collective cultures. This difference leads to variable patterns of consumer behaviour towards the purchase of luxury goods. This will be demonstrated in the later part of this chapter, when consumer behaviour in specific countries are examined.

The theory serves to guide strategies for the marketing of luxury brands. For example, in collective societies the focus of advertising is about status, symbolism, prestige and other social benefits that the luxury goods can bring to the purchaser; the marketing messages should ideally highlight the social approval and high prestige associated with the purchase of the product. Whilst in individualistic societies the focus should be on product features, design, performance and other functional benefits, as well as on using the internet as the major media for promotional messages (Nayeem, 2012).

Subculture

Subculture is defined as "the groupings based on demographic, geographic or psychographic divisions" (Rix, P. 2011). This part looks at how differences in social class, age, gender, income level and geographic regions affect consumer decision making when purchasing luxury goods.

- **Social Class:** Consumers in each country can be divided into social classes based on their income, education, occupation and area of residence (Rix, P. 2011), and while people from all social classes purchase luxury goods, the reasons for their purchase vary greatly.

Research conducted in China (Ma, 2010) identified three different luxury market segments - super rich, middle class and "overdraft" consumers, with each segment purchasing different types of luxury goods for different motivations. The super -rich consumers have more understanding of luxury brands and do not purchase to aggrandise themselves; they are attracted to high-end luxury goods by their high quality, unique design or special features. The middle-class consumers, however, would consider luxury purchases very carefully, often purchase based on others' recommendations and tends to buy mid to high-end luxury goods. The "overdraft" consumers feel that owning luxury goods helps to build their image as successful people; they tend to spend money on mid to low end luxuries including small hand bags, ties and accessories (Ma, 2010).

- **Regional Differences:** Northern Indians prefer conspicuous consumption through which their social status can be recognised; it's important for them to be noticed when shopping for luxury products, according to Sanjay Kapoor (2010), who has remarked that they get enquiries in their store in Northern India from consumers, asking when the store is most crowded so they can come to shop then and maximise their exposure. Whereas Southern Indians don't like to show their wealth; they call stores to find the least crowded times so they can shop then.

Research has also identified regional differences within China, as noted by the brand Shanghai Tang. When the brand sent vouchers to its VVIPs - consumers spending more than $ HKD 80,000 per year- the consumer in northern China tended to spend four or five times the voucher value, while consumers from southern China would spend as close to the voucher value as possible (KPMG, 2013). The research also noted differences in the symbolism of colour between regions in China in selecting products and developing marketing materials (KPMG, 2013).

In China, major cities such as Beijing and Shanghai have seen market saturation for luxury brands; new growth areas will come from the tier 2 (many of which are provincial capitals such as Chengdu and Wuhan, or important commercial cities such as Tianjing and Shenzhen) and below cities (Chow, 2014).

- **Age:** Age has been found to be a significant predictor for luxury consumption. Pak et al. (2008) believed that the process of younger consumers exhibiting unique social values in their consumption decisions is part of their identity formation. This finding has been supported by research conducted in Korea (Pak et al. 2008), Vietnam (Euromonitor 2014) and China (Wong & Ahuvia, 1998), where young consumers are more attracted to Western luxury brands.

The Chinese luxury market differs from Western ones as people aged between 20 and 40 constitute the main source of luxury consumption, while in Western developed countries people aged between 40 and70 comprise the largest segment for luxury purchases (Wong & Ahuvia, 1998).

More recent data from Passport (2013) showed that luxury consumers' ages vary greatly: in Australia the dominant luxury consumers are in their 60s; in Indonesia the majority of luxury consumers are in their 30s; while in China people aged in their 40s constitutes the majority of luxury consumers.

Overall, in Western countries older consumers – those aged over 60 – are the key customer base for luxury goods, and they certainly cannot be ignored. They fuelled the explosion of luxury markets in the 1990s, and are accustomed to buying luxury goods (Khan, 2010). As the population is aging in many Western countries and in Japan, the size of this market segment is growing rapidly; at the same time these consumers are still in good physical shape, live longer and are still young at heart (Khan, 2010), and they have the disposable income that other market segments in these countries may not have to spend on luxury goods.

- **Gender:** BCG (2010) estimated that women influence 80% of a household's spending on luxury purchases, with much of this their buying for themselves. As a result, womenswear remains the largest category of luxury designer apparel sales. But the trend forecast by Passport (2013) has come to pass – demand for luxury designer menswear has grown strongly. Brands such as Zegna, Burberry and Mulberry have adopted strategies to promote their men's tailoring and bespoke services.

- **Reference Groups:** In high individualistic societies the influence of reference groups such as peers, colleagues and family on luxury purchase decision making is usually insignificant; whereas in high collectivism societies they play very important roles.

Chinese consumers, for example, place group values and interests above individual ones, so before making a purchase decision they usually seek family or friends' opinions. They are also more likely to be influenced by celebrity endorsement of what and where to buy (Lukkarinen & Wei, 2012). Eng and Bohaert (2010) showed that Indian consumers' perceptions of luxury are susceptible to reference efforts, so for them others' opinions are important in choosing the "right" luxury goods. Moroccan consumers also displayed similar behaviour with their luxury consumption being influenced by social representation and their position being associated with luxury processions (Nwankwo, Hamelin & Khaled, 2014).

Psychological Factors

This group of *internal factors* strongly influences the consumer decision-making process when purchasing luxury goods.

Motivation

Motivation is the force that prompts action (Pinder, 1998) and drives people to make purchases (Lukkarinen & Wei, 2012). Shopping itself is a form of self-expression; consumers define themselves through their purchase behaviours – how they shop, where they shop and what they buy demonstrates their feelings, desires and personality, and gives themselves a sense of accomplishment (Tatt, 2010). Buying luxury brands serves various consumer needs and motives such as the desire to portray oneself in a specific social class, communicate a desired self-image and provide self-concept reinforcement, and a visible proof that the consumer can afford higher-priced products (Nia & Zaichkowsky, 2000). Luxury goods have the potential to satisfy private and social, physical and emotional needs.

Apart from functional utility, luxury goods are believed to bring esteem and prestige to the owners (Vigneron & Johnson, 2004). The symbolic and social value associated with luxury consumption may, however, vary across cultures (Wang, Sun and Song, 2011). Purchasing luxury goods is not a simple act of engaging with the product or the brand; it has much deeper meaning for many consumers because it offers them an opportunity to temporarily shift the standpoint from which they relate to the rest of the world. It allows them to adjust temporarily their relationship with the world (Wegrzyn, 2013). Luxury goods have the ability to tap into the human's natural quest for happiness. So obtaining a luxury item after a long wait and which has been difficult to acquire is a landmark in the perpetual pursuit of happiness (Wegrzyn, 2013).

Social motivation explains consumers craving to achieve higher social value and be part of a more elitist class (Vigneron & Johnson, 2004). Jung and Shen (2011) identified status consumption as the motivational process by which individuals strive to improve their social standing through conspicuous consumption, so some consumers purchase luxury goods to assert their social position.

Examples in the following country-specific discussions will demonstrate that consumers from the more mature luxury markets, such as the US, Japan and Europe, tend to have more of the hedonic and perfectionism values. Their luxury consumption is less focused on price as an indicator of prestige; while the luxury consumers in emerging markets such as China, India and Russia tend to place greater emphasis on price as an indicator of prestige because their primary objective of their purchase is to impress others.

Perception

Coco Chanel (1883-1971) has said that "Luxury is a necessity that begins where necessity ends".

What is perceived as "luxury" is subjective and multidimensional; it may differ between individuals, it is situational contingent and depends on the experience and individual needs of the consumer (Wiedmann, Hennings & Siebels, 2007).

To acquire information on consumer motives and value perception, and to offer explanations for luxury consumption, a four-dimensional model was established by Wiedmann, Hennings & Siebels (2007, 2009). The model looks at the financial, functional, individual and social value dimensions of luxury, as displayed in Figure 1:

The financial dimension deals with direct monetary aspects such as price, resale costs, discounts and investment; the functional dimension measures a product's quality, features, usability, reliability

Figure 1. Dimensions of luxury value perceptions
Source: Hennigs, et al., What is the value of luxury? A cross-cultural consumer perspective. Psychology and Marketing, (12): p. 1021 (December, 2012)

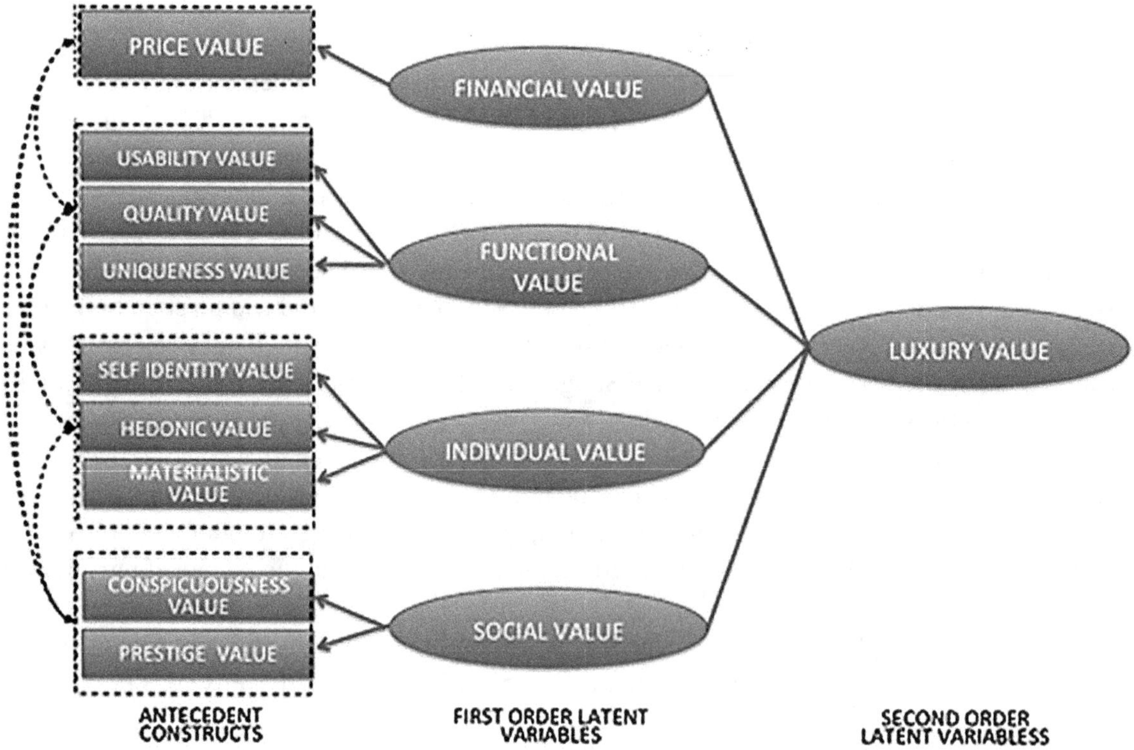

and durability; the individual dimension is based on customers' personal orientations, such as materialism, hedonism and self-identity; and the social dimension focuses on the conspicuousness and prestige consumers acquire by owning the luxury goods (Hennings, Wiedmann & Klarmann, 2013).

A cross-cultural study involving 10 countries in America, Europe and Asia concluded that the conceptualisation of luxury value perception that encompasses the financial, functional, individual and social aspects of luxury brands and products was valid across countries (Hennigs et al., 2012). Further research involving middle income families in America, Europe and Asia concluded that the distinct stage of economic development, the political and legal system and the educational environment means that the luxury value perception encompassing the financial, functional, individual and social aspects of luxury products varies significantly across countries (Hennings, Wiedmann & Klarmann, 2013). This is despite increased global mobility and better communication and media distribution contributing to the homogeneity of the world (so that the perceived importance of the four value dimensions would be expected to be cross-cultural stable). For example, in the purchase of luxury cars, Italians believe that financial aspects are the most important concern while Indians think social aspect are the top priority; for fashion and accessories, Spaniards do not put much social value on such acquisitions, Italians consider the functional aspects to be the most important factor, and Japanese believe that individual aspects are the priority (Hennings, Wiedmann & Klarmann, 2013).

Luxury is not a concept based on rationality; luxury consumers do not make purchase decisions based purely on the assessment of product quality. For example: the cost of a Hermes bag (which will be between £10,000 and 100,000 pounds) is certainly far more than a handbag can rationally be 'worth". The role of luxury goods therefore is not to make life easier but rather to fulfil deep desires (Wegrzyn, 2013). There can be a long waiting period to acquire some luxury items;, this, added to the desire for the product, gives purchasers a sense of achievement when the item finally arrives.

Luxury brands producers need to understand that the whole concept of luxury is illogical; appealing to consumers' rationality will not be effective (Wegrzyn, 2013). Luxury is a lifestyle, and many luxury brands are making efforts to build an entire lifestyle experience around their core identity in order to retain their loyal customers and to attract new customers – Amani has opened a luxury hotel resort in Dubai; Bulgari, well known for its jewellery, has successfully established a chain of resorts in London, Bali and Milan, with another to be set up in Shanghai in 2015; and Versace is planning to build a casino resort in Macau (Ko, 2013).

Attitude

Attitude has been identified as an important dimension of consumer psychographics, and as a focus for market segmentation analysis (Belch and Belch, 2009). Consumers from collectivistic cultures may hold different beliefs and attitudes towards luxury consumptions, compared with consumers from individualistic cultures.

Research (Wang, Sun & Song, 2011) into Chinese luxury consumers' attitudes identified three different market segments: *the elitists* believe that luxury products should be owned only by few well-educated people with good taste; they tend to buy luxury goods for self-actualisation, social comparison and special occasions. The *democratic* group tend to believe that everyone should be able to have access to luxury goods, which should not be reserved for 'refined", well-educated people. This group also believe that luxury goods can be mass produced and should be available in supermarkets. The third group is the *distance* group, which are the consumers who believe that luxury belongs in a different world, one in which they do not belong; they will buy luxury products only for others as gifts.

Situational Factors

Situational factors include temporary characteristics of the individual that are induced by the environment, such as time pressure or a too crowed store (Neal, Quester & Hawkins, 1999). These *temporary factors* affect consumer purchase decisions.

Where Consumers Buy

Many luxury good purchases are made by consumers on international visits where product choices can be better and the prices lower. Some consumers are also beginning to purchase luxury products online in order to get better deals.

Luxury brands have enjoyed the benefit of favourable global tourism trends; the fast growing middle class in emerging economies has benefited sales in the more developed countries such as the US and Europe, where luxury brands have the strongest presence. Travel by these consumers is boosting luxury products' sales. This phenomenon is not only attributed to the superior product selection and availability in the world capitals, but more importantly better prices due to high import tariffs in the travellers home countries, (Deloitte, 2014). US, France and the UK were the favourite shopping destinations, especially for BRIC (Brazil, Russia, India and China) travellers, with Chinese global shoppers being the highest spending nationality and Russians the second (Deloitte, 2014). Luxury stores such as London's Harrods have installed Chinese credit card readers and have seen significant sales increases (Deloitte, 2014).

Consumers from many countries, particularly the emerging economies of China and India, prefer to purchase luxury goods while travelling. The rising prosperity and awareness of the outside world through exposure to books, films and news from the West, as well as the easing of official restrictions on foreign travel, have allowed millions of Chinese consumers to fulfil their ambitions to see the world and to shop for the luxury goods that may not be available in China, or are too expensive (The Economist Intelligence Unit, 2013).

Passport (2013) projected that much of the luxury goods market growth in the developed world will be driven by mainland Chinese and Russians, who are frequent visitors to luxury hotspots and who regard them mainly as shopping destinations. Their domestic prices for luxury goods can be 30-50% higher than in Europe and Hong Kong, due to high levels of consumption tax (Passport, 2013).

WTO information reveals that China has surpassed Germany and the US as the world's largest source of tourism by expenditure. In 2012, the number of international trips by Chinese travellers exceeded 83 million, with 90% of them being under the age of 45. The WTO estimated that the number of Chinese travelling overseas will exceed 100 million annually by 2015, and the average traveller spends 34% of their travel budget on shopping.

What Consumers Buy

Depending on the country, the culture, the subculture, etc. consumers purchase different luxury products for different purposes. Consumers in some areas spend more on luxury cars or watches; others may spend more on apparel or cosmetics.

Chinese luxury consumption is item-driven or product-driven; the consumption is more focussed on personal products such as cosmetics, bags, jewellery and watches, while in more developed markets consumers tend to seek experience through luxury family vacations and time saving services (Wang, Sun and Song, 2011).

Bain's study (2014) identified that accessories are expected to be the strongest driver of luxury market performance, followed by jewellery, watches and other "hard" luxury goods. D'Arpizio (2014) found that beauty products and apparel will have modest growth while men's bags and apparel will have the greatest momentum.

Consumer Behaviour by Country and Region

Consumer behaviour is culturally specific; knowledge about consumers in one country may not be totally useful for planning marketing activities in another, because luxury buying behaviour tends to vary significantly across countries (Lukkarinen & Wei, 2012).

In this part, some country/regional specific consumer behaviour in luxury goods markets is presented, using statistics and case studies. The strategic marketing implications for the promotion of luxury goods in some countries/regions are also discussed.

Europe

The traditional luxury houses are primarily from France and Italy, with a rich history and long heritage of craftsmanship in product categories such as fashion, leather goods and accessories (e.g. Louis Vuitton, Gucci and Chanel). Many other luxury goods are also homed in Europe such as cars (Ferrari), jewellery (Cartier) and watches (Rolex) (Wiedmann, Hennings & Siebels, 2007). Being the origin of many global luxury brands, European consumers tend to have a better understanding of luxury brands' histories and stories. Their purchase behaviour tends to be more rational, selective and for their own enjoyment.

Western Europe

Passport's data (2013) shows that Western Europe accounted for 32% of world luxury sales in 2012, which has made it the biggest region in value terms. The Eurozone economic crisis is the source of the greatest risk to global luxury goods growth, Spain and the Netherlands were among the worst performing luxury markets globally but Italy, Germany and France showed resilience, due in large measure to cash rich tourists' shopping and the increased penetration of affordable luxury goods and their diffusion brands (Passport, 2013). The UK luxury goods industry is also under fierce pressure, as inflation climbs and wages are frozen, which has prompted the middle class to trade down in their choice of goods (Passport, 2013).

Cross-cultural research (Hennigs et al., 2012) showed that French consumers place higher value on the financial dimension of luxury goods, and believe that few people own a truly luxury product. German consumers, on the other hand, are more focused on the functional dimension of luxury goods; they will not buy luxury goods that do not meet their own quality standard; Spanish and Italian luxury consumers purchase whatever product they like and are not concerned about what others think of them (Hennigs et al., 2012).

As the home to most of the world's luxury brands, Europe attracts large numbers of tourists and shoppers, these tourists spend a high percentage of their travel budget purchasing luxury goods. Bain's study (2014) showed that Western Europe can expect continuing strong tourist luxury shopping, with a strong influx of Chinese and Middle Eastern shoppers, but fewer Russian and Japanese.

Eastern Europe

Passport (2013) believed that Eastern European markets offered the opportunity for luxury goods sales despite a strong saving culture, as consumer confidence was running high among an expanding middle class. However, substantial differences exist between countries, indicative of uneven levels of income, spending powers and attitudes. For example, Polish consumers tend to spend rather than save during crises, whilst Romanian consumers' luxury spending slowed down dramatically during the Global Financial Crisis (Passport, 2013).

Russia

After the collapse of the Soviet Union, luxury goods became available to ordinary people in Russia, as long as they had the money to pay for them. With a rapid increase in the middle class, the consumption of luxury goods in Russia became a salient social phenomenon (Kaufmann, Vrontis & Manakova, 2012). However, the Russian market is highly polarised between the rich and the poor, as well as along regional lines, Moscow bears strong resemblance to other luxury goods capitals such as Milan and Paris in its luxury markets, but the regional middle class has only limited purchasing power (Passport, 2013).

Kaufmann, Vrontis and Manakova (2012) argue that Russian luxury consumers are the most glaring example of the concept of conspicuous consumption and status-seeking. Well-to-do Russians generally like to spend their money for ostentatious purposes and because their wealth has been acquired over a short period of time, there is a lack of personal financial management culture in the country (Peshkova 2013). Also, in an economically volatile society such as Russia consumers believe that saving money for the future is not a safe choice (Kaufmann, Vrontis & Manakova, 2012). Another important factor is that many successful business people are in their 30s and 40s; they grew up in an environment where there was limited supply of consumer goods. Now they have money, exaggerated consumption and a desire to show-off is a natural psychological response to their past (Peshkova, 2013).

Research conducted by Kaufmann, Vrontis and Manakova (2012) concluded that there was a positive relationship between the purchasing of luxury goods and consumers' need for uniqueness, status and personal identity in Russia. Although most Russians want to avoid similarity in purchases, they also want possessions which symbolise personal and social identity. In particular, the concept of identity has significant bearing on luxury goods consumption in Russia; they use luxury goods purchases to show the rest of the world who they are (Kaufmann, Vrontis & Manakova, 2012).

As the country's economy develops and more luxury brands are becoming available, Russians have turned into more sophisticated consumers. They are well travelled therefore are fully aware of the broad range of international luxury brands (Peshkova, 2013).

Bain's recent study (2014), however, forecast that the luxury goods market in Russia will suffer a strong contraction, due to political instability, a deteriorating economy and devaluation of the Russian currency.

USA

The US luxury market remains the world's largest and accounts for over a quarter of the overall value of luxury goods sales in 2012 (Passport, 2013). Sales of personal luxury goods were estimated at €62.5 billion ($71.35 billion USD) in 2013 (Unity Marketing, 2014).

American affluent consumers are becoming more selective, more pragmatic, more demanding and much more careful about what luxury brands they buy and how much they spend (Unity Marketing, 2014). Research shows that in today's luxury market, consumers' income demographics are less important than psychographic factors, ie which describe one's willingness to spend, and that is more influenced by the consumer's age. High income ($US 250K+) and younger (under 45) are the highest –spending consumer group in the luxury market today (Unity Marketing, 2014).Their purchases are focused on home luxuries, personal luxuries and automobiles/experiential luxuries.

Excellent customer service has greatest significant impact on American luxury consumers. Research (Edwards, G. & Probst, E. 2011) showed that one in three luxury consumers consider highly trained employees to be the most important factor when making a luxury purchase. The same research also showed that as a strongly individualistic society American luxury consumers obtain purchase information mainly by researching online (71%), followed by visits to stores (57%), reading online reviews (48%), speaking with the sales person (44%), and, lastly, seeking advice from friends and family (27%) (Edwards, G. & Probst, E. 2011) .

Unity Marketing's *Luxury Report 2014* established a psychographic profile of five distinctive luxury market segments, which provides a guide for understanding the US luxury brands market.

1. Extremely affluent who spend the most on luxury and is mostly likely invested in luxury living.
2. Butterflies that have emerged from their luxury cocoons with a passion to reconnect with the outside world. They are less materialistic but have strong spending potential for the right brand experience.
3. Luxury Cocooners who focus their luxury spending on home-related purchases.
4. Aspirers who have not yet achieved the level of luxury to which they aspire; they are more materialistic and believe that what they own is who they are.
5. Temporary Pragmatists who in general are not involved in luxury lifestyles but may have the potential to become luxury consumers in the future.

Bain's study (2014) projected strong growth in the US luxury goods market, due to a strong economy and a large influx of tourists. The major growth will be focused on European brands, leather goods, jewelry and men's wear (D'Arpizio, 2014). Around 50% of US luxury consumers have shopped online (Edwards, G. & Probst, E. 2011).

Asia

Asia is the most populous continent, with its 4.3 billion inhabitants accounting for 60% of the world population. The world's two most populated countries, China and India, together constitute about 37% of the world's population.

With a younger demographic, fast growing middle class and increased international travel opportunities for duty free purchases, Asia is the fastest growing market for luxury goods. Research shows that currently there are over 900 million affluent consumers and there will be an increase of over a billion in Asia over the next decade. This is a group no luxury brands can afford to ignore (Chow, 2013). In particular, a new generation of aspirational, ambitious and affluent young Asians (aged between 18 and 34) who are working hard and then rewarding themselves with luxury products is becoming a major purchasing force in the luxury goods market (Chow, 2013). Passport's statistics (2013) showed that India, China, Malaysia and Indonesia were the four fastest growing markets for luxury goods in 2012.

Research suggests that Asian's luxury consumption is mainly influenced by factors such as Confucian collectivism, individual or group needs and the value attached to being modest and thrifty (Wang, Sun and Song, 2011). They further noticed that Asians are more likely to place importance on the symbolic value as opposed to the hedonic value of luxury goods, especially under conditions of consuming in public. Consumers in Asia purchase luxury goods to secure social recognition and to show their status because the culture emphasizes hierarchy and status (Gao et al., 2009).

Passport (2013) believed that Asia Pacific remains the most dynamic region in the luxury goods industry, with a forecast growth rate almost twice that of any other region.

However as Asia is so large, consumers in Asia are heterogeneous. Mature and economically developed markets such as Japan, Hong Kong and Singapore are more sophisticated while developing markets such as China and India require more nurturing.

China

Global economic growth is increasingly driven by trends in China. Over the past two decades China has seen the penetration of the Western lifestyle and the rise of consumer buying power, so it is becoming an attractive market for all luxury brands (Wang, Sun & Song, 2011). According to a report by Fortune Character Institute (2014), Chinese consumers bought 47% of all world purchases of luxury goods in 2013, with total spending of $ US102 billion. Despite of the GFC there was still an annual increase of 3% in 2013.

Overtaking the UK in 2011, China became the fifth largest market in the world's luxury goods consumption rankings (Passport, 2013). However more than half of Chinese luxury goods purchase occurs outside of China (in 2013 China displaced Germany and the US to become the world's largest source of tourism by expenditure). Most of the purchases were made in Hong Kong and Macao, while less than 40% took place in mainland China (Research report, 2013).

A comparative study by Lukkarinen and Wei (2012) found that within its highly collective culture, Chinese consumers tend to place group values and interests above individual ones; therefore when making luxury goods purchases Chinese consumers are usually very concerned about other's opinions and attitudes. This not only includes family and friends but also celebrities and other opinion leaders. By following other people's opinions the consumers hope to gain social acceptance, recognition and status.

Over the last three decades, as the economy has developed, consumer behaviour changed dramatically. Traditionally, China is a high collectivism society. So for a long period of time the predominant motive for purchasing luxury goods was ostentation, status and social recognition. As its culture changes Chinese consumers are becoming more independent and individualistic; the attitude is changing from ostentation to rational luxury goods consumption with a more mature consumption concept. The Chinese luxury goods market is expected to show steady growth in the future (Research report, 2013).

Another source of luxury demand comes from the social obligation of gift giving (Ma, 2010). Gift giving is ingrained in Chinese culture (Walker, 2013). Consuming expensive gits reflects the social hierarchy as well as maintenance of the balance between group needs and individual needs (Wong & Ahuvia, 1998). The strong collective ties are reflected through the ritual of gift-giving, and luxury goods are recognised symbols to communicate esteem for the recipient and thus bring honour to the giver (Ma, 2010).

A large proportion of the luxury goods purchased by Chinese are for gift-giving., Recipients include government officials, where the gift is intended to smooth pathways for business deals, or other "Guanxi" (interpersonal ties or connections) to develop or maintain social networks for the future. They also include family and friends in order to gain "face" or recognition.

Chinese culture values harmonious interpersonal relationships so gift or favour exchange contributes significantly to the maintenance and expansion of such relationships (Wang, Sun & Song, 2011). Chinese consumers tend to believe that the more expensive the gift, the more recognition will be gained, the more "face" will be obtained and a better relationship will be developed (Wang, Sun & Song, 2011). As a result, Louis Vuitton, Cartier and Hermes are the top three gift selections for Chinese (Walker, 2013). Although the Chinese Government's crackdown on corruption in the past two years has reduced demand, the gift-giving culture will continue though at a lower level.

Chinese consumers pay close attention to the brand name and country of origin of luxury goods, and tend to prefer well known foreign luxury brands with popular logos (Wang, Sun & Song, 2011). Instead of buying 'the right products' Chinese consumers tend to buy 'the expensive ones' in order to impress others or to gain social status (Ma, 2010).

Research shows that Chinese luxury consumers tend to be younger (20 to 40) than with Western luxury goods consumers. The older generation values saving and being thrift, and while the younger generation may not always have purchasing power, it is prepared to go "overdraft' to purchase items that help improve their self-image and social status.

Research also indicated that in the last few years changes are occurring with Chinese luxury consumers: as the consumers are becoming younger and better educated, the luxury consumption culture and patterns are changing. They are following the familiar pattern of economies as they develop with a growing middle class so that the luxury consumption is shifting from goods to experience, including travel (Barley, E. 2014). For affluent consumers, quality is becoming more important than quantity; they want to consume the best brands and services available for the money they can afford in order to satisfy their desire for a "lifestyle upgrade" (Chow, 2014).

This change also encompasses consumers looking for more differentiated products, to aid them in standing out from the crowd. It is estimated that 80% of luxury consumers use online research to source information before buying a luxury item, but the purchases are rarely made online as people enjoy the shopping experience. It is a part of the process of buying expensive brands (Chow, 2014). Although consumers in China are becoming more individualistic and more discerning, they are still buying luxury products as a confirmation of social success (KPMG, 2013)

Bain study, "Luxury goods worldwide market study, Spring 2014", projected that China's international purchasing patterns and consumer profiles would evolve rapidly, with significant tourist flows to all regions of the world. D'Arpizio (2014) predicted that China's spending growth on luxury goods would be the fastest in Asia Pacific.

According to Passport (2013), the main reasons for Chinese shopping for luxury goods overseas are: availability - many luxury labels are not available in China and, in particular, many second and third tier cities have limited access to luxury goods; price - many international luxury brands choose to price their products higher in China in order to create a feeling of exclusivity in the world's most populated country, and there is a higher sales tax imposed on luxury items; status – although the number of Chinese who travel internationally has increased dramatically, compared with its large population base the travellers are still a minority; so, travelling overseas is a symbol of status and the ability to show off by purchasing luxury items exclusive to international outlets adds the glamour (Passport, 2013).

Japan

Japan is the second largest luxury goods market in the world. Being a high collectivism society with a well-developed economy and strong western influence, Japanese consumers display unique buying behaviours. Unlike in the West, where luxury branded goods are an expression of social class, income and refined taste allowing consumers to distinguish themselves from the mainstream, in Japan luxury branded goods represent the mainstream (Howard et al., 2007). Japanese consumers are willing to pay high prices for quality products, and their love of brands sparked the emergence of a mass-luxury market where owning expensive, exclusive products seemed essential rather than aspirational (Salsberg, 2010). Over the years luxury goods in Japan evolved from status symbols into social codes, identifying the owner as belonging to the larger collective group (Howard et al., 2007).

Although the Japanese luxury goods market is shrinking due to a combination of changing demographics and a stagnant economy, McKinsey and Company's research (2013) notes that Japanese consumers remain some of the most discerning, loyal and important luxury customers in the world. Renowned for their appreciation of craftsmanship and quality, Japanese luxury shoppers are also looking for products that will hold their value over time and that offer value commensurate with their price. Research data collected over three decades by Japan Market Research Network on luxury goods purchasing behaviour show five trends in this market (Howard et al., 2007).

1. From "me too" to "me first". In an era of individualism, consumers are seeking out unique products regardless of price. As a result traditionally popular luxury brand such as Louis Vuitton are losing momentum to unique brand such as Bottega Vaneta.
2. Consumers are looking for enriched brand experiences that involve their mind, body and soul. Japanese consumers have always expected exceptional interpersonal service and are seeking much deeper connections with the brands they purchase. To cater for this trend many luxury brands are offering limited and special editions in Japanese market, as well as signature cafe (Mercedes-Benz, Cadillac), spa (Cosme Decorte), restaurant (Chanel), Bar (Baccarat Crystal) or special events to make their consumers feel special (Bollen & Salsberg, 2013).
3. Diversity in brand lifestyle. With a combination of increased confidence, shifting life stage priorities and an adapted definition of value, Japanese consumers are increasingly mixing "high" and "low' lifestyles, and accepting that less expensive brands can also deliver value in terms of quality and functionality. This means a person can drive a BMW but shop at a 100Yen shop; or carry a Louis Vuitton bag but wear Uniqlo coordinates.
4. Authenticity matters. Luxury brands commanded a premium based on the promise of high quality linked to country –specific artisan skills. However, in the past decade many luxury brands (Burberry, Celine, and Louis Vuitton) have moved their manufacturing facilities to China. Japanese consumers believe that "a brand's tradition is important to its value", so there is already evidence that Japanese consumers will not continue to pay premiums for luxury products made in China.
5. Japanese luxury consumers are highly technological; they live online and want to see their favourite brands there. Many luxury brands are quick to take measures to meeting these customers' needs. Burberry Japan actively manages search engine optimization; Cosme Decorte, Estee Lauder and Cartier direct consumers from paper based (such as magazine ads) to online mobile pages using QR codes; and Ermenegido Zegna has used tablet computers like iPad to show customers how custom order suits and jackets will look when combined with a specific shirt or tie. Social media is also

widely used by luxury brands in Japan in order to engage with the customer: Louis Vuitton Japan uses tailored and localized social media to connect with its customers; Mercedes-Benz leverages external bloggers in Japan to write about their products; and Gucci makes use of Smartphone apps and YouTube to keep their customers interested (Bollen & Salsberg, 2013).

Bain's study (2014) estimated that the growth in Japan's luxury goods market will be reasonably positive, due to the currency devaluation which is spurring record growth in local markets.

India

Worth $US8.5 billion in 2013, the Indian luxury goods market managed a growth rate of 25-30% in 2013 (Chaturvedi, 2014). A young demographic profile, increasing disposable incomes and a heightened awareness of brands, as well as a burgeoning urban middle class with a penchant for Western brands, are all helping to fuel a spurt in the country's luxury goods market (Roberts, 2014).

Affected by Indian traditions entwined with a strong British influence, India's consumers display some distinctive characteristics when purchasing luxury goods, informed by regional differences, culture, levels of wealth and experience. For example, the Indian culture is less individualistic compared with Western countries, so the purchase decision for important items such as luxury goods is usually shared among family or friends. It is particularly relevant when the luxury item is purchased for a wedding (Puddick & Menon, 2012). Weddings in India have deep cultural significance and are regarded as one of the primary touch points with luxury. As family and guests spend days celebrating it is a good opportunity to exhibit their wealth and status through the possession and display of luxury goods.

Regional differences is another important factor as the country is geographically large; northern Indians indulge more in luxury spending, as they communicate their status in society through conspicuous consumption. Lavish possessions such as jewellery and cars are used to demonstrate their wealth (Puddick & Menon, 2012). The southern Indian is more subtle in their luxury spending. As intellectual strength has been historically prized by southerners, there is a greater tendency towards knowledge and appreciation of the luxury products than use of them to self-aggrandise (Puddick & Menon, 2012).

Similar to other emerging markets, Indians in their 30s and early 40s are the highest income earners in the country; they are the driving force behind the consumer expenditure growth and demand for luxury products (Roberts, 2014). To target this particular market, BMW positioned itself as an aspirational brand in India, redesigning its market strategy to give its vehicles a youthful image so as to connect with the younger demographic (Chaturvedi, 2014).

The traditional Indian custom of personal adornment has led to strong demand for luxury accessories, luxury jewellery and timepieces and designer clothing and footwear (Roberts, 2014). Embellishment and decoration has been a sign of wealth and prosperity throughout Indian history and complements traditional Indian attire (Puddick & Menon, 2012).

Brand such as Swarovski are doing well in selling jewelry, diamonds and other accessories in India. As with the affluent class in all emerging economies, luxury goods are perceived as an investment in India. Research by Kearney (2011) found that luxury consumers in India devoting a great share of their income to the purchase of jewelry, with this decision being mostly influenced by the increasing prices of gold and diamonds. Value-conscious shopping is ingrained in Indian culture; they are unashamedly value seeking, know the price of items in different markets and will shop around for the best deal. Rooted in India culture is an understanding of the value of products that are precious, exotic, rare and handcrafted. An item is considered to be more luxurious if it is purchased abroad; buying brands from their country of origin means more prestige (Puddick & Menon, 2012). Most wealthy Indians travel overseas frequently, they have access to luxury shopping destinations globally and with import tariffs of up to 30%, luxury goods are usually cheaper outside India. Wealthy Indians are privileged enough to travel, so buying luxury goods from their source of origin means more value for money but also provides them with a heightened sense of legitimacy (Puddick & Menon, 2012).

Euromonitor International has predicted that India will achieve the fastest real growth in luxury goods sales of all emerging markets between 2014 and 2018 (Roberts, 2014), providing great opportunities for luxury brands. However, luxury brands need to look at the changes taking place in India's luxury goods market, and provide not only quality products but also exquisite individual services. They need to relate to local culture and heritage; tap into the Indian love for celebration; connect with the digital age; and not just focus on the big cities (Puddick & Menon, 2012). The potential market for luxury goods in India is huge and the future for luxury goods brands is very positive.

Australia

A small market in comparison with the USA, Europe, Japan or China, the Australian luxury goods market is valued at $9 billion Australian dollars ($US7.1 billion) in 2013. This includes designer clothing, footwear and beauty products, as well as designer luggage and handbags (Ganter, 2013). In the past the supply chain and logistical issues of reaching the Australian market deterred many international luxury brands, but since 2011 many have moved into Australia and are serving the Australian market effectively (O'Rourke, 2012).

The growing retail presence in Australia of many new global luxury brands indicates the viability of the luxury market. There has been a marked increase in the number of luxury brands opening in Australia; and a substantial expansion of well-established brands which are moving into larger retail premises and/or to other retail centres. Louis Vuitton, Chanel, Prada, Gucci and Burberry have all considerably expanded their retail floor space in the country recently.

The luxury market boom in Australia is particularly significant in the resource-rich states – Queensland and Western Australia. These saw international luxury brands such as Zegna, Salvatore Ferragamo, Bulgari, Gucci, Chanel and Hermes opening stores in central Brisbane and Chanel and Prada opening stores in Perth (O'Rourke, 2012).

Research conducted by the Director of MO Luxury, Melinda O'Rourke (2012), indicates that today's Australians are more knowledgeable about luxury brands than ten years ago, and there is a democratisation of luxury goods in Australia (such that they are no longer the privilege of just a wealthy elite, but available to a wider middle class with a growing disposable income) which is the key driver to growth in the sector. It also found that the Australian luxury market proved to be resilient to the global downturn. In 2009, against the global luxury industry's decline in sales, the market in Australia experienced growth of 22% for fashion and accessories and 14% for watches and fine jewellery. The research also identified a rise in the number of luxury consumers within the segments 29 years old and younger, as well as the 30-39 years old segment, whilst a slight decrease in the old consumer aged 50-59 (O'Rourke, 2012).

The 2013 Travel and Tourism Competitiveness Index (TTCI) reveal that Australia ranked third in the world in terms of travel and tourism competitiveness. As an attractive tourist destination, it receives large and fast growing numbers of tourist, especially from Asian countries such as China and Indonesia (O'Rourke, 2012). Asian visitors contribute 30-40% of luxury goods sales in Australia. They spend large amount buying luxury goods to take home as gifts (O'Rourke, 2012).

Middle East and Africa

Consumers in Middle Eastern countries such as the United Arab Emirates, Qatar and Oman have high disposable incomes and the means to buy luxury products. Data published by the World Bank show that some of the Middle Eastern countries have high per capita income, for example, Qatar ($ US136,727), Kuwait ($US88,259), UAE ($US59,842) and Oman ($US45,797). The tradition of Arabian extravagance, the influence of Western lifestyle combined with the economic benefits of their oil reserves have contributed to Middle Eastern countries develop a consumption culture which favours Western produced luxury goods.

Most GCC (Gulf Cooperation Council) markets possess a "label me" culture, where brands are regarded as symbols of social status and success (Battern, 2013). This culture has created a strong demand for luxury brands, and as a result all major luxury brands have presence in this market.

In the Arab world, the display of wealth is a social indicator (O'Cass and Frost, 2002). Individuals are especially concerned about the impression they make on others in society, so luxury goods which enhance their physical appearance become a means to gain approval from society (O'Cass & Frost, 2002). The consumer motivation therefore for purchasing luxury goods is primarily to satisfy the need for social recognition. Consumers in the UAE display their social status and wealth through wearing highly visible items such as Rolex watches or driving Ferraris (Vel. et al., 2011).

Researchers have identified that Middle Eastern consumers are highly materialistic; they consider possessions and money symbols of success and an important source of personal happiness and social status (Predergast & Wong, 2003). Conspicuous consumption is undertaken to improve one's status and social class. Research has revealed that those who clearly show wealth are rewarded with favoured treatment by their social contacts (Vel. et al., 2011). As a result, designer clothing and footwear is the largest market segment for luxury goods sold in the Middle East, with Louis Vuitton, Gucci, Chanel, Christian Dior and Burberry being the most popular luxury fashion brands. Bottega Veneta, Longchamp, Salvatore Ferragamo, Bally and many other luxury brands have also expanded their retail presence in the Middle Eastern market. Swarovski has nine locations in the UAE alone, because Swarovski Crystal Elements are a very popular embellishment for the women's traditional abayas and sheilas, mobile phones and even cars, as they are visible signs of wealth.

Social class is another factor which affects the consumption of luxury goods in the Middle East. An individual's purchases symbolises his/her social class, and many Middle Easterners prefer to be associated with either their own social class or the social class they aspire to (Park et al., 2002). They purchase brands that convey affluence, wealth and style, and view global luxury brands as symbols of all of these.

Family is the central pillar around which factors such as personality, religious beliefs and ethics are built (Barakat, 1993). It also plays a prominent role in purchase decision making as the choice of goods is a reflection of a family's standing in society. Family members are considered to be the main reference group when it comes to making purchase decisions for luxury goods. When any decision has to be made, the entire family and its reputation are taken into consideration (Vel. et al., 2011).

Opinion leadership is another factor affecting the consumption of luxury goods in the Middle East. Arabic culture is high collective (with the UAE's Individualism Index being 25) and word of mouth is a major means of marketing communications. When consumers decide to purchase a new luxury product, they are most likely seeking advice from a friend who knows what and where to buy. Celebrity endorsement also helps consumer decision making on the purchase of luxury goods.

Passport's data (2013) indicated that the Middle East and Africa were the second most dynamic regions in terms of luxury consumption over the period of 2007-2012, and demand in the regions is forecasted to grow by 37% over the five years from 2012.

Why Consumers Buy Counterfeit Luxury Goods

Counterfeit goods are any kind of unauthorized product that infringes upon intellectual property rights - brand names, patents, trademarks, and copyright (Chakraborty et al., 1996).

Although Nia and Zaichkowski (2000) noted that the majority of consumers "did not believe that counterfeits decrease the demand for original, luxury brand name products" (Nia & Zaichowski 2000, 494), the significant growth in luxury consumption has in fact been accompanied by an increase in pirated and counterfeited goods, which account for about 10% of total world trade (Hennigs, et al., 2012).

Globalisation means that consumers as far apart as those in Shanghai, London, Mumbai and Moscow are now completely familiar with luxury brands; they want these brands but many cannot afford to purchase the legitimate items. This has given rise to the supply of counterfeit products (Chaudhry & Zimmerman, 2013).

The Guardian (2014) reported that in Europe alone almost 40 million products were impounded by EU customs in 2012, with an estimated value of €1bn ($US1.14 Billion), according to the EU Commission's annual report on customs actions. It stated that counterfeit goods have gone mainstream in countries like UK, a report by PricewaterhouseCoopers (PwC) reveals that British adults admitting that they regularly buy fake designer clothes, bags, accessories and perfumes (The Guardian, 2014). The less affluent buy more fakes and young people are more likely to buy counterfeit goods.

Research on Chinese consumers confirmed that their attitude towards counterfeit goods affects their willingness to buy such goods. The study found a relationship between consumer vanity characteristics and intention to purchase counterfeits (Sheng, et al., 2012). And because the main counterfeit objects in China are well-known Western brands, Chinese consumers may hold the view that consuming counterfeit goods made by domestic enterprises is somehow supporting local businesses (Sheng, et al., 2012).

Other research has found that integrity has no significant negative impact for emerging countries, such as China and Romania, where trademark law was established only recently and its implementation is somewhat sporadic. The availability of typically low-priced counterfeits lowers the reference price for genuine brands in the consumer's mind (Swoboda et al. 2014).

Chaudhry and Zimmerman (2013) suggest that consumers are willing to buy counterfeit products even when they know the products are fake, the reasons include a perception that the counterfeit goods are as good as the authentic versions; support for the counterfeit market as a means of expressing anti big business sentiments; and lax attitudes about the legal protection of intellectual property (Tom et al., 1998). Some research (Eisend & Schuchert-Guler, 2006) has suggested that both demographic and psychographic variables can identify the types of consumers who are more receptive to counterfeit products.

More recent research has concluded that demographics and national origins are poor predictors. Rather, product features such as price and quality as well as the purchase situation and mood have the greatest impact on consumer attitudes towards the purchase of counterfeit products (Chaudhry & Stumpf, 2011).

FUTURE RESEARCH DIRECTIONS

As the luxury goods market continues to expand globally, it is crucial for marketers to understand the consumer decision making process and the factors influencing their purchase decision. Culture may well be the single most important factor for luxury brands as it directly and indirectly affects consumer motivation, perception and attitudes. In a global economy where consumer demands for luxury goods is ever changing, and in which low-cost counterfeits are easily available, luxury brands marketers should identify and concentrate on the specific value dimensions which are regarded as the most important drivers of consumption for luxury goods. They should use this knowledge to aid the design of their controllable marketing mix elements, in order to address the different consumers groups across the globe and continue to grow the luxury goods market.

CONCLUSION

This chapter provides readers with an overview of the global consumer behaviour in luxury goods markets; research findings presented in this chapter clearly identified the impact of different culture, subculture, consumer motivation, perception, attitude and situational factors on luxury consumer behaviours around the world. As the global luxury goods market continues to grow, more challenges are presented to the luxury brands; many luxury brands are taking steps to address these factors in order to provide better satisfaction to their consumers.

REFERENCES

Adams, R. (2011). The utility of prestige: Chinese and American hedonic ratings of prestige goods. *Journal of Global Marketing*, *24*(4), 287–304. doi:10.1080/08911762.2011.602320

Barakat, H. (1993). The Arab family and the challenge of social transportation. In H. Mighissi (Ed.), *Women and Islam: critical concepts in Sociology*. Routledge.

Barley, E. (2014). Understanding the Chinese luxury market: three competing notions of self-worth. *Warc*. Retrieved January 3, 2015, from http://www.warc.com/Content/ContentViewer.aspx?MasterContentRef=ba80d55d-ee0e-47d0-a37c-80b98b22c8fb&CID=A103222&PUB=EVENT-REPORTS

Batten, A. (2013). *UAE Luxury goods market boosted by strong taste for designer clothing, Passport*. Euromoniteor International.

Belch, G., & Belch, M. (2009). *Advertising and promotions, an integrated marketing communications perspective*. New York: McGraw Hill Irwin.

Bellaiche, J-M., Mei-Pochtler, A., & Hanisch, D. (2010). *The new world of luxury, caught between growing momentum and lasting change*. The Boston Consulting Group.

Bollen, K., & Salsberg, B. (2013). *Luxury goods in Japan: 2013 preview*. McKinsey and Company.

Brink, A., & Berndt, A. (2009). *Relationship marketing and customer relationship management*. Juta Publications.

Brun, A., & Castelli, C. (2013). The nature of luxury: A consumer perspective. *International Journal of Retail & Distribution Management*, *41*(11/12), 823–847. doi:10.1108/IJRDM-01-2013-0006

Cateora, P. R., Sullivan Mort, G., D'Souza, C., Taghian, M., Weerawardena, J., & Graham, J. (2012). International Marketing (2E). Melbourne: McGraw Hill.

Catry, B. (2003). The great pretenders. *Business Strategy Review*, *14*(3), 10–17. doi:10.1111/1467-8616.00267

Chakraborty, G., Allred, A. T., & Bristol, T. (1996). Exploring consumers' evaluations of counterfeits: The roles of country of origin and ethnocentrism. *Journal of Advances in Consumer Research*, *23*, 379–384.

Chang, L. Y. (2014, February 21). China world's biggest luxury consumer, *China Daily*.

Chaturvedi, P. (2014). The changing face of India luxury. *Warc*. Retrieved January 4, 2015, from https://www.warc.com/Content/ContentViewer.aspx?MasterContentRef=2d8ac3e1-17e0-4c5b-9ad1-a324a1a5a42d&CID=A102922&PUB=EVENT-REPORTS

Chaudhry, P., & Stumpf, S. A. (2011). Consumer complicity with counterfeit products. *Journal of Consumer Marketing*, *28*(2), 139–151. doi:10.1108/07363761111115980

Chaudhry, P., & Zimmerman, A. (2013). Protecting your intellectual property rights, Management for professionals. Springer Science + Business Media. doi:10.1007/978-1-4614-5568-4

China Real Time. (2014, June 10). China now has more millionaires than any country but the U.S. *The Wall Street Journal*.

Chow, L. L. (2013). Meeting the needs of affluent Asian consumers. *Warc*. Retrieved January 5, 2015, from https://www.warc.com/Content/ContentViewer.aspx?MasterContentRef=328d023a-6d41-406c-b283-81e8833a7a37&CID=A99788&PUB=EVENT-REPORTS

Chow, L. L. (2014). Rebunking six myths about the Chinese luxury consumer. *Warc*. Retrieved January 5, 2015, from https://www.warc.com/Content/ContentViewer.aspx?MasterContentRef=af044722-504b-48e4-affa-5f751f8b045c&CID=A101665&PUB=EVENT-REPORTS

CII & A.T.Kearney (2011). *India luxury review*. CII and A.T. Kearney.

Cox, A., Granbois, D. H., & Summers, J. (1983). Planning, search, certainty and satisfaction among durables buyers: Alongitudinal study. *Advances in Consumer Research. Association for Consumer Research (U. S.)*, *10*, 394–399.

D'Arpizio, C. (2014). *Luxury goods worldwide market study spring 2014.* Bain and Company.

Datagraphic. (2013). Luxury goods landscape: USA, Passport. *Euromonitor International.*

Deloitte. (2014). *Global powers of luxury goods 2014, in the hands of the consumer.* Deloitte Touch Tohmatsu Limited.

Doran, K. B. (2002). Lessons learnt in cross-cultural research of Chinese and north American consumers. *Journal of Business Research, 55*(10), 823–829. doi:10.1016/S0148-2963(00)00222-8

Doran, S. (2013). How well do we really know the Chinese luxury consumer? *Luxury Society.* Retrieved January 3, 2015, from http://luxurysociety.com/articles/2013/02/how-well-do-we-really-know-the-chinese-luxury-consumer

Dudovskiy, J. (2013). *Consumer Decision Making Process: a detailed analysis.* Retrieved Jan http://luxurysociety.com/articles/2013/02/how-well-do-we-really-know-the-chinese-luxury-consumerurary

Edwards, G., & Probst, E. (2011). Empathica Consumer Insights Panel Analysis of U.S. & Canadian Consumer Behaviours in Luxury Purchases. *Wave, 2*, 2011–2012.

Eisend, M., & Schuchert-Güler, P. (2006). Explaining Counterfeit Purchases – A Review and Preview. *Academy of Marketing Science Review, 06*(12), 1–25.

Eng, T., & Bogaert, J. (2010). Psychological and cultural insights into consumption of luxury Western brands in India. *Journal of Customer Behaviour, 9*(1), 55–75. doi:10.1362/147539210X497620

Forbes. (2013). *Inside The 2013 Billionaires List: Facts and Figures.* Retrieved January 7, 2015, from http://www.forbes.com/sites/luisakroll/2013/03/04/inside-the-2013-billionaires-list-facts-and-figures/

Ganter, C. (2013). In the name of luxury. *Insight,* (9).

Gao, L., Norton, M. J. T., Zhang, Z., & To, C. K. (2009). Potential niche markets for luxury fashion goods in China. *Journal of Fashion Marketing and Management, 13*(4), 514–526. doi:10.1108/13612020910991376

Hanmann, D. W., Jr., & Omar, M. (2007). Branding strategy and consumer high-technology product. *Journal of Product and Brand Management, 16*(2).

Hennings, N., Wiedmann, K-P., & Klarmann, C. (2013). Consumer value perception of luxury goods: a cross-cultural and cross-industry comparison. In *Luxury Marketing*. Springer Fachmedien Wiesbaden.

Hennings, N., Wiedmann, K.-P., Klarmann, C., Strehlau, S., Godey, B., Pederzoli, D., & Oh, H. et al. (2012). What is the value of luxury? A cross-cultural consumer perspective. *Psychology and Marketing, 29*(12), 1018–1034. doi:10.1002/mar.20583

Hoe, L., Hogg, G., & Hart, S. (2003). Fakin'it, counterfeiting and consumer contradictions. *European Advances in Consumer Research, 6*, 60–67.

Hofstede, G. (2001). *Culture's consequences: comparing values behaviours, institutions and organisations across nations*. London: Sage Publications.

Hofstede, G., Hofstede, G. J., & Minkov, M. (2010). Cultures and Organizations: Software of the Mind (3rd ed.). McGraw-Hill USA.

Howard, D., Nomoto, M., Yamaguchi, T., & Kopf, C. (2007). *Japan's changing consumer: driver of change for luxury brands.* JMRN Insights Briefing.

Hudders, L., Pandelaere, M., & Vyncke, P. (2013). Consumer meaning making: The meaning of luxury brands in a democratised luxury world. *International Journal of Market Research*, *55*(3), 391. doi:10.2501/IJMR-2013-036

Husic, M., & Cicic, M. (2009). Luxury consumption factors, *Journal of Fashion marketing and Management. International Journal (Toronto, Ont.)*, *13*(2), 231–245.

Jung, J., & Shen, D. (2011). Brand equity of luxury fashion brands among Chinese and U.S. Young female consumers. *Journal of East-West Business*, *17*(1), 48–69. doi:10.1080/10669868.2011.598756

Kaufmann, H. R., Vrontis, D., & Manakova, Y. (2012). Perception of luxury: Idiosyncratic Russian consumer culture and identity. *European Journal of Cross-Cultural Competence and Management*, *2*(3/4), 2012. doi:10.1504/EJCCM.2012.052594

Khan, M. A. (2010). How can luxury brands survive lasting changes in consumer behaviour? *Luxury Daily.* Retrieved January 2, 2015, from http://www.luxurydaily.com/how-can-luxury-brands-survive-lasting-changes-in-consumer-behavior/

Khraras, H., & Gertz, G. (2010). *The new global middle class: a cross-over from West to East.* Wolfensohn Centre for Development at Brookings.

Ko, N. (2013). Luxury brand marketing: designer extension. *Warc*. Retrieved January 3, 2015, from http://www.warc.com/Content/ContentViewer.aspx?MasterContentRef=2f8b3502-acd5-4460-91e7-f1af73745fd8&CID=A100570&PUB=ADMAP

Lukkarinen, S., & Wei, X. (2012). *Luxury consumer behaviour-a comparative case study of emerging luxury markets in China and Finland.* The Swedish School of Textiles, University of Boras.

Ma, D. (2010). *Luxury shopping behaviour of Chinese consumers.* China Europe International Business School.

Markus, H. R., & Kitayama, S. (1991). Culture and self: Implications for cognition, emotion and motivation. *Psychological Review*, *98*(2), 224–253. doi:10.1037/0033-295X.98.2.224

Nagashima, A. (1970). A Comparison of Japanese and U.S. attitudes towards foreign products. *Journal of Marketing*, *34*(1), 68–74. doi:10.2307/1250298

Nayeem, T. (2012). Cultural influences on consumer behaviour. *International Journal of Business and Management*, *7*(21), 2012. doi:10.5539/ijbm.v7n21p78

Neal, C., Quester, P., & Hawkins, D. (1999). *Consumer behaviour, implications for marketing strategy* (2nd ed.). McGraw Hill, Irwin.

Nia, A., & Zaichkowsky, J. L. (2000). Do counterfeits devalue the ownership of luxury brands? *Product and Brand Management*, *9*(7), 485–497. doi:10.1108/10610420010351402

Nwankwo, S., Hamelin, N., & Khaled, M. (2014). Consumer values, motivation and purchase intention for luxury goods. *Journal of Retailing and Consumer Services*, *21*(5), 735–744. doi:10.1016/j.jretconser.2014.05.003

O'Cass, A., & Frost, H. (2002). Status brands: examining the effects of non-product related brand associations on status and conspicuous consumption. *Journal of Product and Brand Management, 11*(2).

O'Rourke, M. (2012). *Australian* Luxury *Market Nearing 1 Billion Dollars, MO Luxury.* Retrieved January 7, 2015, from http://www.moluxury.com.au/themodown/australian-luxury-marketing-nearing-1-billion-dollars/

Oeshkova, A. (2013). *Symbolic consumption of luxury goods: example of fashion luxury market in Russia.* (Master thesis). University of Kassel, Germany.

Park, H. J., Rabolt, N., & Jeon, K. (2008). Purchasing global luxury brands among young Korean consumers. *Journal of Fashion Marketing and Management*, *12*(2), 244–259. doi:10.1108/13612020810874917

Passport. (2013). Luxury goods: global trends and prospects, Passport. *Euromonitor International.*

Perrey, J., & Spillecke, D. (2011). *Retail Marketing and Branding: A Definitive Guide to Maximising ROI.* John Wiley and Sons.

Pinder, C. C. (1998). *Work motivation in organisational behaviour.* Upper Saddle River, NJ: Prentice Hall.

Predergast, G., & Wong, C. (2003). Parental influence on the purchase of luxury brands of infant apparel: An exploratory study in Hong Kong. *Journal of Consumer Marketing*, *20*(2).

Puddick, M., & Menon, P. (2012). Contemporary lustre: marketing luxury brands in India. *Warc.* Retrieved January 5, 2015, from https://www.warc.com/Content/ContentViewer.aspx?MasterContentRef=80ec1950-9867-49bd-9b77-f79e96017bc7&CID=A99837&PUB=ATTICUS

Research Report. (2013). *China luxury apparel and accessories market report, 2012-2015.* MOZ. Retrieved January 7, 2015, from http://www.researchmoz.us/china-luxury-apparel-and-accessories-market-report-2012-2015-report.html?vsmaid=505

Rix, P. (2011). *Marketing, A Practical Approach.* McGraw Hill Australia.

Roberts, F. (2014). *Inside India's challenging high-growth luxury market, Passport.* Eurompnitor International.

Salsberg, B. (2010). The new Japanese consumer. *The McKinsey Quarterly.*

Schimidt, J. B., & Spreng, R. A. (2006). A proposed model of external consumer information search. *Journal of the Academy of Marketing Science*, *24*(3), 246–256. doi:10.1177/0092070396243005

Sheng, J., Song, L., Wang, Q., & Wang, J. (2012). *The relationship between the willingness of buying counterfeit goods and consumer personality traits, ICPM-2012.* Crisis Management in the Time of Changing World.

Sheth, J. N., Mittal, B., & Newman, B. (1999). *Customer behaviour: consumer behaviour and beyond*. Fort Worth, TX: Dryden Press.

Shiffman, L., O'Cass, A., Paladino, A., & Carlson, J. (2014). *Consumer behaviour*. Pearson Australia.

Shukla, P. (2012). The influence of value perception on luxury purchase intentions in developed and emerging markets. *International Marketing Review*, *29*(6), 574–596. doi:10.1108/02651331211277955

Solomon, M. (2006). *Consumer behaviour: A European perspective* (3rd ed.). Prentice Hall/Financial Times.

Sun, G., D'Alessandro, S., & Johnson, L. (2014). Traditional culture, political ideologies, materialism and luxury consumption in China. *International Journal of Consumer Studies*.

Swoboda, B., Pennemann, K., & Taube, M. (2014). Purchasing the Counterfeit: Antecedences and Consequences from Culturally diverse Countries. *European Retail Research*, *27*(I), 23–41. doi:10.1007/978-3-658-05313-0_2

Tatt, K. E. (2010). *Factors influencing consumer buying behaviour of luxury branded goods*. University Sains Malaysia.

The Economist Intelligent Unit. (2013). *Asia: the Chinese are coming*. Retrieved January 6, 2015, from www.eiu.com/industry/article/.../asia-the-chinese-are-coming/2013-10-1

The Guardian. (2014). *Surge in purchases of counterfeit goods*. Retrieved January 8, 2015, from http://www.theguardian.com/money/2013/oct/02/counterfeit-goods-surge-uk

Tom, G., Garibaldi, B., Zeng, Y., & Pilcher, J. (1998). Consumer Demand for Counterfeit Goods. *Psychology and Marketing*, *15*(5), 405–421. doi:10.1002/(SICI)1520-6793(199808)15:5<405::AID-MAR1>3.0.CO;2-B

Unity Marketing. (2014). *Luxury report 2014: the ultimate six-year guide to the U.S. affluent consumer market*. Unity Marketing. Retrieved January 9, 2015, from http://www.unitymarketingonline.com/catalog/product_detail.php/pid=72~subid=1/index.html

Vel, K., Captain, A., Al-Abbas, R., & Al Hashemi, B. (2011). Luxury buying in the United Arab Emirates. *Journal of Business and Behavioural Sciences*, *23*(3), 145–160.

Vigneron, F., & Johnson, L. W. (1999). A review and a conceptual framework of prestige-seeking consumer behaviour. *Academy of Marketing Science Review*, *1*, 1–15.

Walker, R. (2013). *China's luxury gift culture: dead or alive?*. Euromonitor International.

Wang, P. Z., & Waller, D. S. (2006). Measuring consumer vanity: A cross-cultural validation. *Psychology and Marketing*, *23*(8), 665–687. doi:10.1002/mar.20123

Wang, Y., Sun, S. J., & Song, Y. P. (2011). Chinese luxury consumers: Motivation, attitude and behaviour. *Journal of Promotion Management*, *17*(3), 345–359. doi:10.1080/10496491.2011.596122

Wegrzyn, N. (2013). Luxury brand marketing: making a luxury brand. *Warc*. Retrieved January 10, 2015, from http://www.warc.com/Content/ContentViewer.aspx?MasterContentRef=218ee660-b9e6-487e-817b-caa9a23540fe&q=marketing+-+brands+and+branding+-+brand+strategy&CID=A100567&PUB=ADMAP

Wiedmann, K.-P., Hennings, N., & Siebels, A. (2007). Measuring consumers' luxury value perception: A cross-cultural framework. *Academy of Marketing Science Review*, *7*, 1–21.

Wiedmann, K.-P., Hennings, N., & Siebels, A. (2009). Value-based segmentation of luxury consumption behaviour. *Psychology and Marketing*, *26*(7), 625–651. doi:10.1002/mar.20292

Wong, N., & Ahuvia, A. (1998). Personal taste and family face: Luxury consumption in Confucian and Western societies. *Psychology and Marketing*, *15*(5), 423–441. doi:10.1002/(SICI)1520-6793(199808)15:5<423::AID-MAR2>3.0.CO;2-9

World Economic Forum. (2013). *The Travel and Tourism Competitiveness Report 2013*. Author.

Yaprak, A. (2008). Culture study in international marketing: A critical review and suggestions for future research. *International Marketing Review*, *25*(2), 215–229. doi:10.1108/02651330810866290

Yi, S. (2013). Luxury brand marketing: socially affluent. *Warc*. Retrieved January 10, 2015, from https://www.warc.com/Content/ContentViewer.aspx?MasterContentRef=b242be78-9890-4506-87a9-cc4c1f4a4822&CID=A100571&PUB=ADMAP

Zhang, B. P., & Kim, J. H. (2013). Luxury fashion consumption in China: Factors affecting attitude and purchase intent. *Journal of Retailing and Consumer Services*, *20*(1), 68–79. doi:10.1016/j.jretconser.2012.10.007

ADDITIONAL READING

Roosevelt, M. (2015). *New models for luxury marketing*, Warc. Retrieved February 27, 2015, from https://www.warc.com/Content/ContentViewer.aspx?MasterContentRef=06d21ac3-29f6-47e7-80f0-1bed204c8d20&CID=A103765&PUB=ADMAP

Samuel-Camps, E., & Haldan-Jones, M. (2013). *Luxury brand marketing: The seamless consumer journey,* UM London, Warc. Retrieved February 27, 2015, from https://www.warc.com/Content/ContentViewer.aspx?MasterContentRef=d011f6f3-b961-4ff9-abd3-704074bf9538&CID=A100568&PUB=ADMAP

Wang, J., & Foosiri, P. (2010). *Factors related to consumer behaviour on luxury goods purchasing in China*. University of Thai Chamber of Commerce.

KEY TERMS AND DEFINITIONS

Collectivism: The belief or principle which gives the needs of a group, a society priority over individual ones.

Consumer Behaviour: The behaviours consumer display in the process of searching for, purchasing and consuming products and services.

Consumer Decision-Making Process: A 5-stage process consumers normally go through when making important purchases, it include need recognition, information search, alternative evaluation, purchase and post-purchase behaviour.

Cultural Dimensions: A theory created by Geert Hofstede which divides different cultures according to Power distance, individualism, uncertainty avoidance, masculinity.

Culture: A combination of values, customs, norms, beliefs and behaviour of a society.

Individualism: The pursuit of individual rather than collective interests; a society favours individual's independence and the rights of his/her immediate family.

Luxury Goods: Good are not necessities but can provide buyers with extra sense of pleasure, they tend to be well made and more expensive therefore usually purchased by people with high disposable income.

Chapter 2
Consumer Behaviors and Contemporary Attitudes in Luxury Markets

Gemma García Ferrer
Rey Juan Carlos University, Spain

ABSTRACT

This chapter analyzes the differences in consumer behavior and attitudes towards Luxury Goods. The established bond of the consumer with the luxury brand, as derived from a psychological process, is strong, and characterized by the emotional. The Luxury Brand is a symbol of personal and social identity, it expresses the individual's personality and lifestyle, strengthens the projection of self-image, status and self-concept. This chapter will analyze the buying decision process, customer retention and loyalty. The chapter will study the role of envy in the buying decision process of Luxury Goods, within a context of social comparison. As well as advertising messages and their strategies (of which envy is commonly used). The personality of the Luxury Retail Store will be analyzed. It will review the most important scientific contributions paying special attention to research done in the field of Neuromarketing and Neurobiology of Beauty.

INTRODUCTION

Throughout the chapter the following questions will be answered: what are the key differences of consumer behavior in Luxury Good's markets? In what respect does the buying process differ, the retail store selection process, the post-purchase process, customer retention and loyalty?

This is the starting point, the variables which integrate the global models both for individual or internal structure level (perception, experience and learning, decision criteria, personality, lifestyle and attitudes) and external influences level (economic environment, culture, social class and reference groups).

The relationship that a client establishes with a brand is a bond derived from a psychological process, whose scope is even stronger in the case of the Luxury Good. The Luxury Good becomes a symbol of personal and social identity, a mean of expressing the personality and lifestyle of the individual, which

DOI: 10.4018/978-1-4666-9958-8.ch002

helps to strengthen the projection of self-image, social status and self-concept. The individual reinforces self-esteem through purchasing and using these goods numerous times. These types of purchases directly affect the individual's socialization processes and influence one's state of mind.

As opposed to conventional goods, in order to explain the consumption and purchasing behavior of Luxury Goods, their emotional component needs to be taken into account –including negative emotions such as envy-, as well as the hedonic effect, materialism, the quest for status and social acknowledgement, the self-esteem reinforcement or the experiential dimension.

As for the Luxury Good, the brand plays a major role. A Good with an outstanding design and quality but from an unknown brand will not produce the same feelings as one from a well-known brand.

The Luxury Brands provide tangible, intangible, functional and emotional benefits, but certainly the intangible and emotional are those which create demand and drive success. The search for experiences, sensation seeking, identity, desires, whims and cravings, ultimately the need to feel better through consumption.

Consumerism as escapism creates an entire imaginary universe in the mind of the consumer.

For many years now, Marketing Research had emphasized the study of emotions in the determining of consumer behavior. Emotional Marketing is broadly discussed in academic literature. The emotions relate to the irrational side of the individual and are supposed to work within their subconscious. Despite the difficulty involved in customer subconscious analysis, business practice and marketing have shown that it is easy to win clients over with dynamization of emotions. In this regard, the lines of communication within companies appeal, to a large degree, to emotions against messages based on rationality. The advertising is conceived as a source for generating emotions. In the case of Luxury Goods, the role of emotions and its use in the creation of marketing mix is even stronger. Taking into account the importance of social status and the opinion of reference groups for this type of consumption, the implications of envy and social comparison will be studied. Envy has not been one of the most addressed emotions in academic literature, perhaps because of its negative nature, but it is evident that it clearly influences in the desire of possession, in the characteristics of purchased goods and in the assigned role of acquired brands. In this regard, a clear reference to Veblen's conspicuous consumption theory will be undertaken.

When resources and advertising messages used for engaging the individual are analyzed it will be demonstrated how envy and social comparison are a recurring mean. Luxury Goods are closely linked to the world of culture, art or beauty (for instance fashion, jewelery, etc.). As an example of this, one could note the event and show organized not so long ago in Wall Street by a well-known Luxury Brand, which even involved the restoration work of a historic building for the occasion, to make it look like a French mansion, and gathered clients, celebrities, people of the art world and fashion editors. Due to the relation between these types of products and beauty and art, special attention will be paid to studies related to neurobiology of beauty, among of which it is necessary to mention those conducted by the researcher Semir Zeki.

The emotional component of the Luxury Goods' consumer behavior boosts the role that Neuroscience could play in this field of study. The objectives of this chapter, which in some way have been expressed throughout the introduction, are: to describe the peculiarities of the Luxury Goods' Consumer Behavior from the perspective of a global model (including aspects such as decision making, post-purchase, customer retention, satisfaction and loyalty), to define the role of emotions considering the case of envy (understanding it in a context of social comparison), to assess the impact and psychological effect of the Luxury Brand purchase (self-esteem, mood), to analyze the role of the retail store and its personality (suggesting a way to measure attitudes towards the store), to identify resources and advertising messages, to compile the principle scientific investigations published in recent years, to determine the possibilities of neuroscience in the investigation of this trend, and to define the role of the neurobiology of beauty in the study of the Luxury Goods market.

In order to reach the conclusions explained in this chapter, the author has based her research on different fields: the influence of emotions on decision-making, for the specific case of envy; product distribution which is directly applied to the area of fashion; and finally, the personality of business establishments, which brings us to luxury products and boutiques.

BACKGROUND

Possessions are a reflection of the individual's identity which is expressed based upon them (Belk, 1988). This reality is strongly present in the consumption of Luxury Goods. (Vigneron, F., & Johnson, L. W., 1999; Vickers, J. S., & Renand, F., 2003; Nelissen, R. M., & Meijers, M. H., 2011)

Any definition of what a Luxury Goods is implies it must be done from the understanding of what they mean to the consumer. Hence the importance of this chapter. The Luxury Good will be defined to understand the behavior of its consumers.

Sekora (1977, p.23) defines Luxury as 'anything unneeded'. This definition is implicitly referring to Luxury Goods' Consumer Behavior, who will not seek satisfaction based on the functional characteristics of a good considered as needed. The purchase of a Luxury Good will fill in other gaps: emotional refuge, pleasure seeking and creation of the individual's self-image. In the social dimension of Luxury Goods consumption it is necessary to allude to conspicuous consumption: prestige seeking or characteristics of social class.

Any brand, regardless of being Luxury or not, includes for the consumer an expression and meaning in terms of identity, functionality, symbolism, value creation, psychological attributes and experiential dimension. For the Luxury Brand these contents are specially magnified for non-functional aspects.

Throughout the reviewed literature there appeared a large number of terms, which claimed to identify the characteristics of a Luxury Good. Among these it could be quoted: with aesthetic refinement, with art, of high-price, craftsmanship, of unique nature, authentic, singular or unusual (Kapferer, 2012), original, creative, beautiful, innovative, with excellence, of perfectionism, exclusive, outstanding quality, scarce, superfluous, long-lasting, lifetime, with history, exempt from normality, oneiric related, aspirational, intellectual, artistic, innovative and renewed. It even referred to the magic and charismatic aura around the creative directors of Luxury Brands (Dion & Arnould, 2011). All these characteristics explicitly imply motivations for consumer's purchase.

In the business realm (both consulting groups and organizations) a special effort has taken place for determining the characteristics of a Luxury Good (such is the case for IE Business School and the Premium and Prestige Business Observatory) which does not differ notably from those addressed in the academic world. It is again spoken about outstanding quality, history and craftsmanship, the career of creative directors and designers, big financial investments in creativity and innovation (as reinforcement to the aesthetic dimension), an exclusive distribution channel, international scope and connected to world-renowned brands. Their clients are usually part of an exclusive group, bearers of values, recognized as opinion leaders.

The Altagamma Foundation, which provides data for the industry, has established a Luxury Goods' categorization (of approximately 200 brands in the Personal Luxury Goods Market). The Personal Luxury Goods Market corresponds to categories such as cosmetics, fashion, personal accessories, fine watch-making and jewelry. Along with the categories of wine, hotels, restaurants, furniture, yacht and luxury vehicles it constitutes the total market.

Regarding the Luxury Goods' consumer profile, a large number of them are individuals with a very high purchasing power (at the top of this country's distribution of wealth pyramid). Nevertheless, there are also other consumer groups. People witnessed, over the last few years, a democratization of Luxury, which will be discussed further in later epigraphs.

MAIN FOCUS OF THE CHAPTER

Issues, Controversies, Problems

1. Luxury Goods Consumer

When providing a context for the Luxury Good and the consumer behavior it is necessary to keep in mind the Luxury Goods Industry strategy: in the creation of the Luxury Good one combines the best designs, best materials, best packaging and best merchandising (Ko & Megehee, 2012). The Luxury is out of the ordinary, the Luxury Brands aim to produce astonishment, to transmit an ideology of beauty (Dion & Arnould, 2011).

The consumer of Luxury Goods will be seduced, and is going to suffer from Buchanan's syndrome. Buchanan is the surname of Daisy, the woman with whom Gatsby is in love, the protagonist of the novel The Great Gatsby. This syndrome alludes to an extreme aesthetic sensitivity to Luxury, it refers to a scene of the novel in which Gatsby invites Daisy over to his Palace. During the visit, he opens his wardrobe and shows her his extensive collection of different colored shirts. Daisy starts crying saying: "I've never seen such beautiful shirts".

It is obvious: attractive prices will not be the determinant for the consumer of Luxury Goods. On the contrary, Luxury Goods belong to the category of Veblen's Goods, those whose demand is proportional to their price.

The Luxury Goods consumer behavior will be associated with their characteristics and determined by what the consumer seeks with their purchase: to strengthen emotional ties, to find a symbol for personal and social identity, to express oneself, to boost status, to project an image, to improve self-esteem (Truong & McColl, 2011), to offset loneliness, to live experiences (Atwall & Williams, 2009), to satisfy whims and cravings, to gift to oneself, to increase pleasure or hedonic search (Hagtvedt & Patrick, 2009). The Luxury Good is the fruit of desire and will be purchased assiduously (Okonkwo, 2007). Behind the consumption of a Good and a Luxury Brand the search of self-congruence with the individual's self-image will prevail, an element which will determine loyalty (Liu, Li, Mizerski & Soh, 2012).

The Luxury Goods consumer behavior could likely be explained in a context which prioritizes materialism: the importance of possessions considered as a symbol of success and buying in pursuit of happiness (Richins & Dawson, 1992). Nevertheless, Luxury consumption should not only be understood from the conspicuous consumption and materialism, as part of a highly pejorative concept. Other desires could exist: to forget about oneself, to relax and find oneself (Campuzano, 2003). The Luxury is also associated with activities for personal enrichment and improvement of quality of life.

Fernandez Moya (2012) mentions ten motivations for acquiring Luxury Goods: uniqueness (distinctive image versus common goods), conformity (because the goods are consumed by people who belong to a relevant group), self esteem, hedonism, utilitarianism (provides useful benefits), materialism, legacy (intention of leaving it to someone after death), investment, habit or loyalty and variety seeking.

Silverstein and Fiske (2003) define four consumer emotional groups which could easily explain the behavior of the Luxury Goods consumer: first "to take care of oneself", those who want to gift to oneself due to an excessive work situation and lack of time, second "to explore", those who are in search of experiences which serve as a challenge in order to define oneself for themselves and for others, third "to connect" focus on personal relations, and the "individual style" in which sophistication prevails, to demonstrate success and express personal values and individualism.

2. Global Models of Consumer Behavior for the Case of Luxury Goods Consumption

For a few years now the study of consumer behavior has been approached with a multidisciplinary approach in which there are many social sciences included: economy, sociology, psychology or anthropology help to light the way towards understanding the consumer. On the other hand, the market research techniques, from the simpler theories (for instance, observation), to the more traditional ones (such as focus group, in-depth interviews or surveys), to the more complex (all those derived from neuroscience) or those which aid in the understanding of a mediatized consumer from a virtual environment (netnography, "on-line ethnography"), they are combined in order to analyze the individual. A large part of market research done is aimed at the consumer (García Ferrer, 2012). Many people consider that consumer knowledge and understanding, as well as other aspects, are the company's main competitive advantage (Alonso & Grande, 2004). The global models of consumer behavior (Howard & Sheth, 1969; Engel Blackwell & Kollat, 1968; Nicosia, 1970) try to depict reality from a multidisciplinary perspective. Alonso and Grande (2004) implement their own development parting from these models, classifying the variables that influence the consumer behavior in external and internal.

A. External Variables of Consumer Behavior

The external variables or unrelated conditioning (Ruiz de Maya and Grande, 2013) will be the demographic and economic environment, culture, social stratification and the reference groups (Dubois, B., & Duquesne, P., 1993). With reference to economic environment, an economist could explain demand of a Luxury Good in terms of elasticity, notwithstanding, the consumption of such goods are not easily explained using only economic factors. Certainly, income level is a necessary condition but not enough to explain the purchase (Dubois & Duquesque, 1993). One thing is certain, the success of a Luxury Good includes the fact that the consumer perceive enough added value in such a way that it compensates the high-price paid, especially in economic recession periods (Tynan, McKechnie & Chhuon, 2010).

In connection with demographic aspects, the population composition in respect to age, gender, educational level or occupation could be decisive for understanding the Luxury Goods consumer.

Regarding gender, Stokburger-Sauer and Teichmann (2013) determine that women have a more positive attitude towards Luxury Brands and are more receptive to its singularity (uniqueness), hedonic and status value. Differentiating by genders, equal behaviors will not be found in relation to the emotional meaning that the consumer seeks in the purchase: women are much more emotional and their feeling of envy is stronger than men's, regarding the possession of products which could contribute to beauty enhancement and improvement of self-esteem (Habimana & Masse, 2000). There are even scientific investigations (Wang & Griskevicius, 2014) which indicate that women compete with other women through the conspicuous consumption, protecting themselves from possible threats to their relationships (therefore, a matter of jealousy). Men are possibly more susceptible to the Luxury Technology Market. However, research suggests that technology companies with a focus on design, are more accepted among women with a clear influence, direct or indirect, in buying decision process.

Regarding age, education and occupation, the Luxury Market has experienced the emergence of new sectors such as the case of 'dink' (dual income, no kids) whose purchase is much more individualistic and aspirational, they are hedonists and seek personal well-being, or are the segment of youth with high education, access to a first-time job and the absence of family responsibilities, which have become an emerging segment of these goods.

Regarding cultural patterns, these also have an impact on Luxury consumption in cultures which promote the conspicuous consumption. In the case of Chinese culture, for instance, there is a great predisposition to acquire highly innovative technology such as the wearable computer. In the Chinese market the Luxury Market expectations are very high, they travel a lot and also have access to Luxury Goods via the Internet. On more than one occasion the Luxury Goods research has focused on the Chinese client (Li, Li & Kambele, 2012).

Western cultures have traditionally defined the Luxury Goods consumer as those who likes to show great opulence, this category is common for the Western world. In the Socialist Chinese Market, the centralized power formally rejects the creation of individual wealth and the consumer adopts a smart and more subtle approach, living in luxury in a more intimate and discreet way, far from any eccentricity (Zhan & He, 2012).

Research shows that the country of origin is fundamental in determining the evaluation criteria for consumers and their perception of the Luxury Good (Ko & Megehee, 2012). The conception of Luxury varies according to culture, history and religion. The more elaborate, ostentatious French Luxury had its roots in the catholic religion, the more discreet and minimalist American Luxury is associated with the protestant culture.

Democratization of Luxury, or the trend of "Mass Luxury", is not unrelated to the phenomenon of demographic factors, which reveals how middle-class and high-class consumers are willing to pay a surcharge for acquiring a series of products which provide an emotional compensation (Colombo & Castrillón, 2010). Nonetheless, despite this phenomenon, reality also says that a Luxury Goods loses prestige if stops being only attainable for a few people.

In line with this, consumption of a Luxury Good is an expression of social status in order to differentiate social class. A high social class constitutes the quintessential segment of Luxury Goods market.

Within reference groups one favors the desire of emulation or imitation and the feelings of envy and being envied. Luxury Goods play an important role in these desires and feelings. The opinions of reference groups contribute to the creation of the individual's image. Finally, inside a group it is common that individuals consume the same goods and brands. The Luxury brands help to define segments of consumers who share values, beliefs, personality traits and lifestyles.

B. Internal Variables of Consumer Behavior

The internal variables refer to cognitive faculties and one's personality, their feedback about their experiences: perception, learning and memory, personality and lifestyle and attitudes. (Truong, 2010).

Perception is in charge of capturing, selecting and assessing the stimuli that originates from the exterior. An individual's perception could be radically different if we are talking about a charismatic and well-know brand against one which is not. Positioning of different Luxury Brands will be a reflection of a perceived reality.

Wiedmann, Hennings and Siebels (2007) analyze four dimensions (Dimensions of Luxury Value Perception) in relation to the process of consumer perception of Luxury Goods: financial value (price willing to pay), functional value (refers to utilities: usability values, quality values and uniqueness values), individual value (materialism hedonic and self-identity value) and social value (conspicuousness and prestige value).

The purchasing process establishes a learning process that determines the feelings and attitudes towards a good and its selection. The sum of what is learned stays in the individual's mind thanks to their memory. If the satisfaction of a Luxury Brand has appropriate levels, the consumer behavior will maintain stable and therefore loyal.

Personality traits of individuals will indicate their preferences towards the Luxury Goods and their favorite brands. If one works with a personality model like Big Five, it will not be difficult to find differences regarding the different personality dimensions among the consumers of different Luxury Brands. The Luxury Brands themselves define their target segments based on personality traits.

Regarding personality, the research has focused on personifying brands and even retail stores (AAker, 1997; D'Astous & Levesque, 2003). In the case of a Luxury Brand, the extent in which individuals express themselves through the goods they purchase measures personality, in terms of adjectives of human personality it could be helpful to identify the subtle differences among brands.

Lifestyle will show those areas of life that are important for the individual, what they like to do, like to buy or invest their free time in. Through a classification such as VALS (Values, Attitudes and Lifestyles developed by SRI International) it would be possible to identify the characteristics of Luxury Goods consumers.

Attitudes are defined as a positive or negative feeling towards a good and are modified over time. Some studies segment the Luxury Goods consumers according to their attitude. Dubois, Czellar and Laurent (2005) define three segments based on an attitude scale of 33 items. Therefore defining the presence of three attitudes: elitist, who considers Luxury Goods to be only for a select few, democratic, who believes in an accessible Luxury which is not reserved for a minority, and distant, people who show no interest on Luxury.

In relation with the change of attitudes, over the last few years, there has been a change in the middle-class consumers, who began seeing Luxury as something plausible and less distant.

A new consumer profile has re-emerged (Truong, McColl & Kitchen, 2009) described as "masstige" (from 'mass' and 'prestige'), consumption of highly priced, though not prohibitive, Luxury Goods. Masstige is a terminology used in the book "Trading Up: The Transforming Power of New Luxury" (Silverstein, Fiske & Butman, 2008).

Big Luxury companies have noticed the influence of this new business model, which made "fighter brands" or "combat brands" flourish, second brands created by the big Luxury Brands which are more affordable and open to the public. Along with Outlets these fighting brands transmit an aura of Luxury to the middle-class for an affordable price.

3. Buying Decision Process

In contrast to conventional goods, the buying decision process for a Luxury Good will not arise from a functional need but rather an emotional need, in order to satisfy a desire. The process of searching for information and evaluating alternatives it will be crucial brands follow the positioning strategy as well as what reference groups consume. The point of sale (physical or virtual) will be key in the buying decision process.

After post-purchase evaluation, the wealth of experiences and the satisfaction of desires will define the achievement of the customer retention and loyalty processes.

4. The Role of Emotions in the Luxury Goods Purchase: The Power of Emotional Communication

Today, the role of neurosciences is unstoppable, being one of its main focuses in the analysis of emotions. The Descartes' somatic marker hypothesis is key, defined as the bodily changes that reflect an emotional state of the individual. It is "changes in vegetative, muscular, neuroendocrine and neurophysiological systems, which could provide unconscious signals that precede, facilitate and contribute to decision making". On the contrary, the absence of, alteration and weakening of the somatic markers lead to inappropriate and disadvantageous decision making (Martínez Selva, Sanchez Navarro, Becharra & Román, 2006, pp 411).

The influence of emotions in the purchase of Luxury Goods is very great and determining far above the rationality that could exist during the purchase of a necessity good. The Luxury Goods point of sales and the communications strategies will continuously appeal to emotions and not exclusively to positive ones. Within the negative emotions, envy, has a great effect on the Luxury Goods purchase and it is used on many occasions as an advertising appeal.

Furthermore today's marketing highlights the sensory dimension over the emotional dimension: in fact Luxury food offers a sensory, olfactory, gustatory and even tactile experiences. Later on oncoming epigraphs when the role of point of sales is analyzed there will be a reference to sensory retail strategies.

5. Envy and Social Comparison in Luxury Goods Consumer Behavior

A study of social comparison and envy is conducted based on the search of Veblen's conspicuous consumption theory. This economist defined these terms in his work *the theory of the leisure class* (1899). Behind the ostentation lies the desire of creating envy and showing a higher social status.

The Luxury Goods' buying decision processes are highly influenced by social comparison processes with individual's of higher success whom they would like to imitate. Certain brands are identified as symbol of such success (Mande, Petrova & Cialdini, 2006). From the social comparison processes emerge, from the frustration, feelings of envy. Envy is a negative emotion, a feeling that one considers to have a clear influence on the buying behavior and on the desire for possession (it could even explain behavior based on brands), but which has not specially addressed in marketing literature. Unlike envy which has been analyzed a lot in the field of Psychology as a social emotion (triggered in the context of social comparison).Envy's painful nature is associated with anxiety, depression and low self-esteem. Envy is felt over aspects related with what one considers as relevant domain of life for the individual (Smith, 2004; Parrot & Smith, 1993): that is to say something really important to them and where one considers it inferior for another. Along with its treatment in psychology it has being pointed out the difficulty of measuring envy by its shameful character and low social desirability (that hinders the recognition of it from the individual). The malignant envy has been differentiated, this generates very hostile feelings, and the benign envy, triggers a desire of emulation. Equally envy has been differentiated as a stable personality trait (more pathologic) and envy episodic (motivated by a specific and more related situation with any that all individuals could feel at a given time). In the field of marketing, and particularly for the Luxury Goods purchase, the feeling of envy interests in all aspects, though perhaps benign envy should stand out accompanying the desire to imitate the other (for instance, buying the same Luxury Brand that the other has) and that which is provoked by a particular situation (referring to an exceptional state and not to a personality trait). In many occasions these particular situations refer very to the buying decisions of the envied person.

For marketing, one of the most explicit references to envy is made by Belk (1984). The author connects this emotion to another construct much more analyzed: materialism. Belk creates a scale to measure constructs related to materialism considering three dimensions: possessiveness, non-generosity, and envy. In particular, the subscale of envy is composed by eight items, some of which make an implicit reference to Luxury alluding to very rich people and those who can buy all that they want. Instruments for measuring materialism in Belk's subsequent work (Richins & Dawson, 1992), despite acknowledging the relation between materialism and envy, does not include an exclusive format for it. Regarding materialism, it indicates that it maintains a close relationship to luxury consumption as shown by scale items which were used to measure it.

Belk (2011) analyzes the concept of envy relating it with marketing, conspicuous consumption and Luxury Buying. He even establishes a classification of the envious consumer differentiating from benign, malignant and mixed envy. He notes that benign envy is the engine of consumption.

Van de Ven, Zeelenberg and Pieters (2011) notes that envy has a direct effect on the increase of purchases, indicating and demonstrating from different experiments that benign envy induce paying a higher price for Goods.

Luxury Brands elicit envy, one envies and is envied through its possession.

Currently, the author of this chapter has adapted two tools to measure envy. This includes both envy as a stable personality trait and episodic envy, which can be felt by anyone after a situation that causes it. It is being analyzed how both types of envy influence purchasing decisions, and a clear connection with this negative emotion has been found. In future research, in the field of neurobiology, facial electromyography and evoked potentials will be applied as a brain measure, in order to analyze the influence of envy on decision-making.

6. The Role of the Retail Store on the Luxury Goods' Consumer Attitude: Atmosphere and Personality of the Store

The choice of distribution channel will be key in the Luxury Good's buying decision process. Its contribution to the experiential dimension in the Luxury Good consumption will be highly relevant.

Despite the predominant role of the physical point of sale, the virtual channels on Luxury Brands distribution has taken center stage. Luxury consumption on the Internet is increasing.

The retail store constitutes a key stimulus for the individual's perception. The result of this perception process will be a key answer inside the buying process. It is known that positioning and the product image could be modified according to the type of store which is selling them. This is evident in any product category, but for Luxury Goods it is even more decisive.

The Luxury Goods Consumer will not find their satisfaction only in the product itself, but in their desires, emotions, search for pleasure and aspirations will extend to the event of “going shopping”, an act that will be accompanied by a great quantity of sensory stimuli which the point of sales will provide (music, smell, chance of seeing and touching the product, opportunity of enjoying a given environment, the possibility of interacting with the sales rep, ...). Walk down a commercial street dedicated to Luxury Brands it is assumed that coming into contact with the most emblematic places of cities satisfies not only the desire to shop, but also gets the individual closer to the world of architecture, culture, history and art. For this reason, the sensory stimuli are not exclusively produce in the retail store.

The physical marketing channel is a fundamental axis for the consumption and buying experience, and allows one to be in contact with the real atmosphere of the brand.

The presence of Luxury can be done through their own stores or corners in shopping centers. In addition to commercial streets, Luxury shopping centers and Duty-free commercial spaces are added.

On commercial streets dedicated to Luxury, brands have their own retail store and extend the brand concept to their own store. In this regard one-brand stores will take extreme care in extending their brand image to the window, decoration, furniture and product placement.

The flagship store is a common concept, a powerful communication tool supported on geomarketing studies. The flagship brands are located in emblematic locations of big cities, busy streets (both locals and tourists) and constitute avant-garde innovation and creative design. The favorite cities are Tokyo, New York, Paris and London. The term flagship comes from nautical terminology and was employed for the first time in the fashion world to define stores “that can properly represent the brand’s image”. With an area of approximately 1500 to 2000 meters, its architecture gets the individual closer to culture, art and glamour of refurbished and air conditioned historic buildings. Its interior boasts painstaking decoration, and allows one to see the latest collections as well as some past collections and use advanced technology such as interactive presentations with augmented reality. More services are offered to their clients that increase the experiential and hedonic value in the buying process: private zones, spa, art gallery, cafeteria or a restaurant, live music, exhibitions, fashion shows, talks or tastings, among others. As an example one could mention an important brand that creates an area for drinking coffee and relaxing in its flagship based on the memories recalled by its own designer around the smell of coffee and experiences with family and friends. In conclusion, all that contributes to magnifying the perceived Luxury by the client. The power of communication and stimulus of a flagship is so high that even brands used the restoration works of these stores as promotional marketing of the brand.

Pop-up stores (de Lassus & Freire, 2014): are stores of ephemeral nature which open short-term, they are also trendy in the Luxury Market. They are considered not only a retail store, but a show, something special and eccentric. It allows for the transmission of the brand image with a low risk investment and low costs. Their temporary locations are usually emblematic seeking a strong influx of people.

Both flagship stores and pop up stores are commercial formats which are recognized in the distribution of luxury goods. These terms are used by managers and experts and information about them can be found on the web, which shows us several examples of this kind of establishments.

As with the concept of brand personality, the store personality, especially Luxury, is liable to be measured by giving a subtle methodology to identify differences among different companies. In the case of the Luxury Retail Store it would be possible to adapt a tool for measuring the store personality (García Ferrer & García 2013) to the specific case of Luxury.

7. A Luxury Goods Costumer Analysis from the Neuroscience Approach: Neuromarketing and Neurobiology of Beauty

Neuromarketing has revolutionized the traditional world of market research through subject analysis and their emotions through their brain and physiological responses to stimuli. The decision processes and the role of emotion on it is studied using powerful neuroscience techniques (evoked potential, magnetic resonance imaging, facial electromyography and other physiological measures of peripheral character). Luxury Goods' buying decision process is susceptible to being analyzed using these techniques.

In addition, it is possible to discuss about the neurobiology of beauty. Current marketing tries to excite and stimulate the senses. Marketing strategies are closely related to beauty. A communication campaign could measure their reply from neuroaesthetics, similar to what is done with a filmmaking, an advertising poster, packaging, all the iconographic elements of a brand, the decoration of a retail store, their own product, all that is wished to be considered as beautiful by the consumer, with a similar reaction to what it feels like when admiring a piece of art.

Individuals search for beauty in the all their surroundings and try to achieve, obtain and enjoy it. It is a continuous search, both in the definition of their own-self, and their surroundings, it becomes a constant recreation.

As stated before, the search for beauty is closely linked to the strategic objectives from a marketing action. If in the case that a conventional product pursues beauty in its packaging, in the iconographic aspects of the brand, the atmosphere and decoration of the retail store or in an advertising poster (which is still considered an artistic expression), to a greater extent this will happen for a Luxury Good. Luxury Brands set a close relationship with the world of art and culture. Nobody can deny the artistic value of a jewel, but this can be extended to other Luxury Goods, for example fashion, where the aura of top creative directors and designers make their collections into art, sometimes even exhibited in museums.

Regarding neurobiology of beauty or neuroaesthetics, some authors (del Blanco, 2012) establish the concept of beautiful brands and their psychological effects on the consumer: an increase in optimism, strengthening of self-control and self-esteem, the capacity to tolerate frustration and the impact on happiness. This author uses the example of women's shoe shopping (making references to Luxury Brands) noting it as a product historically associated as a reflection or indicator of social class.. The purchase of shoes, which in some cases could be addictive, allows women to recreate fantasies immersed in a paradise of their own imagination. Something as simple as heels and the consequent increase of height is related to power and status. It has been shown that with the purchase of shoes produces a woman's brain secretes dopamine which consequently improves mood, an area in the prefrontal cortex of the brain is activated and even generates a small dose of adrenaline, something similar happens to the collector when he acquires a unique piece. Finally, the author states that the brain "is structured to associate the feet with sex" because "the area of the brain that communicates with the genitals is next to the one which coordinates the feet". This neurological link determines, from words of Del Blanco (2012, pp 68), "a certain implicit eroticism".

Semir Seki is the pioneer of neuroaesthetics. In his studies he measures the subject's neuronal responses to different stimuli such as paints or photos and analyzes the areas of neuronal activity that have increased as result of perceiving beauty (Kawabata & Zeki, 2004). Another research pioneer in this field was the neurologist Vilayanur S. Ramachandran.

SOLUTIONS AND RECOMMENDATIONS

The consumer behavior is a complex issue determined by a large amount of variables. In the case of Luxury Goods it is necessary to establish differences with regard to the consumption of a conventional product.

The Luxury Goods consumer behavior should start with the description of the characteristics these types of goods that allow for an understanding of the economic concept of "Luxury Good", especially in respect to functional attributes, motivations and wants of its buyers. The emotional component (including negative emotions such as envy), the hedonic effect, the search for status and social recognition, the reinforcement of self-esteem or experiential dimension will be some of the aspects to consider.

The Luxury Consumer study should be addressed from a multidisciplinary perspective and from the adaptation of global behavior models.

In the study of Luxury consumer behavior the application of conventional and modern market research techniques are recommended: to the traditional in-depth interview, focus group, to the survey or observation one can add the relatively new netnography (on-line ethnography) or the more sophisticated neuromarketing techniques. Nor should it be forgotten, in this regard, the contribution of neurosciences for the study of emotions, as well as the aesthetic dimension (application of neurobiology of beauty).

FUTURE RESEARCH DIRECTIONS

The future lines of investigation about the study of consumer behavior and all the aspects dealt in this chapter are many. One of them could be the measurement of envy and its influence on the Luxury Goods buying decision process. For this it will be necessary to have an instrument or survey which helps to differentiate envious people from non-envious people to then submit them to laboratory tests where it can be determined their brain activity and physiological responses to decision processes: evoked potential, magnetic resonance imaging, facial electromyography, skin conductance or heartbeat could be some of these methods. It is thought that the brain's reward system, dopamine and certain areas of the prefrontal cerebral cortex participate in the decision making process.

Other future direction for the Luxury Goods' consumer behavior would be in relation to beauty and neuroaesthetics analyzing the neuronal responses to the perception of Luxury Goods as if they were works of art.

In regard to more traditional lines of investigation, many of them addressed by the researchers mentioned along this chapter, is important that these lines find continuation: study of perceptions, attitudes, brand personality and retail store personality, cultural differences, demographic differences, study of trends related with Luxury (such as materialism or hedonism), Luxury Clients segmentation based on psychographic variables, and so on. It is possible to say that all these have a long path.

CONCLUSION

Throughout the chapter different academic contributions to the consumer behavior and attitudes analysis have been analyzed. The perspective has been based on the singularity of Luxury Goods and a global consumer behavior model to establish differences opposite to conventional consumption. The internal and external variables that determine the behavior has been described, affecting the buying process.

Significant attention was given to emotions and, particularly, to envy, typified by social comparison processes. A special focus on the Luxury Retail Store as communication axis and key element for the buying experience. Finally, future trends for investigation have been described from neuromarketing and neurobiology of beauty.

REFERENCES

Aaker, J. L. (1997). Dimensions of brand personality. *JMR, Journal of Marketing Research, 34*(3), 347–356. doi:10.2307/3151897

Andreu, L. (2003). Emociones del consumidor. Componentes y consecuencias de marketing. *Estudios Sobre Consumo,* (64), 9-26.

Atwal, G., & Williams, A. (2009). Luxury brand marketing–the experience is everything! *Journal of Brand Management, 16*(5), 338–346. doi:10.1057/bm.2008.48

Belk, R. W. (1984). Three scales to measure constructs related to materialism: Reliability, validity, and relationships to measures of happiness. *Advances in Consumer Research. Association for Consumer Research (U. S.), 11*, 291–297.

Belk, R. W. (1988). Posessions and the Extended Self. *The Journal of Consumer Research, 15*(2), 139. doi:10.1086/209154

Belk, R. W. (2011). Benign envy. *AMS Review, 1*(3-4), 117-134.

Campuzano García, S. (2003). *El Universo del lujo: una visión global y estratégica para profesionales y amantes del lujo*. Spain: Mc Graw Hill.

Colombo, D., & Castrillón, F. (2010). Comunicación de marcas de lujo. El deseo de generar deseo. *The Journal of PR Consejo Profesional de Relaciones Públicas de la República Argentina, 1*(1), 61–85.

D'Astous, A., & Lévesque, M. (2003). A scale for measuring store personality. *Psychology and Marketing, 20*(5), 455–469. doi:10.1002/mar.10081

de Lassus, C., & Freire, N. A. (2014). Access to the luxury brand myth in pop-up stores: A netnographic and semiotic analysis. *Journal of Retailing and Consumer Services, 21*(1), 61–68. doi:10.1016/j.jretconser.2013.08.005

del Blanco, R. M. A. (2012). Diálogo con la belleza: perspectiva de neuromárketing. *Harvard Deusto Márketing y Ventas*, (113), 62-68.

Dion, D., & Arnould, E. (2011). Retail luxury strategy: Assembling charisma through art and magic. *Journal of Retailing, 87*(4), 502–520. doi:10.1016/j.jretai.2011.09.001

Dubois, B., Czellar, S., & Laurent, G. (2005). Consumer segments based on attitudes toward luxury: Empirical evidence from twenty countries. *Marketing Letters, 16*(2), 115–128. doi:10.1007/s11002-005-2172-0

Dubois, B., & Duquesne, P. (1993). The market for luxury goods: Income versus culture. *European Journal of Marketing*, *27*(1), 35–44. doi:10.1108/03090569310024530

Engel, J. F., Kollat, D. T., & Blackwell, R. D. (1968). *Consumer behavior*. Holt, Rinehart and Winston, Inc.

Fernández Moya, M. E. (2012). *Purchase and consumption of luxury goods*. (Unpublished doctoral dissertation). University Carlos III, Madrid, Spain.

García Ferrer, G. (2012). Investigación comercial. Spain: Esic Editorial.

García Ferrer, G., & García, C. (2013). *Construcción y validación inicial de una escala para medir la personalidad de los establecimientos comerciales (No. 1305)*. Catedra Fundación Ramón Areces de Distribución Comercial.

Habimana, E., & Massé, L. (2000). Envy manifestations and personality disorders. *European Psychiatry*, *15*, 15–21. doi:10.1016/S0924-9338(00)00501-0 PMID:11520469

Hagtvedt, H., & Patrick, V. M. (2009). The broad embrace of luxury: Hedonic potential as a driver of brand extendibility. *Journal of Consumer Psychology*, 19.

Howard, J. A., & Sheth, J. N. (1969). *The theory of buyer behavior* (Vol. 14). New York: Wiley.

Kapferer, J. N. (2012). Abundant rarity: The key to luxury growth. *Business Horizons*, *55*(5), 453–462. doi:10.1016/j.bushor.2012.04.002

Kawabata, H., & Zeki, S. (2004). Neural correlates of beauty. *Journal of Neurophysiology*, *91*(4), 1699–1705. doi:10.1152/jn.00696.2003 PMID:15010496

Ko, E., & Megehee, C. M. (2012). Fashion marketing of luxury brands: Recent research issues and contributions. *Journal of Business Research*, *65*(10), 1395–1398. doi:10.1016/j.jbusres.2011.10.004

Li, G., Li, G., & Kambele, Z. (2012). Luxury fashion brand consumers in China: Perceived value, fashion lifestyle, and willingness to pay. *Journal of Business Research*, *65*(10), 1516–1522. doi:10.1016/j.jbusres.2011.10.019

Liu, F., Li, J., Mizerski, D., & Soh, H. (2012). Self-congruity, brand attitude, and brand loyalty: A study on luxury brands. *European Journal of Marketing*, *46*(7/8), 922–937. doi:10.1108/03090561211230098

Mandel, N., Petrova, P. K., & Cialdini, R. B. (2006). Images of success and the preference for luxury brands. *Journal of Consumer Psychology*, *16*(1), 57–69. doi:10.1207/s15327663jcp1601_8

Martínez-Selva, J. M., Sánchez-Navarro, J. P., Bechara, A., & Román, F. (2006). Mecanismos cerebrales de la toma de decisiones. *Revista de Neurologia*, *42*(7), 411–418. PMID:16602058

Nelissen, R. M., & Meijers, M. H. (2011). Social benefits of luxury brands as costly signals of wealth and status. *Evolution and Human Behavior*, *32*(5), 343–355. doi:10.1016/j.evolhumbehav.2010.12.002

Nicosia, F. M. (1970). *La decisión del consumidor*. Barcelona: Gustavo Gili.

Okonkwo, U. (2007). *Luxury fashion branding: trends, tactics, techniques*. Palgrave Macmillan. doi:10.1057/9780230590885

Richins, M. L., & Dawson, S. (1992). A consumer values orientation for materialism and its measurement: Scale development and validation. *The Journal of Consumer Research*, *19*(3), 303. doi:10.1086/209304

Rivas, J. A., & Esteban, I. G. (2004). *Comportamiento del consumidor: decisiones y estrategia de marketing*. Esic Editorial.

Ruiz de Maya, S., & Grande Esteban, I. (2013). *Casos de comportamiento del consumidor: Reflexiones para la dirección de marketing*. Esic Editorial.

Sekora, J. (1977). *Luxury: the concept in western thought, Eden to Smollett*. Johns Hopkins University Press.

Silverstein, M. J., & Fiske, N. (2003). Luxury for the masses. *Harvard Business Review*, *81*(4), 48–57. PMID:12687919

Silverstein, M. J., & Fiske, N. (2003). Lujo para las Masas. *Harvard Business Review. America Latina*, 3–11.

Silverstein, M. J., Fiske, N., & Butman, J. (2008). *Trading up: Why consumers want new luxury goods--and how companies create them*. Penguin.

Smith, R. H. (2004). Envy and its transmutations. *The Social Life of Emotions*, 43-63.

Smith, R. H., & Kim, S. H. (2007). Comprehending envy. *Psychological Bulletin*, *133*(1), 46–64. doi:10.1037/0033-2909.133.1.46 PMID:17201570

Stokburger-Sauer, N. E., & Teichmann, K. (2013). Is luxury just a female thing? The role of gender in luxury brand consumption. *Journal of Business Research*, *66*(7), 889–896. doi:10.1016/j.jbusres.2011.12.007

Truong, Y. (2010). Personal aspirations and the consumption of luxury goods. *International Journal of Market Research*, *52*(5), 653–671. doi:10.2501/S1470785310201521

Truong, Y., & McColl, R. (2011). Intrinsic motivations, self-esteem, and luxury goods consumption. *Journal of Retailing and Consumer Services*, *18*(6), 555–561. doi:10.1016/j.jretconser.2011.08.004

Truong, Y., McColl, R., & Kitchen, P. J. (2009). New luxury brand positioning and the emergence of Masstige brands. *Journal of Brand Management*, *16*(5), 375–382. doi:10.1057/bm.2009.1

Tynan, C., McKechnie, S., & Chhuon, C. (2010). Co-creating value for luxury brands. *Journal of Business Research*, *63*(11), 1156–1163. doi:10.1016/j.jbusres.2009.10.012

Van de Ven, N., Zeelenberg, M., & Pieters, R. (2011). The envy premium in product evaluation. *The Journal of Consumer Research*, *37*(6), 984–998. doi:10.1086/657239

Veblen, T. (1965). *The Theory of the Leisure Class. 1899*. AM Kelley.

Vickers, J. S., & Renand, F. (2003). The marketing of luxury goods: An exploratory study–three conceptual dimensions. *The Marketing Review*, *3*(4), 459–478. doi:10.1362/146934703771910071

Vigneron, F., & Johnson, L. W. (1999). A review and a conceptual framework of prestige-seeking consumer behavior. *Academy of Marketing Science Review*, *1*(1), 1–15.

Wang, Y., & Griskevicius, V. (2014). Conspicuous consumption, relationships, and rivals: Women's luxury products as signals to other women. *The Journal of Consumer Research*, *40*(5), 834–854. doi:10.1086/673256

Wiedmann, K. P., Hennings, N., & Siebels, A. (2007). Conceptualization and Propositions: Determinants of a Consumers' Luxury Value Perception. A Cross-cultural Framework. *Journal of Marketing Science*, (7).

Zhan, L., & He, Y. (2012). Understanding luxury consumption in China: Consumer perceptions of best-known brands. *Journal of Business Research*, *65*(10), 1452–1460. doi:10.1016/j.jbusres.2011.10.011

ADDITIONAL READING

Belk, R. W. (1995). Collecting as luxury consumption: Effects on individuals and households. *Journal of Economic Psychology*, *16*(3), 477–490. doi:10.1016/0167-4870(95)98956-X

Han, Y. J., Nunes, J. C., & Drèze, X. (2010). Signaling status with luxury goods: The role of brand prominence. *Journal of Marketing*, *74*(4), 15–30. doi:10.1509/jmkg.74.4.15

So, J. T., Parsons, A. G., & Yap, S. F. (2013). Corporate branding, emotional attachment and brand loyalty: The case of luxury fashion branding. *Journal of Fashion Marketing and Management*, *17*(4), 403–423. doi:10.1108/JFMM-03-2013-0032

Truong, Y., Simmons, G., McColl, R., & Kitchen, P. J. (2008). Status and conspicuousness–are they related? Strategic marketing implications for luxury brands. *Journal of Strategic Marketing*, *16*(3), 189–203. doi:10.1080/09652540802117124

Vigneron, F., & Johnson, L. W. (2004). Measuring perceptions of brand luxury. *The Journal of Brand Management*, *11*(6), 484–506. doi:10.1057/palgrave.bm.2540194

KEY TERMS AND DEFINITIONS

Buying Decision Process: Stages in the process of searching for and the acquisition of a given good.

Emotions: Affective state that creates a somatic response (bodily changes) and affects the individual's decision making processes.

Envy: Social emotion of shameful character and low social desirability. On its benign dimension has been tested a great effect on the purchase of goods.

Neurobiology of Beauty: Measuring of the individual's neuronal responses to beauty.

Neuromarketing: Use of neurosciences and their methods for marketing and in particular to the study of emotions.

Self-Concept: The individual's belief about himself or herself, also including the perceived image that other people have about himself or herself.

Social Comparison: Process through which the individual compares him or herself with others in aspects that belong to relevant domains of life.

Symbol of Identity: Refers to a product that allows the individual to express one-self.

Chapter 3
Consumer Behavior Regarding Luxury Perfumes:
Key Elements for Marketing Strategy Design

Mónica Díaz-Bustamante
Complutense University of Madrid, Spain

Sonia Carcelén
Complutense University of Madrid, Spain

ABSTRACT

Due to the importance of the fragrances segment within the luxury market and the limited academic and professional literature available regarding the same, this chapter offers a detailed description of the basic characteristics of this segment. Therefore, based on the analysis of primary and secondary information (quantitative and qualitative) regarding the Spanish market, the key elements of luxury fragrance consumer behavior have been described, examining the principle explanatory factors leading to decision making processes for their purchase and use; in other words, the motivations to purchase and consume these products. This knowledge is decisive to permit luxury fragrance brands to appropriately design their global marketing strategies and formulate the appropriate marketing-mix.

INTRODUCTION

Perfume and cosmetics is one of the most important product categories within the luxury market, responsible for 20% of the same (Bain & Company, 2015).

In fact, for many consumers, fragrances, treatments and make-up are the access ways to a luxury brand that offers accessible products for the majority of the population. As suggested by C. Antúnez de Mayolo (2009, p.47): *a secretary who earns five hundred dollars a month cannot afford to buy a four-hundred dollar Gucci bag, but she can purchase a perfume made by the same brand.*

DOI: 10.4018/978-1-4666-9958-8.ch003

Euromonitor (2015) valued the global market of perfumes and cosmetics at 277.6 billion euros, retail price. Within this market, the weight of selective or luxury perfumes and cosmetics is around 31% although it varies based on the country.

In Spain, data from Stanpa[1] (2015) has revealed the importance of the luxury fragrance market based on its weight in the Spanish luxury perfume and cosmetics market (54.6%) as well as in the market for all fragrances in Spain (73.7%).

Furthermore, growth registered for this specific market in Spain according to data from Stanpa (2000-2014 historical series) once again reflects the strong penetration rate of this luxury product in the Spanish population.

However, despite the importance of this market, academic and professional literature regarding the marketing of luxury fragrances remains quite limited.

Therefore, this chapter presents the results of a study aimed at identifying and analyzing luxury fragrance consumer behaviors and motivations for purchase and use. This knowledge of consumer behavior allows the corresponding brands to design and apply the most efficient strategies when marketing their products and allows them to improve their competitive position.

METHODOLOGY

Based on an applied methodology perspective, the content of this chapter is based on the following research activities:

- Identification, search for and analysis of secondary information on the luxury phenomenon and its characteristics, perceptions of luxury brands, the luxury fragrance market and its characteristics and consumers, in general, and luxury fragrance consumers, specifically.
- Critical analysis of said documentary sources via comparison with opinions of sector professionals, obtained through five in-depth interviews conducted with managers of the Spanish selective perfume and cosmetics industry (three manufacturers and two distributors of Spanish subsidiaries of multinational leaders of the sector).
- Development of qualitative research via focus groups with luxury fragrance purchasers and users.

Participants were deliberately selected based on researcher's criteria, to guarantee the presence of male and female luxury fragrances consumers, and intentionally, to ensure the participation of individuals with different occupations, income levels, lifestyles, etc., that are traditionally linked to the different age groups.

Therefore, six focus groups were conducted, in which 35 luxury-fragrance consumers in Spain participated (distributed between men and women and grouped by age: between 18 and 29, 30 and 44, and 45 and older) and were selected using the snowball sampling method. Look at the profile of participants in Table 1.

This phase of the research allowed for an understanding of the keys to luxury fragrance consumer behavior, inquiry into their purchasing motivations and identification of the benefits resulting from their purchase and use.

Table 1. Profile of the focus groups' participants

Studies Level	Basis = 35
12 K/School graduate	14.3%
Higher Education/Vocational Education and Training	28.6%
Undergraduate studies	45.7%
Master and PhDs' degrees	11.4%
Main Activity	**Basis = 35**
Student	37.1%
Stay at home	5.7%
Actively employed	60.0%
Pensioner	2.9%
Unemployed	8.6%
Present or Last Occupation	**Basis = 25**
Executive/manager in private or public sector	44.0%
Professional, scientific and technical worker	16.0%
Support service employee	12.0%
Administrative employee	4.0%
Other	16.0%
No answer	8.0%
Gross Average Annual Income Per Household	**Basis = 35**
Less than 30,000 €	5.7%
From 30.000 to 39.999 €	14.3%
From 40.000 to 59.999 €	17.1%
From 60.000 to 79.999 €	17.1%
From 80,000 to 100,000 €	5.7%
More than 100.000 €	22.9%
No answer	17.1%
Interests	**Basis = 35**
Travel	91.4%
Sports	62.9%
Reading	65.7%
Nature	28.6%
Arts	54.3%
Other	8.6%
Age	**Basis = 35**
Between 18 and 29 years old	31.4%
Between 30 and 44 years old	37.2%
Older than 44	31.4%
Gender	**Basis = 35**
Male	49%
Female	51%

- Development of quantitative field research carried out in 2012 via a structured personal survey completed by 520 luxury fragrance consumers (treated final sample) selected in a non-random manner based on defined gender and age quotas. Look at the data sheet in Table 2.

Thanks to this research stage, it has been possible to describe and analyze the behavior of the luxury fragrance consumers regarding these types of products, their purchase motivations and the benefits that, according to the consumers, result from their purchase and consumption.

Furthermore, based on the previous results, different groups of consumers have been identified through multivariate analysis techniques.

THE SPANISH LUXURY FRAGRANCE MARKET

Data from Stanpa (2014 Report based on the AC Nielsen and IMS) reveals that in 2014, the Spanish luxury fragrance market value was 702.3 million euros; this represents 54.6% of the Spanish market of selective or luxury perfume and cosmetics, and 72.9% of the total Spanish fragrance market.

Also, according to the previous source, two large segments are distinguished within the Spanish luxury fragrance market: feminine perfumes–whose value reached 445.5 million euros-, and masculine perfumes–with a value of 256.8 million euros-.

As this data reveals, the feminine market is some 73.5% larger than the masculine one, 63.4% of the total luxury fragrance market in Spain in 2014. According to sector professionals, this may be explained by various reasons; first, the average price of feminine perfumes is higher than that of the masculine fragrances, second, women buy more fragrances than men and are less faithful than men to their usual fragrance and, finally, the purchase of feminine fragrances as gifts is considerably more frequent amongst men than the purchase of masculine perfumes.

Upon analyzing the 15 top luxury fragrance brands in Spain (see Table 3 with data obtained from Shiseido Spain, 2015), it is found that only one of them (Lancôme) is strictly a "cosmetics" brand; the fourteen others are brands that originated in the fashion world. It is also interesting to note that these 15 brands represent 63.8% of the overall luxury perfume market.

Table 2. Data sheet from the survey carried out

Data Obtaining	Technique	Structured Personal Survey
	Questionnaire	Structured-305 Variables
Universe	People from 18 years old, medium and upper class, luxury fragrances consumers and living in Madrid	
Sampling	Sample Size	520 People
	Sampling Method	Non-random quotas sampling (according to sex and age) by simple allocation
Field Work	Period	Jun-12
	Place	Households and Work Centres
Data Analysis	Statistical Techniques	Simple and cross tab
		Cluster analysis
	Software	SPSS 19

Table 3. Top luxury fragrances brands in Spain. Market share (%).

Brands	2013	2014
Chanel	7.3	6.9
Paco Rabanne	5.2	6.2
Loewe	5.9	5.7
Calvin Klein	5.7	5.1
Christian Dior	5.0	4.9
Giorgio Armani	4.4	4.7
Hugo Boss	4.3	4.5
Dolce & Gabbana	4.4	4.5
Carolina Herrera	4.4	4.4
Adolfo Dominguez	3.7	3.6
Lancome	3.2	3.5
Rochas	3.2	3.1
Yves Saint Laurent	2.7	2.9
Cacharel	1.9	1.9
Jean Paul Gaultier	2.0	1.8
Sub Total 15 Brands	63.2	63.8

Source: Shiseido Spain 2015

Another noteworthy aspect, is the relative to advertising investments made in this market: really important (12.5% of figures of total fragrances sales, 13.4% of total feminine ones and 10.9% of total masculine's) and highly concentrated in the television media (see Table 4 with data obtained from Shiseido Spain, 2015).

THE FRAGRANCES: BASIC DESCRIPTION AND CHARACTERISTICS

Perfume is invisible and manifest...
It is an accomplice of the night, hope and the voice of the day.
Perfume is a symbol, a dream... It stimulates desire, evokes enthusiasm and provokes desire.
Perfume embellishes life ...Perfume is life... (Jean-Yves Gaborit, 1985, p.7)

Table 4. Advertising investments in the Spanish market of luxury fragrances. Euros.

2014	Total Media	Tv	Magazines	Outside	Digital	Supplements	Newspapers	Cinema	Radio
Total Fragrances	88.003.580	59.487.643	10.723.753	9.182.839	2.824.833	3.804.513	547.767	1.379.456	52.775
T. Feminine	59.890.473	37.803.982	9.609.152	7.109.263	1.313.189	2.765.125	142.099	1.094.887	52.775
T. Masculine	28.113.107	21.683.661	1.114.601	2.073.576	1.511.644	1.039.388	405.668	284.569	

Source: Shiseido Spain 2015

The characteristics of the fragrances are presented below as manufacturers of luxury fragrances are exposed largely of brands product training courses (L'Oreal Luxury Products Division).

A perfume (or fragrance) is a mixture of aromatic essential oils, ethyl alcohol, water and a fixative that offers a pleasant and long-lasting aroma to the human body.

The quality and uniqueness of the perfume's ingredients determines the quality of the same, which, in most cases, is also related to the intensity and duration of the fragrance.

However, these two qualities, intensity and duration, of the top fragrances, are directly proportional to their "fragility", that is, the more intense and long-lasting a fragrance is, the more it shall deteriorate under the environmental effects of light, sun and air.

Perfumes are commercialized in a variety of concentrations that are defined by the percentage of essential oil aromatics contained in each and the type of alcohol used. Thus, the following concentrations are distinguished which, for the most part in the luxury fragrance market, are commonly referred to by their French names[2]:

1. ***Parfum* or Perfume Extract:** Is that containing the maximum content of the fragrant components (15-40%) diluted in very pure ethyl alcohol (96%). They are typically sold in very small packages (7.5-15 millimeters), given that the fragrance is so intensely concentrated and long lasting, but their prices are also very elevated. They tend to be used at night due to their high intensity, duration and fragility.
2. ***Eau de Parfum* (EDP):** This is one of the most commonly sold concentrations in the luxury fragrance market, making up 10-20% of the fragrance components diluted in alcohol that is 90% pure. It is typically presented in a package or container with a vaporizer and has a capacity of between 30 and 100 millimeters[3].
3. ***Eau de Toilette* (EDT):** This is another of the most popular concentrations of the luxury fragrance market. It contains 4-10% of the fragrance components diluted in an alcohol that is 80-90% pure. The presentation of the Eau de Toilette tends to be similar to that of the Eau de Parfum, although still today, mainly in the case of masculine fragrances, this concentration tends to be packaged in containers without a vaporizer. The characteristics of the Eau de Toilette (lightness of the fragrance and resistance to the effects of light, air…) make it very appropriate for use during the day (although it is not very long lasting).
4. ***Eau de Cologne*:** In general, it contains between 3-5% of the fragrance components diluted in alcohol that is 70% pure. Very few luxury fragrances are sold in this concentration and usually those that do so, market them as a "Limited Edition" for the summer season. This concentration does not exist in the American market.

In addition to the previously described concentrations, some brands market their fragrances in a version without alcohol. Very few fragrances of the selective market do this since, although their lightness may be very highly valued (particularly in hot climates), the very limited duration of the same as well as their milky and less pleasant appearance decrease their demand considerably.

One fragrance may appear in all of the previously described concentrations, although this is not always the case. In fact, many perfumes are presented in only one or two concentrations (usually EDP and/or EDT). This depends on the target audience, the geographic area where it is marketed, the time of year…and basically, the nature of the fragrance.

As for the nature and type of fragrances, they tend to be classified into fragrance families, in accordance with the dominant "note" of the fragrance. The principle fragrance families are the following:

1. Feminine families:
   a. Floral.
   b. Oriental or amber.
   c. Citrus.
   d. *Chypre*.
   e. Fern.
   f. Leather.
2. Masculine families:
   a. Aromatics.
   b. Woody.
   c. Citric.
   d. Oriental.

This classification of the olfactory families is rigorously used by the "noses"[4] and perfume brand manufacturers, but it is generally unknown by most fragrance consumers. Thus, a consumer demanding an oriental or floral fragrance does not mean that it is really from this family. It may be interesting to analyze consumer perceptions with respect to whether or not a fragrance is floral, oriental, citric, etc.

This same reflection may be made with regards to whether a perfume is considered to be light and fresh or intense and heavy. Perfume manufacturers suggest that the consumer is unable to distinguish whether or not a fragrance is fresh or intense. But it is not about the consumer "being correct" or not when qualifying a fragrance as fresh; it is about whether or not they perceive it as being fresh.

Another fundamental element of fragrances is the olfactory pyramid that structures the perfume's composition in three stages (see Figure 1):

Figure 1. Olfactory pyramid of a perfume

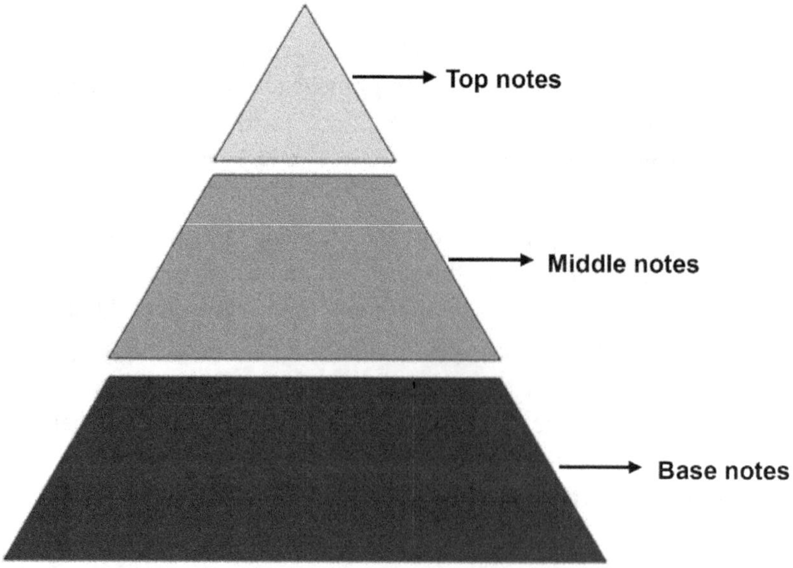

The "top notes" are the first notes that are appreciated in a fragrance. They only last for a few seconds and provide the fragrance "hit" when trying on a perfume.

Next are the so-called "middle notes" that follow the top notes and give body to the perfume. They last one or two minutes.

Finally there are the "base notes" that are those that remain on the skin and provide the final aroma.

A good perfumer should harmoniously combine these three groups of notes.

Another factor to consider with respect to the fragrances is that a same fragrance may be perceived differently depending on the temperature and humidity level of the surroundings and according to the skin on which it is applied.

In this respect, the nose, Emilio Valeros, suggests that "scents are perceived differently according to the climate and, furthermore, they develop differently. With heat, we find that it smells stronger". This is quite logical if we consider that temperature clearly influences the degree and speed of evaporation of the alcohol in the fragrance as well as the degree of skin perspiration.

Another nose, Alberto Morillas, affirmed that the degree of humidity also affects fragrances and that "the greater the humidity, the stronger the fragrance shall seem, therefore in tropical locations, all of the aromas are more intense and heavier".

Therefore, we can say that there are perfumes that are more appropriate for the summer and others that are more appropriate for the winter months.

There are fragrances for day and others for night, however, while it is certain that there are aromas that are clearly defined for different times of the day (as occurs with clothing), in other cases, the increased or decreased appropriateness of a perfume for the day or night may depend upon its concentration (*parfum, eau de parfum, eau de toilette*, etc.).

CRITERIA DEFINING THE FRAGRANCES IN THE ACCESSIBLE LUXURY FRAGRANCE MARKET

The "distribution" criterion for considering the marketed brand products to be selective or luxury is used by FCT Forecasts, Stanpa, Colipa[5], etc. This means, first, that the selective distribution in the area of cosmetics is reduced to specialized perfume shops or department stores having a specialized section of specialized perfumes. Second, the brand or manufacturing or distributing company authorized by the manufacturer (never retailer), signs a contract with the retailer authorizing the sale of their products (all or some of the same) in their point of sale. If the retailer has various points of sale, this authorization should refer to each specific point of sale and does not necessarily include all of them. This is essential for all of the companies operating in the sector in Spain. What varies from one company to another are the conditions by which the product sale is authorized: exposure and merchandising, promotion, advertising, economic conditions, etc.

However, exclusive use of the "distribution" criteria to qualify the marketed brands as "luxury" seems insufficient. First, this is because this is a criterion imposed from the offer side and does not consider the opinion of the demand side or the consumers. Second, because it groups brands and products together in the same category, although they are quite different from one another.

Why then is it agreed that selective fragrances are accessible luxury products?

First, this is the case because their consumption allows for a large part of the population to access the luxury brands. Second, because they comply with all of the criteria suggested by Allérès (1990) and Campuzano (2003) for defining accessible luxury: overall, they are declinations of inaccessible or intermediary luxury, they are manufactured in unlimited industrial series, they serve the needs of the consumers, their quality is essential, their price is quite high and is established in function of cost and those of the competition, its distribution is selective, advertising is carried out cautiously to maintain the prestige of the brand, marketing is carried out via select media, public relations are important, it has a large number of consumers, they are extremely aspiring, there is a controlled imitation market and finally, a large part of their sales are for gifts.

Furthermore, each of the following characteristics proposed by the mentioned authors has been examined for the luxury products in regards to the selective fragrances:

Perfection

Allérès (1990) suggested that perfection is basically reflected in the innovation and creativity in the product concept and its quality.

Innovation applied to a specific product is a short term concept; that is, the innovation that a product offers the market is no longer innovative as soon as other similar products are included in the market. Thus a product that is innovative today may no longer be innovative tomorrow. However, the qualification of innovative brand tends to be linked to those brands that continuously offer innovative products to the market.

This allows us to propose that a fragrance brand is luxurious whenever it is an innovative brand. Thus, the more innovative, the more luxurious the brand shall be.

On the other hand, creativity in product conception refers to the fact that the product is conceived and developed thanks to the talent of a genius creator or artist. This is of particular interest in the field of selective perfumes. The majority of the selective fragrance brands have their origins in the fashion world, that is, they are brands that are signed by prestigious designers recognized as a creative talent. Furthermore, the perfumes are developed by "noses" who are considered to be artists and some of whom have received great international prestige.

Thus it is agreed that those perfumes signed by a prestigious creator are luxurious. And the more prestigious and recognized the creator, the more luxurious the perfume.

As for product quality, undoubtedly a luxury product should be of excellent quality based on their component raw materials and creation process. These criteria allow for the clear definition of different levels of luxury fragrances, especially those based on the exceptional basis of the raw materials used. In this way, we should note that the value of certain fragrances is based on the fact that the raw materials making them up are unusual and extraordinary.

Thus, the fragrances are considered to be luxurious if they are made of exceptional raw materials of great quality. And the higher the quality of the raw materials and the more exceptional they are, the more luxurious the fragrance.

Finally, regarding the more or less artisanal nature of the fragrance creation or manufacturing process as a determining factor for being considered luxurious, the following may be deduced: 1) it is not probable that a luxurious fragrance may be always made in an artisanal and limited manner, particularly taking into account that the majority of the selective fragrances are manufactured in unlimited industrial series while controlling the number of specimens–as indicated by Allérès (1990) and Campuzano (2003) for the accessible luxury products-, and 2) if the inaccessible luxury and intermediate luxury products are created in an artisanal or limited series manner–Allérès (1990) and Campuzano (2003)-, this may clearly influence whether or not the fragrances are perceived as being more luxurious than others. Thus it may be affirmed that the more artisanal and limited the creation of a fragrance, the more luxurious it is considered to be.

Exquisite Presentation

This characteristic is particularly important for fragrances and basically refers to the packaging of the same, that is, to the packaging and container.

The packaging of a fragrance has always been considered a determining factor of the product and, in many cases, is even more important than the fragrance itself. The packaging makes the quality of the perfume tangible[6] and it may become a collector's item.

The quality of the perfume's packaging is mainly determined by the quality of the same and by the quality of the materials that makes it up.

As for the packaging design, creativity and originality have no limits (shaped like an amphora, woman's body, dove, sun, flower…curved or straight lines, avant garde or traditional, minimalist or sophisticated). In fact, there are fragrance packages considered to be true works of art and design; for example, *Mon Parfum* by Paloma Picasso, displayed at the *Musée des Arts Decoratifs* in Paris, or Chanel No. 5, at the *Museum of Modern Art* in New York.

As for the materials used, the range of possibilities is broad: glass, metal, porcelain, vinyl, leather, etc., but whatever material is used in the luxury fragrance packaging, it should be of good quality. The materials used also offer different quality levels: Baccarat or Lalique crystal, use of precious and semi-precious stones, gold and silver impressions, etc.

Given the importance of the luxury product packaging, and specifically that of selective fragrances, it should be noted that these packages are the object of design created with high quality materials. The greater the value attributed to the design and the more precious the materials used, the more luxurious the fragrance.

As for the box and the other packaging, quality imperatives demand the best impressions and care in all carton packaging elements attached to the cellophane that protects the fragrance (Campuzano, 2003).

Value in Transaction

As affirmed by Allérès (1990) and Campuzano (2003), although an expensive product is not necessarily a luxury product, luxury products are always expensive. Thus, luxury perfumes should comply with the prices which are always high in comparison with non-luxury ones. The higher is the price, the more luxurious is the fragrance.

Select Distribution

As previously described, selective distribution is the criteria used by manufacturers, distributors and organisms of the perfume and cosmetics sector to qualify and classify fragrances in the luxury sector. But this criterion, as suggested by Allérès (1990) and Campuzano (2003) is also a determinant for consumers.

In the world of luxury, the difficulty involved in attaining a specific product implies the value attributed to the same. Thus, the distribution of luxury fragrances is always limited. And the more reduced the distribution, the more luxurious the fragrance.

Select Communication

Recently, there has been a profound change in regards to the communication means and media used for the luxury brands.

If those brands traditionally considered luxurious (Mercedes, Chanel, Dior, etc.) utilize means other than the mass media for the communication of their products, upon extending their commercial offer to include luxury products, they have also begun to use the mass media to reach the middle social classes that are available to purchase their products.

For this, it may not be said that the communication of luxury fragrances should be categorically selective but it is believed that selectiveness in the communication of the fragrances allows for them to be perceived as being more or less luxurious. Thus, the more selective is the communication, the more luxurious is the fragrance.

The Strength of Differentiation

Differentiation is desired by most brands –both luxury and non-luxury brands – when developing their products and the more differentiated the product with respect to its competitors, the more extraordinary and valued it shall be by consumers.

While differentiation is not an exclusive quality of luxury products, all luxury products should attain some degree of differentiation. Thus, for a fragrance to be considered luxurious, it should possess some qualities and attributes that identify it and differentiate it from its competitors. And the more differentiated that it is perceived to be by consumers, the more luxurious the fragrance.

Internationally Distributed

This criterion highlights the need of the luxury brands to be internationally recognized. As is the case with differentiation, international recognition is not exclusive of luxury brands.

Thus, it is understood that this refers to international recognition of the special value of a luxury brand or product. So the more internationally recognized or valued the luxury brand or product, the greater is its perceived value and therefore, the more luxurious it is considered to be. Thus, the more internationally valued it is, the more luxurious the fragrance.

Part of a Large Brand

Belonging to a luxury brand is not only one of the characteristics included by Campuzano (2003) for luxury products, but is also a fundamental criterion for many executives of the luxury sector.

Along these lines, there is agreement regarding the idea that the brands that transform products into luxury products, through a process of brand value transfer to each product in question. This idea is also supported by executives of the perfume and cosmetics industry in Spain.

This criterion is fundamental in defining luxury products; any product signed by a luxury brand automatically becomes a luxury product since all of the attributes associated with the brand are to be incorporated into the product. Therefore, fragrances signed by a luxury brand are luxury fragrances. And the more luxurious is the brand, the more luxurious is the fragrance.

LUXURY FRAGRANCE PURCHASE AND USE BEHAVIOR

The consumer behavior includes, among others, the activities done by the individuals when they purchase and use products to satisfy their needs (Rivera, Arellano & Molero, 2009; cited by Martínez Moreno, Ruiz, Lozano & Verján, 2015).

Based on this definition, the content of this heading focuses on describing the basic activities related to luxury fragrances purchase and use behaviour based on the results of the survey referred to in the paragraph of "Methodology" of this chapter.

Thus, as for the locations where luxury fragrances are most frequently acquired (see Figure 2), there is no doubt that this category is led by the large department stores. The next type of establishment that is the most typical for the purchase of luxury fragrances are the specialized perfume stores, followed by airport shops and/or airlines, traditional perfume shops and finally, the Internet, although for this last channel, the purchase of luxury fragrances is growing at a very rapid rate due to the increase in websites offering these products at rates that are more advantageous than the other channels.

Figure 2. Luxury fragrance purchase sites

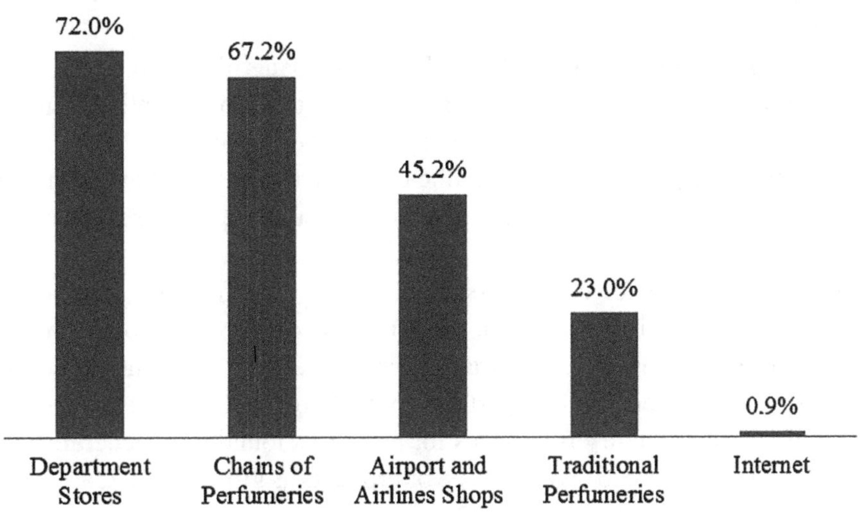

As for luxury fragrance consumer habits, it is interesting to note the differences based on consumer age. The youngest of consumers use the fragrances mainly for special occasions and as their age increases, this fragrance is used regularly throughout the day, every day. So, younger users combine the use of luxury fragrances for special occasions with non-selective fragrances for everyday activities, while as the age increases, only the higher level or selective fragrances are used.

Thus, the number of luxury fragrances used tends to be higher in the older age groups, who alternate some fragrances with others depending on the activity that they carry out, the occasion for use, the season of the year, or even, their mood.

It should also be noted that women have more high quality fragrances than men.

Finally, it is noteworthy that men over the age of 45 tend to use complementary treatment and hygiene products (after-shaves, deodorants, shower gels, etc.) more frequently, that is, those having the same aroma as the fragrance.

LUXURY FRAGRANCE PURCHASE AND USE MOTIVATIONS

If human motivation "refers to the drives, urges, wishes or desires which initiate the sequence of events known as behaviour" (Bayton, 1957, p.282), it could be consider that the consumers' products purchase and use motivations refer to everything that drives individuals to buy and use products to satisfy their needs and desires.

The academic literature distinguishes between extrinsic and intrinsic motivations. The extrinsic motivations are the motivations "to perform an activity because it is perceived to produce valued outcomes that are distinct from the activity itself" (Webster & Martocchio, 1992; cited by Garrity, O'Donnell, Kim & Sanders, 2007, p.21). In contrast to this, intrinsic motivations are the motivations "to perform the activity due to the direct reinforcement of performing the activity per se" (Garrity et al, 2007, p.21).

The knowledge of consumer's motivations implies studying in depth the basic motives for which the man behaves like a consumer (Britt, 1950). In relation to this, "motive is common motivation directing consumer behavior to fulfill its requirement". There are two types of motives in consumer behaviour: utilitarian and expressive. Utilitarian oriented at functional benefit from one product or brand; while expressive oriented at benefit social-symbolic or self-image from product or brand". (Nurcahyo, Nur'ainy & Sariyati, 2011, p.236).

In this context, "fragrances have no significant functional benefit" (Bush, 2003; cited by Toncar & Fetscherin, 2012, p.56). Therefore, "fragrance marketers speak to people's fantasies and attempt to create a sensual "mood"". (Toncar & Munch, 2001; cited by Toncar & Fetscherin, 2012, p.57).

Thus, below are the extrinsic motivations and the expressive motives linked to the purchase and use of luxury fragrances and resulting of the qualitative and quantitative studies that are referenced in the paragraph of "Methodology" of this chapter.

The majority of luxury fragrance consumers acquire them both for their own personal use as well as for gifts. Only a minority– curiously enough, made up of two opposing groups, the youngest women and the oldest men- never purchase selective fragrances for their use since they use fragrances that are gifts or that are purchased for them by their partners– who know their preferences regarding the same.

Also, as for the purchase of luxury fragrances for gifts, it is found that, generally speaking, as consumer age increases, the reluctance to give this type of products as gifts also increases, as it is considered something very personal and difficult to correctly determine; this reluctance decreases if the purchaser knows the fragrance used by the gift recipient or if their preferences in the same are known.

In this context, when giving someone a luxury gift, consumers coincide in that it is fundamental that the fragrance brand be well known and recognized as a luxury brand, so that the gift is valued by its recipient and therefore, the gift giver comes off well and the economic effort made is recognized. There is also agreement that it is important that the age, personality and style associated with the fragrance correspond with those of the recipient of the same.

Furthermore, many purchasers of this type of products place great importance on the presentation and packaging of the fragrance (so that they are as visible as possible) when they are given to another individual as a gift. And, many women (particularly the youngest) also value the specially designed gift packages.

In the scenario of personal use purchases, there is no doubt that the most important motivation for all fragrance purchasers is their liking the aroma of the fragrance. Then, there are the following purchase motivations: that the price is accessible, that they can try out the fragrance or receive a sample of the same prior to purchasing it (valued more significantly by women) and that others like the fragrance (considerably more important for men).

On the other hand, many women, when acquiring a fragrance, place great importance on recommendations and testing the fragrance in the store where it is being sold, and the youngest of female consumers also very positively value receiving a practical, pretty and high quality gift when making the purchase. For men, on the other hand, the oldest of the male consumers recognize the influence of fragrance placement in the sales establishment when making their purchase decision.

As for motivations of use, all luxury fragrance consumers coincide in that they love it when they are told that the fragrance smells good (or that they smell good thanks to the fragrance) and when they are recognized for the fragrance that they are wearing; but while, for the youngest of purchasers, these are determinant factors in the purchase, use and faithfulness to a fragrance–if others do not like the fragrance they may stop using it, even if they themselves like it -, as the consumer's age increases, the relative importance of these factors decreases.

Regarding the previous, the youngest wearers grant the luxury fragrance a fundamental role in the art of seduction and value them as elements that reinforce their personal attractiveness and self-esteem. They also significantly value that the fragrance is part of a well-recognized brand such as the luxury and prestigious brands, since this gives them a special status from a social point of view. Thus, they particularly appreciate the brands associated with fashion designers since these are the most well-known and are those that they can only (or almost only) access through the fragrances of the same.

To the contrary, while all consumers feel it essential to like the fragrance that they use, the relative importance of this factor increases with age, to the point where some of the oldest users are uninterested in whether or not others like the fragrance, with the most important factor being that they themselves like it.

For all users, it is essential that the fragrance that they use corresponds to their style and personality and, in addition, for the more extreme age groups (the youngest and the oldest) it is equally important that it also corresponds to their age. In this sense, most users recognize that their assessments regarding the personality, style and age associated with a fragrance are constructed mainly based on advertising and the different communication elements of said fragrance. These suggest lifestyles or personalities that are masculine or feminine, romantic, formal, sporty, traditional, modern, etc.

Another attribute that is required by all individuals regarding luxury fragrances –and that, furthermore, serves as the basis for evaluation of the fragrance's quality – is its duration. There is agreement regarding this attribute: everyone seeks the longest possible duration and considers that the longer the duration, the better the quality of the fragrance.

Also, in general, most consumers prefer light and fresh fragrances, although some prefer more intense ones and everyone recognizes that these have ideal situations for use.

Likewise, with the increase in age, there is an increased importance given to the exclusivity of the fragrance (used by a small number) and the originality of its aroma.

THE LUXURY FRAGRANCE CONSUMER

Description of the Perfume and Cosmetics Sector in Spain

It is curious how luxury fragrance brands manage to go from the most succinct and almost telegraphic description to the most ambiguous and poetic when defining their real and potential consumers.

In the media plans of the principle luxury fragrance brands, the target consumer of these perfumes tends to be defined by four variables: gender, age, social class and residence.

As for gender, luxury fragrance consumers are both male and female, since masculine, feminine and unisex fragrances exist. However, if possible to deduce, based on the manufacturer's sales statistics (European Forecasts, 2011), the sales of feminine fragrances are clearly superior to those of the masculine fragrances, explained for a variety of reasons: because the average price of feminine perfumes is greater than those of the masculine ones and because women buy more perfume than men and more often. These reasons, while widely accepted in the sector, are not supported by scientific studies or global market data.

As for age, although there are some luxury perfumes that are used by children– such as Tartine et Chocolat by Givenchy or Bulgari Petits et Mamans-, it is estimated that the use of luxury fragrances tends to begin between 15 and 18 years of age and extends beyond the age of 65. Furthermore, the greatest use of luxury perfumes is considered to occur between the ages of 25 and 45.

On the other hand, although, when launching a perfume, the brands tend to define an age range in order to identify their target public, this age group is not absolutely rigid; in fact, there are many perfumes that are directed at youth (15 to 18 year olds) a priori, but that are also used by older consumers and vice versa.

It is also of interest that in Spain, retail sales establishments tend to be associated with a type of consumer based on age; the large perfume chain stores (Bodybell, Sephora, Douglas, etc.) are associated with younger consumers than the department stores (El Corte Inglés) or traditional perfume shops. Again, we refer to opinions that are widely agreed upon by sector manufacturers and distributors, based mainly on the observation and experience, but that have not been scientifically proven by data.

There are no scientific studies regarding social class and residence of the luxury fragrance consumers. However, it is agreed that the consumption of luxury fragrances begins in the middle social class and extends, according to fragrance type, to the upper class. It is also agreed that the luxury fragrance consumer is situated mainly in cities with populations of over 50,000 residents having a greater presence the greater the number of inhabitants. Therefore, the large cities are the sites of the largest concentration of luxury fragrances exists.

In addition to the previously mentioned variables, the luxury fragrance brands, in many communications, describe perfume consumers based on completely subjective and intangible qualities. The following examples illustrate this:

- **Anaïs-Anaïs by Cacharel:** "For a multi-faceted woman, an evasive woman that does not fit into the usual patterns" (Gaborit, 1985, p.18).
- **Calèche by Hermès:** "Elegant with refined taste, the Calèche woman has a serene beauty that comes with confidence. Natural or sophisticated, athletic or romantic, she knows how to seduce without warning. She wants her perfume to have the same personality and to reveal the subtle charms of her radiant femininity" (Gaborit, 1985, p.64).
- **Mania by Giorgio Armani:** "For a modern, elegant and discreet woman. Feminine, unique and full of contrasts" (Press kit for fragrance launch).
- **Romance for Men by Ralph Lauren:** "For a romantic man who does not hide his feelings. A man seeking sensuality, confidence and sweetness in his partner" (Press kit for fragrance launch).

Ultimately, according to the opinion of the selective perfume and cosmetics sector, the Spanish luxury fragrance consumer tends to have the following profile: an individual over the age of 18, primarily between 25 and 45, of the middle to middle-upper class living in cities with over 50,000 residents and in large part, of the female gender.

Types of Luxury Fragrance Consumers Based on Their Personal Use Purchase Motivations

Based on data from a survey conducted in 2012, and after Cluster analysis carried out on the motivations of fragrance purchases for personal use by the studied individuals, it is found that there are two clearly differentiated consumer groups (see Table 5).

Those of group 1 are characterized by placing a greater importance on the fact that the brand is very well known, that the fragrance's advertising corresponds to their age, that the packaging is attractive, original and of good quality, that a practical, pretty and top quality gift is offered with the purchase of the fragrance, that it is presented in a special gift bag or package and finally, that the fragrance's advertising corresponds to their lifestyle and personality.

Therefore, projecting the market segmentation of luxury consumers from the Wiedmann, Hennings and Siebels model (2009, p.640-644) to the individuals studied, it is possible to identify group 1 as that of functionalists seeking fragrances that are selective in terms of quality as well as reaffirmation of the identity.

As for group 2, this group maybe identified as that of the hedonists who only seek personal pleasure provided by the acquired fragrance.

As for the socio-demographic profile of the individuals belonging to groups 1 and 2, this is shown in Tables 6, 7, 8 and 9.

Table 5. "Cluster analysis." K-means algorithms. Cross tabulation of means and standard deviations of the variables in the generated groups. (With Snedecor's F-distribution / ANOVA table).

		Total sample	Groups starting from the division: Group 1	Group 2	Intergroup sum of squares (variance explained): 3,966.07 % of variance explained by the division in 2 groups: 25.56%
No. of members:		**341**	**136**	**205**	
Sum of squares:		**15,516.85**	**4,718.33**	**6,832.45**	
Identification of variables	**Statistics**	**+: Group with highest mean -: Group with lowest mean**			**Snedecor's F**
'That the fragrance's advertising reflects the world of luxury'	Mean: Std. Dev.	2.43 1.66	3.65 + 1.59	1.61 - 1.10	F(1, 339) = 195.22 p = 0.0000
'That I like the aroma of the fragrance'	Mean: Std. Dev.	6.77 0.82	6.58 - 1.19	6.89 + 0.39	F(1, 339) = 11.79 p = 0.0007
'That the price is accessible'	Mean: Std. Dev.	5.12 1.57	5.36 + 1.44	4.96 - 1.63	F(1, 339) = 5.33 p = 0.0217
'That the brand is very well-known'	Mean: Std. Dev.	3.08 1.71	4.31 + 1.59	2.26 - 1.23	F(1, 339) = 178.06 p = 0.0000
'That the fragrance's advertising corresponds to my age'	Mean: Std. Dev.	3.27 1.91	4.60 + 1.54	2.39 - 1.60	F(1, 339) = 159.77 p = 0.0000
'That is a brand of a prestigious designer'	Mean: Std. Dev.	2.74 1.70	3.94 + 1.64	1.95 - 1.19	F(1, 339) = 167.64 p = 0.0000
'That the bottle is pretty, original and top quality'	Mean: Std. Dev.	3.60 1.78	4.61 + 1.52	2.94 - 1.62	F(1, 339) = 91.29 p = 0.0000
'That they offer a practical, pretty and high quality gift for buying the fragrance'	Mean: Std. Dev.	3.50 1.98	4.63 + 1.71	2.75 - 1.79	F(1, 339) = 93.06 p = 0.0000
'That the fragrances comes in a special gift bag or container'	Mean: Std. Dev.	3.18 1.84	4.49 + 1.59	2.32 - 1.45	F(1, 339) = 167.43 p = 0.0000
'That others like the fragrance'	Mean: Std. Dev.	4.69 1.91	5.65 + 1.30	4.05 - 1.99	F(1, 339) = 68.17 p = 0.0000
'That the fragrance's advertising corresponds to my lifestyle and personality'	Mean: Std. Dev.	3.64 2.00	5.10 + 1.39	2.67 - 1.73	F(1, 339) = 187.54 p = 0.0000
'That it is a fragrance that is trendy'	Mean: Std. Dev.	2.67 1.63	3.93 + 1.43	1.82 - 1.14	F(1, 339) = 226.68 p = 0.0000
'That the fragrance is very well positioned in the establishment where it is being sold'	Mean: Std. Dev.	2.63 1.79	3.90 + 1.76	1.79 - 1.21	F(1, 339) = 172.78 p = 0.0000
'That I am recommended the fragrance in the establishment where it is sold'	Mean: Std. Dev.	3.06 1.66	3.89 + 1.52	2.50 - 1.52	F(1, 339) = 67.81 p = 0.0000
'That I am given a sample or allowed to try the fragrance before purchasing it'	Mean: Std. Dev.	5.11 1.84	5.59 + 1.50	4.80 - 1.97	F(1, 339) = 15.84 p = 0.0001

Table 6. Group 1 profile (Base of 136 individuals)

Gender		Age		Education Level		Principle Occupation	
Value	**%**	**Value**	**%**	**Value**	**%**	**Value**	**%**
Men	40.44	18 - 29	34.56	Basic education	4.41	Housewife	8.82
Women	59.56	30 - 44	37.50	Average studies (ESO/ high school diploma)	17.65	Unemployed student	22.79
		45 ó +	27.94	Degree / FP	27.21	Employed student	11.03
				University degree	36.03	Retired	0.74
				Master's or doctorate	13.97	Unemployed	2.94
				Don't know/don't answer	0.74	Active worker	52.94
						Don't know/don't answer	0.74
	100.00		100.00		100.00		100.00

Table 7. Group 1 profile (Base of 136 individuals)

No. of Individuals Making up the Family Unit		Mean Gross Income of the Family Unit		Social Class	
Value	**%**	**Value**	**%**	**Value**	**%**
One	7.35	Less than 30,000 €	13.24	High	4.41
Two	19.85	30,000 – 39,999 €	12.50	Medium-high	34.56
Three	18.38	40,000 – 59,999 €	10.29	Medium	58.82
Four or five	45.59	60,000 – 79,999 €	6.62	Other	1.47
More than five	8.09	80,000 – 100,000 €	10.29	Don't know/don't answer	0.74
Don't know/don't answer	0.74	More than 100,000 €	8.09		
		Don't know	15.44		
		Don't answer	23.53		
	100.00		100.00		100.00

Types of Luxury Fragrance Consumers Based on Their Motivations for Use

The Cluster analysis has allowed us to once again identify the two groups that include the cases with the greatest distances to the average values for level of agreement or disagreement with respect to the variables measuring motivations for use of luxury fragrances by their consumers (see Table 10).

As seen in Table 10, the motivations for consumption of the luxury fragrances are, primarily, similar in the two identified groups, although the level of agreement and therefore, the relation to said attitudes is always significantly higher for subjects from group 1 than for those of group 2.

This cluster analysis reveals the differences between the two groups in regards to the positive or negative sense of identification with the studied attitudes. That is, it is interesting to note that for certain statements (linked to the consumption of luxury fragrances) subjects from group 1 were more or less in

Table 8. Group 2 profile (Base of 205 individuals)

Gender		Age		Education Level		Principle Occupation	
Value	**%**	**Value**	**%**	**Value**	**%**	**Value**	**%**
Men	43.90	18 - 29	25.85	Basic Education	2.44	Housewife	4.88
Women	56.10	30 - 44	41.95	Average Studies (ESO/ High school diploma)	22.93	Unemployed student	11.71
		45 6 +	32.20	Degree/ FP	23.90	Employed student	9.76
				University degree	41.46	Retired	0.49
				Master's or doctorate	8.78	Unemployed	3.90
				Don't know/don't answer	0.49	Active worker	68.78
						Don't know/don't answer	0.49
	100.00		100.00		100.00		100.00

Table 9. Group 2 profile (Base of 205 individuals)

No. of Individuals Making up the Family Unit		Mean Gross Income of the Family Unit		Social Class	
Value	**%**	**Value**	**%**	**Value**	**%**
One	7.32	Less than 30.000 €	16.59	High	2.93
Two	16.10	30,000 – 39,999 €	9.27	Medium-high	38.05
Three	20.98	40,000 – 59,999 €	19.51	Medium	55.61
Four or five	47.32	60,000 – 79,999 €	7.80	Other	0.98
More than five	7.80	80,000 – 100,000 €	6.83	Don't know/don't answer	2.44
Don't know/don't answer	0.49	More than 100,000 €	8.29		
		Don't know	12.20		
		Don't answer	19.51		
	100.00		100.00		100.00

agreement (and the mean corresponding values were below 3), while subjects from group 2 were more or less in disagreement (and the mean corresponding values were above 3).

Thus, while individuals from group 1 use luxury fragrances, alternating them according to their mood and time of use or the activity engaged in, individuals from group 2 did not share these behaviors and attitudes.

Likewise, subjects from group 1 seem to be willing to change their fragrance if others do not like them, while those from group 2 do not care about this. In other words, those from group 1 are much more sensitive to third party opinions when deciding to use a luxury fragrance.

This is also corroborated by the fact that members of the first group claim to use the fragrance as an element of seduction (to flirt) while those from the second group do not use it for this purpose.

Thus, the first group may be identified as the group of seducers and prestige seekers (Wiedmann, Hennings & Siebels, 2009, p.640-644) while the second group is considered to be the more distant users

Table 10. "Cluster analysis". K-Means Algorithm. Cross tabulation of means and standard deviations of the variables in the generated groups (With Snedecor's F-distribution / ANOVA table).

		Total sample	Groups starting from the division		Intergroup sum of squares (variance explained): 1280.87
			Group 1	Group 2	
No. of members:		460	269	191	% of variance explained by the division in 2 groups: 14.96%
Sum of squares:		8,559.68	3,772.15	3,506.67	
Degree of agreement or disagreement with the (from 1 to 5) with respect to the following statements	Statistics	+: Group with highest mean -: Group with lowest mean			Snedecor's F
'I use various fragrances and I alternate them depending on my mood'	Mean: Std Dev.	3.18 1.40	2.44 - 1.12	4.24 + 1.01	F(1, 458) = 308.96 p = 0.0000
'I use various fragrances and I alternate them depending on the time of use (day or night) or the activity that i am going to carry out'	Mean: Std Dev.	2.51 1.45	1.68 - 0.83	3.68 + 1.33	F(1, 458) = 391.80 p = 0.0000
'It is important that the fragrance used is very long-lasting'	Mean: Std Dev.	1.69 0.88	1.57 - 0.74	1.87 + 1.02	F(1, 458) = 13.43 p = 0.0003
'I especially value that the fragrance used belongs to a brand that is known for being luxurious'	Mean: Std Dev.	3.45 1.16	3.32 - 1.13	3.64 + 1.17	F(1, 458) = 8.93 p = 0.0030
'I like that the fragrance I use is used by a lot of people'	Mean: Std Dev.	4.05 0.98	4.04 - 0.96	4.07 + 1.00	F(1, 458) = 0.09 p = 0.7693
' I love when people recognize me for the fragrance that I use'	Mean: Std Dev.	2.19 1.18	1.83 - 0.95	2.70 + 1.28	F(1, 458) = 70.04 p = 0.0000
'I love when people tell me that the fragrance smells very good or that I smell good'	Mean: Std Dev.	1.46 0.78	1.24 - 0.53	1.78 + 0.94	F(1, 458) = 61.25 p = 0.0000
'If others do not like my fragrance I may stop using it or change it for another'	Mean: Std Dev.	3.06 1.23	2.86 - 1.18	3.35 + 1.24	F(1, 458) = 18.05 p = 0.0000
' I don't care if others like my fragrance or not, the important thing is that I like it'	Mean: Std Dev.	2.47 1.26	2.58 + 1.27	2.32 - 1.24	F(1, 458) = 4.48 p = 0.0349
'It is important that the fragrance that I use makes me happy, that I enjoy it'	Mean: Std Dev.	1.99 1.04	1.70 - 0.81	2.41 + 1.18	F(1. 458) = 58.69 p = 0.0000
' I use the fragrance as a means of seduction or to flirt'	Mean: Std Dev.	3.10 1.29	2.75 - 1.19	3.59 + 1.26	F(1, 458) = 53.10 p = 0.0000
'I like fragrances with original or different aromas'	Mean: Std Dev.	2.61 1.09	2.41 - 1.08	2.90 + 1.05	F(1, 458) = 23.05 p = 0.0000
'It is necessary that the fragrance that I use corresponds to my age'	Mean: Std Dev.	2.67 1.21	2.37 - 1.14	3.09 + 1.18	F(1, 458) = 43.88 p = 0.0000
'It is fundamental that the fragrance that I use corresponds to my lifestyle and personality'	Mean: Std Dev.	2.08 0.99	1.74 - 0.78	2.57 + 1.05	F(1, 458) = 94.79 p = 0.0000

(Dubois, Czellar & Laurent, 2005, p.122). The former acquire the luxury fragrances to impress others and for the value associated with their use on different occasions. On the other hand, the latter have a more distant attitude regarding the degree of luxury associated with the fragrances.

As for the socio-demographic profile of the individuals belonging to groups 1 and 2, they are seen in Tables 11, 12, 13 and 14.

Table 11. Group 1 profile (Base of 269 individuals)

Gender		Age		Education Level		Principle Occupation	
Value	%	Value	%	Value	%	Value	%
Men	37.55	18 - 29	33.46	Basic education	4.09	Housewife	7.06
Women	62.45	30 - 44	37.92	Average studies (ESO/ high school diploma)	19.33	Unemployed student	19.70
		45 or older	28.62	Degree / FP	25.28	Employed student	11.52
				University degree	39.78	Retired	1.12
				Master's or doctorate degree	10.78	Unemployed	3.72
				Don't know/don't answer	0.74	Active worker	55.76
						Don't know/don't answer	1.12
	100.00		100.00		100.00		100.00

Table 12. Group 1 profile (Base of 269 individuals)

No. of Individuals Making up the Family Unit		Mean Gross Income of the Family Unit		Social Class	
Value	%	Value	%	Value	%
One	7.43	Less than €30,000	14.50	High	4.09
Two	18.22	€30,000 – €39,999	9.67	Medium high	34.94
Three	18.96	€40,000 – €59,999	16.73	Medium	57.25
Four or five	46.84	€60,000 – €79,999	6.32	Other	1.49
More than five	7.81	€80,000 – €100,000	6.32	Don't know/don't answer	2.23
Don't know/don't answer	0.74	More than €100,000	7.81		
		Don't know	18.59		
		Don't answer	20.07		
	100.00		100.00		100.00

In these profiles, it is seen that subjects in group 1 are primarily female (62.45%), and under the age of 45 (71.38%), while subjects from group 2 tend to be male (61.78%) and over the age of 29 (70.16%).

CONCLUSION

Based on that which has been presented in this chapter, it is found that selective fragrances are accessible luxury products, since, first, their use allows a large majority of the population to access a luxury brand that, in other markets, would be considered inaccessible. And second, the selective fragrances comply with all of the criteria described by Allérès (1990) and Campuzano (2003) in defining accessible luxury.

Table 13. Group 2 profile (Base of 191 individuals)

Gender		Age		Education Level		Principle Occupation	
Value	**%**	**Value**	**%**	**Value**	**%**	**Value**	**%**
Men	61.78	18 - 29	29.84	Basic education	4.71	Housewife	2.09
Women	38.22	30 - 44	33.51	Average studies (ESO/ high school diploma)	20.42	Unemployed student	17.80
		45 or older	36.65	Degree / FP	26.18	Employed student	8.90
				University degree	40.84	Retired	2.09
				Master's or doctorate degree	7.33	Unemployed	4.19
				Don't know/don't answer	0.52	Active worker	64.40
						Don't know/don't answer	0.52
	100.00		100.00		100.00		100.00

Table 14. Group 2 profile (Base of 191 individuals)

No. of Individuals Making up the Family Unit		Mean Gross Income of the Family Unit		Social Class	
Value	**%**	**Value**	**Value**	**%**	**Value**
One	4.71	Less than 30,000	18.85	High	1.05
Two	12.57	€30,000 – €39,999	13.09	Medium high	34.03
Three	22.51	€40,000 – €59,999	10.47	Medium	62.30
Four or five	51.83	€60,000 – €79,999	8.38	Other	1.05
More than five	8.38	€80,000 – €100,000	8.90	Don't know/don't answer	1.57
Don't know/don't answer		More than €100,000	7.33		
		Don't know	10.47		
		Don't answer	22.51		
	100.00		100.00		100.00

Furthermore, if a fragrance has the characteristics recognized for luxury products, it may be affirmed that this fragrance is luxurious. Different levels of luxury may even be defined, based on the values attributed to the characteristics defining a fragrance as luxurious.

On the other hand, and regarding the purchase motivations for luxury fragrances of personal use, the most important motivation of purchasers-users of these products, regardless of their gender and age, is that they like the aroma of the perfume; next, is that the price is accessible, that they can try a sample of the fragrance before purchasing it (particularly for women) and that others like the fragrance (significantly more important for men and the youngest of users).

In addition to the previously stated, it should also be noted that women place more value than men on receiving a practical, pretty and high quality gift when purchasing a fragrance, and they value that the advertising is evocative and representative of their lifestyle and personality. The younger the consumers the more sensitive they are to the fragrance advertising when purchasing for their own personal use.

Thus, based on the purchase motivations for personal use, two groups of purchasers have been identified: a) the functionalists who, when buying luxury fragrances, seek both quality and reaffirmation of their own identity, and b) the hedonists who only seek personal pleasure provided by the acquired fragrance. As age increases, the functionalists move on to become hedonists.

As for motivations for the use of the luxury fragrances, the most notorious motivation refers to the desire for recognition from others through the use of the fragrance; next is fragrance duration, with the personal pleasure offered by its use (particularly for women and the two older groups) and its correspondence with the user's style and personality (particularly for the young group).

Also, the younger the age, the use of the fragrance as a means of seduction is highlighted as well as the importance attributed to the fragrance's correspondence with consumer age.

Finally, two consumer groups have been identified based on motivations for use of the luxury fragrances: a first group, seducers and prestige seekers, characterized by women and those under the age of 45, and a second group, the distanced users, made up mainly of men and those over the age of 29. Thus, individuals from the first group use a variety of fragrances and alternate them based on their mood, the time of use and the activity to be carried out, are willing to change the fragrance if others do not like it and recognize that they use the fragrance as a weapon of seduction or to flirt. Individuals from the second group do not share these attitudes.

All of this should be considered by the luxury fragrance brands when developing products that will best respond to the different consumer motivations based on gender and age and when designing a marketing-mix that allows for the most effective marketing of these products to the different segments identified.

REFERENCES

Allérès, D. (1990). *Luxe...Stratégies Marketing*. Economica.

Antúnez de Mayolo, C. (2009, July). Marcas de lujo. ¿Por qué crece el valor de los bienes suntuarios en todo el mundo? *Business*, 46-47.

Bain & Company. (2015). *2015 Worldwide Luxury Markets Monitor 2015 Spring Update*. Retrieved from www.reportlinker.com

Bayton, J. A. (1958). Motivation, cognition, learning--basic factors in consumer behavior. *Journal of Marketing (Pre-1986), 22*(1), 282.

Britt, S. H. (1950). The strategy of consumer motivation. *Journal of Marketing (Pre-1986), 14*(5), 666.

Campuzano, S. (2003, 2007). *El universo del lujo*. España: McGraw-Hill Interamericana de España.

Dubois, B., Czellar, S., & Laurent, G. (2005). Consumers Segments Based on Attitudes Toward Luxury: Empirical Evidence from Twenty Countries. *Marketing Letters, 16*(2), 115–128. doi:10.1007/s11002-005-2172-0

Euromonitor. (2015). *World All Cosmetics and World Premium Cosmetics Market-Retail Value*. Author.

FCT Forecasts S.A. (1997-2011). *European Forecasts Selective Distribution in Spain*. Author.

Gaborit, J. Y. (1985). *Parfums: Prestige et haute couture*. Fribourg: Office du Livre.

Garrity, E. J., O'Donnell, J. B., Kim, Y. J., & Sanders, G. L. (2007). An extrinsic and intrinsic motivation-based model for measuring consumer shopping oriented web site success. *Journal of Electronic Commerce in Organizations*, *5*(4), 18–38. doi:10.4018/jeco.2007100102

L'Oreal Luxury Products Division. (n.d.a). *Dossiers of fragrances training courses*. Author.

L'Oreal Luxury Products Division. (n.d.b). *Press Kits of fragrances launches*. Author.

Martínez Moreno, O.C., Ruiz Andrade, J.G., & Lozano Ramírez, Mª C., & Verján Quiñones, R. (2015). El comportamiento del consumidor en internet bajo el modelo psicológico social de Veblen. *Revista Global de Negocios*, *3*(5), 101–112.

Nurcahyo, B., & Nur'ainy, R., & Sariyati. (2011). Effect of intrinsic motivation on consumer brand evaluation: The influence of motive, involvement, and need for cognition. *Global Business and Management Research*, *3*(3), 231–246.

Shiseido Spain (2015). *Reports on the Spanish market of luxury fragrances*. Author.

Stanpa. (2015). *Información del Sector: Canales Vs Productos (2000-2014)*. Retrieved from http://www.stanpa.es/estadistica/42/ZonaAsociados.aspx

Stanpa. (2015). *Panel de Consumo: Cierre 2014*. Retrieved from http://stanpa.com/estadistica/92/PaneldeConsumo%28Cierre2014%29.aspx

Toncar, M., & Fetscherin, M. (2012). A study of visual puffery in fragrance advertising. *European Journal of Marketing*, *46*(1), 52–72. doi:10.1108/03090561211189239

Wiedmann, K. P., Hennigs, N., & Siebels, A. (2009). Valued-Based Segmentation of Luxury Consumption Behavior. *Psychology and Marketing*, *26*(7), 625–651. doi:10.1002/mar.20292

KEY TERMS AND DEFINITIONS

Accessible Luxury: Also known as affordable luxury, it is the luxury that is accessed by the "general public" (represented by the middle class) basically to achieve recognition and social status.

Cluster Analysis: Multivariate statistical technique that allows for the formation of groups of elements (individual, organizations, objects, etc.) referred to as clusters (groups, classes, conglomerates). The obtained clusters are homogenous (the elements or members of each group are similar) and heterogeneous (the elements or members of each group are very different from the other groups).

Consumer Motivations: Reasons why individuals purchase and/or consume goods and services.

Consumer Purchase Behavior: Set of behaviors that are carried out by individuals during the acquisition of goods and services.

Consumer Use or Consumption Behavior: Behaviors of individuals linked to the use or consumption of goods and services.

Fragrance or Perfume: Mixture of essential aromatic oils, ethyl alcohol, water and fixative that offers a pleasant and lasting aroma to the human body.

Sell-In: Sale of goods and services that are made to intermediary organizations in the distribution channel of said goods and services (e.g.: manufacturer sale to distributors). It's the opposite of *sell-out*, which refers to the sales of goods and services to final consumers. In both cases, the sales may be expressed in physical units of sold products (e.g.: 100 perfume bottles) or in monetary units (e.g.: 5,000 euros).

ENDNOTES

1 Spanish Cosmetic Toiletry and Perfumery Association.

2 The characteristics cited in regards to the presentation, sales and times of use of the different concentrations, are specific of the luxury fragrances marketed in the selective market.

3 This does not include promotional sizes used for samples, miniatures or travel sizes.

4 In the perfume industry, "nose" is the title given to fragrance creators. They were previously referred to as "perfumists", but currently this name may lead to confusion since, while previously the perfume creator also marketed the product, today, the two figures are clearly separated (creator and seller) and the term perfumist is often used to refer to the perfume seller.

5 Colipa: The European Cosmetics Association. Colipa is a European association created in 1962 to represent and act in the interests of the perfume, cosmetics and hygiene industry. Colipa consists of 25 active national associations, 20 large international companies and five accredited members. Furthermore, it represents over 2,000 companies, from large international companies to small family businesses that often operate in market niches. The cosmetics industry employs more than 500,000 individuals in the European Union.

6 Fragrance or perfume manufacturers refer to the mixture of alcohol, oils or essences and fixatives making up the fragrance as "juice".

Chapter 4
Analyzing Countries for Their Luxury Potentials:
A Macromarketing Approach

Taşkın Dirsehan
Marmara University, Turkey

ABSTRACT

This study attempts to fill in the gaps in the international marketing literature about international marketing entry decisions for luxury products. With this in mind, a macromarketing approach is used to segment countries according to the basic luxury consumption criteria based on the literature review. These criteria include population, GDP, GINI coefficient, total female labor force, and cultural dimensions. These indicators are listed for a total of 60 countries and multidimensional scaling analysis (MDS) is conducted to see whether some countries form groups. Finally, five groups are determined and are discussed for their luxury potentials.

INTRODUCTION

The possession of "beautiful goods" usually makes the owners of the goods happy. Nowadays, people are willing to spend higher amounts of money on luxury products (Husic & Cicic, 2009).In order to succeed in the luxury sector; brands need to build strong images. Thus, luxury brands are now some of the most remarkable and valued brands in the world (Kapferer & Bastien, 2009). As the luxury consumption trends change in today's world, brands need to consider entering new markets. However, entering new markets raises questions that need to be analyzed. This is why luxury consumption has become an interesting area for marketers.

Researchers approach luxury consumption from two theoretical directions: the first is based on social psychology and aims to understand social motivations; and the second one is personally oriented (Godey et al., 2013). Hudders et al. (2013) propose two main categories for luxury brands based on their physical and psychosocial attributes: characteristics referring to exclusivity and characteristics referring to excellent quality and aesthetics. These characteristics are mostly individual.

DOI: 10.4018/978-1-4666-9958-8.ch004

On the other hand, when companies plan to enter a new market, they should first consider macro indicators to select a market and should then focus on individual characteristics after reducing the number of potential markets. Therefore, this study focuses on the macro characteristics of luxury consumption rather than the psychological ones.

Companies operating internationally should collect information about (1)economics and demographics, (2) the cultural, sociological, and political climate, (3) the overview of market conditions, and (4) a summary of the technological environment and the competitive situation (Cateora et al, 2009). This study tries to provide a tool for international market evaluation of the luxury sector including its dynamic structure.

BACKGROUND

Definition and Determinants of Luxury Consumption

As Godey et al. (2013) indicate, even though there is a lack of substantial definitions of luxury, some characteristics of luxury brands have emerged such as beauty, rarity, quality, and price. For luxury brands, the ratio of functional utility to price is low, however, the ratio of intangible and situational utility to price is high (Nueno & Quelch, 1998). Luxury has its roots in the history associated with wealth, exclusivity, power, and satisfaction of non-basic necessities. It was considered negatively until the fourteenth century among the common people. In Europe, with the emergence of the bourgeoisie, luxury was defined as "sumptuous surroundings" that made life more comfortable (Brun & Castelli, 2013).

Grossman and Shapiro (1988) define luxury goods as "goods for which the mere use or display of a particular branded product brings prestige to the owner, apart from any functional utility."As explained in the introduction, prestige is created at personal and societal levels. According to Heine's (2012) definition (p. 60):

Luxury brands are regarded as images in the minds of consumers that comprise associations about a high level of price, quality, aesthetics, rarity, extraordinariness and a high degree of non-functional associations.

Husic and Cicic (2009) report Vigneron and Johnson's (1999) prestige-seeking consumer behaviors, as follows.

1. *The Veblen effect – perceived conspicuous value.* Veblenian consumers attach greater importance to price as an indicator of prestige, because their primary objective is to impress others.
2. *The snob effect – perceived unique value.* Snob consumers perceive price as an indicator of exclusivity and avoid using popular brands to experiment with inner-directed consumption.
3. *The bandwagon effect – perceived social value.* Relative to snob consumers, bandwagon consumers attach less importance to price as an indicator of prestige but will place greater emphasis on the effect they make on others while consuming prestige brands.
4. *The hedonic effect – perceived emotional value.* Hedonist consumers are more interested in their own thoughts and feelings and thus will place less emphasis on price as an indicator of prestige.

5. *The perfectionism effect – perceived quality value.* Perfectionist consumers rely on their own perception of the product's quality and may use price as further evidence of quality.

In parallel with these social and personal approaches, previous research studies have revealed psychometric properties of Vigneron and Johnson's Brand Luxury Index scale (Christodoulides et al., 2008) including: psychological and cultural factors in shaping luxury consumption (Eng & Bogaert, 2010); the role played by income and culture in the acquisition of luxury goods (Dubois & Duquesne, 1993); luxury customer value factors (Choo et al., 2012);and travel motivations and perceptions of a luxury tourist destination (Prayag & Hosany, 2014). Even though some of these research studies compare different cultures, a gap in the literature remains: Do secondary data about countries' socioeconomic and cultural characteristics serve for segmenting international markets?

Segmenting International Markets

Macromarketing research is needed in today's globalization-driven, increasingly integrated world (Stump, et al., 2008). This is the reason why country segmentation studies attract the attention of researchers and managers. For market segmentation, a researcher should make an effort to differentiate homogeneous groups of customers that may be targeted in a similar way because they have similar preferences and needs (Wedel & Kamakura, 2002). On the country level, clustering a set of specified countries on the basis of a wide array of macroeconomic variables represents country segmentation (Helsen et al., 1993). Although clustering based on macro indicators has been criticized because it neglects specific product/service market indicators, a preliminary market assessment based on aggregate data is still a necessary initial step (Cavusgil et al., 2004). After determining which countries to enter, further segmentation analyses can be conducted to reveal segments based on product or service specific criteria.

International market segmentation is important in developing, positioning, and selling products throughout the world (Ter Hofstede et al., 1999). Budeva and Mullen (2014) list the advantages of segmenting countries as:

1. Helping companies to apply a uniform set of marketing decisions to a group of countries (Sethi, 1971);
2. Selecting appropriate markets to enter (Cavusgil et al., 2004); and
3. Transferring previous experience in one country to similar markets (Sethi & Holton, 1973).

Two bases of segmentation are countries and consumers. In the country-based segmentation, each country represents a segment (Helsen et al., 1993; Kale, 1995). This macro segmentation uses information based on aggregated consumers' data at the country level. The limitation of this approach is that it considers the individuals from one country as homogeneous. Thus, many studies attempt to segment markets on the basis of individual data (Boote, 1983; Urban and Hauser, 1993) to reveal groups of individuals across countries (Belvaux & Guibert, 2012). Steenkamp and Ter Hofstede (2002) distinguish between these two segmentation approaches. The country-level segmentation bases include a combination of economic, political, geographic, and demographic information (Huszagh et al., 1986; Helsen et al., 1993) or cultural variables (Hofstede, 1980; Steenkamp, 2001), whereas the bases of individual-level segmentation include domain-specific characteristics such as attribute evaluations (Moskowitz & Rabino, 1994), attitudes(Verhage et al., 1989), and risk or brand loyalty ratings(Yavas, et al., 1992).

It's important to remember that the results of the study of Budeva and Mullen (2014) support the notion that country segment membership is unstable when it is analyzed over the course of a decade. Thus, international market segmentation is dynamic and should be repeated over time in order to follow the changes in the segments.

Country-Based Luxury Studies

As global markets are more easily reachable today, companies may consider reaching new markets in the luxury sector to extend their potential niche markets with more potential. Thus, global markets need to be analyzed in detail to explore the main differences among countries. In particular, the trends in the luxury markets should adopt a macro view.

There is an especially strong relationship between European luxury big business and East Asian markets. Japan in 1980-2000 and China since 2000 were key outlets for luxury products (Donzé & Fujioka, 2015).It's noticeable that the sales of luxury brands are increasing in emerging markets such as Brazil, Russia, China, India, Mexico, and the Middle East. With this growth rate, the joint revenues of luxury sales in these countries are predicted to surpass those of more developed markets within the next decade (Okonkwo, 2009).However, in terms of entering these markets, it is challenging to preserve a global image within the local cultures (Peng Cui et al., 2015). For instance, in China it's suggested that global brands do not adapt their products but keep their international status. The reason for this is that Chinese consumers desire an authentic, western product representing a "link" to the western world's definition of success (Willis, 2006).Since China is considered to be the most rapidly growing market for luxury goods (Mosca et al., 2015), remarkable studies have considered China to be a special case in terms of its growth in luxury sales. In China, luxury spending grew at an annual rate of 15-20 percent between 2005 and 2010 (Peng Cui et al., 2015). In 2013, China/Hong Kong was the leader in composite luxury sales growth with 33.4 percent growth (Deloitte, 2015). In addition, it's estimated that by 2015, it will represent over 20 percent of the world's luxury consumption (Atsmon et al., 2011).It has also been reported in Euromonitor that India will grow by 86 percent in constant value terms between 2013 and 2018. Luxury markets in China, Malaysia, and Indonesia are also expected to grow by 74, 62, and 59 percent, respectively, over the period (Chandran, 2014). In order to look at the countries' positions in the luxury sector, the distribution of the top 100 companies in 2013 is illustrated in Table 1.

After determining the markets (the countries in this case) to enter, companies should carefully analyze the customer structure in those markets. For instance, although in general female consumers are the target segment in luxury fashion, men constitute the majority of consumers in luxury fashion expenses in China (Chevalier et al., 2009).Another example is the age of luxury consumers. While in Europe luxury consumers are mostly older people who have a higher disposable income, American luxury consumers are younger consumers who are willing to experiment with different luxury products (Okonkwo, 2007). Dubois et al., (2005) identify three segments of consumers based on their attitudes toward luxury: democratic, elitist, and distance. People with elitist attitudes believe that only few consumers may own luxury products. In contrast, people with democratic attitudes believe that luxury is open to a larger audience and everyone should be able to access it. People with a distance attitude believe that luxury is a different world; these consumers are not very attracted by luxury and are less interested in it (Dubois et al., 2005).

The literature on luxury strategies in terms of international differences has focused on the following areas:

Table 1. Country profiles for luxury consumption

	Number of Companies	Average Luxury Goods Size (US$mil)	Share of Top 100 Companies	Share of Top 100 Luxury Goods Sales
China/Hong Kong	7	$3,455	7.0%	11.3%
France	11	$4,513	11.0%	23.2%
Italy	29	$1,222	29.0%	16.5%
Spain	5	$637	5.0%	1.5%
Switzerland	11	$2,882	11.0%	14.8%
United Kingdom	6	$980	6.0%	2.7%
United States	15	$2,927	15.0%	20.5%
Other Countries	16	$1,268	16.0%	9.5%
Top 100	100	$2,142	100.0%	100.0%

Source: Deloitte (2015). "Global Powers of Luxury Goods 2015: Engaging the Future Luxury Consumer", Deloitte Touche Tohmatsu Limited, http://www2.deloitte.com/content/dam/Deloitte/ch/Documents/consumer-business/ch-en-cb-global-powers-of-luxury-goods-2015.pdf, p. 24.

- Achieving global brand consistency across countries (Matthiesen & Phau, 2005);
- Success factors in a supply chain context that need to be assessed before entering the luxury fashion market in China(Khan, 2015),
- Balancing the standardization-localization dilemma of brand communications for luxury fashion in China (Liu et al., 2015); and
- Distribution strategies of luxury companies in the Chinese market (Mosca & Re, 2014).

Therefore, after determining which market to enter, it's necessary to conduct a second segmentation analysis to determine the groups to focus on.

Indicators for Luxury Consumption Potential

Luxury consumption is affected by several macro-environmental factors including globalization and cultural convergence (Chadha & Husband, 2006), the emergence of new market segments (Okonkwo, 2007), and a rise in the number of wealthy consumers (Seo & Buchanan-Oliver, 2015).

In order to fill the gap in the literature (to segment international markets in terms of luxury potential indicators), some cues or indications can be used in segmenting international markets according to luxury consumption potentials.

1. In their effort to segment the market for luxury goods, Dubois and Duquesne (1993) indicate that conspicuous consumption is primarily related to an ostentatious display of wealth. Luxury products are traditionally consumed by the wealthiest circles in society (Grossman & Shapiro, 1988). However, there has been a rapid expansion of the customer base to include modest social classes, while a larger circle of consumers can now afford luxury products (Truong et al, 2009). This trend is called the "democratization of luxury" (Evrard & Roux, 2005).Thus, the consumption of luxury products has diversified across different social segments (Seo & Buchanan-Oliver, 2015). Therefore,

economic levels should be considered when it comes to segmenting the luxury market. For this reason, the *Gross Domestic Product (GDP)* and *Population* of countries are taken into account in the segmenting countries. These indicators are taken from the World Bank Database. The World Bank defines GDP as:

the sum of gross value added by all resident producers in the economy plus any product taxes and minus any subsidies not included in the value of the products. It is calculated without making deductions for depreciation of fabricated assets or for depletion and degradation of natural resources. Data are in current U.S. dollars. Dollar figures for GDP are converted from domestic currencies using single year official exchange rates.

Total population is defined by the World Bank as:

Total population is based on the de facto definition of population, which counts all residents regardless of legal status or citizenship--except for refugees not permanently settled in the country of asylum, who are generally considered part of the population of their country of origin. The values shown are midyear estimates.

2. Cultural norms shape the motivation of consumers to buy and consume luxury goods while the differences in culture affect the symbolic traits of the brand (Christodoulides et al., 2009).

As a result of globalization and multicultural influences, consumers begin to appreciate luxury brands in Asia, BRIC, or other developing countries (Kapferer, 2012). Therefore, the customer base of luxury products becomes more culturally diversified (Seo & Buchanan-Oliver, 2015).

Eng and Bogaert (2010) and Teimourpour and Hanzaee (2011) relate luxury consumption to Hofstede's (1980) three cultural dimensions. First, *high power distance (PDI)* is supported by the perceived social status of luxury goods consumption. A high PDI is an indicator of high inequality, meaning there are only some people who can afford to buy luxury products. Second, *collectivism* (the opposite of individualism-IDV) is related to perceptions of luxury as social representation. Third, *uncertainty avoidance (UAI)* is linked to preference for norms or structured cultural practices of luxury consumption. These dimensions for each country have been taken from Hofstede's website (http://geert-hofstede.com/countries.html). They are explained on the website as follows:

PDI expresses the degree to which the less powerful members of a society accept and expect that power is distributed unequally. The fundamental issue here is how a society handles inequalities among people. People in societies exhibiting a large degree of Power Distance accept a hierarchical order in which everybody has a place and which needs no further justification.

The high side of IDV, called individualism, can be defined as a preference for a loosely-knit social framework in which individuals are expected to take care of only themselves and their immediate families.

The UAI dimension expresses the degree to which the members of a society feel uncomfortable with uncertainty and ambiguity.

3. In their research into gender comparisons, Stokburger-Sauer and Teichmann (2013) found that women have higher purchase intention in terms of luxury brands versus non-luxury brands compared to men. In addition, luxury brands provide more uniqueness, status, and hedonic value than non-luxury ones for *female consumers*. Thus, it was decided to include working women in the segmentation analysis. Thus, the total female labor force is calculated by multiplying "Total Labor Force" with "Female Labor Force (% of total)."The World Bank defines total labor force as follows:

Total labor force comprises people ages 15 and older who meet the International Labour Organization definition of the economically active population: all people who supply labor for the production of goods and services during a specified period.

4. Teimourpour and Hanzaee (2011) point out that one of the factors affecting luxury product consumption is the income gap, which is showed by the *Gini coefficient*. A Gini value of 0 (zero) stands for a total equality while 1 (one) equals maximal inequality. According to the World Bank:

Gini index measures the extent to which the distribution of income or consumption expenditure among individuals or households within an economy deviates from a perfectly equal distribution. A Lorenz curve plots the cumulative percentages of total income received against the cumulative number of recipients, starting with the poorest individual or household. The Gini index measures the area between the Lorenz curve and a hypothetical line of absolute equality, expressed as a percentage of the maximum area under the line. Thus a Gini index of 0 represents perfect equality, while an index of 100 implies perfect inequality.

5. In terms of education, Bock et al. (2014) reveal that more educated consumers are more motivated to consume for status. Furthermore, Teimourpour and Hanzaee (2011) indicate that an increase in education in women causes a change in the consumers' desire and makes them want to benefit society. Economic freedom gives a chance to turn these desires into action and they are interested in luxury goods. Therefore, this dimension is considered together with working women in the measurement of the total female labor force.

After determining the macro characteristics to measure luxury market potentials, this paper uses statistics from various sources.

RESEARCH METHODOLOGY FOR COUNTRIES' LUXURY CONSUMPTION POTENTIALS

Research Problem

The main purpose of this research is to reveal the luxury consumption potentials of countries and to understand whether they form some distinct groups. For this purpose, indicators are determined according to the relevant literature, and countries from which secondary data could not be found are excluded from the research. Thus, a total of 60 countries are analyzed for their luxury potentials. These countries are selected from the IMF's list of Advanced Economies and Emerging Markets and Developing Economies.

Preparing the Data

The final data used to compare selected countries include population, GDP (US$), GINI Coefficient, Labor Force, Female Labor Force, PDI, IDV, and UAI. These data are collected from the official websites of the World Bank and Geert Hofstede. The data are presented in Tables 2, 3, 4, and 5. Accordingly, it's possible to state that among the selected countries:

- The United States is the most populated country among advanced economies. It also has the highest figures in terms of GDP, GINI, and total female labor force.
- China, as the most populated country in the world, also leads in terms of GDP and total female labor force.
- The highest GINI value belongs to South Africa among all countries.
- The highest GDPs belong to Brazil in Latin America, Iran in the Middle East, Nigeria in Sub-Saharan Africa, and Turkey in Central and Eastern Europe (CEE).

Table 2. Selected socioeconomic factors for advanced economies

Economy Group	Countries	Population	GDP (US$) (2013)	GINI Coefficient	Total Female Labor Force
Advanced Economies	United States	316,128,839	16,768,100,000,000.0	40.8	7,343,916,980.40
	Germany	80,621,788	3,730,260,571,356.5	28.3	1,926,441,130.50
	Italy	59,831,093	2,149,484,516,711.8	36.0	1,055,354,737.80
	Spain	46,647,42	1,393,040,177,013.7	34.7	1,055,327,871.30
	Netherlands	16,804,224	853,539,351,964.5	30.9	413,648,984.30
	Belgium	11,195,138	524,805,525,215.2	33.0	226,869,475.60
	Austria	8,473,786	428,321,897,648.2	29.2	204,212,223.60
	Greece	11,032,328	242,230,333,768.9	34.3	212,396,355.20
	Finland	5,439,407	267,328,613,728.3	26.9	129,911,079.00
	Ireland	4,595,281	232,077,419,240.0	34.3	97,198,118.00
	Slovak Republic	5,414,095	97,707,323,420.1	26.0	121,770,734.50
	Slovenia	2,060,484	47,987,303,637.8	31.2	46,772,375.40
	Luxembourg	543,202	60,130,847,623.6	30.8	11,510,457.20
	Estonia	1,324,612	24,880,264,958.1	36.0	34,219,152.00
	United Kingdom	64,097,085	2,678,454,886,796.7	36.0	1,505,608,908.30
	Canada	35,158,304	1,826,768,562,832.0	32.6	917,934,932.80
	Sweden	9,592,552	579,679,985,303.4	25.0	242,667,477.50
	Switzerland	8,081,482	685,434,185,074.1	33.7	217,484,156.60
	Norway	5,084,190	512,580,425,531.9	25.8	127,240,228.20
	Israel	8,059,400	290,550,599,943.2	39.2	172,431,624.20
	Lithuania	2,956,121	45,931,968,473.7	37.6	76,777,235.40
	Mean	***31,483,721.57***	***1,592,347,369,535.32***	***32.49***	***768,556,868.47***

Source: Extracted from World Bank, Indicators. http://data.worldbank.org/indicator?display=default.

Table 3. Selected socioeconomic factors for emerging market and developing economies

Economy Group	Countries	Population	GDP	GINI Coefficient	Total Female Labor Force
Latin America	Argentina	41,446,246	609,888,971,036.2	44.5	771,338,050.40
	Brazil	200,361,925	2,245,673,032,353.8	54.7	4,639,613,224.30
	Chile	17,619,708	277,198,774,856.8	52.1	348,877,748.80
	Colombia	48,321,405	378,415,326,790.1	55.9	1,005,629,237.20
	Costa Rica	4,872,166	49,621,089,476.1	50.7	85,689,407.50
	Ecuador	15,737,878	94,472,679,000.0	49.3	303,992,802.00
	Jamaica	2,715,000	14,362,262,584.9	45.5	56,952,896.00
	Mexico	122,332,399	1,260,914,660,977.1	47.2	2,074,981,870.50
	Peru	30,375,603	202,349,846,974.4	48.1	740,269,981.80
	Venezuela	30,405,207	438,283,564,814.8	44.8	557,285,104.80
Middle East	Egypt	82,056,378	271,972,822,883.4	30.8	671,358,965.20
	Iran	77,447,168	368,904,351,626.5	38.3	489,661,720.00
	Jordan	6,459,000	33,678,500,148.0	35.4	32,788,678.50
	Morocco	33,008,150	103,835,702,813.6	40.9	324,708,453.00
	Pakistan	182,142,594	232,286,781,110.6	30.0	1,449,091,254.00
Central and Eastern Europe	Albania	2,773,620	12,923,240,278.3	34.5	49,854,176.70
	Bulgaria	7,265,115	54,479,873,099.9	28.2	155,755,374.00
	Croatia	4,252,700	57,868,674,297.5	33.7	84,678,698.40
	Hungary	9,897,247	133,423,898,611.9	31.2	201,181,306.50
	Latvia	2,013,385	30,956,691,627.6	34.8	51,957,900.00
	Poland	38,530,725	525,865,974,814.9	32.7	838,590,519.60
	Romania	19,963,581	189,638,162,013.3	27.4	427,208,191.40
	Turkey	74,932,641	822,135,183,160.0	40.0	844,865,749.90
Common-wealth of Independent States	Russia	143,499,861	2,096,777,030,571.3	40.1	3,779,587,001.20
Developing Asia	China	1,357,380,000	9,240,270,452,047.0	42.1	34,588,213,758.00
	India	1,252,139,596	1,876,797,199,132.6	33.9	11,645,910,086.80
	Indonesia	249,865,63	868,345,652,474.9	38.1	4,583,026,635.30
	Malaysia	29,716,965	313,159,097,400.7	46.2	503,482,921.40
	Nepal	27,797,457	19,294,348,174.0	32.8	770,158,178.10
	Philippines	98,393,574	272,066,554,886.0	43.0	1,673,111,167.20
	Thailand	67,010,502	387,252,164,290.8	39.4	1,816,165,840.80
Sub-Saharan Africa	Angola	21,471,618	124,178,241,815.7	42.7	364,549,970.40
	Ghana	25,904,598	48,137,027,487.2	42.8	551,313,712.90
	Kenya	44,353,691	55,243,056,200.7	47.7	803,657,402.20
	Nigeria	173,615,345	521,803,314,653.8	48.8	2,297,925,240.00
	Senegal	14,133,280	14,791,699,008.6	40.3	274,859,370.00
	South Africa	52,981,991	350,630,133,297.4	63.1	868,071,475.60
	Tanzania	49,253,126	33,225,037,489.7	37.6	1,205,234,600.40
	Zambia	14,538,640	26,820,870,558.9	57.5	284,979,972.50
Mean		***114,156,580.72***	***632,254,921,662.54***	***41.71***	***2,108,117,401.11***

Source: Extracted from World Bank, Indicators. http://data.worldbank.org/indicator?display=default.

Table 4. Selected cultural factors for advanced economies

Economy Group	Countries	PDI	IDV	UAI
Advanced Economies	United States	40	91	46
	Germany	35	67	65
	Italy	50	76	75
	Spain	57	51	86
	Netherlands	38	80	53
	Belgium	65	75	94
	Austria	11	55	70
	Greece	60	35	100
	Finland	33	63	59
	Ireland	28	70	35
	Slovak Republic	100	52	51
	Slovenia	71	27	88
	Luxembourg	40	60	70
	Estonia	40	60	60
	United Kingdom	35	89	35
	Canada	39	80	48
	Sweden	31	71	29
	Switzerland	34	68	58
	Norway	31	69	50
	Israel	13	54	81
	Lithuania	42	60	65
	Mean	***42.52***	***64.43***	***62.76***

Source: Extracted from *The Hofstede Center,* http://geert-hofstede.com/countries.html.

- The highest GINI belong to Colombia in Latin America, Morocco in the Middle East, Turkey in CEE, and Malaysia in Developing Asia.
- The most individualistic country is the United States.
- Slovak Republic has the highest score in PDI. As stated in the web site of Hofstede:

In societies scoring high on Power Distance it is perfectly accepted that some people have more power than others. It is accepted and expected that these people also use their power. Not in a negative way but to create clarity and structure for people around them. The ideal boss can therefore be compared with a 'good father' who supervises you, is highly visible and tells you what to do. Hierarchical organizations are normal. A key issue for foreigners to understand is that in spite of the very high score on PDI, a manager still has to prove him or herself in order to make people respect and accept decisions from above or the (foreign) headquarter. Visibility and showing results is key.

- Greece has the highest score in terms of UAI. The Hofstede website comments on this score, as follows:

Table 5. Selected cultural factors for emerging market and developing economies

Economy Group	Countries	PDI	IDV	UAI
Latin America	Argentina	49	46	86
	Brazil	69	38	76
	Chile	63	23	86
	Colombia	67	13	80
	Costa Rica	35	15	86
	Ecuador	78	8	67
	Jamaica	45	39	13
	Mexico	81	30	82
	Peru	64	16	87
	Venezuela	81	12	76
	Egypt	70	25	80
	Iran	58	41	59
	Jordan	70	30	65
	Morocco	70	46	68
	Pakistan	55	14	70
Central and Eastern Europe	Albania	90	20	70
	Bulgaria	70	30	85
	Croatia	73	33	80
	Hungary	46	80	82
	Latvia	44	70	63
	Poland	68	60	93
	Romania	90	30	90
	Turkey	66	37	85
Commonwealth of Independent States	Russia	93	39	95
Developing Asia	China	80	20	30
	India	77	48	40
	Indonesia	78	14	48
	Malaysia	100	26	36
	Nepal	65	30	40
	Philippines	94	32	44
	Thailand	64	20	64
Sub-Saharan Africa	Angola	83	18	60
	Ghana	80	15	65
	Kenya	70	25	50
	Nigeria	80	30	55
	Senegal	70	25	55
	South Africa	49	65	49
	Tanzania	70	25	50
	Zambia	60	35	50
Mean		***69.62***	***31.36***	***65.64***

Source: Extracted from *The Hofstede Center,* http://geert-hofstede.com/countries.html.

At 100, Greece has the highest score on Uncertainty Avoidance, which means that, as a nation, Greeks are not at all comfortable in ambiguous situations: the unforeseen is always there ready to 'lay an ambush.' The 'sword of Damocles,' impending over the head of all of us, can illustrate this anxious and stressing feeling about life.

Research Findings: Evaluating Groups of Countries

As the main research purpose of this study is to evaluate countries' luxury potentials, multidimensional scaling (MDS) is used asa research technique. The result obtained from MDS, which is also known as a perceptual or spatial map, visualizes the relative positions of all the objects (Hair, 1998). MDS can produce information to be used in marketing for image measurement, market segmentation, new product development, assessing advertising effectiveness, pricing analysis, channel decisions, and attitude scale construction (Malhotra, 2007). In this paper, MDS is used to detect the differences between country groups or, in other words, to segment countries at the macro level for their luxury potentials.

The data presented in Tables 2, 3, 4, and 5 are used to conduct MDS analysis. Two-dimensional and three-dimensional results are examined. Stress value is 0.22 and RSQ is 0.91 in the case of two-dimensional results, and stress value is 0.126 and RSQ is 0.96 in the case of three-dimensional results. Therefore, the three-dimensional solution is considered because its stress value indicates a fair fit. A linear trend can be observed between distances and disparities in Figure 1.

The graph presented in Figure 2 visualizes countries' positions in a three-dimensional space according to a Euclidean distance model.

Figure 1. Scatterplot of linear fit

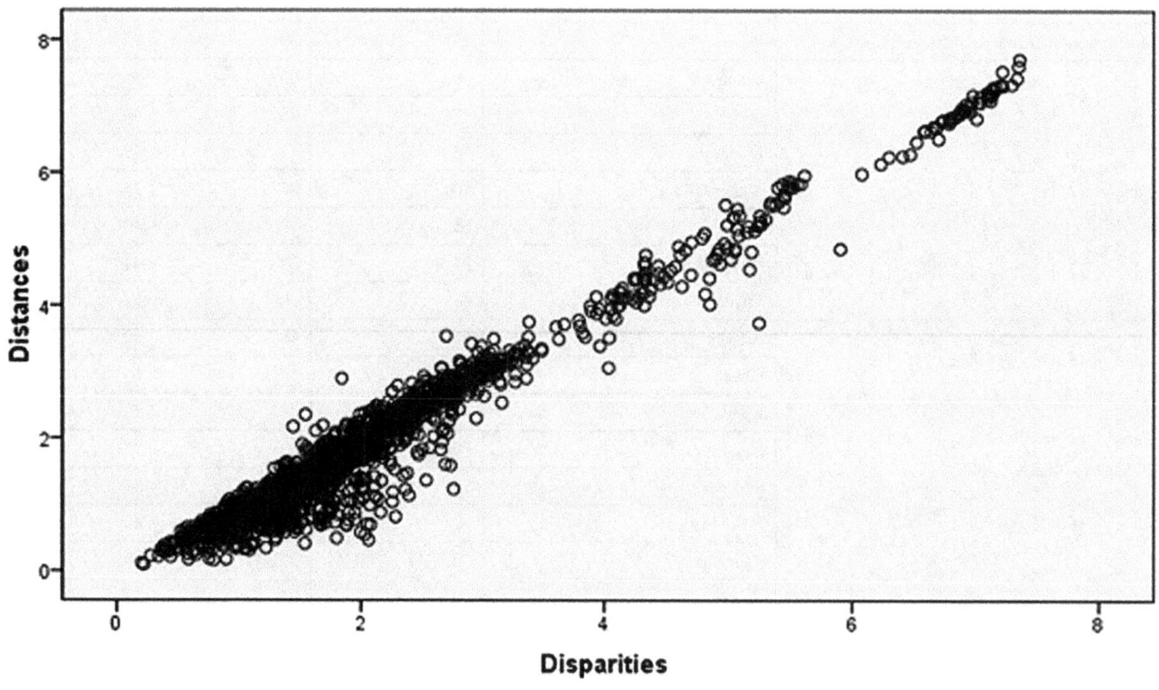

Figure 2. Graph according to Euclidian distance model

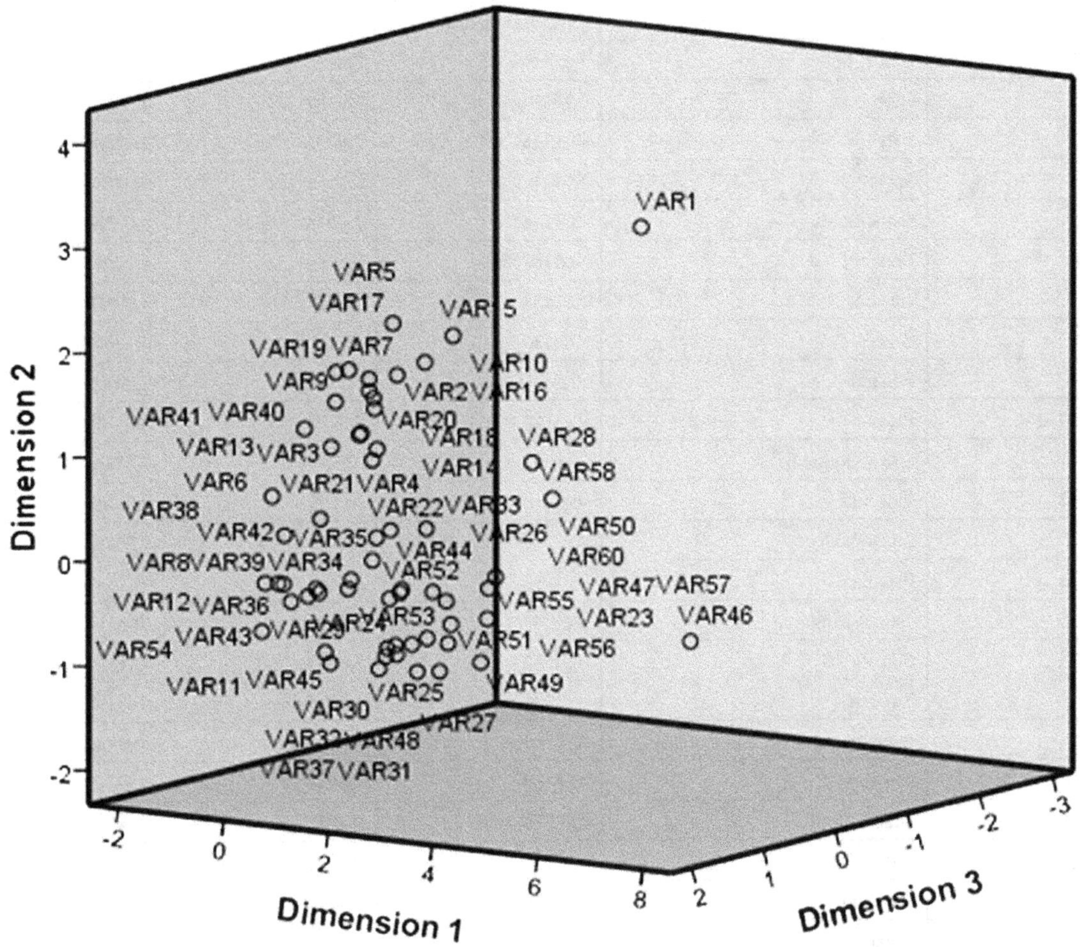

When analyzing the coordinates obtained as a result of three-dimensional MDS analysis, it's possible to observe that some countries can be grouped. The coordinates are indicated in Table 6. Accordingly, five different segments can be proposed as a result.

1. The United States, China, and India can be grouped according to dimension 1. These countries have large populations and large female labor forces. Thus, the main luxury potentials of these countries result from their size.
2. Colombia and Ecuador can be grouped according to dimension 2. These Latin America countries have similar medium-level GINI-values (55.9 and 49.3) and are characterized by low IDVs (13 and 8). Therefore, these countries have luxury potentials based on their collectivist cultures, which create some high-income segments due to the medium-level GINIs.
3. Germany, Italy, Netherlands, Austria, Finland, Ireland, Luxembourg, Estonia, the United Kingdom, Canada, Sweden, Switzerland, Norway, Israel, Lithuania, Hungary, and Latvia can be grouped according to dimension 2 again. The countries in this group are not attractive for luxury products

Table 6. Stimulus coordinates

Stimulus Name	Represented Country	Dimension 1	Dimension 2	Dimension 3
VAR 1	United States	***3,5770***	3,0196	-0,8695
VAR 2	Germany	0,1699	***1,4699***	0,3983
VAR 3	Italy	-0,1395	***1,0249***	0,2849
VAR 4	Spain	-0,4039	0,2535	0,6589
VAR 5	Netherlands	-0,3244	***1,4946***	0,0474
VAR 6	Belgium	-0,6782	0,5366	1,1251
VAR 7	Austria	-0,7558	***1,5580***	0,1960
VAR 8	Greece	-0,7426	-0,3274	0,9960
VAR 9	Finland	-0,5451	***1,3106***	0,3501
VAR 10	Ireland	-0,3162	***1,5201***	-0,7128
VAR 11	Slovak Republic	-0,1852	-0,1914	***1,5726***
VAR 12	Slovenia	-0,6110	-0,5082	0,9146
VAR 13	Luxembourg	-0,6180	***0,8750***	0,3578
VAR 14	Estonia	-0,4936	***0,7695***	-0,1843
VAR 15	United Kingdom	0,2831	***1,8171***	-0,6719
VAR 16	Canada	-0,0552	***1,5133***	-0,1461
VAR 17	Sweden	-0,2531	***1,9819***	-0,2298
VAR 18	Switzerland	-0,4102	***1,1776***	-0,0885
VAR 19	Norway	-0,4554	***1,6049***	0,2317
VAR 20	Israel	-0,8974	***1,1922***	-0,4254
VAR 21	Lithuania	-0,5152	***0,6696***	-0,1336
VAR 22	Argentina	-0,5548	-0,0911	-0,2179
VAR 23	Brazil	0,7464	-0,8943	-0,7986
VAR 24	Chile	-0,4557	-1,1794	-0,6318
VAR 25	Colombia	-0,1973	**-1,4585**	-0,8279
VAR 26	Costa Rica	-0,7712	-0,7858	-1,1446
VAR 27	Ecuador	-0,2009	**-1,4093**	-0,5239
VAR 28	Jamaica	0,0404	0,3666	***-1,9149***
VAR 29	Mexico	0,1467	-1,1288	0,0065
VAR 30	Peru	-0,4278	-1,2257	-0,2525
VAR 31	Venezuela	-0,2151	-1,2926	-0,0075
VAR 32	Egypt	-0,3298	-0,4450	0,8830
VAR 33	Iran	-0,1596	0,0201	-0,1261
VAR 34	Jordan	-0,3847	-0,4011	0,2510
VAR 35	Morocco	-0,3081	-0,2544	0,0143
VAR 36	Pakistan	-0,0710	-0,3893	0,9122
VAR 37	Albania	-0,3457	-1,0255	0,6372
VAR 38	Bulgaria	-0,5902	-0,3188	1,0316

continued on following page

Table 6. Continued

Stimulus Name	Represented Country	Dimension 1	Dimension 2	Dimension 3
VAR 39	Croatia	-0,5056	-0,4260	0,6485
VAR 40	Hungary	-0,6963	***1,0998***	0,6660
VAR 41	Latvia	-0,5206	***0,9412***	0,0396
VAR 42	Poland	-0,5133	0,1604	1,0754
VAR 43	Romania	-0,4872	-0,7008	***1,4024***
VAR 44	Turkey	-0,2764	-0,4624	0,3691
VAR 45	Russia	0,3446	-1,0176	1,0594
VAR 46	China	***6,5548***	-0,5235	0,5872
VAR 47	India	***3,5972***	-0,0799	1,2182
VAR 48	Indonesia	0,4851	-0,9842	-0,1707
VAR 49	Malaysia	0,3054	-1,3770	-1,0228
VAR 50	Nepal	-0,1159	-0,0435	-0,5899
VAR 51	Philippines	0,4011	-1,0978	-0,5152
VAR 52	Thailand	-0,0401	-0,6126	-0,0276
VAR 53	Angola	-0,1267	-1,0884	-0,1701
VAR 54	Ghana	-0,1709	-1,1057	-0,0898
VAR 55	Kenya	0,0110	-0,7628	-0,7703
VAR 56	Nigeria	0,4296	-0,9200	-0,5348
VAR 57	Senegal	-0,2038	-0,6108	-0,2891
VAR 58	South Africa	0,0719	-0,0207	***-2,1656***
VAR 59	Tanzania	-0,0280	-0,5528	-0,1881
VAR 60	Zambia	-0,0677	-0,6639	-1,4935

compared to others. Since all of their PDIs are low (PDI<50), they are individualistic countries (IDV>50)and their GINIs are low (GINI<39). The reason for their luxury sales should be different nations of target groups.

4. Jamaica and South Africa can be grouped according to dimension 3. They share an average PDI (45 and 49). Lastly,
5. Romania and the Slovak Republic can be grouped according to dimension 3 again. While these countries seem to be attractive according to their high PDIs (90 and 100), their low GINIs (27.40 and 26) make their potentials questionable.

CONCLUSION AND FUTURE RESEARCH DIRECTIONS

With the advance of globalization, more companies are operating across national frontiers. Therefore, luxury brands benefit from finding niche markets in different countries and expanding their customer portfolio. However, they have to consider which market to enter. For this strategy, they may start with two consecutive segmentation steps: segmenting the global market and segmenting customers in target countries.

Segmenting the global market may be realized in two ways. Each country may be thought of as one case, and a classification of these cases may be conducted to reveal similarities and discrepancies among them. This is the method applied in this study. As an alternative, consumers may be thought of as global citizens and a primary research study may be conducted to create groups of customers without thinking about national boundaries. This method may reveal global customers based on customers' motivations, values, characteristics, and intentions, etc. However, this second approach is more costly and requires a longer time. However, the first approach can be applied to secondary data and is more practical even though it does not consider the differences in each country, which is its main limitation.

In this chapter, a macromarketing approach is implemented to determine whether countries can be segmented according to their luxury potentials. In the case of this study, 21 developed and 39 emerging countries are taken into consideration. Data to be analyzed are selected based on the literature, and the countries' luxury potentials are analyzed according to these data. As a result, five groups are identified, with the first group comprising the United States, China, and India. This group seems to be more attractive for luxury market entry because of the large populations and high female labor forces of the countries that comprise it. The characteristics of the country groups are illustrated in Figure 3.

Figure 3. Groups of countries for their luxury potentials

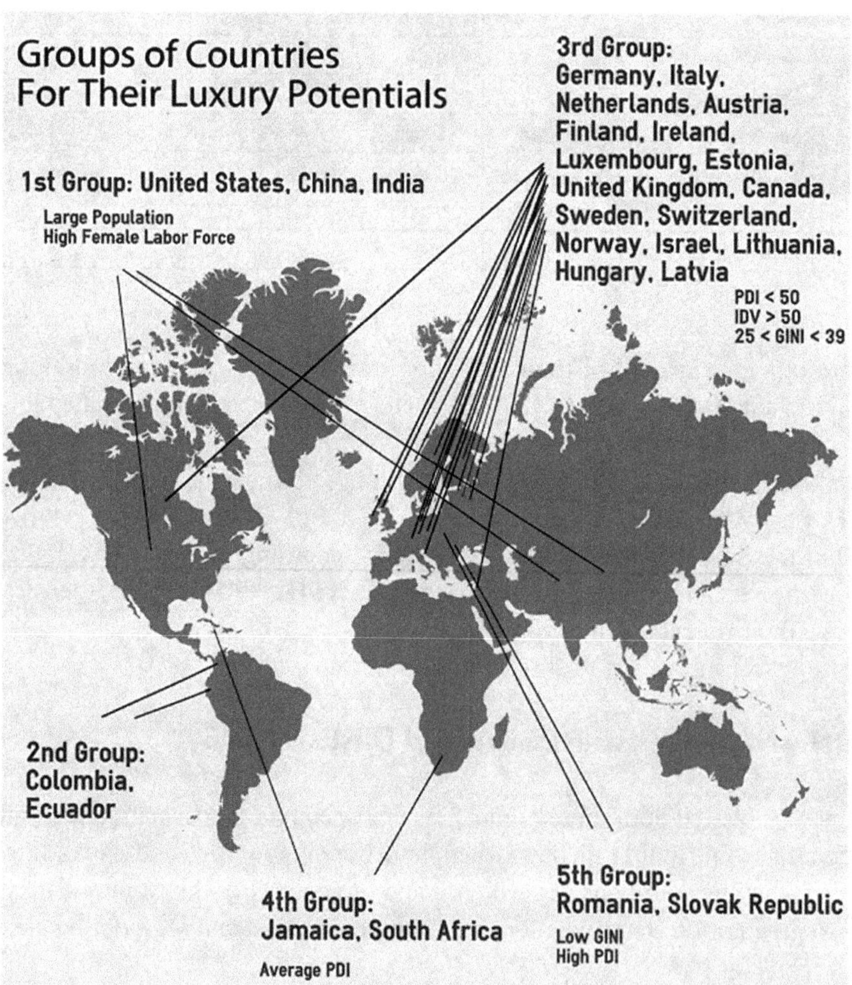

This study should be evaluated as exploratory. Other specific indicators may be used for different specific luxury sectors. The reason for this research is to fill in the gaps in the international marketing literature so as to determine marketing entry decisions for luxury products. As managerial implications, this study should be preliminary; however, besides segmenting the countries in terms of their indicators, it is obvious that there are additional factors affecting brands' choice of markets such as competition, culture, proximity for logistics, and human resources, etc.

In terms of academic implications, this study is expected to encourage new research about segmenting countries according to different criteria for international market entry strategies. Further research studies may consider new indicators to segment luxury markets, as the luxury market is not a distinct market but is composed of different product types. Thus, for each product category, a unique place in the luxury exists, and factors will differ according to the specific features of the category. In addition, individual-based segmentation can reveal different segments based on individual characteristics to complete the market entry strategy.

REFERENCES

Atsmon, Y., Dixit, V., Leibowitz, G., & Wu, C. (2011). Understanding China's growing love for luxury. *McKinsey Insights China*. Retrieved from https://solutions.mckinsey.com/insightschina/_SiteNote/WWW/GetFile.aspx?uri=/insightschina/default/en-us/aboutus/news/Files/wp2055036759/McKinsey%20InsightsChina%20-%202011%20Luxury%20Consumer%20Report_7fbe9eff-0bfd-4cea-8bc5-2dff874db6d0.pdf

Belvaux, B., & Guibert, N. (2012). International Segmentation: Towards a Third Path between Global and National. *International Journal of Market Research*, *54*(1), 111–127. doi:10.2501/IJMR-54-1-111-127

Bock, D., Eastman, J., & McKay, B. (2014). The Impact of Economic Perceptions on Status Consumption: An Exploratory Study of the Moderating Role of Education. *Journal of Consumer Marketing*, *31*(2), 111–117. doi:10.1108/JCM-10-2013-0725

Boote, A. (1983). Psychographic Segmentation in Europe. *Journal of Advertising Research*, *22*(6), 19–25.

Brun, A., & Castelli, C. (2013). The Nature of Luxury: A Consumer Perspective. *International Journal of Retail & Distribution Management*, *41*(11/12), 823–847. doi:10.1108/IJRDM-01-2013-0006

Budeva, D., & Mullen, M. (2014). International Market Segmentation: Economics, National Culture and Time. *European Journal of Marketing*, *48*(7/8), 1209–1238. doi:10.1108/EJM-07-2010-0394

Cateora, P., Gilly, M., & Graham, J. (2009). *International Marketing* (14th International Edition). New York: McGraw Hill/Irwin.

Cavusgil, S., Kiyak, T., & Yeniyurt, S. (2004). Complementary Approaches to Preliminary Foreign Market Opportunity Assessment: Country Clustering and Country Ranking. *Industrial Marketing Management*, *33*(7), 607–617. doi:10.1016/j.indmarman.2003.10.005

Chadha, R., & Husband, P. (2006). *The Cult of the Luxury Brand: Inside Asia's Love Affair with Luxury*. Boston, MA: Nicholas Brealey Publishing.

Chandran, N. (2014). Forget China, This is the Next Big Luxury Market. *CNBC*. Retrieved from http://www.cnbc.com/2014/09/24/forget-china-this-is-asias-new-luxury-market.html

Chevalier, M., Xiao Lu, P., & Toledano, S. (2009). *Luxury China: Market Opportunities and Potential*. John Wiley and Sons.

Choo, H.-J., Moon, H., Kim, H., & Yoon, N. (2012). Luxury Customer Value. *Journal of Fashion Marketing and Management*, *16*(1), 81–101. doi:10.1108/13612021211203041

Christodoulides, G., Michaelidou, N., & Li, C.-H. (2009). Measuring Perceived Brand Luxury: An Evaluation of The BLI Scale. *Brand Management*, *16*(5/6), 395–405. doi:10.1057/bm.2008.49

Deloitte. (2015). *Global Powers of Luxury Goods 2015: Engaging the Future Luxury Consumer*. Deloitte Touche Tohmatsu Limited. Retrieved from http://www2.deloitte.com/content/dam/Deloitte/ch/Documents/consumer-business/ch-en-cb-global-powers-of-luxury-goods-2015.pdf

Donzé, P.-Y., & Fujioka, R. (2015). European Luxury Big Business and Emerging Asian Markets, 1960 – 2010. *Business History*, *57*(6), 822–840. doi:10.1080/00076791.2014.982104

Dubois, B., Czellar, S., & Laurent, G. (2005). Consumer Segments Based on Attitudes Toward Luxury: Empirical Evidence from Twenty Countries. *Marketing Letters*, *16*(2), 115–128. doi:10.1007/s11002-005-2172-0

Dubois, B., & Duquesne, P. (1993). The Market for Luxury Brands: Income versus Culture. *European Journal of Marketing*, *27*(1), 35–44. doi:10.1108/03090569310024530

Eng, T.-Y., & Bogaert, J. (2010). Psychological and Cultural Insights into Consumption of Luxury Western Brands in India. *Journal of Customer Behaviour*, *9*(1), 55–75. doi:10.1362/147539210X497620

Evrard, Y., & Roux, E. (2005). *Culture vs Luxury: The Paradoxes of Democratisation*. Puyricard: CEROG.

Godey, B., Pederzoli, D., Aiello, G., Donvito, R., Wiedmann, K.-P., & Hennigs, N. (2013). A Cross-Cultural Exploratory Content Analysis of The Perception of Luxury from Six Countries. *Journal of Product and Brand Management*, *22*(3), 229–237. doi:10.1108/JPBM-02-2013-0254

Grossman, G., & Shapiro, C. (1988). Foreign Counterfeiting of Status Goods. *The Quarterly Journal of Economics*, *103*(February), 79–100. doi:10.2307/1882643

Hair, J., Anderson, R., Tatham, R., & Black, W. (1998). *Multivariate Data Analysis* (5th International Edition). Prentice Hall.

Heine, K. (2012). *The Identity of Luxury Brands*. (Doctoral Dissertation). Kassel University, Germany.

Helsen, K., Jedidi, K., & DeSarbo, W. (1993). A New Approach to Country Segmentation Utilizing Multinational Diffusion Patterns. *Journal of Marketing*, *57*(October), 60–71. doi:10.2307/1252219

Hofstede, G. (1980). *Culture's Consequences: International Differences in Work Related Values*. Beverly Hills, CA: Sage.

Hudders, L., Pandelaere, M., & Vyncke, P. (2013). Consumer Meaning Making: The Meaning of Luxury Brands in a Democratised Luxury World. *International Journal of Market Research, 55*(3), 391–412. doi:10.2501/IJMR-2013-036

Husic, M., & Cicic, M. (2009). Luxury Consumption Factors. *Journal of Fashion Marketing and Management, 13*(2), 231–245. doi:10.1108/13612020910957734

Huszagh, S., Fox, R., & Day, E. (1986). Global Marketing: An Empirical Investigation. *The Columbia Journal of World Business, 20*(4), 31–43.

IMF. (2013). *World Economic Outlook: Transitions and Tensions*. International Monetary Fund, Publication Services.

Kale, S. (1995). Grouping Euroconsumers: A Culture-Based Clustering Approach. *Journal of International Marketing, 3*(3), 35–48.

Kapferer, J. (2012). Abundant Rarity: The Key to Luxury Growth. *Business Horizons, 55*(5), 453–462. doi:10.1016/j.bushor.2012.04.002

Kapferer, J., & Bastien, V. (2009). The Specificity of Luxury Management: Turning Marketing Upside Down. *Journal of Brand Management, 16*(5), 311–322. doi:10.1057/bm.2008.51

Khan, O. (2015). Luxury Consumption Moves East. *Journal of Fashion Marketing and Management: An International Journal, 19*(4), 347–359. doi:10.1108/JFMM-10-2014-0076

Liu, S., Perry, P., Moore, C., & Warnaby, G. (2015). The Standardization-Localization Dilemma of Brand Communications for Luxury Fashion Retailers' Internationalization into China. *Journal of Business Research.*

Malhotra, N. (2007). *Marketing Research: An Applied Orientation* (5th International Edition). Pearson Prentice Hall. doi:10.1108/S1548-6435(2007)3

Matthiesen, I., & Phau, I. (2005). The 'HUGO BOSS' Connection: Achieving Global Brand Consistency across Countries. *Brand Management, 12*(5), 325–338. doi:10.1057/palgrave.bm.2540229

Mosca, F., Bertoldi, B., & Giachino, C. (2015). Development Strategies for International Distribution in Luxury Industry. *International Journal of Management Cases, 17*(3), 4–18.

Mosca, F., & Re, P. (2014). International Development Strategies of Luxury-Goods Players in China. *The China Business Review, 13*(6), 367–381.

Moskowitz, H., & Rabino, S. (1994). Sensory Segmentation: An Organizing Principle for International Product Concept Generation. *Journal of Global Marketing, 8*(1), 73–93. doi:10.1300/J042v08n01_05

Nueno, J., & Quelch, J. (1998). The Mass Marketing of Luxury. *Business Horizons, 41*(November-December), 61–68. doi:10.1016/S0007-6813(98)90023-4

Okonkwo, U. (2007). *Luxury Fashion Branding: Trends, Tactics, Techniques*. Palgrave Macmillan. doi:10.1057/9780230590885

Okonkwo, U. (2009). Sustaining the Luxury Brand on the Internet. *Journal of Brand Management*, *16*(2), 302–310. doi:10.1057/bm.2009.2

Peng Cui, A., Wajda, T., & Walsh, M. (2015). Luxury Brands in Emerging Markets: A Case Study on China. *Entrepreneurship in International Marketing*, *25*, 287–305.

Prayag, G., & Hosany, S. (2014). When Middle East Meets West: Understanding The Motives and Perceptions of Young Tourists From United Arab Emirates. *Tourism Management*, *40*, 35–45. doi:10.1016/j.tourman.2013.05.003

Seo, Y., & Buchanan-Oliver, M. (2015). Luxury Branding: The Industry, Trends, and Future Conceptualisations. *Asia Pacific Journal of Marketing and Logistics*, *27*(1), 82–98. doi:10.1108/APJML-10-2014-0148

Sethi, P. (1971). Comparative Cluster Analysis for World Markets. *JMR, Journal of Marketing Research*, *8*(3), 348–354. doi:10.2307/3149574

Sethi, P., & Holton, R. (1973). Country Typologies for the Multinational Corporation: A New Basic Approach. *California Management Review*, *15*(3), 105–118. doi:10.2307/41164444

Steenkamp, J.-B. (2001). The Role of National Culture in International Marketing Research. *International Marketing Review*, *18*(1), 30–44. doi:10.1108/02651330110381970

Steenkamp, J.-B., & Ter Hofstede, F. (2002). International Market Segmentation: Issues and Perspectives. *International Journal of Research in Marketing*, *19*(3), 185–213. doi:10.1016/S0167-8116(02)00076-9

Stokburger-Sauer, N., & Teichmann, K. (2013). Is Luxury Just a Female Thing? The Role of Gender in Luxury Brand Consumption. *Journal of Business Research*, *66*(7), 889–896. doi:10.1016/j.jbusres.2011.12.007

Stump, R., Gong, W., & Li, Z. (2008). Exploring the Digital Divide in Mobile-phone Adoption Levels across Countries: Do Population Socioeconomic Traits Operate in the Same Manner as Their Individual-level Demographic Counterparts? *Journal of Macromarketing*, *28*(4), 397–412. doi:10.1177/0276146708325386

Teimourpour, B., & Hanzaee, K. (2011). The Impact of Culture on Luxury Consumption Behaviour Among Iranian Consumers. *Journal of Islamic Marketing*, *2*(3), 309–328. doi:10.1108/17590831111164822

Ter Hofstede, F., Steenkamp, J.-B., & Wedel, M. (1999). International Market Segmentation Based on Consumer-Product Relations. *JMR, Journal of Marketing Research*, *36*(1), 1–17. doi:10.2307/3151911

The Hofstede Center. (n.d.). Retrieved from http://geert-hofstede.com/countries.html

Truong, Y., McColl, R., & Kitchen, P. (2009). New Luxury Brand Positioning and the Emergence of Masstige Brands. *Journal of Brand Management*, *16*(5), 375–382. doi:10.1057/bm.2009.1

Urban, G., & Hauser, J. (1993). *Design and Marketing of New Products*. Prentice Hall.

Verhage, B., Dahringer, L., & Cundiff, E. (1989). Will a Global Strategy Work? An Energy Conservation Perspective. *Journal of the Academy of Marketing Science*, *17*(2), 129–136. doi:10.1007/BF02723371

Vigneron, F., & Johnson, L. (1999). A Review and a Conceptual Framework of Prestige-Seeking Consumer Behavior. *Academy of Marketing Science Review*, (1): 1–15.

Wedel, M., & Kamakura, W. (2002). Introduction to the Special Issue on Market Segmentation. *International Journal of Research in Marketing*, *19*(3), 181–183. doi:10.1016/S0167-8116(02)00075-7

Willis, M. (2006). To Adapt ot to Standardise: Testing Asian Views about Purchasing Western Luxury Products in Seven Asian Locations. *Journal of East-West Business*, *12*(1), 65–94. doi:10.1300/J097v12n01_05

World Bank. (n.d.). *Indicators*. Retrieved from http://data.worldbank.org/indicator?display=default

Yavas, U., Verhage, B., & Green, R. (1992). Global Consumer Segmentation versus Local Market Orientation: Empirical Findings. *Management International Review*, *32*(3), 265–273.

Section 2

Integrated Marketing Communication and New Social Systems in the Luxury Markets

Chapter 5
Managing Integrated Brand Communication Strategies in the Online Era:
New Marketing Frontiers for Luxury Goods

Fabrizio Mosca
University of Turin, Italy

Cecilia Casalegno
University of Turin, Italy

ABSTRACT

Since the spread of digital environments has certainly helped to broaden the spectrum of possibilities for managing channels, while opening new areas of competitive confrontation, is to assume that new technologies have contributed to the definition of a hybrid environment in which pre- and post-digital-revolution habits coexist. The aim of the present chapter is to show how this kind of hybrid channels, want to meet the two requirements to communicate and sell - through the use of media platforms that appeal to each other, meet and complement each other – is nowadays managed and how it can be used in the future to reach business and awareness goals in luxury markets. The analysis has been based on ways through which global luxury goods firms integrate their communication and selling tools each other, by focusing the attention on web and social strategies.

INTRODUCTION

Spaces and environments are places of consumption, but they also provide communication opportunities to the final consumer who, in turn, uses consumption as a communication system that is expressed through a variety of languages (Mosca et al., 2013). The more layers there are in a society, which brings many different linguistic expressions, the more complex it is to analyze consumption dynamics. This is particularly true for luxury goods (Chevalier & Mazzalovo, 2012) that are sold and communicated in markets that are difficult to define, but in which it is possible to find various layers of media attitudes.

DOI: 10.4018/978-1-4666-9958-8.ch005

In fact, it is possible to say that the traditional consideration whereby businesses serve as the exclusive source of communication messages and brand-related content, designed to influence the behavior of consumers and create brand equity, is overtaken. This is due to the fact that marketing and communication strategies, together with the instruments and actors involved in their planning processes, need to take into account the evolution of technology, the transformation of consumer behavior and media attitudes, the fact that stakeholders constantly communicate each others and this kind of communication is difficult to manage by firms. The communication works in attracting people's interest toward a certain brand, but, at the same time, it works as shield for the corporate reputation and a springboard for spreading corporate values.

As a topic that is largely discussed in various areas of interest, it is important to underline that in the last 10 years, technological evolution has been leading mass media to a decline in their ability to attract people's (audiences') attention. Of course, this is due, above all, to changes in the attitudes of generation Y toward the media, together with the growing interest in new media content generated by people (mostly young individuals) – the so-called user-generated content (UGC), such as blogging, podcasting, online videos (eg: YouTube, Vimeo), and social networking (Facebook, Twitter, Pinterest, Google Plus). So, even when we talk about luxury players, it is fundamental to understand that the Internet is now the real "backbone of the media system" (CENSIS, 2013).

In order to respond to the aforementioned trends, organizations are generally dealing with developing a communication plan that can integrate all those tools with which they intend to interface with their stakeholders (Schultz, Tannenbaum & Lauterborn, 1993; Romano, 1988; Krugman et al., 1994; Collesei, 2002; Duncan & Mulhern, 2004; Aiello & Donvito, 2005; Collesei & Ravà, 2008; Belch & Belch, 1998, 2009). Moreover, in order to reach their target audience, the concept of integrated communication becomes inseparable from common value sharing with stakeholders; people are more worried about values and how responsible a given firm is. This is supposed to assume an attitude of protection toward the environment (geographical, economic, and social), upon which a firm should intend to develop its strategic action. Globalization, the fast development of communication technologies, the continuous research of information by people, and the economic and financial global crisis that started in 2008 represent some of the primary factors that have contributed to the increase in stakeholders' expectations and their awareness toward goods and services. Customers, above all, feel more involved in purchases; they pay attention to the product process, when they can, and they want to be notified about everything concerning the firm through which they are buying products. As a consequence, companies have to rethink their offers, as well as their social and environmental impacts, and build a new system of values that respond to the reference community and to society at large. According to the 2013 Consumer Trend Report (2), nowadays, products are being asked to give back a specific set of expected and shared values. Porter and Kramer refer to the fact that firms and stakeholders can co-create value (2011); they regard the sharing of values between the business community and the organization as the main key to holding a competitive advantage.

Turning to the changes made in technology, as well as taking into account the macro-environment factors considered above, we discover that stakeholders (from the luxury goods and players' perspectives) are willing to share values; they want to participate in the content generation of every firm's story. They aim to be a part of an exclusive group; this sentiment has been stronger in the last few years, especially since these individuals have lived in a period of crisis. This is increasingly felt as we talk about the digital age. It is the digital age that is pushing these aforementioned trends; for luxury products, their success can come only when two conditions are fulfilled: personalized identification and provision of a multi-sensory experience. The response to these conditions has led luxury companies to take to online strategies, without forgetting that the concept of a traditional store always plays a major role in the experience of buying luxury goods.

Since the spread of digital environments has certainly helped to broaden the spectrum of possibilities to managing channels, while offering new areas for competitive confrontation, it is possible to assume that new technologies have contributed to define a hybrid environment in which pre- and post-digital revolution habits coexist. The first research question that this chapter seeks to answer is the following: Can we talk about a certain type of "reverse multichannel marketing"? The aim, indeed, is to show how this kind of hybrid distribution and communication channel – which wants to meet the two requirements of communicating and selling through the use of media platforms that appeal to one another, while complementing each other – is currently managed, and how it can be used in the future to reach business and awareness goals in luxury markets.

Considering the particular sector that the present chapter wishes to analyze, the concept of multichannel marketing has been translated in physical and digital channel integration, with the aim of enhancing consumer and audience engagement. Is multichannel marketing just a fad that follows contemporary media attitudes, or does it represent a new strategy? This is the other research question the present chapter seeks to answer through a case analysis. If this is a novel strategy, it means that the logic underlying the development of the digital channel for luxury players is therefore one of integration with the physical channel; it is not to be viewed as a standalone distribution channel, but as one that completes the physical one.

Moreover, this chapter wants to emphasize the importance of the concept of consistency, since in every marketing book, authors say that luxury market players follow different rules than their competitors in terms of consumer goods. We talk about communicative coherence and the ability of companies to decline providing such consistency across all those channels at their disposal to reach their intended audience, considering that, for luxury goods above all, the selling point has always been the first way to communicate the brand's identity and its real essence. Is this consistency reached even if luxury players are mixing their classical channels with those channels that are always exploited by players in every kind of market?

COMMUNICATION AND DISTRIBUTION INTEGRATION AS A LOGICAL MULTICHANNEL LAST STEP

The real challenges for every firm relate to new communication trends on the one hand, and changing buyers' attitudes on the other. Nowadays, one of the most important marketing paradigms refers to the fact that the more consumers perceive that the firm's values are closely aligned with what they think, trust in, and feel, the more they are likely to buy. In particular, this has been brought about by constant communication; stakeholders steadily talk to each other. They are more informed and they want to know everything about the organizations in which they are involved. This is particularly true in highly symbolic value goods markets; information technology increases development (Rifkin, 2000), while the continuous compression of the product life cycle reinforces new consumption mechanisms that will be focused not only on the possession of the product, but on the sharing of wealth and consumption experiences. Moreover, in recent years, researchers and managers have found that various consumption forms exist together, especially when we talk about luxury markets, which range from more traditional buying behaviors (well described in the Conspicuous Consumptions Veblen Model) to the birth of connoisseurs (Corbellini & Saviolo, 2007). This is due to the ongoing changes related to purchasing schemes used by customers, who are defined as smart, well informed, and always looking for brand new experiences and relationships (Okonkwo, 2010).

The aforementioned findings highlight that a lot of the traditional marketing logic has changed in these last few years. Even if the concept of "multichannel marketing" is not new, here we can find roots of another trend: the integration of distribution and communication platforms. This is due to the increase in the penetration of digital environments, which feed customers' associations of new activities when compared to the more traditional rituals of consumption. It common practice to look for information about a product through blogs, social networking pages, and online groups before making a buying decision; people want to understand from other people how good a certain brand is, where to buy a certain product, and how long lasting the materials or textiles of a certain good are. As a result, it is also possible to observe that the same person buys a product by using more than one channel, depending on the product and its availability, price, time, and service (Venkatesan et al., 2007).

When we talk about multichannel marketing, we refer to a strategy concerning the use of more than just one channel for placing information and products/services on the market – even in the aftermarket – and the result is a major public commitment and a higher degree of customer engagement (Rangaswamy & Van Bruggen, 2005). Customers, in particular, perceive that they have the chance to interact with brands; they can generate content, and they can ultimately affect the future of a certain brand (Osmonbekov et al., 2009).

Managers can exploit the advantages stemming from multichannel marketing strategies; they can increase the customer perception of brand equity through concrete actions associated with client retention. A firm that uses multichannel marketing is able to segment and manage the increasing variety of demand; in this way, it is aided by digital innovation. Market management can be easier, and there is a major opportunity to augment the awareness of a corporate brand (Mosca, 2014). Specifically, there are no geographical barriers when we talk about online strategies and, at the same time, the integration of communication and distribution channels (online and offline) is possible.

Moreover, by leveraging the digital environment, it is possible to collect data surrounding consumers' habits and fads, both new and uncommon, and this can offer the ability to make a decisive contribution to the acquisition of other geographical markets. Since one of the so-called "lost opportunities" (Kotler et al., 2009) is represented by the impossibility of finding a product in a local market, online distribution provides companies with a chance to exploit brand communication to sell more products and at a lower cost (Osmonbekov et al, 2009). At the same time, firms can benefit from the results coming from customer relationship management (CRM) when they carefully handle channels; it is possible to collect new and infrequent information on what customers prefer, when they decide to make a purchase, and what the behavior leading the purchase itself is (Ricotta, 2009). Of course, the customer will be incentivized to maintain a relationship with that brand, generating an increase of value for him/her that stems from the available variety, the customization of channels, and the rise in adaptations following personal predilections (Ricotta, 2009).

The arrival of online and social platforms has created another profound change: the upside-down use of communication and distribution strategies. More precisely, when considering the term "social media" – which gained popularity in 2005 – it has been used to describe different types of digital content that have been developed for interactive advertising; this offers audience members the possibility to generate content around a specific brand. Here, we talk about *user-generated contents* (UGC), as argued by Kaplanand and Haenlein in 2010. Consumers become leading actors, and firms can develop measures of engagement and take advantage of word of mouth referrals with a proactive and dynamic approach. This dynamic approach indicates that another trend is becoming important: online selling through mobile channels. Luxury players, above all, can benefit from this growing trend in other markets (KPMG, 2013). Given that authors have previously talked about the integration of channels, we must now point out that the instruments have traditionally been used for distribution, they are now being used and designed to achieve the objectives of establishing competence, which has previously been assigned to communication functions. Vice versa, web and mobile, designed to spread the communication at the beginning, are now becoming the main distribution channels.

Considering what was described above, managers have to approach new strategies through the understanding of how customers use different platforms, after having analyzed them through a new demand segmentation model, as represented in Table 1. This table provides an output of previous researches (Mosca *et al.,* 2013, 2014). The considered dimensions (empathy, expression, and enhancement, which originated from the study of people's attitudes toward online and offline media) are valid for every kind of market, but the interesting thing is that they are also valid for luxury goods (in mature markets). By matching these dimensions with new customer/audience attitudes toward media, it is possible to outline new profiles. Table 1 illustrates a scheme that can be helpful when determining the best method through which to integrate distribution and communication channels; it provides a complete overview of customer behaviors. It is possible to highlight three types of profiles: the Traditionalist, the Multimedia lover and the Eager about social media. Every profile presents, as it is possible to see in the table, a different tendency in using the web and the other screens and a specific reason driving his/her interaction with brands.

Table 1. Online users' profiles (mature markets) (Mosca et al., 2013)

	Traditionalist	Multimedia Lover	Eager about Social Media
	He/she lives the brand communication primarily through its above the line (ATL) media effectiveness. He/she prefers printed paper and specialized magazines as tools through which to enjoy communication and to find information on products and luxury brands.	The ATL advertisement triggers a mechanism that sees this individual interacting with the brand and its products through the use of multiple screens. He/she spontaneously remembers integrated communication campaigns, becoming – in some cases – a means of communication him/herself by sharing content (institutional or not) such as videos, photos, and articles.	Actively contributes to the promotion of messages and information, often becoming an active user not only in the process of diffusion, but also in the process of content creation through the use of comments, links to external sites, or providing additional information through blogs, etc. These individuals are major users of exclusive content made available by companies.
Empathy	✓	✓	✓
Expression	×	✓	✓
Enhancement	×	×	✓

The research questions that were posited in the present chapter now have their first answers. We are talking about the definition of a strategy that concerns the integrated use of communication and distribution channels, which is the answer that players are giving to markets changes. We are not talking about a "fad" or a quick trend; rather, we are talking about a strategy that gains the confidence of the target audience. This phenomenon had its birth in 1994, and it has become viral in recent years, thanks to the increased sales in mobile devices. The first example of such "reverse multichannel marketing" comes from the mass market. In fact, it is possible to analyze a particular case study: Made.com. In early 2015, the UK furniture selling Web site opened its fourth showroom in Soho. The aim of this strategy was to enable people to have hands-on experiences. As is already known, the biggest bug in online selling revolves around the impossibility of trying or touching goods prior to purchase. Made.com can avoid this problem by offering physical places in which nothing is for sale, but where people can test a product, see its real colors, view textiles, and assess their dimensions. As such, we are talking about a space that is not a shop – no cash is exchanged on the way out; rather, this space offers a sort of physical complement to the online purchasing experience. The outfit features 1:1 goods projections to show how possible combinations can be realized when requested by customers. Visitors are equipped with a tablet to gather information on specific products. They can also project their place's spaces, create wish lists, and buy desired products.

This case illustrates how some important elements are fundamental when effectively integrating distribution and communication channels:

- People are encouraged to constantly use screens; they want to optimize the free time they have through screen technology;
- People are willing to make purchases, but only when they know the materials, textiles, and dimensions of the goods they want to try;
- Since technology can help managers in this way, the interaction between communication and distribution channels can bring about positive results, but it is possible to sell only when people perceive that a certain degree of consistency exists among the various channels used;
- A customer may decide to make an online purchase via a physical point of sale if the technology experienced in the physical place can lend value to the purchase itself;
- The audience and possible customers never "go to sleep"; this refers to the idea that the Web and the marketing strategy must consider that this platform does not have geographical barriers; and
- The integration of virtual and physical channels has been reinvented with upside-down logic: the online channel is not additional or an accessory to the physical one; rather, both channels are part of the same process. The physical place is the communication channel and the online space is the selling one.

The above case shows that the spread of digital environments has helped broaden the spectrum of channel possibilities, and this can serve as a new area of competition. If we think that technology and its new horizons have redefined something, it is possible to refer to this as a hybrid exchange environment in which managers can study the coexistence of well-established and growing habits. Moreover, the increasing synchrony between distribution and communication channels can enhance the reassurance felt by customers and, as a consequence, it can further bolster client loyalty (Berger, 2006). When a firm is able to surround its target market, the result will be engagement and long-range profit.

ONLINE AND OFFLINE INTEGRATION ENHANCEMENT: HOW LUXURY FIRMS EXPLOIT THE CONCEPT OF MULTICHANNEL MARKETING

The luxury market's competitive landscape in recent years has been changing, primarily due to the rise in user-generated content. Firms have to revise their strategies to implement a "hold" concept: multichannel marketing is increasing in importance, as international media trends are operated by an ever-more demanding and informed audience.

International research initiatives (KPMG, 2013, for instance) have probed into the situation that luxury firms are facing with a high degree of success: a phenomenon that is known as the "digital challenge". These firms try to integrate both online and offline communication tools and, as a result, they recourse to a plurality of channels that are used to sell, but that are also primarily implemented to tell a story, to enhance the perception of product quality. This is interesting if we think that brands like Burberry, Chanel, Bottega Veneta, Gucci, and Ferrari are using the same channels (digital ones) that mass market firms are using. However, digital channels are a necessity even for luxury goods, since the most frequently used exchange platforms are currently online. Again, is this just a passing trend or a real competitive strategy?

The integration of different platforms in contemporary times revolves around the Web. The age of 2.0 has led the luxury goods players, as will be discussed below, to adopt the same strategies and tactics taken by the actors in mass markets; this has been a revolution, especially if you think that traditional marketing has always considered luxury and mass markets as two competitive environments with totally different mixed marketing strategies. Yet, the Web is able to bridge these two worlds without upsetting them and without having the various players fail their promise of consistency. Data relating to social media serve as examples of what was said earlier: in the middle of 2013, social media was compared (Mosca et al., 2013) between a number of brands (like Chanel) and more famous brands to the consumer (such as Benetton). It turned out that the number of likes and shares for the luxury fashion player was twice that of those in the mass market. This finding is as relevant as ever, as it indicates the short amount of time it took for brands like Chanel to develop their own social presence online.

Considering the necessity of using digital platforms to reach and engage people as a standpoint, it is useful to underline that digital channels are a way better method through which to interact with the audience. Consequently, digital platforms take on a double connotation: a digital channel is a tool through which to inform and persuade individuals, like other older media; at the same time, it represents a way through which to sell a product, using both physical and virtual contact modes. According to this idea, it is possible to say that the benefits coming from online and offline integration strategies interest both luxury firms, as well as their audience members. First of all, the public's attention can be easily captured through the interactions caused by the nature of Web 2.0 (Ricotta, 2009); this pertains to UGC, which was previously discussed, and its power to enhance people's engagement. Moreover, pushing the simultaneous use of different screens – which is called "interactive multimedia" (Casalegno, Li, 2012) – provides luxury firms with some advantages, including the following: long-lasting customer loyalty, especially since the audience is surrounded by a certain message from the firm; the pulse of customer's experience as the result of the interaction; sales increase given that the more a customer has confidence in a brand, the more he or she is going to buy it; and employee retention, since the first customer of a firm is the employee him/herself. On the other side, even customers can benefit from a multichannel strategy; they can customize the product they want by providing feedback to firms, they save time when comparing products and during the purchase process, they feel involved in the exchange process, and they can receive the product in a shorter amount of time through online purchasing.

According to this perspective, even the development of a digital channel for luxury players has to consider integration with the traditional distribution channel; it is not to be viewed as a standalone distribution channel, but as one that complements the physical channel, as will be argued below, and as various examples in the text can show.

Traditional and physical stores always play a major role in the experience of buying luxury goods, but the huge success of the digital channel turns it into an inescapable variable for players in the market for highly symbolic value goods. Nowadays, a Web strategy is essential for a luxury brand (Mosca et al., 2013, 2014). In order to provide a clearer idea of how powerful the method of selling online is becoming, one must consider the Digital Luxury Experience (DLE) 3rd edition. The results of this research project – jointly developed by the Fondazione Altagamma and McKinsey in 2012 – confirm that the online sales of luxury products reached €7.5 billion, accounting for 4% of the total selling. For 2017, the study forecasts an increased incidence of 6% with an increase in sales of €17 billion. Another interesting result concerns the highest growth shown in multi-brand sites when compared with market products at full price. This shows that Web channels today can no longer be regarded as virtual spaces in which consumers hunt for bargain purchases. Luxury customers are involved in services and the breadth of offering, as they are when they buy products in a physical place. Another important finding is that there is confirmation of the increasing role of Smartphones and tablets; in fact, 50% of luxury consumers conduct online searches from a mobile device, and there is also an increasingly strong correlation between the increase in sales and the number of Web pages visited. For companies with a page per visit above the panel average, the sales increase is 16%. Another study published by KPMG indicates that 70% of Chinese customers make purchases online at least once a month (KPMG, 2013).

In fact, especially in this particular competitive environment, consumers are looking for a deep and intimate relationship with brands that emphasize recognition, respect, dialogue, and collaboration with their costumers (Mosca et al., 2013). On the other hand, costumers tend to reject those brands that do not regard their involvement, nor that provide the attention they require. So, they tend to abandon those firms that are not able to convey their experiences, values, and excellent product concepts in a way that is consistent between the real world and the online environment. From this perspective, integrated communication has gained importance in the management of luxury brands. These brands have already exploited their online potential in communication, and they are beginning to approach the Web as a means through which to sell products by leveraging their unique values. Table 2 summarizes the shared content belonging to the most major luxury firms in the past year (2014).

Table 2. Online/social shared luxury firms' contents (analysis conducted by the authors)

	Heritage	Storytelling	Events & Celebrities	Entertainment
Automotive	25%	35%	20%	20%
Fashion	15%	30%	40%	15%
Wine and spirits	40%	10%	15%	35%
Jewelry and watchmaking	35%	20%	30%	15%
Perfumery and cosmetics	35%	15%	15%	35%

Focusing attention on the third research question, it is necessary to consider the ways in which luxury players can maintain consistency in their brand's identity, the new communication and distribution channels that are adopted, and the efforts to reach a certain brand positioning. In this scenario, which is dominated by a stronger relationship between people and technology, communication, and the Web, the marketing of luxury goods requires a new communication model based on the 7Es (4Es + 3Es): Experience, Exclusivity, Engagement, and Emotion, in addition to the other 3Es that have arisen from the opportunities that the Web affords. In particular, the 3Es that have emerged from the social Web have brought the following to communication: Expression, Enhancement, and Empathy. This strategy is described below.

THE "7ES" STRATEGY FOR A MAJOR BRAND'S CONSISTENCY: OUTFITS AND RESULTS

The 7Es strategy was already considered in previous researches (Mosca et al, 2013, 2014), but the interesting thing is that these seven elements are still being considered, and the channels through which luxury players market their products has been based on this model in the last four years to enhance their positioning and the consistency of their brand's identity. As has already been argued, it is very uncommon for luxury players to employ marketing and communication strategies using the same communication and distribution channels already used by mass market firms. One must examine what it is about the "sense of elite" that comes from the unique experiences of a customer, and how this could be received from a selling point. What about the services given by shops and showroom employees? What about the rules that were already studied and applied by managers until a few years ago? Consistency, "sense of elite", and brand engagement can be enhanced through Web communication and online selling if luxury firm managers consider the following elements.

Experience. During the recession and post-recession, and unlike in other markets, the traditional luxury goods customer has not significantly limited his or her consumption. As a result, luxury goods markets have not been heavily affected by the crisis; rather, it can be highlighted that purchasing trends have shown the opposite pattern. While the luxury market and spending on luxury goods has grown, on the other side, luxury consumers have become more selective, informed, and a little bit more cynical. Today, the luxury consumers' purchasing decisions revolve around the question, "Is it worth it?" In this scenario, luxury companies have to provide unique and engaging experiences. Some authors have observed how the next decade will be characterized by the centrality of the experience. Attention is no longer paid to what you buy, but how you buy. This stems from the fact that the selling point has become the focus of a luxury brand's marketing strategies, and it now constitutes a central element in the process of integrated communication, which is capable of influencing, through its tangible and intangible elements, the brand's image. It also ensures that the consumer is provided with a unique and engaging experience.

Burberry

This fashion luxury player – with an allocation of 60% of available resources for digital marketing –opened its flagship store on September 14, 2012 in the heart of London. The flagship store, thanks to the technology developed by the brand, is designed to increase customer engagement and purchasing through a digital and tactile experience in store, which shows the historical and artistic heritage of the brand. The 44,000 square-foot store on Regent Street was developed as the physical expression of Burberry.com; in fact, the rooms in the flagship store follow the sections of the Website that are available online, allowing customers to dive into a combined digital and physical experience. This experience is enhanced by features such as the presence of 100 screens, the installation of the largest indoor advertising screen in the world (22 ft), and 500 speakers that support the playing of movies and exclusive videos of this luxury maison in Britain. Regarding merchandising and inventory, Burberry's flagship store features completely innovative technology. Alongside the RDIF chips sewn into the clothing and accessories, which provide a range of multimedia content related to the products, employees of the British luxury maison – thanks to a series of iPad applications designed for the sales staff – are able to access information about a customer's purchase history and their preferences, thus providing customers with a personal and customized shopping experience. In conclusion, the strategy put in place by Burberry not only allows a costumer to increase his or her perceived value of the brand, thus improving his/her shopping experience, but it also enables the brand to increase its permanence in terms of the amount of time spent in the store, creating the customer's desire to return and repeat the experience.

Exclusivity

In marketing, exclusivity is considered to arise from the second P of the marketing mix: price. Exclusivity, however, has always been the cornerstone of a luxury firm's strategies, and no concept has ever been more intensely protected. Is widely believed that the use of digital marketing in luxury marketing strategies could "put in jeopardy the exclusivity of the brand"; however, on the contrary, it could offer a real opportunity and an elegant way through which to control and develop such exclusivity, simultaneously increasing the visibility of a brand. As a result, the players of the luxury market have created exclusive platforms for consumers, as for instance the virtual community. This expedient has been used, for example, by Burberry for its "Art of Trench". In fact, each maison has a special icon that distinguishes one from the other – similar to, for instance, the Hermès Kelly. For Burberry, this icon is its trench coat. As its symbolic garment, Burberry's creative director, Christopher Bailey, has created a real fashion social network that collects photo shoots of characters, famous and not, who wear the company's icon. The British maison has developed a platform that combines high-quality content produced by the brand with those of its users by allowing users to communicate with the company and with one another. To launch the project, Christopher Bailey has hired Scott Schuman, the world-famous photographer, to take the first hundred pictures; later, users have responded to the initiative by uploading thousands of their own photos.

Engagement

In the realm of luxury goods, engagement is granted and often evoked by one thing: the story. Any video, online experience, or a simple post on Facebook, which is equipped with engaging content, constitutes a story that arouses emotions and involves the viewer in a unique experience. Today, in the luxury market, convincing the consumer to buy is not sufficient. Convincing them, however, to participate in an exclusive trip with and within the brand is the key to success, and that is what stories achieve. In addition, it is known that these stories "sell".

Tiffany

The jeweler reported a significant increase in sales after the public and the press enthusiastically greeted the microsite developed by the brand, What Makes Love True, and the mobile application, Engagement Ring Finder. These two elements of digital marketing conveyed the powerful and engaging history of the Tiffany brand in achieving true love. Tiffany has decided not to focus only on selling products, but on an entire way of life. In fact, the brand has invested heavily in the What Makes Love True campaign. What Makes Love True offers videos, stories, and content from Web users/customers that follow the stages of how the main characters of the stories met and fell in love in a mix that also involves film and romantic songs. What Tiffany did was create an environment that embodies the lifestyle of the brand. The site also offers sections where customers and fans of the brand can share their love stories and a map, thanks to a tracking system, all of which are in place in New York, where a major event has happened.

Emotion

The combination of the 3Es described above takes a fourth element of luxury marketing into account: emotion. Without the proper application of this key variable, the success of luxury brands is not sustainable in the long run. The reason is simple: luxury firms have consumers that can buy almost anything they want. In this context, the physical product acquires secondary importance in favor of what luxury consumers are really looking for: a more personal experience or an engaging story that will evoke in them a particular emotion.

With respect to these basic Es, which have been identified through a literature review (Luan, 2008; Corbellini & Saviolo, 2007; Okonkwo, 2010; Kapferer & Bastien, 2014), it is evident that in order to complete the model, it is necessary to add the 3Es that are linked to consumer empowerment (Mosca et al., 2013).

Enhancement

This is the enrichment of luxury content through the provision of exclusive content; this content could be shared, but it is used to increase the consumer's experience.

Expression

The Internet provides consumers with the opportunity to manage the amount of time they communicate. This has given way to a communication style that is more charming, elegant, and dream-like, and that is able to reach a specific target market which, until now, was not possible with only above the line media.

Cartier

The first luxury brand to use a social network in its marketing strategy was Cartier which, in 2008, created its first official page on MySpace to advertise one of its brands (Love) and its charity campaign. From 2008 onward, Cartier has leveraged the power of the Web, creating opportunities through which to enhance the brand's expression. Nowadays, Cartier is present on Facebook, Pinterest, YouTube, Twitter, and LinkedIn. Moreover, the Web site features an online shopping page. To augment consumer engagement and provide a sense of membership, the various Web pages present the same picture (Cartier's symbol, the jaguar).

Empathy

UGC media are able to provide luxury firms with personal information about their customers, allowing companies to establish a more intimate relationship with their clients. This practice is in line with the inversion of the traditional communication scheme that has influenced the current scenario in almost all markets.

Chanel

Although Chanel has already been mentioned as being very active in social networks, this famous player has not offered sales channels online to date. The company's online presence has been developed to attract customers to its traditional stores. Why? Chanel says that if you do not try on clothes, you cannot buy them. The online catalogue is not used to sell products through the Web; rather, it serves as a tool through which to push its in-store sales. Finally, the company's online and social presence was established to create a sense of empathy, which was already explained. The brand aims to tell a story: the story of Madame Coco. That story can affect people, and this is an effective way through which to establish a more intimate relationship with the customer. In this instance, we are talking about a case of integrating online and offline channels, of course, but the two platforms, the distribution as well the communication one, are not changing their rules, at least so far.

FUTURE DIRECTIONS: BENEFITS AND RISKS FOR CONSUMERS

The potential impact of online stores on a customer's purchase behaviors represents an interesting area of discussion. Are people changing their habits and attitudes in such a way that pushes every luxury firm to consider online selling? So far, as has already been shown, some luxury players have not decided to sell online, but what about tomorrow? Managers can try to provide solutions to the aforementioned questions by considering that online selling features risks and benefits. On the one hand, an online shop can augment the 7Es, and the 7Es can be exploited to encourage people to buy online. It is also worth considering that in the future, generation Y will represent the luxury target market, and studies on their attitudes toward buying and media are showing a strong predilection for online tools (both for buying and for gathering information). Moreover, we have already considered that customers can benefit from online purchasing methods (they can customize their future purchases, they can experience the brand, and they can interact with and gather major information about the firm itself); in addition to these benefits, customers are also provided with the added convenience of receiving products directly to their door (Voyer, Tran, 2013), and customers are also able to monitor online product stocks (usually when a certain product is scarce, people know).

On the other side, online sales feature risks. From a customer's perspective, the first risk is linked to the nature of the online environment: you cannot try to think, you cannot see the clothes or purses live, and the screen on your laptop/PC can provide you with a poor image resolution. Moreover, if the value of a luxury product is high given its selective distribution, how does the online environment change this – especially since Web pages have no barriers? Eventually, from the firms' perspective, the online environment can create conflict among distribution channels.

Finally, managers need to face the pros and cons of online strategies and, consequently, they have to consider if their target market is ready to accept online products. At the same time, they need to consider that people love, above all, to experience products in luxury markets.

CONCLUSION

Digital technology has brought about a radical change in the dynamics of marketing, and it is becoming increasingly important. The spread of social media and mobile media offers firms new business opportunities; these firms have the potential to create viral communication campaigns and to reach, thanks to the potential of new media, multiple market segments, providing the ability to customize messages. While the Web experience is based on exchange, sharing, and collaboration, consumers of luxury goods in mature markets are certainly not immune to this revolution. Hence, firms need to have an online presence, not only through Web sites, but they should also provide content and services to the expanding virtual community. All businesses, including those operating in the field of luxury goods, are conscious that in order to be on the Internet, "showcase Web sites" are being overtaken by the real leading players in the creation and exchange of information and experiences, offering dedicated spaces, content, and additional services to users and fans of the brand.

Luxury firms thus address their system of offerings to consumers with a view of producing any number of functional benefits. With this in mind, the physical quality of the goods, while important, is instrumental in the creation of the emotions that are sought and shared. This can enhance a new concept called "reverse multichannel marketing". What has primarily been a communication platform thus far is now transforming into a selling place, while what has always been a selling platform is now becoming a "showcase" where people can gather information on and experiment with what they can buy online. This represents an interesting and fruitful area for future research for both academics and managers.

REFERENCES

Aiello, G., & Donvito, R. (2005 January). Comunicazione integrata nell'abbigliamento: strategie di marca e ruolo del punto vendita nella distribuzione specializzata statunitenses. *Workshop Le Tendenze del Marketing in Europa*. Ecole Supérieure de Commerce de Paris ESCP-EAP.

Atwal, G., & Williams, A. (2009). Luxury brand marketing–The experience is everything! *Journal of Brand Management*, *16*(5), 338–346. doi:10.1057/bm.2008.48

Belch, G. E., & Belch, M. A. (1998, 2009). Advertising and Promotion. An Integrated Marketing Communication Perspective, New York: McGraw-Hill.

Brondoni, S. (2007). *Market-Driven Management e mercati globali*. Turin, Italy: Giappichelli.

Casalegno, C. (2012). *Pubblicità: istruzioni per l'uso*. Milan, Italy: Franco Angeli.

Casalegno, C., & Li, Y. (2012). *Tendenze evolutive in atto: la comunicazione integrata*. Academic Press.

CENSIS. (2012). *Decimo Rapporto sulla Comunicazione*. Milan: Franco Angeli.

Chevalier, M., & Mazzalovo, G. (2012). *Luxury brand management*. Singapore: Wiley. doi:10.1002/9781119199168

Collesei, U. (2002). Comunicazione e capitale simbolico d'impresa. *Sinergie*, *59*(2), 53–61.

Collesei, U., & Ravà, V. (2008). *La comunicazione d'azienda*. Turin, Italy: Isedi.

Corbellini, E., & Saviolo, S. (2007). *L'esperienza del lusso*. Milan, Italy: Etas.

Duncan, T. (2002). *IMC: Using Advertising & Promotion to Build Brands*. Boston: McGraw Hill.

Duncan, T., & Moriarty, S. E. (1997). *Driving Brand Value: Using Integrated Marketing to drive Shareholder Relationships*. New York: McGraw Hill.

Duncan, T., & Mulhern, F. (2004). *A White Paper on the Status, Scope and Future of IMC*. New York: McGraw-Hill.

Duncan, T., & Ouwersloot, H. (2008). *Intergrated Marketing Communications*. Maidenhead, UK: McGraw Hill.

Fabris, G. (2008). *Societing*. Milano: Egea.

Kapferer, J. N. (2004). *The New Strategic Brand Management. Creating and sustaining brand equity long term*. London, UK: Kogan Page.

Kapferer, J. N., & Bastien, V. (2009). The specificity of luxury management: Turning marketing upside down. *Journal of Brand Management*, *16*(5-6), 311–322. doi:10.1057/bm.2008.51

Kaplan, A. M., & Haenlein, M. (2010). Users of the world, unite! The challenges and opportunities of Social Media. *Business Horizons*, *53*(1), 59–68. doi:10.1016/j.bushor.2009.09.003

Kastenholz, J., Kerr, G., & Young, C. (2004). Focus and Fit: Advertising and branding join forces to create a star. *Marketing Research*, *16*(4), 16–21.

Kotler, P., Adam, S., Denize, S., & Armstrong, G. (2009). Principles of Marketing (4th ed.). Pearson Education.

Krugman, D. M., Reid, L. N., Dunn, S. W., & Barban, A. M. (1994). *Advertising: Its Role in Modern Marketing*. Fort Worth, TX: Dryden Press.

Mosca, F., Casalegno, C., & Feffin, A. (2013, October*). Nuovi modelli di comunicazione nei settori dei beni di lusso: un'analisi comparata.* Paper X Convegno della Scuola Italiana di Marketing, Milano.

Mosca, F., Casalegno, C., & Feffin, A. (2014, September). Last Marketing Communication Challenges In Luxury Brand Markets: A Comparative Analysis. In *7th Annual Conference of the EuroMed Academy of Business*.

Okonkwo, U. (2009). Sustaining the luxury brand on the Internet. *Journal of Brand Management, 16*(5), 302-310.

Okonkwo, U. (2010). *Luxury Online. Styles, Systems, Strategies*. Basingstoke, UK: Palgrave Macmillan. doi:10.1057/9780230248335

Osmonbekov, T., Bello, D. C., & Gilliland, D. I. (2009). The impact of e-business infusion on channel coordination, conflict and reseller performance. *Industrial Marketing Management*, *38*(7), 778–784. doi:10.1016/j.indmarman.2008.03.005

Porter, M., & Kramer, M. (2011). Creating Shared Value. How to reinvent capitalism and unleash a wave of innovation and growth. *Harvard Business Review*, *89*(1/2), 62–77.

Rangaswamy, A., & Van Bruggen, G. (2005). Opportunities and challenges in multichannel marketing: An introduction to the special issue. *Journal of Interactive Marketing*, *19*(2), 5–11. doi:10.1002/dir.20037

Ricotta, F. (2009). *Marketing multicanale*. Milan, Italy: Pearson.

Rifkin, J. (2000). *L'era dell'accesso*. Milano, Italy: Mondadori.

Romano, D. (1988). *Immagine, marketing e comunicazione*. Bologna, Italy: Il Mulino.

Schultz, D. E. (1992). Integrated marketing communications. *Journal of Promotion Management, 1*(1), 99–104. doi:10.1300/J057v01n01_07

Schultz, D. E., Tannenbaum, S. I., & Lauterborn, R. F. (1993). *Integrated Marketing Communications*. Chicago: NTC Business.

Venkatesan, R., Kumar, V., & Ravishanker, N. (2007). Multichannel Shopping: Causes and Consequences. *Journal of Marketing*, *71*(2), 114–132. doi:10.1509/jmkg.71.2.114

Voyer, B., & Tran, V. (2013). *Risks and benefits in selling luxury goods online: should Chanel, the icon of timeless fashion, open an e-boutique?* ESCP Europe, case study 3. Retrieved from www.casecenter.org

ADDITIONAL READING

Annie Jin, S. A. (2012). The potential of social media for luxury brand management. *Marketing Intelligence & Planning*, *30*(7), 687–699. doi:10.1108/02634501211273805

Chaffey, D., Ellis-Chadwick, F., Mayer, R., & Johnston, K. (2009). Internet marketing: strategy, implementation and practice. Pearson Education.

Fuchs, C., Prandelli, E., Schreier, M., & Dahl, D. W. (2013). All that is users might not be gold: How labeling products as user designed backfires in the context of luxury fashion brands. *Journal of Marketing*, *77*(5), 75–91. doi:10.1509/jm.11.0330

Lu, W., & Stepchenkova, S. (2015). User-generated content as a research mode in tourism and hospitality applications: Topics, methods, and software. *Journal of Hospitality Marketing & Management*, *24*(2), 119–154. doi:10.1080/19368623.2014.907758

Ye, Q., Law, R., Gu, B., & Chen, W. (2011). The influence of user-generated content on traveler behavior: An empirical investigation on the effects of e-word-of-mouth to hotel online bookings. *Computers in Human Behavior*, *27*(2), 634–639. doi:10.1016/j.chb.2010.04.014

KEY TERMS AND DEFINITIONS

Engagement: A promise, obligation, or other condition that binds. This is the aim of firms want to serve people for a long while.

Exclusivity: In marketing exclusivity is considered as arising from the second p of marketing mix: the price. The exclusivity, however, has always been the cornerstone of luxury's strategies and no appearance has never been more intensely protected.

Luxury Markets: Places in which it is possible to sell or buy a material object, service, etc., that brings physical comfort or rich living, but is not a necessity of life.

Mobile Sale: Smartphone, tablet or dedicated wireless device that performs the functions of a cash register or electronic point of sale terminal. It represent a possibility to buy things by using the device.

Multichannel Marketing: Is the ability to interact with stakeholders on various platforms. In this sense, a channel might be a print ad, a retail location, a website, a promotional event, a products package or even word of mouth.

Social Networks: Digital platforms in which it is possible to find network of social interactions and personal relationships.

Values: The abstract concepts of what is right, worthwhile, or desirable; principles or standards.

Chapter 6
Conceptualizing and Measuring Content Marketing in Luxury Firms:
An Exploratory Analysis

Elisa Rancati
University of Milan – Bicocca, Italy

Niccolo Gordini
University of Milan – Bicocca, Italy

Alexandru Capatina
University of Galati, Italy

ABSTRACT

Luxury marketing has gone through some major changes over the past couple of decades. The power is moving away from luxury firms to luxury consumers, who are playing a more significant role than ever before. These challenges in global markets have sparked a growing interest by practitioners and academics in the content marketing and in the metrics to measure its impact on luxury firm performance. However, the literature is still fragmented. Trying to fill this gap, this chapter has two main objectives. Firstly, it reviews the existing literature on content marketing and the main metrics used. Secondly, it analyses the degree of use and effectiveness of content marketing strategies, tools and metrics on a sample of 218 luxury firms. The results of the study revealed that content marketing is seen by luxury firms as marketing communications strategy that provides valuable and helpful information to a clearly defined target audience with the aim to increase sales.

INTRODUCTION

The introduction of digital technology and the spread of the Internet have led to radical changes in the way luxury firms meet the expectations and interests of its stakeholders (Okonkwo, 2010; Mosca, 2008, 2010, 2012) and in corporate communication (Okonkwo, 2007). In digital luxury, compared to conventional one, marketing has focused on the content. Content is one of the main competitive factor

DOI: 10.4018/978-1-4666-9958-8.ch006

of e-marketing mix model (Lauterborn, 1990) that offer the optimal value to the online customer. The contents of a luxury brand's website are significant in sustaining the brand's image. The corporate, product and services information provided on the website should be up-to-date and highly interesting (Okonkwo, 2007). "Content is king" is, in fact, one of the most popular slogan in the digital economy. Focus on content involves analyzing new communication models, very different than the usual format used by luxury firms. Content marketing (CM) attracts potential consumers and increases their engagement and empowerment (Kucuk & Krishnamurthy, 2007) through the creation, dissemination and sharing of free content, relevant, meaningful, valuable and able to inspire confidence in existing and potential customers. However, although CM is an up-to-date and hot concept it is actually as old as any other marketing initiative, but CM is still in the beginning phase as not all companies are making the most of it (Pulizzi, 2012). Despite the great attention CM is getting, literature is still fragmented. Many of the marketing journal articles focus on social media and digital marketing tools, and the changes these tools bring to marketing, but do not discuss the topic of content marketing itself. Several authors (Kaplan & Haenlein, 2010; Henning-Thurau, Malthouse, Friege, Gensler, Lobschat, Rangaswamy & Skiera, 2010, 2013; Wymbs, 2011; Weinberg & Pehlivan, 2011) focus on social media and digital marketing, and most do not even mention CM. A recent study (Rowley, 2008) suggests that there is a need for further research in the area of digital CM. Thus, clearly more academic attention is required in the field of CM. A few more contributions (Keyes, 2006; Rowley, 2008; Pulizzi & Barrett, 2009; Halvorson, 2010; Handley & Chapman, 2010; Gunelius, 2011; Lieb, 2011) try to define CM, and, above all, to measure its impact on luxury firms performance. Consequently, this chapter theoretically and empirically examines the evolution of the concept of CM in luxury firms. In doing so, this chapter especially contributes to the research on luxury goods marketing in two ways. First, authors review the literature about the concept of CM and the main metrics used for its measurement. Second, authors analyze the degree of use and effectiveness of CM strategies and metrics by a sample of 218 luxury firms. Actually, the findings of this study suggest that CM as opposed to the conventional communication strategies leads to significantly higher value creation.

In the remainder of this chapter background reviews existing literature on CM concept and metrics. This is followed by an empirical analysis of 214 luxury firms. Sampling, data collection and findings are outlined. The chapter concludes with a discussion, managerial implications and directions for further research.

BACKGROUND

This paragraph as a whole provides a review of the literature, which this research is based on. Although CM is the main subject of this study, it is crucial to explain the broader field which CM is part of in order to fully understand the theme of this research. Firstly, CM is a tool of integrated marketing communications (Keller, 2009; Ewing, 2009), which is the base of the marketing literature where authors find CM. Secondly, the concept of digital marketing (Hauer, 2012) is essential for CM as most of the CM tools today are digital. After these two important concepts have been discussed in the light of marketing literature, the concept of CM is tackled from a few different perspectives; e.g. concept itself, content and channels.

The Concept of Content Marketing

The use of the content as a marketing strategy has recently undergone a deep evolution thanks to the spread of digital communications and social networks. The digital dimension, in particular, has led to the birth of terms such as digital CM (Rakic, Beba & Mira, 2014) that focus on the changes that technological innovation has produced on creation, delivery and content management. Consequently, in recent years, studies on CM (Keyes, 2006; Pulizzi & Barrett, 2009; Halvorson, 2010; Handley & Chapman, 2010, 2012; Gunelius, 2011; Lieb, 2011; Nelli, 2012; Jefferson & Tanton, 2013; Rahimia & Hassanzadeh 2013) are significantly increased without reaching a clear and unique definition of this concept and of metrics for its measurement. Thus, the trying to systematize the literature review on this topic seems particularly relevant. In particular, the review, according to other recent systematic reviews within the management field (Newbert, 2007), focused only on double peer-reviewed journals articles, regardless of their impact factor. The computer based research was performed in August 2015 by using the academic journals within the Ebsco-Host database. Choosing the most suitable research keywords mostly derived from the reading of leading journals articles and books on CM. Authors have conducted a 5 phase research. In the first phase authors have researched papers that contain in their abstract the keyword CM, selecting 382 articles. In the second phase, the relevance of the articles was ensured by requiring that the articles selected in the previous phase also contained at least one of the following keywords (concept* or definition or theor* or framework) in their abstract. The asterisk at the end of a keyword allowed for different suffixes (e.g. theory or theoretical). This phase outputted 110 papers. In the third step the 110 articles' relevance was ensured by requiring that those articles also contained at least one of the following three keywords (literature reviews or background or synthesis) in their abstract. This phase outputted 26 articles. In the fourth step, these 26 papers were further scanned by reading all their abstracts and texts, thus controlling their connection with the research topic. This phase outputted 3 articles. Finally, in the last phase, the snowballing technique (Atkinson & Flint, 2004; Iacobucci & Churchill, 2010) was adopted for integrating the results from the previous phase with papers, book chapters or books, relevant to our research topics, but not found in the EBSCO-Host database. This phase outputted 23 papers and books as shown in Table 1.

Distinctive Features of Content Marketing

After analyzing these 23 papers and books, it has been possible to identify three pillars that characterize CM: 1) contents; 2) customers engagement and 3) goals. Only a synergistic vision of all these elements enables an understanding of the sources of competitive advantage generated by the CM. This definition raises a particular interest as it allows you to focus on a fundamental question for the survival of the company: which contents are able to create a competitive and long-lasting (content longevity) advantage, generating higher performance than competitors? Literature identifies the creation and sharing of unique content, meaningful, valuable, dynamic and relevant to the competitors one of the load-bearing characteristics for competitive advantage. The proposed content must: 1) be able to generate interest, involving, but also informing and educating the customer; 2) express all those values that identify the company in terms of uniqueness, consistency, quality and relevance; 3) be pro-active, that is able to evolve over time: the company must push the community and every visitor to interact, edit content, stimulate conversation, improve and enrich the information (Fantini, 2013). The second basic element of the CM is the consumer engagement. CM encompasses all forms of content that add value to consumers, directly

Table 1. Studies regarding the concept of CM

Author	Paper/Book	Definition
Chaffey D., Mayer R., Johnston K., Ellis-Chadwick F. (2000)	Internet marketing, Pearson Education, Edinburgh.	Content is the design, text and graphical information that forms a web page. Good content is the key to attracting customers to a web site and retaining their interest or achieving repeat visits.
Keyes J. (2006)	Knowledge management, business intelligence and content management, Auerbach Publications, Broken South Parken.	CM is usually focus on intranet-based or internet-based corporate content, including data and knowledge bases.
Pulizzi J., Barrett N. (2009)	Get content. Get customers, McGraw Hill, New York	CM is a marketing technique of creating and distributing relevant and valuable content to attract, acquire, and engage a clearly defined and understood target audience – with the objective of driving profitable customer action. CM is owning, as opposed to renting media. It's marketing process to attract and retain customers by consistently creating and curating content in order to change or enhance a consumer behavior.
Halvorson K. (2010)	Content strategy for the web, New Riders, Berkeley	Content strategy is the practice of planning for the creation, delivery, and governance of useful, usable content.
Handley A., Chapman C.C. (2010)	Content Rules, John Wiley, New York	CM is anything an individual or an organization creates and/or shares to tell their story. What it isn't: A warmed-over press release served as a blog post. It is conversational, human and doesn't try to constantly sell to you. It also isn't a tactic that you can just turn on and off and hope that will be successful. It has to be a mindset that is embraced and encouraged. You've got to start thinking like a publisher and use that to plan and execute your entire marketing plan which content of any variety should be a part.
Gunelius S. (2011)	Content Marketing for Dummiers, Wiley, New York	CM is the process of indirectly and directly promoting a business or brand through value-added text, video, or audio content both online and offline. It can come in long-form (such as blogs, articles, e-books, and so on), short-form (such as Twitter updates, Facebook updates, images, and so on), or conversational-form (for example, sharing great content via Twitter or participating in an active discussion via blog comments or through an online forum).
Lieb R. (2011)	Content Marketing: think like a publisher. How to use content to market online and in social media, Que Publishing, Indianapolis.	CM, in other words, is nothing new. Companies having been creating and distributing content for many years, both to attract new business and to retain existing customers. However, here's the point of differentiation from more traditional forms of marketing and advertising: using content to sell isn't selling. It isn't advertising. It isn't push marketing, in which messages are sprayed out at groups of consumers. Rather, it's a pull strategy—it's the marketing of attraction. It's being there when consumers need you and seek you out with relevant, educational, helpful, compelling, engaging, and sometimes entertaining information.
Cashman J., Treece M. (2012)	Content marketing essentials for small business, Create Space Independent Publishing Platform, London.	CM is the process of creating video, articles, e-books, how-to-guides, social media updates, picture galleries, infographs, webinars, or other forms of media about your business or brand. Creating content, posting it on your website, then promoting it via social media.
Crestodina A. (2012)	Content chemistry: an illustrated handbook for content marketing, Orbit Media Studios, New York.	CM is the art and science of pulling your audience toward your business. It is based on the concept that there are relevant prospects looking for your product or service right now. Content marketers create and promote useful, relevant information with the goal of attracting and engaging website visitors, and then converting those visitors into leads and customers. Content marketing is sensitive to the behaviors and psychology of potential buyers.
Jefferson S., Tanton S. (2013)	Valuable content marketing, Kogan Page, New York.	CM as it the approach has become known is the focus of the most successful marketing today – driving results for all kind of companies and a real differentiator for independent firms and small businesses. CM is an approach that puts your clients first. It's about sharing information that is relevant and valuable to those who buy your services, so people choose to come to you.

continued on following page

Table 1. Continued

Author	Paper/Book	Definition
Clay B., Newland M. (2014)	Content marketing strategies for professionals, Create Space Independent Publishing Platform, North Charleston.	CM achieves business objectives by strategically creating and sharing content.
Didner P. (2014)	Global content marketing, Mc-Graw Hill, New York.	CM is the process of creating video, articles, e-books, how-to-guides, social media updates, picture galleries, infographs, webinars, or other forms of media about your business or brand. Creating content, posting it on your website, then promoting it via social media.
Fishbein M. (2014)	Growth hacking with content marketing, Create Space Independent Publishing Platform, London.	CM, social media marketing and growth hacking are cheap, efficient and effective!
Gordini N., Rancati E. (2014)	Content marketing e creazione di valore. Aspetti definitori e metriche di misurazione, Giappichelli, Turin.	CM is a marketing strategy associated with creating, communicating, distributing, and exchanging content in digital communication that has value for the firm.
Holliman G., Rowley J. (2014)	Business to business digital content marketing: marketers' perception of best practice, Journal of research in Interactive Marketing	Digital CM is the activity associated with creating, communicating, distributing, and exchanging digital content that has value for customers, clients, partners, and the firm and its brands.
Lancaster C. (2014)	Content marketing: turn content into powerful marketing tool, Pogo Book Publishing, London.	CM is used to sell something, but at the same time, you need to educate, encourage and help the targeted audience so they can realize the need and importance of that information in their life.
Lilly M.C. (2014)	Content marketing essentials for small business, Create Space Independent Publishing Platform, London.	Though it goes by many names, CM is defined as publishing content that empowers, engages, educates, and connects readers. To explore it much further, there are five pillars of CM: editorial based (otherwise known as long-form, it is content that tells both a relevant and valuable story. The point of editorial content is to be informative, educational, and/or entertaining); marketing-based (businesses have marketing and sales objectives that they seek to accomplish, and this is no different when it comes to content. Businesses on line have an underlying goal with the content they publish); behavior driven (content seeks to maintain or alter a reader's/consumer's behavior. Having relevant and valuable content accomplishes this); multi-platform (this means that content comes in a variety of media, including print, digital, audio, video, events, etc. It can, but does not necessarily have to be, connected across all platforms); targeted (like all good marketing, knowing your audience is key to having a successful strategy. Know your audience down to the particulars)
Pulizzi J. (2014)	Epic content marketing. Mc Graw Hill, London.	CM is the marketing and business process for creating and distributing valuable and compelling content to attract, acquire, and engage a clearly defined and understood target audience – with the objective of driving profitable customer action. A CM strategy can leverage all story channels (print, online, in-person, mobile, social, and so on); be employed at any and all stages of the buying process, from attention-oriented strategies to retention and loyalty strategies; and include multiple buying groups.
Ramos M. (2014)	Content Marketing: insider's secret to online sales and lead generation. One Night Expert Publishing New York	CM is a marketing technique that uses high-quality, relevant content to educate, engage, and acquire your target customer. CM is not just creating content for the sake of producing content: its objective is always sales. The true potential of CM lies in its ability to provide a conversion path for your leads to follow on their own schedule and at their convenience.
Rotsztein B. (2014)	Content marketing ideas, Creative force publishing, London.	The term "CM" is a catch-all that means different things to different people. Its meaning comes down to a matter of perspective. The author defines CM as the creation and distribution of editorial content used to achieve visibility, credibility and conversions.

continued on following page

Table 1. Continued

Author	Paper/Book	Definition
Slater V. (2014)	Content marketing: recycling and reuse. How your best online content can engage and attract new customers, i30 Media Corporation, New York	CM is a dynamic way to get customers. It is the process of sharing expertise and knowledge online to attract potential customers and establish a relationship with them. CM has to be focused on creating, publishing, and sharing suitable content. However, many CM often overlook a readily available source of content – articles, case studies, blog, posts, videos, images, and other assets that were created years before yet still have the potential to draw new customers.
Van Lieshout L. (2014)	Content marketing for professionals. CreateSpace Independent Publishing platform, London.	CM is any marketing that involves the creation and sharing of media and publishing content in order to acquire and retain customers. This information can be presented in a variety of formats, including news, video, white papers, e-books, infographics, case studies, how-to guides, question and answer articles, photos, etc. CM has been defined in multiple ways. The meaning of the term depends a lot on the purpose and context. One of the most used definition states that CM is the technique of creating and distributing relevant and valuable content to attract, acquire and engage a clearly defined target audience in order to drive profitable customer action. CM creates interest in a product through educational, entertaining or informative material. Successful CM relies on providing "consistent, high-quality content that solves people's problems".
Jarvinen J., Taiminen H. (2015)	Harnessing marketing automation for B2B content marketing, Industrial Marketing Management	CM is a new paradigm that leads potential buyer to interact with their company.

Source: Our Elaboration

or indirectly thereby promoting a business, brand, product, or services. It occurs both online and offline, but the free and simple tools of the social web have opened up the ability for companies of all sizes to compete alongside one another, not for market share but for voice and influence (Gunelius, 2011). The centrality of consumer's role is therefore reflected in the content management system, creating a logical customer centric based on research of a constant adaptation of content to the needs and preferences of customers. On the other hand, customers are increasingly participating in the process of creating value through frequent interactions with the company (value co-creation). This leads implicitly to abandon the traditional concept of the market as a physical exchange of goods and services, separate from the concept of value. The reasons for the occurrence of this model must first be sought in the technological process: Internet, in particular, has accelerated the process of democratization of consumption, making the final customer more and more informed, interconnected with the company and with other customers, and thus more central. Transferring power to customers (customer empowerment) becomes inevitable to allow CM to co-create value through constant dialogue between customers and businesses. Customers can shop provide content is to contribute to company or product-specific discussions forums or communities (Chaffey, Mayer & Johnson, 2000). According to this definition, then, the distinctive characteristics of the CM not only exist on the types of content produced, but in the fact that they add value for customers and potential than competitors, attracting them, creating empowerment and involving (engagement). In this regard, social networks play a key role, being the main meeting place with users, where conversations and exchange of opinions multiply and information is the starting point for each interaction. CM means to produce quality content (Handley & Chapman, Lieb, Jefferson & Tanton, Rose & Pulizzi). When a user posts a message, that user is effectively adding content about the product being discussed, as several authors argue that the Web is a pull medium where the customer decides which content to view (Hoffman, Novak & Yung, 2010). Finally, the third element relates to the objectives pursued by the CM that does not lead back to the single action of operational marketing, but concern the creation, capture, delivery, customization and management of content across an organization. Luxury firms use digital CM to support the implementation of multiple business objectives, such as brand awareness, attraction of customers, creating the leads, maintaining of customer relationships/loyalty (Rakic, Beba & Mira, 2014). According with literature review and with the three main features identified in this study the authors define the CM in luxury firms as a tool to share content, but also to create value and high returns and financial means of the customers distribution, attraction, involvement, acquisition and retention.

Content Marketing Formats

CM strategies enable real commitment of the target group and create an authentic relation with the group (Rancati & Gordini, 2015). CM formats are numerous and articulated. Understanding that different people have very different learning capabilities, seeing, hearing, knowing, it's fundamental for luxury firms try to get the most value from every piece of content by reusing the content in different formats (Jefferson & Tanton, 2013). There are four different groups of CM formats: print, digital, social and live.

Print formats are relevant, well-written and well-designed print publications can make a dramatic impression on company's audience (Pulizzi & Barrett, 2009). There are four categories of print format: magazines, newsletters, white papers and reports.

Today, with news technologies and Internet, there are different options and it is easier for companies connect with customers and clients (Jennifer & Tanton, 2013). Thanks to user-friendly Web tools are easy to get started and to add an additional Web presence. Many of these tools enable companies to begin an ongoing dialogue with them prospects and will improve acquisition and retention. (Pulizzi & Barrett, 2009). Digital formats analysed in the literature are websites, microsites, digital magazines, e-newsletters, FAQ, video, photo-gallery, storytelling, podcast, webinar and mobile App. Social formats are social network and blogs. The main benefits for companies in the use of social media are efficiency: social media used to achieve business objectives allow to implement strategies much more efficient than traditional media and allow a significant reduction of costs in the search for information (Kazim & Karahan, 2011); awareness of the brand: the spread of the brand easier thanks to the large number of users connected to social media; create community: social media enable companies to combine users, far apart geographically, thanks to shared interests by creating groups where users can express their thoughts (Weber, 2009); word of mouth: users through word of mouth become major players in the content's distribution business. Blog represents the earliest form of social media. Live formats are events. In the last twenty years, corporate events, conventions and presentations have begun to be rationally incorporated by companies within the strategies of communication and dissemination of business content. These tools have thus become effective methods able to spread content and information about company, consolidating the company's image at the various stakeholders and establish relations with the territory (Nelli, 2012).

Content Marketing Metrics

Define the CM as a value added activity with a significant relationship on firm performance requires the development and adoption of appropriate system of metrics (Giachetti et al., 2013). Hovewer, CM is one of the many revolutionary aspects of the web is that we are now able to measure with some precision how people interact with our content online (Halvorson, 2010), the identification of such system is a complex, sophisticated and under constant revision, activity, which assumes the simultaneous use of different measurement methodologies. Marketing metrics literature has often been criticized for its limited diagnostic capacity, for its attention to the short term, for the excessive number of different indexes not comparable, for the lack of attention to the creation of shareholder value (Doyle, 2000). All these issues bring to define the marketing metrics as one of the aspects of marketing more "resistant to conceptualization, definition or application" (Bonoma & Clark, 1988). CM cannot be measured with a single metric, because no one metric can successfully or satisfactorily explain whether company goal is achieving. Instead, companies need to create an array of metrics. It is possible to summarize CM metrics in four main categories: consumption, sharing, lead generation e sales (Linn, 2012; Gordini & Rancati, 2014; Rancati & Gordini, 2014; Rancati & Gordini, 2015a; Rancati & Gordini, 2015b). These four categories, independent but at the same time strictly related to each other, allow companies to measure the contribution of the three pillars of CM to value creation, identifying any gap between the results obtained and planned and, consequently, implementing corrective actions in order to achieve the goals. Consumption metrics help marketing manager to measure brand awareness and website traffic generated by the content. This category help to measure the effect of the first pillar of CM. Consumption metrics are the most fundamental type of content metrics and they are generally easy to measure through Google Analytics or similar. Some of the more prominent consumption metrics are: page views, video views, document views, downloads; social chatter; visitors; visitors returns; time on page. These metrics may also be combined each other by providing more specific information such as, for example, the page views/visitor or the number of pages viewed by each visitor. Sharing metrics measure the level of content sharing by consumers with their network of people with a direct and significant impact on the engagement. Thus, these metrics are a useful tool for the measurement of the second pillar of the CM. Examples of sharing metrics are likes, shares, tweets, +1; email forwards; inbound links. These metrics are extremely useful for measuring the diffusion and the sharing of content amongst a large number of consumers and their network of people. However, these metrics do not provide any information on the real economic return generated by the CM. Lead generation metrics create a list of potential contacts interested in the products or services offered by the company. Through these metrics the companies obtain information and data included in a specific database that will be used to contact potential consumers and turn them into actual customers. A few crucial examples of these metrics are: form completions & downloads; email subscriptions; blog subscriptions; blog comments; conversion rate. The sales metrics help marketers to measure the impact of CM on firm performance, finding out how CM impacts customer acquisition and sales goals. Example of these metrics are online and offline sales; customer retention; cost saving; content marketing ROI.

RESEARCH METHODOLOGY

To understand how luxury firms perceive CM and measure its effects on performance, the authors have administered an online questionnaire to the marketing manager. The authors selected a sample of 800 luxury firms covering a broad range of luxury consumer goods (wine and spirits, perfume and cosmetics, fashion and accessories) and luxury durable goods (watches, cars, yachts, jewelry, home design). Authors relied on four well established luxury brand rankings, namely Brand Networks (2014), Brandz (2014), Interbrand (2014), and World Luxury Association (2012) as well as Okonkwo's (2010) list of best practice luxury brand websites to select luxury firms for the sample. The questionnaire consists of 20 items divided into two sections: the first, consisting of 5 multiple choice items, allows to reach general info about the sample (e.g. gender and the age of the respondent, size, business sector, geographical area). The second, consisting of 15 items measured by a Likert scale, analyze: 1) the use of CM and how marketers rate the effectiveness of their organization's use of CM; 2) the main goals of CM strategies; 3) the main tactics used by CM to achieve goals; 4) the amount of total marketing budget in CM and 5) the knowledge and the use of the four categories of metrics previously examined. The initial response rate to this survey was 24% (132 firms). To increase the number of respondents, a follow-up was sent out. The final response rate was 28% (224 firms). In addition, authors have performed checks for potential nonresponse biases by dividing our respondents into early and late respondents. This procedure is performed under the assumption that late respondents are more similar in nature to non-respondents than early respondents. No statistical differences between the early and late respondents had observed, which suggests that nonresponse bias was not a major problem (Kanuk & Berenson, 1975). Finally, we have eliminated all questionnaires with missing data, obtaining a final sample of 218 luxury firms. Table 2 shows our sample.

FINDINGS

Results have been analyzed first at aggregate level and, then, according to the typology of the luxury goods, that is luxury consumer goods and luxury durable goods.

Results show a good use of CM between luxury firms (Table 3). 85% of our sample has claimed to know and use tools of CM in carrying out their activities. In analyzing how marketers rate their organization's use of CM, results show that respondents consider CM to be very effective in 25% of cases, effective in 55%, low effective in 9% and not at all effective in 11% of the cases. The effectiveness is measured by asking respondents if they believe the tools of CM effective and efficient for easier achievement of corporate objectives and increased performance.

When the analysis is conducted by typology of luxury goods, results show that both firms operating in luxury consumer goods sector and in luxury durable goods sector consider CM a very effective tool. Noteworthy, luxury consumer goods make a wider use of CM compared to durable goods.

Table 2. Composition of the sample

	Percentage	Number of Luxury Firms
Cars	16%	34
Watches	14%	31
Home design	9%	20
Jewellery	12%	26
Yachts	12%	26
Fashion and accessories	20%	44
Perfume and cosmetics	11%	24
Wine and spirits	6%	13

Source: Our Elaboration

Table 3. Percentage of luxury brands respondents using content marketing and how marketers rate the effectiveness of their organization's use of content marketing

	Use (%)	Effectiveness (%)			
		Very Effective	Effective	Low Effective	Not at All Effective
OVERALL	85%	25%	55%	9%	11%
Luxury Durable Goods					
Cars	15%	9%	30%	28%	33%
Watches	17%	12%	40%	30%	18%
Home design	8%	10%	32%	30%	28%
Jewelry	9%	10%	27%	33%	30%
Yachts	11%	8%	32%	42%	18%
Luxury Consumer Goods					
Fashion and accessories	22%	10%	41%	34%	15%
Perfume and cosmetics	12%	14%	38%	28%	20%
Wine and spirits	6%	8%	28%	40%	24%

Source: Our Elaboration

Among top goals of CM (Table 4), content marketers cite brand awareness (90%), customer acquisition (75%) and sales (78%) as the main goals for content marketing in luxury industry. Other goals are customer retention/loyalty (50%), lead generation and lead management/nurturing (respectively 54% and 42%), website traffic (30%) and thought leaders (45%).

By type of luxury goods (Table 4), the firms of luxury consumer goods primarily use CM for brand awareness, customer acquisition and lead generation, whilst the firms of luxury durable goods for sales and customer retention.

Although at the aggregate level, 85% of luxury firms use CM and 25% considers it useful or very useful in achieving better performance, only 58% carefully plan a content marketing strategy, based, for example, on industry trends, company characteristics, profile of individual decision makers, analysis of content strategies of competitors. These data are confirmed analyzing the sample for typology of luxury goods (Table 5). In particular, firms of luxury durable goods tend to not adopt a well-planned CM strategy or, in alternative, a strategy based on industry trends and profile of individual decision makers. Firms of luxury consumer goods, instead, tend to make a wider use of a well-planned CM strategy, principally based on industry trends and analysis of content strategies of competitors.

In addition, only 43% of luxury firms have a human resource specifically dedicated to oversee CM activities, whilst outsource CM activities. Breaking down this figure by typology of goods, our results show that firms make a more extensive use of human resources specifically dedicated to CM in the fashion and accessories, perfume and cosmetics.

The figures and tables below examine at the aggregate level and for each typology of luxury goods, 1) the most used CM tools to achieve the goals outlined above (Figure 1 and Table 6), 2) the most used platforms of the most used tool (social media content) (Figure 2 and Table 7) and 3) how firms judge these platforms in terms of usefulness and effectiveness (Figure 3 and Table 8).

Table 4. Goals pursed by CM

GOALS	Brand awareness	Customer acquisition	Sales	Customer retention/ loyalty	Lead generation	Lead management/ nurturing	Website Traffic	Thought leadership
OVERALL	**90%**	**75%**	**78%**	**50%**	**54%**	**42%**	**30%**	**45%**
Luxury Durable Goods								
Cars	12%	12%	16%	15%	10%	6%	9%	11%
Watches	13%	11%	22%	21%	18%	13%	13%	17%
Jewelry	11%	12%	18%	15%	11%	10%	9%	8%
Home design	10%	12%	15%	16%	12%	11%	4%	14%
Yachts	12%	10%	14%	15%	5%	8%	10%	8%
Luxury Consumer Goods								
Fashion and accessories	25%	22%	12%	15%	25%	14%	11%	12%
Perfume and cosmetics	28%	24%	14%	18%	18%	22%	15%	14%
Wine and spirits	19%	16%	6%	7%	16%	10%	7%	9%

Source: Our Elaboration

Table 5. Factors influencing the adoption of a well-planned CM strategy for type of luxury goods

	Industry Trends	Company Characteristics	Profile of Individual Decision Makers	Analysis of Content Strategies of Competitors	No Strategy
Luxury Durable Goods					
Cars	23%	10%	18%	14%	35%
Watches	18%	12%	16%	14%	40%
Home design	18%	6%	18%	13%	45%
Jewelry	21%	13%	15%	12%	39%
Yachts	22%	15%	15%	10%	38%
Luxury Consumer Goods					
Fashion and accessories	20%	18%	12%	26%	24%
Perfume and cosmetics	21%	16%	16%	25%	22%
Wine and spirits	16%	17%	22%	27%	18%

Source: Our Elaboration

As shown in Figure 1, to achieve their objectives, the firms in the sample mainly use the following tools: social media content (96%), blogs (84%), eNewletters (79%), articles on the website of the company (77%), video (75%), infographics (71%) or online presentations (70%). The videos, infographics and online presentation, in which luxury firms operating in the fashion and accessories take percentages greater than or equal to 90%, are instead recorded in other sectors lower values (respectively 72%, 60%, 57%, 54%, 46%, 41%, 32%).

Table 6 confirms the findings obtained at the aggregate level, demonstrating that for both types of luxury goods, the most used tools to achieve the objectives analyzed above are: social media, blogs, the eNewletters, the articles on the website of the company, videos, infographics and online presentations.

Figure 1. The most used content marketing tools

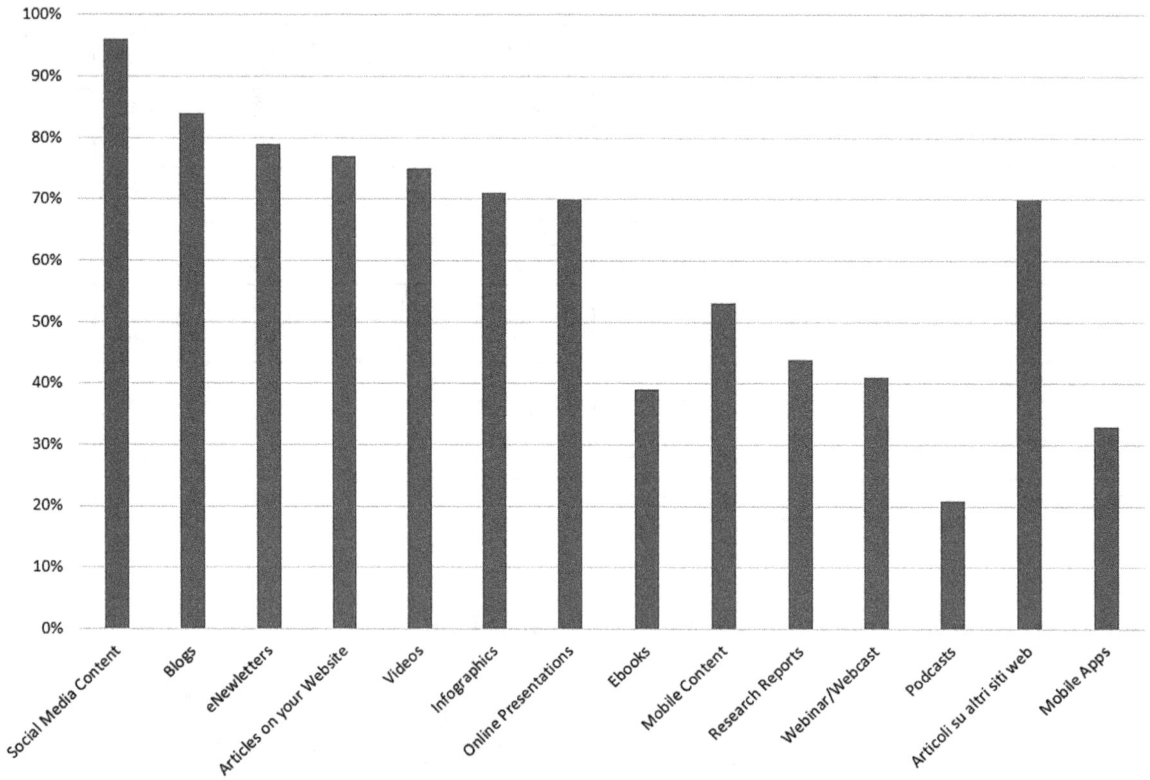

Figure 2. The most used social media platforms

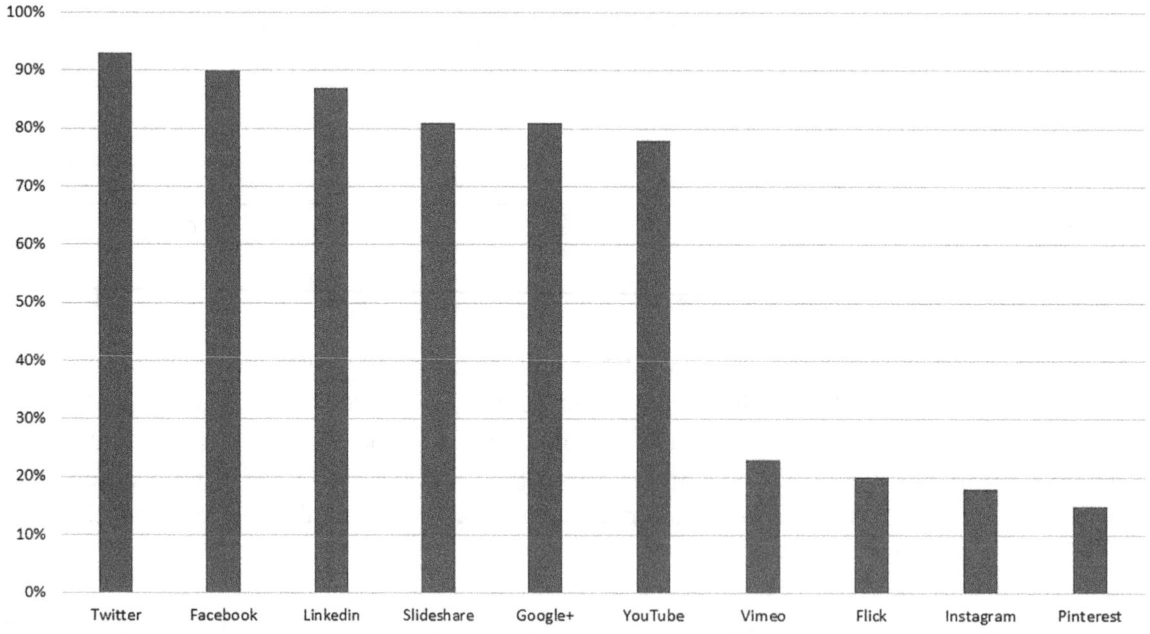

Table 6. The most used tools of content marketing for type of luxury goods

	Social Media	Blogs	eNews	Articles on own website	Videos	Infographics	Online presentations	Ebooks	Mobile content	Research reports	Webinars/ Webcasts	Podcasts	Articles on other website	Mobile Apps
Luxury Durable Goods														
Cars	11%	8%	7%	8%	6%	9%	4%	6%	6%	12%	12%	5%	2%	4%
Watches	13%	10%	9%	3%	7%	7%	7%	9%	8%	8%	7%	9%	1%	2%
Home design	9%	6%	3%	8%	11%	2%	7%	2%	10%	8%	8%	7%	4%	15%
Jewellery	6%	4%	2%	9%	8%	3%	3%	5%	11%	6%	10%	12%	12%	9%
Yachts	8%	6%	4%	11%	5%	6%	9%	8%	10%	8%	8%	6%	7%	4%
Luxury Consumer Goods														
Fashion and accessories	12%	6%	8%	3%	9%	1%	6%	3%	9%	5%	9%	4%	7%	18%
Perfume and cosmetics	11%	9%	7%	8%	7%	8%	6%	8%	9%	7%	4%	5%	4%	7%
Wine and spirits	7%	3%	8%	8%	12%	9%	8%	2%	8%	8%	9%	4%	10%	4%

Source: Our Elaboration

Table 7. The most used social media platforms for type of luxury goods

	Twitter	Facebook	Linkedin	Slideshare	Google +	YouTube	Vimeo	Flick	Instagram	Pinterest
Luxury Durable Goods										
Cars	58%	71%	59%	30%	29%	45%	12%	7%	5%	9%
Watches	56%	72%	58%	26%	23%	49%	11%	8%	13%	17%
Home design	52%	74%	58%	27%	27%	34%	12%	9%	12%	13%
Jewellery	16%	18%	16%	7%	10%	49%	12%	7%	12%	14%
Yachts	10%	11%	9%	13%	12%	30%	10%	9%	6%	10%
Luxury Consumer Goods										
Fashion and accessories	67%	67%	69%	41%	30%	45%	11%	9%	7%	9%
Perfume and cosmetics	69%	63%	62%	49%	34%	46%	10%	11%	12%	14%
Wine and spirits	68%	62%	65%	41%	33%	32%	13%	9%	8%	9%

Source: Our Elaboration

Figure 3. Percentage of total marketing budget spent on content marketing activities by luxury firms

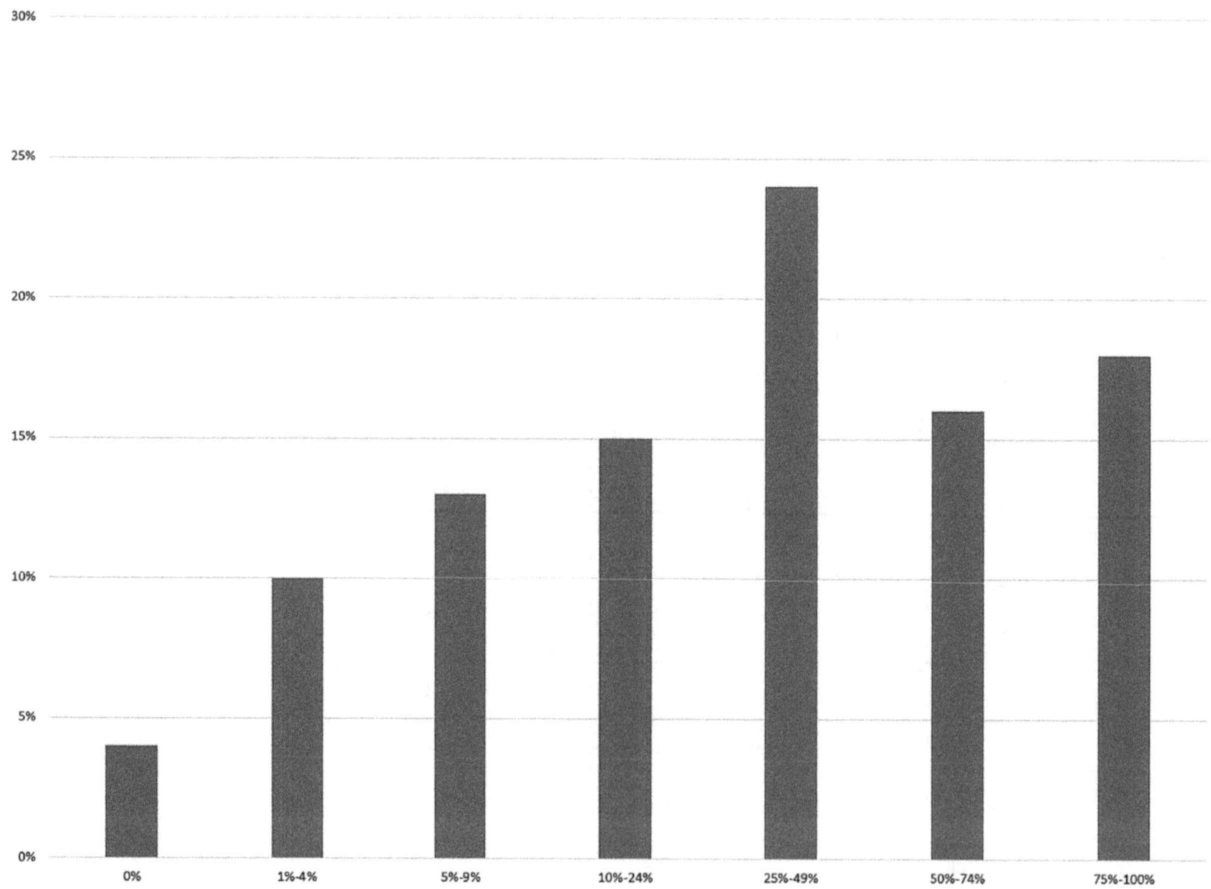

Table 8. Percentage of total marketing budget spent on content marketing activities for type of luxury goods

	99%-75%	74%-50%	49%-25%	24%-10%	9%-5%	4%-1%	0%	I do Not Know
Luxury Durable Goods								
Cars	5%	19%	10%	9%	16%	12%	15%	11%
Watches	16%	21%	14%	9%	7%	8%	18%	7%
Home design	15%	18%	9%	14%	11%	9%	13%	11%
Jewelry	12%	19%	10%	12%	11%	9%	10%	17%
Yachts	9%	15%	10%	12%	13%	13%	12%	16%
Luxury Consumer Goods								
Fashion and accessories	16%	30%	16%	15%	9%	6%	2%	6%
Perfume and cosmetics	19%	25%	13%	11%	8%	7%	9%	8%
Wine and spirits	10%	20%	9%	10%	10%	11%	14%	16%

Source: Our Elaboration

Analyzing the intensity with which respondents make use of the various platforms that constitute the social media (the tool most widely used), most of them makes a very significant use of Twitter (93%), Facebook (90%), Linkedin (87%), Slideshares (81%) or Google + (81%), i.e. the platforms most popular, easy to use, and that do not need huge investments or advanced skills which would require a resource specifically dedicated to CM, as demonstrated by previous results (Figure 2).

Figure 3 analyzes the 2013 investment in CM activities, calculated on the total expenditures of communication. Results confirm that the interest of luxury firms in CM is constantly growing and how companies are increasingly willing to invest in these activities a significant part of their budget.

When the analysis is conducted by typology of luxury goods (Table 8) results shows that firms of luxury consumer goods invest more in CM activities than firms of durable goods. In particular, firms of fashion and accessories are those who spend most of their budget in CM activities of CM, followed by companies in the perfume and cosmetics.

Finally, we have analyzed whether the firms use the four categories of metrics previously analyzed both at the aggregate level and for type of luxury goods (Table 9). In agreement with the literature, our results show: 1) an extensive use of consumption (on average 87% of the sample) and sharing (on average 75%) metrics, i.e. metrics that measures the returns of the activities of publishing and sharing, that are easily calculable in terms of both time and cost and that do not require high skills and competencies; 2) an average use of lead generation metrics (on average 54%); and 3) a low use of sales metrics (on average 31%), i.e. metrics that give a clear economic quantification of the strategies of CM. The analysis conducted for type of luxury goods confirms these data. In particular, firms of durable goods mainly use consumption and sharing metrics, whilst firms of consumer goods also use lead generation and sales metrics.

These results show, both at the aggregate and disaggregated level, a very significant use of consumption and sharing metrics rather than lead generation or sales metrics, allowing us to make some considerations that should lead luxury firms to rethink the role of the CM.

Table 9. Percentage of usage of the four categories of metrics at aggregate level and for type of luxury goods

	Use (%)	Luxury Durable Goods					Luxury Consumer Goods		
Metrics		**Cars**	**Watches**	**Home Design**	**Jewelry**	**Yachts**	**Fashion and Accessories**	**Perfume and Cosmetics**	**Wine and Spirits**
Consumption Metrics	Average	Average	Average	Average	Average	Average	Average	Average	Average
	81%	12%	15%	11%	13%	10%	21%	12%	6%
Page views	76%	10%	17%	11%	12%	12%	22%	10%	6%
Visitors	82%	16%	12%	12%	6%	11%	24%	12%	7%
Video views	84%	12%	15%	11%	14%	14%	18%	13%	3%
Time on page	82%	7%	17%	9%	16%	13%	19%	12%	7%
Document views	81%	11%	15%	12%	15%	11%	20%	11%	5%
Downloads	79%	8%	16%	7%	13%	15%	25%	8%	8%
Page views/ visitor	82%	19%	15%	11%	10%	5%	23%	13%	4%
Visitors returns	85%	15%	13%	10%	15%	6%	22%	14%	5%
Time on page/visitors	75%	11%	19%	12%	15%	4%	20%	11%	8%
Sharing Metrics	Average	Average	Average	Average	Average	Average	Average	Average	Average
	67%	16%	15%	11%	12%	10%	22%	10%	5%
Likes, share, tweets, +1, retweets, pins	79%	18%	18%	11%	11%	6%	21%	9%	6%
Mail forward	64%	16%	15%	11%	12%	9%	24%	8%	5%
Inbound Links	58%	13%	12%	10%	14%	14%	21%	13%	3%
Lead-Generation Metrics	Average	Average	Average	Average	Average	Average	Average	Average	Average
	48%	14%	15%	10%	11%	9%	23%	12%	7%
Form completions	61%	15%	15%	8%	11%	9%	24%	8%	10%
RSS feed	58%	14%	16%	11%	10%	5%	20%	15%	9%
Blog Comments	55%	11%	14%	8%	13%	13%	21%	15%	5%
Email subscription	52%	14%	14%	10%	8%	8%	28%	10%	8%
Newsletter subscription	45%	15%	17%	7%	8%	9%	29%	10%	5%
Qualitative feedback dai consumatori	42%	11%	14%	11%	12%	11%	20%	11%	10%
Blog subscription	39%	13%	19%	14%	9%	9%	17%	15%	4%
Conversion rate	35%	20%	8%	9%	14%	8%	23%	15%	3%

continued on following page

Table 9. Continued

Metrics	Use (%)	Luxury Durable Goods					Luxury Consumer Goods		
		Cars	Watches	Home Design	Jewelry	Yachts	Fashion and Accessories	Perfume and Cosmetics	Wine and Spirits
Sales Metrics	Average	Average	Average	Average	Average	Average	Average	Average	Average
	36%	15%	15%	8%	12%	11%	23%	11%	6%
Offline sales	81%	19%	14%	10%	11%	10%	23%	8%	5%
Online sales	72%	12%	17%	9%	10%	16%	20%	11%	5%
Customer retention	15%	11%	16%	6%	15%	11%	24%	10%	7%
Cost saving	8%	15%	15%	4%	12%	10%	25%	13%	6%
Content Marketing ROI	6%	18%	14%	10%	11%	9%	22%	11%	5%

Source: Our Elaboration

In fact, the greater use of consumption and sharing metrics compared to the others two categories show how luxury firms consider CM. The great importance given to consumption and sharing metrics highlights that, especially for firms of durable goods, CM is still considered simply as a activity of publishing and sharing content, without recognizing, therefore, at CM a key role into value creation process. The prevalent use of these two categories of metrics may be due to their ease of use, to their low cost and to the fact that they do not require high skills and competencies. However, in increasingly dynamic and hyper competitive market, CM must be considered as a value creation strategy and not only as a strategy for publishing and sharing contents.

DISCUSSION AND CONCLUSION

The picture that emerges from the analysis is interesting: the CM permeates the activities of most of the luxury firms. However, despite this positive result, luxury firms are yet too anchored to a reductive concept of CM which qualifies it as a tool for publication and sharing of content, and not as a key factor for value creation. At the conclusion of this study it is, therefore, possible to trace the three main trends for luxury firms:

1. In the aggregate the luxury firms demonstrate a good use of the CM, shall evaluate them positively oriented and invest a significant portion of their budget to boost such activities. At the same time, however, does not take careful planning of these decisions, do not invest on the training of human resources and make extensive use of metrics designed to measure aspects of publishing and content sharing rather than a metric to assess the 'economic impact of CM sign, this, that you have not yet realized the strategic importance of this tool for the acquisition of a lasting competitive advantage;
2. The field of activity affecting the use of the tools of CM. On a one hand, results show that the luxury firms operating in the fashion and accessories, watches and perfume and cosmetics use CM, find it very effective and efficient to achieve their objectives; adopt a well-planned CM strategy, have

human resources specifically dedicated to CM activities; invest more than 50% of their budget for communication costs in activities of CM; also begin to use metric to measure economic aspects of CM;

3. Opposite trend reversed, however, there is the luxury firms of wine and spirits sectors, cars, yachts, jewelery, home design. In particular these companies: they record the almost total lack of careful planning strategies CM and use of lead generation and sales metrics; to recognize such instruments a low level of utility; use mainly to familiar tools and easy to use (such as Facebook or Twitter) that do not require dedicated human resources or huge investments, but can be managed internally by the entrepreneur or by a member of the company responsible for other functions.

To sum up our results suggest that: 1) luxury firms show a very good use of CM, rate it effective, allocate between the 50% to 75% of their total marketing budget to CM. However, they don't develop a documented and planned content strategy and not investing on the training of human resources dedicated to CM activities. This is a first evidence that luxury firms do not recognize yet a strategic role to value creation at CM; 2) luxury firms make an extensive use of metrics designed to measure aspects related to the publication and sharing of content, but, at the same time, a low use of metrics to evaluate the economic-financial impact of the CM strategies and tactics. This is a further evidence that luxury firms do not have yet fully understood the centrality of CM to obtain and sustain a competitive advantage. Thus, these two results suggest that luxury firms do not have still recognized the strategic role of CM in the value creation process.

The results of our study suggest some managerial implications to develop the debate on the CM as a strategy to increase performance and create value. In particular, CM managers should 1) quit the idea of the CM as a simple tactic to publish and share content; 2) begin to carefully plan CM strategies, using human resource dedicated to this activity; 3) increase the use of economic-financial metrics (i.e. lead generation and sales metrics) to properly assess the impact of CM on value creation.

LIMITATIONS AND FURTHER RESEARCH DIRECTIONS

The main limitations of the study are:

1. The small size of the sample. Furthermore, global luxury firms for the sample were selected from Brand Networks (2014), Brandz (2014), Interbrand (2014), and World Luxury Association (2012) as well as Okonkwo's (2010). As there is no official listing of the best global luxury firms who do CM, the sample could have also been constructed of another set of luxury firms. However, the sample of global luxury firms analyzed are all involved in CM and were therefore able to contribute interesting results to this study;
2. The exploratory analysis cannot rely on statistical inference (Dubois & Gadde, 2002). Therefore, another researcher might have had different conclusions from the same data as no descriptive statistical conclusions can be made. Reliability and validity are used to evaluate this research (Iacobucci & Churchill, 2010). The first dimension refers to the extent to which the measure or procedure generates the same results: many similarities were found both between this research and between the studies found in the literature (Gordini & Rancati, 2014), not in luxury markets. In addition, the concept of CM is variable as mentioned earlier and in a few years the perceptions of

CM might be different even within the luxury firms. Thus, even though a repeated study might not draw exactly identical conclusions, similar findings would most probably be found in this period of time. The second dimension used to evaluate research agree with the goal of this study: get a corporate perspective on CM in luxury firms;

3. The perspective of the luxury firm was selected and studied due to the research gap rising from the literature and empirical data. However, CM can and should be studied from the customer perspective as well. CM has so far gained fairly little academic attention, further research could be conducted in order to examine the concept of CM from a customer point-of-view. Based on the current literature and also on the findings of this study, customer has a very central role in CM. Thereby, more information is definitely needed from consumer and customer perspective. Previous studies in luxury firms confirm that customer understanding is a difficult, yet one of the most important aspects of CM (for example in webatmosphere). Although CM is a great tool to engage with customer, luxury firms still have to use time on speculating which are the important themes and contents that should be discussed. Thus, research, insight and tools should be developed in order to make it easier for luxury firms to actually figure out what are the contents and stories that the customer needs and wants (storytelling).

Moreover, based on this research, the role of customers in luxury content creation is expected to increase. Consumers make their own meanings of brands they use in their daily lives and that they are in fact co-creators of the brand stories (Gensler, Völckner, Liu-Thompkins & Wiertz, 2013). In fact, for some luxury firms it is valuable to reduce their own branding efforts and rely more on the consumer-generated brand stories, because if the story is told by a consumer instead of the company, it can be perceived as clearer and more reliable (Gensler, Völckner, Liu-Thompkins & Wiertz, 2013). Therefore, the interrelations between the role of consumer in CM and the luxury brand perception might create and interesting foundation for future research. Furthermore, another intriguing future research theme could be to examine the effects of CM on intangible assets in luxury firms for example. One of the main objectives of luxury firms competition in global markets is to increase sales and build strong brand using online and offline communication tools. For example, a study could be conducted, maybe even with these same luxury firms, to see whether their CM efforts actually make a difference in brand perception in customer perspective. Finally, this study show many differences in the ways CM is used. Some luxury firms found it to be a great tool to increase awareness and arouse interest whereas others emphasized it to be very effective in engaging the customers. Thus, further research could be developed to find out whether CM is more suitable for luxury firms objectives.

REFERENCES

Atkinson, R., & Flint, J. (2004). *Snowball Sampling. The SAGE Encyclopedia of Social Science Research Methods*. London: SAGE Publications.

Bonoma, T. V., & Clark, B. H. (1988). *Marketing Performance Assessment*. Boston: Harvard Business School Press.

Cashman, J., & Treece, M. (2012). *Content marketing essentials for small business*. London: Create Space Independent Publishing Platform.

Chaffey, D., & Ellis-Chadwick, F. (2012). *Digital Marketing–Strategy, Implementation and Practice*. Edinburgh: Pearson Education Limited.

Chaffey, D., Mayer, R., Johnston, K., & Ellis-Chadwick, F. (2000). *Internet marketing*. Edinburgh, UK: Pearson.

Clay, B., & Newland, M. (2014). *Content marketing strategies for professionals*. North Charleston: Create Space Independent Publishing Platform.

Crestodina, A. (2012). *Content chemistry: an illustrated handbook for content marketing*. New York: Orbit Media Studios.

Damian, R. & Calvin, J (2013). *Marketing digitale: trarre il massimo vantaggio da e-mail, siti web, dispositivi mobili, social media e PR online*. Bergamo: Tecniche nuove.

Didner, P. (2014). *Global content marketing*. New York: Mc-Graw Hill.

Doyle, P. (2000). *Value-Based Marketing*. Chichester, UK: Wiley.

Dubois, A., & Gadde, L. E. (2002). Systematic combining: An abductive approach to case research. *Journal of Business Research*, *55*(7), 553–560. doi:10.1016/S0148-2963(00)00195-8

Fantini, M. (2013). *Content Marketing, image, notorietè, conquete, fidelisation: boostez voster webmarketing par la contenu*, Paris: Eni editions Peterson E.T.

Fishbein, M. (2014). *Growth hacking with content marketing*. London: Create Space Independent Publishing Platform.

Foglio, A. (2013). *Il marketing comunicativo dell'impresa: dalla pubblicità alla comunicazione offline e online al consumatore*. Milan: Angeli.

Gensler, S., Völckner, F., Liu-Thompkins, Y., & Wiertz, C. (2013). Managing Brands in the Social Media Environment. *Journal of Interactive Marketing*, *27*(4), 242–256. doi:10.1016/j.intmar.2013.09.004

Giachetti, C., Spadafora, E., & Bursi, T. (2013). Internazionalizzazione, performance delle imprese e crisi economiche: i produttori di piastrelle di ceramica del distretto di Modena e Reggio Emilia. *Mercati e competitività, 2*, 37-58.

Gordini, N., & Rancati, E. (2014). *Content marketing e creazione di valore. Aspetti definitori e metriche di misurazione*. Turin: Giappichelli.

Gunelius, S. (2011). *Content Marketing for Dummies*. New York: Wiley.

Halvorson, K. (2010). *Content strategy for the web*. Berkeley, CA: New Riders.

Handley, A., & Champman, C. C. (2012). *Content marketing: fare business con i contenuti per il web*. Milan: Hoepli.

Handley, A., & Chapman, C. C. (2010). *Content Rules*. New York: John Wiley & Sons.

Hauer, C. (2012). Marketing in the Digital Age. *Editors' Bulletin*, *7*(3), 77–79.

Hennig-Thurau, T., Malthouse, E. C., Friege, C., Gensler, S., Lobschat, L., Rangaswamy, A., & Skiera, B. (2010). The Impact of New Media on Customer Relationships. *Journal of Service Research*, *13*(3), 311–328. doi:10.1177/1094670510375460

Henning-Thurau, T., Hofacker, C., & Bloching, B. (2013). Marketing the Pinball Way: Understanding How Social Media Change the Generation of Value for Consumers and Companies. *Journal of Interactive Marketing*, *27*(4), 237–241. doi:10.1016/j.intmar.2013.09.005

Holliman, G., & Rowley, J. (2014). Business to business digital content marketing. *Journal of Research in Interactive Marketing*, *8*(4), 269–293. doi:10.1108/JRIM-02-2014-0013

Iacobucci, D., & Churchill, G. A. (2010). Marketing Research: Methodological Foundations (10th ed.). Mason, OH: South Western Cengage Learning.

Jarvinen, J., & Taiminen, H. (2015). (in press). Harnessing marketing automation for B2B content marketing. *Journal of Industrial Marketing Management*. doi:10.1016/j.indmarman.2015.07.002

Jefferson, S., & Tanton, S. (2013). Valuable Content Marketing. How to make quality content the key of your business success, London: Kogan Page: London.

Kanuk, L., & Berenson, C. (1975). Mail Surveys and Response Rates: A Literature Review. *JMR, Journal of Marketing Research*, *12*(4), 440–453. doi:10.2307/3151093

Kanuk, S. U., & Krishnamurthy, S. (2007). An analysis of consumer power on the Internet. *Technovation*, *27*(1-2), 47–56. doi:10.1016/j.technovation.2006.05.002

Kaplan, A. M., & Haenlein, M. (2010). Users of the world unite! The challenges and opportunities of Social Media. *Business Horizons*, *53*(1), 59–68. doi:10.1016/j.bushor.2009.09.003

Kazim, K., & Karahan, F. (2011). To be or not to be in Social Media Arena as the Most Cost Efficient Marketing Strategy after the Global Recession. *Procedia: Social and Behavioral Sciences*, 24.

Keller, K. L. (2009). Building on strong brands in a modern marketing communications environment. *Journal of Marketing Communications*, *15*(2-3), 139–155. doi:10.1080/13527260902757530

Keronen, K., & Tanni, K. (2013). *Johdata Asiakkaasi Verkkoon*. Helsinki: Talentum Media Oy.

Keyes, J. (2006). *Knowledge management, business intelligence and content management. Broken South Parken*. Auerbach Publications. doi:10.1201/9781420013863

Kucuk, S. U., & Krishnamurthy, S. (2007). An Analysis of Consumer Power on the Internet. *Technovation*, *27*(1/2), 47–56. doi:10.1016/j.technovation.2006.05.002

Lancaster, C. (2014). *Content marketing: turn content into powerful marketing tool*. London: Pogo Book Publishing.

Lauterborn, R. (1990). *New marketing litany: 4Ps passé; 4Cs take over*. New York. *Advertising Age*.

Lieb, R. (2011). *Content Marketing: think like a publisher. How to use content to market online and in social media*. Indianapolis, IN: Que Publishing.

Lilly, M. C. (2014). *Content marketing essentials for small business*. London: Create Space Independent Publishing Platform.

Linn, M. (2012). *A Field Guide to the 4 Types of Content Marketing Metrics*. Retrieved 15 November 2014 from www.contentmarketinginstitute.com

Malthouse, E. C., Haenlein, M., Skiera, B., Wege, E., & Zhang, M. (2013). Managing Customer Relationships in the Social Media Era: Introducing the Social CRM House. *Journal of Interactive Marketing*, *27*(4), 270–289. doi:10.1016/j.intmar.2013.09.008

Mosca, F. (2008). Market-driven management in fashion and luxury industries. *Symphonya. Emerging Issues in Management*, *1*, 53–78.

Mosca, F. (2010). *Marketing dei beni di lusso*. Milano: Pearson.

Mosca, F. (2012). *Product concepts and heritage per i beni ad elevato valore simbolico*. Turin: Giappichelli.

Nelli, R. P. (2012). *Branded Content Marketing*. Milan: Vita e Pensiero.

Newbert, S. L. (2007). Empirical research on the resource-based view of the firm: An assessment and suggestions for future research. *Strategic Management Journal*, *28*(12), 121–146. doi:10.1002/smj.573

Okonkwo, U. (2007). *Luxury fashion branding*. Hampshire, UK: Palgrave. doi:10.1057/9780230590885

Okonkwo, U. (2010). *Luxury online*. Hampshire, UK: Palgrave. doi:10.1057/9780230248335

Parikh, A., & Deshmukh, S. (2013). Search Engine Optimization. *International Journal of Engineering Research & Technology*, *2*(11), 324–348.

Prandelli, E., & Verona, G. (2011). *Vantaggio competitivo in Rete: dal Web 2.0 al Cloud Computing*. Milan: McGraw-Hill.

Pulizzi, J. (2012). The Rise of Storytelling as the New Marketing. *Publishing Research Quarterly*, *28*(2), 116–123. doi:10.1007/s12109-012-9264-5

Pulizzi, J. (2012). *Six Useful Content Marketing Definitions*. Retrieved 21 February 2015 from http://contentmarketinginstitute.com/2012/06/contentmarketing-definition/

Pulizzi, J. (2014). *Epic content marketing*. London: Mc Graw Hill.

Pulizzi, J., & Barrett, N. (2009). *Get content. Get customers*. New York: McGraw Hill.

Rahimia, F., & Hassanzadeh, J. (2013). The impact of website content dimension and e-trust on e-marketing effectiveness: The case of Iranian commercial saffron corporations. *Information & Management*, *50*(5), 240–247. doi:10.1016/j.im.2013.04.003

Rakic, R., Beba, R., & Mira, R. (2014). Digital Content Marketing for organizations as buyers. *Ekonomika. Journal of Economic Theory and Practice and Social Issues*, *1*, 109–123.

Ramos, R. (2014). *Content Marketing: insider's secret to online sales and lead generation.* Expert Publishing.

Rancati, E., & Gordini, N. (2014). Content marketing metrics: Theoretical aspects and empirical evidence. *European Scientific Journal, 10*(34), 92–104.

Rancati, E. & Gordini N. (2015a). Gli strumenti di misurazione delle strategie di content marketing: un confronto tra imprese italiane e inglesi. *Mercati e competitività, 1*, 45-74.

Rancati, E., & Gordini, N. (2015b), Content marketing: conceptualizing and measuring. Evidence from a sample of Italian firms. In *Proceedings of the 44th EMAC Conference: Collaboration in Research.*

Rose, R., & Pulizzi, J. (2011). *Managing Content Marketing. The real-world guide for creating passionate subscribers to your brands*. Cleveland, OH: CMI Books.

Rotsztein, B. (2014). *Content marketing ideas*. London: Creative Force Publishing.

Rowley, J. (2008). Understanding digital Content Marketing. *Journal of Marketing Management, 24*(5-6), 517–540. doi:10.1362/026725708X325977

Ryan, D., & Jones, C. (2009). *Understanding Digital Marketing – Marketing Strategies for engaging the digital generation*. London: Kogan Page Limited.

Scott, M. D. (2014). *Le nuove regole del marketing. Come usare social media, video online, app mobile, blog, comunicati stampa e marketing virale per raggiungere i clienti*. Milan: Hoepli.

Slater, V. (2014). *Content marketing: recycling and reuse. How your best online content can engage and attract new customers*. New York: i30 Media Corporation.

Van Lieshout, L. (2014). *Content marketing for professionals*. London: CreateSpace Independent Publishing Platform.

Venkatesh, R., & Chatterjee, R. (2006). Bundling, Unbundling, and pricing of multiform products: The case of magazine content. *Journal of Interactive Marketing, 20*(2), 54–78. doi:10.1002/dir.20059

Vescovi, T. (2007). *Il marketing e la Rete. La gestione integrata del Web nel business, Comunicazione, E-commerce, sales management, business to business*. Milan: Il Sole 24 Ore.

Weinberg, B. D., & Pehlivan, E. (2011). Social spending: Managing the social media mix. *Business Horizons, 54*(3), 275–282. doi:10.1016/j.bushor.2011.01.008

Winer, R. S. (2009). New Communications Approaches in Marketing: Issues and research directions. *Journal of Interactive Marketing, 23*(2), 237–256. doi:10.1016/j.intmar.2009.02.004

Wymbs, C. (2011). Digital marketing: The time for a new "academic major" has arrived. *Journal of Marketing Education, 33*(2), 93–106. doi:10.1177/0273475310392544

ADDITIONAL READING

Rahimia, F., & Hassanzadeh, J. (2013). The impact of website content dimension and e-trust on e-marketing effectiveness: The case of Iranian commercial saffron corporations. *Information & Management, 4*, 124–145.

Savar, A. (2013). *Content to Commerce: Engaging Consumers Across Paid, Owned and Earned Channels, New Jersey*. Somerset: Wiley.

Zahay, D. (2014). Beyond interactive marketing. *Journal of Research in Interactive Marketing*, *8*(4), 32–46. doi:10.1108/JRIM-08-2014-0047

KEY TERMS AND DEFINITIONS

Consumption Metrics: Measurement of brand awareness and website traffic generated by the content.

Content Marketing: The marketing and business process for creating and distributing valuable and compelling content to attract, engage, acquire, educate and connect a clearly defined target audience with the objective of driving profitable consumer action and creating firm value.

Lead Generation Metrics: Measurement of number of leads generated.

Sales Metrics: Measurement of the impact of CM on firm performance, finding out how CM impacts customer acquisition and sales goals.

Sharing Metrics: Measurement of the level of content sharing by consumers with their network of people with a direct and significant impact on the engagement.

Chapter 7
The Relative Importance of the Different Relationship Platforms (Physical and Virtual) in the Consumer Experience of Luxury Brands:
How Has It Changed from the Company Perspective?

Paola Peretti
IULM, Italy

Mohanbir Sawhney
Northwestern University, USA

ABSTRACT

Managing luxury brands nowadays is complex (Wiedmann & Hennigs, 2012). On the one hand, luxury brands built their development through a strategic use of physical relationship platforms, making the customer experience inside points of sale an indispensable element for their growth. On the other hand, over the past 10 years, we have seen leading global luxury brands embrace virtual platforms in various ways to re-imagining consumer experiences. Blending these new elements can present challenges. The purpose of this chapter is to understand the relative importance of the different relationship platforms (physical and virtual) in the consumer experience of luxury brands and how has it changed. Results are able on the one hand to expand the theory of luxury branding and on the other hand to highlight some key implications for luxury brand managers.

DOI: 10.4018/978-1-4666-9958-8.ch007

INTRODUCTION

Today's consumers, who can still spend quite a bit on luxury brands, no longer require formal attire or attitudes; immediacy and flexibility are necessary to establish links with their loved brands, but it's difficult to offer a unique and integrated experience (offline and online) if there's no control on the brand tone of voice and image. The challenge is how to find the right balance of awareness, engagement and purchase between the different platforms. (Marketing Manager of a Luxury Brand)

This is just one of the quotes gathered in the questionnaire that interviewed 35 marketing managers of luxury brands, based in Italy, who belonged to a sample of luxury companies identified by the Fondazione Altagamma and Pambianco. The ambition of this chapter is to look further into these challenges and answer one key research question: *What is the relative importance of the different relationship platforms in the consumer experience of luxury brands, and how has it changed, from the company perspective?*

1.1 Literature Review

In recent years the development of virtual platforms (online and mobile) has generated important changes among consumers, market dynamics, marketing pro-cesses and communication.

Consumers have become the real players of this era. Thanks to the Internet's global reach and the growth of social media worldwide, consumers have much better control over access and use of information than in the past (Shankar et al, 2011). They are interconnected and they can communicate by exchanging multimedia content and opinions (Rothaermel & Sugiyamab, 2001; Goldsmith & Horowitz, 2006). The Internet is now an integral part of people's lives: through the Internet consumers communicate, compare, try, buy and express themselves; it has also become the bridge by which organizations can create a lasting, two-way and peer-to-peer relationship with customers through their brands (Martin & Todorov, 2010). This change in roles and the spread of the Internet have led to the rise of Web 2.0, which is discussed in the literature of various disciplines, especially in terms of information technology. As far as marketing is concerned, various scholars have stated that Web 2.0's evolution is the basis for a true revolution in the discipline (Deighton, 1997; Hoffman, 2000; Kotler et al, 2010). In particular, this issue is now flanked by the concept of "consumer empowerment" (Wathieu, et al., 2002, Pires et al, 2006, Wright et al, 2006, Cova & Pace, 2006), both as regards the role and impact of conversations and e-Word of Mouth (e-WOM) on purchase intent and decisions, and on effects in terms of brand loyalty and image (Brown et al, 2007). In addition, it is useful to point out that consumers on a global scale are changing demographically and in terms of expectations and desires (United Nations, 2000) are less likely to be loyal to brands, are more affected by other consumers than by traditional media and their behaviour is less predictable (Svensson, 2002, eMarketer, 2011).

From a business perspective, these phenomena imply a swift change in the approach towards consumers, as the relationship and interaction with them turns into a highly personalized and steady message exchange (Deighton & Kornfeld, 2009; Michelsson & Heinonen, 2010) both off- and on-line (Keller, 2010) in a multichannel context (Simons et al, 2002).

However, from the point of view of the market a double phenomenon is taking place: on the one hand the rise of globalization, which, as investigated historically (T. Levitt, 1984), leads to a cultural convergence as brands and production are standardized (Bellman et al, 2006); on the other hand, the increasing use of the Internet is raising the question a how to manage virtual platforms in the processes of consumer engagement.

Furthermore, the methods of conducting marketing, as noted above, are going through a profound change. In the traditional view, considering the approach introduced and improved by Philip Kotler, marketing is seen as a circular process de-signed to generate value. The ongoing evolution (Kotler et al, 2010) can be summarized in three steps: from marketing as a process "to market" (marketing 1.0, moves products to markets, a functional approach and a "one-to-many" relationship), to that of "marketing to" (marketing 2.0, designed for consumers, differentiation and a "one-to-one" approach), and, finally, to "marketing with" (marketing 3.0, with consumers considered co-creative resources, where values and emotions are important and relationships are "many-to-many"). In the logic of marketing 3.0, brands, to be effective, must try and build a relationship with consumers by creating experiences that generate engagement and consistent use of the Internet will strengthen the brands' promises. This situation creates challenges and opportunities in terms of brand management (De Chernatony, 2004), which organizations must take into account.

In a global market where consumers play an active role in the development of virtual platforms, organizations especially in the luxury industry, that have direct access to consumers through physically related platforms, face a complex challenge. Stores are considered the main platform through which brands are experienced, places where products can be distributed and sold and, at the same time, where superior customer experiences can be created. Particularly in the fashion and luxury sectors, brands have become "experience providers" (Schmitt, 1999), active parts in people's lives and networks, with retail outlets transformed into "relational platforms" (Pellegrini, 2011) where it is possible to represent the brand by engaging consumers in emotional experiences. In fact, luxury, as a business sector and management discipline (Okonkwo, 2009), has become increasingly important, not only in terms of market value, but also for strategic retail use in order to build global brands. In response to a decade of growing demand in the luxury sector, organizations have developed extended market coverage as a major business strategy, with the opening of unique selling points representing the brand's characteristics in terms of status, exclusivity and experience (Fionda & Moore, 2008).

Therefore, luxury can now be considered a dynamic concept which increasingly relates to consumer's experience both online and offline. Particularly in the last few years, brand management literature has analysed thoroughly the aspects relating to luxury, its scope and the reasons behind purchasing a luxury brand. In the retail sec-tor attention has been paid to the points of sale and the crucial role that they play in transmitting the experience of luxury brands. Recently, in the field of marketing, attention has been given to the role of social media and the accent was often placed on the need to understand what the challenges and implications are, especially for luxury brands, yet there is a gap in the literature with regard on how luxury companies are managing these two platforms and how digital is shifting their marketing strategies, aspects on which this study intends to focus. In addition further investigation needs, on this topic, have emerged and are mentioned in several publications and fields of study, in particular: Luxury Online (Okonkwo, 2009, Palgrave Macmillan, 2009), Luxury Brand Management (Wiley, 2008, Kapferer, Bastien, 2009), Luxury Strategy (Kogan Page, 2008) and Luxury Brand Marketing (Vickers, Renand, 2003, Atwal, Williams, 2008).

Given the developments among consumers and virtual platforms, luxury brands' marketing strategies, in fact, need to switch from the "top-down" relationship of the past years to a "bottom-up" one, where customers have become as important as products and the brand itself (Okonkwo, 2009). A further confirmation of this need comes from the first study on this topic "Digital Luxury Experiences" (Altagamma Foundation, 2011, p.3), carried out in order to understand the "state of the art of how luxury brands use the network, the web and social media's dynamics evolution, the potential of mobile and e-commerce". The emerging scenario confirms that virtual platforms are becoming increasingly important to communicate with a variety of consumers, who are heterogeneous and much more aware and informed, and who positively consider the purchase of luxury brands online. Consumers themselves declare that social media are the basic platform for dialogue between a luxury brand and themselves, 37% of respondents believe them to be the "principal source of information for fashion/luxury products", with this percentage rising to 58% in China. In 2012, the same study (Altagamma Fondazione, 2012) showed some important trends: luxury brands'social media presence is increasing (+63% Facebook and +422% Twitter vs. 2011), multichannel marketing is emerging as a driver of distinctiveness, customer experience is becoming more sophisticated and in 12% of cases companies declared that they are progressively integrating online and offline platforms. Finally, in line with our previous considerations, 11% of offline sales are generated by online presence, plus 20% of sales are influenced by online presence. The integration of virtual and physical platforms seems to be increasingly important; in fact, 36% of customers buy the same day after carrying out an online search (in 25% of cases they buy online and 11% in store). This phenomenon is affecting how luxury brands are marketed.

According to Grau (2010), in his report on the results of an empirical study conducted by eMarketer, luxury *players* have been slower than other sectors in launching integrated websites and virtual platforms in line with the size of the brand. This study points out, in fact, that luxury brand consumers expect to be able to buy and have superior online experiences through visual content and VIP treatment. However, in this area the luxury brands have used different approaches and it is not yet clear how these tools may generate value and how they can naturally be integrated with off-line activities, except for a few brands, Burberry for example. In fact, in the last five years the British company has decided to innovate by integrating the virtual into every aspect of marketing and within the point of sale, making the concept of a natural convergence of physical and virtual relationship platforms a source of competitive advantage. Burberry was the first example of a luxury brand that tried to merge digital and physical experiences together as one and in demonstration of this it converted the resources use by investing 60% of its marketing budget in digital as early as 2011 (Baker, 2011).

What are the other luxury brands doing? How do marketers see this challenge? What should we expect in the next few years? Is growth through virtual relationship platforms compatible and sustainable for luxury brands? One element is certain in today's market; luxury brands are tasked with creating a new level of relationship to capture customer attention. These experiences, both physical and virtual, are crucial for showing what makes the brand unique, which is a key factor for success in order to satisfy an audience that is constantly evolving.

In this scenario, it seems that brand experience is no longer restricted to a traditional marketing mix, but more and more consumers are playing an active role in strengthening relationships and brand advocacy. One of the main challenges for luxury companies will be to define the right mix of integration between physical and virtual platforms in order to have a high level of consumer engagement and advocacy, but, at the same time, to protect the unique dimensions of their brands. This challenge will require a broad-based cultural change within luxury companies and new models of marketing and brand management.

The results arising from the literature analysis emphasize the existence of a very complex system of relational tools that presents different exploration possibilities for those who want to analyze it. In fact, starting from the "first contact or awareness" up to the time of purchase and after purchase (loyalty), this relationship tends towards convergence and natural integration without a special distinction between physical and virtual, from the point of view of consumers. In luxury brands this aspect could invalidate the brands' marketing strategies that have remained partially unchanged in recent years and would open up significant challenges. In addition, if one considers the development of luxury brands in emerging countries, this issue acquires even greater significance. For example, in China, which is the most significant market for luxury brands (both as a result of its value and its exponential increase in recent years), consumers expect to be able to find out about, assess and even purchase luxury brands both online and offline; therefore, companies have to work out how to do this in the best and most consistent manner.

Given the changes among consumers and the adoption of social media, the challenge for luxury brands (with intangible dimensions, purchase tied to status and exclusivity) is to integrate platforms and understand how to implement their mix to ensure an adequate experience. The main questions that arise with respect to the analysis are as follows:

- What is the role of virtual platforms?
- What is their role in the integration process with physical ones?
- How can companies decide which configuration to give to different platforms?

The aim of this chapter is to investigate: what is the relative importance of the different relationship platforms in consumer experience of luxury brands from the company perspective, and how has it changed? Specifically, the scientific interest is directed at pursuit of:

- **Motivation:** What reasons have led to the need to combine traditional and virtual platforms in order to deliver the experience of luxury brands?
- **Principles:** What are the underlying principles to support these changes?
- **Resources:** What share of the marketing budget is dedicated to online vs. offline? How has the progression been in recent years and is it possible to see a % of balance that is imaginable for the future?
- **Threats:** Are there threats associated with the use of virtual platforms for the construction of luxury brands?
- **Opportunities:** What are the benefits and opportunities that arise from the use of virtual platforms integrated with physical ones?
- **Direction of Evolution:** What is the direction of change?

1.2 Focus and Methodology

This chapter, as we previously specify, investigates some potential factors, related to existing and possible opportunities coming from the use of the different relationship platforms that are affecting luxury brand marketing strategies. When reviewing the literature, no empirical studies were found concerning the role of physical and virtual platforms in the consumer experience of luxury brands. However, different pieces of research (McKinsey, 2011; Research Center Foundation Altagamma, 2011) have emphasised main trends: the different changes among consumers and the adoption of social media; the challenges for luxury brands that need to integrate the ultimate experience linked to physical points of sale with the evolution of virtual platforms; the potentials for growth linked to the use of virtual relationship platforms. In order to carry out the analysis, the topic being studied was divided into six areas, which corresponded to various questions in the questionnaire that was used to gather data (Figure 1). Analysis was carried out for each of these areas, with various techniques for measuring and representing the results.

A structured questionnaire was sent via e-mail to a representative sample of marketing managers, who are based in Italy and work in the luxury industry. The final database counted 110 managers (N=110) from 88 companies. The response rate was 31.8% (n=35 respondents). Respondents were all from different companies. Respondents were promised anonymity.

The choice of statistical technique used considered a series of factors including the objective of the analysis and the nature of the piece of information, or the type of variable observed. The study started with a univariate analysis of the data and subsequently, it moved on to a bivariate and multivariate analysis for the search of relationships between groups of variables. It should be specified that the data collected are of an ordered qualitative nature in particular (e.g. opinions on a 5 point Likert scale). Various methodologies were used to analyse the questionnaire: basic descriptive statistical analysis; prediction for identifying groups: a cluster analysis.

1.3 Analysis and Results

The analysis of the literature revealed a complex scenario. On the one hand, luxury brands built their development through a strategic use of physical relationship platforms, making the customer experience inside points of sale an indispensable element for their growth. On the other hand, over the past 10 years, we have seen leading global luxury brands embrace virtual platforms in various ways, from simple websites, to e-commerce and social networks, to re-imagining consumer experiences. Blending these new elements within a brand's equity model can present challenges that we analysed, in details, in the next paragraphs.

Figure 1. Structure for analysis of luxury managers' survey

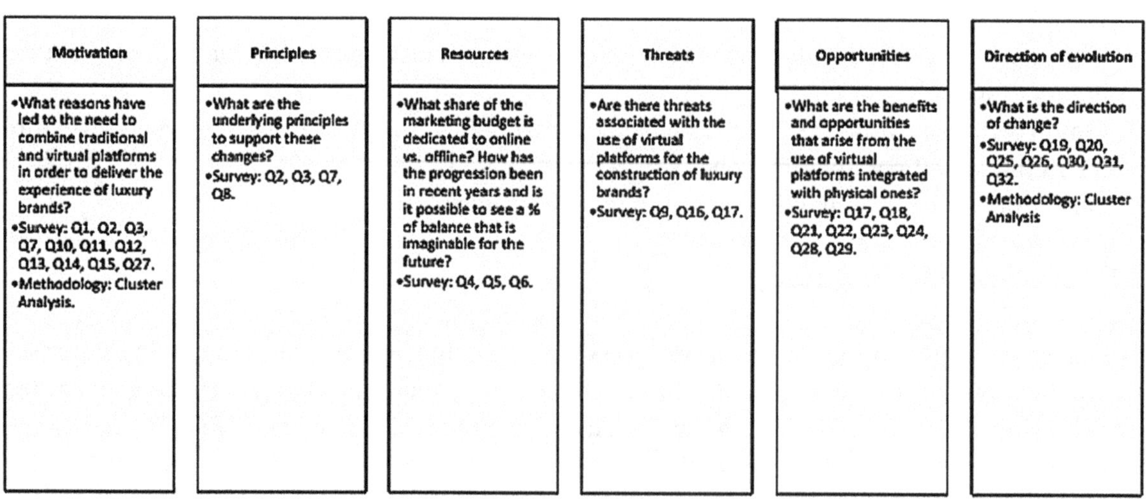

1.4 Motivations for Integrating Physical and Virtual Platforms to Deliver the Experience of Luxury Brands

Specific assumptions were developed on the basis of the analysis of literature and the objective of this empirical investigation is to analyse them in detail trying to understand what it happening, particularly with regard to luxury players in the Italian market. The starting point of the study was on the motivations that are at the basis of the management marketing choices linked to integration. Pro-integration factors were considered (e.g. new marketing tools, the development of technology, new behaviours by consumers and lesser effectiveness of traditional communication methods) together with factors that hinder integration instead (e.g. the cost of adoption of virtual platforms, unique dimensions of the luxury brands which are not easily manageable online, internal culture and requirement for a new organisation to make integration effective).

1.4.1 Pro-Integration Factors

In order to carry out the study, various items in the questionnaire were grouped together in the four macro factors which, on the basis of the assumptions made previously, may facilitate the integration of physical and virtual relationship platforms.

The pro-integration factors were divided and ranked and it emerges that the main thrust towards placing virtual platforms side-by-side with off-line ones, was required first of all by the evolution of technology (Strongly Agree, 50%). Therefore, luxury brands try to follow the natural adoption of virtual platforms by consumers (e.g. e-commerce and social media). Technologies that are evolving have enabled luxury brands to get closer to their consumers and this is considered by marketers to be a significant boost towards their adoption (54.3% (19) Agree, Total cases: 35). "The corporate website, it's the best virtual platform to convey the brand's image and social networks are places where we can build a different experience, still unique but more personal", asserted one interviewed marketing manager. Therefore, in confirmation of the route taken, it can be shown how the managers moved from the Internet to social platforms trying to follow a route that may remain consistent with the touchpoints used off-line (points of sale and the use of traditional means of communication). However, we are still in a phase in which the requirement to test new marketing methods is noticed (Strongly Agree, 46.7% both in terms of promotion, and integrated with 4P, Strongly Agree 37.1%).

Finally, the managers interviewed were divided in their assessment of the fall in effectiveness of traditional communication methods, which for 44% (Strongly Agree/Agree) was a push towards adoption and for the remainder was not.

1.4.1.1 Technological Evolution (e.g. E-Commerce, Social Media, Etc.)

To analyse in more detail the variable linked to technological evolution, it is useful to cite some quotes given by interviewed managers:

- *Technology will evolve quickly and all luxury brands will have to adapt and be present, in a rigorous way, to keep meeting expectations and the "social" needs of a digitally mature audience*;

- *Virtual platforms, like Facebook, maybe one day they will also become transaction channels; but by definition it would be important for us to guarantee our presence but still remain a mass type platform, not suitable for selling our luxury brands where exclusivity is everything;*
- *Unless it becomes highly customizable, I do not think that possible forms of e-shop, on mobile for example, will ever be important for luxury brands un-less we are able to integrate them with our shops.*

Technological evolution is an element that has triggered the requirement to adapt the choice of relationship platforms through which consumers can be reached, not without some resistance. It is precisely the new technologies that have brought luxury brands closer to their consumers, encouraging marketers to use them, although with great caution and fear. The limits that seem to prevail, in using virtual relationship platforms, seem to be the ones that, on the one hand, protect the dimensions of the luxury brands and, on the other hand, support the marketers' requirement to control the experience.

1.4.1.2 New Marketing Tools

Find the right balance between "do-not-interact" with the audience, just releasing institutional messages, and real interaction with consumers.

According to managers of luxury brands, the second factor that has led to the use of virtual relationship platforms alongside physical ones is the desire to test and use new tools from a marketing point of view (either promotionally Strongly Agree 51.4% (18); or integrated into 4P, Strongly agree/Agree, 85.7% (31), Total cases: 35). "Surely Facebook is currently the most important virtual platform, since it is the most used and widely spread but we are trying different forms of marketing tools within the digital space like online media, video channels and social networks like Facebook and Twitter", analysing the data from the survey, it emerges that in the last year the following virtual platforms were used (Figure 2):

- **Social Networks:** Indeed, Facebook proves to be the most transverse (87.9% (29), Total cases: 33) followed by other social network such as Twitter and Pinterest (76.5% (26), Total cases: 34). Video channels can be added to these (e.g. YouTube) that are used as a medium for directing specific communication campaigns (61.8% (21), Total cases: 34).
- **Online and Offline Integration:** In particular they are an example of the involvement of influencers (e.g. bloggers) within events at points of sale (73.5% (25), Total cases: 34), and the insertion of digital devices (e.g. iPads, touch screens) within flagship stores (55.9% (19), Total cases: 34) to improve and enrich the customer experience.
- **E-Commerce:** A significant piece of information is the launch of an e-commerce site dedicated to a luxury brand (64.7% (22) – Total cases: 34).
- **Online Media:** The placing of off-line media alongside online media is already occurring, in fact 47.1% (16) state that they have planned paid-for visibility activities on virtual relationship platforms (e.g. sponsored links on Facebook and Google).
- **Mobile:** In confirmation of the studies cited previously, this platform is at the embryonic stage in terms of growth. Mobile activities in terms of marketing were used, last year, in 26.5% (9) of cases.

Figure 2. Virtual relationship platforms launched in the last 12 months

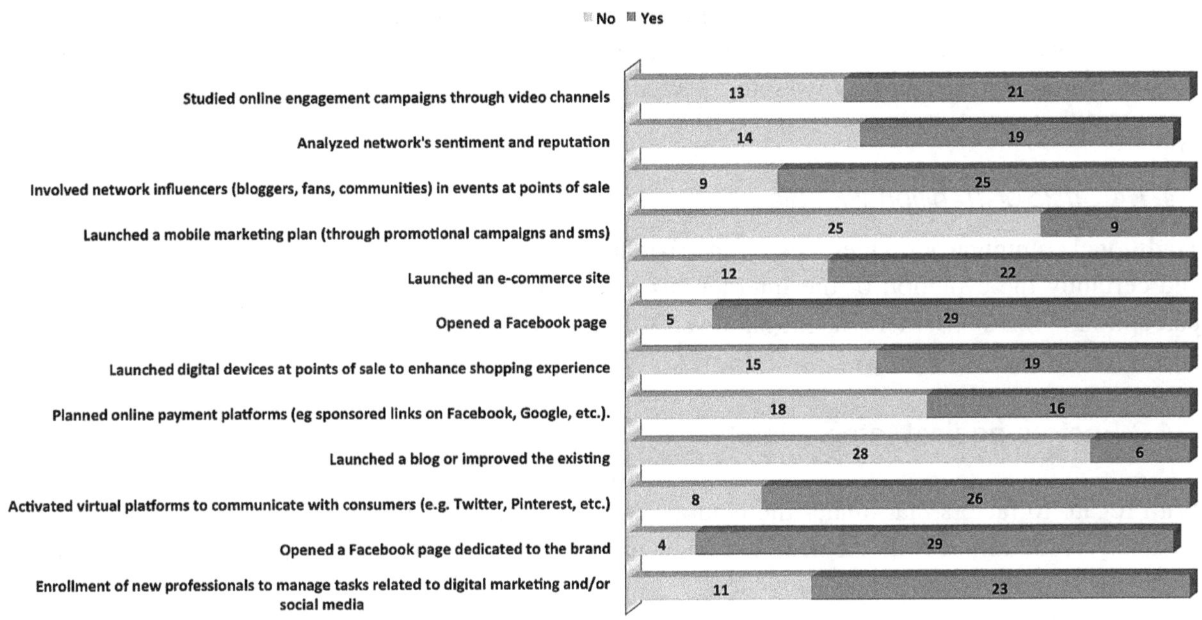

In confirmation of this trend in which the virtual space is growing and transforming, it has emerged that in order to manage virtual platforms new professional figures have been enrolled who are entirely dedicated to virtual platforms (67.7% (23), Total cases: 34). In addition, 57.6% (19) of interviewees declared that they systematically carry out analyses dedicated to online reputation and sentiment.

1.4.1.3 New Consumers' Behaviour

For some luxury goods even Facebook may become an important transactional platform for purchases not exceeding € 2,000/3,000.

It clearly emerges from the study that luxury brand consumers have changed their behaviour in accordance with technological innovation, they have expectations that are targeted with regard to the use of technology and the integration process is leading them towards a natural online and offline convergence. Although initially, within the experience of consumption of luxury brands, relationship platforms could have a crucial role in generating awareness during the discovery and involvement phase, now the propensity to purchase online and via mobile seems to be increasing.

51% (18) of the interviewees maintained that relationship platforms are influencing purchases by luxury consumers, while 17% do not know (a sign that further studies are needed in this area in which there still is not clear evidence). Therefore, the 31% who disagree are clearly in the minority.

In addition, it is interesting to note, in terms of trends underway, that managers essentially consider luxury consumers, particularly loyal ones, ready to purchase both online and offline. Other aspects that are relevant that emerged from the survey are the following ones:

- The awareness and discovery stages are very important online, in particular they are used for information purposes before making a purchase, which in general then takes place offline;
- Luxury consumers seem to be more interested in niche brands compared to the past, they are open to online purchasing, they want to interact with de-signers and find out more about the business that produces the brand in question.

1.4.1.4 Crisis of Traditional Media

Traditional communication methods are in crisis and they do not help to sell as in the past (51.4% (12)), and certainly the evolution of the Internet has made communication complex (47.1%), therefore the perception is that consumers' attention towards offline media has diminished, for 17% quite a lot and 54% a lot.

1.4.2 Factors against Integration

With regard to factors that hinder the natural integration of offline and online relationship platforms the analysis initially reveals the need to review the allocation of resources towards virtual relationship platforms in order not to lose effectiveness.

Another factor that acts as a deterrent for the use of virtual platforms is the unique dimension of luxury brands (Strongly Agree 53.8%, Agree 37.5%). In particular a situation emerges in which there is a desire to find a complex balance between the presence and interaction, between a "top down" approach to communication and a "bottom up" one that starts with dialogue with consumers. Being consistent is the challenge that appears the most complex (Strongly Agree 71.4% (25), Total cases: 35), together with the fear of losing control (Strongly Agree 54.3% (19, Agree 29.4% (10), Total cases: 35). Some examples of quotes taken from the open questions pre-sent in this questionnaire, confirm the trend described above:

- *Reach the compromise between the democratization imposed by social networks and the exclusivity of the brand;*
- *Find the right marketing mix between virtual and physical and how to find in both channels the most appropriate tone of voice;*
- *Luxury brands should be online but it's better not as any form of social commerce (e.g. selling products through social networks like Facebook) because it is a must for us to maintain our own heritage, exclusivity, quality and personality.*

The need to acquire new skills is understood clearly, together with a review of marketing processes and the implications that this may have from an organisation point of view (Strongly Agree/Agree 82.86% (29), Total cases: 35). In addition, lux-ury managers have a need to understand how virtual platforms may help brands to grow. An interesting piece of information is linked to the fact that 62% (21) of them declare that there are luxury brands that thanks to a strategic and integrated use of virtual relationship platforms have managed to acquire a competitive ad-vantage, and they cite Burberry, Tiffany, Gucci and Coach as examples in particular.

1.4.3 Factorial Analysis Regarding Factors for and against Integration

In order to further weigh up these variables, factorial analysis was carried out through SPSS. The procedure used was as follows: a factorial was carried out regarding the "factors pro integration", selecting the 10 items that actually make up this macro factor and require the SPSS to extract just one factor (which automatically includes all 10 items). Therefore, each element contains the weights of the individual items produced by the factorial, all transformed positively. Then, the items were grouped together on the basis of the sub-factors indicated previously and the average "weight" of each sub-factor was calculated so as to assess the impact of various sub factors on the "pro integration" macro factor. The analysis reveals that the sub-factor that weighs the most among the "pro integration factors" is the "need for new marketing tools". With regard to "factors against integration" the same process was followed and in this case the sub-factor with the greatest weight was the one related to costs ("cost of adoption of virtual platforms").

In order to compare the weight of the two macro factors pro and against integration, a cluster analysis was carried out regarding factorial scores produced by SPSS. It emerges from this that about 40% belong to the cluster "factors pro integration" and about 60% to the cluster "factors against integration" (Figure 3).

1.5 Underlying Principles That Support the Integration

We have seen the motivations that may facilitate the adoption of relationship platforms by marketers, now we shall try to understand what are the principles that support this change.

The principles to which the managers refer are as follows:

- **Consumers' Expectations:** According to what was declared in the questionnaire, managers consider luxury consumers to be prepared to purchase both online and offline and to date they believe that online sales (both single brand sites and multi-brand sites) end up accounting for 25% out of the total for Italy. This aspect is fundamental because it gives a push towards integration and increases the relative importance of virtual platforms.
- **Brand Equity Orientation:** "We have to strategically increase the importance of virtual platforms, which can certainly give us a return on sales' volumes, but without penalizing brand equity". It is an aspect that arose from the analysis in an indirect way and which, as we shall see, has very definite implications on the weight to be attributed to the ten characteristics of the luxury brands.

Figure 3. Cluster analysis of factors pro and against integration

		Clusters			
		Frequency	%	%	Cumulated %
Valid	FACTORS PRO INTEGRATION	13	38.2	40.6	40.6
	FACTORS AGAINST INTEGRATION	19	55.9	59.4	100
	Total	32	94.1	100	
	Skipped questions	2	5.9		
	Total	34	100		

- **Resources Progression:** "I'd increase the budget for online activities, concentrating investments in a coherent and integrated way between physical and virtual". "There was no real decline in the budget dedicated to traditional communication in favour of online communication. I would say that traditional communication has been targeted and limited to some channels (more resources to a better focused release schedule). Investments in communication through digital represent a new budget item for our company, with 80% dedicated to offline media and 20% to online". Another point of view: "I wouldn't invest more money on virtual platforms. Costs are still relatively high for traditional media and it's important for a luxury brand to "own" that space. 30% of investment in online activities is about right for me". In summary, there is a budget dedicated to virtual platforms (80%), this budget is separate from offline activities (23 - 71%) and on average counts for less than 30% of the total marketing budget (97%). In some cases it is a budget that was cut from traditional activities (e.g. media press), "We dropped the press budget, increasing the budget in digital channels". In each case, marketers express the need to in-crease investments and consequently the importance of virtual platforms, "I think I would spend more money next year to improve our shopping experience with dedicated services and customization, especially online and integrated in our point of sales".
- **Internal Focus on Innovation:** The request for greater resources, which was analysed above, does not only concern the use of virtual platforms to improve the consumer experience within points of sale, but also the experience linked to the possibility of taking on new skills within the organisations by supporting greater training in this area. "I would invest a good amount of money on training about digital tools for new employees and I'll try different experiments, like for example seeing if we can increase loyalty among potential online buyers in our e-shop or to see if we can strategically use social net-works to increase store traffic offline".

1.5.1 Threats Associated with the Use of Virtual Platforms

The study focused on three variables:

- **Brand Consistency:** As was revealed previously, a significant threat is the one linked to succeeding in ensuring the same consumer experience both online and offline, without luxury products losing their uniqueness (56.3% (18), Total cases: 32). "Keep consistency with the brand's DNA online, tackle the crises of economies and values'" or another threat is considered "High competitiveness online and brand image's protection" (40.6% (13)).
- **Management Process of Consumer Experience:** Talking about the consumer experience, the main threat is related to data management, the flow of information between online and offline and to the fact that they don't enhance their know-how enough (18.8% (6)) and they felt they adopted virtual plat-forms late compare to other industries (25% (8)). "Use digital platforms to organize the work and analyse big data; evaluate the effectiveness of the activities carried out in stores and online; have a faster information and knowledge exchange with colleagues and collaborators within the company". Marketers are scared about not involving consumers enough (28.1%, (9)), Total cases: 33).

- **Selection of Marketing Mix Elements:** "We have to change the marketing mix and use new tools, like for example through private communities within our website we can build an exclusive and unique relationship with our customers and fans". An unsuccessful choice of a marketing mix is seen as a threat, in particular with regard to specific tools linked to virtual relationship platforms such as mobiles (15.6% (5)). Another threat linked to the marketing mix is the observation that luxury brands can be penalised for the excessive importance that is assigned to physical points of sale (25% (8)).

1.5.2 Benefits of the Integration

However, on the other hand, what are the benefits that may increase the relative importance of virtual relationship platforms integrated with physical ones in the management of luxury brands?

- **Enhance Customer Experience:** 75.8% (25), Total cases: 33), together with the possibility of increasing the level of service and customisation (60.6% (20)), the appropriateness of increasing loyalty of consumers over time (45.5% (15)) and the idea of involving younger generations more (42.4% (14)). Customer experience online is seen (Tab. 23) by marketers as "simple" (42.4% (14)) and "different from the other brands" (21.2 (7)); while offline it becomes "emotional and involving" and "traditional" (26.5% (9)).
- **Strengthen Brand Equity:** 36.4% (12), another benefit that can be acquired from the use of virtual platforms together with the benefits revealed above;
- **Boost Innovation:** "Widespread introduction of digital tools in points of sale"; "Completely change the current concept of e-commerce (now considered to be only a showcase of products and not a true distribution channel)". Examples of another benefit associated with the virtual platforms that could in-crease their relative importance if they take on the role of boosting innovation, particularly "beyond online by pushing towards integration in points of sale" and even towards co-creation with consumers (55.9% of the managers interviewed were open to co-creation).

1.6 Luxury Brand Management Challenges: The Direction of Change

The challenge is to deliver content and the shopping experience through all the touch points. Another challenge is to meet the expectations of consumers who are increasingly demanding, critical and selective. Nowadays, effective marketing strategies should render the experience of discovery, purchase and possession unique and unrepeatable, produce strong emotions and engagement both online and offline without becoming banal or, even worse, putting the brand's image at stake. (Marketing Manager of a Luxury Brand)

How can the management of the luxury brands change? How can weights be attributed to the main characteristics of luxury brands? What direction can the integration of relationship platforms take? What are the challenges that marketers have to face and in particular what is their overall attitude with regard to the relative importance of virtual platforms in the consumer experience of luxury brands?

The objective of this last analysis is to answer these questions, focusing on the following aspects in particular:

- **Marketing Approach:** "Propose a suitable offer in terms of quality / price without overpromising but getting closer to the consumer in terms of engagement and social marketing". In order to analyse how the management of luxury brands is evolving (Figure 4) the interviewed managers were asked to rank the strategic importance of the ten characteristics of the luxury brands (Keller, 2009). The three variables that are considered very important, as things stand, are: the maintenance of a premium image; the constant fight against counterfeits and an approach to marketing that sees all aspects of it aligned in order to ensure product and service quality and in particular the uniqueness of the consumer experience of luxury brands. These are followed by (in order of importance): the need to build many intangible brand associations and an aspirational image (both online and offline); the strategy of premium pricing with strong quality and accurate management of brand architecture. On the other hand, aspects that are considered only marginally relevant are: the fact that brand elements (e.g. logos, symbols, packaging) can be important drivers of brand equity; the consideration linked to wider com-petition that would see luxury brands also competing with other category brands and then the element concerning secondary associations from linked personalities or events that can be a driver of brand equity.
- **Integration of Physical and Virtual Relationship Platforms:** The factors that contribute and push towards integration are of two types, those concerning the adoption of digital technologies within points of sale (mobile marketing, QR Code, App, touch screen and digital signage and e-shops in the point of sale) and those linked to the incidence of sales online. In the first case it can be seen that currently, as was revealed above, we are only at a first stage with regard to the adoption of these technologies (62% of interviewees do not use them (20)). With regard to e-commerce 65% of the businesses covered by the study sell online, 6% sell through multi-brand websites, while the remainder declare that they want to activate online sales soon. However, one

Figure 4. Ten characteristics of luxury brands (Keller, 2009) and their relative importance

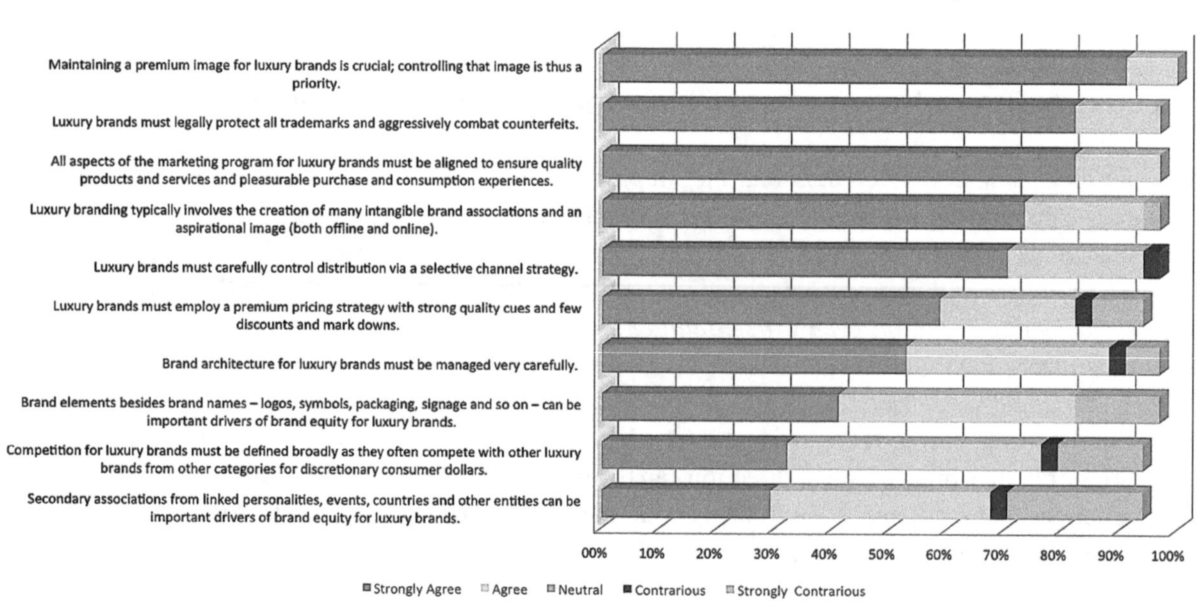

consideration is interesting and opens up to future explorations regarding the direction of change. 70% (23) of luxury marketers (Figure 5) see a trend in action that will lead markets to becoming conversational and in which a purchase may occur within any relationship platform.

- **Cultural Switch:** The markets become fluid and relationship-based and the complexity for whoever manages luxury brands will be precisely finding a difficult balance between the indispensable role of flagship stores, which shall remain the ultimate place to experience the brand (going by the businesses' vision), and the sales that may occur on any platform.

In order to understand in detail the complex attitude of luxury brand managers and analyse the dynamics that are occurring and the various types of attitude with regard to the adoption and importance of virtual relationship platforms, a factorial analysis and a cluster analysis was carried out. With regard to the cluster of managers the process was as follows: all the items of the questionnaire were chosen in which people were asked to express an opinion through an assessment scale. Since there were numerous items, a factorial analysis was carried out to "reduce" the number of items themselves and therefore obtain macro variables. The factorial led to the extraction of 6 factors. On the basis of the factorial points generated, a cluster analysis was then carried out that made it possible to divide the sample into four groups. For each of these clusters a profile was outlined regarding the marketing direction; names were then assigned and calculations were carried out for each one in terms of absolute size % (Figure 6).

The clusters identified may be summarised as follows (Table 1):

- **"Traditionalists" (59%):** To date managers with a marketing direction that can be defined as "traditional" still prevail. They reason in terms of pricing and distribution, they consider intangible elements and brand associations linked to the name and packaging to be drivers of brand equity. For them, virtual platforms still have a very relative importance in the consumer experience of luxury brands.

Figure 5. Conversational markets

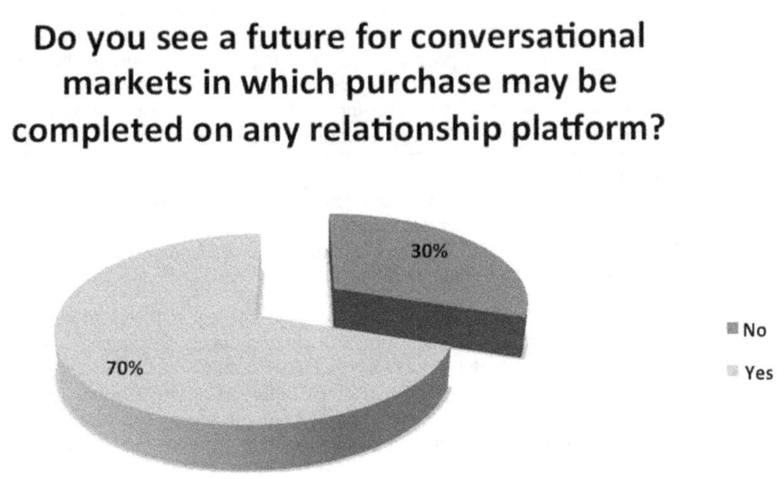

Figure 6. Different clusters and marketing orientation

CLUSTER	NAME	MARKETING ORIENTATION	SIZE	%
1	"Evolved"	Digital marketing oriented	9	**26%**
2	"In the process of evolution"	The point of sale is at the centre of marketing strategies and there is an opening towards the use of social networks.	2	**6%**
3	"Retailers"	The point of sale is at the centre of marketing strategies, but there is not much faith in virtual platforms.	3	**9%**
4	"Traditionalists"	"Old fashioned" marketing	20	**59%**

Table 1. Description of the different clusters

Cluster	Name	Description of Clusters
1	"Evolved"	Members of this cluster consider virtual platforms to be necessary, as they are "interfaces" with consumers who are looking for added value from luxury brands; this additional value is being sought on-line in particular where people are buying things more and more, including impulsively. They believe that there needs to be communication and interaction between stylists and potential buyers, who search online for the criticisms and opinions of other internet users before approaching a brand. The marketing strategies do not have to concern either pricing or distribution channels.
2	"In the process of evolution"	Members of this cluster are aware of the fact that the events organised within the point of sale no longer have the effectiveness that they used to have, and for this reason social networks should be exploited much more, without however abandoning the strategic role of the "physical" point of sale. This should all be done with marketing strategies regarding pricing and distribution channels and actions aimed at increasing the intangible value of the brand.
3	"Retailers"	According to members of this cluster virtual platforms are not needed to interface with consumers, who do not look online for added value from luxury brands. Consumers look for quality and despite technological evolution they are not moving away from physical stores, which are becoming a place to interface with the brand. They have a view of marketing that is oriented towards the traditional: elements of the brand such as name, logo, symbols, packaging etc. will always be the most significant drivers. The internet represents just a very small part of the buying experience.
4	"Traditionalists"	Members of this cluster think that marketing strategies should concern pricing and distribution and should be aimed at increasing the brand's intangible value. They have a "traditional" view of marketing: elements of the brand such as name, logo, symbols, packaging etc. will always be the most significant drivers. The internet represents just a very small part of the buying experience.

- **"Evolved" (26%):** They are aware that the relative importance of virtual relationship platforms is fundamental and growing just like consumers' expectations in this area. They believe the dialogue with consumers to be strategic, there is openness towards innovation and the price and distribution levers are not as binding as in the past.
- **"Retailers" (9%):** Members of this cluster are not moving away from physical stores that are considered the main relationship platforms with consumers. They think that virtual platforms have a relative secondary significance com-pared to physical ones.
- **"In the Process of Evolution" (6%):** In brief these are "retailers" that are moving towards being "evolved". Managers who are aware of the natural integration that will occur through platforms, aware of the loss of effectiveness of some traditional activities that are trying to build a route for reviewing the marketing strategy.

1.7 Managerial Implications

The aim of this chapter was to contribute to the field of luxury marketing by expanding the theory with respect to the characteristics and main challenges and opportunities of luxury brand management. In a constantly transforming global economy, where emerging technologies are personalizing the consumer experience dramatically, in real time and on a global level, luxury marketers face complex challenges: how to integrate consumer experience across the physical and virtual environments; how to deal with an increasing demand for personalized experiences, especially on virtual platforms and finally setting brand strategies and building the right capabilities internally.

Moreover, the unique and constant growth of the luxury sector in the last twenty five years together with the globalization of luxury brands through retail expansion, together with the digitalization of the world (e.g. the explosion of social media and the increase in e-commerce), in fact, has also led to a series of business issues that luxury managers have never experienced before.

This study is just the first step in an area where the need for research contributions, especially from a multidisciplinary perspective, is growing constantly.

What's next? Based on the results of this analysis we can imagine a different scenario with several managerial implications, in particular:

- Integration among different channels will occur and virtual relationship platforms will become the essential; in particular, the opportunity to buy will be provided in a fluid way through all the main virtual relationship platforms, e-shops and including social networks.
- Physical relationship platforms will be spaces in which technology will begin to play a bigger role and will ensure experiences that are consistent with virtual ones. It is likely that luxury centers with multi-brand shops will have greater importance and flagship stores will have a role that is increasingly linked to communication and strengthening of the positioning of the brand. This confirms the strategy of several global brands, like Nike for example, that doesn't have mono-brand stores but flagships in key location worldwide. These flagships are used as communication tools, places where it is possible to experience the brand and leverage all the marketing activities.
- Airports that are growing in terms of purchases could be examples of physical platforms where the use of virtual platforms can be improved in order to offer a more personalized experience and increase customer service on a global level. This could be an interesting situation: luxury consumers may be will be attracted by an "emotional" shopping experience that allow them to order or

to buy the product inside the airport and to receive it directly at home or at another destination. This could be done simply by integrated e-commerce within the point of sales inside the different airports.

- The management of big data in order to offer personalized experiences will become crucial, as will the creation of technological platforms through which a fluid experience and consistency of the brand on a global scale, brand awareness and brand discovery can be ensured.
- In addition, virtual relationship platforms will be places where loyalty with customers can be improved by offering them a private place in which unique and interesting content can converge. Moreover these places can fulfill the need for a two-way but "exclusive" relationship with the brand that consumers consider fundamental.
- Strategies for interactions across the consumer experience journey will be defined and implemented, and for each stage the role and new parameters for measuring the performance will be defined.
- To deliver these new integrated experiences on virtual and physical platforms, luxury managers will rethink the role and structure of the marketing organization and especially how it interacts with other functions.
- Matching investment decisions and priorities with marketing strategies will be given priority by considering both platforms together and also based on new skills that will be developed internally and new processes especially for the use of virtual platforms across the entire consumer experience.

1.8 Research Limits

The study conducted and presented in this research has the following limitations: it refers to the Italian market which, despite being one of the main markets in terms of importance (number of players and market share), provides a specific view, that is only partially representative; the managers' questionnaire could be expanded, for example, by widening the sample.

This study could be extended both in a marketing and retail environment. In addition it would be desirable to widen the study to other disciplines, in particular:

- From a strategic management point of view in order to understand to what extent the role and distribution of virtual platforms may impact on luxury brands' business models and their sustainability over time, in particular by analyzing the predicted growth in emerging countries.
- From a retail management to explore how traditional point-of-sales can be integrated with digital platforms to offer a consistent omni-channel experience.
- From the point of view of corporate communication a series of questions are raised linked to the integration of virtual relationship platforms in internal and external communication activities and how the theory and models linked to the management of stakeholders can vary by taking these developments into account.

The objective, in a general sense, is also to encourage other researchers to use this research as a stimulus to widen knowledge and contribute to the growth of the discipline linked to the marketing management of luxury brands, especially with regard to the use of virtual relationship platforms and their natural integration with the "physical" world in the consumer experience of luxury brand.

1.9 Summary

Luxury brand managers are aware that they are living through a period of fundamental change, in which new skills, new marketing tools and above all a different marketing approach are required, where each relationship platform has to be reconsidered from a strategic point of view. The natural integration of physical and virtual platforms is under way and the factors that are helping this phenomenon are, from the point of view of luxury managers, especially those linked to technological development, which requires new tools to be adopted. Therefore, luxury companies are driven, in their innovation processes, mainly by exogenic factors (new technologies, in particular) and by endogenic factors (the need to adopt marketing strategies that require more effective tools, for example). This process is generating quite a bit of internal resistance; the loss of control and the opening up to direct communication with consumers through virtual platforms is seen as a necessity and not necessarily as an opportunity. Therefore, the idea is to try and replicate experiences, while protecting the luxury brand's dimensions as far as possible, trying to offer content that reinforces brand awareness without going beyond that.

On the other hand virtual relationship platforms are now used by the majority of luxury brands (social networks in particular), which consider them to be a natural extension of physical platforms, without in any case having a precise role in the construction of a relational marketing strategy with consumers. In building these platforms the objective is to partially replicate the "offline" experience, without necessarily considering the behavior of consumers online and in particular the interaction opportunities offered by new technologies.

To summarize the change is occurring in a very conservative way and at a primary level, despite the fact that the majority of marketing managers interviewed are convinced that relationship platforms are having increasing influence in the brand awareness and brand discovery stages and that consumers tend increasingly to want to buy on any of the virtual relationship platforms. So, what are the obstacles to change? Two endogenic factors are considered the main obstacles: the need to reallocate resources and the consequent need to review marketing processes within the company. What stage is this change at? If we consider the managers interviewed, who operate within the Italian market, the cluster analysis carried out reveals that 59% still remain "traditionalists" in their approach to marketing; they are quite open towards virtual platforms but their decisions are driven by traditional logics. However, on the other hand 26% of managers demonstrated that they have an "Evolved" attitude, which is totally digital-marketing oriented. They consider virtual platforms fundamental for growth and they are open to innovation that may also lead to dialogue, greater interaction and co-creation with consumers. In their opinion the traditional levers will continue to be important but it is the fusion between the physical and the virtual that is the only way of meeting the consumers' expectations over time. 6% of managers are "in the process of evolution", they see physical relationship platforms as essential but they are open to a wider use in the various stages of the luxury brand consumer experience, especially in the light of a loss of effectiveness that they highlighted with regard to traditional marketing activities. However, the remaining 9%, the "Retailers", still consider the role of physical platforms to be essential and believe that virtual ones will continue to be secondary even in the next few years.

Therefore, it is possible to assert, in response to the specific question, that the relative importance of relationship platforms is increasing and the process of integration is under way with implications that have an impact on the entire organization.

REFERENCES

Bauer M., Von Wallpach S. & Hemetsberger A. (2011). "My little luxury": A consumer-centred, experiential view. *Journal of Marketing Research and Management, 1.*

Brown, J., Broderick, A., & Lee, N. (2007). Word of mouth communication within online communities: Conceptualizing the online social network. *Journal of Interactive Marketing, 21*(3), 2–20. doi:10.1002/dir.20082

Cova, B., & Dalli, D. (2009). Working consumers: The next step in marketing theory. *Marketing Theory, 9*(3), 315–339. doi:10.1177/1470593109338144

Cova, B., & Remy, E. (2007). I Feel Good: Who Needs the Market? – Struggling and Having Fun with Consumer-driven Experiences. In Consuming Experiences. Oxon, UK: Routledge.

Dall'Olmo Riley, F., & Lacroix, C. (2003). Luxury branding on the Internet: Lost opportunity or impossibility? *Marketing Intelligence & Planning, 21*(2), 96–104. doi:10.1108/02634500310465407

Deighton, J., & Kornfeld, L. (2009). Interactivity's Unanticipated Consequences for Markets and Marketing. *Journal of Interactive Marketing, 23*(1), 2–12. doi:10.1016/j.intmar.2008.10.001

eMarketer. (2012). Consumers' Expectations High for Luxury Brands on Mobile. *eMarketer*. Available at: www.emarketer.com

eMarketer. (2013). Luxury Marketers Investing More in Digital. *eMarketer.* Available at: www.emarketer.com

Fionda, A. M., & Moore, C. M. (2008). The anatomy of the luxury fashion brand. *Journal of Brand Management, 16*(5/6), 347–363.

Grau, J. (2010). Affluent Shoppers and Luxury Brand Retailers Online. *eMarketer*. Available at: www.emarketer.com

Heinonen, K., & Michelsson, T. (2010). The use of digital channels to create customer relationships. *International Journal of Internet Marketing and Advertising, 6*(1), 30430. doi:10.1504/IJIMA.2010.030430

Kapferer, J. N., & Bastien, V. (2009). *The Luxury Strategy: Break the Rules of Marketing to Build Luxury Brands*. Philadelphia: Kogan Page Limited.

Kapferer, J. N., & Bastien, V. (2011). *Luxury Strategy: sovvertire le regole del marketing per costruire veri brand di lusso*. Milano: Franco Angeli.

Kaplan, A. M., & Haenlein, M. (2010). Users of the World, Unite! The Challenges And Opportunities of Social Media. *Business Horizons, 53*(1), 59–68. doi:10.1016/j.bushor.2009.09.003

Keller, K. L. (2003). Understanding Brands, branding, and Brand Equity. *Journal of Interactive Marketing, 5*(1), 7–20. doi:10.1057/palgrave.im.4340213

Keller, K. L. (2009). Managing the growth tradeoff: Challenges and Opportunities in Luxury Branding. *Journal of Brand Management, 16*(5/6), 290–301. doi:10.1057/bm.2008.47

Keller, K. L. (2010). Brand Equity Management in a Multichannel, Multimedia Retail Environment. *Journal of Interactive Marketing*, *24*(2/5), 58–70. doi:10.1016/j.intmar.2010.03.001

Kotler, P., Kartajaya, H., & Setiawan, I. (2010). *Marketing 3.0*. John Wiley & Sons. doi:10.1002/9781118257883

Lent, R. (2009). *Selling Luxury: Connect with Affluent Customers, Create Unique Experiences Through Impeccable Service and Close Sale*. John Wiley & Sons.

Luxury Goods Worldwide Market Study. (2011). Bain & Cuneo. Available at: www.bain.com

Martin, K., & Todorov, I. (2010). How digital platforms be harnessed in 2010, and how will they change the way people interact with brands? *Journal of Interactive Advertising*, *10*(2), 61–66. doi:10.1080/15252019.2010.10722170

Okazaki, S. (2009). Social influence model and eletronic word of mouth. *International Journal of Advertising*, *28*(3), 439–472. doi:10.2501/S0265048709200692

Okonkwo, U. (2009). Sustaining the luxury brand on the Internet. *Journal of Brand Management*, *16*(5/6), 302–310. doi:10.1057/bm.2009.2

Okonkwo, U. (2009). The luxury brand strategy challenge. *Journal of Brand Management*, *16*(5/6), 287–289. doi:10.1057/bm.2008.53

Okonkwo, U. (2010). *Luxury Online: Styles, Systems, Strategies*. London: Palgrave Macmillan. doi:10.1057/9780230248335

Shankar, V., Inman, J. J., Mantrala, M., Kelley, E., & Rizley, R. (2011, July). Innovations in Shopper Marketing: Current Insights and Future Research Issues. *Journal of Retailing*, *87*(1), S29–S42. doi:10.1016/j.jretai.2011.04.007

Shankar, V., & Malthouse, E. C. (2006). Moving Interactive Marketing Forward. *Journal of Interactive Marketing*, *20*(1), 2–4. doi:10.1002/dir.20057

Shankar, V., Smith, A., & Rangaswamy, A. (2003). Customer satisfaction and loyalty in online and offline environments. *International Journal of Research in Marketing*, *20*(2), 153–175. doi:10.1016/S0167-8116(03)00016-8

Shankar, V., & Yadav, M. S. (2010). Emerging Perspectives on marketing in a Multichannel and Multimedia Retailing Environment. *Journal of Interactive Marketing*, *24*(2), 55–57. doi:10.1016/j.intmar.2010.02.003

Tungate, M. (2009). *Luxury World: The Past, Present and Future of Luxury Brands*. London: Kogan Page Limited.

Tynan, C., McKechnie, S., & Chhuon, C. (2010). Co-creating value for luxury brands. *Journal of Business Research*, *63*(11), 1156–1163. doi:10.1016/j.jbusres.2009.10.012

United Nations. (2000). World Population Prospects. *United Nations*. Available at: www.un.org

Verhoef, P. C., Lemon, K. N., Parasuraman, A., Roggeveen, A., Tsiros, M., & Schlesinger, L. A. (2009). Customer Experience Creation: Determinats, Dynamics and Management Strategies. *Journal of Retailing*, *85*(1), 41–41. doi:10.1016/j.jretai.2008.11.001

Vickers, J. S., & Renand, F. (2003). The Marketing of Luxury Goods: An exploratory study - three conceptual dimensions. *The Marketing Review*, *3/4*(4), 459–478. doi:10.1362/146934703771910071

Voller C. & Premo K. (2012). Scaling Up Social Media. *Strategy + Business, 68*, 16-18.

Wright Lee, M. (2011). Fashion Brands Seek New Technologies. *Mashable the Social Media Guide*. Available at: www.mashable.com

Wright Lee, M. (2011). Luxury Brands Seek Social Media Channel Integration. *Mashable the Social Media Guide*. Available at: www.mashable.com

Chapter 8
Strategies for Luxury Fashion Brands' Targeting the Young Audience:
How to Link Celebrity Endorsements and Brand Extensions with Social Media

Carmen Moreno-Gavara
Independent Researcher, USA

Ana Jiménez-Zarco
Open University of Catalunya, Spain

ABSTRACT

The purpose of this chapter is to analyse luxury fashion brands' interactions with consumers, especially on social media. In this sense, we firstly propose a hypothesis relative to how luxury fashion brands can use celebrities (in general, and particularly music and TV idols) and social media to influence on young consumer behaviour. Lately, we try to response this question through a case study based on one of the most South Korean luxury fashion brands. Using members of social media has been a constant in brand strategy. Especially when targeting the young audience. They big consumers and fans of music and audio-visual entertainment products, show a high level of loyalty. This leads them to copy the behaviour and consumption of the same products and brands of their idols. They are big users of social media and the Internet, where they express their feelings, experiences and opinions about their music idols as well as the brands and products they use. This being the case, technology offers empowerment to young people. This allows them not only access to more information but allows the possibility to create their own new content. Thus both roles are important regarding branding. We can use the example of how Korean luxury fashion brands and how they use young music idols to establish a strong emotional relationship with their consumers. They do this by increasing their participation and involvement with their brands in social networks.

DOI: 10.4018/978-1-4666-9958-8.ch008

1. INTRODUCTION

The use of social media members has been a constant in brand strategy. Through a double association and transfer process between the brand and the person -that prescribes a product-, it is possible to create a strong link between them. This link is really important to consumers, especially during image formation. If they consider how the member fits in with the brand, the brand image will incorporate member associations (Chan et al, 2013).

This phenomenon is particularly relevant for brands targeting the young audience. Teenagers constitute a segment of consumers that are very attractive to companies. Teenagers and young people have been an important consumer demographic ever since. According to Akcay (2012), the total amount of money spent by or for teenage consumers is about be $208.7 billion per year. Young people also make such valuable consumers because they influence the purchasing decisions of their friends and family. From a marketing point of view, they are highly influenced by the latest social trends. They are especially, big consumers of music and audio visual entertainment products (music bands, and TV series). As fans, they show a high level of loyalty that leads them to copy the behaviours and consume the same products and brands of their idols. Also, they are big users of social media, where they express their feelings experience and opinions about their music idols and the brand and products they use.

The technology offers empowerment to young people that allow them to play one of two roles: apostle or terrorist. If the brand is able to choose the correct member type it will be able to get young people to associate the brand with their music idol. The idol becomes part of the *universe of the brand.* A strong connection between the young-brand-idol is created. This brand-idol connection gets young people to get involved emotionally with the brand, and act as apostles, and offer favourable opinions about the brand.

Considering the last ideas, this book chapter proposes to analyse how Bean Pole, a luxury south Korean fashion brand, uses k-music idols with a double objective: firstly, by creating a strong relationship between the brand and the consumers, taking advantage of the admiration that young feel for their musical idols. And secondly, by using young people as apostles of the brand, in getting them to use social media as a channel in which to express favourable opinions and experiences about the brand

The chapter is divided into two different sections. The first one reviews the theoretical framework describing how brands can adopt traditional strategies (such as the use of members) to a social media channels, and how social media users can adopt a double role relative to brand: as apostle or terrorist. The second section presents the case of the Bean Pole, a South Korean luxury fashion brand that uses k-music idols to promote their brand, and establish a relationship between the brand and young people. The objective is two-fold: first to create an emotional relationship between the brand and the consumer, and then to use social media as channel to explain positive opinions and experiences about Bean Pole.

2. LUXURY FASHION BRAND STRATEGIES: THE ORIGIN USED AS THE BASIS FOR CREATING A MARKETING POSITION.

The market for luxury fashion is turbulent and dynamic. This means that there is not a clearly defined approach that luxury fashion companies can adopt to attain a sustainable competitive position.

2.1. Fashion Marketing Positioning

The growth of premium fashion brands has fuelled a debate as to the true nature of luxury. The development of luxury fashion brands challenges these conventional views and the nature of luxury. Luxury products are timeless and classic, whereas fashion is ephemeral and transient. Nonetheless, as Jackson (2004) noted there is a 'strong association between the notions of fashion and luxury'. Some luxury brands have become 'fashionable' in people's mind because of their product diversification (Chanel, Yves Saint Laurent). Moreover, 'Contemporary designers reinforce the fashion association' (Jackson, 2004): Tom Ford and Alexander Mac Queen 'provide creative direction' for Gucci, John Galliano and Marc Jacobs for LVMH. Jackson (2004) adds: 'In essence luxury brands have employed high-profile fashion designers to boost the allure of their products at a time in history when more consumers have been able to afford to buy luxury products.' This perspective is reinforced by Baudrillard (1996) who suggests that fashion brands are an essential aspect of the 'cultural capital' of consumers. They reflect and reinforce a sense of identity and allow for the display of 'conspicuous consumption'.

In the field of luxury fashion, the role of the designer can gain iconic status. The design signature of Versace, Alexander McQueen, Tommy Hilfilger, Giorgio Armani, and others can override the importance of other qualities, such as country of origin. Their design signature permeates into other related activities, like perfume, cosmetics, interiors and household products, hotels, restaurants and so on. Internationally renowned fashion designers, such as John Galliano and Marc Jacobs provide a creative direction for the 'grand maison' for LMVH and also produce ready-to-wear collections under their own names. These collections court global media attention through fashion shows in New York, Milan, Paris and London. Galliano has responsibility, not only for fashion of Christian Dior, but for the whole brand, including store design, presentation and advertising. Brand owners, such as Gucci, 'tie-in' notable designers (e.g. Tom Ford and Alexander McQueen) provide direction across a range of their categories and brands. In other words, the marketing and brand development has a creative direction and is closely connected with design. Indeed, the Annual Report of 1999 states that: 'design and product development are the core of Gucci's success and interact with other activities. We consistently strive to maintain a clear brand image' (cited in Moore and Birtwistle, 2005). The luxury fashion brand becomes a lifestyle statement that permeates across other aspects than apparel. Designers become international celebrities whose personal life is the subject of glossy magazines. Their friends, associates and other celebrities are shown in photographs in the UK national press. An example would be Madonna and Stella McCartney attending a function together. Celebrity endorsement is a form of viral marketing and generates international media interest and awareness.

The positioning of the products, namely the luxury brand fashion products which are designed and aimed at upmarket customers in the form of differentiated products may have several forms and varieties. This is to say that the luxury brand fashion products can be positioned in the market based on the usage or function of the product, price of the product, being a substitute product and much more.

According to Callen (2009) luxury brand fashion products may be positioned in the market as substitute products. This is to say that even if there is already a product which is targeting the same upmarket segment; the new substitute product may be offered to add some twists and changes to the product that may also create another niche market within the concentrated or niche market. Even though this market segment tends to be smaller than the original market segment, it still can be profitable and worth positioning by luxury brand fashion products as the prices for the products will be too high compared to other market segments.

Alternatively, Hackley (2009) states that the price may be another focus when positioning the luxury brand fashion products. In the high street clothing industry, the top designer brands usually create their designs first, which is usually copied and launched to the market by other mid-to-low market focusing companies. However, in some cases, a company in the mid-to-low market may launch a product that may trigger the luxury brand fashion company to launch a similar product to the upmarket as an exclusive and unique product as some customers are willing to pay extra for the extra add-ons on the products. The author calls this as copying from midmarket and introducing it to the upmarket that usually have been successful in the high street fashion sector and it is also a common practice.

Klein (2007) explains the "price" based positioning of the luxury brand fashion products by giving an example of focusing on the designers and colors which are usually focused by Laura Ashley's English country patterns and United Colors of Benetton's against an example of Gap 's understated American casual wear that all provide for brand differentiation. However, Doyle (2008) shows that registering a clear brand in the retail industry, particularly luxury brand fashion sector is becoming increasingly difficult and challenging for the companies in the sector. This is to say that the ever increasing competition, media costs, escalation and negotiation between the designers, retailers such as high street giants add extra complexity in the luxury brand fashion products to be positioned accurately and appropriately. However, the theorists also suggest that for luxury brand fashion products to maintain their brand and its identity is very crucial for their survival both in the short and long terms.

Therefore, Luck (2008) states that entering into the luxury brand fashion products sector is becoming more and more complicated given the fact that the market for this products in certain regions is becoming saturated. He mentions about developed countries as already saturated markets for the purpose of positioning luxury brand fashion products as this requires high costs due to high entry barriers into the market. Lockstorm (2007) states that rather than focusing on the developed countries, new market entrants in the luxury brand fashion products are focusing on the developing countries such as China, Malaysia, South Korea in the Asian market which is considered to be very promising for this industry companies. This is to say that the demand for luxury brand fashion products are increasing rapidly due to the improving living standards and increasing consumer spending in the Asian markets which is a next market focus for majority well-established fashion products as well as new market entrants into this industry.

According to Gilbert (2003) the company focusing on positioning their brand in the market has to focus on the following equation:

Brand differentiation X Brand segmentation=Brand position

Even if this equation is a common way of differentiating the product first from other hundreds of product lines in the market and then placing it in the right market segment after identification which leads to a brand positioning, it still may have several issues if the brand is not differentiated properly or the market segment identified is not appropriate.

Baker (2007) states; that when positioning the brand, the company has to identify the gap in the market. Then then will be targeted as a potential market segment for the company. However, in the case of luxury brand fashion products, companies usually focus on the color and design and if it is traditional or modern focused. Further consideration is the size from zero to extra-large and names. This is to say that some companies succeed in positioning their products and brands due to their unique color which can be seen in the case of United Color of Benetton's and Burberry which achieved its successful positioning due the cloth used in making its products.

Therefore, it can be said that when positioning the luxury brand fashion products, the companies have to identify the market segment which is saturated and not very competitive and differentiate their brands in order to fit into the gap in the market segment which leads to effective and successful brand positioning for the companies.

2.2. Western Luxury Brands vs. Local Luxury Brands

Even though the debate between global vs. local brand has been intense and well-documented, there are still some important pending questions regarding the specific impact of perceived global factor on each source of brand equity. This study aims to understand how global brands are in a distinct position to affect loyalty drivers. The analysis is set in three major markets of US, EU and Korea. Evidence includes important attitude and behavioral differences among the consumers in these markets. Results show that consumers prefer global brands to local alternatives in some of the main loyalty drivers, but not in all of them.

Both scholars and practitioners agree the current trend towards globalization is real and accelerating. Consistent with this trend, many companies have changed their strategy from a multi-domestic marketing approach to a focus on global brands. The globalization imperative has been present for more than twenty years (after Levitt's seminal article in 1983), but not many brands can be called truly global. Additionally, in most brand value rankings published by research agencies at the national level, the top positions feature a mixture of global and local brands.

The phenomenon of globalization is explained by several factors. These include the expansion of global media, critical advances in telecommunications (Internet being its best representative), increased feasibility in foreign travel and international investments. All these forces have promoted an increased similarity in lifestyles across the world, giving the emergence of a "global consumer culture" (Alden et al, 1999). On the contrary, other scholars argue that local cultures are still a very powerful force shaping consumers' preferences and still others identify a tendency in consumers to "hybridize" (Holton, 2000), "globalize" (Ritzer and Jurgenson2010)3) or "creolize" as a way to blend global and indigenous cultural forces.

2.2.1. What Is a Global Brand?

There are no formal definitions in the scholarly literature for global brands, but previous studies have defined global as the multimarket reach of products that are perceived as the same brands worldwide by consumers (Johansson and Onkainen, 2005). As for practitioners, the AC Nielsen 2001 study of global brands provided a clear definition considering a brand as global if present in the four major regions of the world, with at least 5 per cent of sales coming from outside the home regions and total revenues of at least $1 billion. According to this definition, the study could identify only 43 brands in the consumer packaged goods industry. From the customer prospective, when a brand is perceived to be marketed in multiple countries it is recognized as global. That perception can be derived from two sources: 1) corporate marketing and communications normally associated with a modern urban lifestyle (Alden et al, 1999); 2) external-based communications such as media exposure, word of mouth or consumers' traveling.

There are important advantages derived from the consumption of global brands, because they are perceived to be more value-added for the consumer, either through better quality (as a function of worldwide acceptance) or by enhancing the consumer's self-perception as being cosmopolitan, sophisticated and modern. Still, in many places, notably Europe, Latin America, and South East Asia, local brands still do well in many fast-moving consumer goods categories. The justification is based on the enhanced ability of these brands to satisfy local needs, hence retaining their local strengths. The global brands that have been dramatically successful mainly stem from the United States of America, Japan or selected European countries. Some authors argue that these brands only "work" because of marketing resources as trade backing from international retailers and massive advertising budgets behind them. However, they may lack the connection to consumers that can sustain a long-term relationship between the consumer and the brand.

Much research analyzing these contrasting forces has been focused on the comparison of Western Societies (especially North America) and Asian countries (Alden et al, 1999, Batra et al, 2000, Alden et al, 2006). However, there is a paucity of research focusing on Latin American consumers. Moreover, most observers tend to assume that Latin America is culturally homogeneous with an outstanding similarity that consumers display in their consumption habits and preferences. This makes these countries the ideal setting for a standardized marketing approach.

2.2.2. The Value of Global Brands for Consumers

Brands play a critical role for consumers in terms of communication and identification. Brands offer a compass to guide them through a purchasing environment typified by too much information. The brand is seen by most consumers as a sign of quality, assisting them to make their purchasing decisions. A brand can also serve as a social business card, expressing membership in a certain group. Premium brands, for instance, can even engender a sense of distinction and prestige. Moreover, in the developed industrial and the newly industrializing countries, brands have actually become part of how people build up their identities and gain fulfillment in their personal lives. Consuming certain brands is also a means to communicate certain values. By opting for particular brands, a consumer demonstrates that he or she embraces particular values; the brand becomes a tool for identity formation.

Brand loyalty is vitally dependent on how the relationship between the brand and the consumer is nurtured and specifically developed. A strong brand brings with it the opportunity to raise the profile of a product and the company that sells it, setting them apart from rivals in the marketplace. That strong brand can also command a price premium for its producer, and can reduce price elasticity, implying a financial stability for the firm (Merino et al, 2006)

As far as global brands is concerned, previous research has concluded that perceived brand globalness is normally associated to brand quality and prestige (Steenkamp et al, 2005), higher esteem (Johansson and Ronkainen, 2005), is having the ability of enhancing the consumer's self-image as being cosmopolitan, sophisticated and modern (Friedman, 1990, Thompson and Tambyah, 1999).

From a cultural point of view, consumers consider global brands to be symbols of cultural ideas (Holt et al, 2004). They use brands to participate in a perceived global identity that they share with other people worldwide. In the process, some of these brands have attained the status of global icons, becoming cultural systems in their own right that speak a universal language.

Despite the previous arguments, local brands still hold important advantages, such as long-standing emotional links that represent a critical proximity to consumer's values, high awareness levels and extensive distribution networks developed through time (Kapferer, 2012)

3. YOUNG PEOPLE AS CONSUMERS: THE INFLUENCE OF YOUNG PEOPLE IDOLS

3.1. Youth People Consumer Process

Adolescence is usually a complex, transitory period that includes rapid biological, social, and cognitive growth. Teens deal with a contradictory ideology; they want to create an individual identity but at the same time, still connect with their own group of friends (Gulland, 2006). In this phase, teenagers are continually learning how to behave appropriately in a new situation or phase of their lives (Steinberg, 1993). Not surprisingly, periods of transition are often accompanied by the need for a variety of products or services to ease the transition (Hartman, Shim, Barber, and O'Brien, 2006).

Not much is known about the spending motivations of this *young group of powerful consumers*, who just a decade ago, were not perceived to be particularly economically important (LaFerle, Edwards, and Lee, 2000). While teens do not earn large salaries, they have more disposable income than adults because most adolescents do not have to pay health insurance, credit card bills, mortgages/rent, supermarket or utilities (Zollo, 1999). Consequently, teens' consumer behaviour gained importance as a research topic due to teenagers' amount of disposable income.

Teens experience role requirements that often require different behaviours. (Hopson and Adams, 1976). According to Moses (2000), teenagers' spending focuses on specific brands that their peers use, sometimes called "the right brands." Teens are shaping their identities, so having the "right" brands is a way to fit into the right group (Moses, 2000). Due to the growing spending power of teenagers, global marketers are trying to understand teenagers' wishes and needs in order to relate to reach this attractive consumer base.

Brand loyalty is widespread in teenagers than in adults and teens often avoid taking risks in appearance-related products given the importance of these products to their perceptions of self (Zollo, 1999).

Branded products are less risky because they are easily recognizable and they serve as a status symbol; this combination makes them a safe choice for teens (Wooten, 2006). Appealing to teenagers is an attractive business strategy because branded product companies hope that teens choose their products as lifetime brands.

Earlier studies explore self as a predictor of a variety of human behaviours, such as motivation, purchase intention, cognition, brand and advertising attitude, (Sirgy, Lee, Johar, & Tidwell, 2008; Tsai, 2006). Adolescents often pass through a stage of identity crisis (Erikson, 1959). Adolescents seek self-identity by acquiring and accumulating selections of consumption objects (Belk, 1988).

Peer pressure may play an important role in a teenager's life, leading to a series of specific behaviours, such as what to eat, how to dress and how to speak. Teens create shared meanings with their friends, so their interpretation of reality is reasonably consistent with that of their peers (Solomon, 1983). Teenagers use their peers to align their values, discussing their personal reflections with friends, while looking for support and mutual understanding (Youniss & Smollar, 1985). Therefore, consumer behaviour research on teens should investigate the influence of peers.

In seeking to explain how teens' view themselves and how the impact of peer pressure affect interest in and attitudes toward luxury brands, consumers' social motivation and materialism are important factors in making purchasing decisions (Heaney et al.,, 2005). In addition, the level of materialism among adolescents is very, high (Roedder-John, 1999). Given that consumers attempt to gain acceptance into social groups through the products that they purchase (Vigneron & Johnson, 2004), findings relating to materialism might explain why the luxury brand market has become increasingly important to teens.

3.2. Fashion Luxury Brands for Young People

Traditionally the market for the luxury brands was considered to be for the ones between the age of 30 and 50 but now younger people are entering the market (Cheong & Phau, 2003). The need for materialism and appearance is not limited to the wealthy consumers but also covers the less-well off young consumers that have a desire for fashion brands. An understanding of consumer attitudes is essential for the marketers to plan their strategy in reaching the target consumers. It is essential for the marketer to understand how consumers think and value a product. There has been a vast increase in the luxury market (Sriviroj, 2007) and attempts are being made to attract the young through different marketing strategies. The young are vulnerable and can easily be attracted by advertising and promotions. They have higher disposable incomes towards spending on luxury. However the attitude of the young towards luxury purchasing is no different than the older adults.

The youth today is not lured by goods that are merely expensive. They want value for money and they purchase luxury goods for self-identity and well-being. Purchasing certain branded luxury goods help them to display their own tastes and values. For some it serves to fulfil the emotional needs where they see luxury as an indulgence of their senses. Luxury goods are premium goods with high quality products, aesthetic design supported by excellent service and purchased by people from the higher income bracket (Cheng, 2006). In the earlier days the term 'luxury' was applied to products that were rare and scarce and available to a small segment of the people (Sriviroj, 2007). The luxury items were out of reach of the ordinary people and considered rare. Today the luxury product market has increased manifold. The young are spontaneously aware of the luxury brands with men focusing on cars and motorbikes and women focus on beauty and food. These reflect the desires and fantasies that are conditioned by the social environment and associations with well-being, comfort, and quality and self- image.

Interpretation of the word 'luxury' depends upon their socio-economic history. The young greatly represent the hedonistic effect in their attitude towards luxury items (Sriviroj, 2007). This implies that they are not influenced by group norms. On the other hand they purchase luxury goods that give them self-fulfillment. They look for exclusive benefits and if products create an emotional value for consumers it represents that the product has been beneficial. The emotional values that the young look for include pleasure, excitement and aesthetic beauty. They indulge in luxury items as it gives them a sense of well-being and self-respect and would also go the extent of using their credit cards for them. They prefer these luxuries against bringing up a child while the elders indulged in luxury only after their basic responsibilities were fulfilled (Hamilton, 2004). The elders seek more than value when considering purchasing a luxury brand. They try to balance the product's tangible and intangible value with price. They assess discretionary purchases as either dispensable or indispensable, based on more deeply held core values (Salzman, 2009). While the young focus on increasing their influence, power and wealth. Elders seek new priorities driven by the fundamentals of human development. The traditional materialistic values are less important for the elders. The elders look for self-actualization in the luxury brand which as per Maslow's hierarchy of needs comes only after all the other needs have been satisfied.

Culture has a strong impact on the purchasing decisions. The young are well aware of the luxury brands in areas like perfumes, clothing, fashion, leather goods, accessories, costume jewelry but not so in tableware. However they are very conscious of modern sports cars and other models of cars that emerge every day. The attitude of the young towards cars has definitely undergone a sea change from the 1980s. Marketing communications used by car companies like BMW and Volvo are largely responsible for creating awareness of these brands among the youth. The young consumers in the 25-34 age range are looking for cars that are more luxurious than entry level. The young adult market has changed from the 1980s because there are now many more non-family households. The young have more disposable income to spend on luxury items. The companies offering cars to the young target advertisements to appeal to the mind-set of the young, something like 'pretty cool' thereby appealing to their lifestyle (Kostecki, 2005). As far as tableware is concerned the attitude of the young has evolved in a different direction than that for cars. Even though household income has risen since the 1980s, and replacement is also fairly frequent, the availability of cheap functional tableware has changed the attitude of the young. The demand for fine crystal is not as it used to be. Young consumers do not perceive such crystal ware as relevant to their lifestyle (Researchandmarkets, 2005). They seek more contemporary products. Besides, they would consider buying tableware only when they have ample resources.

The youth in most countries have become inclined to purchase Italian luxury brands. In Australia, the Italian luxury brand in apparel is considered to be superior to the local Australian brand. Brand name has become important in the luxury market as the status seeking customers are more likely to buy apparel from countries with good brand names. The Italian bard is significantly better on three attributes – quality, fashionableness and brand name (Phau & Leng, 2008). The Italian brands have learned to touch the emotional needs of the target market (Xiao, 2005). They realize that is no longer to be sufficient to be elegant, consistent and effective. Such a self-centred approach does not work anymore. It is now important to know the customer and understand the high-end value proposition. For the young, luxury brands represent their lifestyle and not the income. The young Indian consumer prefers the Italian brands because they have an international high-profile image (Nielsen, 2008). Consumers opt for brand and values – the image that the brand communicates.

A study by Seringhaus (2002) found that luxury brand awareness and purchase is not linked to age, gender, marital status and location of residence. It is more likely to be connected with income, education and occupation. They found that luxury goods are bought for '…what they mean, beyond what they are.' There are three main external effects that influence the purchase of luxury goods. These include the Veblen effect – individuals use product price to display wealth, the snob effect – the item is purchased because of its scarcity and the bandwagon effect – when consumers buy goods because it conforms to a social group (Seringhaus, 2002). Cultural values are significant in determining the luxury system of symbols for young Americans, Asians and Europeans. Wealth display is important for the American consumer culture as they demonstrate their personal affluence through consumption, while Europeans believe that wasteful expenditures diminish the overall quality of life. The Europeans' purchasing habits display a much lesser Veblen effect compared to the Americans while the Asians display the bandwagon effect.

The Eastern culture is based on interpersonal self-concepts which largely depends on the outer self, group decisions, norms, family, relatives and friends (Sriviroj, 2007). The West on the other hand has a foundation of personal self-concepts that relates to the inner http://paramountessays.com5 self and independent decisions. Asians focus on visible possessions like designer labels, expensive cars or jewellery. Cultural differences override the economic prosperity which is also seen in the four cultural dimensions by Hofstede - Power Distance, Uncertainty Avoidance, Masculinity - Femininity and Individualism -

Collectivism. Individual and power distance both increase with economic growth whereas masculinity-femininity is independent of prosperity (Bhosale & Gupta, 2006). The individual – collectivism index is low even in wealthier countries like Japan, Singapore, Hong Kong and South Korea and hence this dimension is independent of economic affluence. The Asian society in general has collectivist values. It is a masculinity driven society where self-control and spirituality continue to exert powerful pressure. For the Europeans, brands are a means of communicating who they are. They recognize that they no longer have one common belief system and hence they seek brands that create a similar vision of life (Christensen). A brand that is self-evident and communicates that life can be difficult and full of challenges but is more appealing to the young in Europe. They want brands that communicate simplicity, purity and harmony. For the Americans, comfort is very important and they prefer brands that represent the "clean cut, all American" way of life (Parker, Hermans & Schaefer, 2004). Self-expression is very important to them. They have more access to credit cards and technology. For them shopping is a social activity. In clothing they give preference to comfort and trendiness while they gave no importance to having same clothing as friends or celebrities. They give lot of importance to fashion specially females.

The buying behaviour of the young has been influenced to a large extent by the marketing campaigns and communications used by the marketers. To attract the young consumer companies usually use talent –celebrity endorsement like movie actors, models, athletes or famous people (Bergeström & Skärfstad, 2004). Young consumers like responding to catwalks and celebrity fashion shows (Newman & Patel, 2004) because a charismatic personality signifies a strong, deep, long-lasting relationship between the consumer and the brand personality (Milas & Mlačić, 2007). Brands have personalities or images, and consumers seek those brands that match their self-image or the image they would like to project to others (Goldsmith, Moore & Beaudoin, 1999). Self-concept is important to the young as self-perceptions motivate behaviour, giving control and direction to human performance (Goldsmith, 2002). The elders on the other hand are less idealistic than they were. They are easily turned off by advertising, stores and shopping malls. They prefer informative-intensive ads that identify a product's benefits rather than image-oriented marketing that targets young consumers (Roberts & Manolis, 2000).

The young consumers are not conformist. They do not want to conform to societal or group norms and are individualistic in their choice, although minor differences can be found in different societies of the world. The young are evolutionary as they give importance to self-concept; the brand must communicate a sense of well-being and self-respect. They are trendy and modern – they want luxury brands that match their lifestyle. They are very conscious of the luxury labels available and they have access to them as the young have higher disposable incomes. What was considered rare and precious has become an object of compulsive buying if it matches the self-image of the young. The buying behaviour of the young has evolved since the 1980s as they go for products like modern cars while objects like tableware does not hold importance. While the elders give importance to self-actualization the young focus on self-concept.

3.3. The Idols Influence on Young People Consumer Behaviour

Celebrity endorsements are among the most successful marketing communication practices used by marketers around the world, especially in breaking message clutter, increasing the credibility and effectiveness of advertisements (Bailey, 2007), enhancing brand recognition (Petty et al., 1983), stimulating positive attitudes towards brands (Kamins, 1989), and finally, increasing sales and profits (Erdoğan,

1999; Choi et al., 2005; Pringle and Binet, 2005). Conveyed through the mass media, celebrities with worldwide popularity are used in celebrity endorsements to overcome the prejudices against messages being advertised. Consumers are likely to build fewer defences against celebrities compared to corporate messages such as advertising, the commercial intentions of which consumers are aware. In contrast, selling products is not seen as the primary aim of celebrity endorsement.

Although being a powerful strategy in marketing communications, in order to reap its benefits, a careful examination and application of celebrity endorsement is required. One of the most important decisions to be made in the planning of this strategy is to choose the right celebrity to be used in the marketing campaign. Defined by McCracken (1989: 310) as "any individual who enjoys public recognition and who uses this recognition on behalf of a consumer product appearing with it in an advertisement." The celebrity endorser plays a key role in the process with her/his attractiveness, popularity, personality, and lifestyle. In consideration of unsuccessful applications of celebrity endorsements which lose millions of dollars, it is necessary to ask which factors contribute most to the effectiveness of this strategy. As a part of this inquiry, considerable academic attention is devoted to defining the characteristics important in explaining the effectiveness of celebrity endorsements.

The effects of celebrities on young people will be explored. One of the main reasons for selecting the young segment is the dominant idea in the marketing literature that the young is a prototypical global segment, having similar practices and desires (Kjeldgaard and Askegaard, 2006). In their search for new alternatives to create their identities, the young serve as social agents through which global products and practices can enter into the local context. However, they also serve as agents of globalization (Thompson and Arsel, 2004) by adapting these practices according to their own cultural norms. Youth therefore act as agents in the process of globalization. Insight into this process may be provided by examining the different effects of local and global celebrities on young people.

In addition, as stated by McCracken (1989), passing through a role change and identity construction process, young people are influenced by celebrities more than other segments of society. Greene and Adams-Price (1990) say that in the transition from childhood to adulthood, young people try to disengage from parental authority in order to construct and define their own identities and lifestyles. Yet, this self-determined construction of the adult identity needs to be socially acceptable as well. This complex process directs young adolescents to search for references within their social environment, namely to peer groups to explore different traits to be adopted. In addition, according to Miles et al. (1998), in a world of weakening bonds between family members and increasing alienation, young people are drawn to peers, and in order to be socially acceptable and likable, they try to conform to the general expectations of peers in terms of consumption preferences. As well as peer groups, celebrities also play a similar role in the identity construction process of young people as individuals who have already constructed their identities successfully (Greene and Adams-Price, 1990; Erdoğan, 1999). Celebrities are an especially important medium in inspiring consumers' idealized images of self, presenting images of seduction for the regular people to esteem and to follow (e.g. Lipotevsky, 1987). The idealized images of the celebrities communicate the traits to be adopted and guide the way to the idealized self in the process of identity construction.

In a similar vein, Boon and Lomore (2001) state that as well as families and peers, young people form secondary attachments to celebrities portrayed in the mass media. It is argued that these attachments play a crucial role in the transition to adulthood through the development of an adult identity. Also the celebrities guide this process through their behaviours, attitudes, and values, and their degree of influence depends on the degree of intimacy of the secondary attachment (Caughey, 1978).

Considering the last ideas we propose the next hypothesis:

H1: Luxury fashion brands use celebrities to engage young audience with the brand.

From a marketing point of view, and considering the impact of celebrity endorsement on the young generation, consumption behaviour in constructing their identities, this study aims to explore the relative favourability of different traits of global and local celebrities in light of the cultural influences.

4. INTERNET AND SOCIAL NETWORKS IN FASHION IN FASHION LUXURY BRANDS MARKETING STRATEGIES

In last sections we have shown how luxury fashion brands use celebrities as way to engage young audience with a brand. Now, we analyse how Internet and social networks are used to increase and strong the role that young people idols' have on consumer-brand relationship.

Note that young audience are big users of social media and the Internet, where they express their feelings, experiences and opinions about their music idols as well as the brands and products they use. This being the case, technology offers empowerment to young people. This allows them not only access to more information but allows the possibility to create their own new content. Thus both roles are important regarding branding.

4.1. Internet and Social Networks in Fashion Luxury Brand Strategies

The fashion context is deemed to be particularly revealing when studying social media usage, as fashion itself is known to spread through network effects (Easley & Kleinberg, 2010). One reason why fashion exists is that it is 'necessarily public . . . a secret fashion is a contradiction in terms' (Reynolds, 1968, p. 44). Not only do fashion trends follow a diffusion curve, but they are also adapted throughout their lifecycle to fit in better with the users' norms, values, and preferences. In fact, it can be argued that trends are co-created by consumers who not only perpetuate but also adapt them along the way. Such network effects mean that when a trend is adopted successfully by a number of people, it impacts the perceived value of the product for another user, in a positive or negative way, depending on the reference point. Fashion is, therefore, a powerful social symbol used to create and communicate personal as well as group identities (Ahuvia, 2005). Kamineni (2005) posits that 'people express themselves through consumption in a myriad of ways, and in this context, product and brands have the ability to communicate messages to others. In that product styles determine how consumers who own a particular product are perceived by others. This has profound implications for peer-to-peer communications about fashion, where users can choose what, when, and with whom they decide to share information, as this in turn impacts their socially perceived identity.

Fashion has been classified as high involvement, which refers to products that are either expensive, rarely bought, linked to personal identity, or carry high risks (social or otherwise). It has been observed that high-involvement products attract a significant amount of conversations online (Hennig-Thurau., 2004). One reason for this high incidence of fashion chatter may lie in the complexity in evaluating its value, particularly its social value. To counteract this, social media users often share style-related information with their peers, with the expectations of receiving feedback on their stylistic choices (Li et al.,

2012). The representation of the fashioned self or self-selected styles has become a critical component of the social web, and opened up a whole new channel to amplify one's fashion preferences and engage with others/brands. The fact that the flow of new fashion or styling choices is never-ending, with the kaleidoscope of products and trends (be it recycled) constantly changing, means there is always a potential element of surprise in user-generated fashion messages. Correspondingly, surprise and newness have been cited as necessary message characteristics for maintaining the interest of a social audience (Knox, 2012).

Fashion brands, especially those in the luxury sector, have also been engaging with viral marketing content, in particular brand-sponsored videos, with the hope Downloaded by [107.203.152.44] at 13:10 10 November 2014 564 Journal of Marketing Management, Volume 29 of attracting the attention of visual influencers. Online pin boards, such as Pinterest, and other visual platforms have become important marketing channels for brands, as they benefit from the network effects of those influencers. Visual content has become, in some cases, its own luxury product (Kondrashova, 2012) and a powerful mode of conveying the brands' desired image. Focusing on the motivations to engage in fashion brand-related eWOM, this research can help fashion brands to understand better how to influence peer-to-peer communications through social media without the use of traditional advertising techniques.

4.2. The Role of Social Networks in Young People Consumer Behaviour

The teenage market has become a very important consumer segment in the U.S. and global markets (Kotler and Keller, 2011). The teenage population is growing at twice the rate of the overall U.S. population. The number of American teenagers is over 32 million (Cohen, 2009). Globally, the number of teenagers is 1.3 billion (Keegan and Green, 2013).

Teenagers spend their free time doing a variety of activities including shopping online, using social media, technology, listening to *music,* and participating in community activities, sports and watching TV. They *appreciate current fashion,* art, cultural and environmental efforts (Carter, 2011). The basic rules for marketing to teenagers are: to be authentic, honest, create a buzz about the company's product, offer cool products, keep your message simple, don't talk down to them, learn their language, offer something that they can use, engage with and solicit feedback from teenage customers (Schiff, 2007; Goodstein, 2007). Teens are realistic and quick to adopt new trends, and both male and female teenagers spend most of their money on clothes (D'Souza, 2010). Their aspirations are nearly identical: they want to graduate from high school, go to and graduate from college. Teenagers look toward to the future, are ambitious, opinionated, influential, and know more about technology than previous generations (Chaet, 2012). They spend more time on the internet, playing video games, *social networking* and surfing the web.

4.2.1. Teenagers Have Significant Buying Power

The average annual income of a 15-17 year old is $4,023; and total U.S. spending on products bought by and for teens is $208.7 Billion (Davis, 2011; D'Souza, 2010; http://statisticbrain.com). Marketers should understand teen purchasing behavior and what influences their purchasing decisions. Teens often have more discretionary income than adults who have mortgages, car payments and other necessary spending. Older teens spend their own money on clothes, jewelry, sports, entertainment, food, health and beauty products for a total $91.1 billion spent in 2011.The annual amount of money families spend on teens for food, apparel, personal-care items, and entertainment is $117.6 billion (http://statisticbrain.com). Teen's spending money is accumulated through paying jobs, allowances, or monetary gifts.

Most teens say that the internet has changed the way they spend their free time and they have integrated technology into their lives (Helmrich, 2004). One out of three view the internet as their primary source of entertainment and 90% use a computer either at home or at school. Most teenagers shop in shopping malls/centers, discount stores, drugstores, electronic stores and department stores (Davis, 2011). According to Nielsen, teenagers average daily media consumption is widely different from any other group of consumers. They spend an average 200 minutes watching television, 52 minutes on a computer,25 minutes playing video games and even more time talking on the phone and exchanging about 96 text messages per day. Marketers reach teenagers in many different ways, mostly through electronic mass media such as: TV, radio, magazines and product placement (Davis, 2011; Carter, 2011).

4.2.2. Social Network and Consumer Behavior

Marketers across the globe are recognizing the importance of understanding consumer behavior as a key element in ensuring success (Sheth and Mittal, 2004). As consumers are moving away from traditional media to new media platforms such as social media, they have become more demanding, more time driven, more information and content intensive and highly individualistic (Sheth and Mittal, 2004).This demanding and changing nature of consumer preferences and tastes have created significant changes in consumer purchasing and decision making as social media platforms facilitate purchase transactions, information seeking and decision making (Raaij, 1998 cited in Ivanauskas, 2009). Constantinides and Fountain (2008 cited in Ivanauskas, 2009) asserted that consumer preferences and decisions are fundamentally formed and based on inputs provided by parties beyond the power of "online" marketers such as friends and family using social media platforms. Users of social media platforms have the ability to exercise great influence over other consumer purchasing patterns and behavior without having any direct contact with them.

The massive growth in user generated "content online", is attributed largely to the emergence of social media, which has resulted in an informational power shift from marketers to consumers. Consumers are now producing and consuming information as they wish (Ritzer and Jurgenson, 2010). For instance, writing blogs have increased from 28 to 44%, creating a social network page has shown an increase from 27.3 to 57.5% and uploading a video clips has increased from 10 to 42% which has produced hundreds of millions of content creators (McCANN, 2008). These developments combined with the declining costs of computing and broadband have enabled a global revolution in consumer publishing which has become a new standard of social media (Treadaway and Smith, 2010). This poses several challenges for marketers as they currently have less control and authority over what information is produced and consumed. With this growth in user generated content, it is believed that "presumption" will increase, which as opposed to earlier forms of capitalism, involves both production and consumption (Ritzer and Jurgenson, 2010). According to Humphreys and Grayson (2008, as cited by Ritz and Jurgenson, 2010), the idea behind "presumption" is to afford "prosumers" autonomy rather than impose control. Thus prosumption supports marketers adopting a stand back approach where there is less involvement with "prosumers", as "prosumers" produce and consume content accordingly. According to Thrift (2005) social media platforms demonstrate the increasingly active role that consumers on these networks are expected to take within these social media platforms. Consumers on these social media platforms are thus responsible for producing commodities that other users are drawn into, such as profiles on Facebook or status updates on Twitter. Hence marketers of brands no longer hold the same type of control over how they communicated as they once did (Stileman, 2009).

The vast majority (80%) of the respondents indicated that social media browsing influenced their purchasing behavior, with 43% indicating that they had purchased items through social media over eight times, 23% purchased items between five to eight times, 10% purchased items between two to four times and, only 4% indicated having purchased once. The aforementioned is supported by research conducted by Universal McCANN (2009) who also reported that social media browsing influences the purchasing behavior of consumers.

Considering the last ideas, we propose the next hypothesis

H2: Luxury fashion brands use social media as a tool to enhance celebrities' endorsement

With the aim of confirming the two hypothesis proposed in the next section we analyse the Bean Pole case study. One of the most famous Korean luxury fashion brands addressed to young consumers.

5. THE BEAN POLE CASE: INNOVATION VS. TRADITION IN KOREAN FASHION LUXURY BRANDS

Over the last decade, Korea has emerged as an influencer for luxury items and lifestyle experiences. Korean style impacts on consumers across Asia Pacific, and foreign luxury fashion brands recognize the benefits to invest in Korea.

Since the last decade Korea has emerged as a new center for the production of transnational pop culture. As a cultural exporter, Korea's success is often attributed to its fashion. Cultural and entertainment products are high quality and incorporate Western elements while never losing its edge through its re-creation of traditional Korean values and cultural identity. Inter-Asian cultural affinity and a lower cultural barrier among Asians to relate to its content also play a significant role in the proliferation of Korean culture overseas.

Local luxury fashion brands, K-pop, television dramas, and movies have gained phenomenal popularity, becoming the newest engine for expanding the country's cultural exports and an integral part of Korea's national image. The booming presence and enjoyment of Korean popular culture has also transformed into preference for other Korean products and lifestyles alike, leading to an increase in Korean product sales in the national and international markets.

In this section will analyse how Korean luxury fashion brands make use of these above items in developing their marketing strategies. And how web 2.0 supports and reinforces the results obtained.

5.1. Dynamics of Korean Fashion Market: Cheil Industry Inc.

South Korea has a market economy which ranks 15th in the world by nominal GDP and 12th by purchasing power parity (PPP), identifying it as one of the G-20 major economies (Chin, 2010). It is a high-income developed country, with an emerging economy,[5]and is a member of OECD. South Korea is one of the Asian Tigers, and is the only developed country so far to have been included in the group of Next Eleven countries.

Korean consumers have long been familiar with Western cultures through travel abroad and mass communications. Korea is a trend-conscious culture in which many foreign fashion brands either entered or re-entered the market after the economic crisis of the 1990s. Now, the Korean fashion marketplace is characterized by two market niches; (a) primarily domestically-produced, inexpensive apparel lines and (b) high-end collections dominated by designer brands imported mostly from the U.S. and Europe (Sung, 2010).

Recently apparel retail industry has shown strong rates of growth in South Korea, increasing its attractiveness to new entrants from foreign retailers. While some retailers selling apparel are highly diverse, many retailers still retain a strong emphasis on clothing, which intensifies rivalry. The country's apparel market trends indicate a favourable import and investment climate for apparel manufacturers and suppliers on a global basis. (Sung, 2010)

With this market trend, many fashion companies endeavour to capture this opportunity, and capitalize on Korea's growing demand for fashion market (Roll, 2005). Top 5 fashion companies (e.g., Samsung Group's Cheil Industries, E-land Group, Kolon, LG Group's LG Fashion, and Sejung) are contributing to increased market sales by performing strategic business focus in fashion industries.

Among the more important fashion companies, Cheil Industries, emerges as the best fashion company by ranking No. 1. During 2012, even in the face of the on-going global financial crisis, their sales reached a record KRW 6010 billion and operating income increased 44.6% year-on-year to KRW 321.7 billion. This implies that the group may deploy a portfolio of successful branding to optimize marketing efforts in the competing fashion market.

Cheil Industries was founded in 1954, as an affiliate of the Samsung Group was created as an initiative company with influence in the development of Korean textile industry. During the first years, the Cheil Industries was a manufacturer of woollen fabrics that in the 1950s, started to export worsted woollen fabrics "Golden Tex" in 1961, and obtained a Korean License for wool mark from International Wool Secretariat (IWS) in 1965 (Yu, 1994).

Today, the company has established a worldwide reputation for high quality and value in the three aspects: (a) leadership of electronic material in the IT area, (b) creating high profit by business structure of chemicals, and (c) gaining competitive fashion brand power. In fact, their objective is to become a leading fashion firm with dominant brand power by launching various brands in domestic as well as foreign markets. For this business mission, the Cheil Industries emphasizes dynamic management policies which includes customer first management, value focused management, responsible management, and establishment of excellent talent pool on HR management.

With respect to organizational structure, Cheil Industries is diversifying to three businesses: (a) chemicals, (b) electronic materials, and (c) fashion. Cheil Industries is showing outstanding outcome in both chemical and IT materials industry. Along with chemicals (43.7%), fashion business continually

Figure 1. Core values of Cheil Industry
Source: http://www.samsungfashion.com/

has been growing, which accounted for 43.5% of total market sales in 2012 (Samsung, 2012). More importantly for the fashion business, the company has implemented an umbrella strategy for two sectors, such as textiles and apparel. Textiles included "Goldentex" and "Lansmere" which are to supply best fabrics in terms of design and technology. The Cheil Industries consist of three business units for apparel: men's wear, women's wear, and casual wear. The other business units are an import team and Gemi plus which are responsible for distributor and licensee of world-famous brands such as Issey Miyake, Mango, and Ninewest.

Today, Cheil Industries is in the midst of entering a new phase: becoming a global top-tier corporation pursuing the highest quality and value. In order to fulfil this vision, they are expanding high value-added businesses and strengthening our presence in the Chinese market with, as always, our strong human resources as a solid foundation. Furthermore, they are aggressively developing new business areas that will determine the company's future while maintaining a strict emphasis on quality that bolsters profitability and elevates their company (See Figure 2). Among their current growth projects, and after a thorough preparation period of (approximately three years), Cheil Industries successfully launched '8seconds', a global SPA brand. '8seconds' consists of five lines, including men's wear, women's wear, denim, lounge wear, and accessories. Its brand concept is for an 'SPA plus concept store' which will mainly target customers in their 20s and 30s. '8seconds' will enable the company to take on overseas SPA brands in the domestic market and to enter the global SPA market, including China, beginning in 2015.

5.2. Bean Pole: A Local Luxury Brand

A Korean casual brand, Bean Pole launched in 1989, is one of best fashion brands with strong brand identity in Korea. Since its launch, Bean Pole has continually increased market sales to above 30% each year, ranking No.1 in the market share in the casual wear sector. In 2011, Bean Pole, rose 18.2 percent

Figure 2. Global presence of Cheil Industries
Source: http://www.samsungfashion.com/contents_eng/presence.jsp

to become the first brand in the Korean clothing industry to post KRW5 00 billion in annual domestic sales (see Figure 3. Currently Bean Pole is expanding to family brands with different product lines. It produces 'neo traditional' family fashion (Bean Pole Men, Bean Pole Ladies, and Bean Pole Kids); as well as accessories (Bean Pole Accessory), golf wear (Bean Pole Golf), and outdoors fashion/equipment (Bean Pole Outdoor).

One critical factor to make a brand strong is building brand salience in that consumer has brand knowledge consisting of brand awareness and brand image (Keller, 2008). Bean Pole is a good example of building a strong brand identity. As a visual element, the logo of Bean Pole with symbols of "Daddy Long Legs" and "Bicycle" plays an important role in the brand awareness.

According to Lee and Oh (2006), consumers' brand association with the Bean Pole's symbol or logo was consisted with favourability, interests, quality, and uniqueness. Uniqueness is critical to the success of brand association or awareness when consumers retrieve brand characteristics from their memory (Keller, 2002). Its brand logo is a 19th century British gentleman riding a bicycle from the early industrial era. This conveys an image of stylish people enjoying the revolutionary items of the time. As part of its efforts to strengthen brand equity, the company invented its own signature plaid pattern and officially registered the design in 2000. Since its establishment, Bean Pole has adjusted its logo, making minor changes since the original. The logo is a depiction of a man riding a penny-farthing bicycle, which represents the brand's image: "a dedication to rise to new challenges and pursue creativity." Furthermore, the logo is to emphasize the British-like style that the brand reflects (See Figure 4).

For fashion products, brand salience may be strongly related to brand image (or concept) including fashion image and style. Bean Pole born as a fusion of traditional and contemporary British fashion culture. Now it is become a fashion-forward brand a contemporary upper-class urban British look, which is derived from Mayfair Street in London. With this brand heritage, Bean Pole ensures identification of an association of the brand in customers' mind with specific product class and consumer needs for fashion and quality. In fact, the Bean Pole embodies contemporary sense and quality, tracking unisex and neo-traditional Bean Pole heritage in the global fashion marketplace. Bean Pole is not a product, but is a brand with prestige and comfortable image in the minds of consumers.

Figure 3. Bean Pole market share

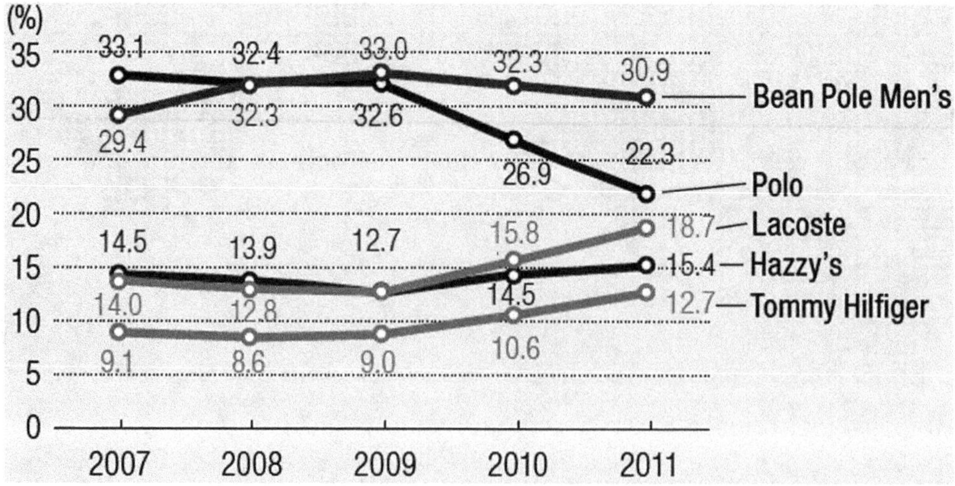

Figure 4. Bean Pole logo evolution

In 2011, and with a 30% of market share in high-end casual wear, the home-grown latecomer tightened its lead over Ralph Lauren's "Polo," the once seemingly unbeatable leader in the market segment. A well-known secret is that Bean Pole was launched in the market with the aim to compete with Polo Ralph Lauren[1].

Bean Pole looks and feels strikingly similar to Ralph Lauren's Polo. Over the last decade, Cheil Industries strategically placed each one of its Bean Pole retailers in close vicinity to Polo retailer within the department store. This practice elevated Bean Pole's image while diluting the Ralph Lauren image and they now seem as direct competitors. Thus, as (Stylianou 2011), shows in his work, globally, Ralph Lauren projects itself as an upper-tier luxury brand it wants to project that same image in South Korea. Ralph Lauren would prefer to be seen as a competitor of Louis Vuitton, or Gucci, for example, rather than Bean Pole. But, the question is really has Bean Pole overcome Ralph Lauren? What are the differences between these two brands? Do they have the same level of recognition and the same brand image associations?

Chun and Kim (2008) compare the brand equity of Bean Pole and Polo Ralph Lauren in respect to Korean consumers' perception. During the summer 2005, the researchers interviewed in Seoul, a sample of 1,014 consumers aged 15 to 34. The study evidences that Polo Ralph Lauren (13.6%) was higher than Bean Pole (13.3%) in the top-of-mind citation, but Bean Pole (46.1%) was higher in the percent of brand recall than Polo Ralph Lauren (40.5%). Polo Ralph Lauren (15.2%) was more frequently mentioned as the most liked one than Bean Pole (9.5%). The perceived quality and brand association show almost no statistically significant difference between the two brands, but Polo Ralph Lauren was evaluated as having a somewhat more affirmative and differentiated image.

Relative to the brand images, both brands were considered highly neat, simple, natural, and sophisticated. Bean Pole was fairly good in its competitiveness according to the brand equity compared to Polo Ralph Lauren, but the latter was highly valued in consumer's preference. Concerning all of the sub brands, the total sales volume of Bean Pole has been higher in the Korean market for several years. However, Polo Ralph Lauren showed a high growth rate again in 2007 thanks to its localized product strategy.

According to Holmquist and Cudmore (2013) the major factor contributing to the Bean Pole success is the balanced combination English and Korean elements of brand image. Bean Pole is characterized by its English name and the uses of English slogans, but also, for the use of Korean and Caucasian models for in its marketing communications. The fusion among European and Korean elements into brand image have led to Korean consumers positioning Bean Pole better that other foreign brands; including

Ralph Laurence. Note that, Korean consumers have the long tradition of regarding 'foreign products' as 'unconditionally good.' Furthermore, a basic popularity of American culture in South Korea (Pyong, 1989) and the high regard of Western products (Synovate, 2009) present themselves as one reason for Korean designers and manufactures to present themselves as Western.

Previous research on the country of origin effect on Korean consumers indicated that they placed greater value on the "Made in Korea" label over products manufactured in other Asian countries. The possible exception is Japanese products. However, regarding American and European products, Koreans viewed them as more luxurious with higher value and quality than products made in Korea (Synovate, 2009). This provides an intriguing basis for further exploration of the increasingly prevalent use of English in Korean advertising. Therefore, quality perceptions may override the natural country-of-origin effects of Koreans.

5.3. Bean Pole Marketing Strategy: Balancing Innovation and Tradition

After decades of rapid economic growth capped by the 1986 Seoul Asian Games and the 1988 Seoul Summer Olympics, Koreans were able to afford and seek a better quality of life. Their shopping needs changed and the domestic clothing industry, which had previously focused on men's and women's suits, began to expand into casual wear. At the time, Korea was still a developing country and consumers tended to hold brands from the US and Western Europe in high regard. International fashion brands like Polo or Benetton represented high-end casual clothing, so instead of directly challenging them, domestic manufacturers felt it would be prudent to position their brands at the low-and mid-price range.

Special strategies were deployed to change Korean consumers' perception of domestic brands and to position Bean Pole as a high-end casual line. Sophisticated designs were emphasized to meet domestic tastes with the watchwords of "high-quality, high-price, and no-discounts. But besides working on brand positioning, Bean Pole has developed other marketing strategies. Based on (a) the brand extension, and (b) the development of communication campaigns aimed at the young audience, these actions are in an attempt to increase the young segment's preference for the brand. Among these marketing actions note, the creation of various lines of clothing and accessories for young segment, or the development of marketing campaigns based in the use of young people's idols. Also, the support of social media, has let the brand to provide an excellent channel to communicate, dialogue and relate with the brand' consumer target. Recently, the success of Korean luxury fashion brands has expanded overseas. Asia-Pacific area has been conquered by Korean brands, which combines perfectly combine luxury Perfection tradition and innovation

5.3.1. Korean's Young Consumer

Since South Korea has widened its market doors to global trade, demand has been continuously on the rise for foreign luxury brands, especially from young South Korean consumers. In fact, Park (2000) points out how consumers in their twenties are rapidly replacing middle-aged consumers as the main consumers of global luxury brands in Korea. They are driving the consumer trendsetters to fashion luxury brands, especially those from the West, which is regarded as a statement of good taste (Nueno and Quelch, 1998).

As young increase their spending power and their western cultural reference points dramatically broaden, foreign and local fashion luxury brands struggle to gain a strong position in the minds and hearts of the young (Louis, 2002). Luxury fashion brand marketers are developing strategies to attract young Korean consumers with moderate income who have never been considered a target market in the traditional sense.

For successful market penetration or expansion into Korea, luxury fashion brand marketers should first identify what leads young Korean consumers to purchase global luxury brands and then devise the most effective strategies based on their findings. Relative to the Korean young consumer profile, some studies developed during the last two decades, show that they are materialistic, and are highly influenced by their reference group (Wong, 1997). They also are defined as consumers who feel the need for uniqueness and place a greater emphasis on publicly possessions that have symbolic meanings and values when consumed in public (Wong and Ahuvia, 1998).

Furthermore, as members of a global segment, young Koreans share some traits with young around the world. Thus they are big consumers of music and audio visual entertainment products (music bands, and soap operas), and as fans, they show a high level of loyalty that leads them to copy the behaviours and consume the same products and brands that their idols do.

In South Korea, the main young idols are k-music singers and soap opera actors. In fact, there is a strong link between both sectors. The principal actors/actress of a young soap opera (also called K-dramas) are also members of a very famous k-music band. Young people admire them, and follow them in and out of social media.

But this phenomenon has reached a global dimension. Oh (2013) defines K-pop and K-dramas are new buzz world in the global entertainment industry. Korean pop singers and actors currently attract unprecedented followers in Asia, Europa and North America. The dominant explanation behind this unique cultural phenomenon, rest on the concept of cultural hybridity of *Pop Asianism* (i.e., continuation and expansion of Japanese, Chinese and Indian subcultures in the global cultural market) (Shim, 2011). But some authors point out that the globalization of K-pop and K-dramas involves a much more complicated process based on the commercial combination of (a) global liberalization of entertainment markets in Asia and the rest of the world, and (b) the rapid advanced of digital technologies like YouTube and social media (Lie, 2012)

Finally, they are part of the so-called generation of digital natives, and are significant users of web 2.0 technologies. In fact, Technology has become an obsession to Korean people (Sang-Hun, 2008; Myungjin, 2005). Fong (2006) points out how South Korea is the most wired nation in the world, and residents switch cell phones more often than anyone else. By capitalizing on that culture, or even playing a role in creating it, phone manufacturers have made getting the newest and latest model a national obsession and point of pride.

This marketing segment has a great attractiveness to companies because of their potential consumers to their products, as well as members with a great capacity to influence the family decision-making process. This is the reason luxury fashion brand designers use this marketing strategy around the product, customizing for prosumers to attract young people's attention.

5.3.2. Bean Pole Casual Lines

The domestic casual clothing market in Korea was created in the 1980s during a brief period when school uniforms were abolished. Since then, the market's growth has paralleled Korea's fast-paced economic development. In the early 2000s, casual wear accounted for over 35 percent of the apparel market, by far the highest among all clothing categories. A gradual nationwide switch to a five-day work week instilled the concept of weekend leisure activity, as well as rising acceptance of informal office wear solidifying the demand for casual clothing across all age groups (see Figure 5).

Bean Pole quickly detected underlying shifts in the market and began to formulate a "total family brand" strategy for the high-end. By leveraging the brand value of its flagship, "Bean Pole Men's," Bean Pole was able to branch out into "Bean Pole Ladies" and "Bean Pole Golf," and then "Bean Pole Kids," "Bean Pole Jeans," and "Bean Pole Accessories." Aspiring to become a lifestyle brand that all family members can enjoy, Bean Pole has continued to create clearly delineated sublines according to target customers' age and gender. It is the first Korean apparel brand that adopted such a brand strategy, and has enjoyed synergy by assigning a single brand to various subline stores.

This strategy of "life stylization" used strong brand equity to create supplementary product lines for the home, including bedding. The 10-year sales record of Bean Pole shows that the highest sales growth was in 2001-2004, the apex of the total brand strategy. In particular, sales exploded by 42 percent in 2003 when the five-day work week was introduced in Korea. Although Bean Pole imitated Polo's strategy, its total brand strategy led to higher success.

5.3.3. The Key Elements of Bean Pole Marketing Communication Strategy: Korean Dramas, K-Music, and Social Media Support

Previously we noted that young people is global consumer segment that easily can be influenced by certain individuals who are socially relevant (Akcay, 2012). In particular, singers, actors or celebrities are admired and followed by young people, turning them into opinion leaders. That is due to young people being big consumers of music and audio visual entertainment products (music bands, and soap operas). They show a high level of loyalty that leads them to copy the behaviours and consume the same products and brands that their idols do.

Figure 5. Market share of clothing categories
Source: Korean Federation of textile industries (2012)

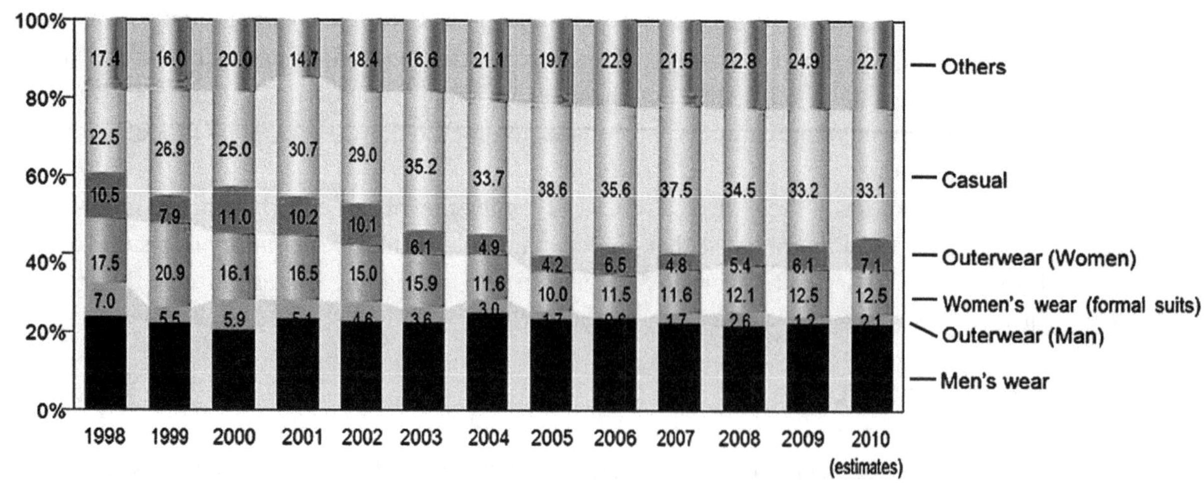

Fashion luxury brands, like Bean Pole, know this phenomenon and therefore design marketing strategies where young idols become spokespersons for the brand. Note, that celebrity endorsements are among the most successful marketing communication practices used by luxury fashion brands as a way to enhance brand recognition and stimulate positive attitudes towards brands (Kamins, 1989), and finally, increasing sales and profits (Pringle and Binet, 2005). In fact, young people are influenced by celebrities more than other segments of society. Celebrities represent all the traits that young people want. They are especially an important medium in inspiring consumers' idealized images of self, presenting images of seduction for the regular people to esteem and to follow (e.g. Lipotevsky, 1987). The idealized images of the celebrities communicate the traits to be adopted and guide the way to the ideal self in the process of identity construction.

Among the main Bean Pole's marketing campaigns highlight two: the one developed by Suzy and Kim Soo-Hyun in winter of 2013, the second, the communication campaign in 2006 starring by Gwenith Paltrowl and Daniel Henney. The last two marketing campaigns of Bean Pole were started by Suzy and Kim Soo-Hyun. Both are South Korean actors, well known for their roles in different TV dramas and movies. Suzy also is member of one of most famous Korean girl's band, *Miss A*.

In 2013, both celebrities signed a contract with the firm Bean Pole to be the public face of the brand. Since then, they have staged different spots, and events conducted by the firm. Both actors have a fresh and youthful, consistent with Bean Pole brand image. Also, this couple enjoys great popularity in Korea, by starring in 2011's drama titled Dream High. The drama was popular among teenagers, and brought` in viewership ratings in the 18 to 20 percent range During ITS two-month run (See Figure 6). Previously, the marketing campaigns of Bean Pole did not address a young public. Thus, during the first half

Figure 6. Bean Pole advertising campaigns
Source: Bean Pole official website

of the last decade, the campaigns were carried out by Gwyneth Paltrow and Daniel Henney. Both are American actors, known internationally. They teamed up late in 2005 for their first Bean Pole advertising campaign. According to a Bean Pole, Paltrow's elegant and intellectual image combined with Henney's exotic features to provide an excellent representation of Bean Pole's premium Collection Line.

Bean Pole also is very active in social networks. Since 2012 it is present in Facebook, and has a total of 135,475 fans. The Bean Pole page not only presents its products, but also inserts the videos of its campaigns. The brand is also presented in twitter. This network is used by some of the celebrities who star in their marketing campaigns to communicate with their fans. Bean Pole is also present in YouTube. It has an official channel with over 8,000 subscribers, which also include institutional communication and includes communication campaigns

Bean Pole uses social media as a channel to interact with its target audience. During 2013, the activity of the brand on Facebook has increased, although as shown in Figure 7, the followers of the brand come mainly from Asia-pacific area.

It should be noted that fans of the brand generate little content about Bean Pole outside Brand's official channels. Even, Korean social networks like Me2day or cyworld have a low activity relative to the brand. The few entries observed about Bean Pole in social networks are relative, or even made by the celebrities starring their communication campaigns.

5.3.4. The South Korean Style: The Key to Fashion Luxury Brands' Success in International Markets

To succeed in Asia-Pacific area, and especially China, luxury brands are getting help from South Korea. Thus Korean style, from viral K-Pop videos to typical food traditions such as fried chicken, are all the rage in China and brands are increasingly using it to reach Chinese consumers (Li, 2014).

The likes of Chanel, Gucci and Louis Vuitton have used product placement in Korean TV dramas to broaden their appeal to young consumers. The draw of Korean is so strong that Chinese producers are trying to make them, complete with Korean actors, so they can fill the sets with Chinese brands.

Korean sitcoms are particularly appealing to the fashion-obsessed young Chinese consumers (Li, 2014). Since Korean drama "My Love from the Star" raked in 34 million viewers in January, Celine dresses and Jimmy Choo shoes worn by Korean actress Jun Ji-hyun have seen big spikes in sales. More affordable items such as lipstick and hairbands are also selling well. The series even sparked a fried chicken and beer craze in China.

The impact has surprised marketers. For instance, Samsonite has viewed the importance of use Korean TV dramas to show its products. Thus the drama actor Kim Soo-hyun was selected to endorse a new leather backpack partly because "My Love from the Star" a Korean soap opera was airing at the time of the product's launch. After Mr. Kim wore the backpack in one episode, Chinese customers swarmed to stores with pictures of him on their phones. Sales of the entire backpack line took off, tripling in February from the same month last year.

The rise of Korean pop culture isn't new. The term *Korean Wave* was coined by Chinese journalists in 1999 to describe the growing appetite for Korean culture exports (Lee, 2012). But Korean TV dramas have only flexed their commercial muscle recently. They help fill a void of high quality original content in several Asia-Pacific countries. Among the success factors of Korean dramas is its r high capacity

Figure 7. Bean Pole fans by county
Source: http://www.socialbakers.com/

Beanpole Fans by Country

	Local Fans	Percentage Of Fan Base
South Korea	120 865	89.2 %
Indonesia	1 787	1.3 %
Taiwan	1 766	1.3 %
Malaysia	1 227	0.9 %
Philippines	1 062	0.8 %
Vietnam	965	0.7 %
United States	909	0.7 %
Thailand	886	0.7 %
Hong Kong	729	0.5 %
Mexico	407	0.3 %
Singapore	383	0.3 %
Peru	307	0.2 %
Japan	281	0.2 %
Australia	266	0.2 %
Canada	225	0.2 %
China	188	0.1 %
United Kingdom	177	0.1 %
France	103	0.1 %
Chile	103	0.1 %
Cambodia	99	0.1 %
Turkey	95	0.1 %
Tunisia	86	0.1 %

to link with local young people, due that they are better than domestic TV dramas at promoting some of traditional culture values: love, family, respect... (Li et al., 2012) But the question is whether that is probably due to Korean soap operas making family values more appealing by wrapping them in designer clothing and cool gadgets.

Luxury brands often prefer Korean actors because they are cheaper to sponsor than Hollywood stars. Still, big brands like Louis Vuitton and Samsonite didn't pay to place their products in "My Love from the Star" because the show, eager to engage style-conscious young viewers, wanted them anyway. Today Korean stars have regional appeal, thus they are well recognized in China, Hong Kong and Taiwan, but also in Singapore to Vietnam.

Yet the Korean wave is a double edge sword for big brands. Along with Korean pop culture, the country's cosmetics and fashion brands are increasingly popular, bringing new competition to global brands (Huang, 2011). Estée Lauder blamed its sales fall in Korea last year partly on competition from domestic brands there. Even, Chinese consumers now go on tours to Seoul for buying the local fashion brands.

Brands like Bean Pole are recognized as direct competition of international luxury fashion brands. However, despite these challenges in the Korean market, and the ever increasing competition from local brands, foreign fashion brands need to stay there because of its influence over the rest of Asia. It is recognized that Korea is an influencer for luxury items and lifestyle experiences. By investing in Korea; they are impacting consumers across Asia Pacific.

6. CONCLUSION

This chapter will discuss how companies can combine different elements to design a successful marketing strategy. In the context of luxury brands, especially those of fashion luxury, companies can use different ways to reach their target audiences. Regardless of the strategy used, it must consider that a 'luxury brand' can be summarized in three dimensions; functionalism, experientialisms and symbolic. From a marketing point of view these translate into three brand image assets: 'brand identity/ awareness', 'exclusivity', 'high quality', 'premium pricing', and 'symbolic value/status'.

Elements like celebrity endorsement, or the intensive social media use as a communication channel with consumers can be drivers of success, especially when the brand is targeted to a young audience. Bean Pole constitutes a clear example of how these three elements influence on brand success, thus confirming the two hypothesis proposed: the influence of celebrities to engage young audiences with luxury brands, and the use of social media as a tool to enhance celebrities' engagement effect.

In Korea, the luxury market is growing and its customers are evolving. The number of young luxury consumers is on the rise, and their values, communication channels, and service demands are different than offer luxury consumers. Korean luxury no longer attaches themselves to a brand supply because of its name or country of origin. Customers seek more and more differentiation and are yielding their loyalty to the brands that can provide the most customization, superior service, and highest value. Korean customers seeking value will also be price-sensitive-shoppers- which can be a huge challenge for luxury retailers who don't use discounting as a sales lever. In the particular case of Bean Pole, a major obstacle is trying to turn this brand in a global one.

During the last decade, Bean Pole has developed some strategies based on the latest developments elements with the aim of changing Korean consumers' perception of domestic brands and to position it as a high-end casual line. Thus, as a highly salient brand in Asia Pacific, and especially in South Korea, Bean Pole is one that has both breadth and brand awareness that customers always recall when making purchases. The Bean Pole has showed a high potential to establish strong brand equity based on the managing of brand strategies in multifaceted ways: (a) brand extension, (b) image positioning linking with celebrity's endorsement, (3) intensive presence and use of social media.

The company has used its strong brand awareness to extend the parent brand to new product categories. The new category to which the brand is extended can be related or unrelated to the existing product categories. A renowned/successful brand helps an organization to launch products in new categories more easily. An existing brand that gives rise to a brand extension is referred to as parent brand. If the customers of the new business have values and aspirations synchronizing/matching those of the core business, and if these values and aspirations are embodied in the brand, it is likely to be accepted by customers in the new line of business. Extending a brand outside its core product category can be beneficial in a sense that it helps evaluating product category opportunities, identifies resource requirements, and lowers risk while measuring the brand's relevance and appeal.

The Bean Pole extension strategy supports a notion that the fit is perceived by the consumer has a positive effect on the product brand image after extension. Thus, the main priority of Bean Pole for managing their brand is that category extension is implementing by applying the parent brand to enter a different product category. Bean Pole has been extending into new product lines with the existing brand value. As a traditional casual brand, Bean Pole has targeting consumers aged 10 to 50. At the same time, Bean Pole develops core benefits of product for selected targets and tries to communicate brand image with customers. The brand are targeting at different segments with various product line: Bean Pole Men's, Bean Pole Ladies, Bean Pole Kids, Bean Pole Golf, Bean Pole Jeans, and Bean Pole Accessory. According to the corporate statement on the website, Bean Pole is the best family brand in Korea that is creating a new lifestyle". Despite its importance, fashion brands on multiproduct extension are relatively limited in Korea.

Obviously, it is suggested that Bean Pole's "categorization approach into brand extension for multi-product brand with different targets is most successful to meet perception of extended brands because the parent brand has already been in consumer's minds. With Bean Pole, it could be said that success of extension is affected by the brand equity and extension in turn has an impact on the brand's equity.

Celebrity's endorsement is the second driver of Bean Pole's success. Celebrities are people who enjoy public recognition by a large share of a certain group of people. Attributes like attractiveness, extraordinary lifestyle or special skills are just examples and specific common characteristics that are observed and celebrities generally differ from the social norm and enjoy a high degree of public awareness. The term Celebrity refers to an individual who is known to the public (actor, singer, sports figure, entertainer, etc.) for his or her achievements in areas other than that of the product class endorsed.

Celebrity endorsement can be profitable advertisement for retail companies. If the company knows about the star power and the image of the celebrity in relation to the power and the functions of the brand it wishes to be associated with. Bean Pole has been aware of this situation. Since 2013 their communication campaigns are being carried out by two of the best known celebrities in Korea. As young idols, they both have a fresh and youthful appearance consistent with Bean Pole brand image, making it easy for people to link the brand and celebrities.

One risk of this strategy is that the company does not realize that the brand should be bigger than the celebrity itself; otherwise it will overshadow the product itself to the point of being obsolete. It defeats the purpose of brand awareness and exposure. From a marketing perspective, using global celebrities in endorsements may not always be an effective strategy in global advertising campaigns as the meanings carried by some of these global celebrities may not be congruent with the core cultural values of the local market. Therefore, the meanings to be transferred should be carefully selected from the pallet of meanings communicated by global celebrities and in return be adapted to the local culture and society. Regardless of the speed of globalization, the preference of many global companies for using local celebrities in their advertisements may stem from this need for adaptation.

Relative to this point, we want note that this study not only confirms some previous findings regarding celebrity influences related to physical attractiveness and personality traits, but also points to new discussions related to their ideology, success, and to values and lifestyles. Our findings also suggest that, despite being a powerful influence on the perceptions of young people, physical attractiveness is not the only reason for positive evaluations. This should be supported with other traits such as personality traits, success, and lifestyles of celebrities in Luxury brands. In addition, the effects of celebrities' physical attractiveness may vary according to gender. We found that especially one high percentage of adolescents participants are influenced by the physical appearance of celebrities, which further affect their desire for identification with the celebrity. It can be concluded that, the socially defined portrayals of status and sense of begin part of, it push to communicate to masses through social agents like media, affects the interpretations of teens regarding the ideal adolescence, and their desire to reach that ideal. In addition to the physical attractiveness attribute, young people's perceptions of celebrities are affected by specific personality traits such as self-confidence, optimism, and determination. Like physical traits, personality traits guide young people's ideal of self-development. Presented as role models in mass media, celebrities are often evaluated as high achievers. Therefore, they are considered exemplary figures according to socially constructed norms and values. Their favorable traits are then internalized by young people in an attempt to reach the ideal self. On the other hand, undesirable personality traits, such as arrogance or self-conceit, result in criticism and disliking as they are contrary to the expression of ideal self and a socially acceptable identity. Thus, when planning celebrity endorsement, marketing practitioners should take into consideration these negative evaluations of consumers towards celebrities and try to understand the undesired personality traits. Another important yet relatively unexplored factor influencing young people's perceptions of celebrities is ideology. The stance of celebrities, for instance, regarding politics and feminism makes an impression on young people. However, rather than a motivation towards activism, they may also choose to reflect their ideological beliefs through commodities, which are consumed by these famous figures. We see that the commoditized representations became an important medium in transferring and communicating the ideology.

Finally, note that the presence in social networks is the third driver of Bean Pole's success. As a means to constitute customer assets through effective communication with consumers, luxury brands have tilted their eyes toward social media. Marketing communication using social media such as Twitter, Facebook, and YouTube has already been evaluated as business take-off tools for luxury fashion brands.

For instance, traditional designer houses such as Louis Vuitton provide live broadcasting fashion shows on their blogs. Ralph Lauren, Chanel, Donna Karan, and Gucci have worked with Apple to create iPhone applications. As many luxury houses, Bean Pole has created its own Twitter accounts or post on Facebook. The old-fashioned one-way communication is changed to interactive two-way direct communication. These channels make possible that Bean Pole and its clients can communicate with each other without any restriction in time, place, and medium.

Social media let luxury fashion brands gain exposure and strengthen relationships with customers. In fact, Social media marketing is a two-way communication seeking empathy with young users, and even enforcing the familiar emotions associated with existing luxury brands to a higher age group. In addition, social media activities of brands provide an opportunity to reduce misunderstanding and prejudice toward brands, and to elevate brand value by creating a platform to exchange ideas and information among people online.

7. MARKETING STRATEGIC DIRECTION AND FUTURE RESEARCH LINES

The methodological contributions of the paper include the development of a research design, which is adapted to the specific requirements of the luxury category. According to the growing consumer-orientation in marketing research, the traits and stimuli originate directly from the consumers. The identification of traits relies on a specific qualitative research approach including the Repertory Grid Method, which is constrained by a theory-based framework, but then again flexible enough to consider the ambiguous and contextual facets of brand personality. In contrast to common practice, the set of stimuli is open for recommendations of survey participants and extended with the ideal brands, which proved to be suitable for the analysis of the luxury brand personality and could also be employed for the analysis of category-specific brand personalities beyond the luxury segment. In addition, the paper explained the benefits of a factor analysis based on individual brand evaluations and oblique rotation specifically for the luxury category and proposed the application of Viral Participant Acquisition.

The results offer substantial insights into the symbolic meaning of luxury brands with a comprehensive overview about the universe of personality traits and their major dimensions, which constitute the first personality framework specifically for luxury brands.

For researchers, these results offer a basis for further research about luxury brand personality and its antecedents and consequences. For example, the personality traits and dimensions could be tested and adapted with further empirical studies for specific luxury categories and consumer segments. In terms of antecedents, future research could analyse strategies for the creation of a luxury brand personality and the impact of specific marketing variables on their perception. In terms of consequences, researchers could employ the framework to uncover the relationships between luxury brand personality characteristics and consumer preferences and to compare different consumer segments.

There are also some practical implications for the management of luxury brands. The framework helps marketers to compare the personalities of different luxury brands and to develop a luxury brand personality, which is the basis to create a luxury brands' aura and magic. On the other hand, the case study evidences that the use of celebrities' endorsement increases the brand recognition and also reinforces the its image transferring to the brand some associations relative to the celebrities, their lifestyle and their preferences. Finally, our research evidences how social media constitutes a powerful tool to enhance the relationship between the brand-the celebrities and the consumers. Internet, and particularly social networks, make possible to create a close, direct and durability relationship among these three actors, that can constitutes the base of a competitive advantage.

Though the research results are limited, it is clear based on this initial study that it is critical for new business models to incorporate ways to connect with customers, build strong relationships, and increasing social engagement to drive growth. Thus, further investigation should be carried out to better understand the social media association with luxury Fashion to build strong customer relationships and to encourage loyalty, and to interact with customers through new channels, formats, or revenue models. It is imperative for luxury marketers to continue building their presence on social media platforms they currently use, and expand to new platforms for engaging audiences. A review of the literature indicates that while researchers have explored the relationship between social media and viral marketing, research has focused on its impact (i.e., on diffusion and sales; Godes and Mayzlin, 2004, 2009; Goldenberg et al., 2009). Less attention has focused on the causes of viral marketing, what drives people to share content, and why certain content becomes viral. Most recently, Burger and Milkman (2012) investigated the link between article characteristics and blogging. Their research suggests that similar factors drive viral marketing and blogging: emotional, positive, interesting, and anger-inducing and fewer sadness-inducing stories are likely to drive the most blogged list. Additionally, they found practically useful content is marginally less likely to be blogged about, which may be partly due to the nature of information. The researchers point out that while movie reviews, technology perspectives, and recipes all contain useful information; it is a commentary so there may be less blogger added value in contributing his or her spin on the issue. Future work should examine how fashion media content characteristics become viral. When attempting to generate word of mouth, marketers often target influential's as in the case of Mercedes Benz Fashion Week attendees (e.g, media professionals, celebrities, socialites). To the extent that these influentials have strong social ties, their influence is greater than others. Rather than targeting these influentials, Burger and Milkman (2012) indicate that it may be more beneficial to focus on crafting contagious content so it becomes viral. Future work might examine the relationship between online content and viral marketing in shaping customer behavior in the luxury marketplace, and incorporating these elements into new innovative business models.

REFERENCES

Ahuvia, A. C. (2005). Beyond the extended self: Loved objects and consumers' identity narratives. *The Journal of Consumer Research*, *32*(6), 171–184. doi:10.1086/429607

Akcay, O. (2012). Marketing to teenagers: The influence of color, ethnicity and gender. *International Journal of Business and Social Science*, *3*(22), 10–18.

Alden, D. L., Steenkamp, J. B., & Batra, R. (1999). Brand positioning through advertising in Asia, North America, and Europe: The role of global consumer culture. *Journal of Marketing*, *63*(1), 75–87. doi:10.2307/1252002

Alden, D. L., Steenkamp, J. B., & Batra, R. (2006). Consumer attitudes toward marketplace globalization: Structure, antecedents and consequences. *International Journal of Research in Marketing*, *23*(3), 227–239. doi:10.1016/j.ijresmar.2006.01.010

Baker, M. J., & Hart, S. (2007). *The Marketing Book*. Butterworth-Heinemann.

Belk, R. W. (1988). Possessions and the extended self. *The Journal of Consumer Research*, *15*(2), 139–168. doi:10.1086/209154

Bergeström, C., & Skärfstad, R. (2004). *Celebrity Endorsement*. Retrieved online 19th March 2009, from http://epubl.ltu.se/1404-5508/2004/193/LTU-SHU-EX-04193-SE.pdf

Bhosale, S., & Gupta, S. (2006). *Tomorrow is a new consumer! Who is the future Asian consumer?*. Retrieved online 19th March 2009, from http://my.acnielsen.com/reports/documents/AsianConsumer.pdf

Boon, S. D., & Lomore, C. D. (2001). Admirer-Celebrity Relationships Among Young Adults Explaining Perceptions of Celebrity Influence on Identity. *Human Communication Research*, *27*(3), 432–465.

Callen, B. (2009). *Managers Guide to Marketing*. Advertising and Publicity, McGraw-Hill Professional.

Carter, B. L. (2011, August). Marketing to Tweens and Teens: Insights, Strategies, and Tactics. The Licensing Journal, 1-3.

Caughey, J. L. (1978). Artificial Social Relations in Modern America. *American Quarterly*, *30*(1), 70–89. doi:10.2307/2712280

Chaet, H. (2012, June 25). The Tween Machine. *Adweek*, 44-47.

Chan, K., Leung, Y., & Luk, E. K. (2013). Impact of celebrity endorsement in advertising on brand image among Chinese adolescents. *Young Consumers*, *14*(2), 167–179. doi:10.1108/17473611311325564

Cheng, C. (2006). *The Impact of Brand Image on Consumer Behaviour of Luxury Goods of Fashion Industry in China*. Retrieved online 19th March 2009, from http://edissertations.nottingham.ac.uk/1585/1/07MSclixss24.pdf

Cheong, E., & Phau, I. (2003). *Young status oriented consumer's evaluation of diffusion brand extensions: The effect of brand loyalty*. Retrieved online 19th March 2009, from http://smib.vuw.ac.nz:8081/WWW/ANZMAC2003/papers/BR03_cheonge.pdf

Chung, I.H., & Kim, I.G. (2008). Comparison of brand equity between two similar global and national brands. *International Journal of Management Cases*.

Cohen, H. (2009). *Eight Ways to Reach Teens*. Retrieved from http://www.clickz.com/clickz/column/1710603/eight-ways-reach-teens

Davis, T. (2011). *The Teen Spending Game: The Complex Marketing Strategy*. Retrieved from http://www.examiner.com

Doyle, P. (2008). *Value-based Marketing: Marketing Strategies for Corporate Growth and Shareholder Value*. John Wiley & Sons.

Easley, D., & Kleinberg, J. (2010). *Networks, crowds, and markets: Reasoning about a highly connected world*. New York, NY: Cambridge University Press. doi:10.1017/CBO9780511761942

Erdoğan, B. Z. (1999). Celebrity Endorsement: A Literature Review. *Journal of Marketing Management*, *15*(4), 291–314. doi:10.1362/026725799784870379

Erikson, E. (1959). Identity and the life cycle. *Psychological Issues*, *1*(1), 13–117.

Friedman, J. (1990). Being in the world: Globalization and localization. *Theory, Culture & Society*, *7*(2), 311–328. doi:10.1177/026327690007002018

Gilbert, D. (2003). *Retail marketing management*. Prentice Hal.

Goldsmith, R. E., Moore, M. A., & Beaudoin, P. (1999). Fashion innovativeness and self concept: A replication. *Journal of Product and Brand Management*, *8*(1), 7–18. doi:10.1108/10610429910257904

Goodstein, A. (2007, August). Teen Marketing: Apple's the Master. *Bloomberg Businessweek*.

Greene, A. L., & Adams-Price, C. (1990). Adolescents' Secondary Attachments to Celebrity Figures. *Sex Roles*, *23*(7-8), 335–347. doi:10.1007/BF00289224

Gulland, C. (2006, July 14). *The ten biggest themes of 'What teens want'*. Retrieved March, 20, 2007, from http://www.ypulse.com/the-ten-biggest-themes-of-what-teens-want

Hackley, C. (2009). *Advertising and Promotion: An Integrated Marketing Communications Approach*. SAGE Publications.

Hamilton, C. (2004). *Money, Marketing and the Innocence of Youth*. Retrieved online 19th March 2009, from http://www.clivehamilton.net.au/cms/media/documents/articles/Money,_Marketing_and_the_Innocence_of_Youth.pdf

Hartman, J. B., Shim, S., Barber, B., & O'Brien, M. (2006). Adolescents' utilitarian and hedonic Web consumption behavior: Hierarchical influence of personal values and innovativeness. *Psychology and Marketing*, *23*(10), 813–839. doi:10.1002/mar.20135

Heaney, J.-G., Goldsmith, R. E., & Jusoh, W. J. W. (2005). Status consumption among Malaysian consumers: Exploring its relationships with materialism and attention-to-social-comparisoninformation. *Journal of International Consumer Marketing*, *17*(4), 83–98. doi:10.1300/J046v17n04_05

Helmrich, E. (2004). *What Teens Want*. YALS.

Hennig-Thurau, T., Gwinner, K. P., Walsh, G., & Gremler, D. D. (2004). Electronic word-of mouth via consumer-opinion platforms: What motivates consumers to articulate themselves on the Internet? *Journal of Interactive Marketing*, *18*(1), 38–52. doi:10.1002/dir.10073

Holmquist, J. P., & Cudmore, A. (2013). English in Korean advertising: An exploratory study. *International Journal of Marketing Studies*, *5*(3), 94–103. doi:10.5539/ijms.v5n3p94

Holt, D. B., Quelch, J. A., & Taylor, E. L. (2004). How global brands compete. *Harvard Business Review*, *82*(9), 68–75. PMID:15449856

Hopson, B., & Adams, A. (1976). Toward an understanding of transition: Defining some boundaries of transition dynamics. In J. Adams, J. Hayes, & B. Hopson (Eds.), *Transition: Understanding and managing personal changes*. London, UK: Martin Robertson.

Huang, S. (2011). Nation-branding and transnational consumption: Japan-mania and the Korean wave in Taiwan. *Media Culture & Society*, *33*(1), 3–18. doi:10.1177/0163443710379670

Ivanauskas, G. (2009). *The evaluation of social media effects on consumers marketing communications*. Retrieved from www.scribd.com

Johansson, J. K., & Ronkainen, I. A. (2005). The esteem of Global Brands. *Journal of Brand Management*, *12*(5), 339–354. doi:10.1057/palgrave.bm.2540230

Kamineni, R. (2005). Influence of materialism, gender and nationality on consumer brand perceptions. Journal of Targeting. *Measurement and Analysis for Marketing*, *14*(1), 25–32. doi:10.1057/palgrave.jt.5740167

Kamins, M. A. (1989). Celebrity and Non-celebrity Advertising in a Two Sided Context. *Journal of Advertising Research*, *29*(3), 34–42.

Kapferer, J.-N. (2002). Is there really no hope for local brands? *Journal of Brand Management*, *9*(3), 163–170. doi:10.1057/palgrave.bm.2540066

Kapferer, J. N. (2012). The New Strategic Brand Management: Advanced Insights and Strategic Thinking (5th ed.). Kogan Page.

Keegan, W., & Marck, G. (2013). *Global Marketing* (7th ed.). Prentice-Hall.

Kjeldgaard, D., & Askegaard, S. (2006). The Glocalization of Youth Culture. The Global Youth Segment as Structures of Common Difference. *The Journal of Consumer Research*, *33*(2), 231–247. doi:10.1086/506304

Klein, G. (2007). *Strategic Marketing*. GRIN Verlag.

Knox, S. (2012). Cerebral advocates: How people are wired to share and advocate. *WOMMA*. Retrieved from http://womma.org/word/tag/creative-wom-ideas/page/2/

Kondrashova, I. (2012). *Digital by design. WOMMA*. Retrieved from http://allthings.womma.org/tag/digital/

Korean Federation of Textile Industries. (2012). *Annual reports of "Korean Fashion Market Trends"*. Prentice-Hall.

Kostecki, E. (2005). *Brand Extension to the Youth and Young Adult Markets*. Retrieved online 19th March 2009, from http://w4.stern.nyu.edu/emplibrary/Erin_Kostecki_honors_2005.pdf

LaFerle, C., Edwards, S. M., & Lee, W. N. (2000). Teen's use of traditional media and the Internet. *Journal of Advertising Research*, *40*(3), 55–66. doi:10.2501/JAR-40-3-55-65

Lee, J. (2012). What is K in K-pop? South Korean popular music, the culture industry and national identity. *Korean Observer*, *43*(3), 339–363.

Lee, M. Y., & Oh, K. Y. (2006). An exploratory study on brand personality: The case of a traditional casual brand in Korea. *Journal of Fashion Business*, *10*(6), 79–90.

Li, G., Li, G., & Kambele, Z. (2012). Luxury fashion brand consumers in China: Perceived value, fashion lifestyle, and willingness to pay. *Journal of Business Research*, *65*(10), 1516–1522. doi:10.1016/j.jbusres.2011.10.019

Lie, J. (2012). What is the K in K-pop? South Korean Popular Music, the culture Industry, and National Identity. *Korean Observer*, *43*(3), 339–363.

Lockstrom, M. (2007). *Low-Cost Country Sourcing: Trends and Implications*. DUV.

Louis, H. (2002). Young Korean consumers wield spending power. *Ad Age Global*, *2*(9), 6.

Luck, D. (2008). *CIM Coursebook Assessing the Marketing Environment*. Butterworth-Heinemann.

LVMH. (2005). *Annual Report 2004*. Retrieved from http://www.lvmh.com/comfi/pdf_gbr/ra_abrege_2004_gbr.pdf

McCracken, G. (1989). Who is the Celebrity Endorser? Cultural Foundations of the Endorsement Process. *The Journal of Consumer Research*, *16*(3), 310–321. doi:10.1086/209217

Milas, G., & Mlacic, B. (2007). Brand personality and human personality: Findings from ratings of familiar Croatian brands. *Journal of Business Research*, *60*(6), 620–626. doi:10.1016/j.jbusres.2006.06.011

Moses, E. (2000). *The $ 100 billion allowance- Accessing the global teen market*. New York: John Wiley & Sons Inc.

Myungjin, L. (2005). *The Social Identities of the 2030 New Generation in South Korea*. Seoul: Samsung Economic Research Institute.

Nueno, J. L., & Quelch, J. A. (1998). The mass marketing of luxury. *Business Horizons*, *41*(6), 61–68. doi:10.1016/S0007-6813(98)90023-4

Parker, R. S., Hermans, C. M., & Schaefer, A. D. (2004). Fashion consciousness of Chinese, Japanese and American teenagers. *Journal of Fashion Marketing and Management*, *8*(2), 176–186.

Petty, R. E., Cacioppo, J. T., & Schumann, D. (1983). Central and Peripheral Routes to Advertising Effectiveness: The Moderating Role of Involvement. *The Journal of Consumer Research*, *10*(2), 135–146.

Phau, I., & Leng, Y. S. (2008). Attitudes toward domestic and foreign luxury brand apparel. *Journal of Fashion Marketing and Management*, *12*(1), 68–89. doi:10.1108/13612020810857952

Pyong, P. (1989). Textbooks for Asian American studies. *Amerasia Journal*, *15*(1), 259–266. doi:10.17953/amer.15.1.7205748t27m84q54

Researchandmarkets. (2005). *Glassware Market Report 2005*. Retrieved online 19th March 2009, from http://72.14.235.132/custom?q=cache:bkESGTvpfrcJ:www.researchandmarkets.com/reports/314492/glassware_market_report_2005.pdf+buying+behaviour+young+tableware&cd=4&hl=en&ct=clnk&gl=in&client=pub-3796354395625809

Reynolds, W. H. (1968). Cars and clothing: Understanding fashion trends. *Journal of Marketing*, *32*(3), 44–49. doi:10.2307/1249761

Ritzer, G., & Jurgenson, N. (2010). Production, consumption, prosumption: The nature of capitalism in the age of the digital "prosumer". *Journal of Consumer Culture*, 163–196.

Roberts, J. A., & Manolis, C. (2000). Baby boomers and busters: An exploratory investigation of attitudes towards marketing, advertising and consumerism. *Journal of Consumer Marketing*, *17*(6), 481–499. doi:10.1108/07363760010349911

Roedder-John, D. (1999). Consumer socialization of children: A retrospective look at twenty-five years of research. *The Journal of Consumer Research*, *26*(December), 183–213. doi:10.1086/209559

Roll, M. (2005). *Asian brand strategy: how Asia builds strong brands*. Palgrave Macmillan. doi:10.1057/9780230513068

Salzman, M. (2009). *Boomers and the Future of Luxury Brands*. Retrieved online 19th March 2009, from http://boomers.typepad.com/boomers/2009/01/boomers-and-thefuture-of-luxury-brands.html

Samsung Corporate Report. (2012). Available on http://sgsg.samsung.com/c/pdf/Cheil%20Industries.pdf

Sang-Hun, C. (2008, June 16). Korea's New Generation of 'Web 2.0' protesters. *International Herald Tribune*, p. 14.

Schiff, J. (2007). *How to Market to Teens: Keep It Real and Simple*. Retrieved from http://www.ecommerce-guide.com

Seringhaus, F. H. R. (2002). *Cross-cultural exploration of Global Brands and the Internet*. retrieved online 19th March 2009, from http://www.impgroup.org/uploads/papers/504.pdf

Sheth, N. J., & Mittal, B. (2004). *Consumer behaviour: a managerial perspective* (2nd ed.). South Western Publishing Company.

Shim, D. B. (2011). *Waxing the Korean Wave. Asia Research Institute*. Working Paper Series, nº. 158.

Sirgy, M., Lee, D., Johar, J., & Tidwell, J. (2008). Effect of self-congruity with sponsorship on brand loyalty. *Journal of Business Research*, *61*(10), 1091–1097. doi:10.1016/j.jbusres.2007.09.022

Solomon, M. R. (1983). The role of products as social stimuli: A symbolic interactionism perspective. *The Journal of Consumer Research*, *10*(3), 319–329.

Sriviroj, S. (2007). *Purchasing Luxury Goods: consumer behaviour of international students in the UK*. Retrieved online 19th March 2009, from http://edissertations.nottingham.ac.uk/1585/1/07MSclixss24.pdf

Steenkamp, J.-B. E. M., Batra, R., & Alden, D. (2003). How perceived brand globalness creates brand value. *Journal of International Business Studies*, *34*(1), 53–65. doi:10.1057/palgrave.jibs.8400002

Steinberg, L. (1993). *Adolescence* (3rd ed.). New York: McGraw Hill.

Stileman, P. (2009). *The extent to which social media changed the relationship between brand and consumer*. Retrieved from www.slideshare.net

Sung, G. (2010). *Korea's apparel industry*. U.S. Departament of Commerce. Online available on http://otexa.ita.doc.gov/webinars/Korea_Apparel_Industry_2010_FINAL.pdf

Synovate. (2009). *Consumers skeptical about quality of 'Made in China' labels*. Retrieved from http://www.marketresearchworld.net/index.php?option=com_content&task=view&id=494&Itemid=77

Thompson, C. J., & Arsel, Z. (2004). The Starbucks Brandscape and Consumers' (Anticorporate) Experiences of Glocalization. *The Journal of Consumer Research*, *31*(3), 631–642. doi:10.1086/425098

Thrift, N. (2005). *Knowing Capitalism: Theory, Culture and Society*. Academic Press.

Treadaway, C., & Smith, M. (2010). *Facebook marketing: an hour a day*. Wiley Publishing.

Universal McCANN. (2009). *Power of the people: social media tracker*. Retrieved from www.slideshare.com

Vigneron, F., & Johnson, L. W. (2004). Measuring perceptions of brand luxury. *Journal of Brand Management, 11*(6), 484–506.

Wong, N. (1997). Suppose you own the world and no one knows? Conspicuous consumption, materialism and self. *Advances in Consumer Research. Association for Consumer Research (U. S.), 24*(1), 197–203.

Wong, N. Y., & Ahuvia, A. C. (1998). Personal taste and family face: Luxury consumption in Confucian and Western societies. *Psychology and Marketing, 15*(5), 423–441. doi:10.1002/(SICI)1520-6793(199808)15:5<423::AID-MAR2>3.0.CO;2-9

Xiao, S. (2005). *What are the critical success factors for luxury goods companies looking to expand in China?* Retrieved online 19th March 2009, from http://www.bimba.org/ips/article.asp?articleid=399

Yeh, Y., & Choi, S. (2011). MINI-lovers, maxi-mouths: An investigation of antecedents to eWOM intention among brand community members. *Journal of Marketing Communications, 17*(3), 145–162. doi:10.1080/13527260903351119

Youniss, J., & Smollar, J. (1985). The individual and relations. In J. Youniss & J. Smollar (Eds.), *Adolescent relations with mothers, fathers and friends* (pp. 160–176). Chicago: University of Chicago Press.

Zollo, P. (1999). Not quite the TV generation. *American Demographics, 21*(5), 35–37.

ADDITIONAL READING

Andrus, D. M., Silver, E., & Johnston, D. E. (1986). Status Brand Management and Gift Purchase: A Discriminant Analysis. *Journal of Consumer Marketing, 3*(1), 5–13. doi:10.1108/eb008149

Arghavan, N., & Zaichkowsky, J. L. (2000). Do Counterfeits Devalue the Ownership of Luxury Brands? *Journal of Product and Brand Management, 9*(7), 485–497. doi:10.1108/10610420010351402

Banerjee, R., & Dittmar, H. (2008). Individual differences in children's materialism: The role of peer relations. *Personality and Psychology Bulletin, 34*(1), 17–31. doi:10.1177/0146167207309196 PMID:17989212

Bickart, B., & Schindler, R. M. (2001). Internet forums as influential sources of consumer information. *Journal of Interactive Marketing, 15*(Summer), 31–52. doi:10.1002/dir.1014

Bloch, P. H. (1986). The product enthusiast: Implications for marketing strategy. *Journal of Consumer Marketing, 3*(3), 51–62. doi:10.1108/eb008170

Burton, J., & Khammash, M. (2010). Why do people read reviews posted on customeropinion portals? *Journal of Marketing Management, 26*(3–4), 230–255. doi:10.1080/02672570903566268

Casalo, L. V., Flavin, C., & Guinaliu, M. (2008). The role of satisfaction and website usability in developing customer loyalty and positive word-of-mouth in e-banking services. *International Journal of Bank Marketing*, *26*(6), 399–417. doi:10.1108/02652320810902433

Christopher, A. N., & Schlenker, B. R. (2004). Materialism and affect: The role of self-presentational concerns. *Journal of Social and Clinical Psychology*, *23*(2), 260–272. doi:10.1521/jscp.23.2.260.31022

Chun, S. H. (2010). *Strategy for Industrial Development and Growth of Major Industries in Korea*. Energy & Mineral Resources Development Association of Korea.

Fuller, J., Mühlbacher, H., Matzler, K., & Jawecki, G. (2009). Consumer Empowerment through Internet-Based Co-creation. *Journal of Management Information Systems*, *26*(3), 71–102. doi:10.2753/MIS0742-1222260303

Hackley, C. (2009). *Marketing – A Critical Introduction*. London: Sage. doi:10.4135/9781446288511

Ho, J., & Dempsey, M. (2010). Viral marketing: Motivations to forward online content. *Journal of Business Research*, *62*(9-10), 1000–1006. doi:10.1016/j.jbusres.2008.08.010

Li, L. (2014). Korean TV show sparks chiken and beer craze in China. *The Wall Street Journal*. (Feb26). Online available on http://blogs.wsj.com/chinarealtime/2014/02/26/korean-tv-show-sparks-chicken-and-beer-craze-in-china/

O'Cass, A., & McEwen, H. (2004). Exploring consumer status and conspicuous consumption. *Journal of Consumer Behaviour*, *4*(1), 25–39. doi:10.1002/cb.155

Oh, I. (2013). The globalization of K-pop: Korea's Place in the global music industry. *Korea Observer*, *44*(3), 389–404.

Park, S. (2000), "Consumers in their twenties are the main target of expensive foreign luxury brands", *Chosun-Ilbo*, May 9, p. 49.

Petit, F. (2006). South Koreans flip for cool phones Having latest model a national obsession. The Globe and Mail (26/06/2006). Online available on http://www.theglobeandmail.com/report-on-business/south-koreans-flip-for-cool-phones/article711911/

Prendergast, G., & Wong, C. (2003). Parental influence on the purchase of luxury brands of infant apparel: An exploratory study in Hong Kong. *Journal of Consumer Marketing*, *20*(2/3), 157–169. doi:10.1108/07363760310464613

Puntoni, S. (2001). Self-identity and purchase intention: An extension of the theory of planned behavior. *European Advances in Consumer Research*, *5*, 130–134.

Sepp, M., Liljander, V., & Gummerus, J. (2011). Private Bloggers' motivations to produce content – A gratifications theory perspective. *Journal of Marketing Management*, *27*(13–14), 1479–1503. doi:10.1080/0267257X.2011.624532

Yoon, K. (2008). Mobile phones, young people, and South Korean culture. *Education about. Asia*, *13*(3), 52–55.

KEY TERMS AND DEFINITIONS

Customer Motivation: The driving force within individuals that impels them to action.

Electronic Word of Mouth (E-WOM): Any positive or negative statement made by potential, actual, or former customers about a product or company, which is made available to a multitude of people and institutions via the Internet."

Korean Wave: The phenomenon of Korean entertainment and popular culture rolling over the world with pop music, TV dramas, and movies. Also known as "Hallyu" in Korean, the term was first coined by the Chinese press in the late 1990s to describe the growing popularity of Korean pop culture in China.

Luxury Goods: Products which are not necessary but which tend to make life more pleasant for the consumer. In contrast with necessity goods, luxury goods are typically more costly and are often bought by individuals that have a higher disposable income or greater accumulate wealth and average.

Social Media: Social media is the collective of online communications channels dedicated to community-based input, interaction, content-sharing and collaboration. Websites and applications dedicated to forums, microblogging, social networking, social bookmarking, and wikis are among the different types of social media.

User Generated Content: User-generated content (UGC) is published information that an unpaid contributor has provided to a web site. The information might be a photo, video, blog or discussion forum post, poll response or comment made through a social media web site.

ENDNOTE

1 Ralph Lauren Corporation is luxury clothing and Goods Company founded by American fashion designer Ralph Lauren specializes in high-fashion luxury clothing for men and women as well as accessories, fragrances, bedding, towels, and housewares. Until recently, Ralph Lauren's presence in South Korea was fully management by its licensee, the Doosan Corporation.

Chapter 9
A Study of the Impact of Social Networking Communities on the Consumption of Beauty Luxury Products

Lynsey E. Macdonald
Glasgow Caledonian University, UK

Irene García Medina
Glasgow Caledonian University, UK

Zahaira F. González Romo
Universitat de Vic, Spain & Universitat Central de Catalunya, Spain

ABSTRACT

The advances in internet technology over the past decade have irrevocably altered the ways in which people communicate – this, in turn, has had an undeniable impact on consumer behaviour. The following chapter set out to explore the phenomenon of blogging and social media communities, and the impact these communities have had on reference group culture, social identity and the buying behaviour of a target group of consumers – women, aged 18-30, who participate in the online beauty community. This research has examined the impact participation in this community has had on the amount of money these consumers spend on beauty and skincare products, and the extent to which it has influenced their attitude towards luxury products. The study confirmed findings from existing literature, in that a connection between purchasing habits and the desire to be considered a member of the community was established. The data collected revealed that participation in the beauty community has an impact not only on the amount of money consumers spend on beauty and skincare items, but that this frequent online communication makes them increasingly more willing to purchase a wider variety of products, both at a high end/luxury and High Street/drugstore level. The study also revealed that regular participation in the community increases consumer knowledge of products, and can eventually lead to their expertise surpassing that of sales staff. The study concludes by outlining recommendations for marketers working with beauty brands, highlighting key considerations to make when approaching the marketing of products via the online community, based on the findings on this study.

DOI: 10.4018/978-1-4666-9958-8.ch009

INTRODUCTION

Research Background

The internet age is one in which global communities can form via web portals, and people from different continents can form groups around particular topics. It has created an interactive platform for people to discuss their thoughts, interests and opinions, and develop an identity based on those who they align themselves with - blogs are one such space (Zhou, 2011). Blogging communities can and have formed around topics from fashion and beauty to food, gardening and gaming, and present people with an opportunity to share their own thoughts while engaging with others with similar interests. The "blogosphere" (Stanyer, 2006, p.406) has grown exponentially over the past decade, and this has had an impact on consumer behaviour. While reference group culture has been studied by academics for decades (Solomon et al., 2013), blogging has created a whole new level of the concept - the wealth of information available online has led to consumers routinely engaging with blogs as part of the decision making process they go through before purchasing a product or service (Johnson & Kaye, 2009). It has been said that consumers are, to an extent, becoming immune to traditional forms of advertising – their daily lives are so saturated with information from brands that they are able to tune out the excess noise (Gerbarg, 2009, p.44). By turning to blogs, consumers can deliberately target brands, services and products that they have an interest in, and in doing so, discuss those products with other consumers who share that interest. This initial search for information can open up an entire community to consumers; something which, over the past few years, has begun to be researched by academics. The potential of blogs to influence buying behaviour has huge implications for marketers and brands.

The internet has also, however, provided consumers with new ways of creating their identity. Social media sites including Facebook and Twitter, in addition to blogs, are utilised by millions of people across the world – the most up to date studies suggest that the percentage of internet users engaging in these sites is currently 74% (Pew Research, 2014). A connection between reference Group culture and creation of the self has been explored many times over by researchers, but the increased popularity of blogging has created a gap in the research, with vast potential to explore the topic from a new angle.

Research Gap

While the impact of blogging has recently begun to be researched in academia in the consumer behaviour field, this particular study will take a targeted look at the impact the blogging trend is having on the consumption of beauty luxury products.

The beauty and cosmetics industry is thriving, and was one of few industries to continue to grow throughout the recent economic crisis with reports estimating that by 2017, revenues in the industry will reach $265billion (Lucintel Report, 2012). The beauty blogging community is also thriving online, with weekly chats scheduled on twitter to bring bloggers across the world together to discuss their love for beauty products. This study will investigate the impact involvement in this community has on the consumption of such products in terms of overall spend, attitudes towards luxury products and levels of consumer expertise. The gap here is to examine the connection between the social identity aspect of blogging (tied to participation in the community) (Arenas-Gaitan et al., 2013), and the buying behaviour of this select group of consumers.

Aims and Objectives

The aim of this study is to investigate the impact participation in the online beauty community through social networking sites such as twitter, and through blogs, has on the purchasing decisions made by consumers in relation to beauty and skincare products. The study will focus on women aged 18 – 30. The research gap has been identified through careful consideration and critique of existing literature around the themes of online communities, social identity, reference group culture and social networking sites – this research will now build on those studies, in line with the following key research objectives:

1. Evaluate whether or not participation in these online communities leads to an increased spend on beauty products within women aged 18 – 30.
2. Evaluate whether or not participation in these communities has an impact on the purchasing of luxury (high end) brands versus High Street (drugstore) brands.
3. Outline recommendations for brands – discuss the impact of key findings of this study on the relationship between consumers and the online beauty community.

LITERATURE REVIEW

This research aims to investigate the impact of participation in social media communities on the buying behaviour of consumers of beauty and skincare products. The advent of social media has been a catalyst which has "irreversibly transformed the communications landscape" (Haddow & Haddow, 2014, p.19), altering the ways in which human beings connect with one another. The relationship between purchasing habits and social networking is one which encompasses theories not only of online communication, but of reference Group culture (Hyman, 1942; Park and Lessig, 1977), social identification (Arenas-Gaitan et al., 2013; Shen and Chiuo, 2009; Tajfel & Turner, 1985), and consumer behaviour (Solomon et al., 2013). The following chapter will examine academic literature exploring each of these themes, and integrate this literature to provide a framework for the data collection and analysis that is to follow. It is through this thorough investigation and critique of what has come before that the research gap can be fully and explicitly identified, and the aims and objectives of the study can be wholly justified (Easterby-Smith et al., 2012, p.102).

The following study explores a relatively new phenomenon – social media and blogging has only, over the past decade, fully emerged and begun to be explored by academics. What exactly constitutes a blog, or weblog, has been debated by theorists throughout the study of the medium (Rettberg, 2008).

The Oxford English Dictionary (OED) defined the term weblog as "A frequently updated Web site consisting of personal observations, excerpts from other sources, etc., typically run by a single person, and usually with hyperlinks to other sites; an online journal or diary." (Cited in Rettberg, 2008, p.22). This notion of "personal observations" is backed up in numerous definitions of the term (Hsu et al., 2012), however, the singularity expressed in the OED definition has been inconsistent. Tan, Na and Ten (2011) defined a blog as "a specialised website that allows an individual or a group of individuals to express their thoughts, voice their opinions, and share their experiences and ideas". This has been identified as a twenty-first century phenomenon, with earlier examples of blogs serving to "[edit] the internet for their readers". (Pedersen, 2010, p.3) A public blog, then, seems to be the general term for an online space over which individuals can communicate their thoughts, set up by anyone with access to the internet (Pedersen, 2010, p.3).

As a recent phenomenon, blogging is, then, an area with great potential for future study – having rapidly grown over the past decade, there is much still to be discovered about this medium, and the motivations behind its use (Pedersen, 2010). Having defined what is meant by the term itself, this section will go on to explore the theories which are so intrinsically tied to it. The themes raised and connections made through the careful evaluation of existing literature will provide a steady foundation for the later stages of this research.

Reference Groups as a Source of Purchasing Information

From as early as the 1940s, the power of reference group culture has been examined by academics in the study of consumer behaviour. The term itself was coined by Herbert Hyman in 1942, in a paper titled "The Psychology of Status".

He went on, over the next two decades, to expand on this term, establishing that reference group theory is based on the notion that humans "use groups to judge ourselves and our attitudes, beliefs, behaviours, and actions (Hyman, 1942), Hyman and Singer (1968)", (Stolley, 2005, p.85). Over time, reference Group theory has progressed and developed, continuing to be observed in studies by a wide range of theorists (Solomon et al., 2013; Bearden & Etzel, 1982). Park and Lessig, in 1977, defined these influences as informational, utilitarian and value-expressive, and this terminology has been carried on through future studies of the subject (Lin & Chen, 2009; Mooij, 2011). According to Park and Lessig's research, informational reference groups involve an "[active] search for information from opinion leaders or from a group with the appropriate expertise" (1977, p.103).

Utilitarian was found to arise when the consumer felt obliged to make a purchase in order to be seen to be meeting the expectations of a particular group, while value-expressive was said to be intrinsically tied to the enhancement of self-concept by alignment with a group which the consumer has a positive psychological image of (p.103). Further studies have contested these definitions by highlighting the difficulty in separating the utilitarian and value expressive influences, instead, jointly classing them as normative influences (Leal et al., 2013; Bearden & Etzel, 1989). While these terms allow for the concept of the reference group to be more fully explored, many of these studies, including Park and Lessig's (1977) original study, and Mooij's work (2011), identified one factor on which all three of these influences are dependent – social interaction between consumers. 2014 saw Pihl refer to a "renaissance for the concept of community" (p.3), a shift which he and others claim has been fuelled by the opportunities granted to consumers by the emergence of internet technologies (Arnould & Thompson, 2005; Muniz & O'Guinn, 2001). Prior to this technology, reference groups were restricted by geography – consumers could (on a day to day basis at least) only communicate with those in their immediate surroundings, including family, colleagues and peers. Now, thanks to social media, consumers can communicate with people not only in their local area, but at the other side of the world. The internet has diminished the limitations of geography, and provided a platform for interaction at a global scale. This interaction leads to the establishment of groups, which can form around an infinite variety of subjects, from fashion and beauty, to lifestyle, gaming or weddings (Shen & Chiou, 2009; Pihl, 2014). Consumers can align themselves with these groups in whichever way they see fit, with the informational influence appearing to be the most basic level at which they can engage with these online communities. Product reviews, situated on blogs or on company websites enable consumers to actively seek out information on a product from trusted opinion leaders before making their purchasing decision (Hsu et al., 2013). As recently as 2013, Hsu et al., noted that 81% of consumers use social sites as a means of seeking advice before purchasing a product, with blogging becoming "a crucial factor before making a purchasing decision" (p.70).

The recommendations of bloggers are viewed as a more reliable and neutral source of information than advertising produced by the marketing department of a brand (Johnson & Kaye, 2009, p.176).

Park and Feinberg (2010) discussed reference group culture in terms of "consumer conformity". They cited "behavioural changes in consumption behaviour due to a reference group (Burnkrant and Cousineau, 1975; Boush et al., 1993; Lascu and Zinkhan, 1999)" (p. 197-198), as a key example of conformity. There is an underlying implication here that engaging with reference groups in an informational sense can lead to the adoption of this group culture, which can influence purchasing behaviour. This behavioural change is closely linked to notions of social identification, literature around which will be reviewed in the following sections of this chapter.

Reference Groups and Impulse Buying

The wealth of information available on the internet has an impact not only on planned purchases, but on impulse buying too. The study of impulse buying has been reframed since online shopping became an option for consumers, with research suggesting that the increased "research opportunities" provided by the internet encourage impulse buys (Ozen & Engizek, 2013, p.80). There is an innate hedonic value to impulse buying, as identified by authors including Hausman (2000). The results of her study confirmed that "consumers engage in impulse buying to satisfy hedonic desires for fun, novelty and variety" (p.413). What she hypothesised, but could not confirm, however, was the notion that this type of shopping behaviour could be influenced by "the need to interact or garner approval from a significant other or a group" (p.408). This is an idea which will be further explored in the results and analysis section of this study – whether or not this is the case when it comes to the beauty community remains to be seen.

Reference groups, then, are of vital importance to any marketing manager. In their work on reference group culture, Solomon et al., suggested that "consumers voluntarily modify what they do and buy in order to identify with a referent.'' (2013, p.398), showcasing the huge power reference groups have over consumer behaviour. While this has been relevant to marketers for decades, the age of the internet has turned what was a localised phenomenon – consumers could only really converse with those around them regarding product decisions – into a global phenomenon.

Online/Blogging Communities: Notions of the Self

In preparing to explore the ways in which online or blogging communities influence notions of the self, we must first identify what exactly is meant by the term online community. While definitions have varied, Chu (2009) provided a useful definition based on the work of Blanchard and Markus – "By online community we refer to communities in which information and communication technologies, particularly the Internet, facilitate the interaction of members, who share a specific objective (Blanchard and Markus,

2004)." (p280). In addition to the knowledge sharing aspect of such virtual communities, theories of social identification and social identity, are prevalent throughout studies of both off and online communities – the notion that communities, virtual or otherwise, attract consumers not only as a source of information, but as a channel to explore the self, create an identity and build meaningful relationships with others is a regular finding in existing literature (Wang et al., (2012), Shen and Chiou (2009)).

The History of Social Identity Theory

Early research by Tajfel and Turner (1985) defined social identity as "relational and comparative" (p16). Research has found that people cultivate a sense of their own identity through the groups they identify themselves with (Li (2011), Arenas-Gaitan et al (2013)), suggesting that consumers create their own sense of identity by interacting with, and comparing themselves to, "desirable peers" (Wang, 2012: p305). Participation in online and blogging communities is, then, a method of establishing relationships with these peers and using this communication to mould social identity. Recent studies have referred to this process of online communication as a form of consumer socialisation, noting that the speed and convenience of virtual communication creates an instantaneous connection with others, and a space in which to begin creating this sense of identity (Wang, Yu and Wei, 2012). Arenas-Gaitan et al. note that membership of such a virtual community provides an incentive to continually "maintain and improve self-image", in an attempt to retain their imagined place within the group (p1153). Social identity is inextricably linked with self concept, meaning that this participation not only aids the construction of identity in the present, but, as argued by Johnson, can help shape the future self (2003, p123). Much of the work on self-concept has examined the way in which consumption can be used to address both the actual self-image and the ideal self-image. If consumers often base their purchasing decisions on what a particular product says about them, this behaviour has the potential to be magnified in a community situation – the overwhelming desire to belong to the group can impact on buying behaviour (Solomon et al., 2013: p398).

There are a number of factors which can impact upon an individual's desire to belong to a particular group. Wichardt (2009) suggested that this pull to align oneself with others can be amplified when "the group is not naturally determined" (p. 870-871). The implication here is that the desire to belong to a community or group which has been deliberately created by others is often stronger than the basic desire to belong to a group you have been born into (including race or gender – groups which, in most circumstances, are predetermined). There is more social pressure associated with the attempt to be accepted by these types of group, which are easier to access today than they were prior to the birth of the internet. The need for belongingness can be linked back to theories of motivation in line with Abraham Maslow's Hierarchy of Needs. Maslow's argument was that once a human's basic safety and physiological needs are met, "needs for love, affection and belongingness" and "self-esteem" emerge. This idea is frequently backed up in studies of behaviour in online communities (Arenas-Gaitan et al (2013), Park et al (2010). In particular, Pihl's ground breaking research on blogging (2014) has highlighted this connection. According to his study, unity and a sense of security within a larger group can be established by the consumer's alignment of their purchases with those of the community in which they are interacting. The purchase of certain products is a means of securing their position within the group – this, again, reflects Sirgy's notions of self-concept, and the "looking-glass self" (1982). In order to fully belong, consumers seek to enhance the image they believe others hold of them, and do so by matching their purchases with those of other community members. This interpersonal influence is said to be a key component of human behaviour (Hsu et al., 2014), and can lead to increased altruistic behaviour in addition to the matching of purchases.

The implication here is that the more time and energy a person expends in an online community, the more confident they will become in actively interacting with other community members. The desire to be seen to be helpful to others becomes stronger, leading to displays of what Hsu et al. (2014) refer to as "prosocial behaviour" – this could include "disseminating positive recommendations" or "convincing out-groups to join the blog" (p. 79). The sense of achievement that has been found to come hand in hand with this apparent behavioural altruism (Wichardt, 2009) encourages members to continue contributing, creating a cycle of content creation, knowledge sharing and social identity building in these communities.

Consumer Behaviour: Consumer Tribes and Collaborative

Consumption

The Notion of Consumer Tribes

The beauty blogging community exists, in 2014, at a global scale. Beauty fanatics communicate on a daily basis across virtual spaces, using the community as a place in which to discuss a common interest – this in itself is not unusual (Dunne, Lawlor & Rowley, 2010; Raacke & Bonds-Raacke, 2008). The difference between a social network and an online community has been debated by authors including Tharon Howard – in his study of online communities in 2010, Howard argued that social networks present weaker ties than online communities, since the individual is at the centre of the relationship on a social network (p.15). In communities, he argues "members have made a commitment to achieve the shared passions and goals of the group", and this makes their tastes and interests easier to predict than that of members of a social network. What we see in the blogging community today, however, is a cross-over between these two ideas. The community is based on shared interests, but, due to the set-up of the comments section on most blogging platforms, the community itself is based predominantly on social networking sites such as Twitter. These are the sites where the communication between members of the community takes place, in the beauty blogger "twitter chats" which are scheduled at the same time every week. Twitter has provided a platform for members of the community to engage in a wider conversation with more members of the community at any one time, than they would be able to if they simply left a comment on a blog post.

Beauty bloggers have, then, formed a very distinct community online over a relatively short space of time, to the point that it could be considered a "consumer tribe" (Cova, Kosinets & Shankar, 2007). There have been various attempts to categorise exactly what constitutes a consumer tribe, but Cova et al. state that "Consumer tribes rarely consume brands and products… without adding to them, grappling with them, blending them with their own lives and altering them" (p.4). Their book Consumer Tribes (2007) includes studies of brand communities, subcultural commodification and e-Tribes, which all explore the ways in which groups of consumers interact together in a tribal, collaborative manner. Other authors have referred to these groups as "hobby tribes" (Kelly, 1998; Wolfinbarger & Gilly, 2001), noting that they combine their passion and experience of a subject or product group to become experts (Kelly, 1998, pp.105-106). The expertise gained from association with such a group raises questions as to whether or not the members of blogging communities can be seen as innovators, in line with Everett Rogers' 1983 Diffusion of Innovation. This model indicates that the bravest and most innovative of consumers, of any product category, make up only 2.5% of the population (Rogers, 2003).

The model measures the rate at which adoption of a new product diffuses throughout a population. In further work on "innovativeness", Rogers discusses the notion that trusted experts/opinion leaders "should adopt new ideas before their followers", but that does not necessarily always mean they are innovators (2003, p.318). Regardless, their combined consumption leads to members of such communities becoming highly informed on the subject, leading them to establish a position as an extremely valued member of the group. The idea here is that consumption itself is not the "sine qua non of contemporary life" (Cova, Kosinets & Shankar, 2007, p.4) but the relationships this consumption cultivates are.

Online Communities and Theories of Collaborative Consumption

The notion of collaborative consumption was described by Felson & Spaeth in 1978 as "those events in which one or more persons consume economic goods or services in the process of engaging in joint activities with one or more others" (p.614). This process can involve direct or indirect contact between consumers - at the time of their study, this included telephone conversations, but today could be seen to include internet forums such as blogs or twitter chats. Critiques of this study in more recent research by the likes of Belk (2014) have dismissed Felson and Spaeth's definition of the term as too broad, and have focused on specific types of contemporary collaborative consumption, such as gaining access to a product (such as a car) via joint activities (such as car sharing) (2014, p.1597). However, when we apply Felson and Spaeth's definition of the term to the behaviour exhibited in the beauty blogging community, it gains a new lease of life. In the tribal sense described by Cova et al., these consumers do not only access online communities as a means of seeking information on a product from an expert before buying it, but the entire process of collaborative consumption is an experience these consumers desire. Through their blogs, and the conversations which take place across social media, bloggers have altered the way consumption is discussed online. Park, Ahn & Kim noted in 2010 that "by creating, sharing and influencing information, they are active creators, owners and managers of symbols and signs of consumption." Their blogs are reflective of the ways in which consumers 'consume', and this joint activity has turned what is for most a hobby, into a rich field for the study of contemporary consumption habits.

What we see here is not a case of joining a forum to seek advice on a particular product, but rather the opposite – purchases are continually made which facilitate an on-going discussion within the community, with no end point in sight (Bagozzi & Dholakia, 1999, p.19). It is an open ended activity which has become a part of community members' daily lives.

Lurking: Differing Levels of Participation

The degree to which members of a community participate in this on-going conversation has been explored over the years, leading to the general consensus that lurkers – those members who read content but do not participate in content creation or routinely engage in conversation – make up the majority of the members of an online community (Sun et al., 2014). Studies have shown that while these community members avoid the social engagement that is sought by others, the amount of information they consume from online platforms such as blogs is often equal to that of more active participants (Ebner and Holzinger, 2005). This has resulted in conflicting approaches to the study of lurkers.

Active participation of members is what keeps the community alive (Bagozzi and Dholakia, 1999), therefore lurkers' lack of contribution has often been considered selfish (Kollock and Smith (1996), Nonnecke and Preece (2001)). On the other hand, research has suggested that many lurkers are unaware that there is any obligation to post, and in some cases, they do not know how to create a post (Preece et al., 2004). In their 2004 study, aptly titled "The top five reasons for lurking", Preece, Nonnecke and Andrews found that both lurkers and posters join online communities for personal reasons (p. 207), and while posters may feel more connected, both groups feel like members of the community despite their differing attitudes towards participation (p207). Lurkers in this study commented that they felt shy, or that they were afraid of being criticised for their lack of expertise (p212) – in terms of the beauty blogging community, this is an area worth exploring. While participation levels seem to be high, the number of lurkers in the community may well be of significant interest to marketers. By reaching out to active community members (who, according to studies, make up only 5.1% of a blogging community), brands have the potential to reach out to the other 95% of members (Nielsen, 2006).

The Advent of Twitter: A New Community Platform

Early Literature on Twitter

Incorporated in 2007, Twitter has only been an active social media platform for seven years (Twitter, 2014). Studies of the site and the ways in which users engage with it are, then, still in the early stages. Jansen et al., researched the power of Twitter in marketing by examining the potential of the site as electronic Word-of-Mouth (eWOM) (2009). They noted that sites such as Twitter have a direct impact on eWOM in that the immediacy of the format and high level of connectivity between people at a global level, allows consumers to share "brand-affecting thoughts" anywhere and to anyone (p. 2170). Twitter has become a natural partner for blogging in that it is considered a "micro-blogging" platform itself (Williams et al., 2013) - the format permits just 140 character updates to be posted by the user, to be seen by all of their followers. Unlike Facebook, unless the user sets their profile to private, anyone can follow anyone – on a public profile there is no option to accept someone's request to follow you. With this being the case, users are more likely to interact with strangers on Twitter than they are on Facebook. The social implications of the site, however, have more recently begun to be explored, with the uses of Twitter being examined in addition to the format.

As a virtual space for communication with others all over the world, Twitter is a platform utilised by over 645million users to date (Statistic Brain, 2014). Studies have explored the use of Twitter as a vehicle for passing on information (Williams et al., 2013); Rudat et al., 2014), with the features offered by the site setting it up perfectly to do so. Liu et al. (2012) explored the use of the Retweet button, which permits users to share content posted by others to their followers, creating a snowball effect - a single tweet can potentially reach thousands of users. Retweeting, and using a hashtag to connect a tweet to an on-going discussion on a topic are the two most powerful ways Twitter encourages users to disseminate information.

Conclusion

Existing literature has examined online communities from a wide range of perspectives. What this literature review has aimed to achieve is a synthesising of this information, with emphasis on the elements which combine the study of social identity with that of consumerism. The revolutionising of reference groups through the internet has altered the decision making process for consumers, presenting them with an opportunity to seek out information from trusted sources before committing to making a purchase. This is a two way process, with consumers looking to blogs for recommendations and bloggers seeking feedback from their followers. This interaction has led to the creation of vast communities online.

Social identity theories are prevalent throughout existing literature, which highlights the already established connection between alignment with an online group or community and the creation of identity. A link between conversations in a particular online community and the purchasing of certain products has, then, already been established. Something that is yet to be explored, however, is the extent to which involvement in this community can impact on the frequency of purchasing, and the types of products members are willing to consume – in the case of this study, this relates to the attitude consumers have to luxury beauty products. If members of a community are willing to conceal or hide information about themselves in order to fit with the desired community (Yoo et al., 2014), there is a possibility that some of the purchasing decisions they make are not on the basis of deeply desiring the product itself, but that buying it provides a means to actively participate in the community and continue association with other members. This research aims to examine the impact the community has on both willingness to spend money on expensive beauty and skincare products, and the frequency of purchasing, building on the studies of reference group culture and online communities which have been explored in this chapter.

METHODOLOGY

Philosophical and Research Approach

The research aims to uncover if a pattern of social interaction across blogs and online communities has an impact on the volume of beauty products purchased by young women in 2014, and investigate the valuable relationships fostered by this consumer behaviour. The data collection will also be of a more qualitative nature – the most significant stage of data collection will be the focus group discussions, which will provide an insight into the varying experiences and perspectives of the beauty community members (Davies & Hughes, 2014, p.27).

In addition to a philosophical stance, the study will take on an appropriate research approach. There are two recognised approaches to the research process. The first is deductive, an approach which sets out to test theories or hypotheses, meaning specific data must be collected in line with what established theories have highlighted as important (Collis & Hussey, 2014, p.7). This study, however, will be based on the opposing approach – inductive research, which allows the theory to emerge from the data (Strauss & Corbin, 1998, p.12). According to Feeney and Heit (2007, p.1), inductive research is a "multifaceted, cognitive activity", which seems an appropriate fit for the data collection and analysis process of this study. Collis and Hussey note that it is often referred to as "moving from the specific to the general" (p.7). The decision to study the connection between online communities and consumption of beauty products was made after a specific pattern of behaviour was observed – social media and blogging has created a new wave of community experience (Pihl, 2014), which has been embraced by beauty product fanatics. The investigation of this subject through the data collection and analysis will then lead to more general observations on the topic, through the shared experiences of the survey and focus group participants.

Methods of Data Collection

Quantitative and qualitative data are the two paths research tends to follow – each aligns itself more closely with a different research paradigm and research approach and together they have been described by Davies and Hughes (2014) as "an algorithm for evaluating how well the research design process fits together." (p.8). More recently, however, increased attention has been given to what Tashakkori and Teddlie (2003) called the "third methodological movement" (cited in Creswell & Plano Clarke, 2011, p.1) – mixed methods research. This is the method this study will utilise.

Mixed methods research involves "[combining] elements of qualitative and quantitative research approaches (e.g. use of qualitative and quantitative viewpoints, data collection, analysis, inference techniques) for the purposes of breadth and depth of understanding and corroboration." (Johnson et al., 2007, p.123). It is a contentious subject - the refining of research questions and the illustration of quantitative data through qualitative findings as some of the benefits to a mixed methods approach, while other academics have consistently found potential "barriers" to success (Bergman, 2008, p.2). Bergman, however, states that "mixed methods research works far better in practice than in theory." (2008, p.2).

In order to conduct this research, both qualitative and quantitative data will be collected. The latter will take the form of an online survey, which will be shared via Twitter to reach relevant participants. Limitations of an online survey have often been discussed by theorists - Lanzar et al. (2010) noted that the inability to ask follow up questions can be problematic, as questionnaires and surveys can lead to "biased data". (p.101). This could be a result of questions which are subject to interpretation or memory (p.101) – for example, a respondent may not recall exactly how many years they have been reading beauty blogs for.

However, there are many acknowledged benefits to such a survey, including but not limited to its ability to be designed specifically to meet the needs of the research project (McNabb, 2010, p.109), the access it provides to unique populations who would otherwise be difficult to reach (Wright, 2005, p.100) and the speed of responses in comparison to traditional postal survey methods (Reynolds, Woods & Baker, 2007; Bryman, 2012). In the case of this research, access to the global beauty community is granted by this type of survey approach – members of the beauty community communicate via Twitter on a daily basis, making it the perfect platform to share the survey on. Through Survey Monkey, an online survey software system, the survey will be published and left open for two weeks to allow time for enough respondents to access it and provide sufficient data for analysis. This survey will provide some basic data on the level of investment of community members, from a sample of the population. Not every member of what is a global community will respond to the survey, but a small sample which is representative of the population (Sapsford, 1999, p.6) will bring valuable data to the research.

This will be combined with the second stage of data collection – focus groups. Two focus group sessions will be conducted, in a neutral location, in order to formulate the remaining data, this time of a qualitative nature. A focus group method was selected as opposed to individual interviews in the interests of mirroring the community aspect which is vital to this study. The most crucial element of this research is to investigate the impact this community has on the buying behaviour of its participants, therefore a community-style, group data collection process seemed an appropriate fit. Focus groups are also seen to be useful in the study of both "habits and usage" and "attitude" (Greenbaum, 1998, pp.10-11), both of which come into play in the exploration of consumer behaviour through online community participation. Additionally, focus group studies enable targeted participants, who will be able to provide more meaningful responses, to be selected (Baker & Hinton, 1999). Once again, this will involve a small sample of the population – Davies and Hughes note that small sample studies, "when they are used cleverly, throw light on feelings, prejudices and subliminal ideas" (2014, pp.168-169). The focus group discussions themselves were scheduled for the 19th and 20th of July 2014, in Edinburgh and Glasgow, respectively. Each focus group consisted of 4 participants – according to Krueger and Casey (2009), focus groups generally vary in size from 4 to 12 participants per group. While smaller groups have the disadvantage of resulting in a smaller pool of ideas, they "afford more opportunity to share ideas" and allow for every participant to share their insights (p.6). Logistically, groups of four or five are deemed advantageous as they are "easily accommodated" in a location such as a restaurant (p.7).

Data Analysis

In order to analyse the data collected through the online survey, the computer software on the Survey Monkey site will be used. Much like the program SPSS, this software can read the data, analyse it and compare results for the user. This will help identify correlations and trends within the collected data – for example, one question in the survey will identify the number of hours per week a participant spends using social media, while another questions how often the participant goes shopping for new beauty products.

This software can examine if there is a correlation between the responses to these two questions.

The focus group data will be analysed thematically, and via a note based technique. As discussed by Beyea and Nicoll, note based analysis involves listening to or watching the recording of the focus group discussion and noting down specific quotes, concluding by transcribing the written oral summaries from the end of the conversations verbatim (2000: p.1281). Full transcripts can be made up if necessary, later in the analysis process. David Silverman discusses Macnaughten's "mapping the woods" approach in his book titled "Interpreting Qualitative Data" (2011, p.212). This approach is similar to that of Beyea and Nicoll – it involves quickly identifying "key passages", "choosing quotations that made a relevant (and repeated) point briefly and in a striking way" and highlighting "quotable themes" (2011, p.212). While this approach will allow the data to be analysed succinctly, and works well for this type of social behaviour analysis, like any data analysis method, it has its limitations. In this case, that drawback is limited focus on the conversation between the researcher and the participants (Silverman, 2012, p.212).

The data will be analysed in terms of the themes raised. According to Braun and Clarke (2013), "A theme 'captures something important about the data in relation to the research question, and represents some level of patterned response or meaning,'" (p.224). Some important questions to ask during the thematic analysis of focus group research were outlined by Krueger (1998, pp.36- 38) – he suggests that the researcher must consider the "Frequency of Comments", the "Extensiveness of Comments", the "Intensity of Comments", the "Specificity of Responses", "What Was Not Said", and finally, must "Find the Big Ideas". By taking these points into consideration when reviewing the recording of the discussions, a more thorough understanding of what the data reveals can be achieved.

RESULTS AND ANALYSIS

The online survey, which was created on Survey Monkey and distributed via Twitter and Facebook, was completed by seventy people. Of the seventy, fifteen were deemed incomplete, meaning that at least one of the twenty six questions was left unanswered. The data which was collected, however, provided some interesting initial results, which deliver some valuable opportunities to compare and contrast with the data collected in the two focus group discussions.

The participants were all members of the online beauty community, who fit the target group for this research (women aged 18 to 30) and they were invited to participate via email after an invitation for volunteer participants was extended via Twitter. The discussions both lasted between 1 hour and 1 hour 20 minutes, and took place in coffee shops, which were deemed a neutral location. All eight participants read through the participant information form and signed consent forms to acknowledge they understood the process, were aware that they could withdraw at any point, and agreed to have the discussions audio recorded for the purposes of analysis. As discussed in the methodology chapter of this study, focus groups were chosen in order to facilitate a group discussion rather than individual interviews, mirroring the community aspect of the beauty community as a whole.

In order to protect their anonymity, the participants will be referred to as A, B, C, D, E, F, G and H throughout the analysis chapter. As the data was analysed thematically, the findings have been broken down into sections which correlate with the objectives of the study, and the themes explored in the literature review. There is, however, a natural interconnectedness in this data, with one theme linking closely to another, which has led to an organic synthesising of the results. In order to maintain readability, it proved unproductive to attempt to rigidly segregate these themes.

Online Community: Levels of Involvement and Motivation to Participate

One of the most interesting observations which can be made in terms of the survey was the information it provided on differing levels of participation in the beauty community (Sun et al., 2014). As discussed in the literature review section of this research paper, Sun et al (2014) noted that lurkers are thought to make up the majority of members of a community. This idea was, to a certain extent, corroborated by the data collected at this stage – despite the fact the survey was tweeted to potential participants using the beauty bloggers hashtag (#bbloggers), 40% of respondents said that they did not write a blog. When asked how long they had been writing their blog for, if applicable, 40.58% of respondents noted that this was "not applicable" to them. In terms of the other responses to this question, 36% said they had been writing their blog for 1-3 years. With over one third of participants indicating that they began writing between 2011 and 2014, there is a suggestion here that this was a period in which beauty blogging really took off. Interestingly, however, when questioned on their participation in the weekly beauty bloggers "Twitter chats", 40.58% of respondents noted that they participate regularly, with 31.88% admitting to participating once or twice – this suggests that over 72% of respondents have engaged in twitter chats at some stage, despite only 59.42% writing a blog of their own. In terms of marketing products, this is something worth noting for brands.

As expected, the two most common reasons cited for participating in the beauty community were as follows – 49% of respondents said that "feeling part of a community of people with similar interests" was their primary reason for reading and/or commenting on blogs, while 32% used this involvement as a means of "researching information on products". These two high response rates are very much in line with two of the main theories explored in existing literature – the informational influence of reference group culture (Park and Lessig, 1977; Mooij, 2011), and Tajfel and Turner's work on Social Identity Theory. This was also reflected in the focus group discussions.

Something which came across heavily in both the focus group discussions and the survey was the insular feeling which seems to exist within the beauty community – while 51.79% said that they discussed beauty products offline with family and friends, 33.93% of respondents said this was a topic they reserved for discussion "mostly online", and the remaining 14.29% said they did discuss beauty products offline, but only with friends they had made through blogging and social media. Interestingly, when using the survey monkey software to compare individual responses, it was revealed that 45% of respondents who said they regularly discussed products offline with family and friends did not write a blog of their own compared with an average of just 13.79% for those who did. This was a subject which was expanded upon in the focus group discussions through incidental comments made by participants. As some of the participants in the focus groups have become friends offline, the following exchange highlighted the circumstances under which participant C was comfortable talking about beauty products:

C: *I'd say I do talk about it offline, but only to you guys! I don't talk about it to my other 'normal' friends!*
D: *Just your internet friends!*

Further on in the discussion, C commented again on the difference between the blogging community and other people, again opting for the term "normal" when referring to non-bloggers owning Real Techniques brushes – a hugely popular brand with bloggers thanks to the range being created by blogging and YouTube stars Samantha and Nicola Chapman:

C: *I still find it a bit weird when normal people have them, and they're like "I've got these brushes" - I always just assumed only bloggers know about them!*
D: *"I've got these new brushes" - no, they're not new! They might be new for you, but not for us!*

This was a discussion which also arose in the second focus group. Participant E noted that she felt the beauty blogger chats had been "infiltrated by a lot of people who don't even necessarily have beauty blogs" – something which the survey results validated. She also described feeling surprised when a shop assistant attempted to sell her a product based on its popularity with blogger and YouTuber Ruth Crilly:

E: *I was like "wow, wait… how do you know about Ruth Crilly?!"*

These discussions reveal an alignment of the community members' behaviour with the work of Widchardt (2009) – his study noted that "when the group is not naturally determined", the desire to become an accepted member is heightened (pp.870-871) – this came across in the focus group discussions. All eight participants across both focus groups said they were overwhelmed by the connections and friendships they had made through the blogging community.

Participant F said she was thrilled to discover how "nice" bloggers were when she began participating in the weekly blogger chats on twitter, while participant B admitted to being initially nervous about attending blogger events because she thought that in real life beauty bloggers would be "really glamorous", and she worried they might not like her. Participant A noted that seeing the communication between other bloggers online was one of the reasons she started blogging in the first place, but that it was "crazy that you feel like you want to meet these people" (referring to more well-known beauty bloggers). In addition to noting that becoming accepted themselves had been important, the verbatim quotes above show the participants voicing their confusion when outsiders attempted to join in discussions on a topic they felt was reserved solely for the established online group. The eligibility of members was most definitely questioned, with the community appearing keen to protect itself as a place solely for those who are genuinely interested in the subject.

Beauty Bloggers as Innovators and Experts

While the insular nature of the community was a definite theme, both the survey results and focus group discussions suggested that this desire for the blogging community to remain a place for only the most passionate of beauty fans was not connected to a desire to be seen as beauty innovators, in terms of the diffusion of innovation (Rogers, 2003). 71% of respondents said no when asked "would you consider yourself a beauty innovator – are you keen to be first to discover a new product?" There is a feeling that what is important here is not being seen as an expert who leads a discussion, but rather being part of an ongoing conversation (Dunne, Lawlor and Rowley, 2010). However, when this issue was raised in the focus groups, it became apparent that while participants did not set out to become beauty experts, or innovators, this seemed to be a byproduct of becoming involved in the community. All four of the participants in the first discussion agreed that blogging had made them willing to try more products, but also made them more confident shoppers who "can't be conned into buying as much stuff now" (participant B). This exchange highlighted the notion of bloggers becoming experts in their own right:

C: *It's always slightly awkward when you know more about the product than the sales staff! I remember I went in to a Benefit counter once and asked for their eye Bright pencil, and she gave me the High Brow one. I wanted the one that you can put on your water line, and she gave me the one for eyebrows. I was like "this isn't what I asked for", and she said "yeah, it's that pencil you wanted", and I was like, "no, it's definitely not"!*

B: *I've noticed that quite a lot actually! I feel like blogging has actually taught us more, and we're becoming a bit more knowledgeable than the actual people working there.*

All eight participants agreed that friends and family see them as a "makeup expert" since blogging, and will come to them for recommendations. Several participants mentioned family members and friends approaching them for advice on what products to buy, from peers to parents, showing an influence across generations.

Social Identity: Community Influence on Purchasing Habits

During the first focus group discussion, the question of how involvement in blogging and social media impacted on their buying habits appeared organically early on in the discussion. Participant B stated: "I feel like it's enabling you to buy things. It's like 'Oh, it's fine, they've all got lots of stuff!'" This was met with collective laughter and agreement from the other participants, and followed up by participant D who stated that "It's okay to have fifteen foundations!" This led into a conversation about the way in which they purchase makeup, and a discussion on the desire to collect makeup rather than simply buy one of each type of product. This was reflected in the second discussion, when participant F acknowledged that only a couple of years ago she owned one blusher and now that she has a blog, she cannot imagine not having a wider choice. The suggestion here is that the more involved members become with the beauty community, the more likely they are to increase their spend on products.

Buying makeup becomes a habitual exercise, rather than something they do simply to replace something they have finished with – participant E noted that she used to only purchase a new cleanser when the previous one was finished. Now, however, she will happily buy three or four to use at the same time.

The connection between the creation of an identity in line with the community (Li, 2011), and this increased purchasing is important to consider. The survey results showed that only 12.5% of respondents had ever made a conscious decision to purchase a product in order to participate in the online conversation surrounding it. However, 84.06% said they had bought a product purely based on the recommendation of a blogger, while 78.26% admitted to having bought a product they did not already want or need simply because there was a buzz around it online. This issue arose in the second focus group discussion:

E: *If someone like Tanya Burr or Zoella, you know, one of these people with millions of subscribers buys something, then, probably because they're quite genuinely friends, the other one buys it. So then you've got those two buying it, and then everyone else starts buying it. So even if you decide you're not really that interested, it then comes up in every blog that you read for the next couple of weeks and...*

H: *And you do feel a bit out of the loop if you don't have it.*

F: *Yeah, like you're missing out.*

There seems to be a pattern of exposure and conformity in this line of discussion. While participants in both focus groups said they felt that the longer they blogged, the more "savvy" they were when it came to making purchasing decisions, the pull to be involved with whatever it is the community at large is discussing is still very much alive. Reading blogs, participating in twitter chats and watching YouTube videos leads to community members being constantly bombarded with images of and conversations surrounding new products. The idea that beauty bloggers do try a wide range of products, and that to be involved at an intense level, you must also be purchasing new products regularly (Pihl, 2014), is reflected in the survey – 67.16% of respondents noted that they had seen an increase in their monthly spend on beauty and skincare products since engaging with the beauty community. Using the survey monkey software to further investigate these figures it was revealed that over 95% of those who answered yes to that question said that they had bought a product purely based on the recommendation of a blogger, 97.78% stated that social media and blogs were their go-to source of information on products and 66.67% acknowledged that feeling part of a community of people with similar interests was their primary reason for reading and commenting on blogs. The desire to belong to the tribe, as discussed by the likes of Hsu et al (2014) then impacts on the amount of money members are willing to spend – the more they spend, the more involved they become.

Consumer Perception: Luxury vs. Drugstore

Two of the key objectives of this study were to explore the impact the online beauty community can have on not only the frequency of purchasing, but participant attitude to high end or luxury products versus lower end/drugstore products. The survey revealed that while 48.48% of respondents felt that participating in online conversations had not changed their attitude towards high end products, 46.97% said that since becoming involved with the community they found themselves more willing to spend money on luxury products – only 4% said they were now less likely to part with money for high end items. The implication here is that if consumer attitude is affected at all by blogging, it is over ten times more likely to be in favour of purchasing luxury goods, rather than a deterrent of such purchases. Other questions in the survey relating to this subject revealed that 55% of respondents buy both luxury and drugstore makeup, and 41% buy both when purchasing skincare items.

When this topic arose during the focus group discussions, participants were asked whether they previously bought more high end or low end products. The response to this question was divided:

C: *I would say drugstore...*
A: *Yeah, me too.*
D: *I'm probably the other way around.*
B: *Same!*

While A and C opted for drugstore and B and D for luxury, all four acknowledged that since blogging, they have found themselves more willing to try a wider range of products and brands. The initial aim of this study was to uncover whether or not consumers were influenced through blogs and social media to buy luxury products – what became apparent here, however, was that social media has just as much power to encourage the purchase of considerably less expensive products:

D: *I think it opens up that whole area that, they might not spend so much money on advertising, but you see it on blogs rather than in magazines...*
A: *Yeah, that's true actually. Like, the eye-shadow palette I wrote about, the Naked 3 dupe? There's no way I would have bought that without reading reviews, because even if I'd stumbled across it online, I'd be like "hmm, it looks really cheap".*

This notion was also reflected in the second focus group discussion. Participant E said that her sensitive skin had always caused her to buy higher end products, but that the blogging community had "opened her eyes to how much drugstore makeup has improved". She followed this up by saying that while she would always have bought high end, she would never have bought the drugstore makeup that she now purchases. She also related this to how much money she is willing to spend, noting that she buys drugstore products more easily now, but she'll "buy seven of them" because the cost per item is so much lower than the cost of individual high end products. Participant F agreed, noting that she often justifies such impulse purchases by planning to write a review of them on her blog and potentially "save someone money". This sort of impulse buying appears to be enabled by the blogging community, because the lives of the members are so saturated with information – the survey results showed that 56.52% of respondents spend over 10 hours per week using social media, with figures of over 60% (some as high as 98%) for usage of specific sites:

An interesting observation which came through on both occasions was the feeling that while the attitude towards buying higher end products might not necessarily have consciously changed, the perception of what actually constitutes an expensive product had most definitely been impacted by the social media community. Following a discussion on how much they used to spend on makeup in comparison to how much they now spend, participant C commented that in the past she "would never have dreamed of spending £40 on a foundation":

Researcher: *Do you think then, having been blogging for as long as you have, your perception of what an expensive product is has been altered?*

Collective Yes.

A: *Yeah, like C was saying, I would never have spent... like for a foundation, I would even say £10 was quite expensive because I was buying drugstore, whereas now, when I look at things, if it's under £30 - if it was £28 - I'm like "oh, that's really good"! And then you think, actually, I could have bought a dress for that! Yet I'm spending it on one makeup item.*

In the second focus group discussion, this idea arose again. When discussing skincare, participant E admitted that the price she deems acceptable for a cleanser has gradually increased since she's been blogging:

E: *There's a Zellens one at £40 that I'm still thinking about... And then when I take myself out of the blogger mind-set and go "that's £40 for a face wash", you realise how bad it is! But then when you're in that mind-set, it just seems okay...*

This revelation could then have an impact on the survey results – the question of attitude towards purchasing higher end products becomes irrelevant if the perception of what constitutes an expensive product in the first place has been altered by these online discussions. In order to further explore this idea, the survey asked participants to select the most money they had ever spent on one individual makeup or skincare item. 36.36% of respondents said that they had spent £50 on one product, while 30.30% said the most they have spent was £25. 6%, however, admitted to spending over £100 on one single item.

RECOMMENDATIONS FOR MARKETERS

Two of the most interesting points to come out of the focus group discussions, when analysed alongside the survey results, were the influence social media and blogs have over the range of high to low end products consumers are willing to purchase, and, even more interestingly, the attitude members of the community have towards product reviews.

The statistics from the survey prove that engaging with bloggers in general is a worthwhile endeavour for brands – 84% of respondents admitted to buying a product purely based on the recommendation of a blogger, and 85% cited social media and blogs as their go-to source for product information today. Even so called lurkers (Sun, Rau & Ma, 2014) are a huge source of potential customers, and their presence is just as strong as that of active participants. A discussion around products being sent by PR companies to bloggers for review, however, revealed that while 'bigger bloggers' – those bloggers who have the largest number of followers – tend to be first in line to test out and review new products, their reviews tend not to be what influences community members to invest in a product. In both focus groups, one participant (B in group 1 and E in group 2) referred to bigger blogs as becoming more and more like magazines. A agreed with this point, noting that often a review on a more well-known blog reads "just like a press release", and it is "obvious they've just been sent a bunch of stuff and need to write about them". E said she felt like the bloggers who now blog as their career might just "do whatever they're told, [...] whatever's going to get them a money." Several participants suggested that they did not trust that a full time blogger really, thoroughly tested the products they are sent before they review them:

F: *I think I'm more likely to trust a part time blogger than a full time blogger, because that's their job.*
E: *Exactly. And they're using affiliate links and they're getting money every time you buy it. I'm sorry, but that changes things, because of course you want to blog about that ASAP so you can make people buy it. If Vivianna Does Makeup blogs about something and everyone buys it from her link, and then Lily Pebbles puts up something a week later, everyone's already bought it from Vivianna's link. So she's not making any money off it. And that does impact on how quickly you want to turn around your reviews. I totally understand it from their point of view, but from my point of view I'm thinking "have you worn that once and you're telling me how wonderful it is?"*

The general feeling across both focus groups was that while 84% of survey respondents admitted to buying a product purely based on the recommendation of a blogger, when it came down to which blogs they were more likely to trust, smaller bloggers swept the board. Participant F said that she makes sure to read several reviews of a product from a range of bloggers before committing to buying it. The community element here also seemed to be an influencing factor.

Participant B said she felt that smaller bloggers "were more on her level", suggesting that the bigger and more famous a blogger becomes, the less relatable they are to members of the community, almost 50% of whom (according to the survey results) engaged with the community in the first place to interact with "likeminded" people. This links to Johnson and Kaye's 2009 work on blogging – they noted that blogs (in terms of reference group culture) were viewed as more neutral sources of information than brands (p.176), something which is clearly impacted by brands and bloggers working together.

For marketers, this presents a slight dilemma – the more followers a blogger has, the further their reach. However, it seems that consumers are unlikely to take a bigger blogger's word for it when it comes to the quality of a product, because it is now common knowledge that they are often paid in one way or another for that review. What sending products to bigger bloggers does result in, however, is discussion of the product online. In order to convince people to purchase the product it is vital that marketers and PR staff for beauty brands also engage with smaller bloggers, with a small but loyal following. By communicating with these bloggers, they can begin to target the wider population and give consumers an opportunity to really trust the reviews.

Secondly, the survey and the discussions revealed that engagement with the beauty community can and does have a genuine impact on not only the level of spending, but the range of products consumers are willing to try out. While the aim of this study, initially, was to investigate the impact the beauty community has on attitude towards luxury products, the focus group discussions revealed that the community has had just as powerful an influence on lower end/drugstore products that consumers may previously have deemed "too cheap" to be effective (Participant A). Three of the eight participants stated that they previously bought high end makeup, mainly because it was what was always advertised in magazines. All eight agreed that they had now purchased drugstore products, as a result of online reviews, that they previously would have dismissed due to the price tag. This notion was reflected in the survey results – when asked if they could think of an example of a product they had discovered via social media and gone on to repurchase more than once, 9 of the 49 respondents who answered the question listed Collection Lasting Perfection Concealer. This is a drugstore product, retailing at £4.19 (Boots.com, 8/8/2014) which has achieved cult status in the beauty community thanks to the consistent high praise it has received on blogs, YouTube videos and twitter. Furthermore, over 46% of respondents admitted to being more willing to purchase high end products thanks to their engagement with the community. Since perception of what constitutes an expensive product has changed, price seems to have become less important than quality.

For both high and low end brands, then, engagement with blogs and social media is a vital way of connecting with potential consumers. While luxury products remain "special" (Participant E), drugstore brands can really benefit from engaging with the population in this manner. Online reviews are what spur the majority of consumers in this community on to purchase a product, to the point that five of the focus group participants admitted to scrolling through reviews and even YouTube videos on their phones in stores before taking a product to the till. Magazines were deemed unhelpful by participants in that they rarely review a product, simply listing them as desirable new items for the upcoming season. By capitalising on this trend, and actively communicating with bloggers, both high and low end brands can secure new customers and widen the reach of their products without relying on traditional advertising.

FINAL CONCLUSION

This study set out to explore the relationship between the online beauty community and the purchasing behaviour of women aged 18 to 30. The key objectives were tied to the impact these communities had on the amount of money participants were willing to spend on products, their attitude towards luxury products and High Street products, and outlining recommendations for marketers.

Previous studies found that the internet age has reinvigorated the concept of reference group culture (Pihl, 2014; Arnould & Thompson, 2005). Existing literature was found to make connections between online communities and the creation of social identity (Arenas-Gaitan et al., 2013; Wang, 2012), and academics have begun to explore the possible influence such communities could have on consumer behaviour (Cova, Kosinets & Shankar, 2007). This research took that idea one step further, with reference to a very specific group – it targeted women aged 18 to 30, who participated in the online beauty community, to explore at a deeper level the impact this community has had on their purchasing habits. Not only did the online survey and focus group discussions back up the findings of the likes of Arenas-Gaitan et al. and Moorley and Chinn in that the online community was found to be both a source of information on products, and a space in which to cultivate friendships and create an identity (Arenas- Gaitan et al, 2013, p.1159), but they also brought to light several new areas of potential study around this subject. Three prevailing ideas which arose throughout the survey and the discussions, which provide some interesting issues for marketers to contemplate, were as follows:

- The increased spend on products witnessed in almost 70% of respondents who participated in the online community, across various social media platforms.
- The increased variety of products consumers are willing to purchase (from low to high end) after participating in the online community.
- The notion that community members are gaining increased knowledge of the industry and products, to the point that their expertise surpasses the staff working for the company.

The importance of incorporating blogging into any marketing plan was summed up concisely by Singh, Veron-Jackson and Cullinane back in 2008 – while there have been vast developments in technology, the proliferation of blogging and social media usage in the six years since their paper "Blogging: A new play in your marketing game" was published, this particular quote remains pertinent:

... Blogging can be viewed as a form of viral marketing because it also uses social networks, user-generated content, and interactivity to spread the message. It shares several advantages with viral marketing, from low cost to voluntary customer participation. (p.283)

This "voluntary customer participation" is the key to unlocking the potential of blogging – consumers are already participating in these online discussions, and the results of this study have confirmed that it is impacting on their buying behaviour. It is now up to marketers to join in the discussion, and engage with potential customers to turn this online conversation into increased sales. The future of blogging is unknown, but if this study is reflective of what is to come, it is an area which will provide fruitful material for research for years to come.

FUTURE RESEARCH DIRECTIONS

This study, much like any other, has its limitations. Geographically, the beauty community is operating at a global level, and while the online survey was available to anyone with an internet connection, the focus group discussions were at a much more local level, and all eight participants were Scottish women. The results, however, highlighted that this is a rich area for further study - similar studies in other countries in the future could lead to an increased understanding of how the community impacts on consumer behaviour on a global scale, through comparison of results from different cultures.

Online communities have been subject to countless studies over the past decade, and will continue to be studied in the future as technology continues to advance. Future studies in the area could build on the results of this study, by exploring the issues of trust in the blogging community – one of the key findings of this particular study was that while over two thirds of consumers do spend more money on products after becoming involved in the beauty community, they are less likely to believe the review of a full time blogger. It would be beneficial to expand on this finding by examining this in more depth in a future study – existing literature on Twitter (Yoo et al, 2014) established a lack of trust developing due to Twitter users "concealing information" about themselves. This research has established that involvement in the blogging community does impact on consumer behaviour, so examining how this impact is further influenced by trust within the community is a logical next step.

Davis et al (2014) said that social media communities "[demand] a shift from marketer led brand[s] to customer ownership and co-creation of meaning" (p.468), something which resonates closely with the results of this study. For marketers, it is clear that engaging with the beauty blogging/social media community is a key method of connecting with potential customers. Theinternet has altered the ways in which brands are able to communicate with consumers (Park and Kim, 2014), and consumers "possess almost unlimited opportunities to engage with brands" (Davis et al, 2014). Not only are consumers able to communicate with the brands themselves, however, but they are able to communicate directly with one another on a daily basis. This creation and sharing of information results in a loss of control for the companies – their products can and will be discussed by this tribe of consumers who are becoming ever more expert in their knowledge, no matter how the brands choose to engage with consumers themselves (Dahlen et al, 2010: p.448). The results of the survey and focus group discussions here suggest that the consumers who invest most highly in their products are no longer responding to traditional methods of advertising through magazines or brand websites, with over 85% of survey respondents listing social media and blogs as their go to source of product information – this is something which can be capitalised on if brands listen to what is making their most fanatical customers tick.

REFERENCES

Arenas-Gaitan, J., Rondan-Cataluña, F. J., & Ramírez-Correa, P. E. (2013). Social identity, electronic word-of-mouth and referrals in social network services. *Kybernetes*, *8*(42), 1149–1165. doi:10.1108/K-04-2013-0081

Arnould, E. J., & Thompson, C. J. (2005). Consumer Culture Theory (CCT) – Twenty Years of Research. *The Journal of Consumer Research*, *4*(31), 868–882. doi:10.1086/426626

Bagozzi, R. P., & Dholakia, U. M. (2006). Antecedents and purchase consequences of customer participation in small group brand communities. *International Journal of Research in Marketing*, *1*(23), 45–61. doi:10.1016/j.ijresmar.2006.01.005

Bearden, W. O., & Etzel, M. J. (1982). Reference Group Influence on Product and Brand Purchase Decisions. *The Journal of Consumer Research*, (9): 1982.

Belk, R. (2014). You are what you can access – Sharing and collaborative consumption online. *Journal of Business Research*, *8*(67), 1595–1600. doi:10.1016/j.jbusres.2013.10.001

Bryman, A. (2012). *Social Research Methods* (4th ed.). Oxford, UK: Oxford University Press.

Collis, J., & Hussey, R. (2014). *Business Research* (4th ed.). Palgrave Macmillan.

Cova, B., Kozinets, R. V., & Shankar, A. (2007). *Consumer Tribes*. Butter-Heinemann.

Creswell, J. W., Plano, C., & Vicki, L. (2011). *Designing and Conducting Mixed Methods Research* (2nd ed.). Sage Publications, Inc.

Dahlen, M., Lange, F., & Smith, T. (2010). *Marketing Communications – A Brand Narrative Approach*. John Wiley & Sons Ltd.

Davies, M., & Hughes, N. (2014). *Doing a Successful Research Project* (2nd ed.). Palgrave Macmillan.

Dunne, A., Lawlor, M. A., & Rowley, J. (2010). Young people's use of online social networking sites – a uses and gratifications perspective. *Journal of Research in Interactive Marketing*, *4*(1), 46–58. doi:10.1108/17505931011033551

Easterby-Smith, M., Thorpe, R., & Jackson, P. R. (2012). *Management Research* (4th ed.). London: Sage.

Feeney, A., & Heit, E. (2007). *Inductive Reasoning: Experimental, Developmental, and Computational Approaches*. New York: Cambridge University Press. doi:10.1017/CBO9780511619304

Felson, M., & Spaeth, J. (1978). Community structure and collaborative consumption. *The American Behavioral Scientist*, *21*(4), 614–624.

Gerbarg, D. (2009). *Television Goes Digital*. Springer. doi:10.1007/978-0-387-79978-0

Greenbaum, T. L. (1998). *The Handbook for Focus Group Research* (2nd ed.). Sage Publications, Inc.

Haddow, G. D., & Haddow, K. S. (2014). *Disaster Communications in a Changing Media World*. Butterworth Heinemann.

Hausman, A. (2000). A multi-method investigation of consumer motivations in impulse buying behavior. *Journal of Consumer Marketing*, *17*(5), 403–426. doi:10.1108/07363760010341045

Howard, T. (2010). *Design to Thrive: Creating Social Networks and Online Communities that Last*. Morgan Kauffman Publishers.

Hsu, C., Chuan-Chuan Lin, J., & Chiang, H.-S. (2013). The effects of blogger recommendations on customers' online shopping intentions. *Internet Research*, *23*(1), 69–88. doi:10.1108/10662241311295782

Hyman, H. H. (1942). The psychology of status. *Archives de Psychologie*, (269): 5–91.

Hyman, H. H., & Singer, E. (1968). *Readings in Reference Group Theory and Research*. Free Press.

Jansen, B. J., Zhang, M., Sobel, K., & Chowdury, A. (2009). Twitter Power – Tweets as Electronic Word-of-Mouth. *Journal of the American Society for Information Science and Technology*, *11*(60), 2169–2188. doi:10.1002/asi.21149

Johnson, T. J., & Kaye, B. K. (2009). In blog we trust? Deciphering credibility of components of the internet among politically interested internet users. *Computers in Human Behavior*, *25*(1), 175–182. doi:10.1016/j.chb.2008.08.004

Kelly, K. (1998). *New Rules for the New Economy – 10 Ways the Network Economy is Changing Everything*. New York: Penguin Books.

Kollock, P., & Smith, M. (1996). Managing the virtual commons – co-operation and conflict in computer communities. In Computer-mediated communication: Linguistic, social, and cross-cultural perspectives. John Benjamins.

Krueger, R. A. (1998). *Analysing & Reporting Focus Group Discussions (Focus Group Kit 6)*. Sage Publications.

Krueger, R. A., & Casey, M. A. (2009). *Focus Groups – A Practical Guide for Applied Research* (4th ed.). Sage Publications.

Lanzar, J., Feng, J. H., & Hochheiser, H. (2012). *Research Methods in Human-Computer Interaction*. John Wiley & Sons Ltd.

Leal, G., Pasinato, A., Hor-Meyll, L. F., & Pessôa, L. A. (2013). Influence of virtual communities in purchasing decisions: The participants' perspective. *Journal of Business Research*, *67*(5), 882–890. doi:10.1016/j.jbusres.2013.07.007

Li, D. C. (2011). Online social network acceptance: A social perspective. *Internet Research*, *21*(5), 562–580. doi:10.1108/10662241111176371

Lin, C. A., & Atkis, D. J. (2012). *Communication Technology and Social Change: Theory and Implications*. New York: Routledge.

Lin, L., & Chen, Y. (2009). A study on the influence of purchase intentions on repurchase decisions: The moderating effects of reference groups and perceived risks. *Tourism Review*, *64*(3), 28–48. doi:10.1108/16605370910988818

Liu, Z., Liu, L., & Li, H. (2012). Determinants of information retweeting in microblogging. *Internet Research*, *4*(22), 443–466. doi:10.1108/10662241211250980

Lucintel Report. (2012). Available at http://www.lucintel.com/market_research_reports.aspx last accessed 02/10/14

McNabb, D. (2010). *Research Methods for Political Science: Quantitative and Qualitative Approaches*. M.E. Sharp, Inc.

Mooij, M. (2011). *Consumer Behaviour and Culture: Consequences for Global Marketing and Advertising* (2nd ed.). Sage.

Moorley, C. R., & Chinn, T. (2014). Nursing and Twitter: Creating an online community using hashtags. *Collegian (Royal College of Nursing, Australia)*, *21*(2), 103–109. doi:10.1016/j.colegn.2014.03.003 PMID:25109208

Muniz, A. Jr, & O'Guinn, T. C. (2001). Brand Communities. *The Journal of Consumer Research*, *27*(4), 412–432. doi:10.1086/319618

Nielsen, J. (2011). *Participation inequality: Encouraging more users to contribute, 2006*. Available at http://www.nngroup.com/articles/participationinequality/

Nonnecke, B., & Preece, J. (2001). Why lurkers lurk. *Americas Conference on Information Systems*.

Ozen, H., & Engizek, N. (2014). Shopping online without thinking: Being emotional or rational? *Asia Pacific Journal of Marketing and Logistics*, *26*(1), 78–93. doi:10.1108/APJML-06-2013-0066

Park, B., Ahn, S., & Kim, H. (2010). Blogging: Mediating impacts of flow on motivational behavior. *Journal of Research in Interactive Marketing*, *4*(1), 6–29. doi:10.1108/17505931011033533

Park, C., & Lessig, P. (1977). Students and Housewives –Differences in Susceptibility to Reference Group Influences. *The Journal of Consumer Research*, *4*(4), 102–110. doi:10.1086/208685

Pedersen, S. (2010). *Why Blog? Motivations for Blogging*. Chandos Publishing. doi:10.1533/9781780631714

Pew Research Internet Project. (2013). *Social Networking Fact Sheet*. Available at: http://www.pewinternet.org/fact-sheets/social-networking-factsheet/

Pihl, C. (2014). Brands, community and style – exploring linking value in fashion blogging. *Journal of Fashion Marketing and Management*, *18*(1), 3–19. doi:10.1108/JFMM-10-2013-0108

Raacke, J., & Bonds-Raacke, J. (2008). MySpace and Facebook: Applying the uses and gratifications theory to exploring friend-networking sites. *Cyberpsychology & Behavior*, *11*(2), 169–174. doi:10.1089/cpb.2007.0056 PMID:18422409

Rettberg, J. W. (2008). *Blogging*. Polity Press.

Reynolds, R. A., Woods, R., & Baker, J. D. (2007). *Handbook of Research on Electronic Surveys and Measurements*. Idea Group Reference. doi:10.4018/978-1-59140-792-8

Rogers, E. (2003). *Diffusion of Innovations* (5th ed.). The Free Press.

Rudat, A., Buder, J., & Hesse, F. W. (2014). Audience design in Twitter: Retweeting behavior between informational value and followers' interests. *Computers in Human Behaviour*, (35), 132-139c.

Sapsford, R. (1999). *Survey Research*. Sage Publications.

Shen, Ch., & Chiou, J. (2009). The effect of community identification on attitude and intention toward a blogging community. *Internet Research*, *19*(4), 393–407. doi:10.1108/10662240910981362

Silverman, D. (2012). *Interpreting Qualitative Data* (4th ed.). London, UK: Sage Publications Ltd.

Singh, T., Veron-Jackson, L., & Cullinane, J. (2008). Blogging: A new play in your marketing game plan. *Business Horizons*, *51*(4), 281–292. doi:10.1016/j.bushor.2008.02.002

Solomon, M., Bamossy, G. J., Askegaard, S. T., & Hogg, M. K. (2013). *Consumer Behaviour – A European Perspective* (5th ed.). New York: Pearson Education.

Stanyer, J. (2006). Online campaign communication and the phenomenon of blogging: An analysis of web logs during the 2005 British general election campaign. *Aslib Proceedings*, *58*(5), 404–415. doi:10.1108/00012530610692357

StatisticBrain. (2014). *Twitter Statistics*. Available at http://www.statisticbrain.com/twitter-statistics/

Stolley, K. S. (2005). *The Basics of Sociology*. Greenwood Press.

Strauss, A., & Corbin, J. (1998). *Basics of Qualitative Research – Techniques and Procedures for Developing Grounded Theory* (2nd ed.). London, UK: Sage.

Sun, N., Rau, P. and Ma, L. (2014). Understanding lurkers in online communities: A literature review. *Computers in Human Behaviour*, (38), 110-117.

Tajfel, H., & Turner, J. C. (1985). The social identity theory of intergroup behaviour. In *Psychology of intergroup relations* (2nd ed.). Chicago: Nelson-Hall.

Tan, L. K. W., Na, J. C., & Theng, Y. L. (2011). Influence Detection between Blog posts through blog features, content analysis, and community identity. *Online Information Review*, *35*(3), 425–442. doi:10.1108/14684521111151450

Twitter. (2014). *About Twitter*. Available: https://about.twitter.com/company,last accessed 18/06/14

Wang, H. (2012). Six P's of youth social media from a young consumer's perspective. *Young Consumers: Insight and Ideas for Responsible Marketers*, *13*(3), 303–317. doi:10.1108/17473611211261674

Widchardt, P. C. (2009). A status based motivation for behavioural altruism. *International Journal of Social Economics*, *36*(8), 869–887. doi:10.1108/03068290910967127

Williams, S. A., Terras, M. M., & Warwick, C. (2013). What do people study when they study Twitter? Classifying Twitter related academic papers. *The Journal of Documentation*, *3*(69), 384–410. doi:10.1108/JD-03-2012-0027

Wolfinbarger, M., & Gilly, M. (2001). Shopping online for freedom, control and fun. *California Management Review*, *43*(2), 34–55. doi:10.2307/41166074

Wright, K.B. (2005). Researching Internet-Based Populations: Advantages and Disadvantages of Online Survey Research, Online Questionnaire Authoring Software Packages, and Web Survey Services. *Journal of Computer-Mediated Communication, 10*(3).

Yoo, J., Choi, S., Choi, M., & Rho, J. (2014). Why people use Twitter: Social conformity and social value perspectives. *Online Information Review*, *38*(2), 265–283. doi:10.1108/OIR-11-2012-0210

Zhou, T. (2011). Understanding online community user participation: A social influence perspective. *Internet Research*, *21*(1), 67–81. doi:10.1108/10662241111104884

Section 3

Old and New Trends in Distribution Strategies for Luxury Players

Chapter 10
Old and New Distribution Channels in the Luxury Sector

Fabrizio Mosca
University of Turin, Italy

Elisa Giacosa
University of Turin, Italy

ABSTRACT

The focus of this chapter is to provide scientific evidence to luxury businesses for competing in a competitive global market, providing for further research opportunities of old and new distribution channels. Thanks to a qualitative method, it emerged that distribution strategies implemented by firms operating in luxury markets are typical and specific with respect to firms in other markets and represent a source of competitive advantage. Four phenomena have characterized distribution in this area in recent years: a growing investment by luxury brands in direct distribution activities; the integration between distribution and communication activities; the development of the digital channel in luxury markets; and lastly, the growing integration between User Generated Content and distribution channels. As the distribution variable influences the constitution of brand identity, old and new distribution channels have to be differently articulated according to the exclusivity of the brand.

INTRODUCTION

Italy and other countries are universally renowned for its strong vocation for luxury. In particular, the Italian and French luxury sectors are important to the Italian and French economy, thanks to a strong tradition in these fields and strong efforts into innovation policy. The market seems to be particularly susceptible to external pushes linked to the socio-demographic, cultural, political and economic context, which impact on to the tastes and desires of individuals and, consequently, to the company's choice.

As the market of a luxury companies is a globalized market, a company has to understand the variables that impact on this marketing mix variable (the distribution variable), and tries to obtain advantages from them. In addition, it is appropriate to place different types of distribution channels into different categories of luxury, in relation to the affordability of a brand (Non affordable luxury and Affordable luxury).

DOI: 10.4018/978-1-4666-9958-8.ch010

Some winning companies permit us to identify successful business models in different luxury sectors, such as the core luxury sectors (fashion, jewelry and watches, perfumes and cosmetics, and cars) and new luxury sectors (wines, spirits and other gourmet products, tourism and catering, and furniture and household items).

The aim of this work is to analyze the distribution strategies of high-symbolic-value goods, highlighting the main trends, and providing scientific evidence to luxury businesses for further research opportunities of old and new distribution channels.

The chapter is structured as follows. The first section analyzes the theoretical background of the distribution variable into the luxury sector. The second section outlines the main focus of the chapter. The third section presents future research directions for this topic. Finally, the last section presents the conclusion, implications and limitations of the study.

BACKGROUND

The luxury business represented a very interesting topic on which many researchers focused.

Luxury in an elitist connotation, but also a social manifestation in a community. A specific target is attracted, firstly, for a status symbol connotation and for intrinsic quality of the products, price, rarity and creative content. More precisely, luxury fashion is divided into non-affordable luxury and affordable luxury, according to the target audience.

Firstly, the *human need* has been analyzed, as luxury companies have to satisfy it. A need is a symptom of what an individual is lacking: it is influenced by his cultural, economic and social context and his expectations and preferences and has different levels (Airoldi, Brunetti & Coda, 2005; Erner, 2004; Giacosa, 2011; Giacosa, 2012; Kemp, 1998). If it is a primary need, the individual seeks to obtain an object that is necessary for his survival and whose purpose is to help him deal with the daily struggle for nutrition, warmth and a certain level of health. When it is a secondary need, the individual is driven by the desire to own a variety of luxury goods that are beyond the simple requirements of daily life. Often, this secondary need will grow until the consumer gains possession of that object, after which the desire diminishes. On this subject, the CEO of Hermès has reconstructed the paradox of luxury: "The more one is desired, the more one grows, but the more one grows, the less desirable" (Thomas, 2011). This paradox is the manifestation that the world of luxury should be considered a phenomenon in its own right, since it is a powerful generator of causal ambiguity (Chailan, 2013; Orton & Weick, 1990; Weick, 1976). The Luxury business falls into the category of secondary needs, and aims to meet several types of needs. First of all, the creative need, namely the need to look a certain way, thanks to thc availability of a particular series of objects designed to enhance the body. Secondly, there is a communicational and social need, namely the need to communicate a given message to the outside world and the feeling of belonging to a social group, through tangible factors (such as a handbag) or intangible ones (such as the brand of the bag). Lastly, there is the need to feel up to date with fashion trends, which is satisfied by possession of objects from the latest designer label collections. Manifestation of a series of secondary needs is to some extent the result of improved economic conditions for a section of the population, and the ageing of the population. Indeed luxury has gained new customers amongst the wealthy sections of the population in emerging countries and amongst the new seniors, that is, those individuals whose good health in adulthood means they can afford higher-quality goods (Duesenberry, 1949; Tynan, McKechnie & Chuon, 2010), a trend that is encouraged by the luxury houses, who have adopted a series of adult testimonials (Demi Moore for Helena Rubinstein, Sharon Stone for Dior, Bono for Louis Vuitton).

Many studies focused on the *environment* in which the luxury companies operate, as the needs perceived by consumers are strongly influenced by the context in which they live, which influences style and membership of a social group. It means that this environment impact also on the company's choices about in terms of distribution. For example, the French, who are the founders of modern luxury, prefer more sophisticated luxury with an emphasis on detail, unlike the Russians who prefer to show off their wealth and this is also seen in the way they dress. Hence, there is no single vision of luxury, rather it is also influenced by environment. The environment in which the consumer lives influences his desires and the demand they generate, just as the environment in which the company operates influences its production. Broadly speaking, environment is everything that surrounds the company, whereas narrowly speaking, the environment is what influences the structure and behaviour of the company and is the source of the company's conditions of life, survival and development (Giacosa, 2011 and 2012). The environment conveys a series of opportunities to the company, but there are also restrictions, which limit the sphere of action. The company may in turn influence the trends that drive consumerism. Trends are influenced by different aspects of the environment, which can be viewed by dividing the environment into many sub-environments, such as social, cultural, economic, political and legislative, physical and natural, and technologic sub-environments (Ferrero, 1987; Mosca, 2010). Some of these sub-environments have a strong effect on the trends that drive consumerism.

First, social sub-environments significantly affects the trends (Amatulli & Guido, 2011; Casaburi, 2011; Nueno & Quelch, 1998), which are generated by the work of companies operating in the sector and by street trends, in other words, they are generated or strongly influenced by individuals. The needs expressed by individuals are influenced by the social groups within society, which identify themselves and the desire. Luxury trend is a tool that conveys, albeit non-verbally, the attainment of a given social status (Paquot, 2007): the more luxurious the item, the higher the social standing conveyed by the individual. Communication of a certain social status by the consumer also requires knowledge of the style of the target opinion leader. In this context, communication from the companies and from the media must promote understanding of the style emerging from the target leader, so that the consumer can properly align himself and feel part of that group. Furthermore, consumer attitudes are influenced by the degree of maturity shown towards luxury (Bourdieu, 1984; Chaudhuri & Majumdar, 2006; Eastman, Goldsmith & Flynn, 1999; Vigneron & Johnson, 1999): if he is particularly accustomed to using luxury items, the consumer's attitude is mature, with every purchase consolidating this habit. On the hand, when his experience of luxury is only occasional, every purchase brings him closer to the world he is discovering and this experience is often enhanced during periods of price reductions.

Even the cultural sub-environments in which the company operates influences expectations and luxury trends alike, owing to the ideologies and cultural values of consumers (Hall & Hall, 1990; Harrisson & Huntington, 2000; Hoecklin, 1996; Kapferer, 1997; Nwankwo, Hamelin & Khaled, 2014; Ritzer, 1999; Yeoman, 2011; Stokburger-Sauer & Teichmann, 2013). Levels of education affecting levels of culture, the importance assigned to religion, lifestyles, the age at which consumers become financially comfortable and the role of women in society are just some of the values that influence consumer choices. This means that different brands may have different value depending on the cultural context. A number of important studies (Hauck & Stanforth, 2007; Mulyanegara & Tsarenko, 2009) have focused on the relationship between luxury and youth, who represent a strong potential for future demand and who should be the key targets of business distribution policies (Banathy, 1996; Choi, 2011; Guercini & Ranfagni, 2012; Jones, 2002; Taplin, 2014).

In terms of the natural sub-environment, a company's operations may also affect the environment in terms of defence and promotion of natural resources and local traditions. When a company aims to use wool from a local breed of sheep that has been conserved, the rarity of the raw material becomes an aspect of the resulting product's exclusiveness. This leads to the concept of sustainable luxury, in ecological and environmental, social and organizational terms (Guercini & Ranfagni, 2013; Guercini and Woodside, 2012; Kapferer, 2012): if the offering is also ecologically and environmentally sustainable (Allen, Walker & Brady, 2012; Jones, Clarke-Hill & Comfort, 2008), then this is perceived as added value that enhances the competitiveness of the offering, especially if customers are sensitive to sustainability issues. Furthermore, when raw materials are authentically linked to a local area, they become a distinctive feature of the product, and as a consequence, the brand. So in addition to being sustainable, luxury is also authentic (Thompson, Rindfleisch & Zeynec, 2006) (because it retains the characteristics of a local area) and this increases its chances of differentiation of the product and the consumers choosing it.

A significant area of research is focused on *distribution* considered as one of the strategic variables in the management of the marketing mix for high-symbolic-value goods. The distribution channel is the combination of organizations through which the product passes to the user or end consumer and plays a key role because it gives consumers access to products and services, putting them in a position to make the purchase. The goal of a distribution system is to effectively realize the contact between consumers and products.

In the luxury context, the distribution represents a fundamental moment of the relationship between a luxury company and its customers, as the boutiques represents the place in which brand expresses itself and where the customer can satisfy their dream and expectations. For understanding the right strategy for selling a luxury product, the details of point of sale have to reflect the customers' needs and perceptions. In other terms, only if the point of sale is perceived as a cathedral of luxury, the customers are sufficiently involved in the shopping experience.

The company has to understand how to sell someone, in addition to sell something (Kapferer & Bastien, 2009). The distribution variable influences the constitution of brand identity, due to how a product is presented and is accessible in terms of availability (Giacosa, 2012; Saviolo & Testa, 2005). In addition, the type of distribution channel depends on the degree of the luxury exclusivity, which consequently impacts on the degree of intensity of the distribution channels (Pellicelli, 2005).The elements of uniqueness and rarity characterizing high-symbolic-value goods must be consistent with marketing and business-development goals (Mosca, 2010). It is possible to identify two opposite, conflicting needs for firms that have to manage the distribution of goods in high-end markets: to preserve and strengthen the brand image and the idea of the uniqueness of the product, and to make products available in an efficient and effective way in the markets of reference (Kapferer & Bastien, 2013). The first requirement leads management to adopt a selective approach to distribution and to prefer choices regarding the control of intermediaries that enable it to maintain leadership in the distribution channel. The second induces management to give the products maximum market presence, via indirect as well as direct options.

It would be wrong to say that firms in the market for high-symbolic-value goods do not view increasing market share through the distribution of their products as a priority; so, if on one hand the easiest option for the businesses we're dealing with here appears to be control of the channel and selection of intermediaries, on the other there is a risk of inadequate presence in markets where management's' choices are too selective.

In this sense, the strategic management of luxury goods' distribution variable involves a balancing act between the two conflicting requirements of preserving the exclusivity of the brand and the product and gaining market share – in other words, between control of the channel and adequate distribution coverage.

Old and new distribution channels state together in the luxury market. The evolution of the distribution system in recent years is characterized by the development of a mixed, direct and indirect system, in which firms flank their networks of directly controlled or franchised single-brand points of sale with new distributive forms (Mosca, 2014) where the communication component and the role of the relational approach with the customer prevail.

Under all distribution options we see a particular emphasis on the ability of the point of sale to stimulate consumers' emotional and sensory side. The downstream vertical integration of the supply chain and the development of relationships with the end customer are the two elements that have most moved the evolution of distribution in the markets concerned toward the current model.

In recent years, the two most significant phenomena that have characterized distribution strategies are:

- International development: firms have increased investments for the opening of new points of sale in growing markets, with a particular focus on the areas of the Far East;
- Streamlining and focusing on profitability. Firms have initiated a process of reorganization of distribution by focusing on profitability at point-of-sale level.

The economic downturn and the consequent contraction of trade margins require firms to assess the formats of distribution under both direct and indirect management, focusing attention on profitability in relation to investment.

MAIN FOCUS OF THE CHAPTER

Issues, Controversies, Problems

The focus of this chapter is to provide scientific evidence to luxury businesses for competing in a competitive global market. In particular, in terms of the distribution channels, we state that old and new distribution channels state together.

In order to achieve the research objective, we developed the following hypothesis:

HP: Non-affordable and affordable luxury products present differences in distribution channel, as the distribution variable influences the constitution of brand identity.

With the aim of exploring the hypothesis mentioned above, the research methodology has been carried out in the following phases:

1. **First Phase**: The hypotheses were analyzed by examining the existing literature about the luxury sector and the drivers in the consumption trend, this highlighted a series of variables that impact on luxury consumption. The findings was illustrated in the previous sentence.

2. **Second Phase**: We made a qualitative analysis. In particular, we analyzed literature on the topic. In addition, we analyzed companies' information of 10 non-affordable companies and 10 affordable companies by using their web sites, journals and newspaper on them. The purpose is to identify the key drivers within the luxury companies and differ considerations in terms of distribution strategy.

The distribution variable is included in the marketing mix (Borden, 1964; Bruner, 1988; Constantinides, 2006; Dixon & Blois, 1973; McCharty, 1964; Pellicelli, 2005). It has to represent the luxury brand, as boutiques interpret the brand's concept: consequently, the place of sell is the network between the customers and the luxury universe. The distribution permits to construct the brand identity, since the point of sales bolsters or undermines the consumer's dream.

For develop our hypothesis, we try to differ the distribution strategy in terms of the luxury typologies (Chevalier & Mazzalovo, 2008; Giacosa, 2011; Okonkwo, 2007):

- **Non-Affordable Luxury:** It represents highly exclusive luxury products, whose price is very high and affordable only for HNWIs (high net worth individuals) (Tartaglia and Marinozzi, 2006). It means that democratization is not for non-affordable luxury. Indeed, the high quality, the exclusive distribution and scarce availability justify the high price; limited editions or, sometimes, single pieces are strongly customised and are linked to the company heritage. Louis Vuitton, Chanel and Hermès for fashion luxury, Ferrari and Rolls Royce for car sector, Gaia and Moët Chandon for wines and spirits, Armani Hotel for travels and holidays, are great examples;
- **Affordable Luxury:** It represents the democratization of the luxury. A wider range of products categories, such as accessories, glasses, perfumes and cosmetics, are inspired by non-affordable luxury, and customers could dream to be part to the luxury universe (Silverstein, 2006; Corbellini & Saviolo, 2009). A sort of "trading up" phenomenon happens (Silverstein, 2006; Gandini & Turinetto, 2009), for which the customer make a sort of zip between luxury products and more traditional ones. Generally, companies of non-affordable luxury are not involved to the phenomenon. Tod's, Gucci, Prada, Mercedes, Audi, are examples of affordable luxury.

In this chapter, we are interested in solving the problem of understanding and identifying successful characteristics of distribution strategy for luxury products, distinguishing in non-affordable or affordable luxury, and in old and new distribution channels.

The Findings

Defining the reference target follows the potential customers' wealth level criterion, it would be interesting to focus on the variable distribution, which is defined according to the different typologies of luxury:

- Non-affordable luxury.
- Affordable luxury.

1. Non-Affordable Luxury

Referring to non-affordable luxury, distribution has to be distinguished in terms of direct, indirect option and old and new channel formats.

The direct distribution channel involves contact between manufacturer and consumer that is not mediated by other entities.

Direct government of distribution activities favors businesses that sell prestige goods in the achievement of certain benefits.

First, the quick, direct flow of information from the market to the firm delivers greater knowledge of consumer needs and a better ability to grasp new trends in consumption even when the signals are still weak and uncertain.

The second advantage for firms that adopt direct distribution is due to the ability to maintain a strong consistency between the brand image and the style of the point of sale because the brand's attributes and values are represented uniformly in all places of direct distribution in order to maximize their effectiveness in the communication process of the firm's supply system.

Other advantages of direct distribution in the high-symbolic-value goods market are: uniform level of customer service in all points of sale, training of specialists in the sale of prestige goods, coordinated management of logistics through a centralized warehouse system for each market with real-time supply, higher profit margins for the manufacturer, control of the disposal unsold products, and integration of the sales system in the firm's information system through the computerized management of the order-sale-reorder flow.

This distribution option for high-symbolic-value goods consists in the direct management of the channel by the manufacturer, without the use of intermediaries, and in the choice of distribution coverage with a limited number of points of sale.

An exclusive direct distribution system is the most extreme form of selective distribution and favors firms that wish to differentiate their products with a policy of quality and prestige, improving their relationships with customers.

The advantages of direct distribution in terms of superior knowledge of the customer, the availability of the best and most reliable information from the market, price control, reduction of intermediation and management margins, brand image consistent with the values offered to the consumer and control of unsold inventory have facilitated the movement of the strategies of the firms under consideration toward this option.

An analysis of the distribution strategies of a sample of firms clearly shows a marked acceleration in exclusive direct distribution, in particular for high end products: the number of points of sale owned by firms and the turnover resulting from them increases as a percentage of sales volumes through independent intermediaries.

Many brands, such as Bulgari, Prada, Armani, Loro Piana, Zegna, Gucci, Tod's, Montblanc, Lancel and Louis Vuitton, have gradually increased their presence in direct distribution by opening new points of sale in major world markets, reducing the percentage of turnover from indirect distribution activities in favor of direct distribution.

It must be noticed that the direct distribution coverage presents some disadvantages.

The main disadvantages and risks of exclusive direct distribution are: insufficient distribution coverage, increased investment in fixed assets, slowing of growth, difficulties in managing human resources.

Old Channels of Distribution

The boutique represents a traditional place where the customer meets the company and an exclusive brand's universe. The distribution of luxury products is exclusive. The limitation of the distribution policy to limited points of sales increases the exclusivity of the brand. For this purpose, the company chooses to commercialise the product through a small number of boutiques with reference to a geographical area, selecting only the main towns to reach the commercial rarity of their products. Although the company boutique requires considerable investment, a selective distribution networks is preferred, privileging mono-brand boutiques, based exclusively on single-brand self-owned boutiques, both for increasing brand image, allowing the customer relationship, skipping the intermediation of wholesalers and agents, and control more directly the distribution system. Exclusive distribution choice, combined to great post-sales services, may be remarkably expensive: for this reason, high prices are necessary for products commercialized in an exclusive manner.

The rareness of the product avoids its value dilution: it means that the company tries to maintain its potential in the minds of the élites who can afford it (Kapferer & Bastien, 2009; Giacosa, 2012). The distribution is exclusive: that is, the company chooses to commercialise the product through a limited number of resellers with reference to a geographical area, who employ highly qualified staff and offer a particular post-sales service. The purpose is to convey the exclusivity of the product, besides carrying out strong control of the distribution system.

Only rareness boutiques may interpret this concept: a small number of exclusive boutiques located in important cities and commercial location means reflect non-affordable luxury; in addition, a small number of product pieces are available on the market. Thinking about Ferrari: the rareness is a strength of the company strategy. Sometimes, the rareness is only virtual: some products are not limited in the quantity, but they are social limited due to their high price. La Prairie caviar essence skin cream is an example: even without a selective distribution and limited editions, this product is perceived as a luxury cosmetic thanks to its price.

Thanks to the featured elements of a brand (Ceriani, 2001), an high involvement of the customer has to happen (Holbrook & Hirschman, 1982; Huang, 2001). Boutiques became a sort of consumption cathedral (Giacosa, 2012; Ritzer, 2000), where the brand (and consequently the products) try to attract the customers in a good-looking way. Customer perception is satisfied in a visual, tactile, olfactory and auditory sense. To reach this purpose, every details of the boutique are extremely studies (Cheng and Chi, 2009; Wang and Ha, 2011): the sign, the furnishings, the lighting, the dummies, the shop window, the fitting room and other elements linked to a virtual communication (Haenlein & Kaplan, 2009) contribute to creating the brand atmosphere (Ceriani, 2001; Parsons, 2011; Pellicelli, 2005; Sacerdote, 2006). To reach this purpose, the internal and external layout is so important, as it strikes the five senses of the customer and increases the desire to buy in a short-term period. When Tom Ford opened in 2007 in Madison Avenue for its haute couture men's collection, a luxurious environment was created: customers found a sort of private residence, where every kind of service was offered, such as personal vendors, butlers, seamstresses, waiters and pattern makers.

In addition, the location choice is significant, as it impacts on a series of factors, such as the budget available to the company and the brand image: 85% of the London stores are located in Bond Street and Sloane Street, and in Madison Avenue and Fifth Avenue for New York (Giacosa, 2012; Moore, Doherty & Doyle, 2010). Boutiques have to be set in the first-tier cities circuit (Jansson & Power, 2010) (Milan, New York, Tokyo and London) or in nouveau riche cities (such as Dubai, Shanghai and Singapore) or well-established stores (such as Galeries Lafayette in Paris), in exclusive touristic places or international airports, as it permits to strengthen the brand image. Only a good location permits to confirm the exclusivity of the brand's universe. Thinking about Montenapoleone street in Milan and Bond Street in London, all is luxury, and all become an experience for luxury: walking along these streets, the consumer's desire is intensified and the attraction by membership of that universe is very high. It happens that a company with several brands prefer to have different locations for each brand to permit a customer and brand differentiation (Corbellini & Saviolo, 2009): for instance, Prada has different location in Milan: the Galleria, via Montenapoleone and Viale Venezia. Tourists mainly frequent the Galleria and via Montenapoleone stores, while residents go to all shops.

A preferential treatment has to be received from regular customers, but also occasional shoppers have to be attracted both from assistant's professionalism and politeness. The shop assistant become the ambassador of the brand: they have to exalt the status of the brand, the company's heritage and all brands details in terms of images, reliability, comfort and scents. For this reason, the shop assistant have to be motivated and trained. In addition, a great post-sales service is offered to increase the brand image. During the interaction with the customers, the price is not a relevant variable, differently from standardized products. On the contrary, competition is based on quality and the protagonist of the relationship are the brand and the customer.

New Channels of Distribution

In addition to traditional channels of distribution, distribution methods are influenced also by the process innovation, which is focused on the introduction of a new operating method, or improving an existing method in the distribution area (Giacosa, 2011; Re et al., 2014). In particular, distribution innovation concerns the types, characteristics and locations of the point of sales, and the other distribution channels. The use of multi-sensorial instruments to attract the consumers permits to attract new consumers and strengthen the retention of old consumers and perfect management of the customer relationship (Binz, Hair, Pieper & Baldauf, 2013; Miller & Le Breton-Miller, 2005; Kapferer, 2002; Poza, Alfred & Maheshwari, 1997; Ward, 1997).

Innovation in distribution could be introduced in different terms:

- **In Strict Sense (i.e. Technological Innovation):** Despite their initial reluctance, non-affordable luxury has been influenced by new technology (Blomback & Ramirez-Pasillas, 2012; Botero, Thomas, Graves & Fediuk, 2013; Ha and Perks, 2005; Micelotta & Raynard, 2011; Mosca, 2014), as the target has a growing confidence with the digital technologies, such as the internet web site and social networks. The website represents an information instrument to present the firm, provide information on location of the sales boutiques and present the collections (Kim & Lennon, 2010; Levy & Weitz, 2006; Macchi, 2011; Okonkwo, 2010; Ries & Ries, 2000; Schlosser, 2007; Yang & Young, 2009), or is also an instrument to sell the products (Guelfi & Giacosa, 2011; Kwon & Noh, 2010; Park & Lennon, 2009; Steinfield, Bouwman & Adelaar, 2002). Gucci was the first, launching Guccieyeweb.com in 2009, a social network site for a new collection of sunglasses targeting digital generation customers, and updating its Facebook site three times a day and tweeting on Twitter. Also Louis Vuitton followed Gucci's example, broadcasting its fashion shows live on its blogs. The social networks may be considered a new distribution channels, but also a communication tool. In strict sense, the social networks like Twitter, Facebook and YouTube represent a great way to benefit from the widespread diffusion of these media in a large section of the clientele (Kim & Ko, 2012; Kim & Lennon, 2010; Levy & Weitz, 2006; Macchi, 2011; Okonkwo, 2007; Okonkwo, 2010; Phan, 2011; Schlosser, 2007; Yang & Young, 2009), to interact with customers both for the growing confidence with the digital technologies and for the low cost of this instrument (Kietzmann, Silvestre, McCarthy & Pitt, 2012; Kim, Choi, Agrusa, Wang & Kim, 2010; Pardo & Tajeddini, 2013; Kaplan & Haenlein, 2010). Chanel, Gucci and Ralph Lauren created some IPhone applications that allow their customers to interact with their brands; Louis Vuitton showed its fashion shows in live broadcasting on its blogs. It emerged that the social networks have a good effects on the brand reputation, as this possibility is perceived as a friendly tool and also stimulates the desire for a brand (Donaldson, 2011; Geerts & Veg-Sala, 2011; Ha & Perks, 2005; Kim & Ko, 2012; Okonkwo, 2009). The examination of numerous cases of this sort among the most innovative currently available has enabled us to take a summary inventory of the technological innovations adopted by luxury brands in their D.O.S.. These include (Mosca, 2014):

- **Smart Labels:** A smart label communicates, via radio signals, with a reading/writing device in a fixed or mobile position up to one meter away. High-end brands are using this technology more and more, as it allows them to facilitate the logistics of the finished product and tends to ensure full traceability of the supply chain. Many brands such as Prada, Gucci and Burberry make extensive use of smart-label technology in their points of sale;
- **Interactive Dressing Rooms:** This is an evolution of the traditional dressing room that allows customers to view all the variants in which the product they are trying on is available on a touch screen; it is also equipped with a responsive screen that permits customers to review all the products previously tried**;**
- **The Technology Associated with RFID Labeling:** Very recently, a well-known American apparel chain equipped its sale points with a technological evolution of the interactive dressing room, *dressing room 2.0*. This kind of dressing room has a webcam inside that lets one send photos and videos of the garments tried to the major social networks. The images or videos are sent to the social network by simply downloading an app that can connect to the mirror of the store. In this way one can ask friends for an opinion in real time. Boucheron, for example, allows prospective customers to try its jewelry on its site using their webcam and face-recognition software. In its New York Epicenter Prada has an interactive dressing room where the customer can change color, light intensity and selected garments;
- **Body Scanning:** Body scanning is an innovative tool that circumvents the need to try garments on physically, giving the client the possibility to observe the garments worn virtually. This is made possible by a 3D body scan that is reproduced on a screen as a digital avatar. It creates a virtual 3D model on which it is then possible to try items of apparel in different sizes and colors. The screen can be of different sizes and offers customers an interactive experience that can configure all the products and accessories in the collection. In addition, thanks to special programs installed on the dressing-room displays, customers can create a personal avatar that can be reused, via a login, each time they go to the point of sale. This system allows the customer to use the personal avatar in any of the brand's stores around the world. The buying experience at the point of sale is completely different from the present one, creating loyalty and above all letting customers avoid wasting time trying on clothes. Body scanners were first introduced in Selfridges and Harrods department stores. A similar service can be enjoyed on the Web, too. This technology is called My Virtual Model and follows the same principle as body scanning, using one's body measurements to create a digital avatar. Luxottica has recently developed, for the Ray-Ban brand, software that combines several models of glasses with a virtual reproduction of the customer's face by integrating a webcam and a facial representation application;

- **Interactive Displays:** The shop window is the first element with which consumers come into contact, making it an ideal tool of brand identity. Until a few years ago, the message it conveyed was one-way: from the brand to consumers. Today, however, firms can directly interact with customers in various ways. One can obtain different information about the products on display and for sale and, in this way, be drawn into the store. Furthermore, it can ensure the function of sale even after hours. The window itself becomes a giant touch screen with which customers can buy and browse the entire offering. The products at the point of sale can be inspected at any time and thus be always available. In addition, *Window Shopping* enables one to customize the content on the screen visible from the outside. Regarding luxury brands, the first to develop this new technology has been Ralph Lauren in its New York and Milan stores, followed by the Pinko store in Antwerp. The famous Parisian Maison Chanel, has set up Window Shopping devoted to the brand's iconic lipstick, Rouge Allure, at fifteen perfume dealers. Consumers can get useful make-up tips through the interactive shop window. The ability to access information on the brand and its history, discover upcoming events, download multimedia content and get news on fashion shows, leaf through new catalogs and even buy when the store is closed – actions reserved in the past only to customers in the digital channel – is now available even in physical outlets;
- **QR Code:** QR – Quick Response – is defined as a two-dimensional matrix bar code. A QR code is made up of black modules arranged in a square pattern. It is used to store information simply and rapidly, generally for retrieval on a mobile phone or smartphone equipped with special reading program. Luxury brands can use QR codes by inserting their logo or other images. This system allows consumers to read web links, images, videos, promotional offers and event announcements. The use of these technologies appropriately integrated with cutting-edge software foster greater awareness while buying and represent new ways of in-shop communication at the time of purchase;

- **In a Wider Sense (Related to the Typologies of Distribution Channel):** Considering innovation in the broad sense, the purpose could be to increase the clientele with new means of distribution, respecting the brand myth and revisiting it. The characteristics of this innovation is to valorize the traditional elements of the brand, but stimulating new desires. When the purpose is to attract new younger customers, new distribution channels have to be used, including:
  - **Flagship Stores:** Flagship stores represent single-brand self-owned sale boutique set in famous locations in the most prestigious cities (in terms of tourism, trade or business) which strengthen the prestige of the brand identity (De Chernatony, 2001; Fabris & Minestroni, 2004; Kapferer & Bastien, 2009; Okonkwo, 2007*;* Ross & Harradine, 2011; Vaid, 2003). Their dimension is variable: they could have a limited dimension and commercial offer, but permitting to increase the visibility of the brand. In addition, limited series of exclusive customised products are created exclusively for the flagship stores, or the products are only displayed and not offered for sale, almost like a museum (Bruce & Hines, 2007; Fernie, Moore & Lawrie, 1998; Kozinets, Sherry, DeBerry-Spence, Duhacheck, Nuttavuthisi & Storm, 2002; Moore, Doherty & Doyle, 2010). Alternately, they are very big, organised on several floors (Kent, 2007). When Renzo Piano projected the Hermès flagship store in Tokyo in the Ginza district, he created a sort of monument for the brand;
  - **Temporary Stores:** They appear suddenly and then close a few months later: they have to test the attraction to the customers about a new product idea, or a new city or an area of the

city probably considered interesting (Giacosa, 2012). Informal style in the boutique and a selection of the products (sometimes created for the pop-up stores) varies according to the characteristics of the customers and the city where the shop is based (de Lassus & Anido Freire, 2014). When the opening of a pop-up store is an event for the city, it means that the brand has a great attraction: we could remember Hermès pop-up stores in Time Warner Center at Columbus Circle across from Central Park in New York, Louis Vuitton in the Dover Street Market in London, and Marc Jacobs in New York. The benefits of temporary stores are manifold. First, they allow the brand to reinforce the perception of scarcity of the luxury product, by limiting consumers' exposure to it in time, through the creation of a unique and unrepeatable event. The event itself facilitates the customization of the product and the strengthening of the brand image. Temporary stores are also useful distribution formats for gathering information and increasing media visibility. In the event that a brand has a need to renovate a store, a temporary store is a solution that allows the companies to boost sales and create movement in view of the subsequent re-opening of the flagship store. The advantages of the development of a system of temporary stores are numerous. First, the firm reinforces the brand image, promoting consumers' interaction with the brand in a less formal context. In addition, temporary stores allow reinforcement of the attribute of scarcity and the perception of rarity and uniqueness of the product. The opening of a temporary store is an event that is important for corporate communication more than distribution, as the media tend to highlight special events created by a brand. Also important to remember is that temporary stores allow management to get in touch with those consumers who follow the brand more closely and to collect strategic information on new trends in less formal contexts. Finally, it can also be used to create unique and unrepeatable events, linked to phenomena that combine fashion, culture and entertainment and support the launch of new products

2. Affordable Luxury

Also for affordable luxury, distribution has to be distinguished in terms of direct, indirect option and old and new channels.

The following point-of-sale formats acquire particular importance in indirect distribution: single-brand boutiques, department stores, corners, duty-free shops and franchised points of sale.

The advantage of this strategic approach is that all charges relating to the costs and risks of internationalization are transferred to and borne by the intermediary. The disadvantage lies in the limited control over the foreign market exercisable by the manufacturer.

Old Channels of Distribution

Competition is based on quality in terms of intrinsic characteristics and distribution, permitting the customer retention with the aim to achieve an optimal trade-off between the rarity and the volume sold (Catry, 2003; Phau & Prendergast, 2000).

This luxury typology abandons exclusive rareness for a selective distribution. It increases the number of boutiques and location in which a wider range of products are sold: a new target is reached through the production and distribution of different merchandise categories (especially accessories) to an affordable price, permitting to customers a belonging to the luxury universe (Danziger, 2005). A limited number of opportunely selected mono-brand or multi-brand points of sale or specialised corners (their own shops or selected boutiques) increase the brand image, favouring the level of customization.

The point of sales represents a traditional channel of distribution. This is fundamental, attracting the attention of new and old customers in several ways: the point of sales is a place in which customers have time to convince themselves to buy (Saviolo & Testa, 2005) and, starting from the windows, the shops is a brand mirror. Armani's megastore in Milan is an example. Via Montenapoleone in Milan, via Condotti in Rome, rue Faubourg St. Honoré in Paris, Ginza quarter in Tokyo, Bond Street in London favour the brand image and increase the customers' desire for a brand.

New Channels of Distribution

Outlets are used to clear stocks, which are multi-brand and owned by third parties or managed directly by the firm, mainly located outside the big centres, in shopping villages or in areas used as factory shops (Giacosa, 2012). The previous years' collections, and a line produced specifically for the outlet, is sold in the outlets. The channel of outlet is not used by non-affordable luxury companies, as it decrease the exclusivity of the brand.

New technological distribution channels are also used for affordable luxury: flagship stores and internet web site are some examples. As for non-affordable luxury, flagship stores permit the customer to enjoy an all-enveloping sense of luxury, where the sensation of luxury is closely connected to the city where the point of sales is located (Giacosa, 2014). The main purpose is not an high return on investment (especially due to the cost of the location), but the brand visibility.

Also digital channels, such as internet web site and social networks, are used by affordable luxury firms. For example, Dolce & Gabbana uses the social media for a direct feedback from their customers: thanks to the collaboration with the fashion bloggers, the fashion shows are instantly uploaded on Facebook and Twitter, and the desire for the that brand increases.

It is to notice that even for more accessible high-end products such as perfume and leather goods, the importance of direct distribution has grown. Various factors underpin the growth, including the strengthening of its management, the proposal of a new distribution concept, the launch of new products and the growth of the global distribution network, particularly in Asia where the leather accessories market is a great success.

The Distribution Strategy of Luxury Goods in the Real World: The Mixed Option

As noted above, selective direct distribution gives the manufacturer strong control over the distribution channel and, consequently, over the relationship with end consumers, avoiding the ever-present risk of a deterioration of the brand's symbolic value.

On the other hand we can say that there are few firms that adopt a selective direct distribution system only; directly and indirectly managed points of sale often coexist, sometimes even in the same market (Mosca, 2014).

The option for mixed distribution was found in all product categories analyzed, although there is a clear differentiation between prestige products in the higher price range, in which the brand's selective direct presence generally prevails, and prestige products in the lower price range, in which indirect distribution prevails over direct. The concomitant presence of direct and indirect distribution options, however, involve, an important consequence for the proper management of the channel: one needs a clear and defined mission for the different categories of intermediaries.

Indirect intermediaries must perform the primary function of ensuring a steady flow of revenues and profits, and an increase in market share. Distribution coverage, even in luxury goods, is always functional to the achievement of market-share objectives. For indirect distribution intermediaries the function of ensuring an adequate and constant flow of information between manufacturer and consumer becomes less important. Direct points of sale, in contrast, must comply with the primary function of communicating and conveying the brand image to end consumers.

That the functions to be performed by indirect intermediaries and direct points of sale are different does not mean that the latter do not have revenue targets: much research has shown that when the enterprise adopts direct distribution this choice often favors the stabilization of its market share. The consequence of the differentiation of functions means that some typical categories of directly managed points of sale are set up and structured with a primary goal of communicating brand values without placing priority attention on sales targets.

Having identified the strategic options in luxury goods along a path that leads from exclusive direct distribution to selective indirect distribution, we can now ask which option is currently most used by market players. Strategic behavior in the distribution of luxury goods is changeable and varies in relation to three main dimensions: multinational extension of the brand, perceived value and brand image, economic value of the product category.

The options are described below:

- **Exclusive Direct Distribution:** The major players in multi-brand luxury for some brands of their very high-level portfolio with positioning at the inaccessible market level and global single-brand players in the same situation tend to adopt primarily an exclusive direct distribution strategy. Exclusive direct distribution is rarely used because firms fear losing market opportunities due to excessive restriction of points of sale in a given geographic area.
    - **LVMH:** The Louis Vuitton Moët Hennessy group has become the world leader in key luxury markets with a diversified portfolio, by integrating a plurality of brands, both in product lines closely related to the group's principal activity, and in unrelated product categories. The group increasingly adopts the exclusive direct distribution option. The points of sale are created with care in order to ensure exclusivity and authenticity of the product and convey its high symbolic value, thanks to a careful conceptual architecture in stores.
    - **Hermès:** Hermès uses a predominantly direct, highly selective distribution with proprietary points of sale exclusively dedicated to its products, including those in different product categories
- **Selective or Exclusive Indirect Distribution:** It is adopted mostly by small firms that do not have the economic resources to make direct investments or by firms that do not wish to get involved in the management of the distribution network because they prefer to concentrate their efforts on the development of brand image and communication activities. Selective or exclusive indirect distribution is adopted by businesses as a strategy to enter new markets with uncertain macro-environmental scenarios. Many Italian luxury firms that maintain a dimension of craftsmanship and have not yet developed financial and/or logistics expertise do not undertake investments in the development of their own points of sale;
- **Mixed Distribution:** Most of the firms that compete in luxury-goods markets adopt a mixed distribution strategy: direct and indirect, selective and/or exclusive. With this approach, firms are

able to achieve a balance between the need to achieve sufficient sales volumes and market shares and the need to preserve and strengthen the brand image to support the premium price. In a mixed option the functions assigned to direct and indirect distribution are well identified. The activities carried out in the directly managed points of sale are intended to communicate the brand's values and products and to ensure shopping experiences to consumers. The activities of the indirect points of sale are mainly aimed at ensuring a steady flow of revenues and adequate margins

A further point to be considered is the balance between direct and indirect distribution.

From an examination of several case studies it is possible to highlight the following:

- **Unstable Balance:** It is not easy to identify a consistent approach or a typical strategy in firms' choice between which part of their revenues can be generated by direct distribution and which by indirect. A presence in key markets with 40% of sales in the direct channel seems appropriate for high-end goods;
- **Brand Image:** Firms that have a higher presence in direct distribution, in general, have a higher perceived brand value, higher sales margins and lower losses in periods of recession. A brand must possess certain characteristics and values, such as a "mythical" value as well as an exchange value, but also an emotional and ethical value. This is the case for example of Hermès and Tod's, which have a significant presence in direct distribution;
- **Balance and Risk:** In markets with higher levels of risk it is advisable to reduce the percentage of direct distribution;
- **Maturity of Consumers:** Mature markets are characterized by the presence of more expert and demanding consumers. In these markets, it is advisable to increase the share of revenue from direct distribution.

The current trend in the distribution of luxury goods goes in the direction of increasing the proportion of sales from direct distribution, although the recent global crisis has led to a slowdown in investment in developing new DOS (Direct Operated Stores) and a focus on formats ensuring sufficient profitability with respect to investment

We said that the distribution variable influences the constitution of brand identity, and this brand identity differs from non-affordable luxury and affordable luxury. Consequently, distribution channels (old and new ones) have to be differently articulated according to the exclusivity of the brand.

HP is confirmed.

FUTURE RESEARCH DIRECTIONS

This study holds theoretical and practical implications. The theoretical implications are linked to an analysis of the distribution in luxury sector, distinguishing between non-affordable and affordable luxury and focusing on the possible actions available to a company. In addition, the analysis of a series of specific features of luxury companies may be useful to better define the optimal distribution strategy.

The practical implications of our study are relevant for companies operating in the luxury context, for those strictly connected with the production and commercialisation of luxury products, and those engaged in allied industries, such as in external R&D and consulting activities. The study revealed the importance of the distribution variable, as it increases the brand identity and consequently increase the competitive advantage of a company.

This study has some limitations. We chose to adopt the qualitative method focusing on distribution strategy in the luxury business. It could be useful to widen the boundaries of the research, by making some successful case studies to analyse the key factors of their success, or making a comparison between luxury context and others.

Business studies need to be increased in this field: while the manufacturing sector has declined in terms of value added, number of companies and employment, the luxury sector has had the opposite tendency. In particular, researchers should analyze its ability to increase the circulation of luxury brands in the world, with the aim of strengthening their consumption. In addition, business researches should encourage politician to increase and facilitate investments in the luxury sector, also in terms of protection of "Made In" against south-Asian countries production.

CONCLUSION

Distribution strategies implemented by firms operating in luxury markets are typical and specific with respect to firms in other markets and represent a source of competitive advantage.

Four phenomena have characterized distribution in this area in recent years.

First, a growing investment by luxury brands in direct distribution activities, with the development of innovative formats – such as flagship stores, DOS and temporary stores – that are used to represent the brand's reference values and the product's symbolic attributes to the consumer in a tightly controlled distribution channel. Here luxury firms enlarge their markets and increase their market share by strengthening their control over the distribution channel. Vertical integration downstream into directly managed distribution activities does not lead luxury firms to abandon indirect distribution options, which they maintain especially in markets characterized by a higher degree of risk and which allow for balanced distributive coverage.

Second, the integration between distribution and communication activities, which finds its most concrete expression in the point of sale managed from an experiential perspective. The consumer has the opportunity to see all the reference values of the brand in the show space, represented by modern means of communication, including multi-media productions, at the point of sale. Numerous distribution formats play an essential communication role, enabling firms to strengthen their long-term relationship with consumers.

Third, the development of the digital channel in luxury markets. This distribution channel has enabled firms to extend their market to new consumers who have different socio-demographic characteristics and are located in emerging countries. High-symbolic-value goods are traditionally considered incompatible with the digital channel; even today some companies that maintain an extreme positioning of their brand believe it inappropriate to develop distribution activities in the digital channel. Most luxury players have developed a direct presence in the digital channel, however, and this strategic distribution option has been successful. The digital channel is increasingly integrated with the activities of physical distribution, and this integration makes it possible on one hand to extend the consumer's shopping experience, and on the other to maintain long-term relationships.

The latest trend concerns the growing integration between User Generated Content and distribution channels. Brand communication in luxury markets has undergone further development with social-media marketing dove-tailed into digital and physical distribution channels. The consumer is ready even in luxury markets to receive information from brands, to share that information and to respond by liking the product and purchasing it in the digital or the physical channel. This growing integration between distribution and effective communication (online and off), following a circular approach in which information channels and their flows surround the consumer, is one of the frontiers of the marketing of high-symbolic-value goods.

REFERENCES

Airoldi, G., Brunetti, G., & Coda, V. (2005). *Corso di Economia aziendale*. Bologna: Il Mulino.

Allen, M. W., Walker, K. L., & Brady, R. (2012). Sustainability Discourse with a Supply Chain Relationship: Mapping Convergence and Divergence. *Journal of Business Communication*, *49*(3), 210–236. doi:10.1177/0021943612446732

Amatulli, C., & Guido, G. (2001). Determinants of purchasing intention for fashion luxury goods in the Italian market: A laddering approach. *Journal of Fashion Marketing and Management*, *15*(1), 123–136. doi:10.1108/13612021111112386

Banathy, H. B. (1996). *Designing social systems in a changing world*. New York: Plenum Press. doi:10.1007/978-1-4757-9981-1

Binz, C., Hair, J. F. Jr, Pieper, T. M., & Baldauf, A. (2013). Exploring the effect of distinct family firm reputation on consumers' preferences. *Journal of Family Business Strategy*, *4*(1), 4–11. doi:10.1016/j.jfbs.2012.12.004

Blomback, A., & Ramirez-Pasillas, M. (2012). Exploring the logics of family brand identity formation. *Corporate Communications: An International Journal*, *17*(1), 7–28. doi:10.1108/13563281211196335

Borden, N. H. (1964). The Concept of the Marketing Mix. *Journal of Advertising Research*, *24*(4), 7–12.

Botero, I., Thomas, J., Graves, C., & Fediuk, T. A. (2013). Understanding multiple family firm identities: An exploration of the communicated identity in official websites. *Journal of Family Business Strategy*, *4*(1), 12–21. doi:10.1016/j.jfbs.2012.11.004

Bourdieu, P. (1984). *Distinction: A Social Critique of the Judgement of Taste*. Cambridge: Harvard University Press.

Bruce, M., & Hines, T. (2007). *Fashion Marketing. Contemporary Issues*. Elsevier Ltd.

Bruner, G. C. (1988). The marketing mix: A retrospective and evaluation. *Journal of Marketing Education*, *10*, 29–33.

Casaburi, I. (2011). China as a Market: Luxury Brand Consumer Behaviour. *Journal of Marketing Trends*, *1*(6), 47–56.

Catry, B. (2003). The Great Pretenders: The Magic of Luxury Goods. *Business Strategy Review*, *14*(3), 10–17. doi:10.1111/1467-8616.00267

Ceriani, G. (2001). *Il marketing moving: l'approccio semiotico*. Milano: Franco Angeli.

Chailan, C. (2013). The role of Art in Luxury Management. In *Proceedings of 6th Euromed Conference of the Euromed Academy of Business, 'Confronting Contemporary Business Challenges through Management Innovation* (pp. 569-574). Nicosia: Euromed Press.

Chaudhuri, H. R., & Majumdar, S. (2006). Of Diamonds and Desires: Understanding Conspicuous Consumption from a Contemporary Marketing Perspective. *Academy of Marketing Science Review*, *11*, 1–18.

Cheng, Y. S., & Chi, L. H. (2009). Salespersons' service quality and customer loyalty in fashion chain stores: A study in Hong Kong retail stores. *Journal of Fashion Marketing and Management*, *13*(1), 98–108. doi:10.1108/13612020910939905

Chevalier, M., & Mazzalovo, G. (2008). *Luxury brand management*. Milano: Franco Angeli.

Choi, T. M. (2011). *Fashion supply chain management: industry and business analysis*. IGI Global.

Constantinides, E. (2006). The Marketing Mix Revisited: Towards the 21st Century Marketing. *Journal of Marketing Management*, *22*(3), 407–438. doi:10.1362/026725706776861190

Corbellini, E., & Saviolo, S. (2009). Managing Fashion and Luxury Companies. Milano: Etas, Milano.

Danziger, P. (2005). *Let them eat the cake*. Dearborn: Kaplan Books.

De Chernatony, L. (2001). *From Brand Vision to Brand Evaluation. Strategically Building and Sustaining Brands*. Oxford, UK: Butterworth Heinemann.

De Lassus, C., & Anido Freire, N. (2014). Access to the luxury brand myth in pop-up stores: A netnographic and semiotic analysis. *Journal of Retailing and Consumer Services*, *21*(1), 61–68. doi:10.1016/j.jretconser.2013.08.005

Dixon, D. F., & Blois, K. J. (1973). Some Limitations of the 4 Ps as a Paradigm of Marketing. In *Proceedings of the Marketing Education Group* (pp. 92-107).

Donaldson, M. S. (2011, October/November). Promoting Luxury Goods in China through Social Media. *MultiLingual*, 29-31.

Duesenberry, J. S. (1949). *Income, Saving and the Theory of Consumer Behaviour*. Cambridge, MA: Harvard University Press.

Eastman, J. K., Goldsmith, R. E., & Flynn, L. R. (1999). Status Consumption in Consumer Behaviour: Scale Development and Validation. *Journal of Marketing Theory and Practice*, *7*(3), 41–52. doi:10.1080/10696679.1999.11501839

Erner, G. (2004). *Victimes de la mode?* Paris: La Découverte.

Fabris, G., & Minestroni, L. (2004). *Valore e valori della marca*. Milano: FrancoAngeli.

Fernie, J., Moore, C. M., & Lawrie, A. (1998). A tale of two Cities: An Examination of Fashion Designer Retailing within London and New York. *Journal of Product and Brand Management*, *7*(5), 366–378. doi:10.1108/10610429810237637

Ferrero, G. (1987). *Impresa e management*. Milano: Giuffré.

Gandini, C., & Turinetto, M. (2009). Lusso necessario alla ricerca del valore per vincere la crisi. Milano: Lupetti, Milano, 2009.

Geerts, A., & Veg-Sala, N. (2011). Evidence on Internet Communication - Management Strategies for Luxury Brands. *Global Journal of Business Research*, *5*(5), 81–94.

Giacosa, E. (2011). *L'economia della aziende di abbigliamento*. Torino: Giappichelli.

Giacosa, E. (2012). *Mergers and Acquisitions (M&As) in the Luxury Business*. Milano: McGraw-Hill.

Giacosa, E. (2014). *Innovation in Luxury Fashion Family Business*. London: MacMillan. doi:10.1057/9781137498663

Guelfi, S., & Giacosa, E. (2011). *Le aziende della net economy*. Torino: Giappichelli.

Guercini, S., & Ranfagni, S. (2012). Social and Green Sustainability and the Italian Mediterranean Fashion Brands. In *Proceedings of Euromed Congress* (pp. 1-15). Nicosia: Euromed Press.

Guercini, S., & Ranfagni, S. (2013). Sustainability and luxury: The Italian case of a supply chain based on native wools. *Journal of Corporate Citizenship*, *52*(52), 76–89. doi:10.9774/GLEAF.4700.2013.de.00008

Guercini, S., & Woodside, A. G. (2012). A strategic supply chain approach: Consortium marketing in the Italian leatherwear industry. *Marketing Intelligence & Planning*, *30*(7), 700–716. doi:10.1108/02634501211273814

Ha, H. Y., & Perks, H. (2005). Effects of consumer perceptions of brand experience on the web: Brand familiarity, satisfaction, and trust. *Journal of Consumer Behaviour*, *4*(6), 438–452. doi:10.1002/cb.29

Haenlein, M., & Kaplan, A. M. (2009). Flagship Brand Stores within Virtual Worlds: The Impact of Virtual Store Exposure on Real-Life Attitude toward the Brand and Purchase Intent. *Recherche et Applications en Marketing*, *24*(3), 57–79. doi:10.1177/076737010902400304

Hall, E. T., & Hall, M. R. (1990). Understanding Cultural Differences. Yarmouth, ME: Intercultural Press.

Harrisson, L., & Huntington, S. (2000). *Culture Matters: How values shape human progress*. New York: Basic Books.

Hauck, W. E., & Stanforth, N. (2007). Cohort perception of luxury goods and services. *Journal of Fashion Marketing and Management*, *11*(2), 175–188. doi:10.1108/13612020710751365

Hoecklin, L. (1996). *Managing Cultural Differences: Strategies for Competitive Advantage* (2nd ed.). Wokingham: Addison-Wesley Publishers.

Holbrook, M. B., & Hirschman, E. C. (1982). The experiential aspects of consumption: Consumer fantasies, feelings, and fun. *The Journal of Consumer Research*, *9*(2), 32–40. doi:10.1086/208906

Huang, M. H. (2001). The theory of emotions in marketing. *Journal of Business and Psychology*, *16*(2), 239–247. doi:10.1023/A:1011109200392

Jansson, J., & Power, D. (2010). Fashioning a Global City: Global City Brand Channel in the Fashion and Design Industries. *Regional Studies*, *44*(7), 889–904. doi:10.1080/00343400903401584

Jones, C., Makri, M., & Gomez-Mejia, L. R. (2008). Affiliate directors and perceived risk bearing in publicly traded, family-controlled firms: The case of diversification. *Entrepreneurship Theory & Practice*, *32*(6), 1007–1026. doi:10.1111/j.1540-6520.2008.00269.x

Jones, R. (2002). *The apparel industry*. London: Blackwell.

Kapferer, J. N. (1997). Managing luxury brands. *Journal of Brand Management*, *4*(4), 251–260. doi:10.1057/bm.1997.4

Kapferer, J. N. (2002). *Ce qui va changer les marques*. Paris: Editions d'Organisation.

Kapferer, J. N. (2012). All That Glitters is not Green: The Challenge of Sustainable Luxury. *European Business Review*, (November/December), 40–45.

Kapferer, J. N., & Bastien, V. (2009). Luxury Strategy. Milano: FrancoAngeli.

Kapferer, J. N., & Bastien, V. (2013). *Luxury Strategy. Sovvertire le regole del marketing per costruire veri brand di lusso*. Milano: Franco Angeli.

Kaplan, A. M., & Haenlein, M. (2010). Users of the world, unite! The challenges and opportunities of Social Media. *Business Horizons*, *53*(1), 59–68. doi:10.1016/j.bushor.2009.09.003

Kemp, S. (1998). Perceiving Luxury and Necessity. *Journal of Economic Psychology*, *19*(5), 591–606. doi:10.1016/S0167-4870(98)00026-9

Kent, T. (2007). Creative Space: Design and the Retail Environment. *International Journal of Retail & Distribution Management*, *35*(9), 734–745. doi:10.1108/09590550710773273

Kietzmann, J. H., Silvestre, B. S., McCarthy, I. P., & Pitt, L. F. (2012). Unpacking the social media phenomenon: Towards a research agenda. *Journal of Public Affairs*, *12*(2), 109–119. doi:10.1002/pa.1412

Kim, A. K., & Ko, E. (2012). Do social media marketing activities enhance customer equity? An empirical study of luxury fashion brand. *Journal of Business Research*, *65*(10), 1480–1486. doi:10.1016/j.jbusres.2011.10.014

Kim, H., & Lennon, S. J. (2010). E-atmosphere, emotional, cognitive, and behavioral responses. *Journal of Fashion Marketing and Management*, *14*(3), 412–428. doi:10.1108/13612021011061861

Kim, S., Choi, S., Agrusa, J., Wang, K. C., & Kim, Y. (2010). The role of family decision makers in festival tourism. *International Journal of Hospitality Management*, *29*(2), 308–318. doi:10.1016/j.ijhm.2009.10.004

Kozinets, R. V., Sherry, J. F., DeBerry-Spence, B., Duhacheck, A., Nuttavuthisi, K., & Storm, D. (2002). Themed Flagship Brand Stores in the new Millenium: Theory, Practice, Prospect. *Journal of Retailing*, *78*(1), 17–29. doi:10.1016/S0022-4359(01)00063-X

Kwon, W. S., & Noh, M. (2010). The influence of prior experience and age on mature consumers' perceptions and intentions of internet apparel shopping. *Journal of Fashion Marketing and Management*, *14*(3), 335–349. doi:10.1108/13612021011061825

Levy, M., & Weitz, B. A. (2006). *Retailing Management*. New York: McGraw-Hill/Irwin.

Macchi, J. (2011). *Lusso 2.0*. Milano: Lupetti.

McCharty, E. J. (1964). *Basic Marketing: A Managerial Approach* (2nd ed.). Homewood: Irwin, Homewood.

Micelotta, E. R., & Raynard, M. (2011). Concealing or Revealing the Family? Corporate Brand Identity Strategies in Family Firms. *Family Business Review*, *20*(10), 1–20.

Miller, D., & Le Breton-Miller, I. (2005). *Managing for the Long Run: Lessons in Competitive Advantage from Great Family Businesses*. Boston: Harvard Business Press.

Moore, C. M., Doherty, A. M., & Doyle, S. A. (2010). Flagship Stores as a Market Entry Method: the Perspective of Luxury Fashion Retailing. *European Journal of Marketing, 44*(1(2), 139-161.

Mosca, F. (2010). *Il marketing dei beni di lusso*. Milano: Pearson Italia.

Mosca, F. (2014). *Distribution Strategies in Luxury Markets: emerging trends*. London: McGraw-Hill.

Mulyanegara, R. C., & Tsarenko, Y. (2009). Predicting brand preferences: An examination of the predictive power of personality and values in the Australian fashion market. *Journal of Fashion Marketing and Management*, *13*(3), 358–371. doi:10.1108/13612020910974492

Nueno, J. L., & Quelch, J. A. (1998). The Mass Marketing of Luxury. *Business Horizons*, *41*(November-December), 61–68. doi:10.1016/S0007-6813(98)90023-4

Nwankwo, S., Hamelin, N., & Khaled, M. (2014). Consumer values, motivation and purchase intention for luxury goods. *Journal of Retailing and Consumer Services*, *21*(5), 735–744. doi:10.1016/j.jretconser.2014.05.003

O'Neal, C. R. (1989). The buyer-seller linkage in a just-in-time environment. *Journal of Purchasing and Materials Management*, *23*(1), 7–13.

Okonkwo, U. (2007). *Luxury Fashion Branding*. New York: Palgrave, Macmillan. doi:10.1057/9780230590885

Okonkwo, U. (2009). Sustaining the Luxury Brand on the Internet. *Journal of Brand Management*, *16*(5/6), 302–310. doi:10.1057/bm.2009.2

Okonkwo, U. (2010). *Luxury Online*. New York: Palgrave MacMillan. doi:10.1057/9780230248335

Orton, J., & Weick, K. (1990). Loosely Coupled Systems: A Reconceptualization. *Academy of Management Review*, *15*(2), 203–223.

Paquot, T. (2007). *Elogio del lusso. Ovvero l'utilità dell'inutile*. Roma: Castelvecchi.

Pardo, P., & Tajeddini, K. (2013). Innovative Marketing Strategies in Family Owned Business: a Work in progress Framework to Integrate Social Media. In *Proceedings of the 6th Euromed Conference of the Euromed Academy of Business 'Confronting Contemporary Business Challenges through Management Innovation* (pp. 2714-2716). Nicosia: Euromed Press.

Park, M., & Lennon, S. J. (2009). Brand name and promotion in online shopping contexts. *Journal of Fashion Marketing and Management*, *13*(2), 149–160. doi:10.1108/13612020910957680

Parsons, A. G. (2011). Atmosphere in fashion stores: Do you need to change? *Journal of Fashion Marketing and Management*, *15*(4), 428–445. doi:10.1108/13612021111169933

Pellicelli, G. (2005). *Il marketing*. Milano: Wolters Kluwer.

Phan, M. (2011). Do Social Media Enhance Consumer's Perception and Purchase Intentions of Luxury Brands? *Vikalpa*, *36*(1), 81–84.

Phau, I., & Prendergast, G. (2000). Consuming luxury brands: The relevance of the 'Rarity Principle'. *Journal of Brand Management*, *8*(2), 122–138. doi:10.1057/palgrave.bm.2540013

Poza, E. (2007). Family business (2nd ed.). Mason, OH: Thompson.

Re, P. G., Giacosa, E., Giachino, C., & Stupino, M. (2014). The management of innovation in the wine business. In *Proceedings of 2nd International Symposium Systems Thinking for a Sustainable Economy. Advancements in Economic and Managerial Theory and Practice* (pp. 1-17). Rome: Business Laboratory System.

Ries, A., & Ries, L. (2000). *The 11 immutable laws of internet branding*. London: HarperCollins Business.

Ritzer, G. (1999). *Enchanting and disenchanted world: revolutionizing the means of consumption*. Thousand Oaks, CA: Pine Forge Press.

Ritzer, G. (2000). *La religione dei consumi. Cattedrali, pellegrinaggi e riti dell'iperconsumismo*. Bologna: Il Mulino.

Ross, J., & Harradine, R. (2011). Fashion value brands: The relationship between identity and image. *Journal of Fashion Marketing and Management*, *15*(3), 306–325. doi:10.1108/13612021111151914

Sacerdote, E. (Ed.). (2006). *La strategia retail nella moda e nel lusso*. Milano: Franco Angeli.

Saviolo, S., & Testa, S. (2005). *Le aziende del sistema moda*. Milano: Etas.

Schlosser, A. E. (2007). Learning through Virtual Product Experience: The Role of Imagery on True Versus False Memories. *The Journal of Consumer Research*, *33*(3), 337–383.

Silverstein, M. J. (2006). *Caccia al tesoro*. Milano: Etas.

Steinfield, C., Bouwman, H., & Adelaar, T. (2002). The dynamics of click-and-mortar electronic commerce: Opportunities and management strategies. *International Journal of Electronic Commerce*, *7*(1), 93–119.

Stokburger-Sauer, N. E., & Teichmann, K. (2013). Is luxury just a female thing? The role of gender in luxury brand consumption. *Journal of Business Research*, *66*(7), 889–896. doi:10.1016/j.jbusres.2011.12.007

Taplin, I. M. (2014). Who is to blame? A re-examination of Fast Fashion after the 2013 factory disaster in Bangladesh. *Critical Perspectives on International Business*, *10*(1/2), 72–83. doi:10.1108/cpoib-09-2013-0035

Tartaglia, A., & Marinozzi, G. (2006). *Il lusso ... magia e marketing*. Milano: Franco Angeli.

Thompson, C. J., Rindfleisch, A., & Zeynec, A. (2006). Emotional branding and the strategic value of the doppelganger brand image. *Journal of Marketing*, *70*(1), 50–64. doi:10.1509/jmkg.2006.70.1.50

Tynan, C., McKechnie, S., & Chuon, C. (2010). Co-creating Value for Luxury Brands. *Journal of Business Research*, *63*(11), 1156–1163. doi:10.1016/j.jbusres.2009.10.012

Vaid, H. (2003). *Branding*. London: Cassel Illustrated.

Vigneron, F., & Johnson, L. W. (1999). A review and a conceptual framework of prestige-seeking consumer behaviour. *Academy of Marketing Science Review*, *9*(1), 1–14.

Wang, C. H., & Ha, S. (2011). Store attributes influencing relationship marketing: A study of department stores. *Journal of Fashion Marketing and Management*, *15*(3), 326–344. doi:10.1108/13612021111151923

Ward, J. L. (1997). Growing the family business: Special challenges and best practices. *Family Business Review*, *10*(4), 323–337. doi:10.1111/j.1741-6248.1997.00323.x

Weick, K. (1976). Educational Organizations as Loosely Coupled Systems. *Administrative Science Quarterly*, *21*(1), 1–19. doi:10.2307/2391875

Yang, K., & Young, A. P. (2009). The effects of customized site features on internet apparel shopping. *Journal of Fashion Marketing and Management*, *13*(1), 128–139. doi:10.1108/13612020910939923

Yeoman, I. (2011). The Changing Behaviour of Luxury Consumption. *Journal of Revenue and Pricing Management*, *10*(1), 47–50. doi:10.1057/rpm.2010.43

KEY TERMS AND DEFINITIONS

Company Environment: It is the context in which a company operates, that affects the company's input–output logic and impacts on the consumption choices of individuals.

Distribution Variable: It represents a fundamental moment of the relationship between a luxury company and its customers, as the point of sale becomes the place where the customer meets the company and the company convinces the customers on the validity of its brand.

Human Needs: They are each individual needs, dictated by perceptions of aspects that are lacking. Such human needs are perceived according to the framework of a mental rating scale: consequently, they could be classify in different categories, such as primary and secondary needs.

Luxury Sector: It is made up of a number of luxury companies that share one or more of the following criteria: the process of acquiring the productive factors; the process of manufacturing goods and services; and the process of distributing them.

Marketing Mix Variables: They are the traditional "4Ps" directly controlled by companies, i.e. product, price, promotion, and place (distribution).

Chapter 11
The Relationship between Fast Fashion and Luxury Brands: An Exploratory Study in the UK Market

Cesare Amatulli
University of Bari, Italy

Vincenzo Speciale
LUISS Guido Carli University, Italy

Antonio Mileti
University of Salento, Italy

Gianluigi Guido
University of Salento, Italy

ABSTRACT

This chapter explores how the luxury sector has been affected by the fast fashion brands in the UK market. In particular, this chapter examines the effects of fast fashion activity on luxury brands and more specifically on how the marketing strategies of luxury brands have been drawn to the fast fashion model. Moreover, it analyzes how co-branding collaborations between luxury and fast fashion brands have positively affected consumer' perception of the luxury brands. The chapter is based on a theoretical review and two studies. Results provide insights for the international fashion business, showing how luxury fashion brands lean towards the fast fashion model and how co-branding collaborations between luxury and fast fashion brands are positive for luxury brands in terms of customer perception.

INTRODUCTION

Walking from London's Knightsbridge up to Old Bond Street, the shop windows of Burberry, Hermès, Louis Vuitton, and Gucci show their latest creations of refined quality materials and unique craftsmanship. Continuing across Oxford Street up to Carnaby Street, one notes pretty much the same designs at the trendy showcases of H&M, Zara, Top Shop, and Forever 21, although at significantly lower prices and quality. Luxury brands evoke rarity, heritage of craftsmanship, exclusivity, premium pricing, and superior quality (Amatulli & Guido, 2011; Chevalier & Mazzalovo, 2008). By contrast, fast fashion ensures permanent assortment rotation, low prices, and accessible variety, but with a great aesthetic content, which derives from those brands' ability to imitate the latest luxury fashion brand catwalk offerings

DOI: 10.4018/978-1-4666-9958-8.ch011

(Byun & Sternquist, 2008; Gabrielli, Baghi, & Codeluppi, 2013). However, today it is not uncommon to find people wearing together shoes from Gucci, jeans from Zara, sunglasses from Dior, shirts from H&M, and bags from Louis Vuitton. Even high-end consumers, typically loyal to luxury brands, are not afraid of such an eclectic mix of fashion and luxury brands (Atwal et al., 2010). The evolution of a mass class of wealthy people and the rapid growth of the Internet have allowed consumers to "trade upwards" and purchase luxury items, mixing these luxury products with fast fashion ones, in a way that seems to lead to the so called "democratisation of luxury" (Okonkwo, 2009). The new fast fashion brands have become competitors of luxury brands through the introduction of limited-edition products, celebrity endorsement, high advertisement expenditure, and store openings in prestige retail locations. Differentiating themselves is becoming extremely important for luxury companies, as they have witnessed great changes from their consumers. Indeed, luxury companies are now considering mass brands as a threat.

However, where are the boundaries between luxury and fast fashion brands? Have luxury fashion brands pivoted towards the fast fashion model? Does co-branding collaboration between luxury and fast fashion brands positively affect consumer perception of the luxury brand? This chapter explores the reactions that fast fashion marketing and merchandising strategies have generated in luxury fashion brands, and more specifically, how luxury brands have tended towards the fast fashion model. Moreover, the chapter also explores how co-branding collaboration between luxury and fast fashion brands has positively affected consumer perception of luxury brands.

The study focuses on the British fashion market, which represents more than 70 per cent of the new luxury brands launched over the last fifteen years (Okonkwo, 2007), and which continuously influences design and fashion styles (British Fashion Council, 2009). The British fashion influence has been propelled by the rise of new designer brands and chains such as Vivienne Westwood, Paul Smith, Stella McCartney, Alexander McQueen, and Alice Temperley and the re-emergence of old luxury brands like Burberry and Mulberry (British Fashion Council, 2009). High levels of creativity and innovation of product design along with solid entrepreneurial skills in retail and brand management are the keys of success of these luxury brands.

THEORETICAL BACKGROUND

Luxury Fashion

A luxury brand can be considered a "coherent system of excellence", a harmonious universe of values, and a perfect system of attributes (Corbellini & Saviolo, 2009). Luxury brands evoke exclusivity, have a well-known brand identity, enjoy high brand awareness and perceived quality, and retain high sales levels and customer loyalty (Phau & Prendergast, 2000). Indeed, a luxury brand can be defined as the sum of feelings and perceptions people have when in contact with a particular company and its products (Chevalier & Mazzalovo, 2008). Therefore, a luxury company brand lives in consumers' mind and its success or failure is based on how it is positioned in the consumer's mind (Parrott, Danbury & Kanthavanich, 2015). Indeed, the creation of brand value is crucial in luxury marketing activities; brand value refers to brand equity, which is an indispensable intangible asset for luxury companies and translates into revenues. The brand value is also relevant to consumers, who achieve an immeasurable level of satisfaction from luxury fashion products. The most visible and symbolic aspect of a luxury fashion brand is the brand name (Okonkwo, 2007); this is due to the fact that it is the "brand name" or "brand logo" that enchants consumers to a brand and generates a relationship between them and their chosen brand (Chevalier & Mazzalovo, 2008). Luxury brands confer much emphasis on creating high brand awareness and the proper brand image with the objective of achieving a high level of brand loyalty and consequently a steady income stream (Amatulli & Guido, 2012). Therefore, luxury brands generally have the advantage of attaining a higher level of global brand awareness than fast fashion brands (Business of Fashion, 2011). The strategy is conceived to assist in developing the global presence and reputation of the brand, and to leverage its status and awareness. Luxury and prestige brands have traditionally embraced the premium pricing strategy to highlight their brand exclusivity (Fionda & Moore, 2009), high quality, and the strength associated with luxury goods, and also to distinguish them from the fast fashion brands. Furthermore brand exclusivity and rarity are essentially maintained through limited production where the aura of scarcity adds to the appeal of luxury brands (Joy et al., 2012; Kapferer, 2004).

The relationship between consumers and a strong brand is a type of bond that begins with a psychological process in the mind of the consumer and is proven through product purchases. As a consequence any luxury brand that attempts to succeed in the competitive luxury market environment needs to understand everything about the luxury consumer (Megehee & Spake, 2012). Indeed, the term "Consumer Behaviour" is defined as the behaviour that consumers display in searching for, purchasing, using, evaluating, and disposing of products and services that satisfy their needs (Schiffman et al., 2008). Thus, consumer behaviour is associated to the consumer's self-concept (Phau & Prendergast, 2000; Guido, Amatulli, & Peluso 2014) and wearing luxury goods is a way to raise the value of the self (Megehee & Spake, 2012). The reason for the purchase of luxury goods is mainly their symbolic value in fulfilling consumer needs and desires. However, research has acknowledged that two main purchasing motives may be identified in luxury consumption: "luxury for others" and "luxury for oneself" (Kapferer & Bastien, 2009; Kastanakis & Balabanis, 2014). Therefore, luxury goods can be purchased for status symbols (i.e., for social statements) or as a means to express an individual style (i.e., for personal pleasure). Vigneron and Johnson (2004) highlighted that the meaning of luxury is determined by a consideration of "interpersonal" versus "personal" perceptions and motives. Amatulli and Guido (2012) introduced the conceptualization of "internalized" versus "externalized" luxury consumption – the former based on the aim of expressing an individual style and the latter based on the aim of showing off a social position. For luxury companies the latter is important to support, given the fact that there should be more people aware of the brand than those who can truly afford to purchase it. If somebody is observing another person and doesn't identify the brand they are wearing, then part of the brand value is lost (Okonkwo, 2007). The luxury brand must be well known and accredited in order to be desired (Chevalier & Mazzalovo, 2008). Luxury consumers are less price sensitive and they buy a complete package of experiences, feelings, and identities, made up of the product and the brand characteristics (Phau & Prendergast, 2000). Luxury consumers acquire their products chiefly in physical stores in order to benefit from a whole product selection and also delight in the luxury retail atmosphere. As mentioned by Okonkwo (2007) there are currently two major segments of the luxury consumer population. The first is the "traditional luxury consumer" who still venerates entrenched brands like Hermès and Christian Dior; and the second segment comprises a considerable proportion of luxury consumers known as the "new luxury consumer" population. This new consumer group is no longer attracted by only brand names but also appreciates a full package of products and services that offer stable value through innovation and an extraordinary experience in every element of the brand (Megehee & Spake, 2012). The current luxury consumer is highly sophisticated, stylish, brand literate, fashionable, and aware of their tastes and preferences (Amatulli, Guido & Caputo, 2011). They have strong values and principles (Schiffman et al., 2008). They are well informed about materials and they also have become highly demanding (Laurent et al., 2001).

Fast Fashion

Fast fashion concerns a consumer-driven approach (Barnes & Lea- Greenwood, 2006), a business strategy which is intended at decreasing the number of processes involved in the buying cycle and lead times for getting new fashion product into stores, in order to satisfy consumer demand (Joy et al., 2012). The term "fast fashion" was first invented by retailers to indicate how fashion styles and trends change rapidly from the catwalk to the store (Brooks, 2015).

The aim of fast fashion is the ability to react quickly to ever-changing fashion trends and consumer demands in order to gain competitive advantage (Barnes and Lea- Greenwood, 2010). Mass retailers such as Zara and H&M have adopted this business strategy and have become recognized for steadily refreshing their product range with new fashion styles, capturing the attention of media and driving customers to visit their stores on a frequent basis (Rosenblum, 2015). As this phenomenon has expanded within the fashion industry, rather than being concerned to mass retailers they have become known as fast fashion brands (Bhardwaj & Fairhurst, 2010). What characterize these brands are the trendy inexpensive clothes, cheaply made designer knockoffs, rapid speed, stylish and up-to-date fashions garments which lure consumers into paying full price now rather than deferring gratification until the year-end sales arrive (Bhardwaj & Fairhurst, 2010; Cohen, 2011; Joy et al., 2012; Rosenblum, 2015). Fast fashion replaces exclusivity, glamour, originality, and luxury with "mass-exclusivity" "massluxe" or "masstige" (Toktali, 2008), by producing products in smaller volumes that usually are not restocked, in order to minimize the risk of inaccuracy and being out of date. As a result, the fashion items change every few weeks. Collections are small and often sell out, creating exclusivity and cutting down on the need for markdowns. According to Barnes and Lea-Greenwood (2006), the fast fashion brands' decisions in producing their products take a lead from luxury fashion brands. What has changed today is not the speed of imitating, but the low cost and large scale at which copies are being made. Fast fashion imitations threaten the innovation process and move the focus of innovation from expressive aspects towards status aspects (Hemphill & Suk, 2009).

Fast fashion is a consumer-driven approach and its persistent demand for novelty is its central force (Bhardwaj & Fairhurst, 2010). Hence, the objective of the fast fashion model is to meet consumer demand by speedily designing, producing, and delivering highly fashionable garments in the shortest possible time (Ertekin & Atik, 2015). Fast fashion customers expect stylish and fresh offerings which results in a high periodicity of fashion turnover and produces a "buy now because you won't see this later" scarcity mentality (Miller, 2013). Updated looks, greater variety and choice, well-designed and limited editions, along with the speed of their availability, have made this industry very attractive to many consumers - appealing both young and mature consumers (Joy et al., 2012). Refined and well-informed consumers, in search of an individual look, have moved towards consumption behaviours such as "mix and match" (Cillo & Verona, 2008; Feitelberg, 2010; Nueno & Quelch, 1998; Yeoman, 2007). Fast fashion allows dreams of luxury to come true. Many consumers will fantasise and dream about owning, wearing and acquiring replicas of catwalk looks or celebrity couture fashions (Miller, 2013).

Fast Fashion Brands vs. Luxury Fashion Brands: Co-Branding Strategies

The success of fast fashion brands has today affected consumer perception as they are no longer regarded as simply "fast fashion" brands but are now "fast premium fashion" brands or, in some cases, "high-end" brands (Bhardwaj & Fairhurst, 2010). Although they remain focused on a mass-market target, it is no longer pertinent to consider these brands as low-end fast brands (Joy et al., 2012). The fast fashion brands have developed new marketing mix strategies and retail tactics that are comparable to those of luxury fashion brands, thus developing a "luxurious appeal" at a better price-value balance (Joy et al., 2012). For fast fashion companies, one of the results of these strategies is the significant rise of their brand asset value. To illustrate, in 2005, Zara featured for the first time on the list of the 100 Best Global Brands (Interbrand, 2005). Indeed, Zara was ranked number 77, with a brand value of $3.73 billion, much higher than the value of luxury brands like Tiffany, Hermès, Cartier, Prada, Bulgari, and Armani. The current year Zara brand value ($12,1 billion) rose to number 36 while the value of the H&M brand has risen to $21.1 billion from $13.8 billion in 2008 (Interbrand, 2014).

For today's luxury consumer, the branded bag or watch is no longer required solely to fulfil one's egotistical needs. Therefore it is no longer a dilemma for wealthy consumers to mix a £25 t-shirt from H&M and a £60 pair of jeans from Zara with a £1,500 bag from Louis Vuitton and a £3,000 watch from Chanel. Consequently, L'Avenue des Champs Elysées in Paris, which is considered as the epitome of a luxury location, currently has stores representing non-luxury brands such as Zara and Naf Naf alongside Louis Vuitton and Cartier. In the same way, London's Knightsbridge is a location chosen by Burberry, Chanel, and Harrods as well as H&M, Zara, Top Shop, and several other fast fashion brands (Bhardwaj & Fairhurst, 2010). The phenomenon of "mix and match" brings together the ideas of luxury and mass-market consumerism (Corbellini & Saviolo, 2009), combining items of fast fashion and luxury fashion. Increasingly consumers of middle or lower class origin are being associated with this phenomenon. Accessories are typically purchased from the luxury brand market, as the price of these longer lasting items is perceived as more affordable (Atwal et al., 2010). Garments, however, as they are being purchased more frequently, are bought from fast fashion companies (Brown, 2011). Mix and match allows the opportunity of creating a more affordable luxury lifestyle and gives the consumer the possibility of gaining a higher prestige within their particular peer group. It is an ever-changing trade that serves to improve personal style, within an economic environment (Atwal et al., 2010).

In an attempt to face up to the competition posed by fast fashion brands, luxury brands are now competing on speed of production and turnover although their high quality and high prices continue to set them apart from fast fashion (Rohwedder, 2004). This guarantees frequent product change into stores and shortens the shelf life of the luxury products in question, so as to give customers a reason to return (Okonkwo, 2007). Some brands like Dolce & Gabbana, Chanel, Versace and Prada have adopted this strategy to reduce seasonality risk. In 2013 Louis Vuitton introduced bold new looks creating an entire Mix & Match Spring/Summer Collection between the Cruise and Icon lines with their own unique styles. Burberry's invested in its supply chain to react rapidly to sales trends and capitalize on bestsellers (Business of Fashion, 2011). Luxury fashion brands have also created more reasonable lower priced diffusion lines mixing haute couture with ready-to-wear. To illustrate, Giorgio Armani developed the Emporio Armani line, a diffusion line aimed at targeting the young adult market. These diffusion lines are mass-produced and designed to appeal to the younger costumer (Armani, 2015). It is important to note that what makes the diffusion lines differ from the principal lines is that whilst still carrying the same brand name, the manufacturing is usually outsourced to cheaper countries, such as China (Plunkett, 2010).

A recent strategic measure adopted by fast fashion brands is to develop collaborations with luxury brands in order to reach new potential customers (Uggla, 2004), elevate their brand status (Okonkwo, 2007), and create unique products (Griffioen, 2011). In 2004, the creative director of Chanel and Fendi, Karl Lagerfeld, designed a limited edition collection for the Swedish fast fashion brand H&M. This strategy was aimed at generating retail innovation, differentiating H&M from competitors, and boosting turnover for both H&M and its luxury brand partner (Amoye, 2011). With this initiative H&M reached sales growth by 12% in the first month after the launch of the collection (Business of Fashion, 2013). After Karl Lagerfeld, H&M collaborated with other fashion designers such as Stella McCartney, Jimmy Choo, Roberto Cavalli, Comme des Garcons, Versace, and Alexander Wang (H&M, 2015). Isabel Marant boosted H&M's total sales by 21 percent at the end of 2013, having a 100 percent sell-out rate and zero discounting (Business of Fashion, 2013).

Other examples of significant collaborations are between luxury brands and other fashion brands include: Italian luxury brand Missoni has collaborated with the mass-market brand Target in the realization of 400-pieces including product categories even outside of fashion, which helped drive Target's net-profits up by 3.7 percent in the first quarter of 2011 (Bickers, 2011); the limited edition collection of boots of UGG Australia and luxury fashion designer Jimmy Choo (WWD, 2010); and the latest sportswear collection designed for Adidas by Stella McCartney to celebrate 10 years of sports performance (Stella McCartney, 2015). Overall, the designer collaborations help the retailer brand get media attention by creating a lot of buzz for both the retailer and the brand; media attention, rather than profits, is often the key measure of success (Friedman, 2014).

Co-branding is a branding strategy that pairs two separate well-known brands together for a unique, collaborative project (Sreejesh, 2012). This could include new or revived products, services or ventures as well as advertising or distribution outlets. Due to the high level of competition and brand protection among luxury brands, the phenomenon of co-branding has been rare in the luxury goods sector. If a co-branding strategy is well managed by combining elements between two brands such as values, visions and wills to generate real synergies, it presents an interesting path towards creating strong brand reputation and differentiation (Rollet et al., 2013). Brands may embrace co-branding for various reasons, depending on whether they are luxury brands or fast fashion brands. If a co-branding strategy is based on consistency and integration between elements of the two brands (e.g., visions and values), it presents an interesting and effective strategy for creating sustainable brand reputation and differentiation for fast fashion brands (Hoffmann & Coste-Manière, 2012). Indeed, for fast fashion brands, the desire to reinforce brand equity is the first motivation behind co-branding activities with luxury brands. For luxury fashion brands, co-branding with fast fashion brands is mainly aimed at increasing their interaction with consumers, in particular younger ones.

Nevertheless, co-branding collaborations offer both great opportunities for success as well as risks for failure. According to Uggla (2004), the characteristic of co-branding is that both associates reach access to the other's customer base and may conquer new segments. Potential disadvantages are that co-branding could harm a luxury brand's image by merging their unique characteristics with a familiar product or a fast fashion brand creating a sense of negative brand perceptions and tending to dilute the brand equity. However, Simonin and Ruth (1998) have demonstrated that under positive co-branding product reviews their association with low-equity brands does not damage high-equity brands. Some authors (Washburn et al., 2000) have stated that when co-branding will stop, the luxury brands that did not collaborate with fast fashion brands will be recognized with higher equity and more exclusive than the ones that decided to co-operate with fast fashion brands. The following table provides an overview of the main opportunities and threats related to co-branding (see Table 1).

Co-branding offers multiple benefits if applied appropriately. It is imperative for the success of the co-branding project that the fit between the associate brands is positive. Indeed, there must be a strategic purpose behind the co-branding activity in order to increase the brand equity (Okonkwo, 2007). According to Uggla (2004), if two incompatible brands undertake a co-branding strategy it can be a failure for one of the brands or for both; their brand identities may be too different, thus generating unclear positioning. Fashion co-operations should always remain limited in order to preserve the perception of luxury (Okonkwo, 2007). However, advertising co-branded luxury goods in a fast fashion store provides a gateway for fast-market customers to penetrate the luxury goods arena. This strategy brings credibility to fast fashion brands, increasing sales revenues, consumer perceived quality and value, as well as high media exposure, differentiation from other fast fashion brands and the positioning of the brand in consumers' mind as more premium (Okonkwo, 2007; Uggla, 2005).

RESEARCH QUESTIONS AND METHOD

A broad range of academic articles and literature have been examined in order to gain an understanding of how luxury on the one hand and fast fashion brands on the other are perceived (Annamma Joy et al., 2012; Barnes & Lea-Greenwood, 2006; Corbellini & Saviolo, 2009; Okonkwo, 2007) and how fast fashion brands have impacted and influenced luxury fashion brands and how the latter have consequently

Table 1. Co-branding opportunities and threats

Author	Research Methodology	Opportunities/ Threats
Simonin and Ruth (1998)	Research paper	• Economies of Scale and Synergies
Washburn et al. (2000)	Research paper	• Brand Equity Improvement • Brand Equity Damage
Washburn et al. (2000)	Research paper	• Efficiency through Creation of New and Unique Consumer Perception of the Co-Branded Product
Vaidyanathan and Aggarwal (2000)	Research paper	• Sales Cannibalization of Existing Products • Product Recalls in Case of Failure
Uggla (2004)	Article	• Media Exposure and Word of Mouth
Uggla (2005)	Descriptive analysis	• Increase of Market • Penetration and Sales • Possible Harm to Brand • Image and Exclusivity
Kapferer (2009)	Descriptive analysis	• Outsourcing of specific responsibilities • Less Risks and Shared Costs
Okonkwo (2009)	Descriptive analysis	• Access to New Markets and Customers • Harm through Environmental Changes

Source: Elaboration of the authors

reacted (Bhardwaj & Fairhurst, 2010; Cohen, 2011; Rollet, Hoffmann et al., 2013). Furthermore, case specific information was secured through contact with managing directors, marketing directors, retail directors, concession and store managers of luxury brands through telephone interviews. This along with other information gave a deeper understanding of the impact of fast fashion brands on luxury fashion allowing one to analyse how the latter have tilted toward the fast fashion model.

The most obvious area being addressed in the luxury fashion industry is the increasing status and production of the fast fashion brands (Okonkwo, 2007). Even as these brands focus their attention on the mass market they will still not be regarded as "low-end" or "middle-end" mass brands. Fast fashion brands are now emanating a "luxurious" appeal (Okonkwo, 2007). These statements served as a basis for the direction of the first part of the research study and have been instrumental in providing the formula for the development of the hypothesis that:

H1: Luxury fashion brands have mainly inclined towards the fast fashion model.

The present research also aims to investigate co-branding collaboration as a consequential strategy resulting from the growth and expansion of mass fashion brands. Uggla (2004) looked at brand connections and the spill-over effect of associate brands upon each other, although not specifically for luxury brands. His theories along with the spill-over concept will be extremely important for the second part of the study in order to analyse consumers' perceptions after co-branding collaborations and thus leading to the investigation of the second hypothesis:

H2: Co-branding collaboration between luxury and fast fashion brands affects positively consumer' perception of the luxury brand.

In fact of analytical relevance to the investigation is the research on consumer behaviour and consumers' perception of the luxury brand. The fast fashion brands have generated a shift of customer's expectations focusing principally on their own interpretation of catwalk styles and trends exhibited by the luxury fashion brands and quickly offering these to consumers in their stores. Today, as expressed by Okonkwo (2007), even the loyal high-end consumer is mixing luxury fashion with fast fashion.

To get an accurate valuation of how luxury fashion brands have inclined towards the fast fashion model and how consumers perceive co-branding collaboration, it was decided to conduct both qualitative and quantitative primary research, through semi-structured interviews for study 1 and a survey for study 2, respectively. The qualitative research provides in depth answers, whereas the quantitative data offers valuable information that will be useful in a broader sphere. Using both qualitative and quantitative data give the research a more comprehensive angle, and this could be used to answer if both the perception in the mind of the consumer has altered but also why luxury fashion brands have inclined towards the fast fashion model with its associated consequences.

Study 1: Qualitative Approach

For this study, qualitative interviews have been conducted (Crouch and McKenzie, 2006) with representatives of luxury fashion brands in order to elicit their point of view. This method allows for more relevant and poignant answers from participants. The criteria used for the selection of the companies in order to conduct the interviews with managers were: a) The brand should be identified as luxury fashion brands from established databases/companies (i.e. Interbrand, Walpole, Euromonitor, and Mintel); b) The potential chosen brands should have been living for a minimum of two years; c) The flagship stores of the luxury brands should operate in prestige locations; d) The potential companies should operate at least one luxury fashion store in the UK.

Seven representatives of different luxury companies agreed to participate: Alexander McQueen, Burberry, Hermès, Giorgio Armani, Ralph Lauren, Stella McCartney, and Versace. A telephone interview was conducted with the store manager, concession manager, managing director, marketing director, and retail director. In order to ensure the quality of the research design, three criteria were put forward: internal validity, external validity, and reliability, which were jointly considered at each stage. Guideline questions were created to provide a higher degree of transparency and external reliability of the study. The interview questions were adapted and reworded according to the specific brand, company and role of the interviewee. Different types of questions were asked ranging from introductory questions to follow-up questions and direct questions, such as: "Are you aware of the increasing influence of fast fashion brands on the luxury fashion industry? - Are you positive or negative about this impact?"; as well as direct questions: "Are luxury fashion brands competing with fast fashion? If yes, what have the luxury fashion brands done in reaction to fast fashion? Do you think that entering into co-branding collaborations with fast fashion brands is a challenging strategy? The interviews were scheduled to take around 20-30 minutes each one.

In a qualitative research the researcher does not try to prove a hypothesis as in a quantitative research, instead he tries to show that the hypothesis is plausible. Since it was a qualitative and not quantitative analysis, the emphasis was not on quantifying the data, but rather to interpret the underlying meaning. So for example when questioning about co-branding collaboration between luxury fashion designers and fast fashion brands, the focus was not on asking how many collaborations there had been, but rather on understanding the reason why these brands or designers had chosen to do these collaborations.

Study 2: Quantitative Approach

The quantitative research consisted of a questionnaire submitted through social network websites and the purpose was to collect and cover a wide range of consumers' perceptions and attitudes towards fast fashion, brand image and luxury fashion brands. The final sample used for this research was represented by two hundred-eighty British respondents. Three main types of data variables were taken in consideration while creating the survey: opinion, behaviour and attribute (Saunders, Lewis and Thornhill, 2009). Opinion reflects how people feel about something, their opinions and attitudes towards the luxury brands and fast fashion brands and the co-branding collaboration itself; behavioural variables describe how people act in relation to the questions posed and these are based on consumers' awareness, association and intention to purchase from the co-branding collaboration between fast fashion and luxury brands, before and after the collaboration; and attribute alludes to the respondents' characteristics, such as if they regularly buy mass-market or luxury clothing items, or a mixture of both. Jointly, the above-mentioned variables allow an evaluation of perception that consumers apply to the luxury and fast fashion brands.

Both open questions, in which respondents could write their own answers, for example "Have the collaborations changed your perception of the luxury brand?" accompanied by the question "Can you explain in terms of quality, luxury appeal, identity etc.?", and closed questions such as, "Have you ever bought any products from the collections of the collaborations between luxury and fast fashion brands?" or "Have the collaborations increased your level of awareness of the luxury fashion brand?" were used. The closed questions were created such that the respondents could answer by deciding from mutually exclusive categories covering all possible responses.

Filtering questions, for example, "Do you think co-branding collaborations are good initiatives?" followed by "why" if the answer given was "yes", were used in order to acquire answers from respondents that could actually give insightful information. Questions, such as "Will you buy products from the main lines of luxury brands after the collaborations?" followed by "no (to the previous question), for what reason?" allowed for elimination of part of the responding population.

The first section of the survey takes into account the general questions of age, gender and income, succeeded by questions concerning the respondent's relationship to fashion brands in order to give a general idea of how high on the hierarchy of needs consumers placed fashion. The third part comprised questions about fast fashion brands and their collaboration with luxury fashion in order to establish whether the general aim of the companies' project had succeeded and whether it had influenced consumers' perceptions and relationship to the luxury brands.

RESULTS AND DISCUSSION

Study 1: Luxury Fashion Brands Have Inclined towards the Fast Fashion Model

The goal of Study 1 was to highlight the effects that fast fashion' activities have produced on luxury fashion brands and specifically on how the latter have inclined towards the fast fashion model. Furthermore, the aim of Study 2 was on how co-branding collaboration between luxury and fast fashion brands have positively affected consumer perception of the luxury brand.

The data gathered through the interviews was collected and divided into different categories in accordance with how the luxury fashion brands have responded to the suggestion that they were being influenced by fast fashion. Trends have been extracted from the research and displayed by for example marking out quotations from the interviews, in order to understand the underlying meaning.

During the interviews in the primary research, the actions and statements from luxury fashion brands have shown that the fast fashion brands have not gone unnoticed. When asked about their awareness of the increasing influence of fast fashion brands on the luxury fashion industry, the interviewees were quite unanimous in their response that in the actual economic situation, fast fashion is a growing entity in the luxury sector. One participant noted that fast fashion brands are succeeding in attracting all kinds of customers without putting off others. The overall view of respondents about fast fashion brands was that they provide inexpensive clothes and are attainable to everyone but they recognised that the quality was significantly lower although many participants agreed that this has improved significantly over the last few years.

In this study it was decided to ask luxury fashion representatives to express their opinion on fast fashion brands, and whether they are positive or negative to their growing presence in the luxury fashion sector. Some participants argued that:

Luxury fashion brands shouldn't see fast fashion as a threat due to their high quality products and their different customer base. And luxury consumers demand a level of service that low-cost stores can't provide. (M-B-SM)[1]

Fast fashion is directed to a totally different customer who is aware of the lower quality of the brand in contrast to that of the authentic designer labels whose items are considered to be unique and original. (F-GA-MM)

But not all the respondents were willing to embrace fast fashion in such a positive light, as they emphasise that luxury brands insist on using only the most expensive materials available and on not developing mass consumption products. According to Rohwedder (2004) fast fashion retailers habitually imitate, manufacture, and ship products to stores much faster and cheaper than established designer brands. Other respondents were also very skeptical about fast fashion brands, commenting that:

I don't like the idea of a bad copy of the main brand and I don't even understand the reason of all this liking for knockoffs. (F-RL-RDD)

The findings in the primary research prove that luxury fashion brands have inclined towards the fast fashion model through the introduction of new practices and techniques. Although during the first introductory questions of the interview most luxury respondents affirmed to maintaining quality and prices high to differentiate themselves from fast fashion, they were feeling pressured to compete with fast fashion brands. Consequently, most luxury fashion makers were competing on speed in order to offer new products more often. This guarantees frequent product change into stores and shortens the shelf life of the luxury products, so as to give customers a reason to return (Rohwedder, 2004). According to one's respondent statement:

The aim and the intention for every luxury company are to keep people coming back into stores offerings new products and styles every four weeks, irrespective of the type of clients that enter to the store; [...] I don't even want loyal customers who visit the store frequently to become bored of not finding something new. (M-B-SM)

The design turnover of luxury products has become higher and their lifecycle has become shorter, which has led to fashion garments changing every few weeks (Bhardwaj and Fairhurst, 2010).

Retailers such as Zara, H&M, Top Shop and so on, have accustomed consumers to this new dynamic business. [...]. Inspired by the success of these new policies, the idea of Burberry has been based on maintaining a dynamic business by improving the entire logistic technology system, every phase from design to the consumer, allowing the company to react quickly to sales trends and to changes in consumption. (M-B-SM)

Another reaction from luxury companies in response to the ever-faster fashion cycle was the offering of complete packages of pre-collections, pre-Fall/Summer collections, cruise and limited edition lines of apparel and accessories in addition to the main season.

The idea of the two traditional Spring/Summer and Autumn/Winter collections is becoming increasingly obsolete. (F-RL-RDD)

Many European design houses, such as Gucci, Prada, Louis Vuitton, Dior, and Saint Laurent have adopted this strategy by speeding up manufacturing and delivering new merchandise to stores more frequently than the twice-yearly schedules of the past (Rohwedder, 2004). Luxury fashion brands have also created more reasonable lower priced diffusion lines mixing haute couture with ready to wear. The diffusion lines are a concrete example of the realisation of a rapid delivery cycle, similar to those of fast fashion brands, with:

Trendier garments arriving to the store every month and labels priced cheaper than the main line. With the introduction of Armani Exchange, the idea was to bring Armani name to another group of customers, younger and looking for the right price; we want to become cheaper in order to make fashion accessible for everybody. (F-GA-MM)

Today's fashion clients are highly involved in the consumption process, they know about brands trends, products - the Internet and social media offers them an unlimited source of information. Tungate (2005) argued that the days when consumers were loyal to brands are long gone.

Designers are facing a very strong reality because fashion consumers constantly desire to update their style and be surprised and satisfied otherwise even loyal clients will get bored of not finding something new; […] luxury companies need to innovate in terms of Information and Computer Technologies in order to attract and retain customers. (M-B-SM)

Mass brands are changing people's views about variety and speed at which this variety changes and that consequently trendy items can be purchased at lower prices and on this regard respondents argued:

Youngsters and young adults increasingly need to reinforce their image through brands, they have a hedonic necessity to express themselves but they often cannot afford to buy the luxury brands because they have limited resources, […] therefore they choose to buy cheap products of mass-market brands. (F-SMC-SM)

Even high-end consumers loyal to brands' labels are not afraid of mixing different fashion and apparel brands, combining both luxuries with mass fashion items. Many wealthy consumers are becoming loyal to fast fashion as well. (F-GA-MM)

Co-branding collaboration is a strategy to attract and satisfy both the consumer that demands quality and design, and the consumer that wants cheap but nonetheless trendy garments. As a consequence, the margins between luxury fashion and fast fashion are weaker today.

The aspect of mixing styles and fashion brands made the decision for luxury brands easier to enter into co-branding collaboration, […] their intention is to offer consumers, through their collaborations, value, quality and design at relatively low prices. (F-AMQ-RM)

Among other strategies, fast fashion brands have tried to enter into new seasonal co-branding collaboration with different designers and celebrities in order to impress their target group of consumers. This results in special and limited collections that generate buzz in a distinctive way. The very first collaborations started in 2004 between H&M and the iconic Chanel designer Karl Lagerfeld, followed by other luxury brands such as Stella McCartney (2005), Viktor & Rolf (2006), the Italian brand Roberto Cavalli (2007), and the Japanese fashion house Comme des Garçons (2008), etc.

When asked about their feelings towards co-branding collaboration with fast fashion brands, the interviewees were in general positive arguing that the fashion industry has been affected by co-branding activities in more than one way. Combining every-day garments with the exclusivity of high-end designer items will result in the development of "mass-exclusivity", "massluxe" or "masstige" collaborations (Tungate, 2005). In the primary research reasons for co-branding with fast fashion brands were found to be:

I think the strategy intensifies awareness among consumers and strengthens the mass brand as an international fashion company as well as the luxury fashion brand. (F-SMC-SM)

Co-branding has an immediate effect on sales revenue and store traffic and generates a lot of publicity for both partners. (M-B-SM)

The short-term collaborative lines are not representative of the luxury brand's main line but they are the designer's interpretation of the partner brand. [...]. If Versace decides, for example, to collaborate with the mass-brand Top Shop, there is a difference between buying Versace and buying Versace for Top Shop items. The latter are not luxury but simply a limited edition collection over a short period of time. (M-V-CM)

The majority of respondents confirmed that image transfer is one of the most significant motive for collaborations, and a major reason for fashion houses to search for strong co-brands. The brand value of a luxury fashion brand would be misplaced if no one identifies the brand that a customer wears. Moreover, interviews revealed that co-branding could help consumers to become more knowledgeable about and familiar with luxury brands.

However, some respondents have voiced their aversion for the co-branding collaborations. The belief was that collaborations with mass-fashion retailers could damage the image of the luxury brand and its core label, perhaps leading to confusion in the mind of customer. In summary, the interviews' participants were generally positive towards the co-branding collaboration and stated that their views of the fast fashion brands changed thanks to the role that collaboration has been having, reinforcing consumer awareness and perception so that the value of both brands is strengthened.

The expectations of the interviewees for the future development of fast fashion in general were optimistic. All respondents expressed confidence that the presence of fast fashion brands will increase, along with its success:

I do think that we are just at the beginning of the expansion of those brands. Because there is a high demand from consumers to bring together products that are trendy and stylish and at the same time accessible and cheap and therefore, I think there will be much more in the future. (F-SMC-SM)

According to the latest findings fast fashion brands are an effective way for fashion houses to reach their consumer targets that would not otherwise be obtainable.

Fast Fashion is really something we have become accustomed to over the last 10 years and we will utilise in the future. (F-GA-MM)

Study 2: Impact of Co-Branding Collaborations on Consumer Perception toward Luxury Brands

After having discussed the views of luxury brands' representatives regarding the impact that fast fashion brands have had over luxury brands, it is furthermore important to understand customers' attitudes to co-branding collaborations between luxury and fast fashion brands. To offer empirical support for this preliminary evidence, the qualitative interviews were used as basis to create a semi-structured questionnaire for a quantitative survey. The aim of Study 2 was to collect and cover a wide range of consumer' awareness and perception towards luxury and fast fashion brands and their associations and intentions to purchase from the co-branding collaborations; the respondents' characteristics, such as if they regularly buy mass-market or luxury clothing items, or a mixture of both.

The co-branding phenomenon is something every consumer asked has an opinion on and the collected data showed that the respondents have generally perceived the co-operation in a positive light. The results of the survey show that all consumers buy clothes as a way to best reflect their personality, although the majority of them (54.3%) purchase a mixture of luxury and fast fashion products. Fashion is thus a way for people to express themselves in an individual way and to define their self-image. They are fashion conscious and when asked how much they usually spend on shopping garments each month, the budget is mostly within the range of £200 to £500 (56.8%). Most believe that fashion should be affordable to everyone and that the co-branding collaboration is successful in providing people fashion trends on a "higher level".

Moreover, 13% of the respondents stated that they purchase luxury fashion, and a further 33% belonged to the category that bought fast fashion items. Of these consumers interviewed, only the 59.3% of respondents stated that they bought products from the collections of the collaboration between luxury and fast fashion brands. Very few luxury consumers have purchased an item from collaborated brands and they were mostly fast fashion consumers or those that were used to mixing both brands. One reason given for this was because of the reliable quality/price ratio and a general comment offered by the majority of the respondents was: *Accessible luxury at affordable prices.* Consumers who purchased products from the collaborations liked the fact that the collection gave them "stylish and trendy items with attractive design". Consumers became excited and curious, wanting to get a piece of a designer's item they would normally not afford.

Another reason given from the younger segment (18-25) in wearing a product from the co-branded collections was the sense of belonging to the luxury brand of the designer responsible for the creation of the collection. This makes consumers feel that they have a personal bond to the luxury brand in question even though the item was produced by and designed for a fast fashion brand. Research among groups of young consumers shown that they would prefer to buy items from fashion collaboration because they had insufficient financial means to allow them to purchase luxury products, but they considered it as a first step toward the world of luxury. The consumers who did not buy items from fashion collaborations were mostly the 13% of people that purchase only luxury products along with others who stated different reasons that were often related to price. They preferred to save a little more money to buy a luxury brand's garment from the original designer rather than an expensive collaborated fashion item from a fast-market oriented brand. Other respondents said that the only reason why they would buy these products would be to mix and match them with the accessories of luxurious brands. However, several respondents believed that many of the fast fashion consumers' feelings and reasons for not purchasing luxury items would remain unchanged. Participants who did not purchase from the fashion collaborations confirmed that they bought limited luxury products because they prefer high-quality materials as well as design and style. Luxury fascinates them and enables to differentiate themselves from the masses feeling more exclusive and unique. However, other participants emphasized that people buy luxury "for their self-image without considering quality" and that they "like the brand logo more than the product it-self", they like "what the brand symbolises".

Consumer perceptions about co-branding collaborations vary; overall the majority noticed that co-operations are good initiatives (67%) and that they have a positive impact on the image of the luxury brand. As shown by the primary research, collaborations were positively perceived by both mass (71%) and luxury consumers (57%) and those activities have increased the overall level of awareness of the luxury fashion brands among consumers (66.4%) by reinforcing the luxury brands' presence in their minds. In general, the respondents underlined that co-branding collaborations "have increased luxury brand awareness". In the event that some respondents were not aware of the luxury brand before the collaboration, they now have a unique opportunity to approach and to enter the world of luxury. Therefore a positive perception together with an increased awareness and understanding of what these brands are, might lead consumers to a desire to buy from the main lines of luxury brands in the future.

Consequently, awareness and change in perception are linked to one another. More specifically 64% of the people who stated that the collaborations have made them more aware of luxury brands also stated that their perception of the luxury brands had changed after such co-operations. 52% of these same people wanted to buy items from the luxury brands' original lines. In other words, these consumers, after becoming more aware, have developed an intention to buy and this in itself presents a more favourable perception of the luxury brands. Of the consumers that asserted that the co-branding co-operations had not made them more aware of the luxury brands, the majority also said that their perception had not changed.

The concept of luxury is not only limited to the quality of the product itself but also to the surrounding environment and the connections to the brand. For this purpose, luxury and fast fashion brands have been brought together through collaborations in a way that the association of one has the potential of spilling over on the other. What one associates with a fast fashion brand, as a consequence of the collaboration, should influence how one perceives the luxury brands. Following this logic, the survey revealed that perceptions of existing and loyal luxury consumers were unaffected and they will continue to purchase items from the main lines of luxury brands after the co-branded co-operations were in place. In the luxury consumers' minds collaborations are something entirely different. Luxury consumers will continue to shop from these brands because their perceptions have not been affected in a negative way by the co-branding collaborations between luxury and fast fashion brands. On the other hand, when asked to explain their perceptions of the luxury brand after collaborations in terms of quality, luxury appeal and identity, a small percentage of the interviewees argued that the co-branded co-operations have influenced the luxury brands in a negative way. Some luxury consumers stated they would not buy any product from the luxury brand after the collaboration with a fast fashion brand because of the resulting loss of exclusivity.

DISCUSSION

The aim of this survey was to investigate how luxury fashion brands have inclined towards the fast fashion model and if co-branding collaborations between luxury and fast fashion brands have affected in a positive way consumer' perception of the luxury brand. Results from two studies provided insights that can be of interest for marketing and merchandising managers involved in developing luxury brands. The purpose of the first study was to show the effects that fast fashion' activities have caused on luxury fashion brands and specifically on how the latter has inclined towards the fast fashion model. To understand if luxury fashion brands have inclined towards the fast model and in which ways they have reacted to the fast fashion phenomenon, qualitative interviews with representatives of luxury brands were conducted. The selection of luxury fashion companies where to conduct the interview in the British market was based on Walpole, Mintel's UK Retail Rankings, Interbrand's 100 Best Global Brands 2013 list, Euromonitor and other leading fashion journals. Seven luxury brands' representatives agreed to participate to the research study and their responses have been discussed in the results section. The literature review showed that fast fashion brands have been successful in entering the fashion industry (Bhardwaj & Fairhurst, 2010; Joy et al., 2012) and according to Okonkwo (2007) these brands have become competitors of luxury brands by offering consumers attractive products at better price-value. Interviews with managers from luxury brands showed that the fast fashion brands have not gone unnoticed and that luxury fashion brands have inclined towards the fast fashion model through the introduction of new practices and techniques, and through the improvement of production and retailing processes.

Results have indicated that investments in the supply chain, Information and Computer Technology (ICT) systems, outsourcing of production, diffusion lines, pre-collections, pre-fall/summer collections, limited-edition lines of apparel and accessories are being used by luxury fashion brands in order to reach consumer needs for speed and variety and to spur product rotation. Retailers such as Zara, H&M, and Top Shop have accustomed consumers to this new dynamic business. Inspired by the success of these new policies, the idea that emerged from many luxury fashion brands representatives has been based on maintaining a dynamic business by improving the entire supply chain and its logistic and information technology systems, every stage from design to delivery to the consumer, allowing these companies to react quickly to sales trends and to changes in consumption by delivering new products in short time. Pre-collections have often a more accessible price point yielding better commercial gains and address the consumer need for "early" and "fast" products prior to the main season fashion collection. Moreover, results have shown that luxury fashion brands have created more reasonable lower priced diffusion lines making fashion accessible to many more consumers thus becoming more competitive with fast fashion brands prices. The research indicates that diffusion lines are an important source of income for luxury fashion brands and help ensure the continued presence of their main lines.

Finally, co-branding collaborations with fast fashion brands are a result of strategic measures adopted by luxury fashion brands to reach out to the masses in a way not possible before. In the primary research, co-branding with fast fashion brands has an immediate effect on sales revenue, marketing budgets, and store traffic, generating publicity and buzz. These short-term limited edition collections with their higher promotional value are useful strategies for image transfer and for strengthening the brand value of both partners. Indeed, companies get the opportunity to communicate with the other brand's consumer base, which can result in an opportunity to reach new, potential customers as shown in Study 2. Interviews revealed that co-branding could help consumers to become more knowledgeable about and familiar with luxury brands too. However, during the interviews in the primary research, reactions from the luxury fashion brands have come out due to the development of fast fashion brands and their strategies. Not all the respondents were willing to embrace fast fashion, as they insist on using only the most expensive materials available and on not developing mass consumption products. They believe that time is needed to create collections in order to achieve authenticity and exclusivity, thus these respondents have not seemed to understand the reasons behind fast fashion being concerned with speed of production, turn-over and the constant development of new affordable designs. Another reaction was about imitating. In fact interviewees complained that fast fashion retailers are used to badly imitate luxury garments and to manufacture and ship products to stores much faster and more cheaply than those of well-established designer brands. In addition, some luxury fashion respondents voiced their aversion for the co-branding. The belief was that collaboration with mass-fashion retailers could damage the image of the luxury brand and its core label and by carrying on these collaborations they would just confuse the customer's mind. They rejected the idea to enter into co-branding collaborations suggesting that designers took the alternative of creating lower-priced line extensions of their own brand in order to keep quality and exclusivity. By contrast, it is better for luxury designers to undertake these collaborations because they can prevent knockoffs of their design from fast fashion brands and they provide a way to increase their value and knowledge among consumers.

The purpose of the second research study was to collect and cover a wide range of consumer' feelings and perceptions towards luxury and fast fashion brands and their associations and intentions to purchase from the co-branding collaborations. To offer empirical support to the study a semi-structured questionnaire for a quantitative survey was conducted in order to reach both luxury and mass consumers' views. Results presented in the survey have shown that respondents in general perceived the co-branded co-operations positively: both mass (71%) and luxury consumers (57%). This could be explained by the fact that the mass consumers became excited and curious, desiring a piece of a designer' item they could normally not afford. This reason makes consumers feel more exclusive and unique as they have a relation to the luxury brands even though the item was produced by and designed for a fast fashion brand. A major reason given by consumers was because of the reliable quality/price ratio and they liked the fact that the collection gave them stylish and trendy items with attractive design.

The majority of the respondents did not believe that the co-branding collaborations negatively affected the luxury brands and results in the survey showed that the overall level of awareness of the luxury fashion brands among customers (66%) had increased as well. A positive perception together with an increased awareness and understanding of what these brands are, might lead consumers to a desire to buy from the main lines of luxury brands in the future. More specifically, people who stated that the collaborations have made them more aware also stated that their perception of the luxury brands has positively changed maturing an intention to buy items from the luxury brands' original lines. On the other hand, the perceptions of existing and loyal luxury consumers were unaffected and they will continue to purchase items from the main lines of luxury brands after the co-branding activities. Reasons were based on the fact that these activities are something not luxury yet still something more special than regular mass fashion clothes. Consequently, luxury consumers will continue to shop from these brands because their perceptions have not been affected in a negative way.

It is also important to note that the effect of co-branding towards the luxury brand strongly relates to how compatible the luxury and fast fashion brands are, as well as to the way that the collaboration is conducted. If a co-branding strategy is well managed by integrating compatible elements between two brands such as visions, values and wills to create real synergies, the collaboration will not affect brands negatively (Rollet et al., 2013). Furthermore, a long-term project may erode and weaken the brand image because consumers may establish lasting conjectures of longevity of the collaboration (Washburn et al., 2000). Therefore, being compatible and not enduring make collaborations somewhat exclusive and this, again, leads to a positive perception of the brand image.

CONCLUSION

Fast fashion has become increasingly important in determining the strategies of global luxury brands. Even if fast fashion brands are focusing their attention on mass markets, they are no longer considered as mass brands, being positioned side by side with luxury fashion brands in the mind of the consumer. It is noteworthy to realize that co-branding is a relevant strategic means for strengthening and revitalizing a luxury fashion brand. In this research, all of the interviewees agreed that collaborations play an increasingly relevant function in luxury fashion industry strategies. However, luxury brands that have decided to enter into co-branding collaborations are not the traditional fashion houses such as Burberry, Gucci or Louis Vuitton, but more recent, less well-established brands with a contemporary and fresh profile. These recent luxury brands with their trendy and stylish designs are fashion conscious, and newcomers to the luxury scene, thus they need more visibility in order to reach higher international recognition. Collaborations with fast fashion brands can be a successful strategy for them if carried out under the right conditions. According to Okonkwo (2007), luxury brands must embrace mass fashion brands as complements rather than competitors. Collaborations are positively perceived by consumers, increasing the overall level of awareness of the luxury fashion brands by reinforcing the luxury brands' presence in consumers' minds. Luxury consumers will continue to shop from these luxury brands because their perceptions are not affected in a negative way by the co-branding collaborations between luxury and fast fashion brands. The high-end brand will gain access to the mass consumerism in a way not possible before. Shared advertising will help ensure extensive market coverage and in addition provide publicity for the co-branding collaborations as well as a quick consumer response. Despite this, the true luxury and prestige brands continue to represent the highest form of heritage and craftsmanship and therefore they remain consistent. Loyal luxury consumers will not be influenced by particular trends so that brand core values will not be compromised (Okonkwo, 2007). Luxury fashion brands should not completely endorse the fast fashion model because that could conflict with the traditional idea of what truly identifies and differentiates luxury itself. Rather, luxury fashion brands must remain innovative and forward-thinking.

REFERENCES

Amatulli, C., & Guido, G. (2011). Determinants of Purchasing Intention for Fashion Luxury Goods in the Italian Market: A Laddering Approach. *Journal of Fashion Marketing and Management*, *1*(15), 123–136. doi:10.1108/13612021111112386

Amatulli, C., & Guido, G. (2012). Externalised vs. internalised consumption of luxury goods: Propositions and implications for luxury retail marketing. *International Review of Retail, Distribution and Consumer Research*, *22*(2), 189–207. doi:10.1080/09593969.2011.652647

Amatulli, C., Guido, G., & Caputo, T. (2011). Strategic Analysis through the General Electric/McKinsey Matrix: An Application to the Italian Fashion Industry. *International Journal of Business and Management*, *5*(6), 61–75.

Amoye, E. (2011). *Questionable Co-branding, Lessons in Luxury*. Retrieved May 30, 2015, from http://lessonsinluxury.com/2011/11/23/focus-focus-focus-through-cobranding/

Armani. (2015). *40 Years of Armani*. Retrieved June 15, 2015, from http://atribute.armani.com/it/atribute-to-history/

Atwal, G., Bryson, D., & von Gersdorff, J. (2010). Luxury brands: Deluxurification is in Fashion As luxury labels continue to diversify into more affordable, mass-market lines, they run the risk of devaluing the whole brand. *Admap*, 44-46.

Barnes, L., & Lea-Greenwood, G. (2006). Fast fashioning the supply chain: Shaping the research agenda. *Journal of Fashion Marketing and Management*, *3*(10), 259–271. doi:10.1108/13612020610679259

Barnes, L., & Lea-Greenwood, G. (2010). Fast fashion in the retail store environment. *International Journal of Retail & Distribution Management*, *10*(38), 760–772. doi:10.1108/09590551011076533

Bhardwaj, V., & Fairhurst, A. (2010). Fast fashion: Response to changes in the fashion industry. *International Review of Retail, Distribution and Consumer Research*, *1*(20), 5–173.

Bickers, J. (2011). *Missoni for Target line sells out, raises questions*. Retrieved June 30, 2015, from http://www.retailcustomerexperience.com/article/184615/Missoni-for-Target-line-sells-out-raises-questions

Brooks, A. (2015). *Clothing Poverty: The Hidden World of Fast Fashion and Second-hand Clothes*. London: Zed Books Ltd.

Brown, A. L. (2011). Fast fashion meets luxury labels. *INSEAD Knowledge*. Retrieved September 15, 2013, from http://knowledge.insead.edu/business-finance/marketing/fast-fashion-meets-luxury-labels-1051

Business of Fashion. (2011). BoF Exclusive: Getting The Luxury Fashion Business Model Right. *The Business of Fashion*. Retrieved September 15, 2013, from http://www.businessoffashion.com/2011/01/bof-exclusive-getting-the-luxury-fashion-business-model-right.html

Business of Fashion. (2013). H&M Could Do More to Catch a Lift From Designer Collaborations. *The Business of Fashion*. Retrieved June 30, 2015, from http://www.businessoffashion.com/articles/news-analysis/hm-could-do-more-to-catch-a-lift-from-designer-collaborations

Byun, S. E., & Sternquist, B. (2011). Fast fashion and in-store hoarding: The drivers, moderator, and consequences. *Clothing & Textiles Research Journal*, *29*(3), 187–201. doi:10.1177/0887302X11411709

Chevalier, M., & Mazzalovo, G. (2008). *Luxury Brand Management: A World of Privilege*. Singapore: Wiley & Sons.

Cillo, P., & Verona, G. (2008). Search styles in style searching: Exploring innovation strategies in fashion firms. *Long Range Planning*, *41*(6), 650–671. doi:10.1016/j.lrp.2008.08.001

Cohen, A. M. (2011). Fast Fashion: Tale of Two Markets. *The Futurist*, *45*(5), 12–13.

Corbellini, E., & Saviolo, S. (2009). *Managing Fashion and Luxury Companies*. Italy: Etas.

Crouch, M., & McKenzie, H. (2006). The logic of small samples in interview-based qualitative research. *Social Sciences Information. Information Sur les Sciences Sociales*, *45*(4), 483–499. doi:10.1177/0539018406069584

Ertekin, Z. O., & Atik, D. (2015). Sustainable Markets: Motivating Factors, Barriers, and Remedies for Mobilization of Slow Fashion. *Journal of Macromarketing*, *35*(1), 53–69. doi:10.1177/0276146714535932

Feitelberg, R. (2010, February 2). Mix and match. Sportswear houses are playing the versatility card. *Women's Wear Daily*, p. 10.

Fionda, A. M., & Moore, C. M. (2009). The anatomy of the luxury fashion brand. *Journal of Brand Management*, *5*(16), 347–363. doi:10.1057/bm.2008.45

Friedman, V. (2010). Assessing the Alexander Wang/H&M collaboration. *Financial Times*. Retrieved June 30, 2015, from http://blogs.ft.com/material-world/2014/04/14/assessing-the-alexander-wanghm-collaboration/

Gabrielli, V., Baghi, I., & Codeluppi, V. (2013). Consumption practices of fast fashion products. *Journal of Fashion Marketing and Management*, *17*(2), 206–224. doi:10.1108/JFMM-10-2011-0076

Griffioen, A. (2011). *Creating Profit Through Alliances: How collaborative business models can contribute to competitive advantage*. Retrieved October 10, 2013, from http://www.allianceexperts.com/images/documents/creating-profit-through-alliances-sq.pdf

Guido, G., Amatulli, C., & Peluso, A. (2014). Context Effects on Older Consumers' Cognitive Age: The Role of Hedonic *vs.* Utilitarian Goals. *Psychology & Marketing*, *2*(31), 103-114.

Hemphill, C. S., & Suk, J. (2009). The Law, Culture, and Economics of Fashion. *Stanford Law Review*, 61.

H&M. (2015). *Campaigns and Designer Collaborations*. Retrieved June 30, 2015, from http://about.hm.com/en/About/facts-about-hm/fashion-for-all/collections/collaborations.html

Hoffmann, J., & Coste-Manière, I. (2012). *Luxury Strategy in Action*. Palgrave Macmillan.

Interbrand. (2005). *The Best 100 Brands*. Retrieved June 30, 2015, from http://www.interbrand.com/en/best-global-brands/previous-years/best-global-brands-2005.aspx

Interbrand. (2014). *The Best 100 Brands*. Retrieved June 30, 2015, from http://bestglobalbrands.com/2014/ranking/

Joy, A., Sherry, J. F. Jr, Venkatesh, A., Wang, J., & Chan, R. (2012). Fast Fashion, Sustainability, and the Ethical Appeal of Luxury Brands. *Fashion Theory*, *3*(16), 273–296. doi:10.2752/175174112X13340749707123

Kapferer, J. (2004). *The New Strategic Brand Management*. London: Kogan Page.

Kapferer, J. N., & Bastien, V. (2009). The specificity of luxury management: Turning marketing upside down. *Journal of Brand Management*, *16*(5-6), 311–322. doi:10.1057/bm.2008.51

Kastanakis, M., & Balabanis, G. (2012). Between the mass and the class: Antecedents of the "bandwagon" luxury consumption behavior. *Journal of Business Research*, *65*(10), 1399–1407. doi:10.1016/j.jbusres.2011.10.005

Megehee, C. M., & Spake, D. F. (2012). Consumer enactments of archetypes using luxury brands. *Journal of Business Research*, *65*(10), 1434–1442. doi:10.1016/j.jbusres.2011.10.009

Miller, K. (2013). Hedonic customer responses to fast fashion and replicas. *Journal of Fashion Marketing and Management*, *2*(17), 160–174.

Nueno, J. L., & Quelch, J. A. (1998). The mass marketing of luxury. *Business Horizons*, *41*(6), 61–68. doi:10.1016/S0007-6813(98)90023-4

Okonkwo, U. (2007). *Luxury Fashion Branding: Trends, Tactics, Techniques*. Basingstoke, UK: Palgrave Macmillan. doi:10.1057/9780230590885

Okonkwo, U. (2009). The luxury brand strategy challenge. *Journal of Brand Management*, (16), 287-289.

Parrott, G. R., Danbury, A. H., & Kanthavanich, P. (2015). Online behavior of luxury fashion brand advocates. *Journal of Fashion Marketing and Management: An International Journal*, *19*(4), 360–383. doi:10.1108/JFMM-09-2014-0069

Phau, I., & Prendergast, G. (2000). Consuming luxury brands: The relevance of the Rarity Principle. *Journal of Brand Management*, *2*(8), 122–138. doi:10.1057/palgrave.bm.2540013

Plunkett, W. J. (2010). *Plunkett's Apparel & Textiles Industry Almanac 2010: The Only Comprehensive Guide to Apparel Companies and Trends*. Houston, TX: Plunkett Research, Ltd.

Rohwedder, C. (2004). Making Fashion Faster: As Knockoffs Beat Originals To Market, Designers Speed The Trip From Sketch to Store. *The Wall Street Journal*. Retrieved September 15, 2013, from http://www.kellogg.northwestern.edu/course/opns430/modules/supply_chain_management/wsjfastfashion.pdf

Rollet, M., Hoffmann, J., Coste-Manière, I., & Panchout, K. (2013). The concept of creative collaboration applied to the fashion industry. *Journal of Global Fashion Marketing*, *1*(4), 57–66. doi:10.1080/20932685.2012.753337

Rosenblum, P. (2015). Fast Fashion Has Completely Disrupted Apparel Retail. *Forbes*. Retrieved June 30, 2015, from http://www.forbes.com/sites/paularosenblum/2015/05/21/fast-fashion-has-completely-disrupted-apparel-retail/

Saunders, M., Lewis, P., & Thornhill, A. (2009). *Research Methods for Business Students*. Harlow, UK: Pearson Education Ltd.

Schiffman, L. G., Hansen, H., & Kanuk, L. L. (2008). *Consumer Behaviour: A European Outlook*. Harlow, UK: Prentice Hall FT.

Simonin, B. L., & Ruth, J. A. (1998). Is a company known by the company it keeps? Assessing the spillover effects of brand alliances on consumer brand attitudes. *JMR, Journal of Marketing Research*, *1*(35), 30–42. doi:10.2307/3151928

Sreejesh, S. (2012). Consumers' Evaluation of Co-Brand Extensions: The Effects of Concept Congruity on the Evaluation of Co-Branded Products, Analyzing the Moderating Role of Task Involvement. *International Management Review, 1*(8).

Stella McCartney. (2015). *Adidas Spring Summer 15*. Retrieved June 30, 2015, from http://www.stellamccartney.com/gb/adidas_section

Toktali, N. (2008). Global Sourcing Insights from the Clothing Industry: The Case of Zara, a Fast Fashion Retailer. *Journal of Economic Geography*, (8): 21–38.

Uggla, H. (2004). The Brand Association Base: A conceptual model for strategically leveraging partner brand equity. *Brand Management*, *2*(12), 105–123. doi:10.1057/palgrave.bm.2540208

Vaidyanathan, R., & Aggarwal, P. (2000). Strategic Brand Alliances: Implications of Ingredient Branding for National and Private Label Brands. *Journal of Product and Brand Management*, *9*(4), 214–228. doi:10.1108/10610420010344013

Vigneron, F., & Johnson, L. W. (2004). Measuring perceptions of brand luxury. *Journal of Brand Management*, *11*(6), 484–506. doi:10.1057/palgrave.bm.2540194

Washburn, J. H., Till, B. D., & Priluck, R. (2000). Co-branding: Brand equity and trial effects. *Journal of Consumer Marketing*, *7*(17), 591–604. doi:10.1108/07363760010357796

WWD. (2010). *UGG Meets Jimmy Choo*. Retrieved October 10, 2013, from http://www.wwd.com/fashion-news/fashion-scoops/ugg-jimmy-choo-team-up-2409232

Yeoman, I. (2007). Pricing trends in Europe's fashion industry. *Journal of Revenue and Pricing Management*, *6*(4), 287–290. doi:10.1057/palgrave.rpm.5160099

ENDNOTE

[1] The first letter refers to the gender of the interviewed (M = Male; F = Female), the second letter to the brand he/she work for (GA = Giorgio Armani; B = Burberry; SMC = Stella McCartney; RL = Ralph Lauren; AMQ = Alexander McQueen; V = Versace; H = Hermès) and the third one to his/her position in the company (SM = Store Manager; RM = Retail Manager; CM = Concession Manager; MM = Marketing Manager; RDD = Retail Development Director).

Chapter 12
The Role of the Founder's DNA throughout Crisis:
The Revitalization of Moncler

Piergiorgio Re
University of Turin, Italy

Bernardo Bertoldi
University of Turin, Italy

Chiara Giachino
University of Turin, Italy

Marta Minopoli
ESCP Europe, Italy

ABSTRACT

In this chapter the authors analyze the Moncler case using concepts link to the family business world. In the luxury industry family businesses are existing entities with a strong DNA created by a founder leader and guided by his vision across generations; the strong link between the founder's DNA, the company and the customers implies a high level of influence on how resources are managed and, consequently, it changes dynamics and results. In the rapid changing luxury industry's business environment it is necessary for the companies to maintain the DNA's heritage. To succeed it is necessary to innovate and to remain linked to the root of the past through innovation and evolution. Moncler perfectly shows how - from the successful vision of the founder to a deep crisis - is possible to reach a second life (with a new re-founder) appealing to the original values and DNA of the company.

INTRODUCTION

Family businesses represent a very important part of many Countries' economic and social scenario (Shanker & Astrachan, 1996; Venter et al., 2005; Lee, 2006). In fact, they are the most common type of ownership structure and company management in the whole world and they often show better performance than public companies (Anderson & Reeb; 2003; Barontini & Caprio, 2005; Lee, 2006; Villalonga & Amit, 2006; Cucculelli & Micucci, 2008).

However, they tend to have a shorter life span and to remain small in size all along: only 30 percent of businesses reach the second generation and a mere 15 percent gets to the third (Matthews et al., 1999;

DOI: 10.4018/978-1-4666-9958-8.ch012

Ibrahim et al., 2009). These studies on family businesses seem to confirm the famous saying *the first generation builds the business, the second enjoys the wealth, and the third loses everything*.

In 1989 Handler stated that *defining the family firm is the first and most obvious challenge facing family business researchers* (Handler, 1989). Since then, researchers, academics and experts in the field have tried to provide a number of definitions that have changed in time. However, as of today, there isn't a universally shared and widely accepted definition of a family business (Littunen & Hyrsky, 2000). For example, Astrachan & Shanker (2003) offered three definitions of family businesses:

- **A *Broad* Definition:** It includes those businesses where a family controls the strategic direction of the firm, and also participates in the business;
- **A *Middle* Definition:** Additionally, the business is run by a founder or descendant, and is intended to remain in the family;
- **A *Narrow* Definition:** It adds the extra criteria of multiple-generation participation in business, and more than one member of the owner's family having management responsibility.

On the other hand, Villalonga & Amit (2009) proposed different definitions of family businesses: *Founder or founding family owned firms*, where *the founder* is the largest shareholder among those individuals who are identified as founders in at least two public sources; *Founding family owned and manager firms*, which restricts the first definition in two ways by including only those firms that are: in their second or later generation and family managed (i.e., those whose CEO is the founder or a member of the founding family); *Individual or family controlled firms*, where the definition of *family* is extended to include not only founding families but also individual investors or families that are not (related to) the founder; *Family controlled and managed firms*, which is the intersection of the second and third definitions, namely, second- or later-generation firms whose CEO is an individual block holder or a member of a block holding family (founding or non-founding).

If it is difficult to define and understand what a family business is and the notion of luxury is not easier to define too, mainly because it is a subjective and multidimensional construct. Key components are *a strong element of human involvement, very limited supply and the recognition of value by others* (Cornell, 2002). Research regarding the definition of luxury is limited and previous studies have demonstrated a lack of clarity with regards to what are the key attributes of a luxury product (Casaburi, 2011).

The word *luxury* derives from the Latin word *luxus* which means *soft or extravagant living, indulgence and sumptuousness, luxuriousness, opulence* (Oxford Latin Dictionary, 1992). Considering its etymology, it implies difference or distance. These meanings are particularly consistent with the belief that consumers can distance and differentiate themselves from one another through the purchase of luxury goods, due to the emotional value that such a purchase conveys (Catry, 2003).

As stated by Dubois and Czellar (2002), it is important to distinguish between the word *luxury* and the word *prestige*. They are often used as synonyms, but in reality they cover different domains in the consumers' mind. On one hand, prestige is *a positive evaluative judgement that consumer form towards products or brands; it can be influenced by accomplishment inherent to the brand or by prestige symbols associated with the brand*. On the other hand, luxury *is linked to perceptions of comfort, beauty and a sumptuous lifestyle; at a symbolic level, consumers can interpret luxury as the prestige symbol of the brand*. Therefore, *prestige* involves purchasing a higher-priced product to embellish one's ego, whereas *luxury* involves purchasing a product that represents value to both the individual and the significant others (Vigneron & Johnson, 2004).

From a consumer perspective, luxury has a social meaning and it encompasses the symbolic dimension of consumption (Casaburi, 2011). The consumer is highly involved in the purchase of goods characterised by a very limited supply; these goods serve as status symbols and convey psychological benefits that play a key role in distinguishing them from non-luxury products. From a product perspective, instead, luxury is often associated with attributes such as excellent quality, distinctiveness, craftsmanship, exclusivity and premium prices.

Luxury and family businesses are strictly interconnected: the luxury sector is characterized by the presence of a lot family businesses. As stated by Carcano et al. (2011) family businesses have some peculiarities that allow them to reach a competitive advantage over non-family businesses.

In this chapter, the authors use the concept of family business in order to describe the fundamental role of the founder of the company, with his/her vision, his/her idea and the strong relationship he/she creates with customers that is link not only to the products but also to the brand.

In fact, family business are existing entities with a strong DNA created by a founder leader and guided by his vision across generations (Chua et al., 1999); the involvement of the founder in the business and in the ownership of the company (Tagiuri & Davis, 1996) shapes the essence of the product, creates the brand with a strong link with the founder, generates the perception of the customer. This strong link between the founder's DNA and the company implies a high level of influence on how resources are managed (Sirmon & Hitt, 2003) and, consequently, it changes dynamics and results.

In the rapid changing luxury industry's business environment it is necessary for the companies to maintain the DNA's heritage, which assure the link with the market and the customers taste, and to change to meet the new challenge of the emerging market. The authors, through the use of a case study, describe how a company mutate from the founder vision to the *next family* or the *next founder* trying to adapt and evolve themselves in the new landscape of the luxury industry, where mutation of the competitive landscape strongly affect the structure of the industry and the behavior of the players.

BACKGROUND

There are two main important concepts to explain: the role of succession and the evolution-adaptation of DNA in a changing environment. The succession is a process that, from the authors' point of view, helps the founder to transmit his DNA to other people (family or non-family members) involved in the leadership of the company. It could happen that there is not a succession process or that the succession process is not successful; in these cases the DNA given to the company, if it is strong and it represents the true essence of the business, survives and remains as an asset ready to be used.

If the DNA is given by the founder, successors (family or non-family members) have the task to recognize it and evolve-adapt it to new business environment.

The succession is the process through which the founder' idea reaches new eras and it is probably the most debated issue in literature.

Many researchers (Handler,1994; Lansberg, 1988; Ward, 1987) agree that succession is the most important step that family firms have to face with, and for this reason, it is one of the most studied topics (Heck et all, 2008). In fact, albeit family businesses pursue a long-term strategy only 30 percent of businesses reach the second generation and 15 percent makes it to the third (Matthews et al., 1999; Ibrahim et al., 2009).

Succession has been defined as *the passing of the leadership baton from the founder-owner to a successor who will either be a family member or a non-family member; that is a professional manager* (Beckhard & Burke, 1983). Many researchers agree that succession is more a process than an event (Churchill & Hatten, 1987; Farquhar, 1989; Friedman, 1987; Handler, 1990). These authors consider succession as a multi-staged process that exists over time, beginning before heirs even enter the business. Aronoff, Ward & McClure (2011) define succession as a *lifelong process of planning and management that encompasses a wide range of steps aimed at ensuring the continuity of the business through the generations.*

The succession in a firm occurs, generally, when the founder or manager retires or decides to leave the firm. But it can also occur because of a sudden inability of the manager to continue with his or her work. The reasons can be various: an injury, serious health problems, or even sudden death of the owner. In some cases, the family business owner may leave the firm to start a new activity.

The succession process may become a very problematic step in business lifecycle since, as many researchers (Churchill & Lewis, 1983; Levinson, 1971; Sonnenfeld, 1987) have stated, it is in the nature of entrepreneurs or CEOs to have difficulty giving up what they have created and managed for a long time. Frequently, owners' sense of immortality and indispensability contributes to problematic successions (Danco, 1982; Sonnenfeld, 1987).

In conclusion, succession is a fundamental step because allows the founder to transmit what he has created to other people (family or non-family members) preserving the core abilities or the essence of the business. Maintain and adapt the essence of the business in the luxury industry is even more complex and important since the strong effects that luxury brands and products create in the customers mind.

At the beginning, as stated by Kapferer (2009), luxury was *the visible result – deliberately conspicuous and ostentatious - of hereditary social stratification.* The kings, the priests and the aristocrats had to differentiate themselves from the crowds and to show off their wellbeing, preserving the social distance.

The purchase of luxury goods can be attributed to two main groups of socio-economic reasons. On one hand, there is the luxury for self, meaning indulging in one's pleasure. On the other hand, there is the luxury for others, meaning demonstrating wellbeing and success (Casaburi, 2011).

The luxury industry's business environment changes very quickly and it is necessary for the companies to maintain the DNA's heritage, which assure the link with the market and the customers taste, and to change to meet the new challenge of the emerging market. A key factor is innovating and be able to be linked to the root of the past, that is possible through innovation and evolution.

Innovation - in all forms – and evolution both of the company and the family is essential to explain the enduring success of luxury brands (even after the loss of the founder) in a changing competitive environment (especially due to the rise of emerging markets). Only by keeping the original company's DNA and evolving responding to a changing competitive landscape a luxury company can leverage the heritage and conquer new markets. The evolution is based on innovation within tradition.

Innovation is a topic widely debated in literature but in the family business context contributions seems to be fewer and sometimes conflicting. For example, Dunn (1996) wrote that family businesses are less creative and innovative, while Craig & Moores (2006) affirmed that the structure of family businesses creates an environment predisposed to innovation. Furthermore, De Massis et al. (2013) underlined how product innovation, for example, is an overlooked topic in existing family business research.

Evolution, on the other side, is a two part process: mutation and natural selection also in the business environment (Fulmer, 2000), and it occurs whenever there is reproduction and competition for finite resources. In the reproduction process the species want to produce exact copies, but it often happens that something change creating a mutant superior or inferior of his parents, giving the start to the natural selection (Darwin, 1909). This approach implies a two ways dynamics: first the company evolves mutating and the result, the mutant, will be stronger or weaker, but, second, the landscape itself changes and the combination of the new landscape and the mutated characteristics will say if the mutant will flourish or perish (Kauffman, 1993).

Evolution is

...the adaptation of species to their surrounding environment(s) over time or as the theory that life on Earth gradually developed from simple to more complex organism. (Svarney, 1995)

From this point of view, the Moncler case well represents the history of a family business with a strong DNA that occurred in a crisis. The new property has understood the fundamental elements of Moncler history and has built on them a new successful story.

THE MONCLER REVITALIZATION

The History of Moncler and Its Revitalization: Maintain, Reinforce, and Manage Brands

Today, imagining an extremely warm but elegant down-padded garment is synonymous of thinking about Moncler. But it was not always like that in the past: Moncler, in its history, has experienced very difficult and tough times.

The brand has actually French origins and takes its name from the contraction of "Monastier of Clermont", where it was founded in 1952 by Renè Remillon.

The first products created by the company were garments and technical tools to camp in the mountains, including tents and sleeping bags. Since the first years of its existence, Moncler revealed a unique involvement in research and innovation, which allowed the brand to deposit some patents, develop new light and warm materials and become the best supplier for all mountain experts. Starting from the expeditions above 8.000 meters, until the Olympic uniforms for the athletes, Moncler was recognised as the best product against the cold.

Furthermore, it started to acquire also a strong popularity outside of the slopes, getting into fashion magazines and invading the urban streets. Its jackets were the flagship of the Italian subculture "I paninari" and the company decided to take advantage of these trendsetters, producing new colours and lines. This positive situation, however, did not last for a long period. In fact, in the 80s Moncler started to suffer and lose market share and audience. The reason was that the company was not ready to that sudden growth and so it was unable to reposition itself correctly. Moncler was no longer a sport brand but not yet a luxury brand. The brand awareness was far too weak to let this double identity live and the management was not able to undertake quick choices to recover this negative situation. In the 90s the company took a breath of air thanks to acquisition of the Italian group Pepper Company Sarl, which started a temp to restore brand equity, but the general situation was still really difficult. In 1998 Fin. Part SpA bought Moncler, with the purpose of create a luxury portfolio of companies and giving new financial resources.

But the turning point was in 2003: Remo Ruffini, already Creative Director, decided to buy the company to re-launch the brand worldwide. The cost of the operations was really low compared to the prestige of the brand, but big investments were required to start a new life cycle.

The Moncler revitalization passed from the development of different lines, characterized by distinct price ranges and materials, to a return to the past, celebrating the marriage between innovation and high quality standards. Remo Ruffini affirms that the mantra of Moncler is to manage its products as *Technological tools* and this strategy lead the company to a new phase of success.

Ten years later, new shareholders have arrived, Remo Ruffini is General Director, CEO and Creative Manager, and the company has reached surprising results:

- From €45 million revenues in 2002 to €585 million in 2013.
- 33% EBITDA margin.
- Presence in 66 countries.
- 107 shops directly managed.
- 24 openings in 2013, which represent 51% of sales.
- 1858 wholesales.
- Decision of going public welcomed enthusiastically by the market.

Remo Ruffini is the new *re-founder* of Moncler: he controls the 31.90% of the company through Ruffini Partecipazioni and he takes the decision on the business.

It is important to underline the active and fundamental role of Mr. Ruffini. He is the true advocate of Moncler *re-born*. He built the strategy and adopted a strong decision-making process, facing fearless even the most difficult challenges. These are the typical characteristics recognized to the founder or to the family by the family businesses studies. Mr. Ruffini objective was to create a precise, consistent, coherent, clear and targeted strategy and he was able to never lose sight of the goal.

Moreover, Mr. Ruffini firmly believes in the past of the company: the DNA of Moncler was fundamental in this re-born and the essence given by Remillon to the brand was to be restored. He bought Moncler because he trusted the history of the brand and the essence created by Remillon that is the starting point of his construction. He wanted to make the most of the past, but made it happen for the future. About this topic, in an interview with Mr. Rezzonico, Mr. Ruffini said:

With my philosophy and strategy in mind, I decided to try it hard: the icon product was there, the skills were there and the know-how was there too. I needed to make Moncler take off again. (Rezzonico, 2013)

In a society that is changing every day faster, characterized by the process of globalization, companies, in order to lead their brands towards a long life, need to be able to combine long-term strategies (the construction of value takes time) with the capacity to adapt quickly.

Firms need to be able to modify their strategy to adapt to the market and learn how to predict what will happen in the future. Moreover, firms must try to change and innovate maintaining a link with the origin. A difficult mission, even aggravated due to the rigidity of the managers, who are struggling to keep what they have built so far, especially if the old strategy brought them to a moment of success.

As Christiansen (2010) wrote, the secret is the ability to be stable and flexible, finding a balance that allows the opposites to coexist.

The image of the brand can be so strong to allow the products to live a second life, just thanks to the connections established with consumers. This connection, as stated before, is even stronger when the founder has the ability to create an essence recognized by customers and used by the company as an asset. In order to take advantage of this condition, it is essential that companies use marketing tools to push on their values and convey the messages they want to consumers. The challenge for companies is to implement these strategies maintaining brand consistency. It is necessary, in fact, to safeguard the source of the brand equity, balancing the trade-offs between marketing activities, and sustaining the product and non-product related associations.

Considering that point, companies must be able to not consider profit as the only goal, but to always protect the value of the brand even sacrificing parts of the actual profits. The two concepts are related: having a brand with a high-perceived value leads the company to enjoy some benefits in terms of savings and revenues. At the same time, companies may be tempted to maximize these benefits without taking care of the fact that the more they capitalize the benefits coming from brand equity, the more the sources of these benefits become valueless.

Marketing managers should however remember that maximizing profits in the short term could lead to make damages in the long term. For this reason, Keller defines the ultimate goal of the company as *creating powerful, unique and positive associations in the minds of consumers* (1999), goal that can be achieved following the four strategies mentioned before. This point is reflected in the behaviour of family businesses, in fact that they tend to maximize profits in the long term perspective.

In order to analyse the key factors which brought back Moncler to its path of success, the authors consider necessary to go back to the reasons why the brand was so strong in the 70's, some years after the launch of the company by Renè Remillon. The triumph of that period hid the causes of the great crisis of the next two decades.

Moncler, in fact, did not start to get popularity and be acclaimed thanks to a clear and defined strategy. On the contrary, the brand was chosen *by chance* by the Italian subcultural movement of *Paninari* and therefore it became "unconsciously" their symbol. Its awareness did not depend on a precise marketing strategy, or on a communication planning, or a precise positioning. Moncler success was mostly decreed by the contact with this trend, which, like all the currents born from fashion, lasted a few years. The crisis came, therefore, as soon as the movement fades away and finds other symbols to express itself. The result of this process was a brand in deep crisis, completely lost, without neither the strong personality of the mountain nor the elegance of the city. In the early 90s there was no more brand identity and the brand associations made by customers were rather negative. The brand did not lose its potential, but it has betrayed itself.

A similar pattern, characterized by a strong loss of success and credibility followed by a great era thanks to a back to basics, was made also by Bottega Veneta.

The fashion company from Vicenza, 2013's revenues leader among luxury brands, has experienced a crisis similar to Moncler's one. Betraying itself and its values it has betrayed the consumer and only a return to the initial DNA has brought the firm back to prosperous periods.

The difference between the two cases is that Bottega Veneta had begun to use low quality materials in its tough period, while Moncler never gave up on quality and did not lowered its standards. The product was always intact, but the consumer did not recognize it anymore. Authors believe that this explanation it is necessary in order to introduce the strategy of revitalization that Mr. Ruffini implemented: the decline of Moncler started where also started its success.

Furthermore, in our actual society, characterized by rapid changes and strong globalization, a failure like the one Moncler experimented in the 80's would have been even faster and more inevitable.

Fashion is everyday more ephemeral and a company that bases its success on affiliating itself to a subculture would encounter its crisis very soon.

To summarize, the success period of Moncler was a moment of sales increase and value prestige decrease.

In the 90's, Moncler has not a precise positioning. People found the products in huge retailers' centres as Decathlon and Cisalfa, but the price was far from being aligned with the kind of products present in these mass-market stores. These shops did not communicate either luxury nor quality or fashion.

Furthermore, the target was too narrow. The brand, without a clear strategy, was focusing on the only category which was still bringing revenues: a female clientele, from 30 to 55, with a passion for winter sports.

At this stage, Moncler was presenting all the symptoms of a brand in the last phase of the product life-cycle.

At this point, it is necessary to start with the real analysis of the factors that brought Moncler to an international success.

How Moncler was able to come back to the past? How it was able to succeed in the crowded and hyper-competitive market of luxury? How they re-built their brand in a period of general crisis?

We can indicate three main dimensions on which Mr. Ruffini worked to re-establish the standard of the firm:

- Product.
- Distribution.
- Communication.

Product

Global Quilted Jacket. In these words is hidden the secret of Moncler.

To start its revitalisation the company has chosen to go back to its core competence: the feathers. *There is not future without past*, stated Mr. Ruffini. For this reason, the first Moncler collection after the crisis included products really alike to the ones of the old collections from 70's. But only the appearance was similar. The products, in fact, were lighter, with a better shape and more wearable. The company was able to change the fit, the style and the materials, creating meanwhile a product able to take the consumer back to the past.

The first purpose of the brand was to fix the lack of positioning. The new message that the firm tried to transmit was that they care about innovation but they do not forget their core values.

Mr. Ruffini was also able to understand the need of extending the use of the down jacket. Its use only on mountain was a strong limitation for the development of the company. So he started to design new products, more fashionable and wearable also in an urban contest, and new lines, studied also for middle seasons and warmer countries. His mantra was to build an easy to wear jacket, really adaptable and contemporary. At this regard, he says: *Our products are not fashionable, because fashion is something that continually changes over time. On the contrary they are contemporary, that means something that belongs to a period of time and this is the entire life*, and he adds: *Products across, of top quality for top people and we want our people to be smart and survive fashion.* In his philosophy, innovation and technology are those elements essentials to drive away the threats of declining. This message was successful, the Moncler down jackets became a must-have for all winter and people were willing to pay a high price for a fashion garment able to last for a long time. The revitalization started from the product. With a return to the product. For this reason, in particular during the first years, Moncler has dedicated many investments to R&D, in order to develop products able to assure great heat in small dimensions. The company has developed a unique technique to fulfil the jackets, which has allowed to have an advantage towards the competition and to obtain more compactness and a 85% higher guarantee of insulation. All the paddings are made with the highest quality feathers on the market, certified 4/4 tufts in quality and removed from the animals with a non-painful technique, dictated by a strict regulation. To certify best quality to the consumer, Moncler uses thorough and rigorous procedures to check its raw materials. All the feathers, for example, pass through a process of selection, elimination, dusting, washing, sterilising, rinsing, and drying.

The next step of the company was to reconsider the target audience of the brand. From a small segment of women between 30 and 55 years old, passionate about sports, to a democratic product, that everyone can desire. Mr. Ruffini wants to create a garment that fits the lady who goes to listen the opera and the young guy enthusiast about skateboard.

In order to do that, the reinterpretation of the produced garments was total. Moncler started to implement different line extensions, in particular upwards, and then it began the development of men and children collections.

Today the collections have a pyramid structure: starting from the base of the pyramid, the products within the larger sections are those that generate more revenues and also have the higher number of models. This huge brand extension improves the capacity of the consumer of making some brand's recalls through new stimulus and connections, covering many usage functionalities.

Moncler implements not only a linked extension, but also a conglomerate extension. Starting from 2013, in fact, the firm has begun the production of sunglasses, shoes and bags to wear both in summer and in winter, both in city and outside.

The success of this brand extension is to be found in having first of all improved the core product. As mentioned previously, in fact, especially for a luxury company can be very risky to implement this kind of strategy without having invested first in its original expertise. At this regard, Mr. Ruffini stated:

We continue to focus on innovation rather than expanding our brand into segments that are not part of our Moncler world, and we are aware that innovating makes our store profitable all year round. It is better to do few things, but excel on them.

From his words, we can understand that he has a clear imagine of the situation and he really understands that it is impossible to move toward new products without a focus on the core value of the company or toward new sectors with no value added for the original one.

To improve its positioning, Moncler has also begun a series of collaborations and partnerships with trend-setters, celebrities and designers.

To conclude this section about the product, a last overview about the fight of Moncler against the counterfeiting is inserted. In order to protect not only its own interests, but also the customers, Moncler has developed a rigorous strategy against the fake products. Each Moncler's garment has a label with an identification code. The customer can verify the originality of the product through a call, a sms or on the Internet. Moreover, Moncler tries to solve the underlying problem, investing large amounts of money in order to shut down the websites of counterfeiting.

Distribution

While Moncler was trying to go back to the original DNA of the product, maintaining its original features, a complete different story happened for the distribution channels.

The company, recognized the total inadequacy of the retails, decided to modify all the system, in order to better reflect the new positioning.

Mr. Ruffini, with the wish of creating an imaginary of luxury around his jackets, realized that was not possible to sell them in big department stores. There are two phases in this process of changing:

- From sport stores (i.e.: Cisalfa in Italy, Decathlon in France) to major luxury department stores (i.e.: Barneys, Bloomingdales, Harrod's) and best specialty stores, in Italy and abroad.
- Aggressive expansion of directly managed retails. First openings in famous ski-resorts, to underline the link with the mountains and the DNA of the brand. Moncler chose towns where the luxury was present and the customers the company aimed at went on vacation.

Then, Moncler continued to open own stores in fashion cities as Paris, Milan, London, New York, Hong Kong and many others. So, at the beginning the distribution of Moncler quilted jackets were centred on the most elite and exclusive retailers all over the world, nowadays the brand counts 107 shops directly owned.

There are many reasons why Mr. Ruffini has chosen this strategy, but we can focus our attention mainly on some of them. Positioning: the brand was willing to convey a new message to the consumer. To be a luxury brand means to be sold in sought after stores. The directly managed shops enable the company to transmit to the customers determinate associations and images without intermediaries. Furthermore, the presence of the logo in very famous streets of shopping combines the image to a sense of exclusivity and transmits positive associations.

Communication: the direct management of the shops allows conveying more effectively the messages of the company. Moreover, Mr. Ruffini would like to reach a larger target, from the elegant woman to the sportive guy. For this reason, a retail controlled by the company is more versatile and democratic. Mr. Ruffini demands also that each shop assistant has a complete knowledge about all the products, the history of the brand and what is going to sale. The average price of the item justifies a careful customer care.

Finally, the new system of Moncler plays also a key role in increasing the occasions of usage. The distribution now covers also the summer and the mid seasons with appropriate products and it serves the Non-European countries that have reversed seasons, guarantying full-year coverage.

Mr. Ruffini ultimate goal would be to split Moncler's sales into four zones of equal proportions: Europe, U.S., Asia and rest of world. The distribution strategy implemented since 2003 has been very successful and it is a good starting point to reach Moncler's goals. Currently, each square meter of store counts for about 30,000 € of turnover and 70% of sales come from abroad, while 30% from Italy. Five years ago, the situation was at the opposite: 70% of sales came from Italy. Moncler currently owns controlled 107 stores and 1858 wholesaler distributors.

Communication

Another cornerstone of the strategy implemented by Moncler starting from 2003 is represented by the communication.

Goal of the company was to involve the consumer and engage him, in order to convey the new positioning of the brand. Mr.Ruffini has recognized the inadequacy of the channels used before 2003 and he has implemented several ways to talk to the customer.

There are some elements that can be analysed.

- **Adv:** Always direct and immediate, very catchy, unusual. The goal is to let the consumer astonished, entertained and engaged in the life of the brand. The wider target chosen by Mr. Ruffini has involved the need to change the channels of communication.

When the brand was more focus on its sport side, the advertising was made on sport magazines or through specific events on the slopes. Now, all the brand communication is more international. In order to amaze the consumer, Moncler almost never uses models or celebrities. Often the protagonists of the adv. are even out of the target, i.e. kids dressing adults' jackets.

The most famous Moncler campaign is the one with a group of dogs wearing down jackets: the company tries to send messages that remain in the mind of the consumer.

- **Events:** In order to reach a very broad target, Moncler needs to organize a wide range of events. Furthermore, the company is specialized in creating unusual moments involving common people and artists. One event, for example, has involved 180 skaters in the New York City centre. The purpose is to create a new language to communicate the beauty and style of Moncler's garments. Moreover, events like this one have strong return on media, Internet and television. The last event organized by Moncler was a choreography studied to celebrate its IPO.
- **Film:** To spread the vision of Moncler, the company produces also video and mini movies that represent the philosophy of the company. The most well-known is the one filmed by Bruce Webber, estimated movie director and photographer who has a strong relationship with the brand. The *Don't steal the jacket* movie-series in 2011 has helped a lot the company to communicate its upward positioning.
- **Web-Communication:** It allows Moncler to be aware of the latest trends, knowing what people like and do, talking directly with them without intermediary, being always present in all the places where are the customers, getting precise feedbacks and making the most of the latest technological innovations before others. Furthermore, the strong presence of Moncler on the web allows the company to better fight the counterfeit.
- **Logo:** The logo plays a very important role because it recalls the past and the history of the brand. In the middle of the image there is a cock, the symbol of the France. Only Moncler can use it, after having been sponsor of the national ski team at the 1968 Olympic Games.

Above there is a pair of ski crossed, which represents the spirit of the mountain: the Moncler logo is a reminder of the DNA of the brand. It is bigger in the basic collections, because the customer is a person who wants to express its social status by buying Moncler. In the high-end collections, vice versa, the logo is smaller and often hidden because the identification is not so important. The typical customer, in fact, looks for the perfect style, the right fit and the possibility of being smart and elegant in every moment of the day. Of course the fact that it is a Moncler quilted jacket gives the guarantee of an exclusive, elite and high quality product, but the client doesn't feel the need to show it off.

To conclude, we can summarize the main strategic points of the revitalisation as following: concentrate on the product; redesign the concepts; reorganize the distribution; go global; focus on research and technology; redesign the communication process; talk to the customer and listen.

Price

Part of the success of the repositioning of Moncler is due to the new pricing strategy developed by Mr. Ruffini.

When the Italian entrepreneur acquired the company, the first objective set by the new management was to transform the down jacket from a sportswear item to a luxury object. In order to achieve so, the average selling price for item has been increased from an average of 300 to 900 Euro.

This strategic operation was necessary to gain credibility and get the access into the luxury department stores. Mr. Ruffini has been instrumental in implementing this strategy, since he was able to build a value proposition strong enough to justify the strong increase of prices.

In the mind of the consumer the down jacket became a product for which it was worth spending, thanks to its versatility (it can be worn either doing sports or living in the city), the strong heritage, the high quality, the excellent technical aspects and the strong attention to style.

After the acquisition of Mr. Ruffini, Moncler has developed a wider range of products, even if the down jacket is always the main focus, with the outerwear representing the 85% of the revenues.

The diversification has been organised in a pyramidal structure. At the bottom we find the bestseller collections, accounting for the major part of the revenues and with the widest range in terms of products. The average price is 800/900€ and they accounts for 75% of revenues.

In the middle, with 15% of revenues, there are all the minor lines, as Children – Accessories – Eyewear – Knitwear, with average price of 300/400€.

Close to the hedge, the high-end haute couture line, with average price of 1200€, but going above for special editions up to more than 5000€. The high price, combined to some specificities of the item, influences also the kind of customer the brand targets. The strategic customer of Moncler is a person that would like to keep his body warm even in winter and who wants to be stylish and comfortable at the same time.

Moncler owns the capability to serve its target better that the others, which are trying to attract the segment with a wider range of products and features.

As a "Focus differentiation leader", Moncler can encounter difficulties if it would decide to enlarge its customer segment or develop new kinds of products: its strength is to have created an item that fits perfectly to its audience.With its distinctive positioning "Born in mountains and living in the cities" concept, Moncler has not direct competitors with same quality, price, and competences. For that reason, we can define the Company as a value innovator, operating in a market where competition against the same segment is minimized. Thanks to its price and characteristics, Moncler has found its "Blue Ocean", creating an uncontested market space and covering a strategic gap in the marketplace.

In order to justify the premium price, Mr. Ruffini poses utmost attention to the customer experience in the retail store.

The first Moncler store directly controlled by the brand was launched in 2001 in St. Moritz, followed by the opening of other strategic-located shops close to well-known ski resorts.

Paris was the first urban city to host a Moncler store in 2007, to underline the French background of the brand. To follow, in less than 7 years, Moncler opened other 107 shops all over the world.

The strategy is clear: the brand understood the risk of depending so much from the European market and in particular from the Italian one. Therefore Moncler has tried to expand its horizons and its popularity abroad, opening up new flagships. This retail expansion strategy has allowed Moncler to pass from 52% of sales generated into the Italian Market to 26% in just 4 years (2008-2012) by focusing the expansion in other EU countries, U.S. and Canada.

Another objective that Moncler planned to achieve was to reduce the percentage of sales originated from wholesales (49% in 2013) in favour of revenues from directly managed retails (70% is the goal for 2016).

In order to reach this result, the company is not only adopting a strategy of stores rollout, but it is also increasing the boutique average size, to showcase a greater number of SKUs (the number of SKUs has increased by 15% per annum over the last few years and each sqm of shop is worth an average of 30.000€).

Moncler is so interested in having more revenues coming from the retail channel instead of the wholesale because the first one grants a gross margin of 80%, while the second just a 50-60%, depending on the specific products.

The retail network is divided in 4 kinds of organization:

- **Free Standing Stores:** Flagships;
- **Concessions:** Shops in department store in which Moncler sells directly to the consumer. The boutique keeps the inventory risk and it receives a percentage of sales;
- **Travel Location:** Mainly in airports;
- **Factory Outlets:** Used to dispose the stocks.

The objective of the company is to open an average of 20 retail shops per year, without closing anyone. The criteria for each launch are the same: return on investment in three years and profit in the first year. The wholesale organization is based on three kinds of shops:

- **Concession to the Department Store (28 All around the World):** The mall bears all the risks of management;
- **Franchise (1 in Seoul):** The owner has to pay a fee and the products at the wholesale price;
- **Multi Brand Shops (1800 in 2013):** The shop decides which item buy and in which quantity. Moncler is forsaking this model in order to build a stronger identity.

FUTURE RESEARCH DIRECTIONS AND CONCLUSION

The results achieved with the Moncler' case can open a discussion on different topics but the authors have identify as interesting link the theory of Christiansen (2010), focused on the creation of timeless products.

Christiansen et al. (2010) theory introduces a theoretical perspective according to which a product's value is the result of the relationships between the firm, the consumer and the product itself. So, companies may be able to create, break and revive these relationships numerous times through strategic marketing, brand identity and brand association. If an enterprise, therefore, is able to achieve this capability, it will also be able to create timeless products. The value of the product, in this analysis, has a strong correlation with the context: it depends on it, it appears thanks to it, and it is dispersed because of it.

The company exploits relationships, mental connections, conflicts, and it attaches, detaches, and reattaches them to the product, creating boundaries with the consumer. In order to achieve its scope, the firm designs and plans processes for the product qualification and requalification.

This new vision of the product life cycle radically changes the process of decision-making performed by managers and companies. Their new scope is to create a product that can adapt itself to innovation without betray its essence. The two key words are: flexibility and solidity.

This oxymoron represents how a product can continue to conquest customers over time, adapting itself, innovating, converting itself to meet modern tastes, while keeping faith with its core values.

The authors found in the Christiansen's theory a new point of view for analysing the family businesses values, where the family essence and the entrepreneurial idea of the founder are transmitted to the company and to the products. This essence is what remains in the company through years and generations; it is a fundamental asset that must be recognised as the starting point of success.

The Moncler case shows how the entrepreneurial idea of the founder in the 1952 gives the life to a very noticed brand in the luxury industry. In this case, the company is not passed through new generations of Remillon's family, but after a deep crisis, was bought by Mr. Ruffini – the new *re-founder*.

The most important thing is that during years the DNA of the company was always there and Mr. Ruffini recognized this point as a competitive advantage. In fact, he said that *the icon product was there, the skills were there and the know-how was there too. I needed to make Moncler take off again.* This sentence underlines how the DNA is a milestone for companies and become necessary to adapt it to the new business environments.

The case of Moncler could be not generalizable, but it is certainly the most successful case of revitalization of the last 15 years in the fashion business. In 2003, the group had revenues for 45 million, but Mr. Ruffini did not care: he was looking for something with a good past story to buy at a low price and make growth. He knew that the Moncler brand had a great story to tell and the core products were strong enough to meet new success. An evaluation of the financial performances incurred in the ten years following the acquisition of Mr. Ruffini is fundamental to give importance to the case study. Starting from the 40-45 million euros of 2003, the company increased its turnover up to 373 million euros in 2009, 429 million in 2010, and 513 million in 2011 up to the 585 million reached in 2013.

It is possible to observe how the company has grown considerably even in times of severe crisis. The reasons are that Moncler was already moving and changing when it faced this difficult period. While the other luxury companies arrived unprepared and blocked in their positions, Moncler was facing a radical change and its structure was flexible and ready to listen the needs of the market.

There is a sentence of Remo Ruffini that clearly represents this situation: *We were driven fast with no hurry, and with a touch of class.*

Many crises arise from a weak governance not ready to change or afraid by challenges. Moncler has proved to be versatile, and, at the same time, rigid in following its clear goals. It has been able to reposition itself on the market, to express its quality, growing up without betraying itself and so it has gained the astonishing results that we see today.

As the authors stated initially *Only by keeping the original company's DNA and evolving responding to a changing competitive landscape a luxury company can leverage the heritage and conquer new markets. The evolution is based on innovation within tradition.* From this point of view, the Moncler case well represents the history of a family business with a strong DNA that occurred in a crisis. The new property has understood the fundamental elements of Moncler history and has built on them a new successful story.

It has to be considered that in the last years, lot of family businesses sold the property of the company to international groups with the risk of losing their tradition, their values and sometimes their way of doing things: e.i. Gucci sold to Gruppo Kering-ex PPR, Gancia sold to Russian Standard Corporation, Sperlari sold to Leaf International BV. The Moncler'case can be used by managers has a good example of how to maintain traditional and successful aspects of a company and build around them new strategies adapted to the new needs. Mr. Ruffini shows how, starting from the heredity of an entrepreneurial family, it is possible to write a new successful story using the same values, and the same competitive advantages that made the company big in the past. Managers have to identify these elements in order to reinforce them.

REFERENCES

Anderson, R. C., & Reeb, D. (2003). Founding-Family Ownership and Firm Performance: Evidence from the S&P 500. *The Journal of Finance*, *58*(3), 1301–1328. doi:10.1111/1540-6261.00567

Aronoff, C. E., Ward, J. L., & McClure, S. L. (2011). *Family Business Succession: The Final Test of Greatness*. Palgrave MacMillan.

Astrachan, J. H., & Shanker, M. C. (2003). Family businesses contribution to the U.S. economy: A closer look. *Family Business Review*, *16*(3), 211–219.

Barontini, R., & Caprio, L. (2005). The effect of family control on firm value and performance: Evidence from continental Europe. *European Financial Management*, *12*(5), 689–723. doi:10.1111/j.1468-036X.2006.00273.x

Beckhard, R., & Burke, W. (1983). Preface. *Organizational Dynamics*, 12.

Carcano, L., Corbetta, G., & Minichilli, A. (2011). Why Luxury Firms are often Family Firms? Family Identity, Symbolic Capital and Value Creation in Luxury-Related Industries. *Universia Business Review*, *4*, 40–52.

Casaburi, I. (2011). China as a Market: Luxury Brand Consumer Behaviour. *Journal of Marketing Trends*, *1*(6), 47–56.

Catry, B. (2003). The Great Pretenders: The Magic of Luxury Goods. *Business Strategy Review*, *14*(3), 10–17. doi:10.1111/1467-8616.00267

Christiansen, J. K., Varnes, C. J., Gasparin, M., Nielsen, S. D., & Vinther, E. J. (2010). Living Twice: How a Product Goes through Multiple Life Cycles. *Journal of Product Innovation Management*, *27*(6), 797–827. doi:10.1111/j.1540-5885.2010.00753.x

Chua, J. H., Chrisman, J. J., & Sharma, P. (1999). Defining the family business by behavior. *Entrepreneurship Theory and Practice*, *23*(4), 19–39.

Churchill, N. C., & Hatten, K. J. (1987). Non-Market-Based Transfers of Wealth and Power: A research framework for Family Businesses. *American Journal of Small Business*, *11*(3), 51–64.

Churchill, N. C., & Lewis, V. L. (1983). The Five Stages of Small Business Growth. *Harvard Business Review*, *61*, 30–51.

Cornell, A. (2002). *Cult of Luxury: The New Opiate for The Masses*. Australian Financial Review.

Craig, J. B. L., & Moores, K. (2006). A 10-Year Longitudinal Investigation of Strategy, Systems, and Environment on Innovation in Family Firms. *Family Business Review*, *19*(1), 1–10. doi:10.1111/j.1741-6248.2006.00056.x

Cucculelli, M., Micucci, G. (2008). *Family succession and firm performance: Evidence from Italian family firms*. Banca d'Italia, n.680.

Danco, L. A. (1982). *Beyond Survival*. Cleveland, OH: The University Press.

Darwin, C. R. (1909). The Origin of Species: Vol. 11. *The Harvard Classics*. New York: P.F. Collier & Son.

De Massis, A., Frattini, F., Pizzurno, E., & Cassia, L. (2013). Product innovation in family versus non family firms: An exploratory analysis. *Journal of Small Business Management*, *53*(1), 1–301. doi:10.1111/jsbm.12068

Dunn, B. (1996). Family enterprises in the UK: A Special Sector? *Family Business Review*, *9*(2), 139–155. doi:10.1111/j.1741-6248.1996.00139.x

Farquhar, K. (1989).*Employee Responses to External Executive Succession: Attributions and the Emergence of Leadership*. (Unpublished Doctoral Dissertation). Department of Psychology Boston University.

Friedman, S. (1987). *The Succession Process: Theoretical Considerations*. Paper presented at the annual meeting of the Academy of Management, New Orleans, LA.

Fulmer, W. E. (2000). *Shaping the Adaptive Organization*. New York: Amacom.

Handler, W. C. (1989). Methodological issues and considerations in studying family businesses. *Family Business Review*, *2*(3), 257–276. doi:10.1111/j.1741-6248.1989.00257.x

Handler, W. C. (1990). Succession in Family Firms: A Mutual Role Adjustment Between Entrepreneur and Next-Generation Family Members. *Entrepreneurship Theory and Practice*, *15*(1), 37–51.

Handler, W. C. (1994). Succession in Family Business; a revew of the research. *Family Business Review*, *7*(2), 133–157. doi:10.1111/j.1741-6248.1994.00133.x

Heck, R. K. Z., Hoy, F., Poutziouris, P. Z., & Steier, L. P. (2008). Emerging paths of family entrepreneurship research. *Journal of Small Business Management*, *46*(3), 317–330. doi:10.1111/j.1540-627X.2008.00246.x

Ibrahim, A. B., Mc Guire, J., & Soufani, K. (2009). An Empirical Investigation of Factors Contributing to Longevity of Small Family Firms. *Global Economy &Finnaca Journal*, *2*(2), 3–4.

Kapferer, J. N., & Bastien, V. (2009). The Specificity of Luxury Management: Turning Marketing Upside Down. *Journal of Brand Management, 16*(5/6), 311–322. doi:10.1057/bm.2008.51

Kauffman, S. A. (1993). *The origins of order: self-organization and selection in evolution*. New York: Oxford University Press.

Lansberg, I. (1988). The Succession Conspiracy. *Family Business Review, 1*(2), 119–143. doi:10.1111/j.1741-6248.1988.00119.x

Lee, J. (2006). Family Firm Performance: Further Evidence. *Family Business Review, 19*(2), 103–114. doi:10.1111/j.1741-6248.2006.00060.x

Levinson, H. (1971). Conflicts That Plague the Family Business. *Harvard Business Review, 49*, 90–98.

Littunen, H., & Hyrsky, K. (2000). The entrepreneurial stage in Finish family and nonfamily firms. *Family Business Review, 13*(1), 41–54. doi:10.1111/j.1741-6248.2000.00041.x

Matthews, C., Moore, T. W., & Fialko, A. S. (1999). Succession in Family Firms: A Cognitive Organization Perspective. *Family Business Review, 12*(12).

Matthews, C. H., Moore, T. W., & Fialko, A. S. (1999). Succession in the Family Firm: A Cognitive Categorization Perspective. *Family Business Review, 12*(2), 159–170. doi:10.1111/j.1741-6248.1999.00159.x

Shanker, M., & Astrachan, J. (1996). Myth and Realities: Family Business Contribuion to US economy – A Framework for Assessing Family Business Statitics. *Family Business Review, 9*(2), 107–123. doi:10.1111/j.1741-6248.1996.00107.x

Sirmon, D.G. & Hitt, M.A. (2003). Managing resources: linking unique resources, management, and wealth creation in family firms. *Entrepreneurship Theory and Practice, 27*(4), 339-358.

Sonnenfeld, J. (1987). *Chief Executives at the Heroes or Villains of the Executive Process*. Paper presented at the meetings of the Academy of Management.

Svarney, P. B. (1995). *The New York Public Library's Science Desk Reference*. New York: Stonesong Press.

Tagiuri, R., & Davis, J. A. (1996). Bivalent attitudes of the family firm. *Family Business Review, 9*(2), 199–208. doi:10.1111/j.1741-6248.1996.00199.x

Venter, E., Boshoff, C., & Maas, G. (2005). The influence of successor-related factors on the succession process in small and medium-sized family businesses. *Family Business Review, 18*(4), 283–303. doi:10.1111/j.1741-6248.2005.00049.x

Vigneron, F., & Johnson, L. W. (2004). Measuring Perceptions of Brand Luxury. *Journal of Brand Management, 11*(6), 484–506. doi:10.1057/palgrave.bm.2540194

Villalonga, B., & Amit, R. (2006). How do family ownership, control and management affect firm value. *Journal of Financial Economics, 80*(2), 385–417. doi:10.1016/j.jfineco.2004.12.005

Villalonga, B., & Amit, R. (2009). Family Control of Firms and Industries. *Review of Financial Studies, 22*(8), 1–56. doi:10.1093/rfs/hhn080

KEY TERMS AND DEFINITIONS

Adaptation: The ability to modify the company's assets and structure in order to remain competitive on the market.

DNA: The *black box* of the company in which is recorded its origin.

Essence: The content of the *black box* that entrepreneur has to leave, the competitive advantage.

Evolution: The ability to read the changing environment and consequently develop the business of the company.

Family Business: A company founded by an entrepreneur and guided by him and/or his family following the original idea of the business and the values (through time).

Revitalization: The ability to identify the company's competitive advantage and leverage it.

Succession: The process through which the entrepreneur has the possibility to continue to survive through the company essence.

Compilation of References

Aaker, J. L. (1997). Dimensions of brand personality. *JMR, Journal of Marketing Research, 34*(3), 347–356. doi:10.2307/3151897

Adams, R. (2011). The utility of prestige: Chinese and American hedonic ratings of prestige goods. *Journal of Global Marketing, 24*(4), 287–304. doi:10.1080/08911762.2011.602320

Ahuvia, A. C. (2005). Beyond the extended self: Loved objects and consumers' identity narratives. *The Journal of Consumer Research, 32*(6), 171–184. doi:10.1086/429607

Aiello, G., & Donvito, R. (2005 January). Comunicazione integrata nell'abbigliamento: strategie di marca e ruolo del punto vendita nella distribuzione specializzata statunitenses. *Workshop Le Tendenze del Marketing in Europa*. Ecole Supérieure de Commerce de Paris ESCP-EAP.

Airoldi, G., Brunetti, G., & Coda, V. (2005). *Corso di Economia aziendale*. Bologna: Il Mulino.

Akcay, O. (2012). Marketing to teenagers: The influence of color, ethnicity and gender. *International Journal of Business and Social Science, 3*(22), 10–18.

Alden, D. L., Steenkamp, J. B., & Batra, R. (1999). Brand positioning through advertising in Asia, North America, and Europe: The role of global consumer culture. *Journal of Marketing, 63*(1), 75–87. doi:10.2307/1252002

Alden, D. L., Steenkamp, J. B., & Batra, R. (2006). Consumer attitudes toward marketplace globalization: Structure, antecedents and consequences. *International Journal of Research in Marketing, 23*(3), 227–239. doi:10.1016/j.ijresmar.2006.01.010

Allen, M. W., Walker, K. L., & Brady, R. (2012). Sustainability Discourse with a Supply Chain Relationship: Mapping Convergence and Divergence. *Journal of Business Communication, 49*(3), 210–236. doi:10.1177/0021943612446732

Allérès, D. (1990). *Luxe...Stratégies Marketing*. Economica.

Amatulli, C., & Guido, G. (2001). Determinants of purchasing intention for fashion luxury goods in the Italian market: A laddering approach. *Journal of Fashion Marketing and Management, 15*(1), 123–136. doi:10.1108/13612021111112386

Amatulli, C., & Guido, G. (2012). Externalised vs. internalised consumption of luxury goods: Propositions and implications for luxury retail marketing. *International Review of Retail, Distribution and Consumer Research, 22*(2), 189–207. doi:10.1080/09593969.2011.652647

Amatulli, C., Guido, G., & Caputo, T. (2011). Strategic Analysis through the General Electric/McKinsey Matrix: An Application to the Italian Fashion Industry. *International Journal of Business and Management, 5*(6), 61–75.

Amoye, E. (2011). *Questionable Co-branding, Lessons in Luxury*. Retrieved May 30, 2015, from http://lessonsinluxury.com/2011/11/23/focus-focus-focus-through-cobranding/

Anderson, R. C., & Reeb, D. (2003). Founding-Family Ownership and Firm Performance: Evidence from the S&P 500. *The Journal of Finance*, *58*(3), 1301–1328. doi:10.1111/1540-6261.00567

Andreu, L. (2003). Emociones del consumidor. Componentes y consecuencias de marketing. *Estudios Sobre Consumo,* (64), 9-26.

Antúnez de Mayolo, C. (2009, July). Marcas de lujo. ¿Por qué crece el valor de los bienes suntuarios en todo el mundo? *Business*, 46-47.

Arenas-Gaitan, J., Rondan-Cataluña, F. J., & Ramírez-Correa, P. E. (2013). Social identity, electronic word-of-mouth and referrals in social network services. *Kybernetes*, *8*(42), 1149–1165. doi:10.1108/K-04-2013-0081

Armani. (2015). *40 Years of Armani*. Retrieved June 15, 2015, from http://atribute.armani.com/it/atribute-to-history/

Arnould, E. J., & Thompson, C. J. (2005). Consumer Culture Theory (CCT) – Twenty Years of Research. *The Journal of Consumer Research*, *4*(31), 868–882. doi:10.1086/426626

Aronoff, C. E., Ward, J. L., & McClure, S. L. (2011). *Family Business Succession: The Final Test of Greatness*. Palgrave MacMillan.

Astrachan, J. H., & Shanker, M. C. (2003). Family businesses contribution to the U.S. economy: A closer look. *Family Business Review*, *16*(3), 211–219.

Atkinson, R., & Flint, J. (2004). *Snowball Sampling. The SAGE Encyclopedia of Social Science Research Methods*. London: SAGE Publications.

Atsmon, Y., Dixit, V., Leibowitz, G., & Wu, C. (2011). Understanding China's growing love for luxury. *McKinsey Insights China.* Retrieved from https://solutions.mckinsey.com/insightschina/_SiteNote/WWW/GetFile.aspx?uri=/insightschina/default/en-us/aboutus/news/Files/wp2055036759/McKinsey%20InsightsChina%20-%202011%20Luxury%20Consumer%20Report_7fbe9eff-0bfd-4cea-8bc5-2dff874db6d0.pdf

Atwal, G., Bryson, D., & von Gersdorff, J. (2010). Luxury brands: Deluxurification is in Fashion As luxury labels continue to diversify into more affordable, mass-market lines, they run the risk of devaluing the whole brand. *Admap*, 44-46.

Atwal, G., & Williams, A. (2009). Luxury brand marketing–the experience is everything! *Journal of Brand Management*, *16*(5), 338–346. doi:10.1057/bm.2008.48

Bagozzi, R. P., & Dholakia, U. M. (2006). Antecedents and purchase consequences of customer participation in small group brand communities. *International Journal of Research in Marketing*, *1*(23), 45–61. doi:10.1016/j.ijresmar.2006.01.005

Bain & Company. (2015). *2015 Worldwide Luxury Markets Monitor 2015 Spring Update*. Retrieved from www.reportlinker.com

Baker, M. J., & Hart, S. (2007). *The Marketing Book*. Butterworth-Heinemann.

Banathy, H. B. (1996). *Designing social systems in a changing world.* New York: Plenum Press. doi:10.1007/978-1-4757-9981-1

Barakat, H. (1993). The Arab family and the challenge of social transportation. In H. Mighissi (Ed.), *Women and Islam: critical concepts in Sociology*. Routledge.

Barley, E. (2014). Understanding the Chinese luxury market: three competing notions of self-worth. *Warc.* Retrieved January 3, 2015, from http://www.warc.com/Content/ContentViewer.aspx?MasterContentRef=ba80d55d-ee0e-47d0-a37c-80b98b22c8fb&CID=A103222&PUB=EVENT-REPORTS

Barnes, L., & Lea-Greenwood, G. (2006). Fast fashioning the supply chain: Shaping the research agenda. *Journal of Fashion Marketing and Management*, *3*(10), 259–271. doi:10.1108/13612020610679259

Barnes, L., & Lea-Greenwood, G. (2010). Fast fashion in the retail store environment. *International Journal of Retail & Distribution Management*, *10*(38), 760–772. doi:10.1108/09590551011076533

Barontini, R., & Caprio, L. (2005). The effect of family control on firm value and performance: Evidence from continental Europe. *European Financial Management*, *12*(5), 689–723. doi:10.1111/j.1468-036X.2006.00273.x

Batten, A. (2013). *UAE Luxury goods market boosted by strong taste for designer clothing, Passport*. Euromoniteor International.

Bauer M., Von Wallpach S. & Hemetsberger A. (2011). "My little luxury": A consumer-centred, experiential view. *Journal of Marketing Research and Management*, *1*.

Bayton, J. A. (1958). Motivation, cognition, learning--basic factors in consumer behavior. *Journal of Marketing (Pre-1986)*, *22*(1), 282.

Bearden, W. O., & Etzel, M. J. (1982). Reference Group Influence on Product and Brand Purchase Decisions. *The Journal of Consumer Research*, (9): 1982.

Beckhard, R., & Burke, W. (1983). Preface. *Organizational Dynamics*, 12.

Belch, G. E., & Belch, M. A. (1998, 2009). Advertising and Promotion. An Integrated Marketing Communication Perspective, New York: McGraw-Hill.

Belch, G., & Belch, M. (2009). *Advertising and promotions, an integrated marketing communications perspective*. New York: McGraw Hill Irwin.

Belk, R. W. (2011). Benign envy. *AMS Review*, *1*(3-4), 117-134.

Belk, R. (2014). You are what you can access – Sharing and collaborative consumption online. *Journal of Business Research*, *8*(67), 1595–1600. doi:10.1016/j.jbusres.2013.10.001

Belk, R. W. (1984). Three scales to measure constructs related to materialism: Reliability, validity, and relationships to measures of happiness. *Advances in Consumer Research. Association for Consumer Research (U. S.)*, *11*, 291–297.

Belk, R. W. (1988). Posessions and the Extended Self. *The Journal of Consumer Research*, *15*(2), 139. doi:10.1086/209154

Bellaiche, J-M., Mei-Pochtler, A., & Hanisch, D. (2010). *The new world of luxury, caught between growing momentum and lasting change*. The Boston Consulting Group.

Belvaux, B., & Guibert, N. (2012). International Segmentation: Towards a Third Path between Global and National. *International Journal of Market Research*, *54*(1), 111–127. doi:10.2501/IJMR-54-1-111-127

Bergeström, C., & Skärfstad, R. (2004). *Celebrity Endorsement*. Retrieved online 19th March 2009, from http://epubl.ltu.se/1404-5508/2004/193/LTU-SHU-EX-04193-SE.pdf

Bhardwaj, V., & Fairhurst, A. (2010). Fast fashion: Response to changes in the fashion industry. *International Review of Retail, Distribution and Consumer Research*, *1*(20), 5–173.

Bhosale, S., & Gupta, S. (2006). *Tomorrow is a new consumer! Who is the future Asian consumer?*. Retrieved online 19th March 2009, from http://my.acnielsen.com/reports/documents/AsianConsumer.pdf

Bickers, J. (2011). *Missoni for Target line sells out, raises questions*. Retrieved June 30, 2015, from http://www.retail-customerexperience.com/article/184615/Missoni-for-Target-line-sells-out-raises-questions

Binz, C., Hair, J. F. Jr, Pieper, T. M., & Baldauf, A. (2013). Exploring the effect of distinct family firm reputation on consumers' preferences. *Journal of Family Business Strategy*, *4*(1), 4–11. doi:10.1016/j.jfbs.2012.12.004

Blomback, A., & Ramirez-Pasillas, M. (2012). Exploring the logics of family brand identity formation. *Corporate Communications: An International Journal*, *17*(1), 7–28. doi:10.1108/13563281211196335

Bock, D., Eastman, J., & McKay, B. (2014). The Impact of Economic Perceptions on Status Consumption: An Exploratory Study of the Moderating Role of Education. *Journal of Consumer Marketing*, *31*(2), 111–117. doi:10.1108/JCM-10-2013-0725

Bollen, K., & Salsberg, B. (2013). *Luxury goods in Japan: 2013 preview*. McKinsey and Company.

Bonoma, T. V., & Clark, B. H. (1988). *Marketing Performance Assessment*. Boston: Harvard Business School Press.

Boon, S. D., & Lomore, C. D. (2001). Admirer-Celebrity Relationships Among Young Adults Explaining Perceptions of Celebrity Influence on Identity. *Human Communication Research*, *27*(3), 432–465.

Boote, A. (1983). Psychographic Segmentation in Europe. *Journal of Advertising Research*, *22*(6), 19–25.

Borden, N. H. (1964). The Concept of the Marketing Mix. *Journal of Advertising Research*, *24*(4), 7–12.

Botero, I., Thomas, J., Graves, C., & Fediuk, T. A. (2013). Understanding multiple family firm identities: An exploration of the communicated identity in official websites. *Journal of Family Business Strategy*, *4*(1), 12–21. doi:10.1016/j.jfbs.2012.11.004

Bourdieu, P. (1984). *Distinction: A Social Critique of the Judgement of Taste*. Cambridge: Harvard University Press.

Brink, A., & Berndt, A. (2009). *Relationship marketing and customer relationship management*. Juta Publications.

Britt, S. H. (1950). The strategy of consumer motivation. *Journal of Marketing (Pre-1986)*, *14*(5), 666.

Brondoni, S. (2007). *Market-Driven Management e mercati globali*. Turin, Italy: Giappichelli.

Brooks, A. (2015). *Clothing Poverty: The Hidden World of Fast Fashion and Second-hand Clothes*. London: Zed Books Ltd.

Brown, A. L. (2011). Fast fashion meets luxury labels. *INSEAD Knowledge*. Retrieved September 15, 2013, from http://knowledge.insead.edu/business-finance/marketing/fast-fashion-meets-luxury-labels-1051

Brown, J., Broderick, A., & Lee, N. (2007). Word of mouth communication within online communities: Conceptualizing the online social network. *Journal of Interactive Marketing*, *21*(3), 2–20. doi:10.1002/dir.20082

Bruce, M., & Hines, T. (2007). *Fashion Marketing. Contemporary Issues*. Elsevier Ltd.

Brun, A., & Castelli, C. (2013). The nature of luxury: A consumer perspective. *International Journal of Retail & Distribution Management*, *41*(11/12), 823–847. doi:10.1108/IJRDM-01-2013-0006

Bruner, G. C. (1988). The marketing mix: A retrospective and evaluation. *Journal of Marketing Education*, *10*, 29–33.

Bryman, A. (2012). *Social Research Methods* (4th ed.). Oxford, UK: Oxford University Press.

Budeva, D., & Mullen, M. (2014). International Market Segmentation: Economics, National Culture and Time. *European Journal of Marketing*, *48*(7/8), 1209–1238. doi:10.1108/EJM-07-2010-0394

Business of Fashion. (2011). BoF Exclusive: Getting The Luxury Fashion Business Model Right. *The Business of Fashion*. Retrieved September 15, 2013, from http://www.businessoffashion.com/2011/01/bof-exclusive-getting-the-luxury-fashion-business-model-right.html

Business of Fashion. (2013). H&M Could Do More to Catch a Lift From Designer Collaborations. *The Business of Fashion.* Retrieved June 30, 2015, from http://www.businessoffashion.com/articles/news-analysis/hm-could-do-more-to-catch-a-lift-from-designer-collaborations

Byun, S. E., & Sternquist, B. (2011). Fast fashion and in-store hoarding: The drivers, moderator, and consequences. *Clothing & Textiles Research Journal*, *29*(3), 187–201. doi:10.1177/0887302X11411709

Callen, B. (2009). *Managers Guide to Marketing*. Advertising and Publicity, McGraw-Hill Professional.

Campuzano García, S. (2003). *El Universo del lujo: una visión global y estratégica para profesionales y amantes del lujo*. Spain: Mc Graw Hill.

Campuzano, S. (2003, 2007). *El universo del lujo.* España: McGraw-Hill Interamericana de España.

Carcano, L., Corbetta, G., & Minichilli, A. (2011). Why Luxury Firms are often Family Firms? Family Identity, Symbolic Capital and Value Creation in Luxury-Related Industries. *Universia Business Review*, *4*, 40–52.

Carter, B. L. (2011, August). Marketing to Tweens and Teens: Insights, Strategies, and Tactics. The Licensing Journal, 1-3.

Casaburi, I. (2011). China as a Market: Luxury Brand Consumer Behaviour. *Journal of Marketing Trends*, *1*(6), 47–56.

Casalegno, C. (2012). *Pubblicità: istruzioni per l'uso*. Milan, Italy: Franco Angeli.

Casalegno, C., & Li, Y. (2012). *Tendenze evolutive in atto: la comunicazione integrata*. Academic Press.

Cashman, J., & Treece, M. (2012). *Content marketing essentials for small business*. London: Create Space Independent Publishing Platform.

Cateora, P. R., Sullivan Mort, G., D'Souza, C., Taghian, M., Weerawardena, J., & Graham, J. (2012). International Marketing (2E). Melbourne: McGraw Hill.

Cateora, P., Gilly, M., & Graham, J. (2009). *International Marketing* (14th International Edition). New York: McGraw Hill/Irwin.

Catry, B. (2003). The great pretenders. *Business Strategy Review*, *14*(3), 10–17. doi:10.1111/1467-8616.00267

Caughey, J. L. (1978). Artificial Social Relations in Modern America. *American Quarterly*, *30*(1), 70–89. doi:10.2307/2712280

Cavusgil, S., Kiyak, T., & Yeniyurt, S. (2004). Complementary Approaches to Preliminary Foreign Market Opportunity Assessment: Country Clustering and Country Ranking. *Industrial Marketing Management*, *33*(7), 607–617. doi:10.1016/j.indmarman.2003.10.005

CENSIS. (2012). *Decimo Rapporto sulla Comunicazione*. Milan: Franco Angeli.

Ceriani, G. (2001). *Il marketing moving: l'approccio semiotico*. Milano: Franco Angeli.

Chadha, R., & Husband, P. (2006). *The Cult of the Luxury Brand: Inside Asia's Love Affair with Luxury*. Boston, MA: Nicholas Brealey Publishing.

Chaet, H. (2012, June 25). The Tween Machine. *Adweek*, 44-47.

Chaffey, D., & Ellis-Chadwick, F. (2012). *Digital Marketing–Strategy, Implementation and Practice*. Edinburgh: Pearson Education Limited.

Chaffey, D., Mayer, R., Johnston, K., & Ellis-Chadwick, F. (2000). *Internet marketing*. Edinburgh, UK: Pearson.

Chailan, C. (2013). The role of Art in Luxury Management. In *Proceedings of 6th Euromed Conference of the Euromed Academy of Business, 'Confronting Contemporary Business Challenges through Management Innovation* (pp. 569-574). Nicosia: Euromed Press.

Chakraborty, G., Allred, A. T., & Bristol, T. (1996). Exploring consumers' evaluations of counterfeits: The roles of country of origin and ethnocentrism. *Journal of Advances in Consumer Research*, *23*, 379–384.

Chandran, N. (2014). Forget China, This is the Next Big Luxury Market. *CNBC.* Retrieved from http://www.cnbc.com/2014/09/24/forget-china-this-is-asias-new-luxury-market.html

Chang, L. Y. (2014, February 21). China world's biggest luxury consumer, *China Daily.*

Chan, K., Leung, Y., & Luk, E. K. (2013). Impact of celebrity endorsement in advertising on brand image among Chinese adolescents. *Young Consumers*, *14*(2), 167–179. doi:10.1108/17473611311325564

Chaturvedi, P. (2014). The changing face of India luxury. *Warc.* Retrieved January 4, 2015, from https://www.warc.com/Content/ContentViewer.aspx?MasterContentRef=2d8ac3e1-17e0-4c5b-9ad1-a324a1a5a42d&CID=A102922&PUB=EVENT-REPORTS

Chaudhry, P., & Zimmerman, A. (2013). Protecting your intellectual property rights, Management for professionals. Springer Science + Business Media. doi:10.1007/978-1-4614-5568-4

Chaudhry, P., & Stumpf, S. A. (2011). Consumer complicity with counterfeit products. *Journal of Consumer Marketing*, *28*(2), 139–151. doi:10.1108/07363761111115980

Chaudhuri, H. R., & Majumdar, S. (2006). Of Diamonds and Desires: Understanding Conspicuous Consumption from a Contemporary Marketing Perspective. *Academy of Marketing Science Review*, *11*, 1–18.

Cheng, C. (2006). *The Impact of Brand Image on Consumer Behaviour of Luxury Goods of Fashion Industry in China.* Retrieved online 19th March 2009, from http://edissertations.nottingham.ac.uk/1585/1/07MSclixss24.pdf

Cheng, Y. S., & Chi, L. H. (2009). Salespersons' service quality and customer loyalty in fashion chain stores: A study in Hong Kong retail stores. *Journal of Fashion Marketing and Management*, *13*(1), 98–108. doi:10.1108/13612020910939905

Cheong, E., & Phau, I. (2003). *Young status oriented consumer's evaluation of diffusion brand extensions: The effect of brand loyalty.* Retrieved online 19th March 2009, from http://smib.vuw.ac.nz:8081/WWW/ANZMAC2003/papers/BR03_cheonge.pdf

Chevalier, M., & Mazzalovo, G. (2008). *Luxury Brand Management: A World of Privilege.* Singapore: Wiley & Sons.

Chevalier, M., & Mazzalovo, G. (2012). *Luxury brand management.* Singapore: Wiley. doi:10.1002/9781119199168

Chevalier, M., Xiao Lu, P., & Toledano, S. (2009). *Luxury China: Market Opportunities and Potential.* John Wiley and Sons.

China Real Time. (2014, June 10). China now has more millionaires than any country but the U.S. *The Wall Street Journal.*

Choi, T. M. (2011). *Fashion supply chain management: industry and business analysis.* IGI Global.

Choo, H.-J., Moon, H., Kim, H., & Yoon, N. (2012). Luxury Customer Value. *Journal of Fashion Marketing and Management*, *16*(1), 81–101. doi:10.1108/13612021211203041

Chow, L. L. (2013). Meeting the needs of affluent Asian consumers. *Warc.* Retrieved January 5, 2015, from https://www.warc.com/Content/ContentViewer.aspx?MasterContentRef=328d023a-6d41-406c-b283-81e8833a7a37&CID=A99788&PUB=EVENT-REPORTS

Chow, L. L. (2014). Rebunking six myths about the Chinese luxury consumer. *Warc*. Retrieved January 5, 2015, from https://www.warc.com/Content/ContentViewer.aspx?MasterContentRef=af044722-504b-48e4-affa-5f751f8b045c&CID=A101665&PUB=EVENT-REPORTS

Christiansen, J. K., Varnes, C. J., Gasparin, M., Nielsen, S. D., & Vinther, E. J. (2010). Living Twice: How a Product Goes through Multiple Life Cycles. *Journal of Product Innovation Management*, *27*(6), 797–827. doi:10.1111/j.1540-5885.2010.00753.x

Christodoulides, G., Michaelidou, N., & Li, C.-H. (2009). Measuring Perceived Brand Luxury: An Evaluation of The BLI Scale. *Brand Management*, *16*(5/6), 395–405. doi:10.1057/bm.2008.49

Chua, J. H., Chrisman, J. J., & Sharma, P. (1999). Defining the family business by behavior. *Entrepreneurship Theory and Practice*, *23*(4), 19–39.

Chung, I.H., & Kim, I.G. (2008). Comparison of brand equity between two similar global and national brands. *International Journal of Management Cases*.

Churchill, N. C., & Hatten, K. J. (1987). Non-Market-Based Transfers of Wealth and Power: A research framework for Family Businesses. *American Journal of Small Business*, *11*(3), 51–64.

Churchill, N. C., & Lewis, V. L. (1983). The Five Stages of Small Business Growth. *Harvard Business Review*, *61*, 30–51.

CII & A.T.Kearney (2011). *India luxury review*. CII and A.T. Kearney.

Cillo, P., & Verona, G. (2008). Search styles in style searching: Exploring innovation strategies in fashion firms. *Long Range Planning*, *41*(6), 650–671. doi:10.1016/j.lrp.2008.08.001

Clay, B., & Newland, M. (2014). *Content marketing strategies for professionals*. North Charleston: Create Space Independent Publishing Platform.

Cohen, H. (2009). *Eight Ways to Reach Teens*. Retrieved from http://www.clickz.com/clickz/column/1710603/eight-ways-reach-teens

Cohen, A. M. (2011). Fast Fashion: Tale of Two Markets. *The Futurist*, *45*(5), 12–13.

Collesei, U. (2002). Comunicazione e capitale simbolico d'impresa. *Sinergie*, *59*(2), 53–61.

Collesei, U., & Ravà, V. (2008). *La comunicazione d'azienda*. Turin, Italy: Isedi.

Collis, J., & Hussey, R. (2014). *Business Research* (4th ed.). Palgrave Macmillan.

Colombo, D., & Castrillón, F. (2010). Comunicación de marcas de lujo. El deseo de generar deseo. *The Journal of PR Consejo Profesional de Relaciones Públicas de la República Argentina*, *1*(1), 61–85.

Constantinides, E. (2006). The Marketing Mix Revisited: Towards the 21st Century Marketing. *Journal of Marketing Management*, *22*(3), 407–438. doi:10.1362/026725706776861190

Corbellini, E., & Saviolo, S. (2009). Managing Fashion and Luxury Companies. Milano: Etas, Milano.

Corbellini, E., & Saviolo, S. (2007). *L'esperienza del lusso*. Milan, Italy: Etas.

Corbellini, E., & Saviolo, S. (2009). *Managing Fashion and Luxury Companies*. Italy: Etas.

Cornell, A. (2002). *Cult of Luxury: The New Opiate for The Masses*. Australian Financial Review.

Cova, B., & Remy, E. (2007). I Feel Good: Who Needs the Market? – Struggling and Having Fun with Consumer-driven Experiences. In Consuming Experiences. Oxon, UK: Routledge.

Cova, B., Kozinets, R. V., & Shankar, A. (2007). *Consumer Tribes.* Butter-Heinemann.

Cova, B., & Dalli, D. (2009). Working consumers: The next step in marketing theory. *Marketing Theory*, *9*(3), 315–339. doi:10.1177/1470593109338144

Cox, A., Granbois, D. H., & Summers, J. (1983). Planning, search, certainty and satisfaction among durables buyers: Alongitudinal study. *Advances in Consumer Research. Association for Consumer Research (U. S.)*, *10*, 394–399.

Craig, J. B. L., & Moores, K. (2006). A 10-Year Longitudinal Investigation of Strategy, Systems, and Environment on Innovation in Family Firms. *Family Business Review*, *19*(1), 1–10. doi:10.1111/j.1741-6248.2006.00056.x

Crestodina, A. (2012). *Content chemistry: an illustrated handbook for content marketing*. New York: Orbit Media Studios.

Creswell, J. W., Plano, C., & Vicki, L. (2011). *Designing and Conducting Mixed Methods Research* (2nd ed.). Sage Publications, Inc.

Crouch, M., & McKenzie, H. (2006). The logic of small samples in interview-based qualitative research. *Social Sciences Information. Information Sur les Sciences Sociales*, *45*(4), 483–499. doi:10.1177/0539018406069584

Cucculelli, M., Micucci, G. (2008). *Family succession and firm performance: Evidence from Italian family firms*. Banca d'Italia, n.680.

D'Arpizio, C. (2014). *Luxury goods worldwide market study spring 2014*. Bain and Company.

Dahlen, M., Lange, F., & Smith, T. (2010). *Marketing Communications – A Brand Narrative Approach*. John Wiley & Sons Ltd.

Dall'Olmo Riley, F., & Lacroix, C. (2003). Luxury branding on the Internet: Lost opportunity or impossibility? *Marketing Intelligence & Planning*, *21*(2), 96–104. doi:10.1108/02634500310465407

Damian, R. & Calvin, J (2013). *Marketing digitale: trarre il massimo vantaggio da e-mail, siti web, dispositivi mobili, social media e PR online*. Bergamo: Tecniche nuove.

Danco, L. A. (1982). *Beyond Survival*. Cleveland, OH: The University Press.

Danziger, P. (2005). *Let them eat the cake*. Dearborn: Kaplan Books.

Darwin, C. R. (1909). The Origin of Species: Vol. 11. *The Harvard Classics*. New York: P.F. Collier & Son.

D'Astous, A., & Lévesque, M. (2003). A scale for measuring store personality. *Psychology and Marketing*, *20*(5), 455–469. doi:10.1002/mar.10081

Datagraphic. (2013). Luxury goods landscape: USA, Passport. *Euromonitor International.*

Davies, M., & Hughes, N. (2014). *Doing a Successful Research Project* (2nd ed.). Palgrave Macmillan.

Davis, T. (2011). *The Teen Spending Game: The Complex Marketing Strategy*. Retrieved from http://www.examiner.com

De Chernatony, L. (2001). *From Brand Vision to Brand Evaluation. Strategically Building and Sustaining Brands.* Oxford, UK: Butterworth Heinemann.

de Lassus, C., & Freire, N. A. (2014). Access to the luxury brand myth in pop-up stores: A netnographic and semiotic analysis. *Journal of Retailing and Consumer Services*, *21*(1), 61–68. doi:10.1016/j.jretconser.2013.08.005

De Massis, A., Frattini, F., Pizzurno, E., & Cassia, L. (2013). Product innovation in family versus non family firms: An exploratory analysis. *Journal of Small Business Management*, *53*(1), 1–301. doi:10.1111/jsbm.12068

Deighton, J., & Kornfeld, L. (2009). Interactivity's Unanticipated Consequences for Markets and Marketing. *Journal of Interactive Marketing*, *23*(1), 2–12. doi:10.1016/j.intmar.2008.10.001

del Blanco, R. M. A. (2012). Diálogo con la belleza: perspectiva de neuromárketing. *Harvard Deusto Márketing y Ventas*, (113), 62-68.

Deloitte. (2014). *Global powers of luxury goods 2014, in the hands of the consumer.* Deloitte Touch Tohmatsu Limited.

Deloitte. (2015). *Global Powers of Luxury Goods 2015: Engaging the Future Luxury Consumer.* Deloitte Touche Tohmatsu Limited. Retrieved from http://www2.deloitte.com/content/dam/Deloitte/ch/Documents/consumer-business/ch-en-cb-global-powers-of-luxury-goods-2015.pdf

Didner, P. (2014). *Global content marketing*. New York: Mc-Graw Hill.

Dion, D., & Arnould, E. (2011). Retail luxury strategy: Assembling charisma through art and magic. *Journal of Retailing*, *87*(4), 502–520. doi:10.1016/j.jretai.2011.09.001

Dixon, D. F., & Blois, K. J. (1973). Some Limitations of the 4 Ps as a Paradigm of Marketing. In *Proceedings of the Marketing Education Group* (pp. 92-107).

Donaldson, M. S. (2011, October/November). Promoting Luxury Goods in China through Social Media. *MultiLingual*, 29-31.

Donzé, P.-Y., & Fujioka, R. (2015). European Luxury Big Business and Emerging Asian Markets, 1960 – 2010. *Business History*, *57*(6), 822–840. doi:10.1080/00076791.2014.982104

Doran, S. (2013). How well do we really know the Chinese luxury consumer? *Luxury Society.* Retrieved January 3, 2015, from http://luxurysociety.com/articles/2013/02/how-well-do-we-really-know-the-chinese-luxury-consumer

Doran, K. B. (2002). Lessons learnt in cross-cultural research of Chinese and north American consumers. *Journal of Business Research*, *55*(10), 823–829. doi:10.1016/S0148-2963(00)00222-8

Doyle, P. (2000). *Value-Based Marketing*. Chichester, UK: Wiley.

Doyle, P. (2008). *Value-based Marketing: Marketing Strategies for Corporate Growth and Shareholder Value*. John Wiley & Sons.

Dubois, A., & Gadde, L. E. (2002). Systematic combining: An abductive approach to case research. *Journal of Business Research*, *55*(7), 553–560. doi:10.1016/S0148-2963(00)00195-8

Dubois, B., Czellar, S., & Laurent, G. (2005). Consumer segments based on attitudes toward luxury: Empirical evidence from twenty countries. *Marketing Letters*, *16*(2), 115–128. doi:10.1007/s11002-005-2172-0

Dubois, B., & Duquesne, P. (1993). The market for luxury goods: Income versus culture. *European Journal of Marketing*, *27*(1), 35–44. doi:10.1108/03090569310024530

Dudovskiy, J. (2013). *Consumer Decision Making Process: a detailed analysis.* Retrieved Jan http://luxurysociety.com/articles/2013/02/how-well-do-we-really-know-the-chinese-luxury-consumerurary

Duesenberry, J. S. (1949). *Income, Saving and the Theory of Consumer Behaviour*. Cambridge, MA: Harvard University Press.

Duncan, T., & Mulhern, F. (2004). *A White Paper on the Status, Scope and Future of IMC*. New York: McGraw-Hill.

Duncan, T. (2002). *IMC: Using Advertising & Promotion to Build Brands*. Boston: McGraw Hill.

Duncan, T., & Moriarty, S. E. (1997). *Driving Brand Value: Using Integrated Marketing to drive Shareholder Relationships*. New York: McGraw Hill.

Duncan, T., & Ouwersloot, H. (2008). *Intergrated Marketing Communications*. Maidenhead, UK: McGraw Hill.

Dunn, B. (1996). Family enterprises in the UK: A Special Sector? *Family Business Review*, *9*(2), 139–155. doi:10.1111/j.1741-6248.1996.00139.x

Dunne, A., Lawlor, M. A., & Rowley, J. (2010). Young people's use of online social networking sites – a uses and gratifications perspective. *Journal of Research in Interactive Marketing*, *4*(1), 46–58. doi:10.1108/17505931011033551

Easley, D., & Kleinberg, J. (2010). *Networks, crowds, and markets: Reasoning about a highly connected world*. New York, NY: Cambridge University Press. doi:10.1017/CBO9780511761942

Easterby-Smith, M., Thorpe, R., & Jackson, P. R. (2012). *Management Research* (4th ed.). London: Sage.

Eastman, J. K., Goldsmith, R. E., & Flynn, L. R. (1999). Status Consumption in Consumer Behaviour: Scale Development and Validation. *Journal of Marketing Theory and Practice*, *7*(3), 41–52. doi:10.1080/10696679.1999.11501839

Edwards, G., & Probst, E. (2011). Empathica Consumer Insights Panel Analysis of U.S. & Canadian Consumer Behaviours in Luxury Purchases. *Wave*, *2*, 2011–2012.

Eisend, M., & Schuchert-Güler, P. (2006). Explaining Counterfeit Purchases – A Review and Preview. *Academy of Marketing Science Review*, *06*(12), 1–25.

eMarketer. (2012). Consumers' Expectations High for Luxury Brands on Mobile. *eMarketer*. Available at: www.emarketer.com

eMarketer. (2013). Luxury Marketers Investing More in Digital. *eMarketer.* Available at: www.emarketer.com

Engel, J. F., Kollat, D. T., & Blackwell, R. D. (1968). *Consumer behavior*. Holt, Rinehart and Winston, Inc.

Eng, T., & Bogaert, J. (2010). Psychological and cultural insights into consumption of luxury Western brands in India. *Journal of Customer Behaviour*, *9*(1), 55–75. doi:10.1362/147539210X497620

Erdoğan, B. Z. (1999). Celebrity Endorsement: A Literature Review. *Journal of Marketing Management*, *15*(4), 291–314. doi:10.1362/026725799784870379

Erikson, E. (1959). Identity and the life cycle. *Psychological Issues*, *1*(1), 13–117.

Erner, G. (2004). *Victimes de la mode?* Paris: La Découverte.

Ertekin, Z. O., & Atik, D. (2015). Sustainable Markets: Motivating Factors, Barriers, and Remedies for Mobilization of Slow Fashion. *Journal of Macromarketing*, *35*(1), 53–69. doi:10.1177/0276146714535932

Euromonitor. (2015). *World All Cosmetics and World Premium Cosmetics Market-Retail Value*. Author.

Evrard, Y., & Roux, E. (2005). *Culture vs Luxury: The Paradoxes of Democratisation.* Puyricard: CEROG.

Fabris, G. (2008). *Societing*. Milano: Egea.

Fabris, G., & Minestroni, L. (2004). *Valore e valori della marca*. Milano: FrancoAngeli.

Fantini, M. (2013). *Content Marketing, image, notorietè, conquete, fidelisation: boostez voster webmarketing par la contenu*, Paris: Eni editions Peterson E.T.

Farquhar, K. (1989).*Employee Responses to External Executive Succession: Attributions and the Emergence of Leadership*. (Unpublished Doctoral Dissertation). Department of Psychology Boston University.

FCT Forecasts S.A. (1997-2011). *European Forecasts Selective Distribution in Spain*. Author.

Feeney, A., & Heit, E. (2007). *Inductive Reasoning: Experimental, Developmental, and Computational Approaches*. New York: Cambridge University Press. doi:10.1017/CBO9780511619304

Feitelberg, R. (2010, February 2). Mix and match. Sportswear houses are playing the versatility card. *Women's Wear Daily*, p. 10.

Felson, M., & Spaeth, J. (1978). Community structure and collaborative consumption. *The American Behavioral Scientist*, *21*(4), 614–624.

Fernåndez Moya, M. E. (2012). *Purchase and consumption of luxury goods*. (Unpublished doctoral dissertation). University Carlos III, Madrid, Spain.

Fernie, J., Moore, C. M., & Lawrie, A. (1998). A tale of two Cities: An Examination of Fashion Designer Retailing within London and New York. *Journal of Product and Brand Management*, *7*(5), 366–378. doi:10.1108/10610429810237637

Ferrero, G. (1987). *Impresa e management*. Milano: Giuffré.

Fionda, A. M., & Moore, C. M. (2008). The anatomy of the luxury fashion brand. *Journal of Brand Management*, *16*(5/6), 347–363.

Fionda, A. M., & Moore, C. M. (2009). The anatomy of the luxury fashion brand. *Journal of Brand Management*, *5*(16), 347–363. doi:10.1057/bm.2008.45

Fishbein, M. (2014). *Growth hacking with content marketing*. London: Create Space Independent Publishing Platform.

Foglio, A. (2013). *Il marketing comunicativo dell'impresa: dalla pubblicità alla comunicazione offline e online al consumatore*. Milan: Angeli.

Forbes. (2013). *Inside The 2013 Billionaires List: Facts and Figures*. Retrieved January 7, 2015, from http://www.forbes.com/sites/luisakroll/2013/03/04/inside-the-2013-billionaires-list-facts-and-figures/

Friedman, S. (1987). *The Succession Process: Theoretical Considerations*. Paper presented at the annual meeting of the Academy of Management, New Orleans, LA.

Friedman, V. (2010). Assessing the Alexander Wang/H&M collaboration. *Financial Times*. Retrieved June 30, 2015, from http://blogs.ft.com/material-world/2014/04/14/assessing-the-alexander-wanghm-collaboration/

Friedman, J. (1990). Being in the world: Globalization and localization. *Theory, Culture & Society*, *7*(2), 311–328. doi:10.1177/026327690007002018

Fulmer, W. E. (2000). *Shaping the Adaptive Organization*. New York: Amacom.

Gaborit, J. Y. (1985). *Parfums: Prestige et haute couture*. Fribourg: Office du Livre.

Gabrielli, V., Baghi, I., & Codeluppi, V. (2013). Consumption practices of fast fashion products. *Journal of Fashion Marketing and Management*, *17*(2), 206–224. doi:10.1108/JFMM-10-2011-0076

Gandini, C., & Turinetto, M. (2009). Lusso necessario alla ricerca del valore per vincere la crisi. Milano: Lupetti, Milano, 2009.

Ganter, C. (2013). In the name of luxury. *Insight,* (9).

Gao, L., Norton, M. J. T., Zhang, Z., & To, C. K. (2009). Potential niche markets for luxury fashion goods in China. *Journal of Fashion Marketing and Management*, *13*(4), 514–526. doi:10.1108/13612020910991376

García Ferrer, G. (2012). Investigación comercial. Spain: Esic Editorial.

García Ferrer, G., & García, C. (2013). *Construcción y validación inicial de una escala para medir la personalidad de los establecimientos comerciales (No. 1305)*. Catedra Fundación Ramón Areces de Distribución Comercial.

Garrity, E. J., O'Donnell, J. B., Kim, Y. J., & Sanders, G. L. (2007). An extrinsic and intrinsic motivation-based model for measuring consumer shopping oriented web site success. *Journal of Electronic Commerce in Organizations*, *5*(4), 18–38. doi:10.4018/jeco.2007100102

Geerts, A., & Veg-Sala, N. (2011). Evidence on Internet Communication - Management Strategies for Luxury Brands. *Global Journal of Business Research*, *5*(5), 81–94.

Gensler, S., Völckner, F., Liu-Thompkins, Y., & Wiertz, C. (2013). Managing Brands in the Social Media Environment. *Journal of Interactive Marketing*, *27*(4), 242–256. doi:10.1016/j.intmar.2013.09.004

Gerbarg, D. (2009). *Television Goes Digital*. Springer. doi:10.1007/978-0-387-79978-0

Giachetti, C., Spadafora, E., & Bursi, T. (2013). Internazionalizzazione, performance delle imprese e crisi economiche: i produttori di piastrelle di ceramica del distretto di Modena e Reggio Emilia. *Mercati e competitività, 2*, 37-58.

Giacosa, E. (2011). *L'economia della aziende di abbigliamento*. Torino: Giappichelli.

Giacosa, E. (2012). *Mergers and Acquisitions (M&As) in the Luxury Business*. Milano: McGraw-Hill.

Giacosa, E. (2014). *Innovation in Luxury Fashion Family Business*. London: MacMillan. doi:10.1057/9781137498663

Gilbert, D. (2003). *Retail marketing management*. Prentice Hal.

Godey, B., Pederzoli, D., Aiello, G., Donvito, R., Wiedmann, K.-P., & Hennigs, N. (2013). A Cross-Cultural Exploratory Content Analysis of The Perception of Luxury from Six Countries. *Journal of Product and Brand Management*, *22*(3), 229–237. doi:10.1108/JPBM-02-2013-0254

Goldsmith, R. E., Moore, M. A., & Beaudoin, P. (1999). Fashion innovativeness and self concept: A replication. *Journal of Product and Brand Management*, *8*(1), 7–18. doi:10.1108/10610429910257904

Goodstein, A. (2007, August). Teen Marketing: Apple's the Master. *Bloomberg Businessweek*.

Gordini, N., & Rancati, E. (2014). *Content marketing e creazione di valore. Aspetti definitori e metriche di misurazione*. Turin: Giappichelli.

Grau, J. (2010). Affluent Shoppers and Luxury Brand Retailers Online. *eMarketer*. Available at: www.emarketer.com

Greenbaum, T. L. (1998). *The Handbook for Focus Group Research* (2nd ed.). Sage Publications, Inc.

Greene, A. L., & Adams-Price, C. (1990). Adolescents' Secondary Attachments to Celebrity Figures. *Sex Roles*, *23*(7-8), 335–347. doi:10.1007/BF00289224

Griffioen, A. (2011). *Creating Profit Through Alliances: How collaborative business models can contribute to competitive advantage*. Retrieved October 10, 2013, from http://www.allianceexperts.com/images/documents/creating-profit-through-alliances-sq.pdf

Grossman, G., & Shapiro, C. (1988). Foreign Counterfeiting of Status Goods. *The Quarterly Journal of Economics*, *103*(February), 79–100. doi:10.2307/1882643

Guelfi, S., & Giacosa, E. (2011). *Le aziende della net economy*. Torino: Giappichelli.

Guercini, S., & Ranfagni, S. (2012). Social and Green Sustainability and the Italian Mediterranean Fashion Brands. In *Proceedings of Euromed Congress* (pp. 1-15). Nicosia: Euromed Press.

Guercini, S., & Ranfagni, S. (2013). Sustainability and luxury: The Italian case of a supply chain based on native wools. *Journal of Corporate Citizenship*, *52*(52), 76–89. doi:10.9774/GLEAF.4700.2013.de.00008

Guercini, S., & Woodside, A. G. (2012). A strategic supply chain approach: Consortium marketing in the Italian leatherwear industry. *Marketing Intelligence & Planning*, *30*(7), 700–716. doi:10.1108/02634501211273814

Guido, G., Amatulli, C., & Peluso, A. (2014). Context Effects on Older Consumers' Cognitive Age: The Role of Hedonic *vs.* Utilitarian Goals. *Psychology & Marketing*, *2*(31), 103-114.

Gulland, C. (2006, July 14). *The ten biggest themes of 'What teens want'*. Retrieved March, 20, 2007, from http://www.ypulse.com/the-ten-biggest-themes-of-what-teens-want

Gunelius, S. (2011). *Content Marketing for Dummies*. New York: Wiley.

H&M. (2015). *Campaigns and Designer Collaborations*. Retrieved June 30, 2015, from http://about.hm.com/en/About/facts-about-hm/fashion-for-all/collections/collaborations.html

Habimana, E., & Massé, L. (2000). Envy manifestations and personality disorders. *European Psychiatry*, *15*, 15–21. doi:10.1016/S0924-9338(00)00501-0 PMID:11520469

Hackley, C. (2009). *Advertising and Promotion: An Integrated Marketing Communications Approach*. SAGE Publications.

Haddow, G. D., & Haddow, K. S. (2014). *Disaster Communications in a Changing Media World*. Butterworth Heinemann.

Haenlein, M., & Kaplan, A. M. (2009). Flagship Brand Stores within Virtual Worlds: The Impact of Virtual Store Exposure on Real-Life Attitude toward the Brand and Purchase Intent. *Recherche et Applications en Marketing*, *24*(3), 57–79. doi:10.1177/076737010902400304

Hagtvedt, H., & Patrick, V. M. (2009). The broad embrace of luxury: Hedonic potential as a driver of brand extendibility. *Journal of Consumer Psychology*, 19.

Ha, H. Y., & Perks, H. (2005). Effects of consumer perceptions of brand experience on the web: Brand familiarity, satisfaction, and trust. *Journal of Consumer Behaviour*, *4*(6), 438–452. doi:10.1002/cb.29

Hair, J., Anderson, R., Tatham, R., & Black, W. (1998). *Multivariate Data Analysis* (5th International Edition). Prentice Hall.

Hall, E. T., & Hall, M. R. (1990). Understanding Cultural Differences. Yarmouth, ME: Intercultural Press.

Halvorson, K. (2010). *Content strategy for the web*. Berkeley, CA: New Riders.

Hamilton, C. (2004). *Money, Marketing and the Innocence of Youth*. Retrieved online 19th March 2009, from http://www.clivehamilton.net.au/cms/media/documents/articles/Money,_Marketing_and_the_Innocence_of_Youth.pdf

Handler, W. C. (1989). Methodological issues and considerations in studying family businesses. *Family Business Review*, *2*(3), 257–276. doi:10.1111/j.1741-6248.1989.00257.x

Handler, W. C. (1990). Succession in Family Firms: A Mutual Role Adjustment Between Entrepreneur and Next-Generation Family Members. *Entrepreneurship Theory and Practice*, *15*(1), 37–51.

Handler, W. C. (1994). Succession in Family Business; a revew of the research. *Family Business Review*, *7*(2), 133–157. doi:10.1111/j.1741-6248.1994.00133.x

Handley, A., & Champman, C. C. (2012). *Content marketing: fare business con i contenuti per il web*. Milan: Hoepli.

Handley, A., & Chapman, C. C. (2010). *Content Rules*. New York: John Wiley & Sons.

Hanmann, D. W., Jr., & Omar, M. (2007). Branding strategy and consumer high-technology product. *Journal of Product and Brand Management*, *16*(2).

Harrisson, L., & Huntington, S. (2000). *Culture Matters: How values shape human progress*. New York: Basic Books.

Hartman, J. B., Shim, S., Barber, B., & O'Brien, M. (2006). Adolescents' utilitarian and hedonic Web consumption behavior: Hierarchical influence of personal values and innovativeness. *Psychology and Marketing*, *23*(10), 813–839. doi:10.1002/mar.20135

Hauck, W. E., & Stanforth, N. (2007). Cohort perception of luxury goods and services. *Journal of Fashion Marketing and Management*, *11*(2), 175–188. doi:10.1108/13612020710751365

Hauer, C. (2012). Marketing in the Digital Age. *Editors' Bulletin*, *7*(3), 77–79.

Hausman, A. (2000). A multi-method investigation of consumer motivations in impulse buying behavior. *Journal of Consumer Marketing*, *17*(5), 403–426. doi:10.1108/07363760010341045

Heaney, J.-G., Goldsmith, R. E., & Jusoh, W. J. W. (2005). Status consumption among Malaysian consumers: Exploring its relationships with materialism and attention-to-social-comparisoninformation. *Journal of International Consumer Marketing*, *17*(4), 83–98. doi:10.1300/J046v17n04_05

Heck, R. K. Z., Hoy, F., Poutziouris, P. Z., & Steier, L. P. (2008). Emerging paths of family entrepreneurship research. *Journal of Small Business Management*, *46*(3), 317–330. doi:10.1111/j.1540-627X.2008.00246.x

Heine, K. (2012). *The Identity of Luxury Brands*. (Doctoral Dissertation). Kassel University, Germany.

Heinonen, K., & Michelsson, T. (2010). The use of digital channels to create customer relationships. *International Journal of Internet Marketing and Advertising*, *6*(1), 30430. doi:10.1504/IJIMA.2010.030430

Helmrich, E. (2004). *What Teens Want*. YALS.

Helsen, K., Jedidi, K., & DeSarbo, W. (1993). A New Approach to Country Segmentation Utilizing Multinational Diffusion Patterns. *Journal of Marketing*, *57*(October), 60–71. doi:10.2307/1252219

Hemphill, C. S., & Suk, J. (2009). The Law, Culture, and Economics of Fashion. *Stanford Law Review*, 61.

Hennig-Thurau, T., Gwinner, K. P., Walsh, G., & Gremler, D. D. (2004). Electronic word-of mouth via consumer-opinion platforms: What motivates consumers to articulate themselves on the Internet? *Journal of Interactive Marketing*, *18*(1), 38–52. doi:10.1002/dir.10073

Hennig-Thurau, T., Malthouse, E. C., Friege, C., Gensler, S., Lobschat, L., Rangaswamy, A., & Skiera, B. (2010). The Impact of New Media on Customer Relationships. *Journal of Service Research*, *13*(3), 311–328. doi:10.1177/1094670510375460

Hennings, N., Wiedmann, K-P., & Klarmann, C. (2013). Consumer value perception of luxury goods: a cross-cultural and cross-industry comparison. In *Luxury Marketing*. Springer Fachmedien Wiesbaden.

Hennings, N., Wiedmann, K.-P., Klarmann, C., Strehlau, S., Godey, B., Pederzoli, D., & Oh, H. et al. (2012). What is the value of luxury? A cross-cultural consumer perspective. *Psychology and Marketing*, *29*(12), 1018–1034. doi:10.1002/mar.20583

Henning-Thurau, T., Hofacker, C., & Bloching, B. (2013). Marketing the Pinball Way: Understanding How Social Media Change the Generation of Value for Consumers and Companies. *Journal of Interactive Marketing*, *27*(4), 237–241. doi:10.1016/j.intmar.2013.09.005

Hoecklin, L. (1996). *Managing Cultural Differences: Strategies for Competitive Advantage* (2nd ed.). Wokingham: Addison-Wesley Publishers.

Hoe, L., Hogg, G., & Hart, S. (2003). Fakin'it, counterfeiting and consumer contradictions. *European Advances in Consumer Research*, *6*, 60–67.

Hoffmann, J., & Coste-Manière, I. (2012). *Luxury Strategy in Action*. Palgrave Macmillan.

Hofstede, G., Hofstede, G. J., & Minkov, M. (2010). Cultures and Organizations: Software of the Mind (3rd ed.). McGraw-Hill USA.

Hofstede, G. (1980). *Culture's Consequences: International Differences in Work Related Values*. Beverly Hills, CA: Sage.

Hofstede, G. (2001). *Culture's consequences: comparing values behaviours, institutions and organisations across nations*. London: Sage Publications.

Holbrook, M. B., & Hirschman, E. C. (1982). The experiential aspects of consumption: Consumer fantasies, feelings, and fun. *The Journal of Consumer Research*, *9*(2), 32–40. doi:10.1086/208906

Holliman, G., & Rowley, J. (2014). Business to business digital content marketing. *Journal of Research in Interactive Marketing*, *8*(4), 269–293. doi:10.1108/JRIM-02-2014-0013

Holmquist, J. P., & Cudmore, A. (2013). English in Korean advertising: An exploratory study. *International Journal of Marketing Studies*, *5*(3), 94–103. doi:10.5539/ijms.v5n3p94

Holt, D. B., Quelch, J. A., & Taylor, E. L. (2004). How global brands compete. *Harvard Business Review*, *82*(9), 68–75. PMID:15449856

Hopson, B., & Adams, A. (1976). Toward an understanding of transition: Defining some boundaries of transition dynamics. In J. Adams, J. Hayes, & B. Hopson (Eds.), *Transition: Understanding and managing personal changes*. London, UK: Martin Robertson.

Howard, D., Nomoto, M., Yamaguchi, T., & Kopf, C. (2007). *Japan's changing consumer: driver of change for luxury brands*. JMRN Insights Briefing.

Howard, J. A., & Sheth, J. N. (1969). *The theory of buyer behavior* (Vol. 14). New York: Wiley.

Howard, T. (2010). *Design to Thrive: Creating Social Networks and Online Communities that Last*. Morgan Kauffman Publishers.

Hsu, C., Chuan-Chuan Lin, J., & Chiang, H.-S. (2013). The effects of blogger recommendations on customers' online shopping intentions. *Internet Research*, *23*(1), 69–88. doi:10.1108/10662241311295782

Huang, M. H. (2001). The theory of emotions in marketing. *Journal of Business and Psychology*, *16*(2), 239–247. doi:10.1023/A:1011109200392

Huang, S. (2011). Nation-branding and transnational consumption: Japan-mania and the Korean wave in Taiwan. *Media Culture & Society*, *33*(1), 3–18. doi:10.1177/0163443710379670

Hudders, L., Pandelaere, M., & Vyncke, P. (2013). Consumer meaning making: The meaning of luxury brands in a democratised luxury world. *International Journal of Market Research*, *55*(3), 391. doi:10.2501/IJMR-2013-036

Husic, M., & Cicic, M. (2009). Luxury consumption factors, *Journal of Fashion marketing and Management. International Journal (Toronto, Ont.)*, *13*(2), 231–245.

Husic, M., & Cicic, M. (2009). Luxury Consumption Factors. *Journal of Fashion Marketing and Management*, *13*(2), 231–245. doi:10.1108/13612020910957734

Huszagh, S., Fox, R., & Day, E. (1986). Global Marketing: An Empirical Investigation. *The Columbia Journal of World Business*, *20*(4), 31–43.

Hyman, H. H. (1942). The psychology of status. *Archives de Psychologie*, (269): 5–91.

Hyman, H. H., & Singer, E. (1968). *Readings in Reference Group Theory and Research*. Free Press.

Iacobucci, D., & Churchill, G. A. (2010). Marketing Research: Methodological Foundations (10th ed.). Mason, OH: South Western Cengage Learning.

Ibrahim, A. B., Mc Guire, J., & Soufani, K. (2009). An Empirical Investigation of Factors Contributing to Longevity of Small Family Firms. *Global Economy &Finnaca Journal*, *2*(2), 3–4.

IMF. (2013). *World Economic Outlook: Transitions and Tensions*. International Monetary Fund, Publication Services.

Interbrand. (2005). *The Best 100 Brands*. Retrieved June 30, 2015, from http://www.interbrand.com/en/best-global-brands/previous-years/best-global-brands-2005.aspx

Interbrand. (2014). *The Best 100 Brands*. Retrieved June 30, 2015, from http://bestglobalbrands.com/2014/ranking/

Ivanauskas, G. (2009). *The evaluation of social media effects on consumers marketing communications*. Retrieved from www.scribd.com

Jansen, B. J., Zhang, M., Sobel, K., & Chowdury, A. (2009). Twitter Power – Tweets as Electronic Word-of-Mouth. *Journal of the American Society for Information Science and Technology*, *11*(60), 2169–2188. doi:10.1002/asi.21149

Jansson, J., & Power, D. (2010). Fashioning a Global City: Global City Brand Channel in the Fashion and Design Industries. *Regional Studies*, *44*(7), 889–904. doi:10.1080/00343400903401584

Jarvinen, J., & Taiminen, H. (2015). (in press). Harnessing marketing automation for B2B content marketing. *Journal of Industrial Marketing Management*. doi:10.1016/j.indmarman.2015.07.002

Jefferson, S., & Tanton, S. (2013). Valuable Content Marketing. How to make quality content the key of your business success, London: Kogan Page: London.

Johansson, J. K., & Ronkainen, I. A. (2005). The esteem of Global Brands. *Journal of Brand Management*, *12*(5), 339–354. doi:10.1057/palgrave.bm.2540230

Johnson, T. J., & Kaye, B. K. (2009). In blog we trust? Deciphering credibility of components of the internet among politically interested internet users. *Computers in Human Behavior*, *25*(1), 175–182. doi:10.1016/j.chb.2008.08.004

Jones, C., Makri, M., & Gomez-Mejia, L. R. (2008). Affiliate directors and perceived risk bearing in publicly traded, family-controlled firms: The case of diversification. *Entrepreneurship Theory & Practice*, *32*(6), 1007–1026. doi:10.1111/j.1540-6520.2008.00269.x

Jones, R. (2002). *The apparel industry*. London: Blackwell.

Joy, A., Sherry, J. F. Jr, Venkatesh, A., Wang, J., & Chan, R. (2012). Fast Fashion, Sustainability, and the Ethical Appeal of Luxury Brands. *Fashion Theory*, *3*(16), 273–296. doi:10.2752/175174112X13340749707123

Jung, J., & Shen, D. (2011). Brand equity of luxury fashion brands among Chinese and U.S. Young female consumers. *Journal of East-West Business*, *17*(1), 48–69. doi:10.1080/10669868.2011.598756

Kale, S. (1995). Grouping Euroconsumers: A Culture-Based Clustering Approach. *Journal of International Marketing*, *3*(3), 35–48.

Kamineni, R. (2005). Influence of materialism, gender and nationality on consumer brand perceptions. Journal of Targeting. *Measurement and Analysis for Marketing*, *14*(1), 25–32. doi:10.1057/palgrave.jt.5740167

Kamins, M. A. (1989). Celebrity and Non-celebrity Advertising in a Two Sided Context. *Journal of Advertising Research*, *29*(3), 34–42.

Kanuk, L., & Berenson, C. (1975). Mail Surveys and Response Rates: A Literature Review. *JMR, Journal of Marketing Research*, *12*(4), 440–453. doi:10.2307/3151093

Kanuk, S. U., & Krishnamurthy, S. (2007). An analysis of consumer power on the Internet. *Technovation*, *27*(1-2), 47–56. doi:10.1016/j.technovation.2006.05.002

Kapferer, J. N. (2012). The New Strategic Brand Management: Advanced Insights and Strategic Thinking (5th ed.). Kogan Page.

Kapferer, J. N., & Bastien, V. (2009). Luxury Strategy. Milano: FrancoAngeli.

Kapferer, J. (2004). *The New Strategic Brand Management*. London: Kogan Page.

Kapferer, J. N. (1997). Managing luxury brands. *Journal of Brand Management*, *4*(4), 251–260. doi:10.1057/bm.1997.4

Kapferer, J. N. (2002). *Ce qui va changer les marques*. Paris: Editions d'Organisation.

Kapferer, J. N. (2004). *The New Strategic Brand Management. Creating and sustaining brand equity long term*. London, UK: Kogan Page.

Kapferer, J. N. (2012). Abundant rarity: The key to luxury growth. *Business Horizons*, *55*(5), 453–462. doi:10.1016/j.bushor.2012.04.002

Kapferer, J. N. (2012). All That Glitters is not Green: The Challenge of Sustainable Luxury. *European Business Review*, (November/December), 40–45.

Kapferer, J. N., & Bastien, V. (2009). *The Luxury Strategy: Break the Rules of Marketing to Build Luxury Brands*. Philadelphia: Kogan Page Limited.

Kapferer, J. N., & Bastien, V. (2011). *Luxury Strategy: sovvertire le regole del marketing per costruire veri brand di lusso*. Milano: Franco Angeli.

Kapferer, J. N., & Bastien, V. (2013). *Luxury Strategy. Sovvertire le regole del marketing per costruire veri brand di lusso*. Milano: Franco Angeli.

Kapferer, J., & Bastien, V. (2009). The Specificity of Luxury Management: Turning Marketing Upside Down. *Journal of Brand Management*, *16*(5), 311–322. doi:10.1057/bm.2008.51

Kapferer, J.-N. (2002). Is there really no hope for local brands? *Journal of Brand Management*, *9*(3), 163–170. doi:10.1057/palgrave.bm.2540066

Kaplan, A. M., & Haenlein, M. (2010). Users of the world, unite! The challenges and opportunities of Social Media. *Business Horizons*, *53*(1), 59–68. doi:10.1016/j.bushor.2009.09.003

Kastanakis, M., & Balabanis, G. (2012). Between the mass and the class: Antecedents of the "bandwagon" luxury consumption behavior. *Journal of Business Research*, *65*(10), 1399–1407. doi:10.1016/j.jbusres.2011.10.005

Kastenholz, J., Kerr, G., & Young, C. (2004). Focus and Fit: Advertising and branding join forces to create a star. *Marketing Research*, *16*(4), 16–21.

Kauffman, S. A. (1993). *The origins of order: self-organization and selection in evolution*. New York: Oxford University Press.

Kaufmann, H. R., Vrontis, D., & Manakova, Y. (2012). Perception of luxury: Idiosyncratic Russian consumer culture and identity. *European Journal of Cross-Cultural Competence and Management*, *2*(3/4), 2012. doi:10.1504/EJCCM.2012.052594

Kawabata, H., & Zeki, S. (2004). Neural correlates of beauty. *Journal of Neurophysiology*, *91*(4), 1699–1705. doi:10.1152/jn.00696.2003 PMID:15010496

Kazim, K., & Karahan, F. (2011). To be or not to be in Social Media Arena as the Most Cost Efficient Marketing Strategy after the Global Recession. *Procedia: Social and Behavioral Sciences*, 24.

Keegan, W., & Marck, G. (2013). *Global Marketing* (7th ed.). Prentice-Hall.

Keller, K. L. (2003). Understanding Brands, branding, and Brand Equity. *Journal of Interactive Marketing*, *5*(1), 7–20. doi:10.1057/palgrave.im.4340213

Keller, K. L. (2009). Building on strong brands in a modern marketing communications environment. *Journal of Marketing Communications*, *15*(2-3), 139–155. doi:10.1080/13527260902757530

Keller, K. L. (2009). Managing the growth tradeoff: Challenges and Opportunities in Luxury Branding. *Journal of Brand Management*, *16*(5/6), 290–301. doi:10.1057/bm.2008.47

Keller, K. L. (2010). Brand Equity Management in a Multichannel, Multimedia Retail Environment. *Journal of Interactive Marketing*, *24*(2/5), 58–70. doi:10.1016/j.intmar.2010.03.001

Kelly, K. (1998). *New Rules for the New Economy – 10 Ways the Network Economy is Changing Everything*. New York: Penguin Books.

Kemp, S. (1998). Perceiving Luxury and Necessity. *Journal of Economic Psychology*, *19*(5), 591–606. doi:10.1016/S0167-4870(98)00026-9

Kent, T. (2007). Creative Space: Design and the Retail Environment. *International Journal of Retail & Distribution Management*, *35*(9), 734–745. doi:10.1108/09590550710773273

Keronen, K., & Tanni, K. (2013). *Johdata Asiakkaasi Verkkoon*. Helsinki: Talentum Media Oy.

Keyes, J. (2006). *Knowledge management, business intelligence and content management. Broken South Parken*. Auerbach Publications. doi:10.1201/9781420013863

Khan, M. A. (2010). How can luxury brands survive lasting changes in consumer behaviour? *Luxury Daily*. Retrieved January 2, 2015, from http://www.luxurydaily.com/how-can-luxury-brands-survive-lasting-changes-in-consumer-behavior/

Khan, O. (2015). Luxury Consumption Moves East. *Journal of Fashion Marketing and Management: An International Journal*, *19*(4), 347–359. doi:10.1108/JFMM-10-2014-0076

Khraras, H., & Gertz, G. (2010). *The new global middle class: a cross-over from West to East*. Wolfensohn Centre for Development at Brookings.

Kietzmann, J. H., Silvestre, B. S., McCarthy, I. P., & Pitt, L. F. (2012). Unpacking the social media phenomenon: Towards a research agenda. *Journal of Public Affairs*, *12*(2), 109–119. doi:10.1002/pa.1412

Kim, A. K., & Ko, E. (2012). Do social media marketing activities enhance customer equity? An empirical study of luxury fashion brand. *Journal of Business Research*, *65*(10), 1480–1486. doi:10.1016/j.jbusres.2011.10.014

Kim, H., & Lennon, S. J. (2010). E-atmosphere, emotional, cognitive, and behavioral responses. *Journal of Fashion Marketing and Management*, *14*(3), 412–428. doi:10.1108/13612021011061861

Kim, S., Choi, S., Agrusa, J., Wang, K. C., & Kim, Y. (2010). The role of family decision makers in festival tourism. *International Journal of Hospitality Management*, *29*(2), 308–318. doi:10.1016/j.ijhm.2009.10.004

Kjeldgaard, D., & Askegaard, S. (2006). The Glocalization of Youth Culture. The Global Youth Segment as Structures of Common Difference. *The Journal of Consumer Research*, *33*(2), 231–247. doi:10.1086/506304

Klein, G. (2007). *Strategic Marketing*. GRIN Verlag.

Knox, S. (2012). Cerebral advocates: How people are wired to share and advocate. *WOMMA*. Retrieved from http://womma.org/word/tag/creative-wom-ideas/page/2/

Ko, N. (2013). Luxury brand marketing: designer extension. *Warc*. Retrieved January 3, 2015, from http://www.warc.com/Content/ContentViewer.aspx?MasterContentRef=2f8b3502-acd5-4460-91e7-f1af73745fd8&CID=A100570&PUB=ADMAP

Ko, E., & Megehee, C. M. (2012). Fashion marketing of luxury brands: Recent research issues and contributions. *Journal of Business Research*, *65*(10), 1395–1398. doi:10.1016/j.jbusres.2011.10.004

Kollock, P., & Smith, M. (1996). Managing the virtual commons – co-operation and conflict in computer communities. In Computer-mediated communication: Linguistic, social, and cross-cultural perspectives. John Benjamins.

Kondrashova, I. (2012). *Digital by design. WOMMA*. Retrieved from http://allthings.womma.org/tag/digital/

Korean Federation of Textile Industries. (2012). *Annual reports of "Korean Fashion Market Trends"*. Prentice-Hall.

Kostecki, E. (2005). *Brand Extension to the Youth and Young Adult Markets*. Retrieved online 19th March 2009, from http://w4.stern.nyu.edu/emplibrary/Erin_Kostecki_honors_2005.pdf

Kotler, P., Adam, S., Denize, S., & Armstrong, G. (2009). Principles of Marketing (4th ed.). Pearson Education.

Kotler, P., Kartajaya, H., & Setiawan, I. (2010). *Marketing 3.0*. John Wiley & Sons. doi:10.1002/9781118257883

Kozinets, R. V., Sherry, J. F., DeBerry-Spence, B., Duhacheck, A., Nuttavuthisi, K., & Storm, D. (2002). Themed Flagship Brand Stores in the new Millenium: Theory, Practice, Prospect. *Journal of Retailing*, *78*(1), 17–29. doi:10.1016/S0022-4359(01)00063-X

Krueger, R. A. (1998). *Analysing & Reporting Focus Group Discussions (Focus Group Kit 6)*. Sage Publications.

Krueger, R. A., & Casey, M. A. (2009). *Focus Groups – A Practical Guide for Applied Research* (4th ed.). Sage Publications.

Krugman, D. M., Reid, L. N., Dunn, S. W., & Barban, A. M. (1994). *Advertising: Its Role in Modern Marketing*. Fort Worth, TX: Dryden Press.

Kwon, W. S., & Noh, M. (2010). The influence of prior experience and age on mature consumers' perceptions and intentions of internet apparel shopping. *Journal of Fashion Marketing and Management*, *14*(3), 335–349. doi:10.1108/13612021011061825

L'Oreal Luxury Products Division. (n.d.a). *Dossiers of fragrances training courses*. Author.

L'Oreal Luxury Products Division. (n.d.b). *Press Kits of fragrances launches*. Author.

LaFerle, C., Edwards, S. M., & Lee, W. N. (2000). Teen's use of traditional media and the Internet. *Journal of Advertising Research*, *40*(3), 55–66. doi:10.2501/JAR-40-3-55-65

Lancaster, C. (2014). *Content marketing: turn content into powerful marketing tool*. London: Pogo Book Publishing.

Lansberg, I. (1988). The Succession Conspiracy. *Family Business Review*, *1*(2), 119–143. doi:10.1111/j.1741-6248.1988.00119.x

Lanzar, J., Feng, J. H., & Hochheiser, H. (2012). *Research Methods in Human-Computer Interaction*. John Wiley & Sons Ltd.

Lauterborn, R. (1990). *New marketing litany: 4Ps passé; 4Cs take over*. New York. *Advertising Age*.

Leal, G., Pasinato, A., Hor-Meyll, L. F., & Pessôa, L. A. (2013). Influence of virtual communities in purchasing decisions: The participants' perspective. *Journal of Business Research*, *67*(5), 882–890. doi:10.1016/j.jbusres.2013.07.007

Lee, J. (2006). Family Firm Performance: Further Evidence. *Family Business Review*, *19*(2), 103–114. doi:10.1111/j.1741-6248.2006.00060.x

Lee, J. (2012). What is K in K-pop? South Korean popular music, the culture industry and national identity. *Korean Observer*, *43*(3), 339–363.

Lee, M. Y., & Oh, K. Y. (2006). An exploratory study on brand personality: The case of a traditional casual brand in Korea. *Journal of Fashion Business*, *10*(6), 79–90.

Lent, R. (2009). *Selling Luxury: Connect with Affluent Customers, Create Unique Experiences Through Impeccable Service and Close Sale*. John Wiley & Sons.

Levinson, H. (1971). Conflicts That Plague the Family Business. *Harvard Business Review*, *49*, 90–98.

Levy, M., & Weitz, B. A. (2006). *Retailing Management*. New York: McGraw-Hill/Irwin.

Li, D. C. (2011). Online social network acceptance: A social perspective. *Internet Research*, *21*(5), 562–580. doi:10.1108/10662241111176371

Lieb, R. (2011). *Content Marketing: think like a publisher. How to use content to market online and in social media*. Indianapolis, IN: Que Publishing.

Lie, J. (2012). What is the K in K-pop? South Korean Popular Music, the culture Industry, and National Identity. *Korean Observer*, *43*(3), 339–363.

Li, G., Li, G., & Kambele, Z. (2012). Luxury fashion brand consumers in China: Perceived value, fashion lifestyle, and willingness to pay. *Journal of Business Research*, *65*(10), 1516–1522. doi:10.1016/j.jbusres.2011.10.019

Lin, C. A., & Atkis, D. J. (2012). *Communication Technology and Social Change: Theory and Implications*. New York: Routledge.

Lin, L., & Chen, Y. (2009). A study on the influence of purchase intentions on repurchase decisions: The moderating effects of reference groups and perceived risks. *Tourism Review*, *64*(3), 28–48. doi:10.1108/16605370910988818

Linn, M. (2012). *A Field Guide to the 4 Types of Content Marketing Metrics*. Retrieved 15 November 2014 from www.contentmarketinginstitute.com

Littunen, H., & Hyrsky, K. (2000). The entrepreneurial stage in Finish family and nonfamily firms. *Family Business Review, 13*(1), 41–54. doi:10.1111/j.1741-6248.2000.00041.x

Liu, F., Li, J., Mizerski, D., & Soh, H. (2012). Self-congruity, brand attitude, and brand loyalty: A study on luxury brands. *European Journal of Marketing, 46*(7/8), 922–937. doi:10.1108/03090561211230098

Liu, S., Perry, P., Moore, C., & Warnaby, G. (2015). The Standardization-Localization Dilemma of Brand Communications for Luxury Fashion Retailers' Internationalization into China. *Journal of Business Research.*

Liu, Z., Liu, L., & Li, H. (2012). Determinants of information retweeting in microblogging. *Internet Research, 4*(22), 443–466. doi:10.1108/10662241211250980

Lockstrom, M. (2007). *Low-Cost Country Sourcing: Trends and Implications.* DUV.

Louis, H. (2002). Young Korean consumers wield spending power. *Ad Age Global, 2*(9), 6.

Lucintel Report. (2012). Available at http://www.lucintel.com/market_research_reports.aspx last accessed 02/10/14

Luck, D. (2008). *CIM Coursebook Assessing the Marketing Environment.* Butterworth-Heinemann.

Lukkarinen, S., & Wei, X. (2012). *Luxury consumer behaviour-a comparative case study of emerging luxury markets in China and Finland.* The Swedish School of Textiles, University of Boras.

Luxury Goods Worldwide Market Study. (2011). Bain & Cuneo. Available at: www.bain.com

LVMH. (2005). *Annual Report 2004.* Retrieved from http://www.lvmh.com/comfi/pdf_gbr/ra_abrege_2004_gbr.pdf

Macchi, J. (2011). *Lusso 2.0.* Milano: Lupetti.

Ma, D. (2010). *Luxury shopping behaviour of Chinese consumers.* China Europe International Business School.

Malhotra, N. (2007). *Marketing Research: An Applied Orientation* (5th International Edition). Pearson Prentice Hall. doi:10.1108/S1548-6435(2007)3

Malthouse, E. C., Haenlein, M., Skiera, B., Wege, E., & Zhang, M. (2013). Managing Customer Relationships in the Social Media Era: Introducing the Social CRM House. *Journal of Interactive Marketing, 27*(4), 270–289. doi:10.1016/j.intmar.2013.09.008

Mandel, N., Petrova, P. K., & Cialdini, R. B. (2006). Images of success and the preference for luxury brands. *Journal of Consumer Psychology, 16*(1), 57–69. doi:10.1207/s15327663jcp1601_8

Markus, H. R., & Kitayama, S. (1991). Culture and self: Implications for cognition, emotion and motivation. *Psychological Review, 98*(2), 224–253. doi:10.1037/0033-295X.98.2.224

Martínez Moreno, O.C., Ruiz Andrade, J.G., & Lozano Ramírez, Mª C., & Verján Quiñones, R. (2015). El comportamiento del consumidor en internet bajo el modelo psicológico social de Veblen. *Revista Global de Negocios, 3*(5), 101–112.

Martínez-Selva, J. M., Sánchez-Navarro, J. P., Bechara, A., & Román, F. (2006). Mecanismos cerebrales de la toma de decisiones. *Revista de Neurologia, 42*(7), 411–418. PMID:16602058

Martin, K., & Todorov, I. (2010). How digital platforms be harnessed in 2010, and how will they change the way people interact with brands? *Journal of Interactive Advertising, 10*(2), 61–66. doi:10.1080/15252019.2010.10722170

Matthews, C. H., Moore, T. W., & Fialko, A. S. (1999). Succession in the Family Firm: A Cognitive Categorization Perspective. *Family Business Review, 12*(2), 159–170. doi:10.1111/j.1741-6248.1999.00159.x

Matthews, C., Moore, T. W., & Fialko, A. S. (1999). Succession in Family Firms: A Cognitive Organization Perspective. *Family Business Review*, *12*(12).

Matthiesen, I., & Phau, I. (2005). The 'HUGO BOSS' Connection: Achieving Global Brand Consistency across Countries. *Brand Management*, *12*(5), 325–338. doi:10.1057/palgrave.bm.2540229

McCharty, E. J. (1964). *Basic Marketing: A Managerial Approach* (2nd ed.). Homewood: Irwin, Homewood.

McCracken, G. (1989). Who is the Celebrity Endorser? Cultural Foundations of the Endorsement Process. *The Journal of Consumer Research*, *16*(3), 310–321. doi:10.1086/209217

McNabb, D. (2010). *Research Methods for Political Science: Quantitative and Qualitative Approaches.* M.E. Sharp, Inc.

Megehee, C. M., & Spake, D. F. (2012). Consumer enactments of archetypes using luxury brands. *Journal of Business Research*, *65*(10), 1434–1442. doi:10.1016/j.jbusres.2011.10.009

Micelotta, E. R., & Raynard, M. (2011). Concealing or Revealing the Family? Corporate Brand Identity Strategies in Family Firms. *Family Business Review*, *20*(10), 1–20.

Milas, G., & Mlacic, B. (2007). Brand personality and human personality: Findings from ratings of familiar Croatian brands. *Journal of Business Research*, *60*(6), 620–626. doi:10.1016/j.jbusres.2006.06.011

Miller, D., & Le Breton-Miller, I. (2005). *Managing for the Long Run: Lessons in Competitive Advantage from Great Family Businesses.* Boston: Harvard Business Press.

Miller, K. (2013). Hedonic customer responses to fast fashion and replicas. *Journal of Fashion Marketing and Management*, *2*(17), 160–174.

Mooij, M. (2011). *Consumer Behaviour and Culture: Consequences for Global Marketing and Advertising* (2nd ed.). Sage.

Moore, C. M., Doherty, A. M., & Doyle, S. A. (2010). Flagship Stores as a Market Entry Method: the Perspective of Luxury Fashion Retailing. *European Journal of Marketing, 44*(1(2), 139-161.

Moorley, C. R., & Chinn, T. (2014). Nursing and Twitter: Creating an online community using hashtags. *Collegian (Royal College of Nursing, Australia)*, *21*(2), 103–109. doi:10.1016/j.colegn.2014.03.003 PMID:25109208

Mosca, F., Casalegno, C., & Feffin, A. (2013, October*). Nuovi modelli di comunicazione nei settori dei beni di lusso: un'analisi comparata.* Paper X Convegno della Scuola Italiana di Marketing, Milano.

Mosca, F. (2008). Market-driven management in fashion and luxury industries. *Symphonya. Emerging Issues in Management*, *1*, 53–78.

Mosca, F. (2010). *Il marketing dei beni di lusso*. Milano: Pearson Italia.

Mosca, F. (2010). *Marketing dei beni di lusso*. Milano: Pearson.

Mosca, F. (2012). *Product concepts and heritage per i beni ad elevato valore simbolico*. Turin: Giappichelli.

Mosca, F. (2014). *Distribution Strategies in Luxury Markets: emerging trends*. London: McGraw-Hill.

Mosca, F., Bertoldi, B., & Giachino, C. (2015). Development Strategies for International Distribution in Luxury Industry. *International Journal of Management Cases*, *17*(3), 4–18.

Mosca, F., Casalegno, C., & Feffin, A. (2014, September). Last Marketing Communication Challenges In Luxury Brand Markets: A Comparative Analysis. In *7th Annual Conference of the EuroMed Academy of Business.*

Mosca, F., & Re, P. (2014). International Development Strategies of Luxury-Goods Players in China. *The China Business Review*, *13*(6), 367–381.

Moses, E. (2000). *The $ 100 billion allowance- Accessing the global teen market*. New York: John Wiley & Sons Inc.

Moskowitz, H., & Rabino, S. (1994). Sensory Segmentation: An Organizing Principle for International Product Concept Generation. *Journal of Global Marketing*, *8*(1), 73–93. doi:10.1300/J042v08n01_05

Mulyanegara, R. C., & Tsarenko, Y. (2009). Predicting brand preferences: An examination of the predictive power of personality and values in the Australian fashion market. *Journal of Fashion Marketing and Management*, *13*(3), 358–371. doi:10.1108/13612020910974492

Muniz, A. Jr, & O'Guinn, T. C. (2001). Brand Communities. *The Journal of Consumer Research*, *27*(4), 412–432. doi:10.1086/319618

Myungjin, L. (2005). *The Social Identities of the 2030 New Generation in South Korea*. Seoul: Samsung Economic Research Institute.

Nagashima, A. (1970). A Comparison of Japanese and U.S. attitudes towards foreign products. *Journal of Marketing*, *34*(1), 68–74. doi:10.2307/1250298

Nayeem, T. (2012). Cultural influences on consumer behaviour. *International Journal of Business and Management*, *7*(21), 2012. doi:10.5539/ijbm.v7n21p78

Neal, C., Quester, P., & Hawkins, D. (1999). *Consumer behaviour, implications for marketing strategy* (2nd ed.). McGraw Hill, Irwin.

Nelissen, R. M., & Meijers, M. H. (2011). Social benefits of luxury brands as costly signals of wealth and status. *Evolution and Human Behavior*, *32*(5), 343–355. doi:10.1016/j.evolhumbehav.2010.12.002

Nelli, R. P. (2012). *Branded Content Marketing*. Milan: Vita e Pensiero.

Newbert, S. L. (2007). Empirical research on the resource-based view of the firm: An assessment and suggestions for future research. *Strategic Management Journal*, *28*(12), 121–146. doi:10.1002/smj.573

Nia, A., & Zaichkowsky, J. L. (2000). Do counterfeits devalue the ownership of luxury brands? *Product and Brand Management*, *9*(7), 485–497. doi:10.1108/10610420010351402

Nicosia, F. M. (1970). *La decisión del consumidor*. Barcelona: Gustavo Gili.

Nielsen, J. (2011). *Participation inequality: Encouraging more users to contribute, 2006*. Available at http://www.nngroup.com/articles/participationinequality/

Nonnecke, B., & Preece, J. (2001). Why lurkers lurk. *Americas Conference on Information Systems*.

Nueno, J., & Quelch, J. (1998). The Mass Marketing of Luxury. *Business Horizons*, *41*(November-December), 61–68. doi:10.1016/S0007-6813(98)90023-4

Nurcahyo, B., & Nur'ainy, R., & Sariyati. (2011). Effect of intrinsic motivation on consumer brand evaluation: The influence of motive, involvement, and need for cognition. *Global Business and Management Research*, *3*(3), 231–246.

Nwankwo, S., Hamelin, N., & Khaled, M. (2014). Consumer values, motivation and purchase intention for luxury goods. *Journal of Retailing and Consumer Services*, *21*(5), 735–744. doi:10.1016/j.jretconser.2014.05.003

O'Cass, A., & Frost, H. (2002). Status brands: examining the effects of non-product related brand associations on status and conspicuous consumption. *Journal of Product and Brand Management, 11*(2).

O'Neal, C. R. (1989). The buyer-seller linkage in a just-in-time environment. *Journal of Purchasing and Materials Management*, *23*(1), 7–13.

O'Rourke, M. (2012). *Australian Luxury Market Nearing 1 Billion Dollars, MO Luxury.* Retrieved January 7, 2015, from http://www.moluxury.com.au/themodown/australian-luxury-marketing-nearing-1-billion-dollars/

Oeshkova, A. (2013). *Symbolic consumption of luxury goods: example of fashion luxury market in Russia.* (Master thesis). University of Kassel, Germany.

Okazaki, S. (2009). Social influence model and eletronic word of mouth. *International Journal of Advertising*, *28*(3), 439–472. doi:10.2501/S0265048709200692

Okonkwo, U. (2009). Sustaining the luxury brand on the Internet. *Journal of Brand Management*, *16*(5), 302-310.

Okonkwo, U. (2009). The luxury brand strategy challenge. *Journal of Brand Management,* (16), 287-289.

Okonkwo, U. (2007). *Luxury fashion branding: trends, tactics, techniques.* Palgrave Macmillan. doi:10.1057/9780230590885

Okonkwo, U. (2009). Sustaining the Luxury Brand on the Internet. *Journal of Brand Management*, *16*(2), 302–310. doi:10.1057/bm.2009.2

Okonkwo, U. (2009). The luxury brand strategy challenge. *Journal of Brand Management*, *16*(5/6), 287–289. doi:10.1057/bm.2008.53

Okonkwo, U. (2010). *Luxury Online. Styles, Systems, Strategies.* Basingstoke, UK: Palgrave Macmillan. doi:10.1057/9780230248335

Orton, J., & Weick, K. (1990). Loosely Coupled Systems: A Reconceptualization. *Academy of Management Review*, *15*(2), 203–223.

Osmonbekov, T., Bello, D. C., & Gilliland, D. I. (2009). The impact of e-business infusion on channel coordination, conflict and reseller performance. *Industrial Marketing Management*, *38*(7), 778–784. doi:10.1016/j.indmarman.2008.03.005

Ozen, H., & Engizek, N. (2014). Shopping online without thinking: Being emotional or rational? *Asia Pacific Journal of Marketing and Logistics*, *26*(1), 78–93. doi:10.1108/APJML-06-2013-0066

Paquot, T. (2007). *Elogio del lusso. Ovvero l'utilità dell'inutile.* Roma: Castelvecchi.

Pardo, P., & Tajeddini, K. (2013). Innovative Marketing Strategies in Family Owned Business: a Work in progress Framework to Integrate Social Media. In *Proceedings of the 6th Euromed Conference of the Euromed Academy of Business 'Confronting Contemporary Business Challenges through Management Innovation* (pp. 2714-2716). Nicosia: Euromed Press.

Parikh, A., & Deshmukh, S. (2013). Search Engine Optimization. *International Journal of Engineering Research & Technology*, *2*(11), 324–348.

Park, B., Ahn, S., & Kim, H. (2010). Blogging: Mediating impacts of flow on motivational behavior. *Journal of Research in Interactive Marketing*, *4*(1), 6–29. doi:10.1108/17505931011033533

Park, C., & Lessig, P. (1977). Students and Housewives –Differences in Susceptibility to Reference Group Influences. *The Journal of Consumer Research*, *4*(4), 102–110. doi:10.1086/208685

Parker, R. S., Hermans, C. M., & Schaefer, A. D. (2004). Fashion consciousness of Chinese, Japanese and American teenagers. *Journal of Fashion Marketing and Management*, *8*(2), 176–186.

Park, H. J., Rabolt, N., & Jeon, K. (2008). Purchasing global luxury brands among young Korean consumers. *Journal of Fashion Marketing and Management*, *12*(2), 244–259. doi:10.1108/13612020810874917

Park, M., & Lennon, S. J. (2009). Brand name and promotion in online shopping contexts. *Journal of Fashion Marketing and Management*, *13*(2), 149–160. doi:10.1108/13612020910957680

Parrott, G. R., Danbury, A. H., & Kanthavanich, P. (2015). Online behavior of luxury fashion brand advocates. *Journal of Fashion Marketing and Management: An International Journal*, *19*(4), 360–383. doi:10.1108/JFMM-09-2014-0069

Parsons, A. G. (2011). Atmosphere in fashion stores: Do you need to change? *Journal of Fashion Marketing and Management*, *15*(4), 428–445. doi:10.1108/13612021111169933

Passport. (2013). Luxury goods: global trends and prospects, Passport. *Euromonitor International.*

Pedersen, S. (2010). *Why Blog? Motivations for Blogging*. Chandos Publishing. doi:10.1533/9781780631714

Pellicelli, G. (2005). *Il marketing*. Milano: Wolters Kluwer.

Peng Cui, A., Wajda, T., & Walsh, M. (2015). Luxury Brands in Emerging Markets: A Case Study on China. *Entrepreneurship in International Marketing*, *25*, 287–305.

Perrey, J., & Spillecke, D. (2011). *Retail Marketing and Branding: A Definitive Guide to Maximising ROI*. John Wiley and Sons.

Petty, R. E., Cacioppo, J. T., & Schumann, D. (1983). Central and Peripheral Routes to Advertising Effectiveness: The Moderating Role of Involvement. *The Journal of Consumer Research*, *10*(2), 135–146.

Pew Research Internet Project. (2013). *Social Networking Fact Sheet*. Available at: http://www.pewinternet.org/fact-sheets/social-networking-factsheet/

Phan, M. (2011). Do Social Media Enhance Consumer's Perception and Purchase Intentions of Luxury Brands? *Vikalpa*, *36*(1), 81–84.

Phau, I., & Leng, Y. S. (2008). Attitudes toward domestic and foreign luxury brand apparel. *Journal of Fashion Marketing and Management*, *12*(1), 68–89. doi:10.1108/13612020810857952

Phau, I., & Prendergast, G. (2000). Consuming luxury brands: The relevance of the 'Rarity Principle'. *Journal of Brand Management*, *8*(2), 122–138. doi:10.1057/palgrave.bm.2540013

Pihl, C. (2014). Brands, community and style – exploring linking value in fashion blogging. *Journal of Fashion Marketing and Management*, *18*(1), 3–19. doi:10.1108/JFMM-10-2013-0108

Pinder, C. C. (1998). *Work motivation in organisational behaviour*. Upper Saddle River, NJ: Prentice Hall.

Plunkett, W. J. (2010). *Plunkett's Apparel & Textiles Industry Almanac 2010: The Only Comprehensive Guide to Apparel Companies and Trends*. Houston, TX: Plunkett Research, Ltd.

Porter, M., & Kramer, M. (2011). Creating Shared Value. How to reinvent capitalism and unleash a wave of innovation and growth. *Harvard Business Review*, *89*(1/2), 62–77.

Poza, E. (2007). Family business (2nd ed.). Mason, OH: Thompson.

Prandelli, E., & Verona, G. (2011). *Vantaggio competitivo in Rete: dal Web 2.0 al Cloud Computing*. Milan: McGraw-Hill.

Prayag, G., & Hosany, S. (2014). When Middle East Meets West: Understanding The Motives and Perceptions of Young Tourists From United Arab Emirates. *Tourism Management*, *40*, 35–45. doi:10.1016/j.tourman.2013.05.003

Predergast, G., & Wong, C. (2003). Parental influence on the purchase of luxury brands of infant apparel: An exploratory study in Hong Kong. *Journal of Consumer Marketing*, *20*(2).

Puddick, M., & Menon, P. (2012). Contemporary lustre: marketing luxury brands in India. *Warc*. Retrieved January 5, 2015, from https://www.warc.com/Content/ContentViewer.aspx?MasterContentRef=80ec1950-9867-49bd-9b77-f79e96017bc7&CID=A99837&PUB=ATTICUS

Pulizzi, J. (2012). *Six Useful Content Marketing Definitions*. Retrieved 21 February 2015 from http://contentmarketinginstitute.com/2012/06/contentmarketing-definition/

Pulizzi, J. (2012). The Rise of Storytelling as the New Marketing. *Publishing Research Quarterly*, *28*(2), 116–123. doi:10.1007/s12109-012-9264-5

Pulizzi, J. (2014). *Epic content marketing*. London: Mc Graw Hill.

Pulizzi, J., & Barrett, N. (2009). *Get content. Get customers*. New York: McGraw Hill.

Pyong, P. (1989). Textbooks for Asian American studies. *Amerasia Journal*, *15*(1), 259–266. doi:10.17953/amer.15.1.7205748t27m84q54

Raacke, J., & Bonds-Raacke, J. (2008). MySpace and Facebook: Applying the uses and gratifications theory to exploring friend-networking sites. *Cyberpsychology & Behavior*, *11*(2), 169–174. doi:10.1089/cpb.2007.0056 PMID:18422409

Rahimia, F., & Hassanzadeh, J. (2013). The impact of website content dimension and e-trust on e-marketing effectiveness: The case of Iranian commercial saffron corporations. *Information & Management*, *50*(5), 240–247. doi:10.1016/j.im.2013.04.003

Rakic, R., Beba, R., & Mira, R. (2014). Digital Content Marketing for organizations as buyers. *Ekonomika. Journal of Economic Theory and Practice and Social Issues*, *1*, 109–123.

Ramos, R. (2014). *Content Marketing: insider's secret to online sales and lead generation.* Expert Publishing.

Rancati, E. & Gordini N. (2015a). Gli strumenti di misurazione delle strategie di content marketing: un confronto tra imprese italiane e inglesi. *Mercati e competitività*, *1*, 45-74.

Rancati, E., & Gordini, N. (2015b), Content marketing: conceptualizing and measuring. Evidence from a sample of Italian firms. In *Proceedings of the 44th EMAC Conference: Collaboration in Research.*

Rancati, E., & Gordini, N. (2014). Content marketing metrics: Theoretical aspects and empirical evidence. *European Scientific Journal*, *10*(34), 92–104.

Rangaswamy, A., & Van Bruggen, G. (2005). Opportunities and challenges in multichannel marketing: An introduction to the special issue. *Journal of Interactive Marketing*, *19*(2), 5–11. doi:10.1002/dir.20037

Re, P. G., Giacosa, E., Giachino, C., & Stupino, M. (2014). The management of innovation in the wine business. In *Proceedings of 2nd International Symposium Systems Thinking for a Sustainable Economy. Advancements in Economic and Managerial Theory and Practice* (pp. 1-17). Rome: Business Laboratory System.

Research Report. (2013). *China luxury apparel and accessories market report, 2012-2015.* MOZ. Retrieved January 7, 2015, from http://www.researchmoz.us/china-luxury-apparel-and-accessories-market-report-2012-2015-report.html?vsmaid=505

Researchandmarkets. (2005). *Glassware Market Report 2005*. Retrieved online 19th March 2009, from http://72.14.235.132/custom?q=cache:bkESGTvpfrcJ:www.researchandmarkets.com/reports/314492/glassware_market_report_2005.pdf+buying+behaviour+young+tableware&cd=4&hl=en&ct=clnk&gl=in&client=pub-3796354395625809

Rettberg, J. W. (2008). *Blogging*. Polity Press.

Reynolds, R. A., Woods, R., & Baker, J. D. (2007). *Handbook of Research on Electronic Surveys and Measurements*. Idea Group Reference. doi:10.4018/978-1-59140-792-8

Reynolds, W. H. (1968). Cars and clothing: Understanding fashion trends. *Journal of Marketing*, *32*(3), 44–49. doi:10.2307/1249761

Richins, M. L., & Dawson, S. (1992). A consumer values orientation for materialism and its measurement: Scale development and validation. *The Journal of Consumer Research*, *19*(3), 303. doi:10.1086/209304

Ricotta, F. (2009). *Marketing multicanale*. Milan, Italy: Pearson.

Ries, A., & Ries, L. (2000). *The 11 immutable laws of internet branding*. London: HarperCollins Business.

Rifkin, J. (2000). *L'era dell'accesso*. Milano, Italy: Mondadori.

Ritzer, G. (1999). *Enchanting and disenchanted world: revolutionizing the means of consumption*. Thousand Oaks, CA: Pine Forge Press.

Ritzer, G. (2000). *La religione dei consumi. Cattedrali, pellegrinaggi e riti dell'iperconsumismo*. Bologna: Il Mulino.

Ritzer, G., & Jurgenson, N. (2010). Production, consumption, prosumption: The nature of capitalism in the age of the digital "prosumer". *Journal of Consumer Culture*, 163–196.

Rivas, J. A., & Esteban, I. G. (2004). *Comportamiento del consumidor: decisiones y estrategia de marketing*. Esic Editorial.

Rix, P. (2011). *Marketing, A Practical Approach*. McGraw Hill Australia.

Roberts, F. (2014). *Inside India's challenging high-growth luxury market, Passport*. Eurompnitor International.

Roberts, J. A., & Manolis, C. (2000). Baby boomers and busters: An exploratory investigation of attitudes towards marketing, advertising and consumerism. *Journal of Consumer Marketing*, *17*(6), 481–499. doi:10.1108/07363760010349911

Roedder-John, D. (1999). Consumer socialization of children: A retrospective look at twenty-five years of research. *The Journal of Consumer Research*, *26*(December), 183–213. doi:10.1086/209559

Rogers, E. (2003). *Diffusion of Innovations* (5th ed.). The Free Press.

Rohwedder, C. (2004). Making Fashion Faster: As Knockoffs Beat Originals To Market, Designers Speed The Trip From Sketch to Store. *The Wall Street Journal*. Retrieved September 15, 2013, from http://www.kellogg.northwestern.edu/course/opns430/modules/supply_chain_management/wsjfastfashion.pdf

Rollet, M., Hoffmann, J., Coste-Manière, I., & Panchout, K. (2013). The concept of creative collaboration applied to the fashion industry. *Journal of Global Fashion Marketing*, *1*(4), 57–66. doi:10.1080/20932685.2012.753337

Roll, M. (2005). *Asian brand strategy: how Asia builds strong brands*. Palgrave Macmillan. doi:10.1057/9780230513068

Romano, D. (1988). *Immagine, marketing e comunicazione*. Bologna, Italy: Il Mulino.

Rosenblum, P. (2015). Fast Fashion Has Completely Disrupted Apparel Retail. *Forbes*. Retrieved June 30, 2015, from http://www.forbes.com/sites/paularosenblum/2015/05/21/fast-fashion-has-completely-disrupted-apparel-retail/

Rose, R., & Pulizzi, J. (2011). *Managing Content Marketing. The real-world guide for creating passionate subscribers to your brands*. Cleveland, OH: CMI Books.

Ross, J., & Harradine, R. (2011). Fashion value brands: The relationship between identity and image. *Journal of Fashion Marketing and Management, 15*(3), 306–325. doi:10.1108/13612021111151914

Rotsztein, B. (2014). *Content marketing ideas*. London: Creative Force Publishing.

Rowley, J. (2008). Understanding digital Content Marketing. *Journal of Marketing Management, 24*(5-6), 517–540. doi:10.1362/026725708X325977

Rudat, A., Buder, J., & Hesse, F. W. (2014). Audience design in Twitter: Retweeting behavior between informational value and followers' interests. *Computers in Human Behaviour*, (35), 132-139c.

Ruiz de Maya, S., & Grande Esteban, I. (2013). *Casos de comportamiento del consumidor: Reflexiones para la dirección de marketing*. Esic Editorial.

Ryan, D., & Jones, C. (2009). *Understanding Digital Marketing – Marketing Strategies for engaging the digital generation*. London: Kogan Page Limited.

Sacerdote, E. (Ed.). (2006). *La strategia retail nella moda e nel lusso*. Milano: Franco Angeli.

Salsberg, B. (2010). The new Japanese consumer. *The McKinsey Quarterly*.

Salzman, M. (2009). *Boomers and the Future of Luxury Brands*. Retrieved online 19th March 2009, from http://boomers.typepad.com/boomers/2009/01/boomers-and-thefuture-of-luxury-brands.html

Samsung Corporate Report. (2012). Available on http://sgsg.samsung.com/c/pdf/Cheil%20Industries.pdf

Sang-Hun, C. (2008, June 16). Korea's New Generation of 'Web 2.0' protesters. *International Herald Tribune*, p. 14.

Sapsford, R. (1999). *Survey Research*. Sage Publications.

Saunders, M., Lewis, P., & Thornhill, A. (2009). *Research Methods for Business Students*. Harlow, UK: Pearson Education Ltd.

Saviolo, S., & Testa, S. (2005). *Le aziende del sistema moda*. Milano: Etas.

Schiff, J. (2007). *How to Market to Teens: Keep It Real and Simple*. Retrieved from http://www.ecommerce-guide.com

Schiffman, L. G., Hansen, H., & Kanuk, L. L. (2008). *Consumer Behaviour: A European Outlook*. Harlow, UK: Prentice Hall FT.

Schimidt, J. B., & Spreng, R. A. (2006). A proposed model of external consumer information search. *Journal of the Academy of Marketing Science, 24*(3), 246–256. doi:10.1177/0092070396243005

Schlosser, A. E. (2007). Learning through Virtual Product Experience: The Role of Imagery on True Versus False Memories. *The Journal of Consumer Research, 33*(3), 337–383.

Schultz, D. E. (1992). Integrated marketing communications. *Journal of Promotion Management, 1*(1), 99–104. doi:10.1300/J057v01n01_07

Schultz, D. E., Tannenbaum, S. I., & Lauterborn, R. F. (1993). *Integrated Marketing Communications*. Chicago: NTC Business.

Scott, M. D. (2014). *Le nuove regole del marketing. Come usare social media, video online, app mobile, blog, comunicati stampa e marketing virale per raggiungere i clienti*. Milan: Hoepli.

Sekora, J. (1977). *Luxury: the concept in western thought, Eden to Smollett*. Johns Hopkins University Press.

Seo, Y., & Buchanan-Oliver, M. (2015). Luxury Branding: The Industry, Trends, and Future Conceptualisations. *Asia Pacific Journal of Marketing and Logistics*, *27*(1), 82–98. doi:10.1108/APJML-10-2014-0148

Seringhaus, F. H. R. (2002). *Cross-cultural exploration of Global Brands and the Internet*. retrieved online 19th March 2009, from http://www.impgroup.org/uploads/papers/504.pdf

Sethi, P. (1971). Comparative Cluster Analysis for World Markets. *JMR, Journal of Marketing Research*, *8*(3), 348–354. doi:10.2307/3149574

Sethi, P., & Holton, R. (1973). Country Typologies for the Multinational Corporation: A New Basic Approach. *California Management Review*, *15*(3), 105–118. doi:10.2307/41164444

Shankar, V., Inman, J. J., Mantrala, M., Kelley, E., & Rizley, R. (2011, July). Innovations in Shopper Marketing: Current Insights and Future Research Issues. *Journal of Retailing*, *87*(1), S29–S42. doi:10.1016/j.jretai.2011.04.007

Shankar, V., & Malthouse, E. C. (2006). Moving Interactive Marketing Forward. *Journal of Interactive Marketing*, *20*(1), 2–4. doi:10.1002/dir.20057

Shankar, V., Smith, A., & Rangaswamy, A. (2003). Customer satisfaction and loyalty in online and offline environments. *International Journal of Research in Marketing*, *20*(2), 153–175. doi:10.1016/S0167-8116(03)00016-8

Shankar, V., & Yadav, M. S. (2010). Emerging Perspectives on marketing in a Multichannel and Multimedia Retailing Environment. *Journal of Interactive Marketing*, *24*(2), 55–57. doi:10.1016/j.intmar.2010.02.003

Shanker, M., & Astrachan, J. (1996). Myth and Realities: Family Business Contribuion to US economy – A Framework for Assessing Family Business Statitics. *Family Business Review*, *9*(2), 107–123. doi:10.1111/j.1741-6248.1996.00107.x

Shen, Ch., & Chiou, J. (2009). The effect of community identification on attitude and intention toward a blogging community. *Internet Research*, *19*(4), 393–407. doi:10.1108/10662240910981362

Sheng, J., Song, L., Wang, Q., & Wang, J. (2012). *The relationship between the willingness of buying counterfeit goods and consumer personality traits, ICPM-2012*. Crisis Management in the Time of Changing World.

Sheth, J. N., Mittal, B., & Newman, B. (1999). *Customer behaviour: consumer behaviour and beyond*. Fort Worth, TX: Dryden Press.

Sheth, N. J., & Mittal, B. (2004). *Consumer behaviour: a managerial perspective* (2nd ed.). South Western Publishing Company.

Shiffman, L., O'Cass, A., Paladino, A., & Carlson, J. (2014). *Consumer behaviour*. Pearson Australia.

Shim, D. B. (2011). *Waxing the Korean Wave. Asia Research Institute*. Working Paper Series, nº. 158.

Shiseido Spain (2015). *Reports on the Spanish market of luxury fragrances*. Author.

Shukla, P. (2012). The influence of value perception on luxury purchase intentions in developed and emerging markets. *International Marketing Review*, *29*(6), 574–596. doi:10.1108/02651331211277955

Silverman, D. (2012). *Interpreting Qualitative Data* (4th ed.). London, UK: Sage Publications Ltd.

Silverstein, M. J. (2006). *Caccia al tesoro*. Milano: Etas.

Silverstein, M. J., & Fiske, N. (2003). Lujo para las Masas. *Harvard Business Review. America Latina*, 3–11.

Silverstein, M. J., & Fiske, N. (2003). Luxury for the masses. *Harvard Business Review*, *81*(4), 48–57. PMID:12687919

Silverstein, M. J., Fiske, N., & Butman, J. (2008). *Trading up: Why consumers want new luxury goods--and how companies create them.* Penguin.

Simonin, B. L., & Ruth, J. A. (1998). Is a company known by the company it keeps? Assessing the spillover effects of brand alliances on consumer brand attitudes. *JMR, Journal of Marketing Research, 1*(35), 30–42. doi:10.2307/3151928

Singh, T., Veron-Jackson, L., & Cullinane, J. (2008). Blogging: A new play in your marketing game plan. *Business Horizons, 51*(4), 281–292. doi:10.1016/j.bushor.2008.02.002

Sirgy, M., Lee, D., Johar, J., & Tidwell, J. (2008). Effect of self-congruity with sponsorship on brand loyalty. *Journal of Business Research, 61*(10), 1091–1097. doi:10.1016/j.jbusres.2007.09.022

Sirmon, D.G. & Hitt, M.A. (2003). Managing resources: linking unique resources, management, and wealth creation in family firms. *Entrepreneurship Theory and Practice, 27*(4), 339-358.

Slater, V. (2014). *Content marketing: recycling and reuse. How your best online content can engage and attract new customers*. New York: i30 Media Corporation.

Smith, R. H. (2004). Envy and its transmutations. *The Social Life of Emotions*, 43-63.

Smith, R. H., & Kim, S. H. (2007). Comprehending envy. *Psychological Bulletin, 133*(1), 46–64. doi:10.1037/0033-2909.133.1.46 PMID:17201570

Solomon, M. (2006). *Consumer behaviour: A European perspective* (3rd ed.). Prentice Hall/Financial Times.

Solomon, M. R. (1983). The role of products as social stimuli: A symbolic interactionism perspective. *The Journal of Consumer Research, 10*(3), 319–329.

Solomon, M., Bamossy, G. J., Askegaard, S. T., & Hogg, M. K. (2013). *Consumer Behaviour – A European Perspective* (5th ed.). New York: Pearson Education.

Sonnenfeld, J. (1987). *Chief Executives at the Heroes or Villains of the Executive Process.* Paper presented at the meetings of the Academy of Management.

Sreejesh, S. (2012). Consumers' Evaluation of Co-Brand Extensions: The Effects of Concept Congruity on the Evaluation of Co-Branded Products, Analyzing the Moderating Role of Task Involvement. *International Management Review, 1*(8).

Sriviroj, S. (2007). *Purchasing Luxury Goods: consumer behaviour of international students in the UK.* Retrieved online 19th March 2009, from http://edissertations.nottingham.ac.uk/1585/1/07MSclixss24.pdf

Stanpa. (2015). *Información del Sector: Canales Vs Productos (2000-2014).* Retrieved from http://www.stanpa.es/estadistica/42/ZonaAsociados.aspx

Stanpa. (2015). *Panel de Consumo: Cierre 2014.* Retrieved from http://stanpa.com/estadistica/92/PaneldeConsumo%28Cierre2014%29.aspx

Stanyer, J. (2006). Online campaign communication and the phenomenon of blogging: An analysis of web logs during the 2005 British general election campaign. *Aslib Proceedings, 58*(5), 404–415. doi:10.1108/00012530610692357

StatisticBrain. (2014). *Twitter Statistics.* Available at http://www.statisticbrain.com/twitter-statistics/

Steenkamp, J.-B. (2001). The Role of National Culture in International Marketing Research. *International Marketing Review, 18*(1), 30–44. doi:10.1108/02651330110381970

Steenkamp, J.-B. E. M., Batra, R., & Alden, D. (2003). How perceived brand globalness creates brand value. *Journal of International Business Studies, 34*(1), 53–65. doi:10.1057/palgrave.jibs.8400002

Steenkamp, J.-B., & Ter Hofstede, F. (2002). International Market Segmentation: Issues and Perspectives. *International Journal of Research in Marketing*, *19*(3), 185–213. doi:10.1016/S0167-8116(02)00076-9

Steinberg, L. (1993). *Adolescence* (3rd ed.). New York: McGraw Hill.

Steinfield, C., Bouwman, H., & Adelaar, T. (2002). The dynamics of click-and-mortar electronic commerce: Opportunities and management strategies. *International Journal of Electronic Commerce*, *7*(1), 93–119.

Stella McCartney. (2015). *Adidas Spring Summer 15*. Retrieved June 30, 2015, from http://www.stellamccartney.com/gb/adidas_section

Stileman, P. (2009). *The extent to which social media changed the relationship between brand and consumer.* Retrieved from www.slideshare.net

Stokburger-Sauer, N. E., & Teichmann, K. (2013). Is luxury just a female thing? The role of gender in luxury brand consumption. *Journal of Business Research*, *66*(7), 889–896. doi:10.1016/j.jbusres.2011.12.007

Stolley, K. S. (2005). *The Basics of Sociology*. Greenwood Press.

Strauss, A., & Corbin, J. (1998). *Basics of Qualitative Research – Techniques and Procedures for Developing Grounded Theory* (2nd ed.). London, UK: Sage.

Stump, R., Gong, W., & Li, Z. (2008). Exploring the Digital Divide in Mobile-phone Adoption Levels across Countries: Do Population Socioeconomic Traits Operate in the Same Manner as Their Individual-level Demographic Counterparts? *Journal of Macromarketing*, *28*(4), 397–412. doi:10.1177/0276146708325386

Sun, G., D'Alessandro, S., & Johnson, L. (2014). Traditional culture, political ideologies, materialism and luxury consumption in China. *International Journal of Consumer Studies*.

Sun, N., Rau, P. and Ma, L. (2014). Understanding lurkers in online communities: A literature review. *Computers in Human Behaviour*, (38), 110-117.

Sung, G. (2010). *Korea's apparel industry*. U.S. Departament of Commerce. Online available on http://otexa.ita.doc.gov/webinars/Korea_Apparel_Industry_2010_FINAL.pdf

Svarney, P. B. (1995). *The New York Public Library's Science Desk Reference*. New York: Stonesong Press.

Swoboda, B., Pennemann, K., & Taube, M. (2014). Purchasing the Counterfeit: Antecedences and Consequences from Culturally diverse Countries. *European Retail Research*, *27*(I), 23–41. doi:10.1007/978-3-658-05313-0_2

Synovate. (2009). *Consumers skeptical about quality of 'Made in China' labels*. Retrieved from http://www.marketresearchworld.net/index.php?option=com_content&task=view&id=494&Itemid=77

Tagiuri, R., & Davis, J. A. (1996). Bivalent attitudes of the family firm. *Family Business Review*, *9*(2), 199–208. doi:10.1111/j.1741-6248.1996.00199.x

Tajfel, H., & Turner, J. C. (1985). The social identity theory of intergroup behaviour. In *Psychology of intergroup relations* (2nd ed.). Chicago: Nelson-Hall.

Tan, L. K. W., Na, J. C., & Theng, Y. L. (2011). Influence Detection between Blog posts through blog features, content analysis, and community identity. *Online Information Review*, *35*(3), 425–442. doi:10.1108/14684521111151450

Taplin, I. M. (2014). Who is to blame? A re-examination of Fast Fashion after the 2013 factory disaster in Bangladesh. *Critical Perspectives on International Business*, *10*(1/2), 72–83. doi:10.1108/cpoib-09-2013-0035

Tartaglia, A., & Marinozzi, G. (2006). *Il lusso ... magia e marketing*. Milano: Franco Angeli.

Tatt, K. E. (2010). *Factors influencing consumer buying behaviour of luxury branded goods*. University Sains Malaysia.

Teimourpour, B., & Hanzaee, K. (2011). The Impact of Culture on Luxury Consumption Behaviour Among Iranian Consumers. *Journal of Islamic Marketing*, *2*(3), 309–328. doi:10.1108/17590831111164822

Ter Hofstede, F., Steenkamp, J.-B., & Wedel, M. (1999). International Market Segmentation Based on Consumer-Product Relations. *JMR, Journal of Marketing Research*, *36*(1), 1–17. doi:10.2307/3151911

The Economist Intelligent Unit. (2013). *Asia: the Chinese are coming*. Retrieved January 6, 2015, from www.eiu.com/industry/article/.../asia-the-chinese-are-coming/2013-10-1

The Guardian. (2014). *Surge in purchases of counterfeit goods*. Retrieved January 8, 2015, from http://www.theguardian.com/money/2013/oct/02/counterfeit-goods-surge-uk

The Hofstede Center. (n.d.). Retrieved from http://geert-hofstede.com/countries.html

Thompson, C. J., & Arsel, Z. (2004). The Starbucks Brandscape and Consumers' (Anticorporate) Experiences of Glocalization. *The Journal of Consumer Research*, *31*(3), 631–642. doi:10.1086/425098

Thompson, C. J., Rindfleisch, A., & Zeynec, A. (2006). Emotional branding and the strategic value of the doppelganger brand image. *Journal of Marketing*, *70*(1), 50–64. doi:10.1509/jmkg.2006.70.1.50

Thrift, N. (2005). *Knowing Capitalism: Theory, Culture and Society*. Academic Press.

Toktali, N. (2008). Global Sourcing Insights from the Clothing Industry: The Case of Zara, a Fast Fashion Retailer. *Journal of Economic Geography*, (8): 21–38.

Tom, G., Garibaldi, B., Zeng, Y., & Pilcher, J. (1998). Consumer Demand for Counterfeit Goods. *Psychology and Marketing*, *15*(5), 405–421. doi:10.1002/(SICI)1520-6793(199808)15:5<405::AID-MAR1>3.0.CO;2-B

Toncar, M., & Fetscherin, M. (2012). A study of visual puffery in fragrance advertising. *European Journal of Marketing*, *46*(1), 52–72. doi:10.1108/03090561211189239

Treadaway, C., & Smith, M. (2010). *Facebook marketing: an hour a day*. Wiley Publishing.

Truong, Y. (2010). Personal aspirations and the consumption of luxury goods. *International Journal of Market Research*, *52*(5), 653–671. doi:10.2501/S1470785310201521

Truong, Y., & McColl, R. (2011). Intrinsic motivations, self-esteem, and luxury goods consumption. *Journal of Retailing and Consumer Services*, *18*(6), 555–561. doi:10.1016/j.jretconser.2011.08.004

Truong, Y., McColl, R., & Kitchen, P. J. (2009). New luxury brand positioning and the emergence of Masstige brands. *Journal of Brand Management*, *16*(5), 375–382. doi:10.1057/bm.2009.1

Tungate, M. (2009). *Luxury World: The Past, Present and Future of Luxury Brands*. London: Kogan Page Limited.

Twitter. (2014). *About Twitter*. Available: https://about.twitter.com/company,last accessed 18/06/14

Tynan, C., McKechnie, S., & Chhuon, C. (2010). Co-creating value for luxury brands. *Journal of Business Research*, *63*(11), 1156–1163. doi:10.1016/j.jbusres.2009.10.012

Uggla, H. (2004). The Brand Association Base: A conceptual model for strategically leveraging partner brand equity. *Brand Management*, *2*(12), 105–123. doi:10.1057/palgrave.bm.2540208

United Nations. (2000). World Population Prospects. *United Nations*. Available at: www.un.org

Unity Marketing. (2014). *Luxury report 2014: the ultimate six-year guide to the U.S. affluent consumer market.* Unity Marketing. Retrieved January 9, 2015, from http://www.unitymarketingonline.com/catalog/product_detail.php/pid=72~subid=1/index.html

Universal McCANN. (2009). *Power of the people: social media tracker.* Retrieved from www.slideshare.com

Urban, G., & Hauser, J. (1993). *Design and Marketing of New Products.* Prentice Hall.

Vaid, H. (2003). *Branding.* London: Cassel Illustrated.

Vaidyanathan, R., & Aggarwal, P. (2000). Strategic Brand Alliances: Implications of Ingredient Branding for National and Private Label Brands. *Journal of Product and Brand Management, 9*(4), 214–228. doi:10.1108/10610420010344013

Van de Ven, N., Zeelenberg, M., & Pieters, R. (2011). The envy premium in product evaluation. *The Journal of Consumer Research, 37*(6), 984–998. doi:10.1086/657239

Van Lieshout, L. (2014). *Content marketing for professionals.* London: CreateSpace Independent Publishing Platform.

Veblen, T. (1965). *The Theory of the Leisure Class. 1899.* AM Kelley.

Vel, K., Captain, A., Al-Abbas, R., & Al Hashemi, B. (2011). Luxury buying in the United Arab Emirates. *Journal of Business and Behavioural Sciences, 23*(3), 145–160.

Venkatesan, R., Kumar, V., & Ravishanker, N. (2007). Multichannel Shopping: Causes and Consequences. *Journal of Marketing, 71*(2), 114–132. doi:10.1509/jmkg.71.2.114

Venkatesh, R., & Chatterjee, R. (2006). Bundling, Unbundling, and pricing of multiform products: The case of magazine content. *Journal of Interactive Marketing, 20*(2), 54–78. doi:10.1002/dir.20059

Venter, E., Boshoff, C., & Maas, G. (2005). The influence of successor-related factors on the succession process in small and medium-sized family businesses. *Family Business Review, 18*(4), 283–303. doi:10.1111/j.1741-6248.2005.00049.x

Verhage, B., Dahringer, L., & Cundiff, E. (1989). Will a Global Strategy Work? An Energy Conservation Perspective. *Journal of the Academy of Marketing Science, 17*(2), 129–136. doi:10.1007/BF02723371

Verhoef, P. C., Lemon, K. N., Parasuraman, A., Roggeveen, A., Tsiros, M., & Schlesinger, L. A. (2009). Customer Experience Creation: Determinats, Dynamics and Management Strategies. *Journal of Retailing, 85*(1), 41–41. doi:10.1016/j.jretai.2008.11.001

Vescovi, T. (2007). *Il marketing e la Rete. La gestione integrata del Web nel business, Comunicazione, E-commerce, sales management, business to business.* Milan: Il Sole 24 Ore.

Vickers, J. S., & Renand, F. (2003). The marketing of luxury goods: An exploratory study–three conceptual dimensions. *The Marketing Review, 3*(4), 459–478. doi:10.1362/146934703771910071

Vigneron, F., & Johnson, L. (1999). A Review and a Conceptual Framework of Prestige-Seeking Consumer Behavior. *Academy of Marketing Science Review*, (1): 1–15.

Vigneron, F., & Johnson, L. W. (1999). A review and a conceptual framework of prestige-seeking consumer behavior. *Academy of Marketing Science Review, 1*(1), 1–15.

Vigneron, F., & Johnson, L. W. (1999). A review and a conceptual framework of prestige-seeking consumer behaviour. *Academy of Marketing Science Review, 1*, 1–15.

Vigneron, F., & Johnson, L. W. (1999). A review and a conceptual framework of prestige-seeking consumer behaviour. *Academy of Marketing Science Review, 9*(1), 1–14.

Vigneron, F., & Johnson, L. W. (2004). Measuring perceptions of brand luxury. *Journal of Brand Management, 11*(6), 484–506.

Vigneron, F., & Johnson, L. W. (2004). Measuring Perceptions of Brand Luxury. *Journal of Brand Management, 11*(6), 484–506. doi:10.1057/palgrave.bm.2540194

Villalonga, B., & Amit, R. (2006). How do family ownership, control and management affect firm value. *Journal of Financial Economics, 80*(2), 385–417. doi:10.1016/j.jfineco.2004.12.005

Villalonga, B., & Amit, R. (2009). Family Control of Firms and Industries. *Review of Financial Studies, 22*(8), 1–56. doi:10.1093/rfs/hhn080

Voller C. & Premo K. (2012). Scaling Up Social Media. *Strategy + Business, 68*, 16-18.

Voyer, B., & Tran, V. (2013). *Risks and benefits in selling luxury goods online: should Chanel, the icon of timeless fashion, open an e-boutique?* ESCP Europe, case study 3. Retrieved from www.casecenter.org

Walker, R. (2013). *China's luxury gift culture: dead or alive?*. Euromonitor International.

Wang, C. H., & Ha, S. (2011). Store attributes influencing relationship marketing: A study of department stores. *Journal of Fashion Marketing and Management, 15*(3), 326–344. doi:10.1108/13612021111151923

Wang, H. (2012). Six P's of youth social media from a young consumer's perspective. *Young Consumers: Insight and Ideas for Responsible Marketers, 13*(3), 303–317. doi:10.1108/17473611211261674

Wang, P. Z., & Waller, D. S. (2006). Measuring consumer vanity: A cross-cultural validation. *Psychology and Marketing, 23*(8), 665–687. doi:10.1002/mar.20123

Wang, Y., & Griskevicius, V. (2014). Conspicuous consumption, relationships, and rivals: Women's luxury products as signals to other women. *The Journal of Consumer Research, 40*(5), 834–854. doi:10.1086/673256

Wang, Y., Sun, S. J., & Song, Y. P. (2011). Chinese luxury consumers: Motivation, attitude and behaviour. *Journal of Promotion Management, 17*(3), 345–359. doi:10.1080/10496491.2011.596122

Ward, J. L. (1997). Growing the family business: Special challenges and best practices. *Family Business Review, 10*(4), 323–337. doi:10.1111/j.1741-6248.1997.00323.x

Washburn, J. H., Till, B. D., & Priluck, R. (2000). Co-branding: Brand equity and trial effects. *Journal of Consumer Marketing, 7*(17), 591–604. doi:10.1108/07363760010357796

Wedel, M., & Kamakura, W. (2002). Introduction to the Special Issue on Market Segmentation. *International Journal of Research in Marketing, 19*(3), 181–183. doi:10.1016/S0167-8116(02)00075-7

Wegrzyn, N. (2013). Luxury brand marketing: making a luxury brand. *Warc*. Retrieved January 10, 2015, from http://www.warc.com/Content/ContentViewer.aspx?MasterContentRef=218ee660-b9e6-487e-817b-caa9a23540fe&q=marketing+-+brands+and+branding+-+brand+strategy&CID=A100567&PUB=ADMAP

Weick, K. (1976). Educational Organizations as Loosely Coupled Systems. *Administrative Science Quarterly, 21*(1), 1–19. doi:10.2307/2391875

Weinberg, B. D., & Pehlivan, E. (2011). Social spending: Managing the social media mix. *Business Horizons, 54*(3), 275–282. doi:10.1016/j.bushor.2011.01.008

Widchardt, P. C. (2009). A status based motivation for behavioural altruism. *International Journal of Social Economics, 36*(8), 869–887. doi:10.1108/03068290910967127

Wiedmann, K. P., Hennings, N., & Siebels, A. (2007). Conceptualization and Propositions: Determinants of a Consumers' Luxury Value Perception. A Cross-cultural Framework. *Journal of Marketing Science*, (7).

Wiedmann, K.-P., Hennings, N., & Siebels, A. (2007). Measuring consumers' luxury value perception: A cross-cultural framework. *Academy of Marketing Science Review*, *7*, 1–21.

Wiedmann, K.-P., Hennings, N., & Siebels, A. (2009). Value-based segmentation of luxury consumption behaviour. *Psychology and Marketing*, *26*(7), 625–651. doi:10.1002/mar.20292

Williams, S. A., Terras, M. M., & Warwick, C. (2013). What do people study when they study Twitter? Classifying Twitter related academic papers. *The Journal of Documentation*, *3*(69), 384–410. doi:10.1108/JD-03-2012-0027

Willis, M. (2006). To Adapt ot to Standardise: Testing Asian Views about Purchasing Western Luxury Products in Seven Asian Locations. *Journal of East-West Business*, *12*(1), 65–94. doi:10.1300/J097v12n01_05

Winer, R. S. (2009). New Communications Approaches in Marketing: Issues and research directions. *Journal of Interactive Marketing*, *23*(2), 237–256. doi:10.1016/j.intmar.2009.02.004

Wolfinbarger, M., & Gilly, M. (2001). Shopping online for freedom, control and fun. *California Management Review*, *43*(2), 34–55. doi:10.2307/41166074

Wong, N. (1997). Suppose you own the world and no one knows? Conspicuous consumption, materialism and self. *Advances in Consumer Research. Association for Consumer Research (U. S.)*, *24*(1), 197–203.

Wong, N., & Ahuvia, A. (1998). Personal taste and family face: Luxury consumption in Confucian and Western societies. *Psychology and Marketing*, *15*(5), 423–441. doi:10.1002/(SICI)1520-6793(199808)15:5<423::AID-MAR2>3.0.CO;2-9

World Bank. (n.d.). *Indicators*. Retrieved from http://data.worldbank.org/indicator?display=default

World Economic Forum. (2013). *The Travel and Tourism Competitiveness Report 2013*. Author.

Wright Lee, M. (2011). Fashion Brands Seek New Technologies. *Mashable the Social Media Guide*. Available at: www.mashable.com

Wright Lee, M. (2011). Luxury Brands Seek Social Media Channel Integration. *Mashable the Social Media Guide*. Available at: www.mashable.com

Wright, K.B. (2005). Researching Internet-Based Populations: Advantages and Disadvantages of Online Survey Research, Online Questionnaire Authoring Software Packages, and Web Survey Services. *Journal of Computer-Mediated Communication, 10*(3).

WWD. (2010). *UGG Meets Jimmy Choo*. Retrieved October 10, 2013, from http://www.wwd.com/fashion-news/fashion-scoops/ugg-jimmy-choo-team-up-2409232

Wymbs, C. (2011). Digital marketing: The time for a new "academic major" has arrived. *Journal of Marketing Education*, *33*(2), 93–106. doi:10.1177/0273475310392544

Xiao, S. (2005). *What are the critical success factors for luxury goods companies looking to expand in China?* Retrieved online 19th March 2009, from http://www.bimba.org/ips/article.asp?articleid=399

Yang, K., & Young, A. P. (2009). The effects of customized site features on internet apparel shopping. *Journal of Fashion Marketing and Management*, *13*(1), 128–139. doi:10.1108/13612020910939923

Yaprak, A. (2008). Culture study in international marketing: A critical review and suggestions for future research. *International Marketing Review*, *25*(2), 215–229. doi:10.1108/02651330810866290

Yavas, U., Verhage, B., & Green, R. (1992). Global Consumer Segmentation versus Local Market Orientation: Empirical Findings. *Management International Review*, *32*(3), 265–273.

Yeh, Y., & Choi, S. (2011). MINI-lovers, maxi-mouths: An investigation of antecedents to eWOM intention among brand community members. *Journal of Marketing Communications*, *17*(3), 145–162. doi:10.1080/13527260903351119

Yeoman, I. (2007). Pricing trends in Europe's fashion industry. *Journal of Revenue and Pricing Management*, *6*(4), 287–290. doi:10.1057/palgrave.rpm.5160099

Yeoman, I. (2011). The Changing Behaviour of Luxury Consumption. *Journal of Revenue and Pricing Management*, *10*(1), 47–50. doi:10.1057/rpm.2010.43

Yi, S. (2013). Luxury brand marketing: socially affluent. *Warc*. Retrieved January 10, 2015, from https://www.warc.com/Content/ContentViewer.aspx?MasterContentRef=b242be78-9890-4506-87a9-cc4c1f4a4822&CID=A100571&PUB=ADMAP

Yoo, J., Choi, S., Choi, M., & Rho, J. (2014). Why people use Twitter: Social conformity and social value perspectives. *Online Information Review*, *38*(2), 265–283. doi:10.1108/OIR-11-2012-0210

Youniss, J., & Smollar, J. (1985). The individual and relations. In J. Youniss & J. Smollar (Eds.), *Adolescent relations with mothers, fathers and friends* (pp. 160–176). Chicago: University of Chicago Press.

Zhang, B. P., & Kim, J. H. (2013). Luxury fashion consumption in China: Factors affecting attitude and purchase intent. *Journal of Retailing and Consumer Services*, *20*(1), 68–79. doi:10.1016/j.jretconser.2012.10.007

Zhan, L., & He, Y. (2012). Understanding luxury consumption in China: Consumer perceptions of best-known brands. *Journal of Business Research*, *65*(10), 1452–1460. doi:10.1016/j.jbusres.2011.10.011

Zhou, T. (2011). Understanding online community user participation: A social influence perspective. *Internet Research*, *21*(1), 67–81. doi:10.1108/10662241111104884

Zollo, P. (1999). Not quite the TV generation. *American Demographics*, *21*(5), 35–37.

About the Contributors

Fabrizio Mosca is Bachelor of Business Management (University of Torino, Italy), MBA (University of Torino, Italy) and took a Ph.D. in Economics and Business Administration at Luigi Bocconi University, Milano, Italy. Fabrizio Mosca has written several articles and books on Strategic Luxury Management and Luxury Marketing. This topic is the main field of his research. Fabrizio Mosca is, presently, a professor at the Business Management Department of University of Torino, where he teaches Marketing, Marketing Advanced and Strategic Management. He is also involved in many different postgraduate and International Master programs, in the Luxury Master of Il Sole24Ore and in the doctoral program. He is also part of the Scuola di Amministrazione Aziendale, the Turin Business School of Management.

Rosalía Gallo is Bachelor of Arts (hons), MBA (IESE, Barcelona) and a Doctor in Economics and Business administration (UPC, Universidad Politécnica de Cataluña). Rosalía Gallo has written several articles and cases on Family Business. She has also contributed to different books. She has published articles on Marketing and teaching methodology and innovation, and has contributed to different congresses and seminars both with presentations and participating in discussion panels. Rosalía Gallo works as a consultant for companies (frequently Family Businesses) in marketing and Management. Rosalía Gallo is, presently, a professor at the Business Economics Department at Universitat Autònoma de Barcelona, where she teaches at the BBA program, in different postgraduate and International Master programs, and in the doctoral progam "Culture production and consumption" where she has taugh the course "Marketing arts and culture", as well the IDEM doctoral program where she has taught the course "Family business" She has also been part of the management the Economics and Business School at Universitat Autònoma de Barcelona.

* * *

Cesare Amatulli, PhD, is Assistant Professor of Marketing at the University of Bari and adjunct Professor of Trade and Retail Marketing at the LUISS University, Rome. He is author of articles appeared on some of the most prestigious journals in the marketing and consumer behavior fields, such as Journal of Business Research and Psychology & Marketing.

Bernardo Bertoldi teaches Marketing and Family Business Strategy at the Department of Management at the University of Turin, and Fundamental of Finance at the Escp-Europe. Bernardo Bertoldi works also as a consultant for companies and in particular for family businesses companies. His main research interests are family businesses and entrepreneurship and he has published a lot of articles and books on these topics. He is collaborator for the Sole24Ore for arguments linked with family business capitalism and the automotive sector.

Alexandru Capatina is PHd. Associate Professor at Dunarea de Jos University of Galati, Romania. His main research and teaching interests are focused on: Customer Relationship Management, Competitive Intelligence, Online Marketing.

Sonia Carcelén, Ph. D. (cum laude), Communication Sciences. Complutense University of Madrid, Spain (2001). Dissertation: Sales promotion as a strategic marketing tool. Marketing and Market Research Department. Professor of Marketing, Marketing and Research Department, Complutense University of Madrid, Spain (September 2000 – present). Research Project like a team leader and team member: She has collaborated on research project funded by private and institutional companies like Shiseido, General Council of Spanish Lawyers, ADT, Spanish Association of Advertising Agencies, Immigration Observatory of Community of Madrid, Ministry of Economics and Finance. Different publications in books, books chapters, journal articles and papers presented at meetings and International Congress. Research Fellowships in The Royal Complutense College, Harvard University. Cambridge (USA) (July-August 2010 and June-August 2012) and in Communications Department, Montevideo University (Uruguay) (August-September 2004).

Cecilia Casalegno, PhD in business administration, is a researcher and lecturer at the Department of Management, University of Turin. She teaches in Marketing, Firm Strategy and Communication courses at the School of Management, University of Turin. Her main fields of research concern the integrated communication and the leadership development strategy. She is author of national and international publications.

Mónica Díaz-Bustamante, PhD Degree in Economic and Business Sciences (Cum Laude) from Complutense University of Madrid and Degree in Economic and Business Sciences from Complutense University and Financial Studies University College (CUNEF) of Madrid. She has worked as Marketing Director and Marketing Manager in Luxury and Professional Divisions of L' Oréal Group, and as Marketing Director in Chantelle Group and Shiseido Group. During last years, she combines the teaching and academic activity with marketing and business development consultancy for different companies. In teaching she is professor of Marketing and Market Research Department in Complutense University of Madrid, in Villanueva University, and in CEU Postgraduate European Institute. She has also taught in the Carlos III University, in ICADE Business School and in Aliter International Business School. It is also relevant her participation in research projects (both in quality of main investigator as a team member) related to the new technologies and consumer behavior, and in international and national congresses and seminars of Marketing and Communication.

Taşkın Dirsehan joined the Faculty of Business Administration (lectured in English) in Marmara University as a marketing research assistant in February 2011. He received his BA in Business Administration from Galatasaray University in 2009, his MA in Production Management and Marketing from Marmara University and PhD in Marketing from Istanbul University. His research and teaching interests are in the areas of sustainability, international marketing, consumer behavior, brand management and marketing research. His research has been published in various national and international journals including Boğaziçi Journal Review of Social, Economic and Administrative Studies. He has also presented his research at various conferences including National Marketing Congress and International Strategic Management Conference.

Gemma García Ferrer, Ph.D. has her doctorate in Business Sciences from UAM (Spain) and Master in Health and Social Methodology of Behavioural Science (UAM, UCM, and UNED, Spain). Gemma García Ferrer also has a Bachelor degree in Business from UAM. Dr. García Ferrer has been dedicated to teaching and researching for over the last 18 years (it includes work in Business Environment and Psychology). Currently, Dr. García Ferrer is Professor of Market Research from URJC (Spain). Author of a book about Commercial Research (Last 2012, was republished its third revised and updated edition in Spain, and in 2013 was co-edited in Latin-America). García-Ferrer's studies in the field of commercial research, retail and consumer psychology have been shown in renowned National and International congress, and published in Scientific Journals as well.

Chiara Giachino is a researcher at the University of Turin, Department of Management. She teaches Marketing, Marketing business to business and Business Strategies. Her main research interests are family businesses, social media, innovation and entrepreneurship.

Elisa Giacosa received a Ph.D. in Business Administration in 2003 and she is currently an Assistant Professor in Business Administration at the Department of Management, University of Turin (Italy), where she teaches Financial Accounting and Net economy (undergraduate). She was Erasmus Visiting Professor in some foreign universities. Her research interests are in family businesses, crisis management, fashion firms, net economy and financial analysis, on which several international publications were focused. She is a Associate Fellow of the EuroMed Academy of Business.

Niccolò Gordini is Assistant Professor of Management at University of Milan-Bicocca (Milan, Italy). He held a PhD in Small Business Management at University of Florence (Italy) and he is qualified as Associate Professor of Management (Italian NSQ 2013). He is a member of the editorial board of several international management journals and reviewer for many international journals, international books and international conferences. He has published, as author or co-author, twenty research papers in international and national journals, seven book chapters, and two books.

Gianluigi Guido (Ph.D., University of Cambridge, UK) is Full Professor of Marketing and Marketing Research at the University of Salento, Lecce (Italy).

Ana Isabel Jimenez-Zarco is Associate Professor at Innovation and Marketing Area Open University of Catalunya) and Part-time professor at Marketing Department at ICADE, Pontificia of Comillas University. PhD in Economics and Business Sciences from the University of Castilla-la Mancha, Spain. She has a Post degree in Building Models in Ecology and Natural Resources Management from Politecnica University of Catalonia. Until 2002, she carried out her teaching and research activities in the Marketing

Area of the University of Castilla la Mancha, and during short periods in East Anglia University, Brighton University (UK) and Chapingo University (Mexico). From 2003 to 2006 she has been the co-director of the Master's Degree Programme in Marketing and Communication Management, and from 2006 to 2012 she was served as Programme Director of the Bachelor's Degree in Business Administration at UOC. As a researcher, her main areas of research interest concern innovation and entrepreneurship, and brand image and identity. She is author of several books and articles on these areas, and serves as a reviewer and associated editor of several international journals in the marketing area.

Yuping Li lectures in marketing at the School of Fashion and Textiles in the Royal Melbourne Institute of Technology (RMIT) University in Australia. Her teaching covers a wide range of marketing related subject areas, including advertising and promotion, consumer behaviour, strategic marketing and global marketing. Ms. Li has a Bachelors degree in Science from Beijing University in China and a Masters of Business Administration from Monash University in Australia. She has been an academic in Australia since 1993. She previously taught at Victoria University in Melbourne and also in China; and has lectured at the University of Turin. Her research interests are in the areas of advertising and promotion, international trade, global marketing and consumer behaviour. Ms Li takes consulting work in the fields of marketing, advertising and promotion, International trade and cross-cultural communication. She has received teaching awards from RMIT University and was awarded the 2010 RMIT TAFE Outstanding Teacher/Trainer of the Year for her excellence in teaching.

Lynsey Macdonald graduated from Glasgow Caledonian University with a Masters Degree in International Marketing in 2014. She previously studied at The University of Glasgow, graduating with an MA Honours Degree in Film and Television Studies in 2011. She has worked on social media projects with a number of companies in central Scotland over the past three years, with particular investment in the blogging and YouTube communites. Her key areas of interest in her academic work lie in the area of digital marketing, with a focus on social media, online communities, branding and blogging.

Irene García Medina, Bachelor of Communication Sciences (Universidad Complutense de Madrid, Spain) and Ph.D. in Marketing (University of Sophia - Antipolis, France) and International Relations (University of Vienna, Austria). As a teacher, Irene has previously taught Marketing and International Business Management at graduate level and master's degree in the Faculty of Business and Economics at the University of Madeira (Portugal), at University Pompeu Fabra (Spain) and at University of Vic (Spain). As a professional, she has worked as Marketing Director of the French company VTDIM, as Consultant for the Portuguese Chamber of Commerce, as Head of Communication and Promotion of CORDIS (European Commission, DGXIII, Luxembourg),...She has given lectures, seminars and workshops in the field of marketing in several countries and has published numerous articles and books.

Antonio Mileti is Assistant Professor of Business Management and Marketing at the University of Salento (Lecce, Italy). He holds a Master of Science (Master Recherche) in Marketing from CUOA (Vicenza, Italy), and a Ph.D. in Law and economics at the University of Bologna. Dr. Mileti has contributed in several national and international conferences and has published a number of articles in major referred journals.

Marta Minopoli is an Italian graduate in Management, specialised in Marketing and Entrepreneurship. She obtained her Bachelor degree in 2011 in Università Cattolica del Sacro Cuore, discussing a thesis about Experienced Marketing. In 2014 she graduated with full marks and distinction at Escp Europe Business School. Trilingual, Marta has gained several marketing experiences in six different countries and three continents. Her research interests center on analysing the product life cycle and the process of brands' revitalization.

Carme Moreno-Gavara is a Senior Marketing Manager professional with exceptional silks and experience in Research and e-Commerce Marketing. Carme has more than 8 years of marketing experience, and three as a Lecturer in Open University of Catalonia. She is an international marketer and a thought leader in digital marketing and multicultural marketing industry, especially in luxury fashion. She is specialist in Marketing Strategy, Digital Marketing (e-WOM), Multicultural Marketing, Consumer behavior, luxury brand. Degree in Economic and Business Science, Degree in Market Research (specializing in On-line Marketing) and, MBA in Business Management in the Knowledge Society. She also holds an Executive MBA in Fashion Retail Management, at the University of Barcelona. In 2012 she finished her studies in Luxury brand management, at London College of Fashion. In 2013 she went on to complete my qualification in PR, Digital Marketing & Social Media for fashion business at London College of Fashion.

Paola Peretti has more than 15 years experience in marketing and communication. She is specialized in digital marketing strategies with a strong international background. Mrs. Peretti is Italian and she lived and worked in Italy, France, Spain, United States and Sweden. She has a Ph.D in Marketing and she was Visiting Researcher at Northwestern University in Chicago and Stockholm School of Economics. She is still working with Prof. Sawhney at Kellogg School of Management, doing research around digital marketing and innovation for luxury brands. In her career Dr. Peretti has worked eight years in Milan mainly for major Italian publishing companies such as Rizzoli-Corriere della Sera (#1 Italian Newspaper), Mondadori and Condé Nast with increasing responsibilities and overview over activities ranging from product management, marketing, e-commerce, event management, corporate communication, PR, media planning. Then she moved to Chicago, U.S where she took a Master of Science in Integrated Marketing and Communication from Roosevelt University and she worked for Alberto Culver. After three years in Chicago Mrs. Peretti, back to Italy, joined the Natuzzi Group, Milan Office, has Chief Corporate Communication Officer, responsible to develop and manage two divisions: corporate communication, plus strategic marketing and business development (with a special focus on the digital marketing strategy worldwide). In 2010 she joined Fleishman-Hillard (an American marketing & pr agency), as Senior Vice President Digital Services (clients: 3M, Nestle, Rocca from Damiani Group, Firmenich, Bulgari, etc.) for Europe and finally in 2011 she was relocated to Sweden, Stockholm where she actually works for Electrolux as Digital Marketing, Manager responsible for Europe, Africa and Middle East. Dr. Peretti holds a Bachelor in Business Administration (Bocconi University - Milan), a Master of Science in International Management (Esade – Bacelona), plus a Master of Science in Integrated Marketing and Communication (Roosevelt – Chicago) and Ph.D. in Corporate Communication (major in Marketing). She won a prize in Sweden for best and innovative research in 2013. Author of two books: "Digital

Marketing" (2011, bestseller) and "Crowdfunding" (2014) she is also President and Founder of a non profit organization called "Crazy4Digital Marketing" that wants to inspire marketers around digital and at the same time collect financial resources to develop projects that will bring technology (e.g. we created Math Melodies – an app that can teach math to 1st to 5th grade blind students) to people with disabilities or special needs to give them the chance to have a better life.

Elisa Rancati is Assistant Professor of Marketing Department of Economics, Management and Statistics (DEMS) University of Milan-Bicocca Piazza dell'Ateneo Nuovo. Research interests include Content marketing, Marketing metrics, and Marketing Research. From 2006 to the present, Elisa has been Assistant Professor of Marketing, Faculty of Economics, University of Milan- Bicocca. From 2002-2005 PhD in Marketing Management, Faculty of Economics, University of Milan- Bicocca. In 2004. Elisa was Visiting Scholar, University of Manchester, UK. From 2002-2005, Elisa served as a Teaching Assistant for the Faculty of Economics, University of Milano-Bicocca. Recent publications include contributors to several conference proceedings and a chapter in an edited book.

Piergiorgio Re is full professor at the Department of Management at the University of Turin where he teaches marketing, marketing business to business and competitive analysis. Piergiorgio Re has written several articles and books on marketing, culture and family business. He is involved in different postgraduate Master programs and research projects; his main research interests are linked with the cultural marketing and family business.

Zahaira F González Romo, PhD. in Advertising and Public Relations by the Autonomous University of Barcelona. Professor of Advertising and Public Relations at the University of Vic Consultant to Advertising and Public Relations at the Open University of Catalunya. She has given lectures, seminars and workshops in the field of marketing and advertising in several countries and has published numerous articles and books. As a professional, she has her own Advertising Agency, and she work as Consultant for several companies in different countries.

Mohanbir Sawhney is a globally recognized scholar, teacher, consultant and speaker in strategic marketing, innovation and new media.His research and teaching interests include marketing and media in the digital world, process-centric marketing, collaborative marketing, organic growth and network-centric innovation. He has been widely recognized as a thought leader. Business Week named him as one of the 25 most influential people in e-Business. Crain's Chicago Business named him a member of "40 under 40", a select group of young business leaders in the Chicago area.He is a Fellow of the World Economic Forum. Prof. Sawhney is the co-author of five books. His most recent books are Collaborating with Customers to Create (2008) and The Global Brain: your Roadmap for Innovating Smarter and Faster in the Networked World (2007). His research has been published in leading journals like California Management Review, Harvard Business Review, Journal of Interactive Marketing, Management Science, Marketing Science, MIT Sloan Management Review, and Journal of the Academy of Marketing Science. He has also written several influential trade articles in publications like the Financial Times, CIO Magazine, and Business 2.0. He has won several awards for his teaching and research, including the 2006 Sidney Levy Award for Teaching Excellence at the Kellogg School, the 2005 runner-up for Best Paper in Journal of Interactive Marketing, the 2001 Accenture Award for the best paper published in California Management Review in 2000 and the Outstanding Professor of the Year at Kellogg in 1998. Students have nominated him as one of the top 5 professors at Kellogg in 2008 and 2009. He was awarded the Distinguished Alumni Award by the Indian Institute of Management, Calcutta in 2011 and he received the Light of India Award in 2011. Prof. Sawhney advises and speaks to Global 2000 firms and governments worldwide. His speaking and consulting clients include Accenture, Adobe Systems, Alticor, Banco Real, Boeing, Celanese, Cisco Systems, Dell, DuPont, Ericsson, Fidelity Investments, General Mills, Goldman Sachs, HCL Technologies, Honeywell, IBM Consulting Services, Infosys, Johnson & Johnson, Juniper Networks, Kellogg Company, Kraft Foods, McDonald's, Microsoft, Motorola, MTV Networks, Nissan Motor, Nomura Research Institute, Raytheon Missile Systems, SAP, Sony, Teradata and Thomson Corporation. He serves on the boards and advisory boards of several technology startup companies, including EXLservice, Bahwan Cybertek, vMock, Cross-Tab Group, Firescope and Pagewell. Prof. Sawhney holds a Ph.D. in marketing from the Wharton School of the University of Pennsylvania; a Master's degree in management from the Indian Institute of Management, Calcutta; and a Bachelor's degree in Electrical Engineering from the Indian Institute of Technology, New Delhi.

Vincenzo Speciale is a London-based worker with experience in the field of communication, PR and marketing. Grew up in Rome, Vincenzo has recently graduated from LUISS Guido Carli University with a bachelor in Economics and Management and a master degree in Luxury and Fashion Management. He has a special interest in luxury and fashion branding and he believes the road to success is trying.

Index

U

V

www.ingramcontent.com/pod-product-compliance
Lightning Source LLC
LaVergne TN
LVHW060419300926
849162LV00006B/1470